Handbook for
Economics Teachers

Handbook for
Economics Teachers

Edited by
David J. Whitehead
Lecturer, Teaching of Economics,
University of London Institute of Education

HEINEMANN EDUCATIONAL BOOKS

Heinemann Educational Books Ltd
22 Bedford Square, London WC1B 3HH
LONDON EDINBURGH MELBOURNE AUCKLAND
HONG KONG SINGAPORE KUALA LUMPUR NEW DELHI
IBADAN NAIROBI JOHANNESBURG
EXETER (NH) KINGSTON PORT OF SPAIN

ISBN 0 435 84902 6

Set, printed and bound in Great Britain by
Fakenham Press Limited, Fakenham, Norfolk

Contents

Section 4: Ways of Teaching Particular Topics

PART THREE: RESOURCES, ASSESSMENT AND ORGANISATION

Section 5: Miscellaneous

List of Contributors

A. G. Anderton	Head of Economics, Codsall High School, Wolverhampton
Clive Baker	Senior Administrative Officer, The Associated Examining Board
Patricia Barden	Economics Teacher, Alleyn's School, Dulwich, London
Jonathan Benjamin Bokor	Economics Teacher, Hasmonean Boys' School, London
Quintin N. Brewer	Head of Economics, Tunbridge Wells Girls' Grammar School, Kent
Richard C. Brierley	Head of Economics, Forest Hill School, London
David R. Butler	Head of Business Studies Department, Eaglesfield School, Woolwich, London
Nigel Carr	Economics Teacher, Brentwood School, Essex
Ralph Cooke	Head of Economics, Walton High School, Stafford
Ann Cotterrell	Part-time Lecturer in Economics, Barking College of Technology, London
Brinley Davies	Head of Economics, Worthing Sixth Form College
Dennis C. Dobbs	Educator, Hillsborough School District, California, USA
Sally Donovan	Economics Teacher, Archbishop Tenison's School, Croydon
R. Ellis	Deputy Head of First Year, Northumberland Park School, London
Carol G. Goodell	Recently completed her Ph.D. in Education at Stanford University, USA
James M. Haywood	Head of Economics, Cardinal Newman School, Luton, Beds
R. Helm	Economics Teacher, Raynes Park High School, London
Gordon Hewitt	Deputy Director, Esmée Fairbairn Research Centre, Heriot-Watt University
Robert F. Hill	Educator, Palo Alto School District, California, USA
J. R. Hough	Senior Lecturer in Education and Economics, Loughborough University
W. E. Jennings	Economics Teacher, Sydenham High School, Ontario, Canada
Myron L. Joseph	Professor of Economics and Industrial Administration, Carnegie-Mellon University
Maurice Knights	Head of Economics, Technical High School for Boys, Tunbridge Wells, Kent
Maureen Lakeman	Senior Teacher, Highams Park Senior High School, London
A. M. Leake	Economics Teacher, Haberdashers' Aske's Boys' School, Elstree, Herts
Peter Leech	Head of Economics, Boston Spa Comprehensive School, Yorks
Kenneth Light	Ohio Council on Economic Education, Ohio, USA
Graham Loomes	Part-time Economics and Business Studies Teacher, Reigate College, Surrey
Stuart Luker	Head of Economics, Charters School, Ascot, Berks
Andrew Maclehose	Economics Teacher, Atlantic College, S. Wales
Keith Marder	Head of Social and Economic Studies, Langdon School, East Ham, London
David L. McDougall	Principal Economics Teacher, Dunfermline High School, Fife
P. M. Morrison	Head of Faculty of Social and Environmental Studies, Brondesbury and Kilburn High School, London
Philip Negus	Lecturer in Social Sciences, Arnold and Carlton College of Further Education, Nottingham
Kenneth J. Neubeck	Assistant Professor of Sociology, University of Connecticut, USA
John Rees	Head of Economics, Harrow School, Middx
Z. S. Starnawski	Lecturer in Legal Studies Method, Monash University, Australia
Linda M. Thomas	Deputy Head, Tamworth Manor High School, Merton, London
Alistair Thomson	Economics Teacher, Haberdashers' Aske's School, New Cross, London
John Tulk	Head of Commerce, Mynyddbach School, Swansea
Jennifer H. Wales	Head of Economics, Passmores School, Harlow, Essex
R. Whelan	Economics Teacher, Woking Sixth Form College, Surrey
Maurice Willatt	Head of Economics, Haberdashers' Aske's Boys' School, Elstree, Herts
John Wolinski	Lecturer in Economics, Brooklands Technical College, Weybridge, Surrey
Keith R. J. Wood	Economics Teacher, Gillingham Technical High School, Kent
Nigel Wright	Teacher, Islington School Support Unit, London

Acknowledgements

The following people and organisations are thanked for granting permission to use copyright material:

Mel Calman, Michael Heath, Myron L. Joseph;

The Daily Mail, The Economist Newspaper Ltd, Mirror Group of Newspapers Ltd, Times Newspapers Ltd;

Barclays Bank Ltd, Centre for World Development Education, Economics Association, Lloyds Bank Ltd, Metropolitan Regional Examinations Board, Ohio Council on Economic Education, Transport and General Workers' Union, The Treasury, Victorian Commercial Teachers' Association;

G. I. Barnett and Son Ltd, Croom Helm Ltd, Forest Press Division, Lake Placid Education Foundation, Hodder and Stoughton Educational Ltd, Hutchinson Publishing Group Ltd, Macmillan London and Basingstoke, New Science Publications, Penguin Books Ltd, Sage Publications Inc.

Preface

'L'embarras des richesses'
Abbé d'Allainval

This is the latest in a series of Handbooks produced in conjunction with the London University Institute of Education. It aims to be an indispensable practical manual for economics teachers in schools and colleges of further education. Unless readers feel it is essential to have it within reach, it will not have achieved its purpose.

A number of influences affected my decision to embark on the considerable task of editing such a book. First, I was roused by the intentionally stirring remark of J. M. Oliver, in his original and thought-provoking monograph, *The Principles of Teaching Economics*: 'When I come right down to it, I hope to live and die an old-fashioned "sock-it-to-them" teacher.'[1] Such a method may be unobjectionable, providing that the pupils can take the 'punishment', but from my counselling of economics method students on teaching practice, I am continually reminded that many cannot. Indeed, it may be that such an approach still persists from the days when economics teachers could expect a reasonably homogeneous 'audience'. A similar dilemma has been noticed in Australia: 'Unfortunately, these teacher activities (oral communication of economic facts, and instruction of students in economic theory dredged from university textbooks) are still commonplace in schools, so much so that one can be forgiven for believing that secondary school students succeed in understanding economic issues and principles despite their teachers rather than because of them.'[2]

Another factor was a certain exasperation with the existing literature on teaching economics. Though excellent sources for writing academic essays on economics curriculum and methodology, their 'paucity of practical suggestions (are) infuriating'.[3] This handbook aims to satisfy J. C. Powicke's objective: 'not for blueprints but for detailed accounts and assessments of what has been tried out in schools so that any reader can make decisions in the light of other teachers' experience as well as his or her own'.[3] It should be viewed as complementary to existing books on teaching economics (a list of which appears in Chapter 51).

I thank: Alan Hornsey, for his invaluable advice in the early stages of planning; the Editorial Board, for their suggestions about content and approach; my past PGCE students (thirteen of whom contribute to the Handbook) for their encouragement and for the humility they have taught me; to Mavis Landen, for secretarial support; to my family, for their forbearance. My chief thanks go to the contributors (almost all of whom are practising schoolteachers) for the wealth of everyday experience they have brought to their articles, and for the patience with which they bore my editorial suggestions. Close reading of the text will provide evidence of a variety of standpoints and assumptions; I hope that at least some will prove provocative.

David Whitehead
October 1977

References

1 Oliver, J. M., *The Principles of Teaching Economics*, (Heinemann Educational, 1973), p 61.
2 Burkhardt, G. A., *Teaching Economics in the Secondary School,* (McGraw Hill, 1976), p 1.
3 Powicke, J. C., Review of *Teaching Economics* (2nd edition), in *Economics*, 12(2), Summer 1976, p 106.

General Introduction

Parts One and Two of the Handbook cover the thirteen to sixteen and sixteen to eighteen age ranges respectively, and Part Three deals with resources, assessment and organisation. Section 1 describes some courses suitable for classes below the fourth year, discusses teaching problems at this level, and how they may be partly solved by the use of a variety of methods and materials. Also, guidance is given on syllabus construction and school-based assessment. Section 2 consists of eleven chapters on the teaching of particular topics and concepts to this age range.

Section 3 contains practical suggestions for dealing with the non 'A' level sixth former and for organising individualised learning. Problems which arise mainly in colleges of further education are discussed, and remedies offered. Advice is given on using speakers from outside the school, on developing an economics trail, and on getting the best from urban study centres. Section 4 has twenty-three chapters on teaching specific topics and concepts to this age range.

Section 5 provides advice on textbooks and other resources for all age groups, and how to catalogue them. Methods of internal and external assessment are explained, and guidance is given on how to run an Economics Department. Finally, a comprehensive list is provided of useful addresses for economics teachers. Most are relevant to resources which are mentioned in Sections 2 and 4.

Most of the topics taught in elementary economics courses are covered in the Handbook. Nevertheless, there are a few omissions. In particular, an anticipated chapter on the teaching of comparative economic systems failed to materialise. Readers are referred to J. R. Coleman's *Comparative Economic Systems – An Enquiry Approach*, (Holt, Rinehart and Winston, 1968) for full treatment of this topic. Another more intentional gap is in coverage of the use of field studies. This has been done so well in B. R. G. Robinson's (ed) *Field Studies in Teaching Economics*, (Economics Association, 1975), that it would be pointless to duplicate it here. Another hoped-for chapter on an individualised 'A' level course did not appear. Despite the possibility of other lacunae, the Handbook has far more comprehensive scope than any comparable publication.

Some errors are bound to infiltrate such an enormously detailed work, and apologies are given in advance for any that have bypassed the editor's scrutiny. Particular organisations are certain to change their portfolio of free pamphlets for example. It might be more advisable, when writing to such bodies, not to ask for specific publications, but to state the area of interest, and ask for any relevant materials available.

It has been difficult to classify a number of resources, so if, for example, the reader is looking for information about what is available on Money and Banking, it is advisable to refer to *both* the relevant chapters (13 and 37). Guidelines for prices of resources are as follows. Wallcharts: either free or not more than £2. Films: between £2 and £10 per day's hire, except that where they are available on free loan, this is stated in the text. Audio tapes: £3–8 each. Videotapes may be hired at approximately the same rates as films. Cassette/filmstrip packs cost from £8. Filmstrips cost from £3.

Part One
Teaching Economics to the 13–16 Age Range

Introduction to Part One

'"Write that down", the King said to the jury, and the jury eagerly wrote down all three dates on their slates, and then added them up, and reduced the answer to shillings and pence.'

Alice in Wonderland,
Lewis Carroll

Very few economics teachers are called upon to teach their subject below the fourth year. Yet in the lower school, humanities or social studies courses are often developed, to which an economics dimension would add value. Keith Wood demonstrates how such a grafting of an economics component may be achieved. In contrast, a third year course devised by David Butler concentrates on economics as a discrete subject, aiming mainly to introduce leading ideas and give pupils a foretaste of full-scale courses which operate from the fourth year. Within most fourth and fifth year economics classes, the range of ability and attainment of literate and numerate skills is now so great, that all teachers must find it a problem how to manage such diversity. Alain Anderton, while suggesting a number of specifics, is sceptical about any remedy which claims total success. He develops his suggestion of individualised learning by explaining how worksheets and similar material may best be produced. The argument is taken further, and related particularly to economics, by John Tulk, with his systematized methods of work which, no doubt in common with most of the contributions, will find a balance of supporters and detractors. Very little has been published on the mechanics of constructing a Mode III CSE course in economics. An actual case study is provided by Linda Thomas, who shows how the course was influenced by current educational thinking. Richard Brierley, in his chapter on the organisation of project work, puts forward proposals for effective implementation of this method.

As mentioned in the General Introduction, the Handbook does not attempt full coverage of the use of field studies. Nevertheless, a number of original approaches are included, because of their everyday relevance to economics teachers. Maureen Lakeman outlines what she considers to be important criteria for the success of visits, and Patricia Barden shows how very localised field studies can be worthwhile if smoothly organised. Section 2 on teaching particular topics begins with the universally taught 'Prices and Markets', in which David McDougall makes a variety of short suggestions for enlivening the topic. Ralph Cooke has gained valuable experience of how to teach about firms from his role in helping to develop the Understanding Industrial Society Project and as AEB Chief Examiner for the 'O' level of that name. He stresses especially the importance of pupils interacting with firms' employees, whether they be those of the local greengrocer or of a public corporation. A science fiction approach to teaching the division of labour is described by Peter Leech, and two American simulations useful for this topic are appended. 'Money and Banking' contains ten unorthodox ways of treating the subject at this level and, as with all these chapters, gives a substantial list of resources at the end. Jennifer Wales' chapter contains topics which pupils do not perhaps find as intellectually demanding as some, but which nevertheless benefit from the treatment she gives them. In contrast, the subjects of employment, unemployment and inflation, although superficially obvious, quickly become complex at the theoretical level. David McDougall's experience with the 'concrete' objects of the Scottish Economics Curriculum Development Project for the first two years of secondary education gives added strength to his suggestions, some of which might otherwise be considered impractical. Pam Morrison highlights the most important aspects of the topic of trade unions and employers' federations. While it can be argued that the law of comparative costs should not necessarily be included in a treatment of international economics, Rod Ellis and Rosemary Whelan consider it appropriate to include it here at this level. They stress how important it is to emphasise the distinction between real and money flows, to avoid confusion with such concepts as 'invisible imports'.

With distribution we return to a largely descriptive topic, but it is one which, as Quintin Brewer shows, can be used as a vehicle for elucidating a number of economic concepts. Teachers frequently aver that for a variety of reasons they find the topic of population difficult to teach. David Butler considers the use of population models and surveys, and examines some interesting and contentious problems which are common with this age group. Finally, Alain Anderton demythologises the Welfare State, which, although not on most 'O' level syllabuses, appears in a large number of other courses which economics teachers are obliged to teach below the sixth form.

Section 1: General

1   Teaching Economics Below the Fourth Form: Content, Methods and Assessment
Keith R. J. Wood

Introduction

Teaching economics to eleven to fourteen year olds within an interrelated social studies context provides a framework for concentration on economic concepts with the bonus of ready appreciation of the relevance of those concepts to the real world.

What follows is an outline of the content and methods of the economics component of a technical high school social studies course. This is a three year course, interrelating the disciplines of economics, sociology, geography and history and including elements of R.E., which is followed by all pupils in years one to three.

The aim of the course is to provide an understanding of the conceptual development of the subjects under the umbrella of a social studies content rather than to integrate fully the content of the disciplines. The benefits of such a course flow from the opportunities created for teachers and pupils to pursue a topic of study in breadth as well as depth.

Economics teachers are fortunate since much has been written on what economics should be taught in the classroom and on the development of economic understanding.[1] It is possible to pursue a developmental approach to economics through a thematic or topic-based social studies course and in this way bring the subject 'alive' for the pupils whilst ensuring an understanding of basic economic concepts.

Content

The aim of the economics component of the course is to teach concepts and principles basic to an understanding of economics using a 'spiral' development[2] (see Figure 1.1). The concepts and principles introduced early on in the course are returned to later at a greater level of complexity and the application is extended to provide continuity within the course.

In year one the basic economic problem of allocating scarce resources in relation to the unlimited demands on them, the need for choice and the opportunity cost involved, and the benefits of specialisation to increase the productivity of resources, are examined initially in the context of a study of early man and the development of primitive societies. The importance of the distribution of the factors of production, location of settlements and trade is also observed in the course of a study of the development of ancient civilisations.

Year two of the course deals with conflict, revolution and change, building upon the concepts already studied. The notion of economic conflict invites the examination of the effects of different factor endowments on the local community and at regional and national levels. The need for specialisation and exchange become relevant topics as does the importance of money. The choice to produce consumer goods or capital goods is considered. Also rich and poor countries are compared.

Contrasting the development of nations dissimilar to our own leads into a detailed case study of the effects of different factor endowments. The 'law' of diminishing returns can be considered in the context of population problems in the Third World and provides a basis for the study of production and supply in year three. Experience suggests that the principle of diminishing marginal utility is readily evoked at this stage and rarely forgotten afterwards and thus is available for work in year three on the interaction of demand and supply in the market.

In year three a study of the nature of man's modern environment, in terms of its institutions and the forces at work within it, leads to consideration of: the market mechanism as a means of allocating resources; commodity and factor price determination; government intervention (e.g. the Welfare State); distribution of income (nationally and internationally); and strategies and scope for further economic development.

Figure 1.1 Development of economics component within a social studies framework

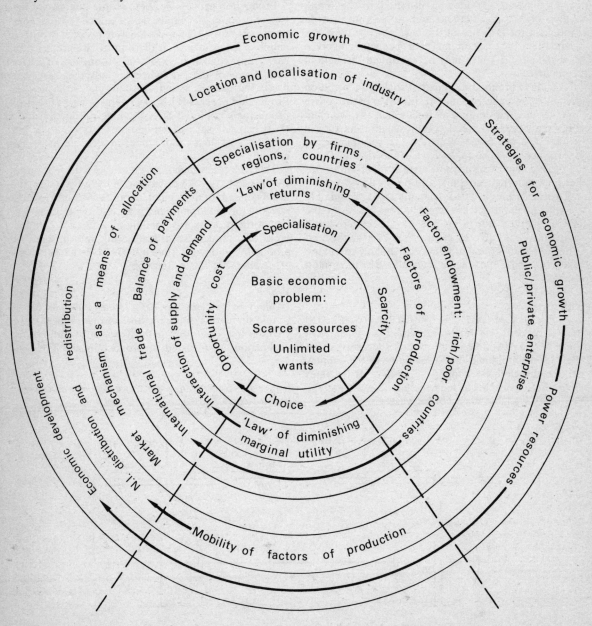

Methods

Some examples of methods which might be used to develop an understanding of economics within the framework of a social studies course for eleven to fourteen year olds follow.

Lack of space precludes a detailed discussion of the ways in which the economic concepts are exemplified by and carry over to the other aspects of the social studies course, but it is possible to indicate briefly how connections may be established. For example, in year one of the course, the study of the bushmen of the Kalahari desert provides an insight into the implications of division of labour and the need to provide capital for the life-style of the bushman, and lays the foundations for an examination of the factors involved in social change which may be continued throughout the course.

The study of modern industrial society (centred on the mixed economy) during the third year of the course involves the consideration of topics such as town planning methods, the effects of industrialisation on the worker and the family unit and the role played by government agencies in the lives of individuals. International comparisons lead to a study of relationships between differing economic and political systems.

Textbooks aimed at CSE students and often suitable for younger pupils are becoming increasingly available (see Resources) but as yet few have been produced which are preferable to careful tailoring of the vast range of resources and simulations available to suit the needs of pupils following an interrelated or integrated course.

Year One
The basic economic problem. The class may be asked to make a list of all the things they would like if they cost them nothing. Adding up the wants soon shows that they are manifold and that if everyone in the country produced such a list it might be endless! It becomes clear that some choice must be made and that the resources available must not be wasted.

The factors of production. The class may be instructed to draw a detailed map of an imaginary desert island, describing it fully, and then to make lists under the headings land, labour, and capital of the types of resources on the island which fit the categories.

Division of labour and specialisation. It is possible to set up side-by-side in the classroom two simple production processes. The design of a product, e.g. a two-dimensional car, may be specified which is to be made with the aid of pencils, rulers, compasses and scissors (see Figure 1.2).

Production process A has the same quantity of factors of production (pupils, desks, rulers, scissors, compasses, paper, etc) as production process B but A employs the principle of division of labour such that each pupil concentrates on the production of a particular part of the car (wheels, windscreen, etc) and passes this on to be assembled at the end of the process. Production process B has each pupil at his or her desk producing completed cars. Running production for a short period, say fifteen minutes, soon shows the advantage of division of labour in terms of increased output.

This exercise, which is best returned to in year three, can be used to evoke discussion of the advantages and disadvantages of division of labour to be found in most introductory economics texts. By altering the technology of the process it is possible to observe the importance of capital. Also, it leads easily into projects on production and work. (See pp. 67–74 for a more complex version of this simulation.)

Year Two
Production and the law of diminishing returns. A simple simulation along the lines of that suggested for year one may demonstrate the importance of the factor proportions to be used in production and the con-

Figure 1.2 Specification for a two-dimensional car (not to scale)

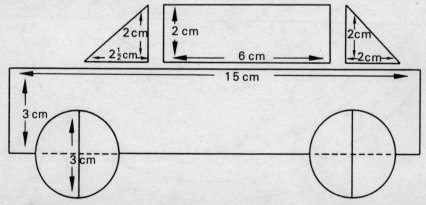

straints imposed on increased production by the inflexibility of the supply of factors of production.

It is possible to use the design for a two-dimensional car above (although other tasks may easily be substituted), but this time production may be constrained by the use of the teacher's desk only, two pairs of scissors, two pencils, two rulers and an unlimited supply of raw materials, i.e. paper. Adding increasing amounts of labour, i.e. pupils, to these factors and

noting output over some fixed time period, say five minutes, will produce results which can be put on a graph. For example one pupil may produce two cars in five minutes, two pupils working together may make five cars in the same time, three pupils nine cars (much depends on how much is remembered from year one about the organisation of production), but eventually, diminishing returns will set in, e.g. four pupils produce only twelve cars. Ultimately production can be made extremely difficult when, say, ten or fifteen pupils are trying to work at one desk and share the other available factors of production.

Graphs of total production, average production and marginal production may be plotted by all pupils and the implications of these observations for the form discussed (see Figure 1.3). For example, the need to increase the land and capital inputs and the time required to achieve this may be discussed. Cost and efficiency considerations may enter the discussion.

Diminishing marginal utility. Pupils initiated into the technique of measurement at the margin may return to a consideration of the determination of consumer choice and value. It is possible to feed selected pupils with homogeneous units of some type of cream-filled chocolate bar and ask them to record their enjoyment of each 'bite' by indicating a score out of ten per unit consumed. Again, graphs plotted showing 'satisfaction' per unit usually evoke comment on the formulation of consumer preferences and can lead into a discussion of value (see Figure 1.4).

It is worthwhile to spend some time on the weaknesses of the method of measuring and recording satisfaction. It is also useful to give some thought to what might lead to ever-increasing or constant satisfaction (e.g. the introduction of a glass of water between 'bites' or the provision of long 'rest' periods) – in other words, what happens if 'other things' do *not* remain the same.

Figure 1.3

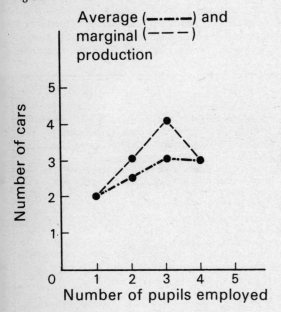

Figure 1.4 Graph to show diminishing marginal utility

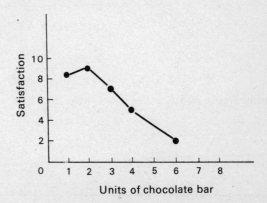

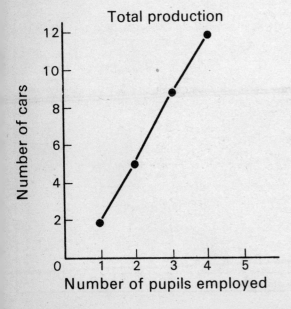

Although there is a very real cost in terms of chocolate bars, experience suggests that the investment is worthwhile since the principle is rarely forgotten afterwards.

Exchange. The importance of money and its essential properties may be discussed at this stage. It soon becomes apparent to pupils that specialisation requires the facility of exchange and that some medium of exchange is essential. An excellent introduction to this topic is the film *The Curious History of Money*. It is fast-moving and somewhat detailed but it is a cartoon which absorbs the audience. It is short enough to be repeated and contains sequences which are easily simulated in the classroom to aid understanding (e.g. shortcomings of barter, and the use of the bill of exchange).

Year Three
The market. An auction may be used to simulate the operation of the market mechanism. This is best dealt with after a discussion of alternative techniques for solving the problem of what should be produced, e.g. the advantages in terms of control over the use of resources, and disadvantages, in terms of lack of consumer choice, under a centrally planned system.

Sums of money are allocated to half of the class members and they are provided with a list of possible prices of some imaginary product which it is assumed they wish to purchase in as great a quantity as possible (see the consumer schedule below). The rest of the class members are producers. They are provided with a schedule showing how much of this commodity each of them as producers may be able to produce, earning

---

How the Market Works

Consumer Schedule
As a potential consumer of a product called *Erk!* you have been allocated £_____ per week and we assume that, under any circumstances, you wish to spend all of this allowance on packs of *Erk!* Fill in the schedule below to show the maximum number of packs that you can buy at the prices listed.

No. of packs per week	Price per week (£)
	1.50
	2.00
	2.50
	2.75
	3.00

Draw a graph to illustrate these statistics. (*Remember*: price per pack on the vertical axis and quantity on the horizontal axis.)

Market Observations

Price per pack	Quantity demanded per week	Quantity supplied per week

Illustrate these statistics on a similar graph.

Producer Schedule
As a producer of *Erk!* your company is a member of a cooperative of ten producers making the same product but selling through a central marketing agency.

As managing director you are involved with the hiring of labour and the purchase of machinery. Your company rents the land on which the factory is built. Your aim is to produce packs of *Erk!* and, after covering the cost of labour, land, machinery, raw materials and power, to make a *profit*.

In the schedule below are shown the various quantities of *Erk!* which your factory can produce in a week and the price per pack at which each must be sold if your company is to make a profit.

No. of packs per week	Price per week (£)
	–

Draw a graph to illustrate these statistics. (*Remember*: price per pack on the vertical axis and quantity on the horizontal axis.)

Market Observations

Price per pack	Quantity demanded per week	Quantity supplied per week

Illustrate these statistics on a similar graph.

normal profit at the range of suggested prices. The teacher should complete the first part of this schedule ensuring that each producer is faced with a different supply schedule indicating different costs and levels of efficiency (see the producer schedule on page 6).

The consumers and producers should be able to draw simple graphs from the data presented to them. This will allow them to estimate easily how much of the product they wish to buy or sell at prices suggested by the 'auctioneer' and declare aloud their wishes.

One member of the class must be reserved for the job of 'auctioneer' and he or she must have an assistant with a calculator. The 'auctioneer' attempts to clear the market, i.e. to equate supply and demand, by suggesting alternative prices and, at each price, having the assistant calculate total supply and demand in the market. In this way the 'auctioneer' can gradually build up the market supply and demand schedules on the board.

The essentials of the problem are soon grasped. At low prices, many consumers are unable to obtain the desired quantities and some producers cease supplying to the market; at high prices, few consumers can afford to buy but many producers are willing to sell. Observation and discussion lead to the realisation that one price must be found which satisfies both consumers and producers and that the easiest way to obtain the solution is to graph the market schedules from the blackboard and observe the price where the lines intersect, i.e. the equilibrium price.

From this simple simulation it is possible to discuss reasons why equilibrium prices once attained might change. On the demand side: more/less consumers (it is easily illustrated that more consumers cause the market demand curve to shift to the right and thus price to rise); more/less money allocated to consumers; alternative goods preferred. On the supply side: more/less producers; changes in the costs of production. In general, from this simulation it is possible for pupils to understand the 'laws' of supply and demand.

A discussion may follow of those markets and commodities where supply and demand do not freely determine price, and where government intervention is important. It is also possible to go on to study the effects of monopoly and advertising. It may be useful to follow up work on the market using case-studies with questions based on them. (See Figure 1.5 below.)

Figure 1.5 Example of a newspaper cutting (from the Sunday Times, *24 October 1976) that might be used as the basis of a case study or as an exercise.*

Boom for jeans, doom for tights

THE FALL of the mini skirt, and the rise of the ubiquitous blue jeans combined last week to close two Courtaulds tights factories, and put 870 people out of work.

In 1972, UK demand for tights was running at a staggering 52m dozen. In the first six months of this year, it had dropped to just 20m dozen and that was mostly before the long, hot summer, when women tended to buy, and wear even less.

Throughout the Common Market the picture is equally as bleak. Last year, the latest figures available, the stockings and tights industry suffered from 45% over-capacity, despite the fact that industry employment had fallen from 78,000 in 1971, to 53,000. Much of the Common Market problem it attributed to imports.

The cheap, one-size end of the market, which is where the Courtaulds plants were operating, has suffered the most. Unbranded tights abound at the 20p price level, and these are sold in retail outlets ranging from petrol stations to newsagents' shops and supermarkets. Not surprisingly, the big tights makers like Courtaulds have been trying to stimulate demand in the upper, more profitable reaches of the market, and Kayser, one of Courtaulds' brand names, will have spent more on advertising this year than all hosiery brands together spent in 1975.

Last year, with the tights market running at about £150m, every woman over 14 bought on average 24.9 pairs. This year, demand has declined some 10% as cheap and cheerful jeans have become virtually a uniform. The trouble with jeans is that women tend not to wear tights under them, though a market has developed for so-called "jeans socks." In fact, in order to maintain a very smooth outline under very tight jeans, many women wear nothing at all — even knickers.

"Bring Back the Mini" might well be the rallying cry of the UK tights industry. The mini required that tights always be perfect, and there really was not any way for a minor ladder or hole to be hidden. As a result, demand soared. Today's lower hem lines mean that small imperfections can be tolerated longer, even by the woman who has opted to wear a skirt instead of trousers. Until a basic change in demand occurs, all British tights manufacturers can do is try to move upmarket, leaving the cheap, one-size slice of the market to imports.

Lorana Sullivan

Questions on the *Sunday Times* article:

1 How has the demand for tights changed in the last five years?
2 What factors have affected the demand for tights?
3 What effect has the change in demand had on the price of tights?
4 How have suppliers reacted to the change in the market?

Introduction to macroeconomics. Having considered the influence of supply and demand on price in goods markets, it is possible to generalise and discuss the influence of aggregate demand on the level of employment and inflation.

Income and wealth. It is not so easy to introduce simulation and role-playing methods to this section but it can be brought to life by the use of carefully chosen examples and exercises. The following suggested methods may help (see Resources):

(a) Begin with an examination of how students spend their pocket money and compare this with national statistics on average expenditure by teenagers.
(b) Use examples from newspaper articles to show the relationship between income level and standard of living.
(c) Students may calculate national income per head from population and national income statistics. International comparisons of income per head provide a basis for a discussion of income distribution and an introduction to the problems of the Third World.
(d) An examination of sources of income can be enlivened by running a 'mini' stock exchange game using the financial press and notional amounts of money, and by setting the task of finding out where to get the highest return on savings.
(e) If the statistics are carefully explained, it is possible to have thirteen to fourteen year olds plot Lorenz Curves to examine the distribution of income and wealth. The Annual Abstract provides the statistics.
(f) The influence of the labour market on the size of incomes may be introduced in the light of previous work on markets through a discussion of (i) differences in natural ability, education and training; (ii) geographical immobility; (iii) occupational immobility; and (iv) social immobility. All of these can be exemplified with reference to experience and with current material from newspapers, etc.
(g) The working of the tax system in its many aspects can be seen through simple calculations of Income Tax and Capital Transfer Tax liability and research on rates of VAT.

Assessment
Evaluation of the gain in economic understanding achieved by such an economics component in a three-year course over that which may develop as a result of other influences anyway is difficult. Test scores of students who have completed the three-year course compared with previous years' students who have not experienced the course are of little value because so many factors will have intervened during the time that will have elapsed. A control group of similar ability and background is required.

However, it is true that a failure to grasp basic concepts at an early stage will show up clearly when the course returns to these concepts in years two and three and on this basis it is possible to evaluate the success of teaching methods. Here (as with any attempt to test understanding at the end of the course), data-response questions, passages with missing words, multiple-choice questions, case-study material and essays all have a role to play in evaluation.

Example of Data-Response Question
The following statistics show the amount of *Erko* – a detergent powder – which would be supplied and demanded at various suggested prices per week.

Price (p)	Quantity demanded (pkts) per week	Quantity supplied (pkts) per week
10	6000	1000
20	5000	2000
30	4000	3000
40	3000	4000
50	2000	5000
60	1000	6000

(a) Draw graphs to represent these statistics and estimate the market price of *Erko*.
(b) Using the graphs that you have drawn, suggest what would be the effect of the government insisting that the price of *Erko* should not be greater than 25p per packet.
(c) With reference to your answer to question (b), explain the existence of very long waiting lists for Council accommodation.

Example of Passage with Missing Words
Fill in the gaps with the words from the list.
The boom in _____ prices in the Medway Towns which came to a halt in the summer of 1973 could be linked directly to the availability of _____ for house-buyers. When there was a ready _____ of such loans the _____ for houses was high resulting in an _____ in house prices and _____ prices.
The _____ for new houses has been seriously affected by the scarcity of loans for home-buyers which has since occurred.
An _____ supply of new houses has developed which has caused the _____ of new houses to _____ and, therefore, a _____ in the number of new houses being built. This has led to _____ for some small building firms and some _____ among building workers.

Missing words:
market, supply, price, reduction, demand, house, land, increase, excess, unemployment, bankruptcy, fall, mortgages.

Some conclusions
The success of an interrelated social studies course depends on continual staff consultation and careful coordination of material throughout its planning and teaching, to ensure continuity of development of the social studies content for the pupils, whilst preserving the conceptual development of the disciplines involved. A major benefit of the interrelated course is that it allows the expertise of individual departments to be used to its fullest extent and thereby provides a variety of experiences for the pupils. Indeed, for the economics component of the social studies course to be taught with the maximum pupil participation and the minimum of staff distress, experience suggests that it must be taught by an economics specialist.

It is sometimes difficult to reach agreement at the planning stage of such a course on what of history, geography, economics, etc. should be included – the opportunity cost of, say, more history may be less economics! Thus it is essential that course planners should be able to see beyond content and appreciate the conceptual interrelationships of their subjects.

The implications of this type of course for later 'O' level and CSE courses in economics are important. Much of the time that might have been spent on an introduction to the course and on internalising basic concepts will be available for greater exploration of those concepts in depth and for case study and project work.

The students will have a better understanding of what they are committing themselves to if they choose to study economics as a fourth-year option. Those students who decide to avoid the subject will, at least, have a basic understanding of the economic forces at work in society.

References

1 See, for example, Lee, N. and Entwistle, H., 'Economics Education and Educational Theory' in Lee, N. (ed), *Teaching Economics*, (Economics Association, 1967); Lumsden, K. G. and Attiyeh, R. E., 'The Core of Basic Economics', *Economics*, Summer 1971; Senesh, L., 'Teaching Economic Concepts in the Primary Grades', in Lee, N. (ed), *Teaching Economics*, (Economics Association, 1967).
2 See Bruner, J. S., *The Process of Education*, (Harvard University Press, 1963).

Resources

General Texts
Davies, B. and Hender, D., *Production and Trade*, (Longman Social Science Studies, 1974).
Davies, F., *Starting Economics*, (Hulton, 1970). These are aimed at CSE students but are certainly of use in a lower school course.
Dunning, K., *Working and Spending*, (Hulton, 1971).
Garrett, J., *Visual Economics*, (Evans, 1966). These books provide an introduction to economics for younger pupils.
Hambling, C. and Matthews, P., *Human Society*, (Macmillan, 1974). This book fits the economics into a social studies framework remarkably well. Especially useful are chapters 2 and 3.

Other Books
Barr, J., Connexions: *Standards of Living*, (Penguin, 1969). This contains many examples of use of newspaper cuttings.
Development Puzzle, (CWDE). This contains a mass of information for teaching about economic development and provides lists of available resources.
Donaldson, P., *Economics of the Real World*, (Penguin, 1973). This is useful for the graphic exposition of income distribution on pages 178–180.
Marsh, J, *Welfare State*, (Harrap New Generation Series, 1975). Other books in this series may also be useful.

Film
The Curious History of Money, (Multilink Film Library). Free loan.

Other Resources
Poverty Game, (Oxfam). Useful simulation to provide insights into problems of economic development in the Third World.
The Humanities Curriculum Project Kit *People and Work* contains some useful material.

2   A Third Year Introductory Course in Economics

David R. Butler

Justifying a course in economics below the fourth year

Possibly the greatest problem which economics teachers will face in introducing an economics course below the fourth year is in convincing Heads that it has a viable place in the curriculum at this level. Indeed, in many schools, economics is still regarded as a subject to be taught only to the academic sixth former. The growth of comprehensive education may well present the economics teacher with the opportunity to 'stake his claim' in the pre-fourth year curriculum. The economics teacher could advance two main arguments in favour of introducing economics at this level, when rebutting the accusation of his Head or Director of Studies that he is simply 'empire building'. First, why should geography and history be taught and not economics? Surely, some knowledge of topics such as inflation, the balance of payments and finance, which the pupil reads or hears about every day, is at least as relevant as knowledge of the Congress of Vienna or sheep farming in the Outer Hebrides. Secondly, how can pupils intelligently decide whether to opt for a subject in the fourth year if they have virtually no idea of what it is about? Pupils at least get a taste of most other option subjects lower down the school.

Economics for a Comprehensive Third Year

The course outlined below has been taught at a London comprehensive school since September 1974 to all pupils in their third year. The nature of the school very much determined the syllabus content and method of teaching and it is presented here as an example of the type of course which has shown itself to be reasonably successful rather than any idealised or all-purpose syllabus. The school is a ten-form-entry boys' comprehensive with three broad bands of ability for teaching purposes. There is a common curriculum up to and including the third year after which there is an option system. Economics was allocated one thirty-minute period per week within a very crowded third year curriculum. Economics teachers proposing to introduce a course below the fourth year need to take account of the nature of the school, the interests of the pupils and the time allocated to the subject. It is likely that a course for third year girls in a rural Independent School will be very different in structure and detail from the one outlined below.

Objectives of the Course

1 To introduce the pupil to certain basic economic concepts.
2 To make the pupil aware of a number of aspects of the commercial and economic world with which he might be concerned.
3 To provide the pupil with some insight into the type of work he might be doing if he opted for the subject at 'O' level or CSE.
4 To provide a background or a first stage in a spiral curriculum to later work in economics.

Content

The course was divided into three main sections: (a) production, (b) exchange and (c) distribution. Each section was designed to take approximately one term. The sections were divided into a number of units which were intended to take about two sessions of thirty minutes each. Details of these units are provided in Appendix I.

The production–exchange–distribution model was chosen because it was felt that it could be easily understood by the pupil and would give some continuity to the course. Continuity is a problem, particularly when the pupils are only seen once a week. Pupils like to see where they are going in a course and to see that it has some type of structure. The 'chain of production' is given to the pupils very early on in the course, as well as a copy of the syllabus, so that they are able to relate the two and see some sort of purpose in the course.

The same basic syllabus content is taught to all pupils regardless of ability. This is very much in line with current educational thinking. The depth to which each topic is taken and the methods used are varied between pupils according to their ability level. For example, top ability pupils at this level may be able to see the application of the division of labour to countries specialising and trading while this will almost certainly be beyond the less able.

Method

Wherever possible, the approach is to relate the content to the pupil's own economic experience and interests. As much use as possible is made of physical models in order to facilitate the understanding of concepts. A considerable number of films, video tape recordings, and simulations are used in order to make the course attractive. Again, it is important to emphasise that the examples chosen and the methods used will very much depend upon the nature and interests of the pupils. At the school where this course is run, the boys have a passion for British-built motorcycles which may not be common to pupils in other schools. Local examples help to stimulate interest and make the course more realistic. Slides of the local high street seem, for some inexplicable reason, to create as much interest as pictures of the most up-to-date American hypermarket.

Resources

Books
There is no one book which is entirely suitable for this level. The main problem is the level of language used, particularly with the more conceptual topics. Most of the standard 'O' level and CSE textbooks have some useful diagrams or short extracts. The new edition of *Visual Economics* by J. Garrett (Evans) is pitched at a suitable level for at least some of the sections. The economics teacher introducing a third year course will find that he will need to produce a considerable amount of his own material in the form of fact sheets and work sheets.

Films
Although such aspects of the course as money are well covered by films, there is a shortage of directly relevant films on many of the sections. There are, however, many films which can be adapted for use by the economics teacher. For this reason many of the films mentioned below need to be carefully previewed by the teacher before use. The pupils need to be instructed carefully in what to look out for in the film. The film *Girl in a Pink Turban*, for example, gives a great deal of technical information about the making of ICI pharmaceutical products, but the pupil's attention needs to be drawn towards how the division of labour is employed, how automation is used, the chain of production from raw materials through to the finished product and distribution etc. This is quite difficult to achieve, particularly with lower ability pupils. Care-

fully stuctured worksheets and questionnaires assist greatly here.

Other Resources
There is a considerable amount of free material available which is often attractively presented. Banks, Consumer Advice Centres, and large companies are often useful. Slides taken in the local area can also add interest.

Assessment

Short tests are conducted each term and there is a longer test at the end of the course. Assessment is important in order to give the teacher some kind of 'feedback' on the course. By and large it has been found that the descriptive aspects of the course were reasonably well grasped but that some of the concepts were less well understood. Not surprisingly perhaps, this was particularly true of the less able pupils. For example, most pupils could explain what the division of labour was and give examples of it. The more able pupils could show why it resulted in a faster rate of production in the experiment carried out (see Appendix II) but very few could relate the concept to trade between two countries.

Evaluation

Small modifications continue to be made each year. The interests of the pupils change as well as those of the teacher. Most pupils have expressed interest in at least some aspects of the course. Different ability levels have shown varying degrees of interest between syllabus sections. Less able pupils have shown a keen interest in aspects of money such as cheques and credit cards whilst more able pupils have often shown a surprising degree of interest in topics such as 'how a large company operates'.

The interest in economics has been reflected in the increased numbers of pupils opting for economics and commerce in the fourth and fifth years. Although it is still early days to form any firm conclusions, it would appear that examination results in the fifth year are improving and this might be due in part at least to the introduction of the third year economics course.

Appendix I: Details of Syllabus

Content	Method and Resources
Section A: Production	
1 What is economics?	
2 The chain of production	Films: *Looking at Steel* (Viscom. BSC), *Girl in a Pink Turban* (ICI). Pupils examine factors of production and construct chain of production diagrams for different products. (This serves as an outline for the whole course)
3 The division of labour	Film: *The Man who Made Spinning Tops* (American cartoon from Rank, also available through ILEA film library), *Division of Labour Game* (see Appendix II)
4 How a large company operates	Film: *Girl in a Pink Turban* (ICI). Use actual example of a large company such as Unilever or ICI
5 Financing a large company	Film: *My Word is My Bond* (Stock Exchange Film – Guild Sound and Vision). Free loan. Simple investment game – pupils each buy 3 shares and follow progress over 6 weeks. Winner is pupil who makes largest per cent gain
Section B: Exchange	
1 Barter	Film: *Curious History of Money* (Cartoon film from Multilink Film Library.) Free loan. Actual demonstration in the class to show problems, e.g. pupils exchange rulers, pencils, etc.
2 Money (a) – qualities, cash, foreign.	Film: *Curious History of Money* (second half)
3 Money (b) – Cheques, credit cards, etc.	Film: *A Piece of Plastic*, (Advertising film from Barclays). Free loan. Pupils fill in cheques, etc.
4 Trade	Pupils construct lists of imported goods in own homes and countries of origin. Bar graphs of UK trade pattern. Simple example of two countries trading
Section C: Distribution	
1 Transport – relative speeds, efficiency, etc.	Exercise where pupils have to work out the cheapest way of moving different cargoes between two places given certain pieces of information. (Geography Department may well have some useful material) Film: *Murex to Darina* (Shell film showing off-loading from large to small tanker – point of economy of scale can be illustrated as well as problems of large tankers). Free loan
2 Wholesaling	Exercise showing the functions of wholesalers. Discussion as to reasons for decline
3 Retailing	Local slides of different types of shops. High street survey. Simple comparison of supermarket prices and corner shop – discussion on reasons for growth Video – *Commerce for Today* (ILEA): (see Resources in Chapter 18 on p. 106 for details)
4 Advertising	Discussion on advertising techniques. Video or audio recordings of actual adverts to illustrate techniques. Pupils construct own poster adverts or possibly Video advert. Video – *Commerce for Today* (ILEA): Advertising. (See p. 106 for details)
5 Consumer protection	Case studies to show rights when shopping. Leaflets from Consumer Advice Centre. Safety labels (Kite Mark, etc.) in home. Talk by someone from Consumer Advice Centre. Film: *A Question of Standards* (British Standards Institute)

Appendix II: Division of Labour Game

Equipment (for each team of five). Twenty ball point pens which can be taken apart and put together again; clock or watch with second hand; time recording sheets; an assembly diagram.

Purpose. (i) To show how the division of labour results in a faster assembly time than individual assembly; (ii) To demonstrate why it is quicker; and (iii) To reveal possible disadvantages which may result.

Method. One member of the team is appointed as timekeeper and checker. In the first assembly the rest of the team assemble five pens by themselves, and the total time is added up and recorded.
In the second assembly the team appoints a production manager who organises them into an assembly line. The twenty pens are assembled using division of labour and the time taken is recorded. (This can be compared to other teams – thus introducing an element of competition.)
The second time is then compared to the first.
Discuss why the second time is faster than the first, and any problems, e.g. hold ups in production – faulty assembly etc.

Notes. Bright pupils may point out that the second time is faster because 'workers' have gained greater skill with the practice. It may therefore be useful to repeat the individual assembly. Occasionally the second time may be slower than the first. This could be used to point out the problems. It is probably better to take the average times for the whole class to prove the point.

3 Problems of Mixed Ability Classes in Teaching Economics

A. G. Anderton

The debate on mixed ability teaching has been going on for a long time, and the move towards comprehensive schools is just one aspect of it. No attempt will be made here to discuss whether or not economics should be taught in mixed ability classes. That problem is copiously dealt with elsewhere in its general context. *Teachers and Teaching* by Morrison and McIntyre[1] gives a good summary of current findings and further references. Rather, teaching strategies for mixed ability teaching below the sixth form in economics will be considered and evaluated here.

One solution to mixed ability teaching is to devise a scheme of individualised learning. Each child follows a course where he covers the work at his own pace. Although a rigid implementation of such a scheme must be a rare occurrence, it is feasible. Its main advantage is that it should enable each pupil to develop and reach his maximum attainment. The slow do not hold the bright back, nor are the slow left behind. Group work can still be accomplished, because several pupils working at roughly the same pace can act together. But the disadvantages for teaching economics in this way at this level are daunting.

1 The resources must be available. There is no commercially produced package and hence the materials will have to be mainly teacher-produced and organised. This is a mammoth task. Moreover, the resources would ideally be multi-media, in order to make the work more stimulating. Tapes, slides, photographs, discussions, games and simulations all need to be provided.
2 Apart from organising the materials, the teacher will also have to encourage the pupils in their work, act as a 'human resource' and provide assessment. Anyone who has tried to work in this sort of context knows that it is far more draining than traditional teaching methods.
3 The theory is based on the assumption that the pupils will want to learn. This, as every teacher knows,

is just not true. In a true mixed ability class of say twenty pupils in an average catchment area, there will probably be at least one pupil with behaviour problems, four or five who will need strong 'encouragement' to work and the rest will also need pressure from the teacher to produce results. No set of economics resources by themselves will motivate all adolescents to learn. The key link, as in all teaching, is the teacher. If the teacher is not totally committed to this approach or is not able to cope with the demands of the situation placed upon him, the whole thing will fall flat on its face.

Traditional teaching methods on the other hand have just as many drawbacks. Most teachers are competent in handling the traditional teaching situation. But at what level should the lesson be pitched? The stock answer is to aim for the middle and hope for the best. That way, both the less able pupils and the bright pupils suffer. Traditional teaching methods, then, are no solution either. Some sort of compromise between traditional teaching and individualised learning is probably a better basis on which to work.

Before these teaching strategies are considered, it would be useful to comment on learning difficulties in economics. Learning economics is not like, say, learning a language. With a language, there must be a thorough understanding of what has gone before, before the learner can pass on to the next stage. In economics, different topics can be taught in isolation. Material on the firm can be taught without the pupils having a prior knowledge of national income or the balance of payments. Of course, pupils will probably have a better chance of tackling a new topic if they have successfully mastered previous ones. Also certain words and concepts will keep on cropping up. On the whole though, all pupils will tend to start each new topic with the same amount of economic ignorance, particularly the nearer it is to the start of the course.

What then are the difficulties which must be overcome in mixed ability teaching so far as economics is concerned? There will be large differences between pupils in motivation; powers of concentration; behaviour; background knowledge; mathematical competence; reading skills; the ability to communicate in a written form; the ability to communicate orally; the ability to grasp concepts; powers of analysis; and being able to form reasoned judgements. Many of these are linked or overlap. For instance, a child unable to concentrate will often be a child with behaviour problems. The above list will now be used to suggest ways of overcoming teaching problems in the mixed ability classroom.

1 *Firm fair discipline in a good working environment* – a prerequisite of all successful teaching. An excellent

book on this, and other practical aspects of teaching, is Michael Marland's *The Craft of the Classroom*.[2]

2 *A wide variety of teaching techniques*. Even adults find it difficult to concentrate for very long. Providing a variety of activities will help increase concentration and be more interesting for the pupil than teaching through one medium, hence increasing motivation. The learner is also exposed in a critical situation to a wide variety of media, some of which like television will be an important source of information for him later on. Pupils who are not very competent in some skills may shine where other skills are required.

3 *Resources geared to the ability of the learner*. This is crucial for all the points mentioned above. Pupils who find the work too difficult will lose motivation and concentration and of course will probably learn very little. Some types of resources – like films and video tapes – have often been designed to cater for a fairly wide range of ability. In others – like discussion work and simulations – the medium automatically adjusts itself to the level of ability of the participants. This is unfortunately not true of the 3 R's – what most people have been conditioned to think of as the real work to be done. So far as written material is concerned there is no easy solution. Low ability children cannot be given 'O' level textbooks. Ideally, written material at different levels should be available. Using several textbooks poses its own problems – no two textbooks cover the same material exactly the same way for instance. Moreover, there is no textbook for the bottom 20 per cent of the ability range. It is very time-consuming for the teacher to write his own material but well worth the effort if done successfully. Writing in simple language, but covering all the ground, it is possible to produce material which can be understood by all pupils except those with severe reading difficulties. The disadvantages are that the poorer pupils are put off by the volume of words and the brighter pupils are not taxed enough linguistically. These are not particularly important disadvantages however. The best solution would be to write the same material at several levels. This is even more time-consuming and expensive, but supplemented with a ricoh-synchrofax tape is the ideal solution. When writing material it is a good idea to get the English department in the school to check it over for ability level. They can see difficult words and sentence constructions which the specialist economist may miss. The maths department can also advise on presentation of graphs and statistics, and how to tackle any elementary maths that may be needed in economics.

4 *Interaction between pupils of all levels of ability*. One of the main claims of mixed ability teaching is that it raises the standards of the lower ability children. It does this partly by producing a better working atmosphere where children are not labelled failures. It also does it because of the interaction between bright pupils

and slower learners. Pupils can learn from each other. In mixed ability classes, subgroups – for discussions or simulation games for instance – should also be mixed ability. To get this, the teacher will have to do a little directing of pupils, but it is well worth the resulting moans of the pupils in terms of the output of each group.

5 *Allowing pupils to progress at different speeds*. It is often said that in mixed ability classes, the bright pupils finish the work first and are held back by the slower learners. Although this might be true of certain subjects, it is often not the case in economics, particularly where the answer cannot be answered 'mechanically'. Give an exercise working out the hire purchase price of an article and the bright will finish before the slow; but ask an evaluative question like 'Is it better to borrow to buy a good rather than save up for it?', and the slow will usually finish before the bright. This does not mean to say that the question is a bad one to ask in the situation. 'What causes inflation?' is as good a question to ask at CSE as at university level. In preparing lessons, the teacher should try to foresee the rates at which different groups are going to work and have ready extra material for those that finish quickly. However, homework can be a particularly difficult problem with mixed ability classes. The pupils think it grossly unfair if some get more homework than others. Yet, as argued above, it is often not necessary to set the bright extra homework in economics because their answers will be far better and often have taken a longer time to prepare than those of the less able. However, as in any class, the teacher needs to ensure that he is extending all the pupils to their maximum ability and extra work for the very bright or a different type of homework for the really less able might be called for.

One thorny problem, often overlooked in the literature on mixed ability teaching, is that of classroom assessment. Pupils have to be assessed, but the teacher does not want in the process to nullify the achievement of the less able because they are compared with the bright. Nor does he want the very bright to sit back and relax because they can see that they are so much better than the rest. Comparing pupil with pupil is sometimes necessary – as in a formal exam for instance. But in normal classroom work, it can be invidious in its effects. The only feasible solution is surely to assess the pupil's actual performance against his potential performance, to assess effort rather than ability. Whatever scheme is chosen, the pupils must be kept informed of their progress, otherwise a vital point of the rationale of assessment disappears. The simple system of having an A to E marking scale where C represents average effort is sufficient, provided the teacher undertakes some readjustments of conditioned reflexes and no longer always gives the brighter pupils B's or A's and the less able C's or D's.

External examinations can present very difficult problems. If the CSE examination is very different in content to that of the 'O' level then it can be argued that mixed ability teaching is impossible without some sort of individualised learning system – the merits and problems of which have been discussed above. A far easier solution is to use a CSE which closely parallels the 'O' level, preferably not only in content but also in assessment. AEB's 'Understanding Industrial Society' 'O' level is matched with a CSE for instance. Writing a Mode III syllabus is another alternative if there are no Mode I or II's suitable (see Chapters 6 and 53). Until a common 16+ examination is introduced, this is really the best solution to the problem.

References

1 Morrison, A., and McIntyre, D., *Teachers and Teaching*, second edition, (Penguin, 1973).
2 Marland, M., *The Craft of the Classroom*, (Heinemann Educational, 1975).

4 The Use of Worksheets and Self-instructional Material

A. G. Anderton

In many circles, teacher-produced worksheets have become a panacea, in others, a symbol of all that is bad in teaching. The truth probably lies somewhere between these two extremes. Teacher-produced material won't solve discipline problems, won't initially be received with any more enthusiasm by pupils than a normal textbook, and won't necessarily be any better than bought material. However there are very important advantages which can be claimed for worksheets:

1 Material can be tailored to suit the needs of the individual situation. Local interests can be catered for. It can be prepared with specific teaching groups in mind. The mixed ability class can be more easily dealt with.
2 It is far less expensive to produce than to buy material. It is also more flexible in that course sections can be added whenever necessary, and parts can be updated without having to throw the whole away. If worksheets are lost by pupils, the cost is minimal – certainly not the case with textbooks.
3 There might be no suitable commercially available material. This is especially true with experimental courses or many Mode IIIs.

There are however important disadvantages with worksheets:

1 However good the reprographic facilities, the best teacher-produced material can never be as good in terms of quality of reproduction as the best books available. It is possible to obtain colour, for instance, on worksheets produced with ink machines, but the process is so laborious and expensive that it is very rarely used. Modern textbooks are making very important strides in the quality of their presentation.
2 Producing worksheets is yet another burden on teachers' time. Worksheets which are worth producing do take a great deal of time to prepare.

The teacher in his or her own situation must make a choice, then, as to what to produce. Often, textbooks will be used in conjunction with worksheets in the overall scheme of materials to be used. Teacher-produced worksheets can be used in a wide variety of ways:

1 As a text, as a substitute for part of a book.

2 As a short passage for use in discussion, comprehension or as an example. It might be a piece of continuous prose, or a set of figures, or purely visual material. Case studies would be included here.
3 As a set of questions and exercises, to be used in conjunction with other material.
4 As a set of instructions or explanations for a task to be performed. Instructions for field work or games are examples.
5 As a guide to other resources available and where to find them.
6 As an individualised learning text, which would presumably contain elements of all the other five points mentioned above. Programmed learning is one way of approaching this.

The *use* of worksheets, though, is for many teachers the least troublesome aspect. Handling resources should be second nature to the teacher. A need arises where commercially produced material is unsuitable or unavailable. A worksheet can fill the gap. Defining the need is simple but producing a worksheet to meet it is far from easy. The following procedure, as summarised in Figure 4.1, might help in the production of worksheets.

The first step is to decide for whom the material is to be provided. The ability of the group being aimed at is crucial. If the material is for sixth form use, for example, the language and presentation can be quite sophisticated. If it is for low ability fourth and fifth years, then the language should be as simple as possible. Most worksheets assume far too great a competence on the part of students below sixth form level. When writing for less able children, try to keep sentences short with few subordinate clauses. Technical terms and long words should be explained.

The next step is to decide on the purpose of the worksheet. Jot down key concepts or ideas. Formulate a set of objectives for the sheet. Think also of the context in which it is going to be used and other resources available which will be used in conjunction. This will lead on to thinking about the type of format to be used – a set of questions or a test perhaps. The format will also be constrained by the reprographic facilities available. A worksheet based on visual material will be difficult if not impossible without a stencil cutter or offset litho equipment. Then go ahead collecting or writing the material. Whilst doing this,

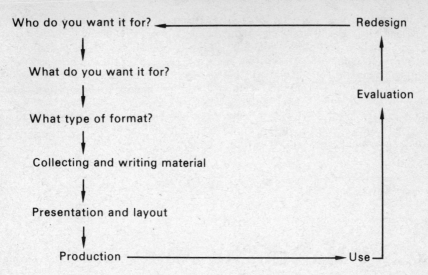

Figure 4.1 Procedure for producing worksheets

remember to bear in mind the ability range of the pupils. Pitching the work at the right level is probably the most crucial factor in the fate of a worksheet. Always take great care with presentation and lay out of material. It is very important that the text should be legible. Pupils who have to decipher words are only being presented with additional difficulties in the learning process. Care should be taken with drawings and diagrams. Typed material is preferable unless the handwriting is excellent. Photographs should have plenty of contrast. Experience is the key to success; learning what the reprographic machines available to you will and will not do. Everything is now ready for production. Once used, the material should be evaluated. It can then be redesigned when the need arises. In most cases, the worksheet will be capable of improvement, however experienced the teacher. Fortunately, it takes little time to do this if the basic structure is sound.

Different types of machine will restrict what can be produced. Many schools now have three different types of equipment: banda machines, ink Roneo or Gestetner machines and offset litho. Photocopying, although giving a good finish, is far too expensive for more than a few copies at a time.

The humble banda is still much used in schools for very good reasons. It can be produced quickly – writing or drawing on to a banda master sheet superimposed on to a banda wax colour sheet. Banda machines are fairly simple to operate. Variety can be obtained by drawing on different coloured sheets – a simple way of improving the quality of material often ignored by teachers. The main disadvantages are that only about 100 to 150 copies can be obtained from one master, and the paper can only be printed on one side. If other means of reproduction are available, the banda is useful for work wanted in a hurry and for short items.

Reproduction on Roneo or Gestetner machines is done through a cut stencil or skin, ink being pushed through the cuts on to the paper. It is possible to write or draw straight on to a skin by using a plastic (or similar) sheet between the two layers of the stencil. Special pencils are available although most people use ordinary biros and pencils. The skin is delicate and can easily tear. For this reason, the banda is preferable if the teacher wants to write directly. Most skins in fact are used for printing. Typing straight on to a skin should be done with a typewriter whose keys are clean, preferably an electric typewriter. The cleaner the cut, the better the quality of reproduction. Mistakes can be rectified by using a special correcting fluid. To reproduce photographs or pictures, use an electronic stencil cutting machine. This is invaluable. Don't expect miracles, but good well-contrasted material will be well produced. The original copy is placed into the machine and a stencil is cut from that. The stencil is then used to reproduce material in the ordinary way. Text can be interspersed with pictures by typing the text on to paper and putting the pictures where desired. Many schools now have ancillary typing staff who will do the required typing, also staff for reproducing the material – a great help to teachers.

Offset litho equipment is a luxury. Its only real advantage over ink duplicating machines is the quality of reproduction, especially of the printed word. Paper or metal plates are used instead of stencils, a photocopier instead of a stencil cutter. The type of material which can be presented is no different to an ink machine with stencil cutter, and is prepared in the same way.

One problem which every producer of material must face is that of copyright. Most schools break copyright laws in one way or another. Publishers would be unlikely to prosecute even if they discovered that a school was pirating material. Ultimately at the moment, the question rests on the morals of the teacher. Certainly copying material which is printed on single sheets (like some sets of case studies) is being unfair on publisher and author. Reproducing magazine or newspaper articles is a minor infringement in comparison. Reproducing large parts of textbooks is, fortunately for the publishers, time-consuming and probably as expensive as buying the textbooks themselves.

As has been mentioned before, worksheets are time consuming to prepare. However, they can add a new dimension, making for more effective teaching. This is being increasingly recognised as schools acquire more and more sophisticated reprographic hardware. It is unfortunate that in many schools these resources are underused.

5   Resource Material for Multi-Ability Use

John Tulk

The preparation of teaching resource material can throw an enormous work load upon the teacher, especially when the resource material is intended for mixed ability use. Indeed, the Nuffield Resources for Learning Project discovered that it took one teacher/editor/writer up to twenty-two hours to produce one hour of independent learning materials for pupils![1]

Thus even the most experienced economics teacher can be expected to recognise the need for the efficient use of teaching resources. Ideally, the basic teaching resource would have the following characteristics:

1 Be capable of multi-ability, multi-age, inter-disciplinary use.
2 Be economically viable in an educational context – in 1974–5, for example, it has been estimated that the average secondary school had only 1p a lesson to spend on books, materials and equipment for each pupil.[2]
3 Allow a degree of control over pupils' work efforts and motivation.
4 Be flexible in use, in a variety of classroom situations.
5 Be up-to-date, and capable of being easily and inexpensively updated.
6 Be 'starter' or 'stimulus' material rather than be curriculum prescriptive – the individual teacher should be able to develop the topic in his/her own way, as opposed to having to conform to a laid-down, rigid pattern.
7 Be of presentable quality.

Chapter 4 outlines one possible approach by demonstrating how teachers can produce their own worksheets, and how these can form a flexible, inexpensive and easily updated form of resource material. Equally, it points out that worksheets can be time-consuming to prepare and produce.

It could be of great advantage to the economics teacher (granted the limitations of finance and preparation time) to attempt to produce *structured worksheets* – i.e. worksheets structured not only in terms of content, but also in terms of classroom utilisation, with each worksheet providing the basis around which a lesson can be structured. A structured worksheet should be designed so that it may be used in a variety of ways in the classroom, and with a variety of different classes, and it should exercise as high a degree of control over the pupils' work efforts as the teacher judges to be necessary.

Economics teachers will already be familiar with the difficulties in presenting a topic in condensed form, without over-simplifying and misrepresenting the subject. This already difficult problem is exacerbated when attempting to produce worksheets for multi-ability use.

It is hoped that the following example of a structured worksheet, together with the accompanying compilation principles and classroom utilisation explanations, will prove of interest and relevance to economics teachers in secondary schools. The topic chosen is that of inflation, which the economics teacher may wish to teach to a number of classes of differing levels of age and ability. These may, for example, range through a sixth form GCE economics class, a fifth form mixed ability social studies class, and a fourth form money management class of less able pupils.

The structured worksheet on inflation is designed to form the basic resource material for all three lessons. Readers are, however, asked to note the following points about the worksheet illustrated.

1 The worksheet is *not* presented as a standard of excellence of content; it represents just one of many hundreds of actual business studies/social studies worksheets produced during the last few years for use in a comprehensive school in a socially deprived area. It has been selected because: (a) it illustrates well the *principles* upon which such structured worksheets are compiled; (b) it was one of the few worksheets reproduced initially on offset litho, and therefore reproduces better for illustration purposes in this book.

2 The worksheet now illustrates the adage 'Today's fact is tomorrow's misinformation', since the content is now in need of updating.

3 Original cartoons, illustrations, headlines, print material, etc. were cut out from newspapers and magazines – refer to the observations on copyright in Chapter 4.

There exists at least one textbook of interest to economics teachers which does expressly permit teachers to duplicate class handout material from its contents. This is Shafto, T. A. C., *Study Notes on Commerce*, (McGraw-Hill, 1973).

Figure 5.1 The structured worksheet

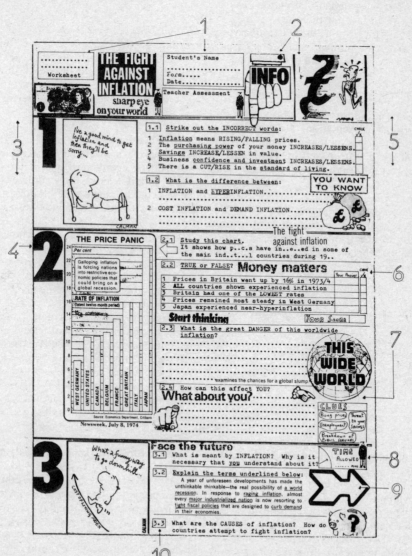

The Structured Worksheet – Compilation Principles

The reprographic production process follows that already outlined in detail in Chapter 4 – make up master draft (type, or write/draw with a technical drawing pen on good quality typing paper, paste in any desired newspaper or magazine cuttings with Cow Gum), and then process (photocopying, electronic scanning) to obtain spirit, ink, or offset litho masters for mass duplication.

The following points are explanations of the arrowed numbers on the illustrated structured worksheet (Figure 5.1):

1 Starter Boxes

'Name, Form, Date' – immediate, attention-ensuring task for pupils.

'. . . . . . Worksheet' – for possible interdisciplinary use.

'Teacher Assessment' – motivational spur, pupils reminded of work standards expected.

2 Media Techniques

Headlines, slogans and illustrations; adds variety and liveliness to visual presentation of information; designed to attract pupils' attention, and motivate further attention and good work effort. Care must be taken, however, that this is not done at the expense of clarity.

3 Programmed Learning Techniques

Although the aim is not to produce a programmed worksheet, many of the techniques of programmed learning can be beneficially incorporated into the worksheet. Examples are:

Breakdown of subject content into small, logically arranged steps;

Immediate feedback of results from objective questioning;

Cues to aid correct responses;

Repetition of subject matter at varying stages of complexity.

All this can contribute a *self-learning element* to the worksheet.

4 Clear Numbering

Clear numbering of sections, sub-sections and questions is vital for effective use of the worksheet in classroom conditions.

5 Response-orientated

Continuous pupil participation is called for by a variety of question techniques; the pupil is required to give written (or verbal if so desired) responses at every stage of the presentation of the subject matter.

Thus, information is effectively and efficiently conveyed to the pupil, who is required to assimilate, analyse and respond in some way; this can be contrasted to the merely passive process of copying dictated or blackboard-presented information.

6 Objective Questions

These often prove popular with pupils; since self-marking is possible, they can provide immediate feedback of results.

7 Self experience and Interests

Attempts can be made to relate the subject content to the real world experience of the pupils. Pupils' own analyses and opinions can also be called for, and class surveys can sometimes be incorporated into the worksheets.

8 Time Box

Adding a time element to pupils' answers allows for flexibility in the teaching approach. It can provide pupils with a guide to the depth of answer required, sometimes add a sense of urgency, and can also be a factor for the teacher to consider in his/her marking assessment.

9 Effective Paper Usage

By requiring answers to be written on the back of worksheets, economical use of paper stocks can be made, and, if desired, the complete lesson can be self-contained on a single sheet. Additional file paper can easily be attached for lengthy answers.

10 Open-ended, Structured Questions Section

The final section on each structured worksheet is always 'open-ended' – i.e. it requires the pupil to respond *individually and unaided*, according to the best of his/her abilities, in the time allowed, on the subject content of the worksheet.

Moreover, a form of 'structured questioning' technique is employed; the questions are presented in descending order of difficulty. Thus less able pupils may, within the time limits set by the teacher, only prove capable of writing a few lines in answer to the first question; the more able pupils may prove capable of writing much more detailed answers, and progressing to the more difficult questions.

The Structured Worksheet – Classroom Utilisation

As already outlined, the aim of producing a structured worksheet is for the teacher to have available basic core print material, which may be used with a number of different teaching groups. This does, however, necessarily imply that the classroom teacher uses his/her professional expertise to assess the particular learning requirements of each group, and accordingly *controls and varies the presentation of the structured worksheet to each teaching group.*

In secondary schools today, two broad general teaching approaches may be delineated. First, it is common for pupils to be taught on a *unified group basis* – i.e. where the whole class is kept in 'lockstep', covering the same ground at the same pace. Secondly, and more rarely employed, pupils may be taught on an *individualised learning basis* – i.e. where pupils are allowed to progress at their own rate on suitable learning materials, seeking individual assistance from the teacher when required. Indeed, some commentators point out that a commitment to mixed ability teaching necessarily implies a commitment to individualised and personalised learning. (See Chapters 3 and 22 on individualised learning.)

Structured worksheets can, with the necessary teacher control and variation, be profitably used in both these teaching approaches. With the unified group approach, the structured worksheet still caters for individual effort in the final, open-ended and structured question section, while with the individualised learning approach, the self-learning elements on the structured worksheet make it suitable for inclusion in the teaching resources.

Some examples of the practical classroom utilisation of structured worksheets are given in Table 5.1. The list is far from exhaustive, containing just a few obvious suggestions for use with different types of ability groups.

Structured worksheets may also be used profitably by the teacher:

for revision and test purposes;
as a 'catch-up' programme for pupils who have been absent;
as 'emergency' work material for pupils if their regular teacher is absent;
to provide an efficient system of immediate marking and feedback of results to pupils.

Ablest Ability Teaching Groups
These pupils may be expected to work quickly through the structured worksheets, and to produce detailed and reasoned answers. Possible teaching approaches using the worksheets include:

1 Starter technique – issue worksheet, pupils attempt independently, teacher check through with class, teacher follow-up on topic.
2 Test technique – teacher gives independent lesson on topic, then issues worksheet in final part of lesson as test/follow-up work.
3 Lockstep technique – issue worksheet, work through with class, section by section, teacher elaboration and addition at all points.

Average Ability Teaching Groups
Any combination of the approaches mentioned above and below, according to teacher's judgement of the learning situation needs.

Least Able Ability Teaching Groups
These pupils may be expected to find the structured worksheets difficult and confusing, and will require teacher guidance and assistance throughout. One approach (in detail):

Issue worksheet, work through with class, section by section.
Any part judged inappropriate can be missed out.
Try by verbal question and answer technique to elicit answers from pupils, write correct answers on blackboard. Encourage pupils to attempt simple, objective-style questions unaided.
Finally, pupils make independent attempts at final section open-ended, structured questions, even though in very many cases only a few lines may be written in answer to the first, easier questions.

Mixed Ability Teaching Groups
These groups may be expected to contain a random selection of the ablest, average, and least able pupils, and thus present the teacher with special problems. Two possible presentation techniques are:

1 Staple several associated structured worksheets together to create a self-learning booklet. After brief introduction, issue to pupils for completion, together with any other aids, e.g. textbooks, leaflets, etc. Pupils may, if teacher desires, be allowed to work in pairs, or small groups. Teacher circulates among pupils, giving individual help and assistance when necessary.
2 Issue structured worksheet to pupils, after brief introduction. Work through at uni-pace, section by section, with class, keeping all pupils in 'lockstep' as a single teaching entity at this stage. Pupils attempt final, open-ended structured questions section on a common, set time basis; this should (for example) enable the ablest pupils to produce in-depth, detailed answers, while the least able pupils should be capable of producing limited answers more slowly in the time set.

Table 5.1 Examples of the practical classroom utilisation of structured worksheets

The *recording of information* is a necessary educational (and social) skill today, yet secondary school pupils receive comparatively little help or guidance in information processing.

To this end, the economics teacher may find it of benefit to prepare a number of *standardised forms* for use by pupils. These are duplicated forms which can be used with all classes, in a variety of subject settings, according to the particular learning requirement. Teachers can design their own standardised forms in accordance with their own individual needs and ideas. They can be produced in the same way as worksheets, but in large quantities – economies of scale apply on longer duplicating runs!

Some examples of standardised forms, used in a large comprehensive school in a variety of different economics, business and social studies lessons, and with classes of varied ages and abilities, are illustrated here, with a brief explanation of their purpose.

The frontsheet (Figure 5.2) is designed to provide a master record sheet for any particular topic. Pupils record details of all work done on the frontsheet,

Figure 5.2 A frontsheet

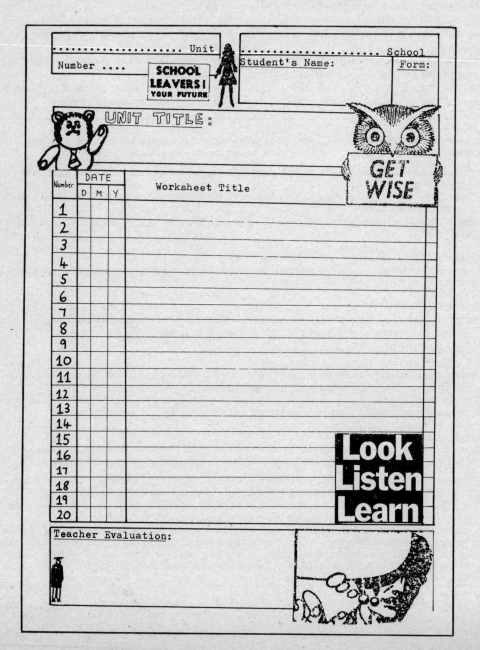

behind which they assemble and staple relevant sheets.

Additional information – e.g. pupils' own notes, revision work, updated information, leaflets, newspaper cuttings, etc. – can be added on at any time. Pupils thus compile a number of *topic units*, which can be kept in a wallet file.

This topic unit approach can be particularly useful when course work assessment is used, as in some Mode III examinations. It is also particularly applicable to subjects like economics, commerce and business studies, where much updating of information and new developments occur during the period of the course. *The checktest* (Figure 5.3) is designed to be used with textbooks, booklets, leaflets, teaching kit materials, etc. Pupils find out answers themselves, using the firm guidelines provided by the teacher.

Figure 5.3 A checklist

The audio-visual aids form (Figure 5.4) is designed to provide a pupil's written record of any audio-visual aids demonstration used. Note the feedback section for pupils' own opinions, to aid the teacher in his/her assessment of the effectiveness of the particular audio-visual aid used.

Figure 5.4 An audio-visual aids form

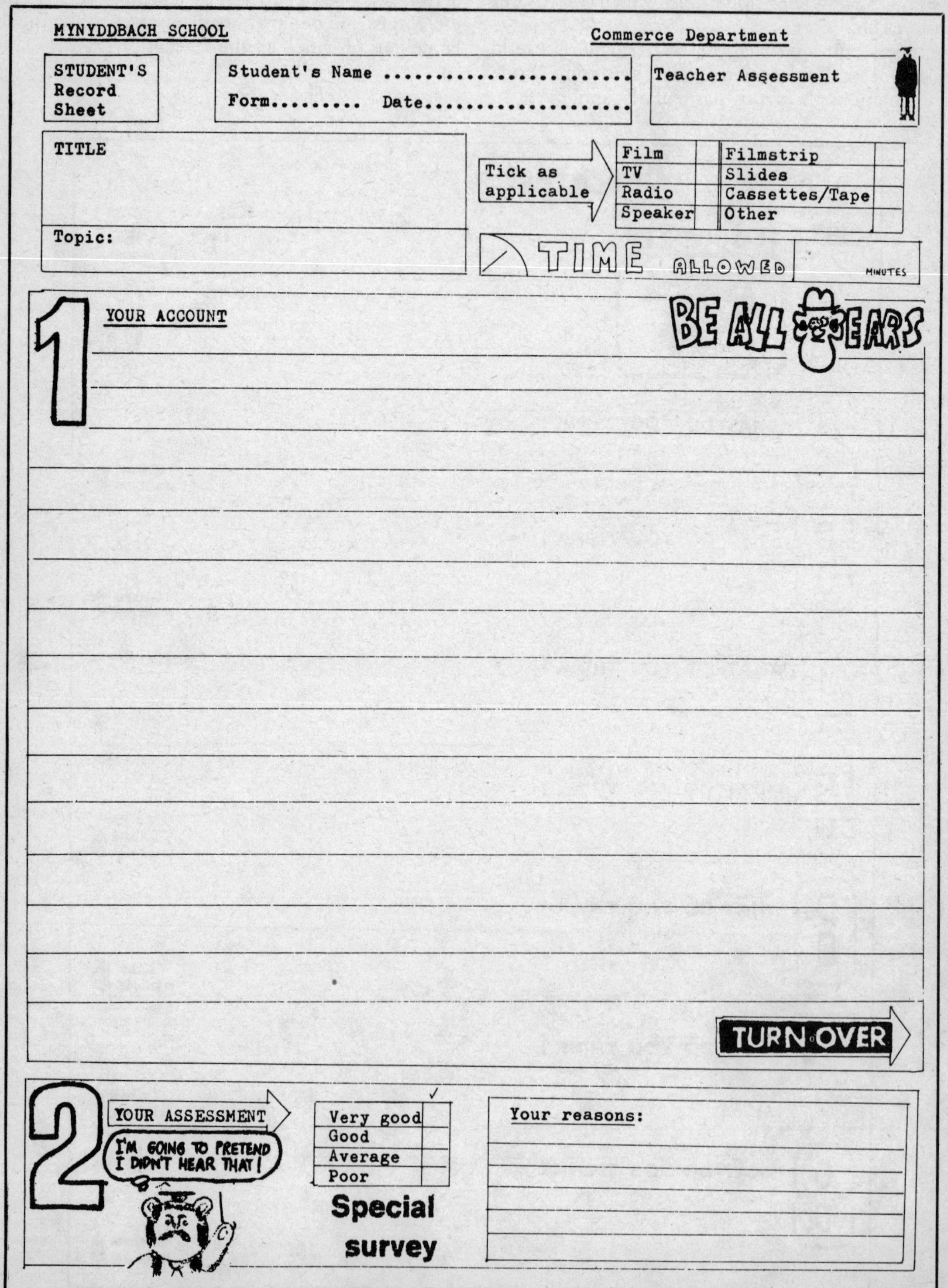

MYNYDDBACH SCHOOL

Commerce Department

STUDENT'S Record Sheet

Student's Name ....

Form......... Date...................

Teacher Assessment

TITLE

Topic:

Tick as applicable

Film		Filmstrip	
TV		Slides	
Radio		Cassettes/Tape	
Speaker		Other	

TIME ALLOWED MINUTES

1 YOUR ACCOUNT

BE ALL EARS

TURN OVER

2 YOUR ASSESSMENT

I'M GOING TO PRETEND I DIDN'T HEAR THAT!

	✓
Very good	
Good	
Average	
Poor	

Special survey

Your reasons:

The essay form (Figure 5.5) is designed for straight-forward essay work. It is intended to provide clear instructions and assistance to pupils, and to facilitate the marking procedure for teachers.

Figure 5.5 An essay form

The visits form (Figure 5.6) is designed for use whenever outside visits are organised by the teacher, and in particular is intended to:

1 Convey visit details and instructions to pupils.

2 Provide pupils' written accounts of the visit.
3 Aid teacher in assessing effectiveness of visit (final feedback section).

Figure 5.6 A visits form

MYNYDDBACH SCHOOL

VISIT ASSESSMENT RECORD

COMMERCE DEPARTMENT

Student's Name........................
Form.................................

VISIT DETAILS 
Organisation...
Organisation Representative..................................
Address...

DATE........................... TIME.......................
MEETING PLACE...
Direction Instructions......................................
....
....
....
Accompanying Staff..

INFO

GET WISE

YOUR ACCOUNT OF THE VISIT

YOU You
Instant report

Continue over (if necessary)⇨

BACK TO YOU
Assessment of visit – did you like or dislike it, find it interesting or uninteresting, etc.

What you say about what we do.

Conclusion

Structured worksheets and standardised forms represent just one attempt made to meet a basic resource need of teachers today – that of the provision of consumable, print handout material of presentable quality, which may be used flexibly by the teacher in the classroom. Moreover, the provision of such core print material can be provided at little, or no, additional financial cost – the production cost of an individual worksheet can be as low as ½p per sheet, and a complete year's course of print material can thus cost less than 40p per pupil; and against this can be offset the saving in exercise book costs![3]

It is noteworthy that some current trends mean that the teacher is becoming increasingly able to produce his/her own print material. These include:

1 Improvements in reprographics technology – typewriters, photocopiers, duplicating processes. For example, a teacher having access to an IBM Selectric 82 typewriter and offset litho duplicating equipment can quickly produce print material comparable in quality to that of commercial printing, yet still at extremely low cost.
2 Improved access to reprographic facilities – the growth of school resources centres (often with ancillary staff), teachers' centres, LEA area resources centres. Additionally, the economics teacher may have more immediate access to reprographic facilities within the business studies department in the school.

The hard-pressed classroom teacher is entitled to look for greater assistance in the onerous, time-consuming and unending task of creating such print material from the various curriculum development and educational research projects, LEA advisory staff services, and in-service training courses. Often, efforts and resources appear to be directed towards theoretical discussion, or dominated by what has been termed the 'Concorde mentality' – i.e. investment in sophisticated and expensive equipment that is of limited use!

Yet, it is indisputable that in schools today one of the most inexpensive, flexible, and educationally beneficial forms of resource material remains the duplicated, printed page. It may well be that this simple and obvious fact merits greater recognition and prescription for priority action.

References

1 Taylor, L. C., *Resources for Learning*, (Penguin Education, second edition, 1972) p 237.
2 Marland, M. & Leslie, I., 'A Penny For All Their Thoughts', *Times Educational Supplement*, 26 March 1976.
3 Cost analysis (1977 LEA consortium prices): one thermal stencil, 8p; 500 sheets A4 duplicating paper, 82p; miscellaneous (ink, wastage, etc.), 10p.

6   Development of a Mode III Basic Economics Scheme – A Case Study

Linda M. Thomas

Background

In September 1971, a South Wales grammar school with a substantial and long standing reputation for scholarship was reorganised and became a 13–18 comprehensive high school. Previously, it drew its pupils from among 11+ successes throughout the whole of the city. To facilitate reorganisation during 1971–72 the previous first form grammar school entry was allowed to continue into the second form. The new entry for 1971 consisted of three third forms, three fourth forms and one fifth form from the secondary modern schools. These were grafted on to the existing four grammar school streams, at each year. However appropriate the traditional curricular framework had been in the context of a grammar school, (see Hirst[1] for a light-hearted but devastating denunciation of much of what was taught), it proved to be less effective in a comprehensive school environment. Some members of staff were impelled to reconsider their approach.

The original scheme was designed for the fourth year intake of seventy pupils, divided into three streams. With very few exceptions these pupils lived in the school's new catchment area in one of the oldest working class areas of the city. There can be little doubt that the pupils' attitudes to school were, at best, utilitarian or apathetic, and, at worst, implied complete rejection of the educational system. This assertion was manifested in the high rate of truancy and absenteeism, in the behaviour and demeanour of the pupils, and in their hostility, which was expressed verbally and physically.

Philosophy

The two members of staff who were mainly concerned with the development and implementation of the scheme were influenced in their planning by three factors.

First, they were impressed by the conclusions expressed in the Newsom report[2], by Schools Council Working Paper No. 2[3], and the Schools Council's Enquiry I[4]. These suggested that the curriculum for less able pupils or for pupils who leave school as soon as possible, should be practical, realistic, and vocational; that it should be a preparation for adult life; and that subjects should, when possible, be linked to pupils' lives outside school so that they could see the value of what was learnt.

On the other hand they were aware of the dangers of this approach. As economics specialists, they were concerned to safeguard the integrity of the subject and were on their guard against the danger of trivialising the material. Oakeshott[5] argues that learning is not equivalent to obtaining a firmer grasp of the familiar, the recognised and the relevant, but a means of initiation into the different and unfamiliar inheritance of understanding and sentiments. Education is offering a release from the immediate, circumscribed nature of the pupil's world, rather than concentrating on reproducing that world, and on providing information already within the pupil's reach. The pupil must be given the opportunity to understand himself in new contexts so as to acquire a more ample identity, rather than to be provoked to see himself more clearly in the mirror of his current world. Education is a means of release from the 'facts of life' and a commitment to involvement in the 'quality of life'. Therefore, while they were aware of the need for relevance, the two teachers were also concerned with the development of rationality. Hirst[6] argues that to have a rational mind is to imply experience structured under some form of conceptual schemes. These schemes, the forms or disciplines of knowledge, are the basic articulations

whereby the whole of experience becomes intelligible to man. This does not mean that it is necessary to protect the logical structures of traditional school subjects or to follow them slavishly. What it implies is that teachers must place more emphasis on building coherent structures, on analysing and attempting to communicate the basic structure and meaning of the discipline. The development of rationality then becomes dependent on cognition of or mastery of conceptual structures.

Lastly, the two teachers were impressed by Bruner's work. Bruner[7] argues that a curriculum must reflect not only the nature of the knowledge itself but also the nature of the knower and the knowledge getting process. He suggests that the concepts which form the structure of the intellectual disciplines should be brought into a relationship with the pupil's developing conceptualising ability. In his 'spiral' thesis, Bruner argues that progression means treating each concept at every stage but in a gradually more sophisticated form as information levels and levels of understanding advance. Rather than progression from simple to difficult concepts, Bruner advocates progression for all concepts from simple to more sophisticated contexts. In this way the integrity of the subject is safeguarded and learning is also related to the child's development.

The following outline of the course reflects these three areas of concern. The content attempts to be relevant; it is structured by means of a conceptual framework; and it is organised spirally. This is the scheme used as a teaching syllabus. (See Appendix I – Category B is a more sophisticated context than Category A.)

Assessment

In this particular case the originators of the course unhesitatingly decided to make the course an externally assessed one. They were convinced that assessment of work is a powerful motivational tool since it provides feedback and reinforcement. Furthermore, the external examination system, perhaps for irrational reasons, has achieved high status in the community, in further education, and with employers. In the situation described above, this was crucial. The decision immediately produced a considerable degree of expectation in teachers and higher levels of self-esteem in pupils. The absence of a CSE Mode I scheme in economics led to the development of a Mode III scheme. Incidentally, this added to the flexibility of the assessment procedure and enabled the teachers to design a package which was suited to the school's particular needs. It contained three sections: continuously assessed work, a project, and an end of course examination, internally set and marked. The three sections were externally moderated.

The examination syllabus, which was submitted to the board, gave the content on which assessment was to be based (see Appendix II). Another example of a submission to an examination board is included as Appendix III.

A more detailed check list, loosely based on Bloom's *Taxonomy of Educational Objectives,*[8] was prepared for use in the continuous assessment and project sections of the assessment procedure (see Appendix IV). Its purpose was to improve the objectivity of the procedures involved (see Chapter 52 of this Handbook). At the end of the course, course work and projects and examination papers were submitted to the moderator, together with the check list of objectives and the mark sheet (see Appendix V). Instructions for filling in the mark sheet were provided by the examination board. The term mark was obtained by averaging the marks obtained for each piece of course work mentioned in the check list of objectives.

Methods

The team of teachers who taught this course made use of a variety of teaching methods and resources. Since the course was firmly based in the real world, teachers used examples from the pupils' own experience to develop understanding of the conceptual scheme outlined in the teaching syllabus.

Use was made of worksheets for presenting necessary information, but these always required pupils to refer to leaflets, booklets, etc. A large resource collection was available which consisted of free handouts from many associations and institutions and of books ánd other material collected by the department.

Films, film strips, visits to outside organisations and visiting speakers were used where appropriate but these were not such an integral part of the course as in the Understanding Industrial Society Project's work (see Chapter 11). The disadvantage of using these particular materials or methods is that they are all fairly sophisticated contexts in which to work. Furthermore, they are usually topic orientated rather than concept orientated. They tend to present in the same package a whole range of concepts at varying degrees of difficulty. On the other hand these methods are an invaluable means of generating interest and of safeguarding the relevance of the course. Therefore care was taken to specify precisely the use to be made of each particular film or visit and to concentrate on that aspect.

Pupils were encouraged to prepare a number of short projects on topics which caught their interest. The teachers found that this technique helped to reduce the tendency to present beautifully prepared, highly polished pieces of work which were all copied from other sources.

References

1 Hirst, P. H., 'The Curriculum' in *Schools Council Paper 12*, (HMSO, 1967).
2 Newsom Report, *Half Our Future*, (HMSO, 1963).
3 Schools Council, *Working Paper 2: Raising the School Leaving Age*, (HMSO, 1965).
4 Schools Council, *Enquiry One*, (HMSO, 1968).
5 Oakeshott, M., 'Education: the Engagement and its Frustration' in R. F. Dearden, P. Hirst and R. S. Peters, *Education and the Development of Reason*, (Routledge and Kegan Paul, 1972).
6 Hirst, P. H., 'Liberal Education and the Nature of Knowledge' in R. F. Dearden, P. Hirst and R. S. Peters, *Education and the Development of Reason*, (Routledge and Kegan Paul, 1972).
7 Bruner, J. S., *The Process of Education*, (Harvard University Press, 1960).
8 Bloom, B. S. *et al.*, *Taxonomy of Educational Objectives*, (Longman, 1956).

Appendix I

I Scarcity

Wants; Resources; Efficiency
Opportunity Cost; Economic Conflict

A *Family wants depend on:* number of children; number of dependants; choices made.
Family wants: are culturally determined; differ in importance between individuals and groups; change and grow with time; are subject to diminishing marginal utility.
Resources: have alternative uses (e.g. time, money); are unevenly distributed (rich and poor families,

skilled and unskilled); may be less than sufficient to meet all wants. If wants exceed resources there is scarcity. If such scarce resources are used at maximum efficiency, greater satisfaction of one want implies less satisfaction of another want.

Thus families: budget; share; borrow; choose (involving opportunity cost). The existence of interpersonal opportunity cost leads to: economic conflict; conflict of interest.

B   The pattern of local wants illustrates the principle that wants differ in importance between individuals and groups. (Comparative study of farming, town, tourist communities in different seasons.)
Resources, especially raw materials, are not evenly distributed geographically.

II Specialisation

A   *Specialisation:*   exists in the family (e.g. role specialisation, job specialisation, hobbies); increases the need for skills and for capital; requires exchange; gives rise to interdependence.

B   *Specialisation:*   occurs regionally; results in urban societies; is used in almost all regions to increase production; requires exchange and money; increases the need for trade and transport; gives rise to interdependence.
Comparative case studies to illustrate: the use of money; the effect of strikes; structural changes; regional unemployment.
Regional specialisation gives rise to interdependence.

III Consumption; Exchange; Production

Wants; Resources; Goods; Services
Diminishing marginal returns

A   *Consumption:*   is the process of 'using up' goods and services to satisfy wants;
is largely organised within households;
results in economic activity (e.g. retail, wholesale trades, advertising, consumer 'protection', resale price maintenance).
Production: is the process of converting resources into a form suitable for the satisfaction of wants;
requires use of labour (who works where?) and enterprise (who organises?); occurs in the home where it is subject to diminishing marginal returns.
Goods are bundles of disembodied services which satisfy wants.
Production largely occurs within firms.
When specialisation and exchange are well developed, the producer of a good is unlikely to be its consumer.
All producers are consumers of some goods and services.
Not all consumers are producers.
Therefore exchange is necessary; for example, barter (reciprocal exchange), market (indirect exchange).
Money is required to facilitate market exchange; intervenes between production and consumption, especially in societies where specialisation and exchange are well developed.

B   *Producing:*   local illustrations of mass production; social costs in local industry; finance of small local firms – importance of insurance.
Comparative studies to illustrate barter *v.* money; banking.
The local authority is both producer and consumer of goods and services.
The national government is both producer and consumer of goods and services.

IV Exchange: Price

A *Market exchange:*
   Price: is the ratio of exchange of one good for another; depends on bargaining power, which is usually related to supply and demand.
   Redistributive exchange: is the collection by an authority followed by redistribution to appropriate members of society; results in prices policy, VAT; results in subsidies, for example, council house rents, agricultural subsidies; involves local transport systems, car parks, entertainment, baths.

V Aggregates

A *Families can spend only:* what they earn; unearned income; what they borrow.
   Money wages; real wages.
   Money income; cost of living; standard of living; inflation.
   Consumption is largely organised within households.
   Production is largely organised within firms.

B Local examples to illustrate the circular flow of goods and services (local shopkeepers).
   Comparative studies to illustrate differences in: regional employment; cost of living.

Appendix II: Syllabus for CSE Mode III Examinations in Basic Economics

1 Spending Money
(a) *Using money*
Money is productive only when used – spending or investing. Spending means choice; decisions should be based on fact, and on knowledge.
(b) *Advertising*
Influence of advertising; motives; advantages; disadvantages; methods of advertising; local and national.
(c) *Consumer protection*
Statutory protection; Consumers Association; British Standards Institute; the Design Centre; British Electrical Approvals Board.
(d) *Budgeting*
Wise choice implies the structuring of a scale of preferences so that essentials are given the right priority, semi-luxuries such as leisure-time activities and holidays are accounted for and luxuries are budgeted for.
(e) *Buying and shopping*
Some points to consider – loss leaders, quality/price relationships, packing/weight relationships, correctness of labelling and pricing, weight/value relationship, change fiddles, impulse buying.

2 Credit
(a) *Purchasing alternatives*
Cash – instant ownership without further commitment;
credit – means continuing legal commitments;

advantages of cash purchases; advantages of credit purchasing.
(b) *Signing an agreement*
Age-limit; references; points to note when signing.
(c) *Hire purchase*
Legislation; agreement; interest.
(d) *Credit sale*
Legislation; agreement.
(e) *Other forms of credit buying*
Credit drapers; cheque and voucher trading; credit clubs; credit cards; budget accounts; instalment salesmen.
(f) *Loans*
Bank loans and overdrafts; interest; money lenders and pawnbrokers.
(g) *Interest rates*
Comparison of interest rates with current examples.

3 Keeping Money
(a) *Savings banks*
Historical development, brief; services provided by the Trustee Savings Bank and the National Savings Bank.
(b) *Commercial banks*
Accounts; services.
(c) *National Giro*

4 Savings
(a) *Savings for the beginner*
Degree of risk involved; ease of withdrawal; convenience; return offered; accumulation.

(b) *National savings*
Savings banks; Premium Savings Bonds; National
Savings Certificates; British Savings Bonds;
Save-as-you-Earn; savings schemes.
(c) *Other forms of saving*
Banks; building societies; unit trusts; investment trust
companies; finance houses; endowment insurance;
stocks and shares and local authority bonds.
(d) *Indirect savings*
Co-operative dividends; trading stamps.

5 Money for the Future
(a) *Life assurance*
Premiums; return offered; endowment.
(b) *Other forms of insurance, e.g. fire, accident*
Principles of insurance.
(c) *National insurance*
Contributions; unemployment benefit; sickness
benefit; maternity grants; death grants; pensions;
family allowance; supplementary benefits; offices.

6 Money for Marriage
(a) *The importance of saving and planning*
(b) *Setting up a home*
(c) *Adding to the family*

7 Money for Housing

(a) *Buying a house*
Costs; finance; estate agents; buying older property.
(b) *Renting a house*
Agreements; legislation; furnished or unfurnished.
(c) *Shelter*

8 Everybody's Money
(a) *Development of a money using society*
Specialisation; barter; money-power and wealth;
industrialisation; more equal distribution of wealth;
dependence.
(b) *Income*
Earned income; unearned income; income from
property and investments.
(c) *Inflation*
(d) *Pooling money*
Before income becomes the individual's spending
money some is pooled to provide public amenities;
taxation; social security payments; rates.

9 Money and Responsibility
(a) *Responsibility of the community*
The budget – nationally and locally – safeguards.
(b) *Responsibility of the individual*
For dependants; to the community; to less wealthy
nations.
(c) *Self-indulgence*

Appendix III: A Mode III Economics Syllabus Used in a London School

Subject: Everyday Economics
Mode   :   III (for first examination in 1976)
Summary of Mark Allocation:

Written examination: Paper A	25%	
	Paper B	25%
Oral examination		15%
Course work		20%
Project		15%
		100%

EVERYDAY ECONOMICS MODE III SYLLABUS

Topic 1:   Personal Budgets

Calculation by each student of his own income and
expenditure, now, in five, and in ten years' time, i.e.
school age, adolescent, and adult patterns of
expenditure. Principle of remaining solvent and the
need for careful planning of budgets. Introduction to
the value of savings. (Treated in depth in Topic 3.)

Effect of inflation on future budgets. Bills to be met
as an adult.
A practical approach to the concept of opportunity
cost through the idea that expenditure on one good
necessitates the sacrifice of not buying an alternative.
The principle that the size of our incomes determines
the size of our share of national output of goods and
services.

Topic 2:   Major Budget Decisions

A   Buying a House or Renting
Comparison between the two; which is the better in
the short and the long term. Main advantages of
buying, e.g. inflation proof, a good investment.
Difficulty of finding houses and flats to rent, shortages
of space when family grows, no tax relief as on
mortgage interest.
Different types of mortgages, sources of mortgages
outlining advantages of each. Principle that the house
is security for the loan. House prices compared locally

and nationally. Practical introduction to demand and supply as forces behind prices.

B Car or Public Transport
Comparison of these alternatives and examination of financial costs.

Depreciation costs, HP, tax, etc – all the yearly costs of car ownership. Cost per week and mile. Different costs for different makes. Principle of fixed and variable costs revealed through the diminishing cost per mile the more miles travelled.

Costs per mile of bus, train, taxi and bicycle; loss of convenience and speed.

C Costs of Children
Concept of opportunity cost may be approached in this section. The loss of wife's income, cost of meeting child's needs. Higher tax allowances, maternity benefits and family allowance.

All of A, B and C to be fitted into case studies of representative families with and without cars, children or their own house.

Topic 3:   Money, Inflation and Savings

Money as a claim on resources. Value of money – goods and services it will buy. Why do we need money? – explained by reference to (a) early man without trade or specialisation, (b) growth of barter, (c) problems of barter, (d) appearance of money, (e) development to paper and bank deposit money.

Functions and characteristics of money.

Inflation. Value of money. The nature and symptoms of inflation, rising prices. A given amount of money buys less goods and services. Causes of inflation. Idea of real income.

Effect of inflation on:

(i) Personal savings;
(ii) The weak, those unable to ensure rise in disposable incomes equal to inflation;
(iii) Prices of houses and other goods in future decades;
(iv) How best to deal with inflation. Buy a house, re-adjust budgets, etc.

Savings. Reasons for saving, future purchases, e.g. house deposit, to buy large goods for cash at a discount, etc., holiday, for retirement, for security.

Different forms of saving, building societies, SAYE, shares, bank and Post Office accounts, insurance policies, pension funds. Income tax, interest, risk and liquidity aspects of each type of saving.

Topic 4:   Banking

Main emphasis on personal services of a bank with a simple sketch of banking structure. Functions of and differences between current and deposit accounts, loans and overdrafts. Procedure for borrowing.

Comparison of bank loans and hire purchase for large loans.

Simple description of standing orders, cheques, credit cards, paying-in slips.

Comparison of different commercial banks, opening hours, charges and services (including co-operative and trustee banks).

Simple outline of commercial bank's functions, Bank of England, the clearing house system.

Alternative provided by Post Office services mentioned but treated in depth in Topic 9.

Topic 5:   Insurance

Early history and development. Fire insurance linked to fire brigade, shipping insurance – misuse of.

Principles of insurance – compensation of unfortunate minority from premiums of majority. Reduces risks facing industry. Third Party insurance.

Types of insurance: motor, house, life, fire, theft, holiday, industrial. Advantages of each type.

Place of insurance companies in the economy. Largest investors in shares. Large foreign earnings. Lloyds.

Topic 6:   Unions and the Economy

What is a union? What are its functions? e.g. wage negotiations, preserving jobs, improving working conditions and fringe benefits (holidays, pensions, subsidised canteen).

Outline of current law on picketing, strikes, 'closed shops', union immunity from lawsuits for damages from industrial action.

Unions and inflation. Argument that union power is a cause of inflation. Argument that unions protect members from suffering from inflation by ensuring equal increases in disposable income. Impact of strikes on the economy.

Government incomes policies, reasons for, recent history of, under Labour and Conservative Governments.

Topic 7:   Foreign Trade and the Balance of Payments

Why Britain needs to trade, need for food and raw material imports, gains from cheap imports, advantages of specialisation.

A description of balance of trade (visible trade, the monthly figures, invisible trade), capital flows, overall balance of payments and the final result as revealed by changes in Britain's foreign currency reserves.

Significance of bad balance of payments figures. The measures the Government is forced to take. Higher interest rates, taxes, devaluation. Impact of these measures on investment and unemployment.

Topic 8:   Foreign and British Holidays

Comparison of foreign and British holidays and the

choices of travel and accommodation. Comparison of package tours, motoring, camping, train journeys, charter flights, channel crossings, etc. Costs of each compared including student, tourist or charter discounts.

Preparing for a foreign holiday, passports, and foreign exchange. All sources of foreign exchange compared for commission costs and convenience. Budgeting spending money, and saving to pay for holiday. Insurance for health, theft, car, etc.

The pound's exchange rate, the role of demand and supply in setting it, meaning and significance of phrase 'the pound is weak'.

Topic 9:   The Post Office

Savings accounts dealt with under 'inflation and savings'. Means of payment, postal order and Giro. Comparison of services to those of banks. Ordinary, registered and express mail. Telecommunication.

Economics of the Post Office. Labour costs in delivering a letter. Demand and supply and capacity aspects of off-peak reductions in telephone charges, and in two-tier letter charges.

Topic 10:   Retailing and Markets

Different types of retailers. Which are growing and why. What type of service does each offer. Position of shopping centres and market stalls in relation to population and transport routes. Practical comparison of prices for some goods in different outlets, especially the discount stores. Economics of these price differences. How to shop wisely, compare prices and price per ounce, etc., savings from comparing prices on large items. *Which?* magazine reports.

Competition and price control. Way in which retail profits are kept low by competition. History of resale price maintenance. Government legislation to improve consumer's position, Trade Descriptions Act, Trading Standards Departments, moves towards unit pricing and date stamping. Laws regarding 'sales' and fair use and guarantee of goods.

Topic 11:   Manufacturing

Small and large firms, structure and economics of each illustrated by visits to both. Economies of scale, division of labour, importance of good positioning of factory. Training schemes and promotion schemes. System of payments, flat wage or piece rates.

Management aims. To avoid bankruptcy, to make profits and expand. Role and importance of profits, arguments for and against profits.

Topic 12:   The Individual and the State

1 Taxation principles. Income, purchase, and value added tax – description and outline of difficulties and advantages of each.

2 Where tax money is spent. Aims of the unbalanced Government budget, to affect demand levels, employment, inflation and balance of payments.

3 Understanding and completing a tax form. Understanding the tax code and how to check it, which allowances can be claimed and how to keep tax liability to a minimum. Progressive rates of income tax.

4 Understanding your pay slip. Tax and National Insurance deductions. The principle of the National Health and Insurance system.

5 Licences, car, dog, marriage, television, local trading, etc.

6 Local rating system. Assessment of rates, evaluation of the system (and any proposed changes).

7 Any current laws or plans affecting individual finance.

Topic 13:   Worldwide Population, Energy, Food and Other Resources

Simple description of problems, rapid population growth in many backward economies, periodic setbacks to harvests causing shortages and famine, malnutrition. Difficulty of development with heavy population pressure.

Different Western situation. Decline in birth rates and most nations approaching population stability. Opportunity cost of having children increasing as we grow richer, but underdeveloped world remains in vicious cycle – poverty causing high population growth which perpetuates poverty.

Balanced study of energy and resources. Rich countries use far more per head than the poor. As Third World develops they try to buy resources and goods so prices rise. The price mechanism as way of ensuring we do not run out of energy and food. High price of oil reduces demand and should lead to massive substitution of alternatives. Higher food prices should encourage larger crops, development should increase Afro-Asian yields to Japanese and European levels. Immense problems of transition leading to temporary shortages, energy and food crisis in future.

Appendix IV

Assessment Scheme   **Course Work and Projects Basic Economics – Check List of Objectives**

Content	Knowledge	Comprehension	Application
Having Money	1 Definition of terms: money, spending; income, saving.	1 Income must be spent or saved: Y=C+S. 2 Appreciation of range of alternatives and of choices which are constantly being made. Choice depends on knowledge.	
Advertising	1 Forms of advertising. Formal knowledge of. 2 Functions of advertising: to persuade and inform.	1 Recognition of advertising gimmicks and the extent of advertising pressure. 2 Ability to recognise two elements of persuasion and information in contemporary advertising.	 3 Connection between: advertising and prices; employment; indoctrination; sales; personal behaviour; news media. Assess value of advertising.
Consumer Protection	Formal knowledge of: 1 1893, 1887–1953, 1955, 1961, 1963, 1968, Consumer Protection Acts. 2 Consumer Association; BSA; Kite Marks; Design Centre; Electricity Council. 3 Credit notes; Complaints procedures. 4 Guarantees.	1 Ability to recognise consumers' rights in practice with regard to sales, prices, offers for sale, contracts, agreements, descriptions, etc. 2 Meaning of value for money, *Which?* best buys. Why consumer bodies are necessary. 3 Where to go for help. 4 The American consumer protection scene.	1 Loopholes in the Acts. 2 *Which?* tests. 3 Analysis of usefulness of guarantee. 4 Future development in consumer protection.
Budgeting	1 Simple budgeting procedure. 2 Rules of wise budgeting: flexibility; knowledge of range of alternatives; planning.	1 Debit and credit. 2 Appreciation of existence of scale of preferences. Essentials and luxuries. Budgeting at different stages with different scales of preference: adolescence, young married family.	2 Survey of some common alternatives: DIY; opportunity cost; leisure – cost of holidays; car expenses. 3 Budgeting and the poor; budgeting and the well-off.
Buying and Shopping	1 Names of kinds of retail outlets: corner shop; supermarket; department store; chain store; multiple chain store; markets.		

Content	Knowledge	Comprehension	Application
		2 Principles of wise shopping: planning, knowledge, checking and complaining, relative prices, ratios of weight/value/price. Influence of displays and advertising by loss leaders.	2 Time *v.* money. Resale price maintenance; recommended prices; shopping around. 3 Deep freezers; convenience foods; exercise in opportunity cost analysis.
Credit	1 Definition of terms: credit, rates of interest.	1 Cash *v.* credit. Arguments for and against. Why interest is paid. Calculation of rates of interest, given certain information. Effect of time factor on interest. Concealed interest rates.	
	2 Means of obtaining credit.		2 Hire purchase. Comparison of current interest rates and sources of borrowing.
Keeping Money	1 Kinds of money.	1 Reasons for existence of banks: safety and convenience and services.	1 Comparison of services provided by TSB, commercial banks, National Savings Bank, Giro.
	2 Definition of terms: notes, coin, cheques. 3 Procedure for opening a bank account. Procedure for use of paying-in slip and cheque.	3 Crossed and uncrossed cheques; crossed and open cheques; advantages of use of cheques. Cost of current accounts *v.* benefits.	2 Travellers' cheques, credit cards, clearing system. 3 Credit transfer, standing order payments, budget accounts, overdrawn accounts.
	4 Simple accounting procedure.	4 Principle of a running balance.	
Saving	1 Definition of terms: saving.	1 Why save? – transactions, precautionary motives. Appreciation of difference between saving money and banking money (current account). Appreciation of connection between saving money and borrowing money (lending).	1 Trading stamps – saving without lending.
	2 Names and descriptions of main institutions and classification into national (government) and private institutions.	2 Importance of savings institutions as channels for small savings.	2 Stock Exchange – market for resale of securities. Comparison of main features of savings institutions. Investment – direct and indirect; bonds and shares.
		3 Principles of wise savings: safety, interest, value, services, simplicity, availability.	

Content	Knowledge	Comprehension	Application
Insurance	Four kinds of insurance. Definitions of terms: insurance, premiums, insurer, insured, underwriter, broker, insurance agent, policy.	Principles of insurance. Appreciation of role of insurance in business and for the individual. Actual procedure involved.	Life assurance, endowment policies.
National Insurance; Health	Contributions and benefits.	Appreciation of concept of welfare state as a safety net. Minimum acceptable standards.	Case studies of welfare state, loophole victims; junkies, very poor.
Money for Marriage	2 How to read pattern books, dimension charts (metric). How to read gas and electric metres. 3 Method of management of household finances. Statement of main items. Filing system. Bills: weekly, quarterly.	1 Revision of principles of saving, budgeting, consumer protection. 2 Shopping for furniture: prices, quality, special features. Kitchen design. 3 Structure of family budget and expenditure. Budget accounts⎫ revision. Joint accounts ⎭	1 Costing exercises on babies, weddings, setting up a home; application of principle of opportunity cost. 2 Gas electricity. Costing exercises and recognition of value judgements made. 3 Women's Lib. and marriage. Financial arrangements after marriage.
Money for Housing	1 Definition of terms: mortgages, deposits, stage payments. 2 Procedure involved in buying a house.	1 Role of the building societies, estate agents, lawyers and surveyors, NFABC. Kinds of mortgages. Other source of finance. Interest rates. Tax position (option mortage scheme).	3 House prices and inflation. Gazumping. Old *v.* new houses (local authority grants). Study of house ownership trends nationwide and dwelling needs.
Renting a House; Shelter	Rent Acts	Agreements. Local authority housing. Private agreements. Needs and functions.	The 'fair rents' row. Renting *v.* buying.
Income	1 Definition of terms: income, wages, rent, interest, profits. 2 Use of block graphs.	1 Distribution of income. 3 Net advantage principle.	3 Trade union activity. Women's wages. Time rates and piece rates.

Appendix V

Mode III Mark Sheet in .... (Name of subject)

School ....   School Number ....

Candidate's number	B(Boy) G(Girl)	Examination CSE 21/2 100	+2 50%	Projects 25%	Term- work 10	×2½ 25%	Total
		1	2	3	4	5	
120	G	47	23½	19	7	17½	60
123	G	36	18	20	6	15	53
125	G	43	21½	20	8	20	61½
127	G	10½	5	5	2	5	15

Signed ....   Signed ....

Headmaster/Headmistress

Date ....

Subject Teacher(s)

7   The Organisation of Project Work

Richard C. Brierley

By dint of the fact that the majority of economics teaching follows examination syllabuses, much of the project work that is attempted is orientated around the specifications laid down by the examining board. It is worth emphasising at once that to ignore these specifications when project work contributes to the final mark awarded in the examination will adversely affect the candidate's chances of success.

The teacher need be in no doubt as to the requirements of the boards in this respect: all issue clear and precise instructions and if doubt should arise, the teacher has only to raise the query with the board. It is the duty of any examining board to ensure that teachers are quite certain about the terms under which candidates are entered for examinations, just as it is their duty to ensure that these terms are adhered to when they come to moderate papers.

If the requirements of the boards are felt to be a constraint on the work of the teacher, it is quite acceptable to propose a Mode III syllabus which may be more specifically suited to the particular requirements of the teacher's classes, though acceptance of these syllabuses is not guaranteed. Again, the boards can supply full information on this procedure. However, in fairness to our examining boards, great care is taken over the syllabuses they offer, and it is rare that the teacher cannot find scope within them to introduce a good degree of individuality and innovation.

Furthermore, there is no reason why project work should be limited exclusively to the preparation of material for examination assessment. It can have a far wider use as a learning aid, and its value rests on the teacher's capacity to use this technique to its best advantage in each particular situation.

The Value of Project Work

It is important to establish the purpose for which project work is being employed, for this, in turn, will determine the manner and method in which it is presented and the value of the end-product when it is completed.

In the case of the more able pupil, the project is the means by which individual research is encouraged, resulting in the opportunity for the pupil to draw personal conclusions on a subject that has absorbed a fair amount of his attention. The teacher is therefore concerned to pose the question 'Why?' rather than 'What, where or how?'.

At once, this demands that the pupil obtains sufficient background information on the chosen subject to allow an assessment of the material available. Conclusions cannot be drawn when only very limited evidence is available. Therefore the choice of subject must be combined with the availability of evidence. The teacher is advised not to rely, on his pupils' behalf, on the willingness of outside agencies to provide that evidence, either as a result of an interview or in reply to a letter. Many frustrations are experienced by pupils, only too anxious to research a subject, when they discover a dearth of information or a reluctance to impart information.

By the same token, it is equally inadvisable for the chosen subject to be so broad in potential scope, that even the ablest and most enthusiastic pupil finds problems in selection of material to use, resulting, as is often the case, in an end-product that is superficial and over-generalised. Moreover, this type of work invariably holds the pupil's interest and attention less readily than a topic of a more personalised nature.

The compromise that is needed takes the teacher back to the original reason for this form of project work: the aim of encouraging individual research. Unless ample time is spent with the individual pupil, establishing interest areas, examining his likely sources of information, and suggesting methods of approach, the teacher cannot expect a great deal of success. With large classes, this style of project work will make exten-

sive demands on the teacher's time. It might well be preferable not to proceed, than to risk members of the class becoming alienated to work which they see as unpleasant but obligatory.

However, there are other approaches to be explored with project work, which, in their own right, can be of great value. An alternative purpose for the use of the project is to allow pupils to learn and understand a given body of information, in their own time and at a rate of progress most suited to each individual. In this instance, while the teacher is primarily posing questions of 'What, where or how?', the opportunity remains for the more interested or capable pupil to also ask 'Why?'.

The emphasis has been reversed. The teacher is asking the pupil to collect information from carefully specified sources, to consider particular questions, and, if the opportunity presents itself, to draw a personalised conclusion. Needless to say, this form of project work is more easily launched, even on larger classes, but runs the risk of pupils resorting to 'hack' copying of information, in order simply to complete the assignment set. Once again, the solution rests on the teacher's involvement with the individuals in the class. The less able pupil may well be making a substantial achievement simply because he has understood the question asked and is copying an appropriate section from an appropriate source; we must not assume this to be any less valuable for that pupil than the effort of the more able in thinking through the question and devising his own answer in his own words. The onus is on the teacher to differentiate the relative skills each individual in his class is capable of using and the standards that each may achieve.

Individual contact in this kind of project work, while as important as for the research-style project, is clearly less time consuming. Both, however, rely on the teacher's knowledge of the group and of the individuals within the group he is teaching.

Finally, any form of project work is of little value unless it contributes to the emphasis that economics is not merely a classroom subject to be learnt from printed matter, but is an alive science, in evidence in many ways in our everyday lives. For example, it is so easy to run through the major imports and exports of the UK, using the latest statistics available, and never direct our pupils to an awareness of the extent to which this involves themselves and their families; but to start by suggesting they assemble a list of all the items in their kitchen at home, and label each with its country of origin, may at least give that sense of involvement that is so essential.

Initial Plans for Project Work

There is little of value that is likely to emerge from

project work which is haphazardly organised or which is not geared to the particular needs and interests of the pupils for whom it is intended.

As teachers, we should be sceptical about the value of project worksheets which are retained from year to year, and used by successive generations of pupils. Of course, it is a burden to re-appraise our approach on an annual basis, especially if we have also to bear in mind the requirements of the examining boards. Moreover, there is nothing more satisfying than to see the whole syllabus's teaching material neatly filed and ready for use at the start of each new year. We become impressed by our own efficiency in having the work laid out for the ensuing twelve or twenty-four months. But what looks good, and may well have worked extremely well with last year's class, may be quite unsatisfying to this year's group: and how can the project work be specific to a class of pupils we may not have met until the start of the new year?

Project work must be the subject of continual re-appraisal. It must be re-adapted to each new intake and reflect the teacher's own concern and enthusiasm if it is to generate a similar response in his pupils.

Until the teacher has come to understand and know the class, albeit on only a fairly superficial level, it is as well to stay clear of project work. Only after several classes will it be possible to begin to devise the kind of work that will be most satisfactory. Then, of course, the preparation of project work may become a feverish effort to keep one week ahead of our classes, but it will at least reflect a sense of immediacy and life far more than material lifted from an appropriate file, dusted and distributed.

Ideally, a compromise is reached. The teacher will have mapped the route he wishes to cover, the aspects that he will want to be treated by the use of project work, and will have the first items under way fairly soon after starting with the group. By the time a mutual understanding has been achieved, the first piece of project work should perhaps only require duplicating. (Of course, it may be that the project work is not accompanied by a worksheet at all, allowing perhaps greater flexibility, but running a number of risks, about which more is said later.)

The batting order, then, is this:

1 Plan the order of presenting material;
2 Decide on areas suited to project work;
3 Get to know the class;
4 Cautiously start the project work with them.

Choosing Suitable Items for Project Work

The examining boards will generally specify only the amount of project work to be completed and the approximate subject area to be covered (or avoided).

While this leaves the teacher with a fair degree of individual choice, it also places on him the burden of making the right choice.

Select items for which there is a good amount of material to fall back on. Even if the pupils are not directed to this in the first place, it will provide reinforcements that will almost certainly be required at some stage.

Even if the pupil is required to undertake a fair amount of individual research, either ensure that he has a good introduction to the topic (probably by teaching in class) or that a subject is chosen with which he is already likely to be familiar, if only at a superficial level. For example, when starting a project on 'distribution', the pupil will either need to know what comprises the various chains of distribution, or he will need to make a start on familiar ground, such as looking at the work of local shopkeepers. Development of project work from a base that is familiar can prove very rewarding, as the teacher is inviting the pupil to answer questions that the pupil himself may ask. 'Why is it that the local shop always seems to have a good supply of Yiddish food, but is so often out of stock of cornflakes?' To seek answers to his own questions will not only spur the pupil's interest in what he is doing, but will bring home to him the awareness that his study of economics is also a study of the world in which he lives.

Select items also that cater for a mixture of abilities. The less able pupil may feel satisfied if he has only drawn a map of the local shopping precinct and commented on the various different types of retail outlet to be found there; the more able pupil will wish to have the opportunity of commenting on the reasons for this, going on to assess the extent to which the shopping precinct is a microcosm of the economy of the area, indicative of the distribution of wealth, the size of the local population, and the types of jobs done. By contrast, it would be difficult to see how 'consumer protection' might offer the same potential range, and, while it might well form the next part of your teaching curriculum, it might not have the flexibility to be handled in project work form.

The final choice, however, will rest on the teacher's own aptitudes and abilities, his resources, the aims he is working towards, and the class with which he is dealing.

Presenting the Project

A verbal introduction to the work may well be found more than sufficient to initiate a project, and this approach, as has been said already, allows the maximum degree of flexibility. However, some form of worksheet to accompany the assignment gives the pupil a ready reference to guide him through his work, and this is important. However attentive pupils may be, they will still benefit from having notes to refer to as they become increasingly involved in the project. If, as project work implies, they are expected to study to a greater or lesser extent on their own, it is reasonable to suppose that the teacher will not always be present in person to answer queries.

This is not to say that the worksheet should replace an introduction to the project itself, in which the nature of the subject and the method of proceeding with it is outlined. Many teachers include this introductory

material with the worksheet itself, which can work very well, so long as it is not allowed to develop into a substitute for teacher–class contact. The extent to which an introduction is needed, either verbally or in writing, will hinge on the familiarity of the pupil with learning in this way. Those unaccustomed to it will probably require a good deal of detailed initial guidance, while those well experienced in project work may require no more than to be told the subject to be tackled and the salient features to be included.

But certain features must be commonplace to any worksheet. In the first instance, it must be a stimulus in itself. Pupils are swift to notice our concern for their

Figure 7.1 Specimen project worksheet. If possible, include an actual newspaper cutting for the first part

NOW THE MINERS JOIN THE STRIKE

The South Wales steelworkers who went on strike last week following the dismissal of one of their shop stewards, were joined today by local miners. As the action spreads, union leaders are seeking urgent talks with the Energy Minister in

INDUSTRIAL RELATIONS

Headlines like these are all too common and it seems that relations between the various sides of British industry are anything but good. But is this really the case?

In this project, you should try to find out about our industrial relations and come to your own decision on how good or bad you think they are.

Read the books and leaflets that are given on the next page, keeping in mind the questions that have been asked. You will find it useful to *take outline notes*.

Then – write about *four sides* on this subject, covering the points raised and making *your own conclusions*. You can include suggestions as to how you think our industrial relations could be improved.
There are at least two *charts of information* that could be usefully included in this project. You will find them amongst the materials listed.

You may also find it helpful to have a word with Mr Smith, who is our school's teachers' union representative.

REMEMBER: to work neatly and clearly throughout.

You have two weeks (until May 14th) *to complete this*.

Industrial Relations Project Worksheet, page 2

Find out precisely what is meant by 'industrial relations'.

Which organisations and groups of individuals are most involved in these relations?

What factors make for 'good' or for 'bad' relations?

> *Refer to:*
>
> *The leaflets on the TUC and the CBI*
>
> *Economic Report No. 123, Problems in British Industry*

How can industrial relations be improved?

What efforts have been made in recent years to improve industrial relations in Britain?

How successful have these efforts been?

> *Refer to:*
>
> Last week's leader article in *The Economist*
>
> Your own notes on the work of the trade unions
>
> Chapter 12 of your textbook

How do we judge how good or bad a country's industrial relations are?

How does Britain compare with other countries?

> *Refer to:*
>
> Pages 12 to 23 in the book, *Britain by Statistics*

IN CONCLUSION: Why do you think good industrial relations are essential for the prosperity of an economy?

work by the care taken in the preparation and visual appearance of material supplied to them. Furthermore, however well produced, material that is obviously inappropriate to the level at which the pupil is working is no less discouraging: it is as ineffectual to over-estimate the capabilities of the pupil by distributing closely typed scripts that are found hard to understand, as it is to insult his intelligence with a sheet that is reminiscent more of a comic than a serious invitation to study. Again, it is the teacher's knowledge of his class that must determine the presentation techniques he uses.

The worksheet should present clear directions as to the scope of work to be covered. To ask loosely for information on the institutions found in the City of London, may result in detailed notes on the history of the Bank of England or a perceptive understanding of the work of a Lloyds underwriting syndicate, either of which may be a justifiable interpretation of the teacher's instructions, but neither of which is strictly required for an economics course. The worksheet must also be clear in the method of approach it expects to be adopted. 'Write a page on the work of the Stock Exchange, using the leaflet provided' is almost a direct invitation to copy out a page from the specified source; whereas, 'Read the leaflet on the Stock Exchange, and, in your own words, write at least a page about its work' at least makes the teacher's intention clear, even if the less able may still have to resort to copying out selected passages. The time limit imposed for the completion of the work should also be made clear. Pupils often quite rightly judge the quantity and quality they are expected to produce by the amount of time they are allocated. The abilities of the pupils should be borne in mind when allocating time for this work, and, given this constraint, it should be remembered that some will inevitably be less successful than others.

Above all, the worksheet should be a signpost and not a destination in itself. It does not contain the information sought, but the sources where the information may be found. It prompts the pupil towards the questions that should be considered, without containing the answers to these questions itself. Preparation of a project worksheet is not to be confused with the preparation of a data response exercise.

Teachers may find the specimen worksheet (Figure 7.1) offers some useful guidelines.

Working through the Project

Because the end-product rests on the pupil's own discovery of information (either from the teacher's prescribed sources or from sources the pupil has researched for himself) it is important that the teacher vets the incoming data carefully and regularly.

In fact, pupils will generally tend to come to the

teacher to ask if their information is correct or if they are approaching the best sources, and the teacher should find this to be one of his busiest, and most rewarding, times in the classroom.

Clearly, however, this approach demands that the teacher not only has a sound command of the information himself, but also a good appreciation of the reliability and availability of its sources. It would be quite erroneous to assume that project work is a method by which the non-specialist can cover his ignorance of the subject.

The approach also requires to some extent (and perhaps the more the better) the adoption of an 'open door' environment, in which pupils have ready access in class time to the school library, the local information centre, the town hall, and so on. The teacher will have organised class visits to places pertinent to the subject in question, but particular visits for individuals may also be required. How better for a group to learn about the services of a commercial bank than to be given an 'interview' by a local bank manager, or to find out about the organisation of a public corporation by making initial enquiries at the local NCB pithead office, or to learn how local government is financed by speaking to an official of their council? The demands on the teacher can be extensive, but the value for his pupils is clear: in reinforcing the awareness that the subject is deeply involved with the world outside the classroom.

Before the pupil moves to complete his project, it is important to ascertain that understanding as well as learning has taken place. There are a number of ways of tackling this, the easiest being to set an objective test on the work that should have been covered. Perhaps, if this is unfair to the less able pupil, it might be preferable simply to discuss each pupil's findings with him individually, posing the occasional question and suggesting he could include an answer in his final draft. Alternatively, a general class discussion could take place, allowing the more able to show their perception of the subject, and giving the less able the chance to pick up a few points to include in their own work. This has the added advantage of clearly illustrating to the 'hack' copiers that the best results are being achieved by those who have thought about the work rather than merely written the prescribed amount, and even the less able, more often than not, raise their standards accordingly, if only to question the relevance of what they have copied.

Concluding the Project

It is essential that the teacher should impress on his class that the initial project that has been written will almost certainly need to be re-drafted and re-written before it can be considered finished. This is particularly so when the completed project is to count towards the final mark in the examination.

The more able pupil will need to have shown that he has appreciated the integrated and involved nature of the subject in the conclusions he has drawn. His work must finally reflect the thinking and research that has gone into it.

The less able pupil will need to review what he has written and to have shown that the better part of it, at least, is original and has been comprehended.

All pupils will need to ensure that a good standard of English has been maintained throughout, that well drawn diagrams, maps or illustrations have been used, as and if appropriate, and that the end-product is a well organised and presented piece of work in which the pupil has invested his best endeavours and from which he has derived the satisfaction of a job well done.

Effectively, for the teacher, this requires an interim marking of the original draft, but this has the benefit not only of his being able to encourage high standards from his pupils, but also of ensuring that the requirements of the examining board have been adhered to.

Submitting Project Work to the Examining Board

The examining board will issue clear instructions on the actual submission of the project work. In the case of CSE work, a collection of short projects, compiled into a single folder, is usually required. These often benefit by being well illustrated throughout, with a list of the individual 'titles' given at the start. As the pupils start to complete projects for later submission, it is well worth encouraging them to keep these at home until the assembled folder is required. Nothing is more disastrous than for a pupil to find his carefully prepared work stolen or defaced because he has left it at school.

At 'O' level, it is more usual for a single 'extended' project or essay to be required. The principles involved are much the same as for the shorter project, but there needs to be a far stronger emphasis on choosing a suitable topic, developing the correct approach and presenting clear and well-argued conclusions. The revision of the first draft will often result in the need to research further information and re-appraise findings. Clearly, at all stages, close consultation between the teacher and the individual pupil is required.

Whenever project work is prepared for submission to an examining board, it is imperative that the teacher allocates adequate time in his curriculum for it to be tackled satisfactorily. A last minute rush is useless in educational terms, depriving the pupil of the opportunity to explore and display his interest and ability in the subject. Pupils must feel that the project is not simply a duty performed for the examination, but is a focal part of the course, providing an invaluable way to learn about the world in which we live.

It is worth mentioning two practical points at this juncture. Teachers are advised to allow for delays in the final submission of work by their pupils, by asking for it at least a couple of weeks in advance of the board's final date. Also, if the teacher is personally required to mark the project on the board's behalf, it is now customary for the board to pay him a small fee for doing so.

Conclusion

If one word were to be given to the organisation of project work, it should perhaps be 'collation' – bringing together material from a variety of sources in such a way that is clear, interesting and informative. Pupils can learn a great deal through project work, but its value is proportional to the time and attention that the teacher gives to it. We must be clear in our minds as to what we expect our pupils to achieve, conversant with the sources we wish them to tap, and informed about and sympathetic to their individual interests, attitudes and abilities.

8 The Application of Field Studies and Factory Visits

Maureen Lakeman

Why Have Visits?

Since lessons at school are normally confined to the classroom, they do not allow pupils to see much of the topic which the teacher is describing, still less experience it or work out for themselves the advantages/disadvantages, etc. inherent in it (for example, in the division of labour). Thus it is worthwhile to take pupils out of school, even bearing in mind the difficulties, which will be discussed later.

The visit has many functions: first, to consolidate the subject-matter already taught in the classroom, as for example having pupils see how cheques are cleared at a bank's head office; secondly, to enable pupils to gain insights into syllabus topics, as for example visiting a clothing factory to see how mass production works; thirdly, to develop their social skills by putting them in situations where they are forced to make conversation with firm's staff, pass round cups of tea, etc.

There is another spin-off benefit, which is that career opportunities can be ascertained and discussed, even rejected, when visiting organisations, where perhaps for the first time in their lives pupils can watch people at work.

Where to Go?

The question of where to go depends to a large extent on what is available in the vicinity of the school; teachers in cities have a huge choice whereas schools in rural areas find it impossible to arrange many varied visits. It is, however, more difficult to organise visits in a time of economic crisis: firms which are not recruiting because staff are not leaving do not react so kindly to requests for visits when they have no immediately foreseeable benefit from the upheaval such a visit creates. The firms who are most generous tend to be banks, insurance companies, retail organisations (but avoid sale times!), large manufacturing concerns and government departments. They can be contacted directly on a trial-and-error basis, or through local Careers Officers, who usually have lists of local firms willing to organise visits. Gradually, the teacher can build up a list of contacts to whom he writes every year. Those firms which are the most helpful, well-organised and friendly go to the top of the list!

Unfortunately, there seems to be a tendency recently for firms to suggest that they might send a representative to the school to teach a specific topic, but this is not the same as a visit, and sometimes can lead to embarrassment, as not all representatives are good communicators or aware of the different levels of intelligence in classes, even when told which exam is being followed.

How to Organise a Visit

(a) Method of Travel
If the school is near a station, then train or underground is very convenient, especially if the party is travelling in a big city, where parking of coaches can be difficult. Cheap party tickets can be had if forms are filled in and left at the station about a week in advance. The only problem when using public transport is in keeping the party together. Always have plenty of time in hand in case anyone gets lost; insist that no one wanders away, and keep checking the numbers in the party.

Coaches which are hired can be unreliable (sometimes not even arriving!) and traffic jams may cause the party to be late, but at least the pupils are kept together. Again, booking should be made weeks in advance, and confirmed nearer the date.

(b) Size of Party
The firm to be visited usually stipulates numbers: it seems twelve to fifteen is the norm. This is an ideal number for one teacher, but check whether the teacher must be male/female according to the sex of the party – different regulations prevail. It is often necessary with a small group to leave half a class behind at school, who then have to be supervised, but if the whole class is taken, two teachers will probably have to accompany it anyway. Taking a whole class, even if allowed by the firm, can be exhausting and nerve-racking – avoid it unless the class is always excellently behaved!

(c) Administration of Visit
The teacher in charge should make a check-list of organisational details and go through them to avoid misunderstandings. These could be: obtain permission

for visits from Head; write to firms asking for visits generally; confirm dates, times, class numbers, level, programme; book transport; tell pupils all details, including money needed; collect permission slips from pupils if used; communicate details to school office, Head, staff, and especially the teacher in charge of day-to-day covers.

It is helpful to the school if visits coincide with the period which is normally used by the teacher to teach the class being taken out, especially if that period is followed by non-teaching time, thus not requiring other teachers to be used. It is also better to arrange all visits by the beginning of the school year, and circulate details, rather than do it piecemeal and interfere with, or be disrupted by, other activities.

(d) Follow-up

If the teacher knows the firm to be visited well enough, he can duplicate a worksheet to be filled in during the visit or afterwards. Sometimes the former is rendered useless, as the person in charge of the group follows a different time-table from the one envisaged! A general worksheet on the lines of 'What did you see?', 'What did you think of ....?' can be given out at the next lesson with that class. A discussion or an essay might be an alternative. These can both be inconvenient if one half of the class has been out but not the other half. Generally, some follow-up is a good idea but the method depends on the circumstances of the visit and the level of ability of the class concerned. It is interesting how much is retained by the pupils, often months after the visit. If they can channel the memories into their exam papers, then it will have been even more worthwhile.

9   The Use of Local Field Studies

Patricia Barden

There are two main methods of using field work in schools: (1) A block system of several days usually at a field study centre involving concentration on a particular area or topic which is later consolidated into reports or projects. It is used mainly at sixth form level in the physical sciences and geography. (2) Using specific places to visit such as museums or factories which can also be used for pupils further down the school. The object here, however, is to explore a further method of exploiting the undoubted educational advantages of field study work which involves the continuous application of it throughout the school year and incorporating it into the normal teaching of the economics curriculum.

This method can also be used at sixth form level, but the pressure of work for the 'A' level syllabus is often too great. Its main advantages are to be seen with 'O' level and CSE pupils.

The aim is either to reinforce what has been studied in class, or to prepare pupils for what will be studied, by giving them an opportunity to go out into the neighbourhood of the school and confront the object of the study at first hand. They may merely be observing or actually collecting their own data. This raises the question of whether there will be enough suitable topics of study in the locality of the school. Schools situated in the middle of a large town or industrial complex are fortunate in this respect, and the problem of the teacher in a school stuck in the middle of a suburb, where the only obvious economic activity appears to be commuting, is appreciated. However, most localities have some other economic activities going on, even if it is just a row of shops and a car park. All the families in the suburbs are economic units with patterns of employment, socio-economic distributions, consumer preferences, and so on. The point is that it would be practically impossible for an economics teacher not to find at least four or five subjects for study in the immediate locality of the school, wherever it is situated.

Planning

Have a good look round the area and decide what is available first and then work out what can be done with it (for a suggestion see the worksheet in Appendix I). Once this has been accomplished it is then possible to compare what material can be used with the required areas of the curriculum and the order in which they can be taught. It is then necessary to plan a working scheme into which the field studies can be incorporated.

Field studies take place outside the school and although most pupils are surprisingly good about returning to class on time, it is wise to make sure that a few extra minutes are available to cover latecomers. Thus ideally, field study lessons should be planned for periods just before breaks, lunch breaks or the last period of the day if double periods are not available. In fact using double periods can be counter-productive, as it is too long a time for this age group to be wandering around out of school, and the rest of the period is not of much use if pupils are over-stimulated from having just returned or over-eager with anticipation of going out! One of the main benefits of this type of method is that it should not encroach upon other teachers' time by requiring permission to miss other lessons or substitutions for the economics teacher.

This method is designed to be used throughout the school year but although some studies can be one-off affairs, such as the comparison of branded and unbranded goods, other topics such as the effects of a new motorway on the area will require larger study, and these are best left to the summer term after the exams (internal) for example, when it is notoriously difficult to keep this age group occupied anyway!

The Preparation of Materials and Aids

Maps of the area are essential and it is most effective to divide up the area into sub-divisions such as residential, commercial, industrial or whatever. 'Real' maps are preferable in accuracy and detail to any teacher's attempts with a Banda sheet. Pupils also respond better to professional-looking materials.

Portable cassette recorders are invaluable for taping pupils' interviews as they often are of interest to the rest of the class. Also, few pupils are able to extract the vital material from conversations while they are actually taking place, and a record of what was said can be listened to at leisure in class later. Apart from that available at the school most pupils are quite keen to bring in their own equipment if they have any.

It is important that each pupil has some form of identification on him while he is out of school. Some sort of card should be made up with his name, form, and the address and telephone number of the school. There should also be some statement to the effect that the pupils have permission to be out of school and why. The more professional-looking these are, the better care will be taken of them, and many pupils find them useful as a means of introducing themselves to people.

The taking of photographs appeals to the pupils but it is an expensive and risky business. However if school equipment is available, it is an excellent method of allowing them to collect information in an interesting way.

The whole class cannot descend on one particular supermarket under the supervision of the teacher. They need to be split up into small groups and sent off to their various tasks (see below). Consequently for most of the time they will be on their own. It is therefore vital to make up the worksheets very carefully so that while working on their own the pupils have as much practical teacher advice with them as possible. It is best not to give too specific instructions as to what they should do, but rather suggestions as to the aspects of a particular object of study they might wish to tackle. The point of this is, apart from the obvious educational advantage of encouraging them to make their own decision and thus increase participation in the learning programme, that it can occur that the pupils are sent off with detailed instructions about the task but find for some reason that they are unable to do it – for example the shop might be shut! If no alternatives are given they will merely do nothing at all. The worksheet should therefore give general instructions as to the object of the study, what they will need in the way of materials and then suggest different things they might do. The worksheet should also provide practical advice on how to approach people for interviews or the best place to position themselves to observe certain behaviour or phenomena.

Work programme sheets should be given to each group with the list of assigned tasks on it. The group leaders can therefore keep track of what they have done and what is still to be done and possibly also the end result they must keep in mind.

Each group leader should be given a folder containing all the worksheets, maps, pictures and so on for which he is then responsible.

It must be stressed that all this material should be pleasantly and efficiently presented and made to achieve maximum response from the pupils. If possible the stationery the pupils use for the work should be in some way different from normal school stock. For example yellow paper instead of white will help to underline the importance and special nature of the work and quickly dispel any hope that it is all one big opportunity to get out of lessons!

A few final aids for the teacher which are of use are a record book to keep track of what has been done by each group as the term progresses and a signing in and out book. The latter is important psychologically as the group leaders should sign their groups out and then sign them in again when they return. This helps to reinforce his sense of responsibility for the group.

Class Organisation

The most effective form of organising the work is in the form of groups with group leaders.

1 It avoids duplication of materials such as maps, folders, tapes.

2 It reduces the number of pupils the teacher has to deal with as he can co-ordinate and instruct the four or five group leaders who can then pass on his instructions to their groups.

3 Once formed the groups are settled, so there is no time-wasting as to who goes where with whom at the start of every field study. Only in exceptional circumstances should the teacher permit individual pupils to change groups.

4 It makes the keeping of accurate records as to who has done what easier for the teacher.

5 Groups quickly develop group identity and purpose which gives the execution of the work increased motivation.

6 Group leaders become teacher substitutes and can make decisions for the group which would otherwise have to be referred to the teacher.

7 Pupils feel more confident in groups.

The actual formation of the groups can be flexible and informal but the question as to whether the teacher should decide who goes in which group or whether they should be allowed to choose for themselves must be considered carefully. The latter method is more desirable as it causes the normal peer groups to coincide with the official groups – a considerable managerial advantage. However the teacher should try to predict in advance what the likely combinations will be as some groupings of 'friends' are potentially disastrous! The appointment of the group leader should be done by the teacher. Correct group formation is essential to the success and effectiveness of this type of work, and as much thought should be given to it beforehand as to any other aspect of the organisation.

It is by no means the most academically able pupils who make the best group leaders. Indeed it is often the less able pupil who possesses the social confidence and common sense necessary for the task. It is also worthwhile considering giving these pupils an opportunity to do something important and active in the subject to increase their motivation by appointing them the group leaders.

Classroom Work

This is where all the effort of preparation and organisation done by the teacher pays off, and the teacher can exploit the benefits of field work. One of the main benefits is that the enthusiasm gained in the field study is carried over into ordinary work. The field work results must be incorporated into the teaching and there are various methods of doing this depending on the skill of the teacher.

Method One
Each group reports to the rest of the class on the work they have done, the results and any economics involved. They will of course need considerable help and it is unwise just to hand the lesson over to them without having checked their material and discussed with them how they intend to present it. This is the method pupils enjoy most, but it is not advisable for an inexperienced teacher to use it right away as it can easily disintegrate without skilled and careful handling.

Method Two
The teacher presents the work prepared by the field groups using any diagrams, tapes and so on which they have made. This is very successful so long as the teacher makes it clear by constant reference that he is using 'Group II's' work or whatever.

Method Three
The groups are instructed to consolidate their work and their findings into reports which can then be filed and used as resources. They can also make up Banda sheets for distribution to the rest of the class.

It is very important that the pupils see some solid end result of their efforts. They often enjoy making wall charts for example.

Throughout the year the teacher should refer back to field work done during normal lessons as often as possible.

Conclusion

Educationally the value of presenting pupils of this age with learning in a concrete form is well proven. However on a more practical level, with economics, much of the objects of study for the pupils are familiar and yet not! For example everyone knows what a supermarket looks like but now for the first time the pupils have looked at it in an analytical and critical way, and they thoroughly enjoy extracting new knowledge from everyday objects. And this is really what it is all about. Too many CSE and 'O' level syllabuses are constructed in such a way as to make economics an arid, unexciting and unrealistic subject with the emphasis on learning facts and definitions. Many of the areas of study are about things the pupils think they know all about anyway – for example market areas, population. So they find it boring. This is an attempt to motivate them, show them the usefulness of the subject and its practical application and allow them, occasionally, to enjoy learning it!

Useful Sources

For methods and suggestions as to what can be studied at a local level see the following:

Robinson, B. R. G. (ed), *Field Studies in Teaching Economics*, (The Economics Association, 1975).
Senesh, L., *Our Working World* series, (Science Research Associates Inc. 1973).
The Oxford Geography Project series, (Oxford University Press).

Appendix I

A Sample Worksheet

A Supermarket
You should not have any problems doing the work for a supermarket so long as you behave quietly and properly while you are inside the store. Remember not to handle the goods for sale – you may end up having to buy them if you do!

It MIGHT be a good idea to buy something in the shop, e.g. a packet of crisps.

A Go round the store and make a rough map of the shelves, counters, etc. and note the different goods that are displayed on them.

B Make a list of the commodities the supermarket is selling plus the brand names, e.g. Heinz, Kelloggs, etc. Try and make a list of the prices.
C Note what special offers the store is having.
D The customers – different types of customers will tend to buy different types of goods. To observe this the best place to stand is at the check-out counters. Make a table of different types of goods and tick off as each customer buys them. See the teacher for details on this.

NOTE: If anyone asks what you are doing show them your card and explain your purpose. If they tell you to leave do so at once.

Class Work

From your rough map make a proper and accurate plan of the supermarket with a colour code for all the different goods.

Make up a brand list and price list to go with your map.

Make your own report about the supermarket – what you observed about things like service, conditions of the goods for sale, e.g. were any packets torn, were any frozen foods above the freeze line, etc?

Write up your consumer report. See teacher for details on this.

Section 2: Ways of Teaching Particular Topics

10 Prices and Markets
David L. McDougall

General Comments

The topic of prices is normally a fundamental part of most courses in economics and can provide the basis for much further development of other topics in the same courses. Teaching the topic to younger pupils requires a fair amount of effort from the teacher. This is not only because the topic itself is important, but also because few textbooks reduce it to a simple enough level to have meaning for people in the age range of thirteen to sixteen years. This means that when teaching this topic the teacher has relatively few aids which he can use and must rely on his own scheme of work. This chapter aims to provide some suggestions for ideas which the teacher could adapt to his own requirements. In the same way, consideration of markets creates difficulties and it may be unrealistic (with pupils in this age range) to adopt a very theoretical approach, unless the pupils are of above-average ability.

Content

The teaching of prices must include demand, supply and their interaction, and the pupils should ultimately be able to explain and analyse changes in demand, supply and prices. The teaching of markets at this level can cover the behaviour of producers in three different situations: (1) where there are many producers; (2) where there are a few producers; (3) where there is only one producer.

Teaching Methods

The following methods suggest a way of approaching these topics either separately or in a series of lessons. It is not anticipated that courses would necessarily cover the whole range of topics included under the heading 'prices and markets' in one block of lessons, but rather that different parts would be covered at different stages of the course. This means that when pupils came to cover some topics, say imperfect competition, they would have a greater background knowledge than when they covered, for example, demand. Most aspects of both prices and markets are covered very adequately in general textbooks from the teacher's point of view, but much of this material then has to be broken down into a form which is usable by the younger pupils. The following sequence has been arranged in such a way that it could be used by a teacher without the pupils having to rely on a textbook until they had reached a stage at which they were thoroughly familiar with the basic concepts involved.

1 Prices in the Real World
Pupils are either given a list of commodities or can compile the list themselves and the teacher informs

them of the price of each item on the list two or three years previously. The class then have to find the current price levels of the items. An example of this is shown in Table 10.1.

The pupils are then required to represent the price changes graphically (see Figure 10.1).

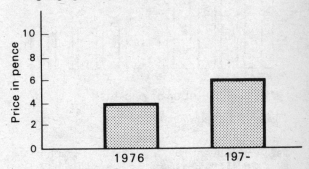

Figure 10.1 Price of local newspapers

The final stage is for pupils to try and explain why each of the commodities has changed in price. This can be done in two ways. Pupils can attempt to think of their own explanations, or the teacher can provide information from which the pupils can extract reasons to explain each of the price changes. Such information can be given in the form of a passage in which several ideas are available for the pupils to find, or the information can be provided by a series of sentences and the pupils have to relate the most likely explanation to the appropriate commodity.

Example. One of the sentences might say 'Shortages of timber in recent years throughout the world have caused the price of paper to rise.' This could be used by pupils to help explain the rise in the price of their local newspaper. On the other hand one factor might be used to explain several of the price changes. The whole exercise leads to considerable class discussion, and the degree of sophistication which is introduced depends both on the teacher and the maturity of the members of the class.

2 The Demand Curve
(a) *Consumer satisfaction*. Pupils are asked to decide on a scale of, say, one to five, how many units of satisfaction they would receive from the consumption of a packet of crisps. The teacher suggests that crisps of any flavour are available and asks how many pupils think they would derive maximum satisfaction of five out of five from the consumption of one packet. The number of units awarded by the class is totalled and noted down (one member of the class can act as a 'scorer'). The procedure is repeated for a second packet and for several more packets until the pupils

Item	Price in 1976	Price in 197—
local newspaper 1 lb potatoes loaf of bread packet of crisps lowest bus fare 20 cigarettes		

Table 10.1

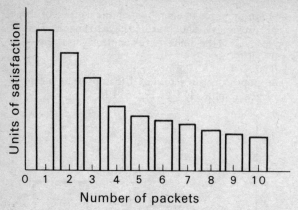

Figure 10.2 *Consumption of crisps*

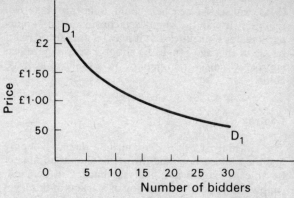

Figure 10.4 *Demand for an LP*

have been offered, say, ten packets. A graph of the class totals is then constructed (see Figure 10.2).
An overall picture of diminishing satisfaction with each successive unit of consumption will emerge. The exercise again provides the basis for considerable class discussion, and the essentially subjective nature of the idea of consumer satisfaction, as well as the differences between consumer tastes, will become evident.

(b) Class demand. The pupils are asked how many of them would buy a packet of crisps if the price was one penny. The price is then increased successively through several price levels to, say, ten pence. This allows a class demand curve to be constructed (see Figure 10.3).

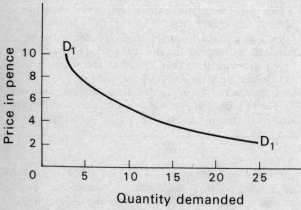

Figure 10.3 *Demand for crisps*

(c) Auction. A commodity is offered to the class for sale by auction. A good example might be a currently popular LP. The class is asked how many would bid ten pence for it. The price is then increased by small amounts with bidders indicating willingness to buy at

each price level by raising their hands (see Figure 10.4).
The same exercise can be repeated for different commodities which might be less popular, thus allowing comparison of a number of curves.

(d) Market research (school survey). The class can organise a survey of other pupils in the school, asking how many would buy a certain commodity over a range of prices. This could be something practical which might actually be sold in the school (for example, a school newspaper). The results are then collected and represented graphically (see Figure 10.5).

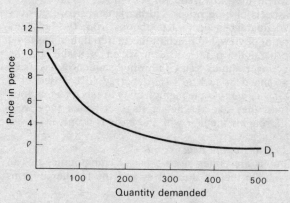

Figure 10.5 *Demand for school newspapers*

3 The Supply Curve
Following the previous example of a market survey concerning the potential sales of a newspaper, the class could try to calculate how many newspapers should be produced and at what price they should be sold. They make out a list of all the different costs involved (for example, paper, stencils, writing materials, printing materials, distribution, advertising) and can be

encouraged to put a value on the time they would have to spend in producing the newspaper. They then work out how much it would cost them to produce a variety of output levels (say, fifty to 500, at intervals of fifty). This allows them to decide how much they would have to receive per copy to induce them to produce each different output level. In other words, it will take longer to produce 500 than fifty, so how much extra will they have to receive per copy to make production and distribution of 500 copies worthwhile? By then posing the question in the form 'If the price is 10p how many copies would we produce?' it is possible to work through the whole range of prices and then to construct a type of supply curve (see Figure 10.6).

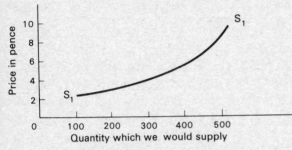

Figure 10.6 Supply of school newspapers

4 Interaction of Demand and Supply

Having calculated the demand and supply curves for newspapers in the school, the two curves can be put together on the same diagram. The pupils are then asked questions relating to the two curves. Examples:

How many newspapers would be put on the market if the price was ten pence?
How many would be demanded at ten pence?
How many extra newspapers would there be if the price was ten pence?
How many would be put on the market at one penny each?
How many would consumers want to buy if the price was one penny each?
How much would the shortage be if the price was one penny?

These and other questions allow the class to develop the idea of an equilibrium price, and once they have completed a practical example like the one above it is possible for them to consider a whole series of examples for various products.

5 Shifts of the Demand Curve

The class is given a demand schedule and asked to draw the demand curve from it on graph paper. They then calculate the effect of: (a) a 10 per cent increase; and (b) a 10 per cent decrease in the level of demand at each

price level. They draw the new demand curves (on the same graph paper) and try to suggest factors which might have caused the shifts in the curve.

6 Effects of Changes in Demand on Price

The class is given a supply schedule and asked to draw the curve for it on the same graph paper as in (5) above. They then answer questions on how the equilibrium price reacted to changes in demand.

7 Shifts of the Supply Curve and its Effects

In the same way as they did for demand in (5) and (6) above, the pupils use graph paper to show how shifts of the supply curve are represented and by relating these to a demand curve assess the effects of changes in supply on the price level.

8 Causes of Price Changes

The class is asked to explain what would happen to price following a series of adjustments to demand and supply (for example, the effect on price of an increase in demand with no change in the supply curve).

9 Exercises

The pupils are asked to draw diagrams to illustrate, and write explanations of, a series of situations. Examples:

1 The effect of an advertising campaign on the price of petrol;

2 Frost destroys much of the world's coffee crop in one year;

3 Football clubs charge higher prices for European Cup matches.

These exercises can also include the examples which were used in (1) above, even if it may be more than a year since the class completed that part of the work.

10 Stock Exchange Game

The purpose of this game is to illustrate the effects of changes in demand and supply on market prices, and perhaps to give the pupils a simplified introduction to the buying and selling of shares. Each pupil has £10 to spend and the object is to make as much money as possible by trading in shares. There are four companies whose shares are available (these can be given names by the teacher to create 'local' interest). The shares of the companies are priced at £2, £1, 75p and 50p respectively. (There is no significance in these particular prices – they could be any prices to start with.) Each company's shares are looked after by a different 'broker' whose job is to distribute share certificates to buyers and collect certificates from sellers. Buying and selling can only take place through a broker.

Each pupil is given a sheet divided as shown in Table 10.2.

Time Period	Price of A	Price of B	Price of C	Price of D
1	£2.00	£1.00	75p	50p
2				

Table 10.2

Each broker has a supply of about 20 share certificates for his company, and in each time period the pupils are not allowed to buy more than one share in each company. (The teacher has to decide the method of allocation if demand exceeds supply.) The teacher announces the prices at the start of each time period. If demand is high (i.e. many buyers) the price will rise in the next time period, but if there are many sellers the price will fall in the next time period. Eventually the brokers may be able to fix their own prices, determined by market forces, and it may be possible to introduce several other 'sophistications' to make the game more realistic.

11 Different Types of Markets
The Stock Exchange game can be extended to introduce pupils to the idea of different types of markets. Instead of having four companies, it is possible to operate with only one company's shares available, but with a larger number of brokers. This introduces a greater degree of competition and can allow experiments to assess the effects on price of a market where there are many buyers and sellers. The same type of experiment could be tried where there are only, say, four sellers, all competing with each other. If the sellers do not of their own volition introduce practices such as collusion or price fixing, the teacher can discreetly suggest to one or two of them that these practices might be attempted. Eventually it is possible to experiment with only one seller who is attempting to maximise his profit. This may lead to some interesting results if the teacher can resist the temptation to interfere, because the seller may at first raise his prices so high that demand for his product disappears. In order to make any money he is then forced to reduce his prices and take account of the demand for the product. This again raises possibilities for considerable class discussion.

12 Historical Survey
The class studies the development of one industry which has progressed from having a large number of relatively small producers to having only a few firms competing with each other. The UK motor industry could be used as an example. The teacher then asks questions about the behaviour of the buyers and sellers in the different market situations, and with some classes it may be possible to construct diagrams to illustrate the different markets. This type of survey allows the class to consider the costs and benefits to consumers, as well as producers, of the markets, and provides the basis for studying other related topics, such as economies of scale, costs of production (and cost curves), government intervention and types of integration.

13 Worksheet
The historical survey in (12) could be done in the form of a worksheet in which the 'story' is presented in a narrative form and the teacher provides a series of questions to follow it. Alternatively a worksheet could be based on very simple diagrams to illustrate different types of markets with questions asked about the behaviour of the producers and consumers in the markets (see Figure 10.7).

Figure 10.7

What would happen if seller B raised his prices above the level of all the other prices?

What would happen if seller D reduced his prices below the level of all the others?

What would happen if sellers L, M, N and O were to group together to fix their prices?

What would happen if sellers E, F, G and H all joined together to produce in one factory?

If all the sellers were charging the same price what steps could seller I take to attract people to buy from him rather than from the other sellers?

These questions provide examples of the way a worksheet on markets could be reduced to a simple level and then built up into a more advanced type of model.

14 Theoretical Background
Having considered several fairly practical approaches to the teaching of markets, the teacher is in a position to be able to relate some of these markets to more theoretical explanations involving cost and revenue curves. The extent to which this is possible will depend on how able the class is to cope with economic theory. Even at the age of sixteen, many pupils will find difficulty in understanding such theory.

Problems

Many pupils have difficulty in appreciating the difference between changes in quantity demanded or supplied (resulting from changes in price) and actual shifts of the demand and supply curves (leading to changes in price).

Average pupils up to the age of sixteen are usually capable of understanding and using demand and supply diagrams, but such pupils may find more difficulty in understanding traditional diagrams relating to the various types of markets.

Use of textbooks is often counter-productive unless the teacher ensures that each step of the textbook is thoroughly understood by the pupils.

Resources

Textbooks
As has been pointed out, very few textbooks simplify their treatment of prices and markets sufficiently to be very useful for thirteen–sixteen year-old pupils. As a result, use of textbooks for this part of the syllabus is not easy. One which provides a good simple framework is *Starting Economics* by F. Davies (Hulton, 1977) in which chapters 5 and 6 introduce pupils to the laws of demand and supply in a simple and interesting way.

A textbook by D. Christie and A. Scott entitled *Economics in Action* (Heinemann Educational, 1977) covers prices and markets in considerable detail, especially in parts 3, 4 and 5.

Written Material
A very simple approach to consumption is available in the Consumption Unit of the pilot course prepared for the Scottish Central Committee on the Social Subjects, available from The Scottish Centre for Social Subjects at Jordanhill College, Glasgow. This is specifically geared towards younger secondary pupils.

Films, Tapes, etc
Tape/filmstrip sequences are available from Audio Learning Ltd on: 1 *Scarcity and Choice* (ECO 001); 2 *Demand* (ECO 006); 3 *Supply* (ECO 007); 4 *Price* (ECO 008).

Available for purchase and hire from Guild Sound and Vision are programmes from the ILEA TV Service on: *The Economic System* (16", 900 9699 0); *Three Economic Systems* (18", 900 9700 9).

Concluding Note

The general tenor of this chapter is to suggest that very little of the existing published material, whether in the form of textbooks or audio visual tapes, is aimed at pupils in the thirteen–sixteen age range. As a result, little of this material can be used to help such pupils in their understanding of prices and markets. The teacher can use parts of textbooks or tapes, but only if these are adapted to be suitable for these younger pupils. With money to buy teaching aids becoming increasingly scarce, the teacher may find that prices and markets are best taught by his own manipulation of the existing resources and not by relying very heavily on audiovisual and other aids.

11   The Firm, as in the 'Understanding Industrial Society Project'

Ralph Cooke

General Comments

The firm is a central concept in any economics course and the topic can be approached in a variety of ways and at a variety of levels. However, at 'O' level and more particularly CSE, it is important that the study should be made in as concrete a fashion as possible. The 'Understanding Industrial Society Project' tries to do this by means of an activity approach wherever possible so that pupils are able, by the use of a variety of techniques, to attempt to grasp the complexities of these basic economic units. Although the project is intended to cover much more ground than the study of the firm, this is an area where the particular methods used may be of some help to teachers of other economics courses in the fourteen–sixteen age group. All the following activities are undertaken with both 'O' level and CSE pupils although the depth necessarily varies with the ability of the pupils.

The project starts by introducing pupils to the advantages and disadvantages of starting their own business and looks at some of the problems involved, for instance, the type of organisation which might be preferred initially, raising finance, pricing and methods of selling the product. Pupils then move on to the opportunities and difficulties presented by the expansion of the business, exploring in particular the following topics:

1 *Finance*. How a private limited company can 'go public'. The function and working of the Stock Exchange. The importance of institutions such as pension funds and insurance companies in the capital market. Reasons for fluctuations in share prices. Calculation of dividends.

2 *The location of a large factory*. Factors affecting choice of location such as the sources of raw materials and components and the location of the market, availability of labour with the skills required, transport, power, land, reputation, etc. Reasons for government intervention and the forms which such intervention might take.

3 *The organisation of a large factory*. This is dealt with in more detail later in the chapter.

4 *Trade unions and industrial relations*. Functions, types and organisation of unions. The Trades Union Congress and the Confederation of British Industry. Types and reasons for industrial disputes.

At this point pupils also look at attitudes which people have to their work, e.g. are they working mainly 'for the money' or are there other reasons as well? Can certain jobs be made more interesting for the people who have to do them and if so, what are the advantages and disadvantages?

5 *Increasing profits*. This may be done by decreasing costs and/or increasing sales. Investigating the former method, pupils use the technique of value analysis, i.e. the product is examined and questions such as the following are asked:

Is the product better than the customer really wants? Can cheaper materials be used? Are all the finishes essential?

Methods of expanding sales are then examined, for example, persuading customers to buy more than one of the product, making the product less durable and more difficult to repair, and fashion changes.

Advertising is dealt with in detail. Apart from learning about the function of advertising and its advantages and disadvantages, pupils follow the stages of an advertising campaign paying special attention to such topics as the identification of the target market, consumer resistance and how it might be overcome, brand images, media to be used and costs.

All these methods of increasing profit are also looked at from the consumer standpoint. To what extent are they advantageous or disadvantageous to the consumer?

The project tries to move as far as possible away from 'chalk and talk' in the teaching of the above topics and incorporates a variety of case studies, written and numerical exercises, points for structured class discussions which may be open-ended, and role play exercises, together with suggestions for films, tapes, speakers and visits.

What follows is intended to give teachers some indication of the way in which a small part of the project might be dealt with.

The Small Business

When pupils begin the project, they are required to decide on a product which they feel is likely to sell, taking into consideration certain restrictions such as lack of capital, technical expertise and competition from established large firms. The class product which emerges is likely to be a simple one, e.g. soft toys or printed stationery, and this is then used as a peg upon which to hang much of the rest of the course.

The initial question must be why should anyone wish to start their own business? Answers may be in terms of the possibility of high profits and the satisfaction of 'being one's own boss', but against this should be set greater responsibility for the success of the venture and consequent worry, not only for the businessman but also for his family. The teacher should be ever watchful for case studies which appear from time to time in the press, on radio and on television.

Examples of Such Case Studies

1 Case study of Gerry Parish's success in setting up the Queensway discount furniture supermarket firm, from the *Sunday Mirror* of 22 June 1975 (see Figure 11.1). Possible questions:

(a) Why do you think Gerry Parish might have wanted to set up his own business rather than work for someone else?

(b) What would you consider to be the reason for Gerry Parish's business success?

(c) Explain the methods Gerry Parish might use to sell furniture and carpets in the same way as supermarkets sell food.

2 A case study of Paul and Teresa Folkes' restaurant

LAYING DOWN SUCCESS—£50 PLUS PLUCK

GERRY Parish did business the hard way.

During the day he was a carpet-layer; in the evenings he borrowed samples from a friend who worked for a carpet firm and went out selling.

Gerry got customers by knocking on doors and advertising in local newspapers. He travelled in his old car or on his bicycle to see people.

Price cuts

Business boomed. Soon his friend began giving him big discounts on the carpets, and he passed the discounts on to customers in price cuts.

That is how Gerry started the big Queensway discount furniture supermarket firm whose sales topped £11 million last year.

In 1967 he opened a shop in Norwich. Within a few months he moved to a disused warehouse near by.

He had only £50, creditworthiness and confidence. His idea was to do with furniture and carpets what supermarkets had done for food. And, like super-

YOUR MONEY MATTERS
By Robert Head

markets, sell strictly for cash.

Today he has twenty-six branches from Devon to Dundee.

Plans include opening six more branches during the next two years.

Discounts are up to 50 per cent., and Queensway also has its own brand of furniture and carpets, called Cannon.

Mr. Parish, who is in his mid-30s, says that for the year ending September, sales should reach £18,500,000 and next year they could hit £25 million. In 1968 they were just over £265,000.

Profits this year are expected to be £1 million compared with £503,600 last year and a £4,600 loss in 1969. He hopes to make £1,500,000 next year.

He aims to offer shares in Queensway to the public as soon as his financial advisers give the go-ahead. I will be watching out for them.

Time to play it cool, investors

I WOULDN'T be in any great hurry to buy lots of shares just now. And if I had made money this year when Stock Exchange prices doubled or trebled, I would be content to take some profits.

The boom was too fast for comfort, and shares have fallen by a tenth since the peak earlier this month.

The immediate outlook is not so hot with inflation and unemployment rising rapidly. Many industries face a slump, with car production, for example, at its lowest ebb for thirteen

Figure 11.1 Reprinted by permission from the Sunday Mirror, *22 June 1975*

The great restaurant dream

Getting away from it all is a great middle-class dream; self-sufficiency in Wales, a pub in the Peak District, a boutique in a market town. In the next few weeks Lifespan will look at some of the dreams and the reality; first, running a restaurant. It's one thing to cook a dinner party for friends, another to cook for profit. For Paul and Teresa Folkes it's a dream beginning; for Maurice and Valerie Vane it's a nightmare which has ended. *Paul Flattery* reports

THE GOOD LIFE

A new entry in the *Good Food Guide* this year, is Kea House Restaurant in Tregony (pop. 600), Cornwall. It has been open for just over a year and is owned and run by Paul and Teresa Folkes. It is especially pleasing for the Folkes since it is their first time in the business.

Paul Folkes gave up being an estate agent in London three years ago. He took his wife, Teresa, and their two small boys to live in Cornwall where, with others, he formed a property company. With the economic climate worsening it collapsed within six months after the banks withdrew their money.

"We then wondered what the hell we were going to do," says Paul. They didn't want to go back to London, and since Teresa was good at cooking they decided to try private catering.

At first it was just pâtés for local delicatessens and cooking for people's freezers, then parties, weddings and business lunches. "It just progressed from there to the restaurant."

With their youngest, William, only three-and-a-half and Alexander just starting school, they needed a place where they could both live and work. It came along in the shape of The Town Arms pub in Tregony. The brewery, which already owned the village's other pub, was closing it down.

Much to the Folkes's surprise, the bank lent them £20,000 to buy and refit it although neither of them had ever had experience in such a venture. After five weeks of alterations and installations the pub became a restaurant. One of the first customers, needless to say, was the bank manager.

Teresa does all the cooking and Paul the managing and buying, as well as running their small but well-stocked bar. The food wasn't too good at the start, Teresa admits. "I had no training, and frankly I didn't know what I was doing."

Paul agrees. "To a certain extent, I don't think we knew what we were letting ourselves in for. If we did, we might have had cold feet. The change between now and when we first opened is quite incredible."

"Cooking food for your friends at dinner parties is all right," says Teresa, "but when you start charging people you wonder how you have the audacity to do it. Partly it's the worry of reaching the quality and partly it's a completely different technique. Instead of doing a set menu for several people at the same time, you are doing lots of different things with five, ten minutes in between."

"The most difficult thing for

Paul and Teresa Folkes: "It's more than business, it's our life"

me," says Paul, "was wondering if everyone was liking it. You become over-attentive to people and I used to upset Teresa a lot by continually asking 'is it all right?'" Hardly anything has ever been sent back, they say, only, oddly enough, plain steak. They now have found a good reliable supplier of meat as they have with vegetables. Paul buys the fish direct from the fishing fleet at Mevagissey.

"People do come to Cornwall expecting fish," he says, "but they only get given sole or plaice. So this year we are trying to specialise in some of the unusual fishes you get around here, like John Dory, Monkfish, Bream and Mullet. Lobster outprices itself but we do crab in the summer, squid and scallops and mussels when we can get them."

The Folkes offer a small but varied menu of eight main courses which changes once a week in the winter and twice in the summer. They do add special dishes when things become available. The restaurant itself is fairly small, with a maximum of 32 people at one time, furnished simply with pine tables and cane chairs. They wait on the tables themselves, with occasional help, and dress quite informally.

"Neither Paul nor I could go around in bow ties with white napkins and do silver service," says Teresa. "One has to make a virtue out of necessity I suppose. Somebody who came in a few times said it felt like going out to dinner with friends. This is what we're trying to do. Being amateurs, we have to have that approach. Yet one doesn't want to trade on that and make it an excuse for not keeping your standards as high as you can. It is a fine balance."

Although Tregony is a tiny

place, it is well situated lying between quite a number of larger towns such as Truro, St Austell and St Mawes. "Right from the start," says Paul, "we didn't count on getting a lot of trade from the village itself. We thought, slightly pie-in-the-sky I suppose, that if the place was any good, people would come to us. It took a long while to start proving that point."

They are now doing well and would be leading a comfortable life if they owned the restaurant outright. But the repayments and interest to the bank make it quite a struggle, especially during the winter when whatever money comes in at night goes out buying things the next morning. Neither of them takes a salary and apart from one week's holiday in Brittany they have only ever taken running costs from the restaurant.

"We can take about £500–£600 a week in the summer," says Paul, "and just less than half of that, £200–£250 goes out on food. Out of the rest comes repayments and interest to the bank – nearly £300 a month – and overheads such as electricity, telephone, rates, the car and wages of occasional help. In the winter takings slip right down to about £150 a week although we had a good Christmas period, taking about £900 in nine days."

"One can't allow a great margin of borrowing," says Paul. "That was perhaps our biggest mistake. The headache of that on top of being tired from the sheer continual hard work becomes a bit much after a while. We could make a hell of a lot more money just serving up steak and chips or plaice and chips, but we couldn't do that."

"There were three things we said we wouldn't do when we started off," says Teresa. "Prawn

cocktail, chips, and steak. Well we very quickly put the steak o: because with a small menu you must have something plain in case someone gets desperate. We have done prawn cocktail, but only for a party who specifically ordered it in advance. And the chips we've done for a little boy who came in for his birthday.

"All we've got is our own style," says Teresa. "This is more than just a business, it's our whole life. It's very hard work – I've never worked so hard in all my life – but it's enjoyable at the same time. Nerve-racking, but it's fun."

Maurice and Valerie Vane: "We hadn't appreciated the hard work"

Figure 11.2 Reprinted by permission from the
Sunday Times, *8 May 1977*

in Cornwall, from the *Sunday Times*, 8th May 1977 (see Figure 11.2). Possible questions:

(a) How did the Folkes's raise money for their business and why do they think this was their biggest mistake?
(b) How else might a person raise money to set up a small business?
(c) What disadvantages do the Folkes see in running their own business? Can you think of any other disadvantages?
(d) List the various costs of running the business which are listed by the Folkes. What other costs are there which they have not included?
(e) Are the Folkes in business solely to make as big a profit as possible or do they have other aims as well?

Pupils should also be warned that not all small businesses are successful and that many end up bankrupt for a variety of reasons, e.g. the wrong product, lack of research into potential markets, bad management, bad luck and so on.

The Small Firm

Part of the project requires an inquiry into the organisation of a small firm and the two basic methods used are a case study (see Resources) and a visit to a firm. The case study is designed to make pupils think about such topics as the organisation of a small firm in terms of personnel and production, the possible advantages of small firms over larger ones in the same type of business, the advantages and disadvantages of concentration both for the firm and the worker, and reasons why employees in a small firm may not feel it necessary to belong to a trade union.

The Large Mass Production Firm

Later in the project, pupils are required to investigate a large mass-production firm and again a case study (see Resources) and visit approach is used. One of the objects of the case study is to show pupils the ways in which large firms differ from small firms, for example, a more complex organisational structure and production flow, the welfare and social facilities provided for the workers, the problems which may be caused by multi-unionism, the dangers of disruption on a mass-production line and the possibility of a wider gap between management and workers. Other topics to be considered include internal economies and diseconomies of scale, how a large firm may try to increase demand for its products and the effects which strong competition may have on the price and quality of its goods.

Outside Visits

While case studies can make a significant contribution to pupils' understanding, it is also vital that pupils should get out of the classroom to visit firms of various sizes so that they can apply this knowledge and get the flavour of industry by meeting management and workers 'in the flesh'.

Preliminary Organisation – Pupils
1 Pupils should have used a case study approach.
2 They should have at least some knowledge of the type of product made by the firm they are to visit.
3 Pupils must be clear as to the information they are attempting to elicit from the firm's personnel and, therefore, the questions they should ask. This can be done by class discussion in which the pupils identify the main areas of inquiry, e.g. labour relations, sales, production, etc., then they break up into smaller 'buzz groups', each group discussing detailed questions in their chosen field. Each group then reports to the class and additional questions can be added at this stage, perhaps with some guidance from the teacher.

Preliminary Organisation – Firms (see also Chapter 8)
1 It is most important that the firm should be told the aims of the visit. It may need to be pointed out, tactfully perhaps, that it is not a 'careers visit'. If the firm is not clear in its own mind what it should be doing with the pupils, then the chances are that it will do the wrong thing, that managers will come armed with the wrong information and that the visit will degenerate into a 'machine watching' exercise. Teachers may get round this danger by sending a list of the sort of questions pupils will ask. This does not necessarily guarantee success but at least managers cannot say that they were not warned beforehand.
2 A preliminary visit to the firm is of great use when management is willing to co-operate. This gives the teacher an opportunity to tell them much more about the objectives, to amplify some of the questions pupils are likely to ask, to discuss in greater detail the structure of the visit and, perhaps most important of all, to get a lot of information about the firm, information which is likely to be useful when it comes to a post-visit discussion.

Some Suggested Questions

1 General Information
What is the history of the firm?
How many factories does the firm own?
What products are made?
Is the firm a limited liability company? Public or private?
What is the present capital structure?
What is the present turnover?

What were the profits last year and what are the expectations for the present year?

Is there a dominant individual or group of shareholders?

Has the company ever been given financial assistance by the government?

What are the prospects for the expansion of the business?

2 Location

What factors had to be taken into consideration when deciding on the location of the factory or factories?

How are raw materials transported to the factory and how are finished goods transported to the market?

Are there any factories in the Assisted Areas, and if so, why did they start or move there?

3 Management Structure

What is the management structure of the firm?

Who plans the production and how is this done?

How large is the research and development department?

4 Production

How many of each article were produced in the last year?

What raw materials are used and in what quantity?

Where do the raw materials come from (domestic or imported)?

What outside services are used by the firm, if any?

Are there any waste products? If so, what happens to them?

What use is made of computers?

5 Labour

How many employees are there?

How many different unions are there? Is there a dominant union? Which one?

What percentage of the employees are members of unions?

Have there been any strikes in the past five years? What were the reasons?

How many of the strikes were (a) official, (b) unofficial?

How is wage bargaining carried out?

What are the normal number of hours worked per week by: (a) unskilled workers, (b) skilled workers, (c) office staff?

Is there any shift work?

What is the usual method of payment for the factory worker: piece rates or time rates? Why is one method of payment chosen rather than another?

What percentage of the workers are (a) male, (b) female?

What is the 'catchment area' of the factory?

What training schemes are run by the firm?

To what extent can the firm be disrupted by workers striking in other firms?

What social and other facilities are there for the workers?

What are the safety regulations in the factory?

6 Competition and Marketing

Who are the main competitors? How does the firm compete with them (e.g. price or non-price competition)?

Are there any competitors nearby? Does it matter?

How much money was spent on advertising last year? Does the firm have its own advertising department? Does it use an agency?

Which media are used most?

What percentage of sales go to (a) other firms, (b) households?

At what time of the year are sales at (a) their highest, (b) their lowest?

What use is made of market research?

How are the products distributed? e.g. wholesalers, direct to retailers, etc.

How many people are employed in the sales department? What percentage of the work force is this?

What percentage of the sales are exported? Where are the main foreign markets?

These are not intended to apply to all firms nor to be exhaustive but merely to give an indication of the sort of information which pupils are likely to find helpful. Doubtless teachers will be able to add many more to this list.

Structure of the Visit

1 Preliminary talk about the firm by a member of the management.

2 Tour of the factory in small groups (six to eight pupils) following the production line.

3 Question and answer session. This is vital and is the opportunity for pupils to ask questions of the type listed if they have not already received the answers to them in stages one and two. Some firms provide at this point a team of management and it is also useful if someone from the union side, say a shop steward, can also be included as he might be able to give a different slant (although tension is highly unlikely to develop between management and union in this sort of gathering). The visit usually lasts for about two and a half to three hours.

Problems which Might be Encountered

1 The management may be loath to discuss some matters, e.g. those relating to trade unions and industrial relations. This, however, can be turned to the teacher's advantage in post-visit discussion, for it does say something about management attitudes and these can be discussed with the pupils.

2 Managers and others involved with the visit may tend to talk above the heads of the pupils; when touring the factory they may only speak to those immediately around them without waiting for others to catch up and they may try to communicate in noisy surroundings. Consequently some pupils may not have a clear picture

of anything that has been going on. For this reason, it is essential to have a de-briefing session.

Post-visit Discussion
At this point many of the loose ends may be tied together and pupils can have gaps in their information and understanding filled. The teacher needs to be knowledgeable about the firm so that he can guide the discussion and tease out the salient points relating to the firm's operations. Pupils can also help each other at this stage by explaining points which others have either not understood or have missed, e.g. some might have

---

Type of job ....*Male/Female*

Married/Single

Ask: 'How important do you consider each of the following?'
Put a tick in one column against each.

	Very important	Fairly important	Not very important	Not at all important	
(a) High wages (b) Working conditions (c) Being able to talk while working (d) Working with friends (e) Interesting work (f) Varied work (g) Responsible work (h) Canteen (i) Social club					

Ask: 'Do you live near any of the people you work with?'
Yes/No

'Do you see any of the people you work with outside work?'
Often/Not often

'Is there any other job you would sooner do?'   Yes/No

If yes, ask 'Why?' and 'Why don't you change to it?'

'Do you expect any promotion?'

'How did you receive your training for your present job?'

Observe for yourself:

Are they able to talk while working?   Often/Not often

Is the work interesting?   Yes/No

Is the work varied?   Yes/No

Is there any opportunity to plan their own work?   Yes/No

Is the work responsible?   Yes/No

Figure 11.3 Questionnaire form, reproduced from
Understanding Industrial Society, *published by*
Hodder and Stoughton

been given information on the tour of the factory which others did not receive.

Written Work on the Firm

Pupils following the 'Understanding Industrial Society Project' now write up their visit to the firm. Given all the information which pupils have collected, they should now be able to organise their thoughts and write a structured account of the firm under, for example, the following headings:

 1 *Brief* history;
 2 General comments, e.g. products made, type of firm, size of firm, capital structure, turnover, profits;
 3 Location of the firm;
 4 Management of the firm;
 5 Raw materials;
 6 Production flow, including diagram;
 7 Office work – a study of an order form from the time it is made to the time it is paid;
 8 Waste products;
 9 Trade unions and labour relations;
10 Structure of the work force;
11 Facilities for workers;
12 Training;
13 Safety;
14 Competition;
15 Market research and advertising;
16 Sales;
17 Prospects for the future;

Pupils are expected to present data in a variety of ways, e.g. tree, flow and other diagrams, graphs, tables, etc.

Questionnaire

If the firm to be visited will allow this, a questionnaire, such as the one in Figure 11.3, put to personnel at a variety of levels (unskilled and skilled labour, office worker, management), will give the pupils useful information about people's attitudes towards their jobs and will provide more raw material for further classroom work.

Post-visit Work on the Questionnaire

1 Collate the information from each group of workers. It is helpful if the questionnaires can be duplicated so that each pupil has a set from which to make the necessary calculations.
2 Contrast different groups of workers in terms of:
(a) What they think are the most important features of their jobs, e.g. high wages or interesting work? Why?
(b) Their propensity to mix with their colleagues outside work.
(c) Differences in training, e.g. on the job, apprenticeship, further and higher education.

(d) Their prospects, as they see them.
(e) How interesting and responsible is the work? Why? What problems can arise from monotony?
(f) How might the workers' jobs be made more interesting? Could this involve higher costs for the firm?
3 It is recommended later in the project that each pupil should take one worker's questionnaire, try to put himself in that person's shoes and write an account of his or her attitude towards work. Pupils should use all the information in the questionnaire but fill it out imaginatively.

The Class Product

When a visit to a small firm has been completed, pupils can be asked to devise the best production line and management structure for a firm manufacturing their product. They should be able to justify all their decisions and this can be a challenging exercise for them.

Visiting Speakers

Speakers from a variety of firms may be usefully brought together, e.g. a sole proprietor and representatives from a small private and a large public limited company. This can be a valuable 'compare and contrast' exercise about raising finance, production flow, opportunity for division of labour, use of profits, labour relations, etc. Managers may also be prepared to talk about their own areas of responsibility, e.g. personnel, marketing.

Bank managers are usually willing to speak about the ways in which banks can help industry, and trade unionists can be used to give pupils an idea of industrial relations as seen from the shop floor.

Management Game

The 'Understanding Industrial Society Project' incorporates a simple business game which is undertaken by fourth year pupils. All such games are a simplification of reality and this is no exception, expecially when one considers that it is aimed at fifteen year old CSE/'O' level candidates. The game is competitive and gives pupils some indication of what it feels like to be the manager of a small firm. Each group has starting cash of £4000. They have to decide the selling price of the good, how much to produce and calculate the total costs for each time period. The umpire will then tell each group how much they have actually sold at that price. Groups then calculate their income, cash in hand and the amount of goods to be brought forward to the next time period. The aim of each group is to maximise profits.

The lessons to be learnt from the game are clearly shown and pupils have found this an interesting and relatively painless method of reinforcing some basic ideas.

Resources

Books
Sanday, A. P. and Birch, P. A., *Understanding Industrial Society*, (Hodder and Stoughton, 1976) Pupils' Book p 224 and Teacher's Guide p 176. This is the core book for the 'Understanding Industrial Society Project' and contains the whole course including case studies of small and large firms. The Teacher's Guide provides a great deal of additional information for those who wish to teach the project, e.g. films, tapes, other resources, syllabuses, specimen questions as well as suggested answers to questions in the Pupils' Book. Many CSE examining boards run Mode III examinations based on the project and teachers should be able to negotiate with their own regional board should it not already have such a Mode III.

The Associated Examining Board's 'O' level examination 'British Industrial Society' covers similar ground in a similar fashion.

Other books do not cover the topic in the same manner but do have particular chapters which provide useful supplementary information.

Baron, D., *Economics: An Introductory Course*, (Heinemann Educational, 1976), p 144. Part III provides information on business units, the Stock Exchange, size of firms and location of industry. It is well presented and provides a variety of questions at the end of each chapter. Suitable for 'O' level and CSE pupils.

Garrett, John L., *Visual Economics*, (Evans, 1976), p 64. Chapter 6 introduces rent, interest and profits. Chapter 9 covers Britain's industries. Chapters 15 and 16 deal with production (including factors of production, types of business enterprise, manufacturing methods and costs of production). Each chapter is two pages in length and will, therefore, require expansion but could provide an introduction to a topic for CSE pupils. While the book uses a variety of visual material, the questions at the end of each chapter are rather unimaginative.

Marder, K. B. and Alderson, L. P., *Economic Society*, (Oxford University Press, 1975), p 256. Generally a well-presented text with good explanatory diagrams. Chapters 3, (sections 2 and 5), 4 and 5 cover classification of industry, division of labour, the organ-isation of firms, economies and diseconomies of scale and reasons for small firms. Needs to be used selectively for CSE pupils.

Nicholson, J. F., *Modern British Economics*, (Allen and Unwin, 1973), p 184. A suggested structure for investigating an industry is provided on pages 21 and 22 and this could be developed in an interesting fashion.

Small Firms Information Centre
This Centre produces several free booklets on aspects of running a firm. Not really suitable for pupils to read from cover to cover, but rather for the teacher to use selectively. For example:

Watkins, D. S., *Starting in Business*. Covers such topics as self-assessment, i.e. what do you want from your business and have you the ability to run it, the choice of business, what marketing involves and its importance, how to raise finance and to whom the small businessman can go for advice.

Watkins, D. S., *Raising Finance for New Enterprises*. This deals with a wide range of methods, e.g. the businessman's own resources such as cash, property, life policy; relatives and friends, bank loans and overdrafts, trade credit, hire purchase and leasing, Industrial and Commercial Finance Corporation Ltd, National Research Development Corporation, Council for Small Industries in Rural Areas and Government help in Assisted Areas.

The booklet also provides information on financial planning, including cash flow calculations.

Cassette Tapes
Sanday, A. P. and Birch, P. A., *Understanding Industrial Society*, (Hodder and Stoughton). Set of three – can be purchased singly. These tapes are intended to complement the core book but they can be used independently.

Cassette 1 track 2. Interviews with people who have set up their own businesses. A builder, three young people who have established a hand-made jewellery business and the owner of a health food shop. These interviews highlight why people decide to set up their own businesses, initial difficulties, raising finance, worries and responsibilities, long hours and hard work, the importance of ploughing profits back into the business and knowing one's market.

Cassette 2 track 1. This includes an interview with the works manager of a medium sized, Coventry engineering firm in which: first, he talks about the development of the firm; secondly, he follows an order through the various planning stages of production; and thirdly, he deals with training workers in the firm and recounts the different types of training necessary for various groups.

Cassette 3 tracks 1 and 2. Interviews with a foreman and a shop floor worker. They talk about their jobs and their attitudes towards work.

A synopsis and teaching points are also supplied with each tape. Aimed at CSE/'O' level pupils.

Tape–Slide Sequences (Cassette or Open Reel)
Manufacturing Large Scale (AVC5). Deals with firms making such goods as machine tools and televisions. Rather a lot of technical information although the commentary also touches on such areas of interest as the importance of planning and control of production, bulk buying, industrial relations and the significance of mass production. The teacher may feel, however, that the gold is buried under rather a lot of dross.

Business Organisation (AVC 18). Starts with a summary of the factors affecting the location of a firm, sources of capital and then looks at a wide range of departments in the firm.

Both these tape–slide sequences (from Student Recordings Ltd), suffer from a rather unimaginative commentary.

Films
Trade It In, Throw It Away, (Concord Film Council), 50 minutes. Directed and narrated by Trevor Philpott

in America for BBC's *Tonight* programme. Made in the mid-60s so certain aspects of the film, e.g. prices, are dated. However, the 'message' is still relevant. Concentrates on planned obsolescence but brings in along the way such topics as wasteful packaging, waste disposal, the size of General Motors, the speed at which raw materials are being consumed and consumer protection. Stimulating, with plenty of material for discussion.

The Industrial Worker, (National Audio-Visual Aids Library), 17 minutes. Teaching notes and questions for discussion are also available. Looks at two American workers, one skilled and the other one unskilled, anxious about automation. The film also points to the benefits of automation for workers.

Filmstrip
The Factors of Production, (Economics Association). A well-structured, sound introduction to this topic. The teacher's booklet is a helpful source of additional information and also contains many well thought out questions (with answers for the teacher).

Wallchart
British Industry (Ref. C 926/7), (Educational Productions Ltd), 2 charts, $37\frac{1}{2}'' \times 25''$. The first (and more useful) chart explains clearly the structure of a modern industrial company. The second chart illustrates some of the achievements of British industry from early days to the present time.

12 Division of Labour
Peter Leech

Introduction

The concept of division of labour is included in most courses at CSE and GCE 'O' level in both economics and commerce. The reason for this is quite obvious. It is, other than language, the key development that enabled our species to rise above all other forms of life on this planet. Teachers realise the importance of the subject, but all too often try to 'get it over with quickly' because pupils find it boring. The idea of this chapter is to show that it need not be so and that it can be taught in an interesting way without simply telling the story of

the economist's standby – Robinson Crusoe. It is hoped that this will make it more likely that this essential concept will then become part of courses other than those already mentioned, such as third year courses and integrated courses in areas such as social studies and humanities.

Teaching Methods

In the following the teaching methods mentioned are put into groups according to the order in which they are usually taught. This does not mean to imply that this structure is rigid or that methods mentioned in one area are not equally applicable to other areas. Indeed many methods must cut across several parts of the topic by the very nature of the work involved.

History and Development
Often the teacher starts by tracing the development of the division of labour from early times to the present day. The idea that poverty is inevitable in an economy where specialisation is absent can be illustrated by telling, or duplicating copies of, a story of how hard it was for a caveman to live when he was trying to be a 'Jack of all Trades'. Indeed our old friend Robinson Crusoe is often brought in at this stage. With lower ability groups, there is a need to personalise the story (e.g. Charlie the Caveman) and to illustrate it, either by humorous episodes or by caricature type drawings (see Figure 12.1). An effective technique with such groups is to build up a story around a small number of cartoon caricatures and use them to show how the life of a caveman became progressively easier as he began to specialise. A variation on this theme would be to provide the pupils with the drawings and get them to tell the story, using these drawings as the stimulus. Most of the teaching would probably come through discussion of the stories. When giving out the pictures there is no reason why they should be put in the right order; indeed the sorting out of the right order could be an important part of the exercise.

As an alternative to this general approach of teaching by stories where all the changes happen to one person, be it Charlie the Caveman, Robinson Crusoe or themselves, the development can be shown by a story involving travel through time. A feasible example is to tell of an advanced alien civilisation which is suffering from the problems of 'over-specialisation'. They use their Time Machine to study the history of specialisation on Earth to try to get a clue as to where they went wrong. This story can be built into a simple teacher-produced multi-media package by tape recording the story, using a variety of different voices to play the various roles and including some space ship sound effects of the type usually available at Teachers' Centres. Slides or drawings could be used to illustrate the story and, as a piece of work to accompany the story, two or three worksheets outlining parts of the stages of development and questions to test pupil understanding could be duplicated. (More detail on how this could be done is included in Appendix I.)

use their local town or other near-by place with which they are familiar.

The Extent of Division of Labour
A second point about the division of labour that pupils need to understand is the extent of specialisation in modern economies. This causes some surprise, particularly among the less able pupils.

Perhaps the obvious starting point is simply to ask what jobs the pupils' friends and relatives have. When

Before specialisation

Figure 12.1

After specialisation

Another interesting piece of work for pupils to do is to explain, either in writing or orally, how they would pass a week on a given location without using anything that had been made by anyone else. The location need not be an exotic desert island. It is far more effective to

listing these on the blackboard, they can be put into various columns for categorisation into primary, secondary and tertiary sectors, or any other classification chosen. This list can then be supplemented by asking pupils to copy the list down and add to it all the other jobs that they know, under the correct column. The total number for the class can then be put together and the variety should surprise most of the class.

To put this type of work into a more concrete context, a picture of the extent of specialisation in the local area can be built up by analysing the 'jobs vacant' columns of local newspapers. If each job advertised is put into a certain group, then these groups can be given a key and plotted on to a map of the area to see if there is any specialisation within the area. The probable result, that most of the jobs in the tertiary sector are in the Central Business District, could prompt discussion of the general reasons for the location of industry. Similarly, by comparing the results with those from the newspaper of a different region, or even another country, the reasons for regional and international specialisation could be discussed.

The 'chain of production' approach can also be used in this context. This can be done by a series of slides or photographs showing the various processes that a given commodity undergoes. Usually the more sophisticated the product the more the extent of division of labour is shown. This type of approach can be extended and improved upon enormously if a local firm can be persuaded to allow itself to be used as an illustration of the productive process. A visit to the factory will show a number of different jobs being done. It will also show much better than photographs how workers are interdependent, as the various stages of production lead to the finished product. Information about the source of raw materials, components and the wholesale and retail outlets can be sought from the management to complete the chain of production for this good. It is even better of course if the area has its own specialisation and a product can be followed through from factory to shop. A good example is bread which can be followed through from a local farm to a bakery and then on to a bread shop. Pupils can be asked to draw their own production flow charts, the degree of sophistication of which can be varied to suit the needs of the individual teacher's requirements and the ability of the pupils involved. Similar flow charts can of course be drawn for other industries where no visit is possible and then compared as an introduction to discussion about why some industries are more specialised than others.

The Advantages of Division of Labour

Pupils find this aspect of the topic most difficult to understand. To give the pupils a list of theoretical advantages to learn appears to have only a short term success. Lasting recall, indicating understanding rather than memory alone, would seem to require a more concrete exposition. This can be provided by giving the pupils a task to perform. A very simple outline of how this can be done is as follows:

1 *The task*. To draw and then cut out a piece of paper 6 cm square within which is drawn a circle of radius 3 cm.
2 *The equipment*. One pair of compasses, one ruler, two pencils, one pair of scissors and several sheets of paper, per group.
3 *Operation*. The class is split into groups of three. Each group is given one set of equipment and told to use no other. Half of the groups specialise with one person doing each of the three parts of the task. The other half of the groups are told to complete the whole of the task individually. The class is then given a specific time period in which to complete as many as they can, possibly subject to some kind of quality control. The follow-up work to this simulation would be a discussion of the advantages of division of labour, usually initiated by a bad loser who thought that the game was unfair. The process could be repeated but with the suggestion that some of the groups devote a part of the allotted time to making some kind of capital equipment such as a cardboard stencil of the circle or square to draw round. (See Appendices II and III for further examples of labour simulations.)

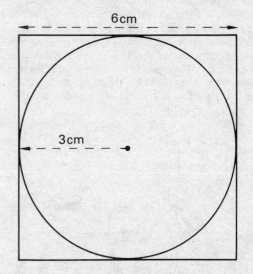

Figure 12.2

Once the idea of specialisation having certain advantages has been put into a concrete context it is easier to expand upon it by generalisation. A good way to do this is to devise a simple comprehension worksheet centred around a home-made poster. This poster is easily made by cutting out a picture to illustrate each of the advantages of division of labour and then sticking them on to a piece of plain paper next to a slogan encapsulating the particular advantage. Figure 12.3 is an example of this.

Figure 12.3

Probably the hardest aspect of all for pupils to understand is the comparative advantage argument. All too often this is shown in the traditional way by showing the comparative costs of producing wine and cloth in England and Portugal. There are other ways of making this relevant without simply substituting Japan and radios for Portugal and cloth. It can also be shown on a more personal level as in this example:

Mr Smith is a baker. He owns a small bakery and works alone. He works for eight hours each day. Six hours are spent actually baking bread and the other two are spent in delivering it. By the time he has paid for the raw materials, power and so on, he can make a profit of 5p per loaf. Each hour he can make fifty loaves.

Summary:

Delivering	2 hours
Baking	6 hours
Loaves baked	300
Profit	300×5p=£15.00

Then John, a schoolboy, comes asking for the delivery job. Mr Smith knows that John is a bit slower than he is and that he could deliver the loaves faster by himself, but decides to take him on at a wage of £1 per hour and spend more time doing what he is best at – baking his bread, which is in high demand. Because John is slower the deliveries take him four hours. The next day this is what happens.

Summary:

Baking	8 hours
Loaves baked	400
Revenue	400 × 5p = £20.00
Minus John's wage	= £ 4.00
Profit	= £16.00

Discuss: 'Why is Mr Smith £1 better off by paying John to deliver bread when he could do it more quickly himself?'

The Disadvantages of Division of Labour

The methods used in the previous section can be expanded upon and used here. The task set for the pupils previously, for instance, could be used as a starting point for discussion about whether or not the assembly line type of production would become more boring than that of performing the whole process individually.

With this age range visual stimulation is very important. Pairs of photographs could be used as a basis for discussion of the disadvantages of specialisation. For example, the pupils could be shown a picture of a craftsman such as a potter and an assembly line mass producing a similar good, and encouraged to discuss why the quality of goods produced by the former should be higher than the latter. It may be possible to get a worker from an assembly line to come into the school to give a more personal talk about his feelings when working in this way. A tape recorded interview might be a more practical alternative to a speaker, but in both cases the exercise would be more effective if linked to a visit to the factory in question. Pupils could then add to the discussion by expressing opinions about how they would feel doing the jobs seen on the visit. The question of whether or not these disadvantages are inevitable could be touched upon by a comprehension exercise on, for example, an outline of the Volvo experiments at their Kalmar plant in Sweden. The text of the exercise could be supplemented by photographs or drawings, if available. It would include a description of the conventional assembly line organisation of car production, and the problems inherent in it such as boredom, absenteeism, poor industrial relations, poor quality goods and so on. There could then follow a description of Volvo's scheme for getting around these problems by introducing, at some extra cost, the idea of organising production in terms of small groups doing more of the processes than on an assembly line. Questions on terminology, understanding and extended discussion points, could be tailored to suit the needs of each individual teacher. (Seminar Cassettes' tape on job satisfaction describes the Volvo experiment.)

Resources

For those who like a conventional textbook, chapter 4 of J. Harvey's *Introductory Economics* (Macmillan, 1971) gives all the advantages and disadvantages of division of labour, going back to Adam Smith's example from the pin making industry. This book is singled out, not for being so much better than all the others of its type, but because it is the classic archetype of the textbook coverage of this topic. The same information is contained in much the same form in a wide variety of introductory textbooks in economics and commerce. This is not to say that such textbooks are universally 'dry'. J. Nobbs, in Unit 16 of his *Social Economics* (McGraw-Hill, 1976), for instance, enlivens the description by including examples of division of labour ranging from that of Jesus being a specialist carpenter, to the 7882 separate tasks performed when producing the Model T Ford – 670 of which could be done by legless men, 2637 by one-legged men, 2 by armless men, 715 by one-armed men and 10 by blind men. B. Davies and D. Hender have a similar section in chapter 3 of *Production and Trade*, (Longman Social Studies Series, 1974). They show how a group of people discover the advantages of division of labour when making paper chains for the decorations for a Christmas party.

Possibly the most varied and interesting coverage of the topic is that given by F. Davies in chapter 4 of *Starting Economics* (Hulton, 1977). In this we are introduced to the character of Fred Flinthead and lightheartedly follow his progress from a poor 'Jack of all Trades' to a more affluent specialist hunter trading with other people. The idea of division of labour is then put into a more up-to-date context by applying the principle to the mailing of a circular letter to the parents of the pupils of a school.

In terms of articles, rather than books for pupils, one well worth reading is that by W. A. Campbell called 'Teaching Division of Labour to Less Able Pupils – A Role Playing Approach', which appeared in *Economics*, 8(6). In this article there is an extended example and discussion of the sort of simple task-performing exercise mentioned in the section above on the advantages of division of labour. As well as giving an outline of the organisation of the exercise, there is some discussion of the points that were made by his pupils and suggestions of areas for extension and integration into other parts of the course.

Student Recordings Ltd have produced two tape and filmstrip packages related to this topic. These two are called *The Division of Labour* (AVC 24) and *Mechanisation* (AVC 26). While providing a good summary, these packages would be too dull and the commentary too dry and verbose to be very useful for any but the most academic pupils of this age.

A new cassette/filmstrip pack from Audio Learning is *Production – Primary, Secondary and Tertiary Activities* (ECO 002).

Guest speakers with practical knowledge of local industry such as personnel managers, may well be prepared to come in to the school. It may even be possible to organise a debate with a local management representative and a production line worker, giving alternative sides to the advantages and disadvantages of mass production methods. A visiting speaker may also be of some help concerning the extent of the division of labour. An official from the local Job Centre for example would be able to talk about the variety of jobs available, problems caused by regional specialisation, differences between local and national labour markets and so on.

Appendix I

The Story of Zee

The advantages of division of labour could be shown through a story of a visitor from another planet coming to earth at various times in a time machine. Such a story might have the following basic outline.

1 Introduction – setting the scene on the alien planet, where the inhabitants have become dehumanised and life too compartmentalised because of over-specialisation on this planet. Zee is a scientist from that planet who is instructed to use their time machine to study the planet earth and to try to find clues as to how the process of specialisation could be halted or reversed.
2 Visit One – description of the position on earth when there was no real division of labour, stressing the poverty.
3 Visit Two – moving from prehistory to early recorded times and the greater division of labour bringing about improvements in the standard of living.
4 Visit Three – to England at the start of the Industrial Revolution, with the greater use of machinery and the harnessing of power.
5 Visit Four – to modern Britain where an unemployed textile worker from a formerly highly specialised area is arguing about the state of the economy with an assembly line worker who is claiming to be on strike to relieve the boredom of his work.
6 Visit Five – Britain in the 1990s where there has been the great compromise between less specialisation and lower output and better quality goods and job satisfaction. This compromise has been brought about by the constraint of limited resources, a step not undergone yet on Zee's relatively resource-rich planet.

Accompanying Work
If the story outlined above were to be tape recorded with bits of dialogue for each of the visits, there could be accompanying worksheets, each outlining one or more bits of the story and then followed up with questions. These questions could range from terminology used in the story to asking why the first characters in the story were so poor compared to the later ones. There could also be questions of the following type: 'Stone Age Sam was poor but he did something different every day. Zee was rich but spent half his life pushing a button on a machine. Describe the life of each of them and give all the reasons that you can for preferring to be one of these two rather than the other.' Other exercises might include tasks such as drawing a picture or series of pictures to illustrate the story.

Other materials to amplify the story could be visual ones, such as pictures and drawings of various scenes throughout history or tools and machines used at different stages of specialisation. These could be used as the starting point for discussion as to the advantages of various degrees of specialisation.

Appendix II: Assembly Line: an Economics Simulation*

Dennis C. Dobbs, Carol G. Goodell and Robert F. Hill

Assembly Line is a simulation that provides a concrete experience of the real world of work and technology. The purpose of the simulation is to provide the learner with a dramatic and dynamic model of a mass production system. It provides first-hand experience with the varying attitudes and feelings that are a part of our mechanised society.

The simulation leads to an understanding of how mass production methods have made possible increased productivity and reduced cost of production. It also provides insights into the social changes that lead to the creation of new jobs, the disappearance of old jobs, and man's sharp increase in his use of natural resources.

Assembly Line further provides players with opportunities to simulate many assembly line working conditions. These include lack of contact with and therefore lack of pride in the final product; monotony resulting from repetitive tasks; demands to speed up or slow down production; and the pressures and responsibilities in man's factory work.

* Reprinted with kind permission from the authors.

General Outline

Setting Up
First transfer the outlines of automobile parts and run off about fifty copies on white paper. A practical sequence of operations is shown in the illustration of the conveyor belt set-up.

Efficiency Engineers
Before playing *Assembly Line*, the teacher should have two or three pupils set up the conveyor belt. In their role as *efficiency engineers* they should arrange the assembly sequence in order to maximise efficiency. These tasks should be done by the pupils. They should have the opportunity to make and correct their own errors, for problem solving is at the core of the learning experience of this simulation.

Demonstration
When it is time to play *Assembly Line*, the teacher may wish to begin by demonstrating how to put together one car before the pupils begin production. Ideally, the pupils who set up the conveyor belt and assembly line layout can provide 'on-the-job' training for others.

Line Supervisor
Line supervisors handle problems that arise and order materials when supplies are low. They also make decisions about changes in the sequence of assembly tasks. Reassigning jobs and seeing to it that defective automobiles are correctly reassembled or salvaged fall under their jurisdiction.

Maintenance Crew
The *maintenance crew* sees to it that the work area is kept clean and that the conveyor belt is in good repair.

Inspectors
Inspectors can be placed at mid-points along the belt and at the end of the line to insure quality control.

Order Blanks
Workers are now ready to receive their first *order blank*. The teacher may make these out in advance, or they can be made out by the *biller*.

Management Procedures
The *order blank* is turned over to a *line supervisor*. At the end of the assembly line the *inspector* compares the final product with the order and signs the blank if the automobile passes inspection.

Workers' Duties
The first few *workers* along the belt rough-cut the sheets of parts along the dotted lines, and place them on the belt. The next several *workers* cut each part out along the solid lines, and return them to the belt. If the parts are reproduced on white paper, the next step is to have them 'painted' by *workers* using crayons, taking care not to colour areas to be glued. The *line supervisor* must know what colours have been specified on the *order blank* so he can pass this information along to the *workers*. The next *workers* on the line paste parts together.

Problem Solving
All will not go smoothly during the simulation experience, nor should it, for this would cut off problem-solving opportunities for the learner. For instance, if there seems to be a snag in the sequence of operations, the teacher can let it go on until a solution is devised by leaders among the pupils; or he can intervene and ask the pupils to describe the problem and proceed to a discussion as to what the alternative solutions might be. Later, research on a field trip could reveal how real assembly line operations deal with such problems.

GOALS

1. Introduce concept of mass production in industry.

2. Gain information about the operation of an assembly line.

3. Experience some of the feelings of workers on an assembly line.

4. Utilize related social and academic skills.

CONCEPTS

Mass production
Division of Labour
Interchangeable parts
Gross income/Net income
Monotony
Job specialization

MATERIALS

1. Tables and chairs or desks with legs on outer corners to permit conveyor to pass on the floor beneath.

2. One to two foot wide roll of paper for conveyor belt. (Improvise)

3. Scissors and paste or glue.

4. Card board for car templates to be used with coloured construction paper, or dittos and white construction paper.

5. Pencils for tracing templates on coloured construction paper, or crayons for "painting" cars on dittoed white construction paper. Do not paint G (glueing surfaces).

ROLES

ASSEMBLY LINE can be adapted for groups from 12 to 40 in size.

Billers (0-2)
Tracers (4-8) (Template)
    or
Rough Cutters (1-3) Ditto
Fine Cutters (3-15+)
Gluers (3-10+)
Inspectors (1-2)
Line Mechanic (1)
Line Supervisors (1-3)
Accountants (1-2)
Maintenance Crew (1-2)

OPTIONAL PLAYERS

Foreman
Auto Dealers
Customers
Design Engineers
Managers
Union Representatives
Salesmen

DIRECTIONS

1. Transfer car diagram to a ditto or trace parts on card board paper to be used as tracing templates.

2. Arrange desks or tables in a long row with seating for workers on each side.

3. Set up a paper conveyor belt. Paper is taped together after being looped over and under the line of tables or desks.

4. Distribute materials and tools.

5. Demonstrate to players the assembly of one car. (Optional)

6. Designate player roles and places.

TIME

45-75 minutes (depending on discussion time)

QUESTIONS TO CONSIDER

PRODUCTION

1. Do some people have harder jobs than others?

2. Is there a more efficient way of increasing the number of cars produced?

3. Does anyone get behind? What can be done about this?

4. What are some other factors hindering productivity?

5. Are there high enough standards of quality in the cars being produced?

6. What are the special problems of workers on the assembly line?

7. How can management improve working conditions?

8. How can costs be cut?

SOCIOLOGICAL

1. How are differences between labour and management settled?

2. What must a worker do in order to be promoted?

3. What is an Equal Opportunity Employer?

4. Could physically or mentally handicapped people work on an assembly line?

5. What should be done about the worker who "just can't do it right?"

6. What are society's responsibilities toward people who can't hold a job?

7. What responsibilities does an individual have in doing what is necessary to make a living?

PSYCHOLOGICAL

1. How are people affected by monotonous tasks?

2. How can a worker be helped to feel that what he does is important?

3. Does a worker's attitude toward his job affect the nature of his work? How?

4. What accounts for many people being "clock watchers" while on the job?

5. Could some people receive a good deal of satisfaction from assembly line work? Who? In what way?

6. When you are older would you want to work on a real assembly line? Why?

ECONOMIC

1. How are income, expenses, and profit determined?

2. Why might a manufacturing company use an assembly line operation?

3. How does demand affect the likely profits of a manufacturing company?

4. What are some of the consequences of a large company having to shut down operation?

5. What are some reasons for workers going on strike?

6. How does mass production affect our supply of natural resources?

7. What happens if a product is defective and is returned?

SWORD MOTOR COMPANY

Makers of the Model B
Oxford, England

Order Number:_____. Date:_____

Dealer's Name:_____

Delivery to City of:_____

Number	Colour(s)	Price

(Add **10**% Sales Tax)

Inspector's Signature:

_____

Total Price:_____

Biller: Do computation on the back of this sheet.

Actual size of manufactured
Automobile before painting

CUTTING DIRECTIONS First rough cut parts on dotted lines. Then all seven pieces should be cut by the fine cutters.

ASSEMBLY DIRECTIONS (SEQUENCE)

1st glue roof tabs to underside of door panel
2nd glue motor compartment to underside of door panel
3rd glue assembled component on to chassis
4th glue fenders and running board to assembled chassis
5th glue wheels on to fender tabs

PAINTING DIRECTIONS

Colour motor hood, door panel, and fenders such that no white paper shows.

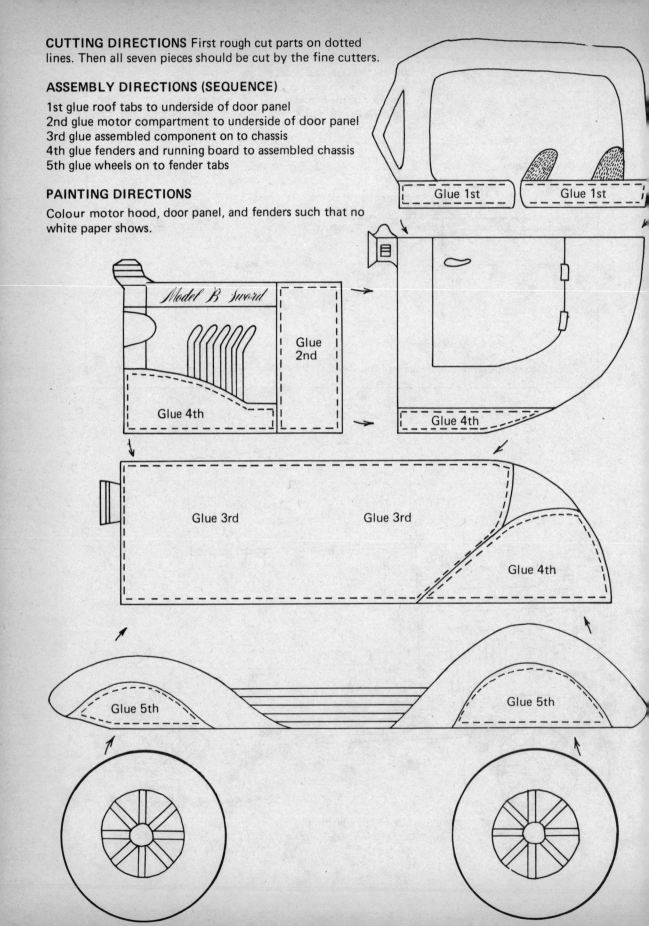

The room is set up so that a piece of paper long enough to provide three feet of working space per student can be pulled by a player (*line mechanic*) across a flat surface and then returned in a circular pattern, much like any standard conveyor belt. Such a surface can be arranged by using desks or tables with chairs on each side. When the inspectors reject a car, they place it on the bottom returning belt for salvage recycling. The paper must be narrow enough to provide work space on each side of the belt. Ideally, the belt should be one to two feet wide.

CONVEYOR BELT
SET-UP

Figure 12.4

Appendix III: The Widget Game*
K. Light

Objectives
To identify four sources of efficiency in the production process, namely (1) specialisation; (2) education; (3) motivation; (4) scale of enterprise.

Materials Required
1 pencil per student
20 boxes of paper clips
1000–2000 5 cm × 5 cm paper squares

* Reproduced with permission from *Adventure: Economics*, (Ohio Council on Economic Education, 1975).

Conduct of Simulation

The simulation is conducted in three sessions, each three minutes long. Distribute ten paper clips, ten 5×5 cm squares of paper, and a pencil to each student. Tell the students they are going to produce widgets. Describe the making of widgets:

A widget is made by taking a 5 cm by 5 cm square of paper and putting an 'X' in each of the four corners, folding the square in half and concealing all of the X's, then clipping (placing a paper clip) the open end of the paper opposite the fold and carefully creasing the fold.

After describing the procedure for making a widget, ask each student to make a widget and wait for further instructions. After each student has made a widget, inspect the products and correct faulty production.

The first production period will be spent with each student making his or her own widget. Tell students their products will be examined at the end of the production period for quality. Each student will begin with one complete widget and materials to make nine more. Additional materials will be available, but carefully instruct students on the orderly pick-up of extra items. No producer may take more than ten sets of production items at one time. Tell students you will count the output of each producer at the conclusion of the production period. Conduct a three-minute production period.

Following the first production period, check all widgets produced. Examine for X's, proper use of paper clips and careful creases. Poorly constructed widgets should be discarded. After the quality check is completed, tabulate the number of widgets made by each student and by the entire class. Have the best widget makers describe their production process.

Before the second production period, students should be grouped in eights. The group should work together to discuss the production of widgets and plan for the second production period. This time, students within the groups of eight may decide to work alone or in groups. Prior to the production period, each student should have ten sets of materials; the groups may combine materials and organise however they wish. Once again, tell students you will count output and measure quality. Conduct the production period and calculate group output and total output. Have the most productive individuals or groups describe their efforts.

In the third and final period, permit students to do group planning in much the same way as in period two, emphasising that a group of eight can divide into smaller groups of any size or work as individuals. However, the final output score will be by group summing the output of the eight individual members. Finally, tell the students that the most productive group will be rewarded with fifteen extra minutes of free-time, or whatever reward best fits your situation. Conduct the production process and calculate group and total output.

Discussion

Following the three production periods, outputs of each period should be compared. Typically, the output per student increases each period. Why?

1 Once students know what to do and how to do it, widget production (increased education) output increases.
2 When students divide their labour and the output increases, it shows that division of labour in simple and complex tasks often increases per man output.
3 The per man production of widgets is usually greatest when two or three students work together. Other sizes (scale of enterprise) are too small or too large. The proper size of plant and manpower depends on the product to be made.
4 When workers are motivated by rewards they often produce more. The motive of many workers is profit or the ability to share the proceeds of increased output.

Many other significant learnings can evolve from this simulation, but emphasise the four listed outcomes.

13 Money and Banking
David R. Butler

General Comments

Money and banking as a topic is included in most 'O' level and CSE syllabuses and might well form part of a course for younger pupils. Some aspects of this topic may appear to be rather 'dry' to the teacher but pupils often show a surprising degree of interest in many aspects of it. It does have the advantage of being a 'live' topic in the sense that pupils can actually see the commercial banks in their High Streets and may well have come into contact with aspects of them such as cheques and credit cards as well as being exposed to the very considerable amount of advertising which these organisations indulge in. Younger pupils seem to be particularly fascinated by the money side of this topic, and an elementary treatment of the development of money including cheques and credit cards is a popular and useful section in a third year basic economics course. (See Chapter 2.)

Content

Most syllabuses require at least some of the following: barter – its problems and the reasons for money; the 'qualities' of money; the development of notes and coins, cheques and credit cards; services and functions of commercial banks; the asset/liability structure of commercial banks; the Bank of England and the control of the commercial banks; merchant banks, overseas banks, and savings banks; the National Giro; saving and borrowing money; insurance.

Teaching Methods

The following suggested methods and approaches have been used to supplement 'chalk and talk' and basic textbooks in an attempt to make the topic more stimulating for the pupil.

1 Barter classroom simulation – two members of the class are picked to represent a ruler seller and a pencil seller. The ruler seller wishes to buy pencils and the pencil seller, rulers. They have to arrange a deal between themselves. The teacher uses this to illustrate the problems of fixing exchange rates and of the objects being indivisible (i.e. they are unable to have an exchange rate of $1\frac{1}{2}$ rulers to five pencils). The situation is then repeated with another two members of the class but this time the pencil seller does not require rulers but wants a rubber. Hence a third member of the class is brought in and the problem of needing a double coincidence of wants (or 'wanting what the other person has to sell') is illustrated. This can be extended to include other members of the class to illustrate the problem of having multiple exchange rates. (See the Resources section at the end of the chapter for a marketed barter game.)

2 Development of coins, notes – the historical

Month	Balance from previous statement	Interest at 2%	Present balance	Minimum payment	Amount paid
	£	£	£	£	£
1	00.00	00.00	100.00	15.00	15.00
2	85.00	1.70	86.70	13.00	13.00
3					
4					
5					
6					

Table 13.1 Credit Card Statement

approach – what things have been used as money (see Resources for references). The example of the German inter-war hyperinflation creates considerable interest and is useful in bringing out many of the fundamental aspects of money.

3 Cheques – younger pupils enjoy filling out cheques, paying in slips etc. Fascimile documents are easily obtained (see Resources) or reasonably realistic ones can be easily constructed.

4 Credit card exercise – you buy a new amplifier costing £100 with your credit card and decide to pay for it over six months. For the first five months you pay the minimum possible (this is either 15 per cent or £6 – whichever is the greater). In the sixth month you pay off all the outstanding balance. Complete the following table (Table 13.1) and answer the questions below:

Questions on Credit Card Exercise
(a) How much do you eventually pay for the amplifier?
(b) How much more is this than the cash price?
(c) Although you have paid more for the amplifier using a credit card, what advantages may there be in buying it this way?

5 Bank services – an ideal topic for project work as there is plenty of material easily available from the banks. Pupils can find out as many services as possible. This works particularly well if linked to a local branch visit (see Resources). Pupils can also carry out a survey amongst relatives and friends as to which bank, if any, is used, and why it is used and whether it is the same as the one where their account is held.

6 Asset/liability structure – the actual figures can be obtained from bank reviews and the *Bank of England Quarterly Bulletin*, and can be used as a basis for discussion with more able pupils.

Questions on the Article shown in Figure 13.1
1 What is meant by 'the minimum lending rate'?
2 How is MLR calculated?
3 Why should a cut in MLR 'increase the pressure on the Building Societies Association to decide in favour of an early cut in their interest rates'?
4 Why has the MLR fallen?
5 What are the advantages and disadvantages of allowing MLR to fall?

The class could also be split into groups each representing a different clearing bank. Each bank is allocated the same amount of money which has to be divided into an asset structure (cash at Bank of England, money at call, advances, etc). The teacher allocates a rate of interest to each asset during the year (the game to run for ten years). During the year the teacher introduces a number of 'effects' e.g. increase in Special Deposits, cash withdrawals by customers of £x million from Barclays, etc. If banks find that they cannot meet Bank of England or customer requirements they have to borrow and are hence penalised by the interest charged.

7 Loans and overdrafts – simulation exercise of different people applying to their bank manager for loans/overdrafts for varying purposes. Pupils need to decide whether they should give loans, what securities might be accepted, etc (see Resources for a marketed simulation).

8 Role of the Bank of England – newspaper articles with questions based on them are useful stimulus material which help to make topics such as MLR and

Figure 13.1 Example of the use of a newspaper cutting which could be used to provide the basis for an exercise on the Bank of England (aimed at top ability fifth years)

MLR pressure for mortgage rate cut

By John Whitmore

The Bank of England has cut its minimum lending rate from 9½ per cent to 9¼ per cent, the second reduction in consecutive weeks. This latest move, coupled with the possibility of a further downward drift in money market rates next week, can only increase the pressure on the Building Societies Association to decide in favour of an early cut in their interest rates at their monthly meeting next Friday.

Although the Bank has been attempting to keep the rate of decline in interest rates to a moderate pace, it has been happy to allow rates slip down a few notches since the Budget.

Concern about the impact of the incomes policy negotiations on overseas confidence may, however, now lead the authorities to decide that rates should be discouraged from slipping much more over the coming weeks.

If, in fact, there is little overseas concern about the pay talks and if money continues to flow into the country on a large scale, the authorities will be left with the choice —assuming they are not prepared to give up their policy of holding down the exchange rate—of either allowing interest rates to fall more quickly or introducing additional exchange controls.

This week's cut in MLR brings the total fall from last October's crisis level of 15 per cent to 5¾ points. The reduction largely reflects the revival in overseas confidence in sterling after the announcement of the sterling "safety net" late last year and the acute depression in the domestic demand for bank advances.

Once again, this week's Treasury bill tender drew heavy applications. Total applications for the £500m of three-month bills on offer amounted to £1,073m. The average rate of allotment fell from 8.7643

per cent the previous week to 8.5179 per cent.

Ronald Kershaw writes: No encouraging signs of early reductions in mortgage interest rates came from the annual meeting of the Yorkshire County Association of Building Societies at Leeds on Thursday. Mr Raymond Potter, general manager of the Halifax and chairman of the association, said that the prior need was to raise lending to a higher rate than at present.

No reduction in interest rates would be desirable until lending was increased, until some liquidity was restored and, most important, until societies were satisfied that the general level of interest rates would continue to fall.

Mr Potter said that at December 31, 1976, the total assets of the Yorkshire societies were £9,500m, out of a total of about £28,000m for the movement as a whole.

Special Deposits a little more 'real' to the pupil. (See worksheet on MLR article.)

9 Savings banks and National Giro – as with the commercial banks, the documents issued by these organisations are easily available and younger pupils do enjoy actually using them. It is possible to set up a National Savings Bank within the school (see Resources for details) which pupils can run themselves under supervision and with which pupils are able to save and invest. Pupils can be given an imaginary £1000 to invest over a period of three to six months, in any type of financial institution, including the Stock Exchange. The winner is the pupil who ends with the most money, net of tax. Alternatively, a set of cases can be presented on a worksheet, describing various individuals' financial situations. The pupils are asked to define what is the best saving plan for them.

10 Other suggestions – set up a mock bank. Trace the life of a cheque through the clearing system. A comparison of the National Giro and commercial banks based on a questionnaire survey of account holders. A study of banks in the local High Street which takes in their location, size, facilities, etc.

Areas where Pupils have Problems of Understanding

(a) Barter – less able pupils have difficulty in visualising an economy without money. In particular they find it difficult to understand that a good may have a 'price' in terms of other goods. A good demonstration in the suggested simulation could assist considerably here.

(b) Money – many pupils regard money as having an intrinsic value (e.g. 'Pound notes have a silver strip in them which is worth £1' is a common misunderstanding). Pupils find it difficult to understand why a £1 note is worth £1 of goods. The illustration of the German hyperinflation helps to demonstrate what 'paper' money depends upon to be of value.

Example
'A 50 Mark note, worth about £1 when issued in June 1919, would then have bought two dozen eggs. A 10 000 000 000 Mark note issued on 1 October 1923 three weeks later bought one-seventh of an egg' (from an article published in *The Times*, 11 October 1974).

Questions/Discussion
 (i) Why did an egg cost so much more in 1923?
 (ii) Why did money become worth so much less?
 (iii) What things were used as money instead of notes?

(c) Asset/liability structures – pupils tend to confuse the terms. Credit creation (although often not required at this level) may be difficult for many pupils to comprehend. A common misunderstanding is to say that a bank lends out eight times its deposits. (This will only be the end result in a multi-bank system and under certain assumptions. No bank lends out more than is put into it.) A simulation may again be of great value here with the teacher introducing a deposit so that the pupils can actually see how it creates credit in the banking system.

(d) Overdrafts – pupils frequently misunderstand how an overdraft works and how it is different from a personal loan. Actual case studies of loans and overdrafts to illustrate what they are used for may help to clarify the differences.

(e) Bank Giro and National Giro – pupils tend to confuse the terms and have problems in understanding how they each work. The use of an actual Bank Giro document and an illustration of its 'journey' should help to distinguish the two in the pupil's mind.

(f) Bills of exchange – there is a lack of good explanation in most textbooks and many do not deal with them at all. Some explanations are given in the film *Curious History of Money* at a basic level although this tends to go rather too quickly and needs reinforcing by the teacher. An actual example of a transaction involving a bill of exchange might also be very useful here.

Resources

Books
The commercial banking aspect of this topic is well covered in most economics and commerce textbooks, as are the banking mechanism and the more descriptive aspects of bank services which many syllabuses require. Many textbooks are weak on merchant banks, savings banks and overseas banks. Understandably, textbooks tend to become out-of-date rapidly on bank charges, interest rates, and the additional services now offered by organisations such as the Trustee Savings Bank and the National Giro.

Stanlake, G. F., *Introductory Economics*, (Longman, 1976), part 6: 'Money and Banking'. Covers development of money, functions/qualities of money, banking mechanism, Bank of England, National Giro and London Money Market. Quite good on merchant banks and bills of exchange.

Nobbs, J., *Social Economics*, (McGraw-Hill, 1976), units 2, 3, 4, 5, and 6. Deals with barter, functions of money, cheques, bank services, savings banks, assets and liabilities, credit creation, Bank of England. Good overall coverage. Good summary of commercial bank services. Quite good on savings and merchant banks.

Nobbs, J. and Ames, D., *Daily Economics*, (McGraw-Hill, 1975), units 3, 4, 5 and 8. Deals with credit, banking services and insurance. Intended for the less able pupil. Well presented and written although a little thin on material.

Thomas, D. J., *A First Course in Commerce*, (Bell, 1976), chapter 4: 'Banks'. Deals with commercial banks, Bank of England, clearing house system, savings banks, merchant banks, post office, Giro. Good presentation of cheques etc. Good diagram on clearing system (p. 38) plus explanation.

Allen, M. (ed), *Save and Prosper Book on Money*, (Collins), chapters 2, 3, and 4. Looks at savings loans, bank services etc from the consumer's viewpoint. Extremely well presented with 'wiseguide' sections giving advantages and disadvantages of loans and investments. Good coverage of National Giro services, Trustee Savings Bank and National Savings Bank. Needs to be carefully adapted by the teacher for examination syllabuses.

Garrett J., *Visual Economics*, (Evans, 1969), chapters 4 and 24. Covers barter, banks and money. Aimed at younger pupil. Might well be used with lower ability groups of thirteen year olds. Not entirely satisfactory but better than a lot of material aimed at this level.

Akers, A. G. and Booth G. L., *Your Bank Account*, (Nelson, 1971). Cartoon approach for younger pupils on this one aspect of banks. Quite well illustrated and points made in simple language.

Barber, W., *Money Matters*, (Nelson, 1974). Aimed at the non-examinee but might be useful at CSE level. Good visual approach to cheques, bank accounts, savings accounts, loans, etc.

Written Material
Bank Education Service. An excellent source of a tremendous amount of material sent freely in multiple copies. Material includes blank cheques, Giro forms, credit slips and statements. Pamphlets: 'A Selection of Facsimile Bank Forms and Documents', 'How to Handle Cheques', 'The Life of a Cheque', 'The Clearing System', 'The Role of the Banks'. Wallcharts – BES produce an excellent series of large wallcharts on several different aspects of the banking system. (Other wallcharts available from National Westminster Bank Advertising Dept (free) and from Pictorial Charts – *Your Money* (F16).)

Life Offices Association. Four excellent booklets available free and in large quantities entitled: 'What is Life Insurance', 'Life Assurance and You', 'People, Protection and Prosperity', and 'Saving and Spending'. They also produce three less useful study kits at 75p each entitled 'Money and Society', 'Money and You', 'Life Assurance and You'. The first kit deals with the development of money and barter. Aimed at younger age group. Workcards and filmstrip. Needs 'back up' by teacher. Parts of the kit might be adapted for a third year course.

Main commercial banks, building societies, insurance and assurance companies, etc. All produce a large number of well presented, if somewhat biased, leaflets. These can easily be adapted for class teaching examples; Barclays Bank 'Why Everyone Should Apply for a Barclaycard', 'A Student's Guide to Banking'. Midland Bank 'How a Cheque Book Works'. Lloyds Bank 'Cash Cards'. National Westminster Bank 6 charts: 'Computer Support', 'How to Secure A Loan', 'The Bank Abroad', 'Personal Service', 'An Investor's Guide', 'Not Only A Bank But Also'.

National Giro. Leaflets, e.g. 'Isn't it Time you Opened a Giro Account?'

National Savings Committee. Leaflets explaining various savings schemes offered. They will also supply wall posters advertising different schemes if asked nicely.

Films, Tapes, etc. The Curious History of Money (Multilink Film Library, free loan) – cartoon film covering barter, coins, notes, cheques, bills of exchange, etc. Suitable for all age groups. Commentary tends to be a little too fast so that plenty of 'back up' by the teacher is required.
The Rise of Parnassus Needy (same source, free loan). – cartoon film dealing with bank loans. Suitable for all ages. Rather dated (talks of £.s.d.) and criteria for giving bank loans somewhat dubious. *A Piece of Plastic* and *A Sign of our Times* (both free loan, same source) – advertising films for Barclaycard showing basic uses (about ten minutes only).
Your Money and Your Life (Royal Bank of Scotland) – guide to bank services, twenty minutes (free loan).
Why We Use Money – US cartoon film aimed at primary school pupils but suitable for other ages. £6, eight minutes. From Rank Film Library (Ref 21 9030).
The Bankers – Daily Life of Bank Managers, 27″ from Multilink Film Library (free loan).
Fly Me to the Bank – shows services Midland performs for its customers – 23″ – Multilink Film Library (free loan).

Cassette tape. Understanding Industrial Society Project (Hodder and Stoughton). Cassette 1, track 1 – 'Trying for a bank loan' – an interview with the bank manager (made in co-operation with Lloyds Bank).

Tape/filmstrip. Student Recordings Ltd – *Money and Banking* (AVC/140) and *Commercial Bank Services*. Factually quite good but rather a dull commentary.

ILEA TV – *Commerce For Today* series. Available on video tape for hire or purchase. From Guild Sound and Vision. Very good programme on credit (900 9692 1). *Banking 1 – Why Bother to Open a Current Account* (900 9703 0). *Banking 2 – Making Use of Your Cash* (900 9704 7). Aimed at about CSE level.
BBC Film Enterprises, *Economics of the Real World – Inflation*, on German hyperinflation.

Talks and Visits
The BES will send visiting speakers. (See also Chapter 24.) These vary considerably and at this level often only duplicate the efforts of the teacher. It is important to stress the age and ability of the pupils. (I have found speakers to be more useful at sixth form level.) The main banks will supply a similar service. Midland Bank will send their caravan which demonstrates the workings of a branch bank to the school for a whole day. Pupils need to be divided into groups of about ten. Works well with fourth year pupils. (Select appropriate programme.)

  Local branch visits. Contact local branch manager to arrange an 'open evening'. The local Barclays branch is extremely co-operative in this. An arrangement which works well is to divide the pupils into small groups and to rotate them around the various branch functions (counter, securities, manager etc) about every five minutes. These evenings are popular with fifth years and can be run jointly with the careers department.

Other Resources
Bank Loan – a simulation by D. Birt and P. Tinniswood (Longman/Lloyds Bank from Longman Group Resources Unit, £2 for ten copies). Gives a number of case studies and pupil has to decide whether to grant loans to each of the customers. Pitched at CSE/'O' level pupils, though a little difficult for some CSE groups. Well produced, interesting case studies.

Newspaper advertising – the more interesting adverts can provide stimulus material for all ages.

Bank Reviews – published quarterly by all the main banks. Plus *Quarterly Bulletin* from Bank of England. Statistics on bank liabilities/assets. (Articles are very useful at sixth form level.)

Sandford and Bradbury, *Case Studies in Economics – Principles of Economics* – case study of hyperinflation in Germany.

Schools Council's History, Geography and Social Sciences 8–13 Project. The Money Unit (Collins) – has two barter simulations and a game simulating conditions in a POW camp where chocolate develops as a medium of exchange. These could certainly be developed for use with older pupils, especially the latter of these. (Price £10.)

Study kit, *Money*, (Jackdaw No. 70). Kit of documents on the development of money over the last 300 years.

14   Industry – Organisation, Finance, Location, and Government Influence
Jennifer H. Wales

Industry is a major subject on most CSE and 'O' level syllabuses, but the range of topics included varies considerably, from business ownership to the location of industry. Whilst Social Economics syllabuses tend to stress the role of the employee, economics courses look at industry from the point of view of production.

  For many economics courses, industry is a suitable starting point, especially for brighter pupils who are capable of working with ideas of which they do not have first hand knowledge. With less able groups, it is advisable to begin with a subject about which they have

personal experience, such as consumption, and work backwards through the distributive processes to industry. It is possible to give them some appreciation of industry through visits but this is unlikely to reach the level of insight that they have into consumption before the course begins.

  Industry generally forms a substantial part of a two-year course. In order to sustain interest, it is essential to employ a wide range of techniques, especially with less able groups. Many of the basic concepts can be acquired initially by discussion and questions such as

'What would you do if . . .', and the ideas can be developed by logical progression. From this point a range of work can be done to expand the preliminary observations. This may vary from visits to factories to the use of textbooks and the mass of free material that is available.

Teaching Methods

1 Business Organisation and Finance

The teaching of organisation and finance has to be integrated as the motives behind each type of organisation are generally financial.

An initial introduction to business organisation can be made simply in class discussion, as the reasons and methods of expansion are straightforward and can be elicited by careful questioning. From this stage each type of organisation needs to be looked at in more detail in order to discover the sorts of business that fall into each category. The Yellow Pages of telephone directories are a very useful resource for doing this, as sole proprietors, partnerships and companies show up very clearly in various sections.

The sole proprietor needs little explanation generally as most people know someone who runs a small business. As homework the class can be asked to find out or to decide for themselves why people run a business rather than working for someone else. The finance of a sole proprietor can be worked out with reference to the class and their experiences as his methods of raising money are similar to their own.

The next development is to enquire how the firm might grow larger and the idea of a partner soon emerges. The class will know that some doctors and dentists work in small groups and this is easily extended to cover others.

Companies form the largest section of this topic. They require a great deal of attention as a considerable amount of detail is often needed for examinations. Companies and their finance lend themselves to the workcard technique as there is a wide variety of material, some of which is available free. The set of cards can be divided into groups, using a different coloured card for each one. The groups might be private companies, public companies, shares, the Stock Exchange, the new issue market and other sources of finance. A final group could be composed of examination questions from both CSE and 'O' level papers. This range means that the less able members of the class will cover perhaps the first three, which will provide them with plenty of material for their examination, while the 'O' level candidates will complete all the sections. Everyone will attempt at least one question from the final group in order to practise the technique required for examinations. The cards in any one group should be designed independently of each other

so that they can be used out of sequence as this will prevent holdups if a particular card is in demand. The most useful material for this work is the range of leaflets and the wallchart that the Stock Exchange provides free of charge. These cover all aspects of the Stock Exchange including its history, trading and a glossary of terms. The latter is particularly useful as some students find the terminology a stumbling block. (See Resources at the end of the chapter.)

A simple buying and selling game based on the Stock Exchange can be worthwhile as long as the group is either proficient at maths or has calculators, as the sums can be very time-consuming and therefore boring. The use of the *Financial Times* can stir interest, partly because of its unusual colour!

An alternative exercise is to plot a graph each week showing the value of shares of local companies. This can be annotated to try to explain price movements.

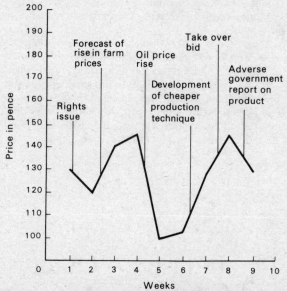

Figure 14.1 Movements in the share price of East Anglian fertilizers

Figure 14.1 illustrates a hypothetical example showing the type of information that can emerge from such an exercise. If a large version of this is made for display purposes a great deal more information can be included. It is a useful exercise because it shows the relationships between different forces within the economy.

Usually the benefits of a visit to the Stock Exchange are social rather than academic, since most of the work can be covered fully in the classroom. But a visit does provide a different environment and this can help the learning process. Students can see quite clearly how brokers work on the floor of the Stock Exchange. They should select a broker and watch him as he moves from pitch to pitch. One of the films that is shown to visitors, *My Word is my Bond*, explains how everyone is involved with the work of the Stock Exchange through insurance, trade unions and pension funds. The film is also available on free loan from Guild Sound and Vision (see Resources).

As this topic is very detailed, it is essential that the information should be set out clearly so that it can easily be learnt and retained. A chart is one way of doing this and it rounds off the topic well. It can be set out in the following way and each member of the class can complete it independently to reinforce what they have learned.

Type of organisation	Number of participants	Source of finance	Limited liability

A story describing the growth of a business from a sole proprietor to a public company forms an interest-ing concluding homework. The class are provided with the initial situation and are asked to expand on it and explain why and how the company developed. This shows very clearly each individual's understanding of the material.

The size and structure of firms can be considered by looking at local industry. A visit to a nearby industrial area can show the variation in size quite distinctly. A worksheet set out as follows will provide the necessary information.

Factory: Name and Product	Size	Reason

The first two columns can be filled in by the students. The final column needs considerable discussion later on, but initial ideas can be suggested by the class for homework as preparation for the follow-up lesson.

This leads on logically to the topic of economies of scale. Most students already understand an elementary statement of the concept as a result of the trend to bulk

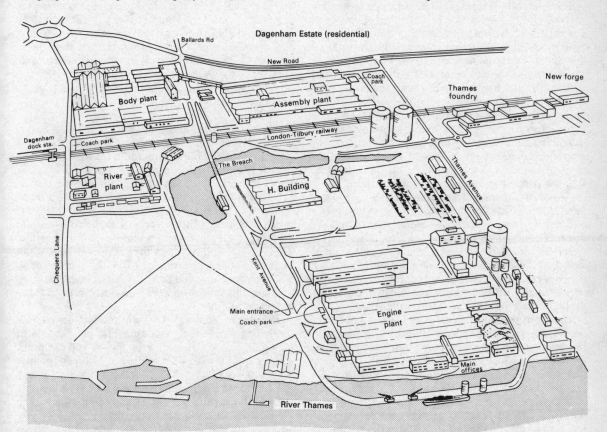

Figure 14.2 Dagenham Estate

buying. More ideas may emerge by asking the group to decide what savings would be made if, for example, two large supermarket chains amalgamated. In a similar way, diseconomies can result.

Understanding of the concept of vertical integration can be tested by showing the class an example like the one in *Economics – An Introductory Course* by D. Baron (see Resources) which depicts a chain of integration from a rubber plantation to a garage selling tyres. The students are then asked to invent their own chains. This exercise proves particularly successful with less able students, who enjoy illustrating their examples, and like to see them displayed on the walls.

2 The Location of Industry

Many students will already have reached some understanding of the concept of the location of industry from the geographical point of view. The Geography Department can provide a fund of material that can be readily adapted to meet the needs of economics. An example of this is the plan of the Ford works at Dagenham in Figure 14.2.

This provides an excellent basis for a lesson on locational factors as it includes many examples, and when put into its national context there are even more. Several economics text books contain fictional examples of industrial location but the advantage of the Dagenham plan is that it is a real situation and many students will have heard of it and may even have visited it.

The BBC produces a series of TV programmes each year called *Location Britain*. These are once again geographically orientated but give a broad look at locational factors. The programmes cover a variety of topics of which the most useful are those on Merthyr Tydfil and aluminium smelting at Lynemouth, Northumberland. The others are about the effects of the change from fishing to North Sea oil on Peterhead, London Airport and the seaport of Liverpool.

Although there are commercially produced tape/filmstrip sets on the location of industry (see Resources), it is preferable for the teacher to build up his own material on this topic, so that he can select examples which are relevant to the local environment as well as those of more general importance. Such sets of slides can be collected quite cheaply over time. The commentary provided by the teacher will be appropriate because he will have visited the sites.

There are several location games which have been developed with geography in mind but are equally relevant to economics. One of the best known of these is the Iron and Steel game (see Resources). The aim of this game is to select new locations for a steel works as the sources of raw materials and production methods change. The students are divided up into groups which represent different companies with a managing director, finance director and other members of the board, so there is some spin-off into areas other than location.

The government plays an important role in the location of industry and provides some useful material for classroom use. The Department of Industry publishes various booklets which contain pictures, charts and maps showing the areas and the grants and benefits that are available. The great advantage of this material is that it can easily be replaced as the legislation changes. Unfortunately the booklets are really designed for industrialists and therefore the Department of Industry is unwilling to part with more than two or three copies in response to each request.

The map in Figure 14.3 is an example of the contents of one of these booklets, *Incentives for Industry*. This material is also available in the form of a wallchart which is also free.

The following case study combines basic locational factors and government legislation. First provide the class with information about various sites, including labour supply, availability of raw materials, cost of transport and details of the grants and incentives in each area. The choice should be between expansion on the home site where space is limited, an intermediate area and either a Development Area or a Special Development Area. If there are too many options, the exercise becomes too complex. Varying factors can be introduced about each site including social as well as economic information to make the situation more realistic. Such a study is well suited to students of all abilities as the depth of answer can vary greatly. It is possible to build in more variables for more able members of the group.

3 The Government and Industry

The government has some influence in all the sections already discussed but it is useful to draw all this information together and to introduce other details to show the overall effect that the government has on industry.

Nationalised industries are covered well by most textbooks. Each industry produces glossy booklets which are free. These vary in their relevance to economics but most contain some useful information. They stimulate interest in the classroom because of their attractive appearance. After the basic ground work has been covered there is a considerable amount of interesting follow-up work that can be related to the nationalised industries.

The idea of monopoly can be introduced on a simple level, by asking the class to work out why most nationalised industries are monopolies and the problems that would exist if they were not. From this point it is easy to work out the disadvantages as almost everyone has some complaint about one of the industries.

Differential pricing can be considered after asking the class to collect tariffs from the gas and electricity boards and leaflets about cheap day returns from British Rail. The resulting information can form the

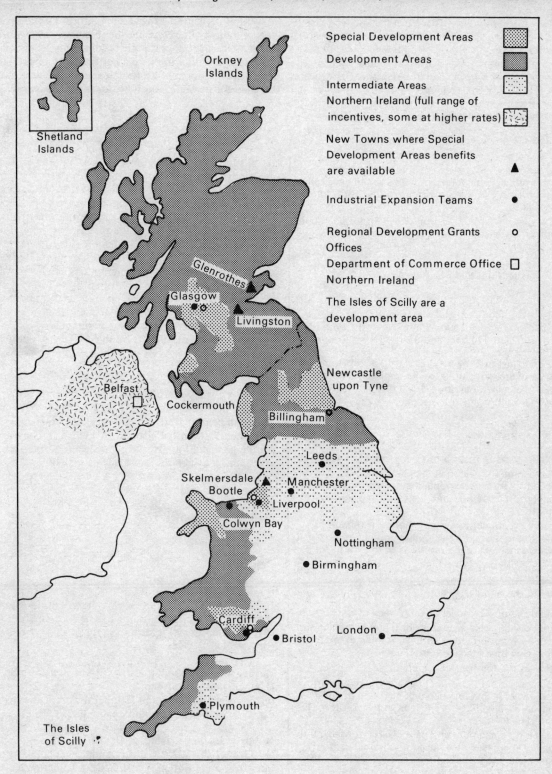

Special Development Areas

Development Areas

Intermediate Areas

Northern Ireland (full range of incentives, some at higher rates)

New Towns where Special Development Areas benefits are available ▲

Industrial Expansion Teams ●

Regional Development Grants Offices ○

Department of Commerce Office Northern Ireland ☐

The Isles of Scilly are a development area

Orkney Islands

Shetland Islands

Glenrothes

Glasgow

Livingston

Newcastle upon Tyne

Belfast

Cockermouth

Billingham

Leeds

Skelmersdale
Bootle

Manchester

Liverpool

Colwyn Bay

Nottingham

● Birmingham

Cardiff

● Bristol

London

Plymouth

The Isles of Scilly

Figure 14.3

basis of discussion and written work about why monopolies charge different prices for the same service.

When looked at in this way, the whole ability range
can understand the reasons. It also helps the less able
students to deal with such material as that below when
they leave school (see Figure 14.4).

A Standard Domestic Rate

A fixed charge in respect of each week of   20p

And a charge for each unit supplied of   2.412p

And an adjustment by way of charge or rebate in
respect of fuel costs for each unit supplied ascertained
in accordance with the provisions of this Tariff for Fuel
Cost Adjustment

Subject to a maximum charge of 6.178p for each unit
supplied, increased or reduced by the fuel cost
adjustment.

B Domestic Night and Day Rate 1

A fixed charge in respect of each week of   26p

And a charge for each unit supplied of 2.645p but
reduced for each unit supplied between the hours of 9
p.m. and 7 a.m. (10 p.m. and 8 a.m. during Summer
Time) to 1.312p

And an adjustment by way of charge or rebate in
respect of fuel cost for each unit supplied ascertained
in accordance with the provisions of this Tariff for Fuel
Cost Adjustment.

C Domestic Night and Day Rate 2

A fixed charge in respect of each week of   26p

And a charge for each unit supplied of 2.575p but
reduced for each unit supplied between the hours of 1
a.m. and 8 a.m. (2 a.m. and 9 a.m. during Summer
Time) to 1.018p

And an adjustment by way of charge or rebate in
respect of fuel cost for each unit supplied ascertained
in accordance with the provisions of this Tariff for Fuel
Cost Adjustment.

D Domestic Slot Meter Rate

A fixed charge in respect of each week of   26p

But reduced, in the case of a slot meter for which the
Board have not provided, or have removed, the lock
on the coin box attached to the meter to   24p

And a charge for each unit supplied of   2.412p

And an adjustment by way of charge or rebate in
respect of fuel cost for each unit supplied ascertained
in accordance with the provisions of this Tariff for Fuel
Cost Adjustment

Subject to a maximum charge of 6.178p for each unit
supplied, increased or reduced by the fuel cost
adjustment, and a charge in respect of each week of
6p reduced to 4p in the case of a supply where the
Board do not provide a lock on the coin box.

Figure 14.4 An example of an electricity board tariff

Textbooks cannot be relied upon for information in
this section, as there are frequent changes in government policy and books rapidly become out-of-date. It is
therefore essential to make a collection of newspaper
cuttings as a source of up-to-date material. These may
be used for personal reference or in the classroom.

Conclusion

At this level, most of the work about industry is very
descriptive and therefore creates few problems of
understanding. The problems that do arise tend to stem
from the volume of information that has to be retained
for examination purposes. As a result it is essential to
make a simple summary of the material at the end of
each section. The methods which provide the clearest
synopsis are charts and diagrams. The incentives for
industry to move to development areas can be shown
most clearly in a chart, for example in a simplified
version of the information given in the Department of
Industry booklet, *Incentive for Industry*. Less able students find the variety of shares and other types of
securities confusing but may be able to remember them
more easily when set out in a chart.

The CBI is appointing a number of regional officers
through the Understanding British Industry Project.
They will be prepared to answer teachers' queries and
help them establish liaison with industry. They are
planning to build up lists of good speakers and useful
visits, and to make the most of these, they have produced a booklet of guidance for teachers and are doing
the same for industry. They have a list of useful
addresses which can be used to supplement the list
produced in Chapter 57.

Resources

Books

Nobbs, J., *Social Economics*, (McGraw-Hill, 1976). A
short but detailed section on business ownership. It
covers the necessary information for social economics
courses.

Baron, D., *Economics – An Introductory Course*,
(Heinemann Educational, 1976). Lays greater stress
on the organisational and structural side of the firm,
e.g. the size of the firm and economies of scale.

Nobbs, J. and Ames, P., *Daily Economics*,
(McGraw-Hill, 1975). A very simple explanation of
industrial organisation – designed for CSE/non-exam
groups.

Barber, W., *Business World*, (Nelson, 1974). A simple explanation of industrial ownership from the business point of view. Set out very clearly. Good for the less able.

Dunning, K., *Working and Spending*, (Hulton, 1971). Covers many basic concepts of production. Suitable for the lower years of the secondary school or low ability fourth and fifth years.

Sauvain, P. A., *Where the Money Goes*, (Hulton, 1976). Approaches each topic in cartoons. Short sections on profit and loss, running a business and the Stock Exchange.

Long, M. and Roberson, B. S., *World Problems: Topic Geography*, (English Universities Press, 1969). A geography textbook containing a useful section on the location of industry.

Watts, D. G. and Jones, S. G., *Industrial Location in Britain and Ireland*, (Ginn, 1974). Many examples of location showing economic and geographic influences.

Graves, N. J. *Geography in Secondary Education*, (The Geographical Association, 1971). Contains the Iron and Steel Game.

Free Leaflets and Wallcharts
The Department of Industry: *Areas for Expansion; Incentives for Industry; Wallchart of Development Areas.*
The Stock Exchange: leaflets describing its work; glossary of terms; wallchart showing its work.

Wallcharts
Careers Consultants Ltd, *British Manufacturing*, (20 photos, 10"×7½", AP 30).
Career Consultants Ltd, *Public Money*, (free), re government revenue and expenditure.
Department of Industry, *The Areas for Expansion* (free). Map of UK with assisted areas shaded.
Educational Productions Ltd, *How the Stock Exchange Works*, (C1237); *How a Company is Formed and Financed* (C1238).

Pictorial Charts Educational Trust, *British Manufacturing*. Shows centres of population and the numbers employed in major industries (A30).

Audio-visual Resources
Guild, Sound and Vision, 16 mm films:
My Word is My Bond – about the Stock Exchange, (18", 127 3967–3, free); *The Launching* – about the New Issue Market, (28", 127 1288–1, free); and *Money Go Round* – Pop View of the Stock Exchange, (37", 127 2021–3, free).

Concord Films Council, *A Long Time Dying* (25"). A look at a condemned pit village in Durham.

ILEA Television service – video tapes for hire or purchase from Guild Sound and Vision:
Business Ownership, (16" 900 9701.6); *Central Government Finance*, (20", 900 9705.4); *Local Government Finance*, (20", 900 9706.1); *The Economic System*, (20", 900 9699.0); *Three Economics Systems*, (20", 900 9700.9).

Educational Productions Ltd, *Types of Business Organisation* (filmstrip).

Student Recordings Ltd (tape/filmstrips):
Business Ownership (AVC/17); *Business Organisation* (AVC/18); *Structure of Economics* (AVC/21); *Location of Industry* (AVC/22); *Production Factors* (AVC/23); *The Public Sector* (AVC/30); *The Private Sector* (AVC/31); *The Joint Stock Company* (AVC/32).

Audio Learning cassette/filmstrip, *Economies of Scale* (ECO 004).

The Understanding British Industry Project: lists of useful addresses.

15 Employment, Unemployment and Inflation

David L. McDougall

General Comments

Most syllabuses for pupils up to the age of sixteen include these topics. However in the world of the 1970s unemployment and inflation are in the news so often that many pupils are interested in them before they ever consider what has to be 'done' for exams. Most textbooks give some kind of descriptive and definitional attention to the whole topic, but unfortunately it is quite common for this part of the syllabus, which may be of immediate interest to thirteen–sixteen year olds (especially the sixteen year old school leaver), to be made boring and tedious. For example, the emphasis may be placed on describing the differences between types of unemployment rather than examining why the unemployment has been caused.

Content

It is often thought that the syllabus places emphasis on understanding the differences between types of unemployment and types of inflation, but it is probably more common for syllabuses to require examination of causes of changes in employment and prices. For example, this part of the Scottish Ordinary Grade syllabus is expressed simply as 'Instability: fluctuations of prices and employment'. This clearly places the emphasis on the fluctuations and puts the topic into a dynamic context.

Teaching Methods

The following suggestions are all intended to supplement and enliven what may be covered by class notes or textbooks. The suggestions do not necessarily have to be inter-related or followed in order, but might provide some ideas which teachers could use to expand particular parts of the whole general topic.

1 Exercise on why people are employed – ask someone in the class to suggest a good or service that they would be willing to pay for. Ask all the other members of the class to write down *all* the different people who would be employed in providing this good or service for the consumer. Example: the consumer wants to buy a camera. People are employed to: sell the camera;

transport the camera to the shop; put the camera in a box; write instructions for the use of the camera; print the instructions on the box; assemble the parts of the camera; make the parts of the camera (how many?); transport the parts to the camera factory.

This list could be extended almost indefinitely to include everyone who is employed, however indirectly, in the production of the camera. Eventually the teacher reminds the class that all these people have been employed because *someone wanted to buy a camera*.

2 Illustration of why people are employed – all the people who were employed in (1) can be combined in a flowchart type of diagram to illustrate how they all inter-relate to produce a camera – to satisfy the demand of a consumer. This can be done on large sheets of paper which can be put on classroom walls. If

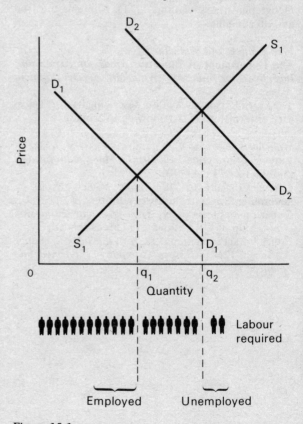

Figure 15.1

the department possesses a kit of materials of the type described in the SCCSS courses for pupils in S1 and S2 it is possible to illustrate the production of a product using this. Plastic men represent workers, matchbox toys can represent transport, boxes can represent buildings, and pieces of Lego can represent materials. The teacher could use these to illustrate how a consumer's demand for a product results in employment of many people, but the pupils (perhaps in groups) could set up their own illustrations of the people involved to produce other products.

3 Explanation of what factors affect demand – having established that the existence of demand for a product results in employment, the pupils can be asked to suggest as many factors as they can which help to explain what influences the level of demand (e.g. advertising, level of wages, tax rates, hire purchase restrictions, rates of interest) and pupils may be asked to illustrate these (perhaps in the form of posters). For example, a poster to illustrate why a person decides to buy a new cooker would provide scope for imaginative pupils.

4 Diagrams – different parts of the syllabus can be related to each other by using diagrams which help younger pupils to understand the connections between them:

(a) Demand for houses and employment in the building industry (see Figure 15.1). The teacher explains that if goods and services are produced then people have to be employed. If demand for houses is D_1D_1 and supply is S_1S_1 then the quantity on the market will be q_1, which requires some people to be employed. If demand increases to D_2D_2 then the quantity on the market will increase to q_2 and this requires more people to be employed in the building industry, thus reducing the number of unemployed building workers. This may help some pupils to understand the relationship between changes in demand and fluctuations in employment levels. For example, they could also be asked to suggest how this change in the building industry might affect employment in other industries.

(b) Income and employment. This is based on a simple circular flow diagram (see Figure 15.2). The teacher can give values to the different flows. For example incomes may be £100 and spending £100. This will mean that all the producer's output is being bought. If then the government takes £20 in tax and consumers save £10, how much will the producers be able to sell? What happens to the level of unemployment?

The teacher can make this type of diagram as complex or as simple as the class can understand by introducing as many different flows as the class are familiar with.

5 Flick cards – a problem with the type of diagram shown in Figure 15.2 is that it is a static representation. In order to overcome this it is possible for groups in the class to make 'movie' type diagrams. By using small cards (even as small as 2 cm by 4 cm) they can illustrate the effects of injections into, and withdrawals from, the circular flow. The three cards shown in Figure 15.3 are intended to illustrate the effect of increased income tax.

Each picture represents a slight movement from the previous one.

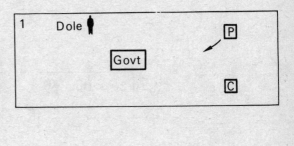

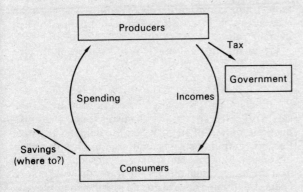

Figure 15.2

Figure 15.3

After about twelve pictures the 'flow' might be complete (see Figure 15.4).

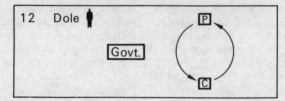

Figure 15.4

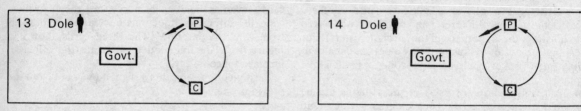

Figure 15.5

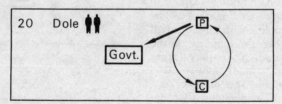

Figure 15.6

The next picture would illustrate money moving to the government (see Figure 15.5).

By the time, say, the twentieth picture is reached the effect of the withdrawal has been to reduce consumer spending by so much that the 'dole' queue is increasing (see Figure 15.6).

When all the cards have been drawn, with a separate picture on each one, they are placed in order in a pile. By holding the left end of the pile and flicking through the right hand end, the pictures give the impression of movement, illustrating how the flows are changing within the economy. The opportunity exists for imaginative groups of pupils to compose their own illustrations of changes in the economy. They can make use of different colours and can adjust the thicknesses of the flow lines to develop their ideas of how to show how changes in these flows affect the level of employment.

6 Practical models – using the type of kit of materials described in (2) above. Different groups in the class can set up production flows for a variety of products, maintaining consistent levels of output. The class can then adjust their models to show what happens when demand falls.

Production of steel can be used as an example (see Figure 15.7).

The class can physically move the iron ore to the steelworks, the coal to the steelworks, and then produce the output of steel. When the demand for steel falls, the output of steel is reduced, thus in turn reducing demand for coal and iron ore. Consequently fewer iron ore miners, coal miners and transport workers are needed, and some have to go and join the unemployed.

This type of exercise can be carried out for the pro-

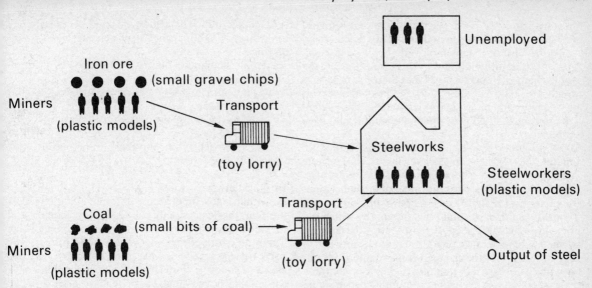

Figure 15.7

duction of different, and more complex, products – e.g. cars, TVs, washing machines.

7 Types of unemployment – it is often difficult to help a class to find out about the different types of unemployment without either telling them or giving them written descriptions of types of unemployment. One way of overcoming this is to give the class a long list of people who are unemployed.

Example: a building worker in the winter;
a former shipyard worker;
a Mediterranean tour guide in the winter;
a former coal miner;
a docker temporarily laid off due to a fall in UK trade;
a fifty-year-old car worker (due to closure of a plant).

The list may include at least twenty people and the teacher can decide on the types of unemployment to be included. The class is asked to study the list and divide it into the number of types of unemployment which the teacher wants to illustrate. They can do this without advice from the teacher at first and then follow up their initial sub-divisions by discussion. The teacher could suggest passages from textbooks to be read to assist with dividing the list into the categories. Gradually the pupils will come to understand the differences in the categories of unemployment until they can explain the distinctions without having to resort to 'parrot' definitions.

8 Historical case study – a good way of illustrating how unemployment can come about and affect particular areas is to carry out a fairly detailed study of one industry in an area near the school. For example, ship-building on the Clyde can be followed from the early nineteenth century up to the 1970s, showing how demand for ships increased the demand for workers in that area, how other industries developed in the same region, how competition developed, how and why workers came to be laid off, how capital began to replace labour, how the ancillary industries suffered, and how the whole region suffered. If the local area can provide an illustration such as this, the pupils will appreciate the significance of each stage of development of the industry in their local area. They will then be able to consider other industries at different stages of development (e.g. the car industry) and discuss why these industries are having problems and relate them to the case study which they have carried out.

9 Effects of unemployment – this type of lesson might be a good way of introducing the topic of unemployment, although it could fit into the series of lessons at any stage. The class is asked to construct a table suggesting how different types of people might be affected by being unemployed.

Example: a boy of sixteen just left school with no qualifications;
a girl just graduated from university with an honours degree in physics;
a married woman of thirty-eight with two children;
a man of forty-six who has been an engineer for twenty-five years.

By considering a wide range of examples the class may come to appreciate the implications for different people of being unemployed. The teacher may even be able to find enough contrasting examples from the local area to make the significance of unemployment even more immediate. The table would simply be a list of the unemployed people concerned, with the class attempting to assess how the person would be affected personally, what their job prospects would be, what they might do to make themselves more employable, how society could help them to find jobs, and what effect their unemployment would have on society.

10 Price survey – as an introduction to the topic of inflation the teacher can ask the class to find out the current prices of a 'shopping basket' of goods. The teacher then gives the class the prices of the same goods from one year previously (see exercises in Chapter 10). The class can then calculate the amount by which the prices have changed, possibly representing the changes by means of diagrams (e.g. bar charts), and try to suggest reasons for the changes. If the pupils are familiar with the use of index numbers they can continue their prices survey over several months, constructing an index of prices in the local shops. This allows an analysis of the price changes to be made on the basis of the pupils' own experience.

11 Effects of inflation – in the same way as the effects of unemployment on different types of people were studied, the class can be asked to assess how various types of people would be affected by a period of rising prices.

Example: a teenager at school with only pocket
            money to spend;
          an unemployed man of twenty;
          a young couple with two children and only
            the husband working;
          a widow in her forties with three children;
          a man who lends money;
          a couple living off a pension.

This allows the class to appreciate how different types of people may suffer more than others during periods of inflation (even if members of the class think that they themselves are relatively unaffected).

The class can also assess the effects of inflation on less personal aspects of the economy to try to appreciate the wider significance of inflation.

Example: a small company with small stocks and low
            profit margins;
          a large company with big stocks and high
            levels of exports;
          a country's balance of payments;
          the amount of tax collected by the government.

This type of list can vary in complexity depending on the extent of the class's knowledge of economics.

12 Causes of inflation:

(a) Demand pull. The class is asked to draw diagrams to illustrate the effects of various changes of demand on price.

Example: demand is higher for European Cup football matches;
          demand for houses has risen in the UK since 1945;
          consumers have more to spend due to tax reductions;
          workers in hospitals are given pay increases.

By considering a variety of examples it is possible to show that many superficially different situations have the same basic economic circumstances, namely that for some reason there has been a rise in demand which has in turn brought about an increase in price.

(b) Cost push. The members of the class are each asked to choose a product. For the product they have chosen they have to make a list of all the costs they can suggest that would be involved in producing that product. They are also asked to allocate an approximate percentage of the total cost to each of the costs incurred (the accuracy of this is not important for the purpose of this exercise).

Example: production of an ice cream

Total cost	100% (selling price)
Labour	20%
Materials	30%
Premises	10%
Transport	15%
Profit	15%
Tax	10%

It is less important to be exact with the detailed proportions of the costs than to illustrate that there are a variety of costs involved. Having allocated the percentages the class is then asked to calculate the effect on the selling price of an increase in one of the costs. For example, how would a 10 per cent increase in the cost of materials affect the selling price of the product?

They can be asked to suggest ways in which increased costs could be absorbed without passing the increase on to the consumer in the form of a higher selling price. If the teacher can provide a detailed costing of the production of an actual good this would be helpful, but it is difficult to maintain such detailed figures for a range of products without having contacts in manufacturing industry.

13 Goods and money simulation – the main purpose is to provide a simple illustration of the relationship between the money supply, output and the general price level.

The class is divided into two groups: consumers and

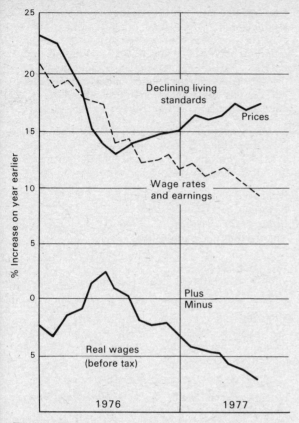

Figure 15.8

producers. There is also a third group – the government – but it is perhaps best if the teacher adopts this role to start with until the class become more sophisticated in the use of the game. All the members of the class keep a record of each time period divided into three sections – money supply, output of goods and services, general price level. (If the class reacts well to the simulation, this can be made more complex by introducing other variables.)

The producers are given blocks of wood to sell, the total number of which is fixed at the start of the time period. The consumers are given money, the total amount of which is controlled by the government. During each time period the consumers try to achieve as high a standard of living as they can by buying as many goods and services from the producers as their money will allow, each block of wood representing a good or a service.

The consumers and producers haggle with each other to fix the prices, and they soon discover that over-pricing will result in unsold stocks, while under-pricing will reduce profits. At the start of each time period the government adjusts either the money supply or the output of goods and services, with everyone in the class noting the totals and the effects on the price level during the time period. Members of the class can try to predict the effects of changes and can suggest means of preventing price rises while still allowing living standards to rise.

It is possible to develop fruitful discussion in several directions out of this simulation, and it is also possible to make it more involved by introducing other factors such as income tax, income distribution, savings, indirect taxes and varying rates of economic growth.

14 Newspaper articles – it is possible to find many articles from newspapers on employment, unemployment and inflation. These can be used to show the class the immediate relevance of their work and to stimulate them to look up references and explanations in their textbooks. This can be done by compiling worksheets relating to newspaper articles and asking questions which will force the pupils to look outside their own knowledge for answers.

For example, the diagram shown in Figure 15.8 was taken from the Business News of the *Sunday Times*, 14 August 1977.

It could give rise to questions such as:

What is meant by 'real wages'?
What is the difference between 'wage rates' and 'earnings'?
How do rising prices affect living standards?
Describe what has happened to living standards since the start of 1976.
What factors have caused prices to rise since 1976?
How could the information in this diagram be used to support an argument against government-imposed wage controls?
The teacher can relate the questions to the specific aspects of the topic which the class have been studying. With pupils in the age range thirteen–sixteen it is probably better not to use lengthy articles, but to choose relevant parts of such articles to direct the pupils' attention to the areas which the teacher wants them to consider in greater depth. This method is also a means of encouraging the pupils to refer to textbooks because they can be asked questions which force them to go and find the answers for themselves if the teacher chooses the article and the questions carefully.

16 Diary of events – a way of developing an awareness of what is happening in the economy is for the members of the class to keep a weekly diary of important developments in the local and national economies (relating if necessary to a wider range of topics than simply employment, unemployment and inflation). This ensures that the class are informed of changes which occur so that they can discuss topics such as 'the causes of inflation in the UK' with a background of information to support their views.

Problems

Probably the most difficult problem with younger pupils is introducing them to the language and definitions of these topics in a way that still allows the topic under consideration to remain interesting and relevant to them. The textbooks generally provide a descriptive background, but it is the teacher's task to make this more lively. One way of helping to achieve this is to refer constantly to what is happening in the 'real' world, both locally and nationally, particularly by references to newspapers and by keeping records.

Another problem is that it is difficult for younger, or less able, pupils to understand some aspects of the topic when they first encounter them. Until they have covered the whole range of 'employment, unemployment and inflation' they may not fully appreciate the significance of certain points. It may therefore be worthwhile spending some time, after the whole range has been introduced, on a few lessons relating different aspects.

Resources

Books

Garrett, J., *Visual Economics* (Evans, 1973), chapter 9 'British Industry'; chapter 15 'Production', chapter 30 'Choosing a Job'. This is a good source of ideas for the teacher and deals with all aspects of the topic which it covers in a very simple way.

Baron, D., *Economics – an Introductory Course*, (Heinemann Educational, 1976), chapter 1 'Who Works?'; chapter 17 'Government Control of the Economy'. Makes these topics understandable for younger pupils.

Donaldson, P., *Illustrated Economics*, (BBC, 1976), chapter 1 'Fuelling Inflation'; chapter 2 'Money's the Problem'; chapter 3 'Is 3 Million Unemployed the Answer?'; chapter 4 'Winners and Losers'; chapter 5 'Savings Standard'. Provides some good ideas and explanations for the teacher, but it is too difficult for most younger pupils.

Christie, D. and Scott, A., *Economics in Action*, (Heinemann Educational, 1977), inflation, pp 101–102; economic policy, pp 131–138; causes of inflation, pp 115–118 and 135–138; weapons against inflation, pp 123–138. Has many useful examples and provides good exercises to help pupils' understanding, but on this topic may be quite difficult for these younger pupils.

Nobbs, J. and Ames, P., *Daily Economics*, (McGraw-Hill, 1975), Starting Work, Topics 1.1, 1.2, 1.3, 1.4. This might be suitable for younger pupils to introduce them to reasons for working.

Wallchart

Pictorial Charts Educational Trust.
British Manufacturing – Population and number employed in major industries.

Tape/Filmstrips

Student Recordings Ltd, *Unemployment Trends*, (AVC/28).

Filmstrips

Five filmstrips: *Basic Economic Concepts, National Income* (2), *Saving and Investment, Money, Prices and Interest*, (McGraw-Hill).

Miscellaneous

Longmans Social Studies Series 3: *The Social Contract; Unemployment and the Unemployed.*
Schools Council: Humanities Curriculum Project, *People and Work* resources box.

The courses prepared in the pilot study under the SCCSS to investigate the teaching of economics to pupils in S1 and S2 provide useful material for very young pupils, or pupils requiring very simplified approaches, particularly in the sixth and final unit entitled 'National Income and the Standard of Living' which deals partly with unemployment and its causes. This material is available from the Scottish Centre for the Social Subjects, Jordanhill College of Education, Glasgow.

16   Trade Unions and Employers' Federations
P. M. Morrison

General Comments

In most CSE and 'O' level courses, trade unions and employers' federations form only a small part of one section and the temptation is to spend far more time on the subject than is warranted by its weighting in the examination framework. It is important to avoid this trap, and yet, at the same time, teach the subject as clearly and concisely as possible. Unlike some other topics in economics, the subject usually creates an immediate interest and it is often viewed with enthusiasm by all the members of the class (particularly in CSE groups) and is seen to be relevant to their own future experience. If the lessons can be built round this feeling of immediacy there can be a considerable bonus in positive feedback from the class.

Content

In economics courses the main emphasis is on the 'functions of modern trade unions', rather than on their history or their present political importance. To identify the economic functions and then to portray them clearly to a class of fifteen year olds can be difficult but satisfying. It must usually be assumed that the history of trade unionism is covered in considerable detail elsewhere in the school, and even if a few of the pupils have not studied it in history or social studies it is only necessary to cover the trade union movement from 1799 to 1920 very briefly. However it can be effective to make use of historical material by way of introduction to the organisation of trade unions, and in the description of how they are run.

Most of the time allocated to the topic should be spent on describing the processes that trade unions are involved in and how this affects the average member on the shop floor. At the same time it should be shown how employers link together in the same manner to meet the employees and to act as a pressure group in the same way as the trade unions.

Finally it should be shown how the role of trade unions and employers' federations is widening as governments increasingly consult them on economic and social policy.

Teaching Methods

In a two year CSE/'O' level course, it is reasonable to assume that three to four weeks can be devoted to the topic. The following approach uses a variety of teaching methods and aims to give each pupil an understanding of what a trade union does, what is expected of a trade union member and an outline understanding of industrial relations in modern society.

What is a Trade Union?

This question is usually guaranteed to start a discussion on many aspects of trade unions, but with no real answers provided. However, if an introductory class discussion on this question is controlled, it can give many insights into the pupils' emotional responses to the subject, which is after all very controversial, and can be a useful basis for simulation games later on in the course. However it is best to move on fairly quickly to answer the question more formally by describing the history of trade unions. Lawton and Dufour in *The New Social Studies*[1] suggest that: 'Detailed step-

by-step narration of events is probably less effective than seizing upon dramatic contrasts and highlights, such as Tolpuddle, the Dockers' Tanner episode ...'. Films can be particularly useful to give emphasis to the 'dramatic contrasts'. This can lead very quickly into the organisation of unions. The three main types of unions (craft, industrial and general workers' unions) can be described, still with some historical references, but also reinforcing the work with examples of modern unions. It is advisable to move on to the internal organisation of trade unions quite quickly. It is often useful to get a local union official into the school, or to ask someone from the local trades council to speak. These people are usually delighted to come into the schools and often have interesting points of view even if they are in relation to one union rather than to several. Most of them are sufficiently sensitive to understand that they must avoid trying to persuade pupils to adopt certain political ideas and treat the topics in an educational manner. Once the pupils understand what a trade union is, it is possible to move on to study the role of trade unions. This again needs to be broken down into small parts. The first stage is to study how unions attempt to improve the conditions of work by collective bargaining, by taking the pupils step-by-step through a dispute, either real or imaginary. This needs to be teacher-directed, but at each stage a discussion should take place on what each side, labour and management, should do. Once the pupils understand all the stages of negotiation, then it can be useful to run a simulation exercise, with pupils cast in the role of managers, workers, officials and government conciliators. (See below and Chapter 36 for examples of such simulations.)

This should make it quite clear how the unions operate and how effective their collective bargaining can be, and it provides a jumping off point for the study of the national organisation of the trade union movement and the employers' federations. This brings in the role of the TUC and its relations with the government, and can show how the trade union movement has extended its sphere of influence in recent years and is now involved in many decisions at national level, sending members to many advisory committees. At the same time the role of the Confederation of British Industry can be explained and it can be shown how both organisations rely to a certain extent on the goodwill of their members. It is very difficult to get over this last point by any other method than 'chalk and talk' but it should be kept as brief as possible.

A Selection of Approaches

1 Case studies. The teacher can duplicate a brief account of a real or imaginary dispute and can set questions on it. A published example of this can be found in *Modern Society* by Jack Nobbs,[2] where a case study of British Leyland is given and some questions asked on the dispute and some of the possible solutions.

2 Newspaper articles. These can be used with nearly all pupils, but are probably most effective with the most able, because the others will find the prose difficult to interpret effectively. However they should only be used at the end of a topic with pupils in this age range. The temptation to use newspaper cuttings plus questions on them as a starting point at this level should be avoided as they can lead to unnecessary confusion.

3 Simulations. As already mentioned, this can be a very effective aid in helping pupils to understand how trade unions operate. To simulate a dispute the only preparation needed is three duplicated handouts.

(i) A general description of the firm and the events leading up to the dispute. This is given to all the pupils.
(ii) A list of alternative courses of action and their probable results for the management side.
(iii) A similar list of the possible actions for the union members given to the union side.

The pupils are issued with the appropriate handouts and they then need to be given the opportunity to meet in their two separate groups to discuss their strategies. The simulation can then begin, with each side acting their parts and modifying their positions as a result of their negotiations, eventually reaching a settlement. This works well with fifteen year olds and obviously the handouts can be modified to make the simulation more or less sophisticated. An additional benefit of this type of game is that it is free, using only a few banda sheets and a little imagination on the part of the teacher.

4 Television and radio. In this country there is usually a dispute in some section of industry and it can be followed on the TV or radio news by all the pupils. It can form the basis of class discussions and focuses the attention of the class on an actual event which is directly relevant to their studies.

References

1 Lawton, D. and Dufour, B., *The New Social Studies*, (Heinemann Educational, 1973), pp 299–302.
2 Nobbs, J., *Modern Society Social Studies for CSE*, (George Allen and Unwin, 1976), p 152.

Resources

Most textbooks cover the functions of trade unions fairly clearly, some of them are not so exact about employers' federations, and most of them are out-of-date as soon as they are published in respect to current developments in industrial relations. Most of them need some explanation first, and all of them need constant reference to current events to utilise fully the interest shown by most classes.

Baron, D., *Economics: An Introductory Course*, (Heinemann Educational, 1976), pp 25–31. This book has all the necessary information for CSE level and some useful questions, but the approach is very dry except for one cartoon illustration.

Harvey, J., *Elementary Economics*, (Macmillan Education, fourth edition, 1976), pp 324–34. Has a long detailed section on collective bargaining, but it is only suitable for the most able pupils.

Harvey, J., *Elementary Economics Workbook*, (Macmillan Education, 1976), pp 47–8. A workbook published as a companion to the textbook mentioned above, this also poses a few questions on trade unions as well as giving examples from past papers.

Nobbs, J., *Social Economics*, (McGraw-Hill, 1975). Has a useful section in chapter 5, and some interesting stimulus material.

Finally, a more comprehensive list of references can be found in *The New Social Studies* (reference 1 above). However, it is important to remember that the best stimulus material comes from:
(a) Current disputes;
(b) The most recent legislation, almost certainly printed in the *Economic Progress Reports* issued by the Central Office of Information;
(c) Local union officials and employers' groups, who will be able to give local examples of the work of unions and the local firms.

Other Resources
TUC *Trade Unions Kit*
Cassette tapes from *Understanding Industrial Society Project*, (Hodder and Stoughton), which contains dialogue between shop stewards, and role of foreman. Students Recordings Ltd: tape/filmstrip, *The Trade Unions* (AVC/27); *Work and Wages*, (AVC/25).

17 Comparative Costs, International Trade and Payments

R. Whelan and R. Ellis

Introduction

Most CSE and 'O' level courses require a knowledge of why countries specialise in the production of particular commodities. This involves teaching some elementary trade theory. Other aspects of international trade are also included in most courses, in particular: balance of payments accounts, the terms of trade, international institutions, exchange rates and international co-operation.

Classroom space may be used to create an appropriate 'atmosphere' for teaching a particular topic. This could be achieved for teaching about world trade by displaying posters and pictures of different parts of the world and their produce. Advertisements in magazines are one possible source e.g. Italian cars, French wines. Other space could be used to display wallcharts used by the teacher and material made by the pupils. For example, it may be possible to make a large graph for display, plotting the balance of payments position over a period of years, that could be added to over time. In addition, spare pin-board space could be used for pinning up newspaper and other article cuttings on new developments.

Specialisation and the Law of Comparative Costs

The concept of specialisation is fundamental to any economics course, and when dealing with international trade this inevitably leads to a discussion of the principle of comparative advantage. Specialisation, in terms of the division of labour, will in most cases have been dealt with prior to international trade, and so pupils will have a basic knowledge of the concept.

Economics textbooks generally tackle this topic by means of a numerical example, and it is well worthwhile studying the various texts in order to find a clear exposition. Alternatively the teacher can easily construct his own, for example:

Countries A and B can both produce tractors and wheat. Using ten units of labour Country A could produce ten tractors or 200 tonnes of wheat. Using ten units of labour Country B could produce twenty tractors or 100 tonnes of wheat. If each Country had twenty units of labour, they could produce in this way:

	Tractors	Wheat (tonnes)	Opportunity cost ratios
Country A	10	200	1:20
Country B	20	100	1:5
Total produced	30	300	

If the two countries decided to trade with each other, they could each specialise in producing the good in which they have the greatest *comparative advantage*. In this case, Country A has the greatest comparative advantage in the production of wheat, and Country B in the production of tractors. Production with specialisation:

	Tractors	Wheat (tonnes)
Country A	0	400
Country B	40	0
Total produced	40	400

If Country A uses all her labour to produce wheat, and Country B uses all her labour to produce tractors, more is produced of both goods.

As with many problems it is often useful to look at the situation in a different way, both to reinforce the original exposition and also as an alternative for those pupils who have difficulty with the numerical explanation. In this case the problem can be explained by means of a simple production possibility line graph.

As an introduction it may be possible to illustrate the advantages of specialisation in a more practical way by constructing a simple class exercise. (See Chapters 1 and 12.)

Imports and Exports

With less able pupils, the teacher must show clearly that a visible import is something coming into a country, but which will involve payment going out of the country. In other words money is flowing in the opposite direction to goods. An example of a simple illustration of this is shown in Figure 17.1.

In the case of invisible imports and exports the emphasis on the flow of money becomes more important. For example, in the case of tourism the UK earns money through invisible exports when a tourist from abroad spends money during his holiday in London, i.e. money flows into this country. The reverse would be true of a British tourist spending money abroad.

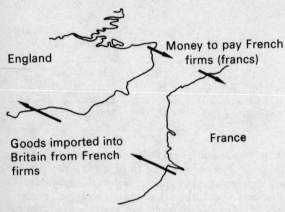

Figure 17.1

Many syllabuses require a knowledge of the composition of trade for one or more particular countries. Younger pupils can do some preliminary research on this. For example they could find out where certain commodities in their home are made and write out a list. It would also be useful to work out what proportions of these commodities were made in EEC countries.

e.g.	Commodity	Country
	Car	
	Shoes	
	Furniture	
	Clothing	
	Tinned food	

The Balance of Payments

The use of a diagram will once again help both the teacher and the pupil to explain and understand this topic, e.g. an illustration using scales to show equilibrium or disequilibrium. For textbooks using this approach see *Starting Economics*[1] and *Elementary Economics*[2].

The diagram can be utilised so that the effect of invisible imports and exports on the balance of payments can be shown.

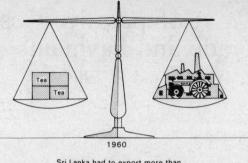

Sri Lanka had to export more than one and a half times as much tea in 1970 as in 1960 to pay for the same amount of imported manufactured goods

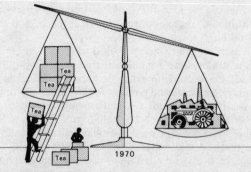

Figure 17.2 Reproduced by courtesy of the Centre for World Development Education

The diagram in Figure 17.2 is taken from *Facts about Development 4, World Trade*, published by the Centre for World Development Education. Alternatively a simple exercise may be used to demonstrate the concept of balance to younger or less able pupils. Borrow a balance from the Science Department. Make small boxes representing both visible and invisible exports and imports.

1 To show a visible balance place an equal number of boxes on each side of the balance.
2 To show a deficit on the visible account place more boxes on the imports side of the balance (similarly for surplus).
3 To show the effect of invisible exports use boxes of a different colour. It is possible to show by manipulation of the boxes for example a situation where a surplus on invisible account can rectify a visible deficit.

As with exchange rates it is helpful if pupils can look at the problem in terms of 'money flow', i.e. money flowing in and out of a country. The difficulties that occur when studying the balance of payments accounts, especially the use of plus and minus signs, are often easier to overcome as soon as the pupil grasps the idea of 'money flows'. Using this approach the teacher can deal with the balance of payments accounts in a simple way to begin with, and then move on (with the more able pupils) to a more detailed breakdown and discussion of the accounts.

Any form of graphical or diagrammatic presentation of the subject will aid the pupil in his understanding of the balance of payments and should be used wherever possible. For example, when explaining the current balance, a graph similar to the one shown in Figure 17.3 would give the pupil a clearer view of the importance of invisible trade in the current account.

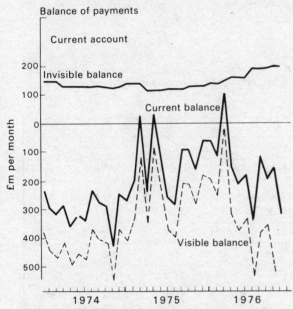

Figure 17.3 Reproduced by courtesy of the Treasury from Economic Progress Report, *87, June 1977, published by the Information Division of the Treasury*

Exchange Rates

The theory of exchange rates is another topic that often causes a great deal of confusion, especially with younger pupils. It is essential that pupils understand the concept of 'money flows' in order to see how one country needs to obtain the currency of another country in order to buy its goods, and a diagrammatic approach is often the most useful.

Once an understanding of the flow is achieved it will be possible to move on to explain how the value of one country's currency can vary in relation to the dollar. A graphical presentation of the problem often enables the pupil to see relationships more clearly, and the more capable pupils should have little difficulty in applying the laws of supply and demand to this problem. Many of the textbooks use a graph for this topic in order that the price (exchange rate) of a currency can be seen to move in accordance with the demand and supply for the currency.

The classroom could be arranged so that the movement in the exchange rate can be plotted on a graph or wallchart. This would help the pupils to see at a glance the relationship between the movements in the exchange rate and events which may take place both at national and international level. It is always a useful exercise to relate daily economic events to the movements in any of the economic indicators, not only to the exchange rate.

The differences between fixed and floating exchange rates can be taught at this level using simple supply and demand analysis. A mathematical example will show how devaluation of a country's currency can make that country's exports more attractive to foreign buyers. For example:

The exchange rate before devaluation is £1=$4, i.e. a British car priced at £10 000 will cost $40 000 in the USA.

After a devaluation of 50 per cent, £1 is now exchanged for $2, i.e. the car will now cost $20 000 in the USA.

A further useful exercise involves getting the class to suggest what assumptions underlie this example.

Terms of Trade

The teaching of the terms of trade and their importance may create problems as it involves some statistical work, in particular the use of index numbers. Pupils would benefit from doing some simple calculations themselves, and the more able pupils could be given actual terms of trade statistics for interpretation.

An example of use of a terms of trade exercise for more able 'O' level pupils follows, using Figure 17.4.

Questions:

1 Are Japan's terms of trade moving favourably or unfavourably?
2 Which countries are in a better position regarding their terms of trade, than in the base year?
3 Describe how the UK terms of trade have moved between 1972 and 1976.

Alternative questions on the graph for less able or younger pupils:

This graph shows how the prices of exports and imports change for different countries. If the curve for a

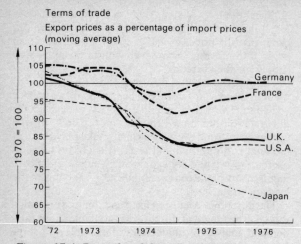

Terms of trade

Export prices as a percentage of import prices
(moving average)

Figure 17.4 Reproduced from Barclays Bank
Review, *November 1976, by courtesy of Barclays
Bank Group Economic Intelligence Unit*

country falls it shows that the prices of goods it sells
abroad are falling compared to the prices of goods it
buys from abroad. This is called an 'unfavourable'
change.

For Japan from 1972 to 1976 the prices of the goods
it sold abroad, for example TVs and cars, fell compared
to the prices of the goods Japan bought from other
countries.

1 Does this mean that the Japanese had to sell more,
or less, cars and TVs to earn enough money to pay for
the goods they wanted to buy?
2 Which country on the graph has a terms of trade
figure in 1976 greater than 100?
3 Which country's terms of trade figure rises after
1972 and then falls again?

Figure 17.5 Reproduced from Barclays Bank
Review, *February 1977, by courtesy of Barclays
Bank Group Economics Intelligence Unit*

World Trade

Exports and imports (at current prices and exchange rates)							
Exports (F.O.B.)							
	U.K.	U.S.A.	E.E.C.	Italy	Germany	France	Japan
$'s thousand million (quarterly data expressed as annual rates)							
1974 3rd qtr	39.7	93.5	275.8	32.9	87.9	44.1	59.9
4th qtr	41.9	108.5	302.0	34.1	96.8	51.5	66.0
1975 1st qtr	43.9	108.8	298.2	32.3	90.1	54.0	53.2
2nd qtr	46.0	106.9	313.0	34.5	94.7	58.1	54.6
3rd qtr	40.9	100.5	271.2	34.9	83.2	46.4	54.8
4th qtr	45.7	114.4	309.3	37.7	92.7	53.8	60.7
1975 1st qtr	46.5	109.4	308.1	32.2	93.7	54.2	57.8
2nd qtr	46.2	118.8	323.5	35.4	98.3	60.2	65.1
3rd qtr	44.2	109.7	313.9	37.8	100.6	51.3	70.2
Imports (C.I.F.)							
1974 3rd qtr	54.6	114.0	295.8		69.7	51.5	61.9
4th qtr	56.2	116.7	308.1	42.4	74.2	55.4	63.4
1975 1st qtr	56.2	104.9	302.8	36.1	72.1	56.0	58.2
2nd qtr	54.4	98.2	310.3	37.4	79.1	56.1	57.1
3rd qtr	51.2	101.5	276.6	36.7	70.2	46.5	56.4
4th qtr	52.2	108.9	315.5	43.3	78.4	57.3	59.8
1976 1st qtr	54.5	117.4	322.3	39.1	80.2	62.1	59.4
2nd qtr	56.2	126.6	342.3	43.3	86.3	64.8	63.0
3rd qtr	55.1	134.9	329.0	41.3	87.2	59.9	67.3

It may not be necessary to teach the construction of index numbers to less able pupils. In teaching the terms of trade it may be adequate to show that a movement above 100 is a 'favourable' change, and a movement below 100, an 'unfavourable' change.

Trade Restrictions

This is a very straightforward section to teach. It involves distinguishing between different types of restriction, and determining which is appropriate in particular circumstances, and overall effects.

The information could be arranged in the following pattern:

Type of restriction	Explanation of how it works	When it is appropriate
Tariffs		
Quotas		
Subsidies		
Exchange control		
Embargo		

To enliven the topic a classroom discussion on the use of restriction could be initiated as follows:

Country X decides to impose an import duty on foreign-produced motor bikes so that it can sell its own. Most motor bikes imported into Country X are produced in Country Y. What will be the arguments for/against this duty of:

(a) the Government of Country X;
(b) a motor-bike producer in Country X;
(c) a motor-bike producer in Country Y;
(d) the Government of Country Y;
(e) a motor-bike purchaser in Country X;
(f) GATT.

The use of these restrictions should also be related to the problem of correcting disequilibrium in the balance of payments. Because it is such a recurring problem in the UK, the teacher can often find relevant material in newspapers and other publications.

Customs Unions, the EEC and International Institutions

These topics involve a large amount of descriptive work. As a result this is often taught by 'lecture' from the teacher and can become very dull. Alternatively, after giving the pupils a brief introductory outline, the teacher could provide material for them to work on their own. For example he could prepare workpacks consisting of resource material, e.g. newspaper and other articles, leaflets, etc.

A useful exercise for pupils to become aware of the spatial aspect of the customs union is to study a map of the area covered. In the case of the EEC the pupils can be given an outline map of Europe and mark on it the member countries. They can also show on the map the size of the populations of each country, and what goods are produced in different parts of the union. Younger pupils particularly enjoy working with maps and take great care over presentation.

The Third World

Trade links between rich and poor countries may also be included in the teaching of international trade at this level. This can be used as a starting point for a wider examination of all aspects of rich world–poor world relationships, if the scope of the course allows.

The distinction between oil-exporting and oil-importing countries may also be made. Pupils should be made aware of the importance of oil in world trade.

There are ever-increasing amounts of material available for use as teacher or pupil resources for this topic. The *Development Puzzle*, published by the Centre for World Development Education, is a useful source-book. It includes a section on trade, with teaching notes and information on films, wallcharts, photographs, games and other resources available.

Oxfam provide an outline of *The Trade Game* which can easily be prepared by the teacher. It is suitable for fifteen year olds and upwards and illustrates the relationship between buyers and sellers of internationally traded commodities.

Use of Statistics

The teaching of international trade and payments involves at least some use of statistics. If pupils can interpret certain basic statistics they will more easily understand news items on trade. Most textbooks can be used as a source of statistics but the teacher can supplement these.

Barclays and Lloyds *Bank Reviews* both provide some current trade statistics. The *Economic Progress Report* shows graphs of overseas trade, balance of payments and the terms of trade. Newspapers can also be used as sources for statistics, in particular *The Times* and *The Financial Times*.

The statistics provided in these publications are mainly in too difficult a form to be understood directly by pupils, but can be simplified and adapted by the teacher, and used for illustration, calculations or exercises. Other sources for consultation are: *Economic Trends* – with articles on latest UK balance of payments position every March, June, September and December; the *Monthly Digest* and the Annual Abstract of Statistics.

An example of an exercise involving interpretation of statistics for 'O' level fifth form pupils follows, using Figure 17.5.

1 Which country has experienced a falling value of imports over the period shown?

2 Which countries in the third quarter of 1976 would have been in surplus on current account, and which in deficit?

3 Use two bar graphs to show the changes in values of UK exports and imports over the period shown.

An example of interpretation of statistics for medium ability thirteen–sixteen year olds follows, using Figures 17.6 and 17.7.

Current account receipts, 1976

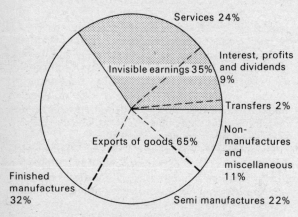

Source: *Monthly Digest of Statistics and Economic Trends, March 1977*

Figure 17.6 Reproduced from the Economic Progress Report, *87, June 1977, by courtesy of the Treasury*

Using Figure 17.6:

1 What does 'invisible' mean here?

2 What is the largest item of Britain's exports?

3 What percentage of total invisible earnings is services?

4 Give some examples of services.

Using Figure 17.7:

1 What do the + and − signs mean?

2 The invisible balance is greater in 1976 than in 1971, but the current balance is lower. Why is this?

3 How much were Britain's invisible earnings in 1976?

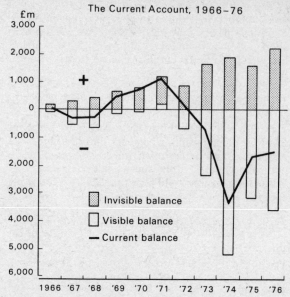

Source: *Economic trends, March 1977*

Figure 17.7 Reproduced from the Economic Progress Report, *87, June 1977, by courtesy of the Treasury*

References

1 Davies, F., *Starting Economics*, (Hulton, 1977), chapter 7. This book is written for CSE courses but it could also be used for younger pupils. The chapter adequately covers the concept of international specialisation and the principle of comparative costs. There are also sections on trade restrictions and the balance of payments but the section on exchange rates is not very satisfactory.

2 Harvey, J., *Elementary Economics*, (Macmillan Education, 1976), chapters 14 and 15. This is more suitable for an 'O' level than a CSE course. The sections on international specialisation, the advantages of trade and government control of trade are particularly useful. There is also a section on UK trade which is necessary for many courses. Statistics are clearly presented. Balance of payments accounting is also covered and methods of correcting an imbalance. A separate chapter reviews the EEC in some depth. This provides background on the aims and institutions of the EEC.

Resources

Books

Baron, D., *Economics; An Introductory Course*, (Heinemann Educational, 1973), chapters 13, 14 and 15. This book is best suited to the lower ability thirteen–sixteen year olds, as it concentrates on a simplified treatment. It is well presented and covers all the necessary topics needed for a study of international trade.

Harbury, C. D., *Descriptive Economics*, (Pitman Publications, fifth edition, 1976), chapter 10. Covers international trade very comprehensively – for example the chapter includes the problems of OPEC and the oil price rise. Some of the sub-topics such as international co-operation are better suited to the older pupil. The diagrams are clearly presented.

Harvey, J., *Elementary Economics Workbook*, (Macmillan Education, 1976), chapters 14 and 15. The workbook is particularly suited for use with the textbook, but it is also useful on its own. These two chapters provide the pupil with a lot of work on trade he can do on his own. The teacher's edition provides answers to questions set in the workbook.

Harvey, J. and M., *Producing and Spending*, (Macmillan Education, 1967), pp 121–34. Aims to cover material for a CSE course in commerce. It explains the need for trade documents involved and balance of payments statistics. At the end of the section there are some very useful 'things to do' for the pupil, including some elementary use of statistics.

Jelley, C., (ed), *Peter Donaldson's Illustrated Economics*, (BBC, 1975), pp 45–53. The section entitled 'Buying British' provides useful teaching material on some aspects of trade. In particular it defines a balance of payments 'problem' and reviews possible solutions. The book was designed for use with the BBC TV series of the same name.

Marder, K. B. and Alderson, L. P., *Economic Society*, (Oxford University Press, 1975), chapters 14 and 15. This book is aimed at 'O' level and CSE pupils. It

outlines some trade theory and Britain's trade position. There is also a brief outline of the structure and aims of the EEC. Chapter 15 covers international payments giving a clear explanation of balance of payments accounting and excellent illustration of trade statistics.

Nobbs, J., *Social Economics*, (McGraw-Hill, second edition, 1976), chapter 7. This is a useful book for both CSE and 'O' level courses. It contains good sections on the terms of trade, the balance of payments and international institutions.

Stanlake, G. F., *Introducing Economics*, (Longman, third edition, 1976), part 9. This revised edition of the book is suitable only for the more able 'O' level pupils. In particular this edition contains detailed analysis of recent developments in the international monetary system. Chapter 26 includes excellent analysis of comparative costs and the terms of trade. Other chapters include particularly useful sections on the workings of the IMF, and the origins, aims and structure of the EEC.

Other Resources
1 Guild Sound and Vision Ltd, *Europe is Happening*, (29″, 350 3112.3), – on the EEC.
2 Bank of Education Service. One chart: *International Trade Settlement*, (free).
3 Audio Learning Ltd Tape/filmstrip pack: *The Theory of Comparative Advantage*.
4 ILEA TV Service. Two 20″ video tapes on international trade. Available for hire or purchase from Guild Sound and Vision. *International Trade 1 – Background Theory*, (900 9711.9). *International Trade 2 – Get Out There and Sell*, (9712.6).
5 ILEA TV Service. One 20″ video tape on the Common Market, (900 9713.3).
6 Careers Consultants Ltd. One chart: *International Trade*, (free).

18   Distribution – Wholesaling and Retailing
Quintin N. Brewer

General Comments

Wholesaling, retailing, transportation and advertising are topics which appear on many economics and commerce 'O' level and CSE syllabuses. They are also suitable topics for inclusion in introductory courses for younger pupils as much of the material falls within their own experience. Pupils will be aware not only of the different types of shops but many may have had experience of working in one. It would be advisable for the teacher to ascertain his pupils' experience in this field so that he can draw on their particular insights, thus stimulating the interest of the whole class.

To put this topic into perspective it is necessary to consider it in the context of the interdependent processes of production and exchange. This approach gives students a better understanding of economic relationships. However, introductory courses for younger pupils may concentrate on topics within the pupils' experience. Whilst a basic knowledge of the types and functions of retailers and wholesalers may be sufficient for commerce students, it does not meet the needs of an economics student. The teacher of economics should emphasise the economic forces which have produced the present pattern of distribution and, in addition, he should consider the reasons for the changes in methods of distribution which have occurred in recent years.

Content

The following aspects of this topic are the ones most commonly included in syllabuses:

(a) Distribution in the context of the production and exchange of goods.
(b) The functions of the wholesaler; the services he provides to the manufacturer and to the retailer; the reasons for the decline of the wholesaler; the ways in which the wholesaler performs a useful economic function at present.
(c) The functions of the retailer; the organisation, finance, and services of the various types of retailers: e.g. independents; voluntary groups; multiple chain stores; supermarkets; hypermarkets; department stores; co-operative societies; mail order firms.
(d) Changes in the distributive trades in the post-war years and an analysis of the reasons for these changes.
(e) The functions and types of advertising; consumer protection.

(f) The importance of transport in the process of distribution. The types and relative advantages of each form of transport. However, this aspect of distribution is generally taught in the context of factors influencing location of industry.

Teaching Methods

Traditional methods of teaching can be supplemented by the following:

1 Case studies may be used to illustrate the process of distribution by reference to local industries, e.g. food processing firm: study of source of raw materials; outline of the range of products; methods of distribution. A comparison of different firms in the area may illustrate a variety of methods of distribution. Students could devise a questionnaire to be sent to a number of firms, analyse the results and supplement this by selected visits. (See Chapter 11 for a suggested questionnaire.)
2 An exercise based on newspaper articles (such as that shown in Figure 18.1) can be used to illustrate the manufacture and distribution of a product. Students could be asked to illustrate the process in the form of a diagram and to explain how the mark-ups of the cloth wholesaler, manufacturer, outworker and retailer are justified and why the retailer's mark-up is so great.
3 The following simulation may be used to illustrate the importance of the wholesaler: Four members of the class may act as manufacturers of different products and another four as retailers. The manufacturers wish to sell their products to all the retailers and the retailers wish to buy products from each of the manufacturers. The rest of the class calculates the number of contacts necessary between manufacturers and retailers in this situation. The teacher can use this to illustrate both the problems and advantages of this method of distribution. Another member of the class may now be introduced to act as a wholesaler who buys the goods from the four manufacturers and sells them to the retailers. Again the rest of the class calculates the number of contacts necessary between manufacturers, the wholesaler and retailers, and the basic function of the wholesaler becomes apparent.
4 Another way of illustrating the importance of the wholesaler is by using a map of Britain as follows. A furniture manufacturer, based in Birmingham, has orders from customers in Margate, Dover, Brighton,

WHO GETS
WHAT OUT
CF A SIMPLE
SUNDRESS
LIKE THIS?

THIS is a break-
down of how
material originally
worth only 35p ends
up as a £6·99 dress
and isn't over-
priced.

THE dresses start
life at the mill as grey
cloth, produced at a
cost of 28p a metre.
Each dress takes 1·25
metres (35p-worth of
cloth).

THE material is
sold to a cloth whole-
saler for 35p a metre.
The wholesaler prints
on the design, which
costs him 35p a metre,
bringing his total costs
to 80p a metre. The
wholesaler then adds
on his mark-up and sells
the cloth to the dress
manufacturer for 80p
a metre.

THE manufacturer
sends the cloth to the
outworker to be
made up into dresses.
The sundress takes
1·25 metres at a cost of
£1. Each dress costs
£1·20 to make (which
includes the
outworker's mark-up
of 5p a dress).

THE finished dress
has now cost the
manufacturer £2·20.
He adds a plastic bag
costing 1p and a hanger
costing 2p. He then
puts on his mark up
which varies from
40 per cent. to 50
per cent.

SO the store buys
the dress for around
£3·30 and adds its own
mark-up of 100 per cent.
plus. The total comes
out at £6·99.
(All prices include
VAT).

PICTURE BY PETER AKEHURST

Figure 18.1 Reproduced from the Daily Mail, *23
May 1977, page 13*

Eastbourne, Hastings and Folkestone. Lines may be
drawn on the map from Birmingham to each of the
above South Coast resorts (illustrating the special
journey which must be made in each case). On a separate map it may be shown how the introduction of a
wholesaler, based at Maidstone, could result in a saving
in transport.

5 To make students aware of the different types of
retailer a survey of the local shopping centre may be
conducted. The exercises in *Descriptive Economics*[1]
contain many useful ideas, e.g. conducting a survey of
the shops classified by what they sell (butchers, bakers,
fishmongers etc). In addition, the following type of
survey may be used:

Name of road	Name of shop	Classification*	Type of goods sold

* Shops may be classified under the following headings: independents; voluntary chains; multiple chain stores; department stores; co-operative societies.

Alternatively this information may be plotted on a local map. From this it is possible to show the key positions in the shopping centre.

Further work could include a classification of those shops which specialise in selling mainly one product and those selling a wide variety of goods, followed by a discussion of the reasons in each case.

6 To illustrate the relative advantages of different types of supermarket, students can survey and report on the following: the range of goods sold; the variety of brands of particular products; whether the supermarket's own brand is available; the prices of certain goods; special offers; layout and display; number of checkouts. (See Appendix to Chapter 9.)

A comparison between independents and supermarkets will also enable students to judge the advantages and disadvantages of shopping in these very different types of retail outlet. Follow-up work can include an analysis of the change in the value of turnover of the main groups of retailer businesses.

7 Case studies of particular retailers can be made. Articles sometimes appear in the newspapers and colour magazines. Many firms are willing to send information and booklets on request. This can form the basis of some interesting project work on, for example, the beginnings of the firm; its development and reasons for its success; how it has changed since it was set up. A special study of this nature can reveal much about the changes which have occurred in retailing in general.

8 Newspaper articles are particularly useful in illustrating recent developments in retailing, e.g. the article shown in Figure 18.2. Such material may be used as a basis for classwork. After the students have read the article, the following questions may be asked:

(a) What factors influenced Tesco's decision to give up Green Shield stamps?

Figure 18.2 Reproduced from The Economist, *14 May 1977, page 126*

BUSINESS : BRITAIN   THE ECONOMIST MAY 14, 1977

Trading stamps

Tesco drops its Green Shield

Stamps or discount, asks the cashier at the filling station. Thanks to the petrol price war, consumers are increasingly often being given the choice. Even when the trading stamps are 5-fold or 10-fold, many drivers are opting for the cash.

Little wonder that their wives, on ever-tighter household budgets, are thinking the same way. And they have won. Tesco, after market research, a study visit to America, and experiments in a number of its stores that operate under the Adsega shopfront, is ending its 14-year-old distribution of Green Shield stamps. It is proclaiming price cuts in its shops, from June 8th, instead.

Tesco says its research showed 90% of customers would prefer cut prices to stamps; and it will now have £20m to play with, which on past form it would have spent on stamps this year, out of its forecast £850m turnover. For comparison, it spends about £2m a year on press and television advertising.

In practice, the break was not due to a simple, heroic change of strategy. Tesco, till now bound by its contract with Green Shield to give stamps in all its stores, had been ready to go on with stamps in a more flexible system, at the right price. But Tesco is a famously tough buyer, and the price it offered (no one is saying how much) did not appeal to Green Shield.

Green Shield, unlike many suppliers squeezed by giant retailers, was prepared to make the break. It says that Tesco for some years has accounted for about 20% of its turnover, which when announced for 1976 will have been a bit over £75m. That suggests a deal worth £15m last year ; Tesco's figures suggest 2.35% on its then £750m turnover, ie about £17½m. Either figure is a huge chunk for Green Shield to lose. But International Stores has already started talking about stamps for another 100 of its stores, previously blocked by Tesco's right to an exclusive franchise wherever it got in first. Green Shield is after other chains too, though in a way that suggests it won't be eager to tie itself too closely again to any one giant pair of apron-strings.

On the garage forecourts it has certainly lost takers, but "5-fold" means many more stamps, and it claims that its throughput in petrol is still holding up.

The consumer organisations are delighted. They have always been against trading stamps, which are of less value than they are made to seem.

Green Shield sells its stamps to retailers at £3 for for a 5,000-stamp pad for a small shop, less for large buyers like Tesco. At that price, the book — 32 pages of 40 stamps apiece—is "worth" almost 77p. To the customer, Green Shield used to claim it was worth fifteen bob—75p. Today, it admits, that figure is 70p—in goods, not the cash option which few customers want. And even today's figure is calculated on manufacturers' recommended retail prices.

Shop around, and you can make the value seem much less. Spend £32 at Tesco and you've filled a book. Take 21 books (hurry, a new catalogue comes out on May 23rd) and you can get a 2 kw Rima fan heater at your Green Shield gift centre. At an Argos catalogue discount store—Green Shield under another hat—the heater costs £10.50. That makes your books worth 50p each. Buy a Moulinex carving knife and that becomes 61p. On some Argos goods you can find a value above 70p. But the lesson holds : trading stamps may be very good value against the prices in Harrods, but cash frees customers to shop where they please. And that makes more difference today than it used to.

(b) Why are the consumer organisations pleased with Tesco's decision?

(c) How is the Green Shield Company reacting to Tesco's decision?

(d) Why do customers saving Green Shield stamps prefer to exchange them for goods rather than for cash?

(e) If Tesco stopped advertising, would prices be reduced further?

9 One method of teaching advertising is by showing some carefully selected advertisements on a video tape recorder, and using these as the basis for discussion on the following lines:

(a) Which adverts were informative and which were purely persuasive?

(b) Which adverts aroused your interest?

(c) Which adverts might influence you to purchase a product?

(d) Which adverts were aimed at particular groups of people?

N.B. It will probably be necessary to show the recording twice, the first time for enjoyment, then an explanation of the purpose of the lesson and finally a re-showing of the advertisements.

Students can be encouraged to bring in examples of different types of advertisements from newspapers, colour supplements and magazines. They can be divided into two categories: those which are mainly informative and those which rely on persuasion and displayed on different sides of the room. In practice it may be difficult to make a complete distinction as many advertisements are partly informative and partly persuasive; in these cases the class may discuss which function appears to be most important. The class may then be divided into two broad groups, one to discuss the advantages and disadvantages of advertising to the consumer and the other to discuss the advantages and disadvantages of advertising to the firm. Further interesting methods of teaching this topic can be found in *Descriptive Economics*, mentioned previously.

10 Consumer protection can be a rather 'dry' topic but interest can be aroused by the use of simplified *Which?* type reports on particular products composed by the pupils. These may be used by the teacher to show how consumers can be exploited. This will provide a useful introduction to legislation on consumer protection which may then be explained by means of case studies, e.g. how consumers are protected against dangerous toys. Films are another useful aid to show the work of particular bodies such as the British Standards Institution (see Resources).

Reference

1 Harbury, C. D., *Descriptive Economics*, (Pitman, 1972), p 157.

Resources

Books
Many economics textbooks give a reasonably good outline of wholesaling and retailing but few give much coverage of the other aspects of distribution e.g. advertising, transport. For these areas, commerce textbooks are more useful.

Baron, D., *Introductory Economics*, (Heinemann, 1973), chapter 5. A simple, concise and well presented outline of the work of wholesalers and retailers suitable for both CSE and 'O' level courses.

Birch, P. A. and Sanday, A. P., *Understanding Industrial Society*, (Hodder and Stoughton, 1976), chapter 6. An interesting chapter on distribution including a study of a department store.

Charnley, A. H., *Retail Trade and Distribution*, (Ginn, 1971). This booklet can be recommended for use with more able students and can be of value to the teacher.

Davies, A. and Coy, J., *Economics from Square One*, (Allen and Unwin, 1973), chapter 4. A good outline of the different methods of distributing products with examples. The work of the wholesaler is covered especially well.

Harbury, C. D., *Descriptive Economics*, (Pitmans, 1972), chapter 6. A comprehensive outline of the work and functions of the wholesaler and retailer; also included are sections on advertising and consumer protection.

Harvey, J., *Elementary Economics*, (Macmillan, 1976), chapter 7. A fairly comprehensive outline of the functions and work of wholesalers and retailers. To complement this book a chapter of questions is included in Harvey, J., *Elementary Economics Workbook*, (Macmillan, 1976), chapter 7. This is a most useful teaching aid containing various types of questions as well as points for discussion and project work.

Lobley, D., *Success in Commerce*, (John Murray, 1975), units 2, 3, 4, 7, 16, 17. A well presented book which covers all the basic aspects of distribution including consumer protection, advertising and transport.

Marder, K. B. and Alderson, L. P., *Economic Society*, (Oxford University Press, 1975), chapter 7. This chapter gives good coverage of wholesalers and retailers as well as a section on consumer protection.

Nobbs, J., *Social Economics*, (McGraw-Hill, 1975), units 9–12 and 24. Suited to both CSE and 'O' level courses, these units cover all aspects of distribution including advertising and transport well.

Written Material
Many stores are willing to supply booklets which can be useful as teaching aids.

Co-op Study Notes are available from London Co-operative Society Ltd.

It is worth writing to stores such as Marks and Spencer, Tesco, Sainsbury and British Home Stores, which produce different types of booklet each year.

The British Standards Institution produces some teaching kits on consumer protection e.g. *BSI and the Consumer* for ROSLA children, and *Standards Make Sense* giving information on British Standards and suggestions for follow-up activities. Other leaflets from BSI are available free of charge.

Wallcharts
Two charts: *Chain Store Organisation* and *How a Chain Store Works* (C1145/1/2) from Educational Productions Ltd.

The Cost of a Bike (C30) – from raw materials to retail outlet; also compares methods of buying a motor bike. Also *Analysing Advertising* (C25). Both from Pictorial Charts Educational Trust.

Four charts on the history and current activities of the Co-operative movement: *The Society* (two charts), *School Co-operative* and *You and Your Co-op*. All free from London Co-operative Society.

Films
British Standards Institution, *A Question of Standards* (15 minutes) showing the use of Kitemark for standardising and safety.

British Standards Institution, *Living Standards* (20 minutes) showing the role of BSI in protecting and safeguarding the community.

BBC Enterprises, *Economics of the Real World*

Programme 12: *Consumers – Masters or Puppets* (25 minutes). Suitable for older or more able students.

Guild Sound and Vision, *Advertising in Perspective*, (50 minutes, 300–7462–2).

ILEA TV series: Video tapes available for purchase or hire from Guild Sound and Vision (13–20 minutes each): *Everyday Contrasts*, (900 9690.7); *Complaining*, (900 9691.4); *Credit*, (900 9692.1); *Advertising 1 – A Gentle Art*, (900 9693.8); *Advertising 2 – A Dangerous Weapon*, (900 9694.5); *Retailing 1 – History of Retailing*, (900 9707.8); *Retailing 2 – Recent Developments*, (900 9708.5); *Transport 1 – Passenger*, (900 9709.2); *Transport 2 – Freight*, (900 9710.2).

Viscom Ltd National Audio-Visual Aids: Potato Marketing Board, *Potatoes Please* (23 minutes, free loan). Also: *A Tradition of Quality* shows lamb production and distribution, (15 minutes, free loan).

Filmstrip/Tapes
The following filmstrip/tapes are all from Student Recordings Ltd:

Transport Systems and Communications (AVC/10); *Unit Shops, Multiples and Chain Stores* (AVC/11); *Department Stores, Supermarkets, and Co-operatives* (AVC/12); *Mail Order, Markets and Mobile Trading* (AVC/13); *Advertising and Marketing* (AVC/16); *The Wholesale Trade* (AVC/38); *Shops and Shopping* (AVC/152 and AVC/153) deals with aspects of advertising, consumer protection, shoppers' rights.

The commentary is rather dry. Therefore they need to be used selectively by the teacher.

Other Material
The following sources may be used in teaching distribution: *Which?* reports; *The Retail Trades Directory*.

19 Population
David R. Butler

Population is often an important section in 'O' level and CSE syllabuses. Teachers frequently experience problems in teaching it and may well find it a rather dull topic. Population does not normally form part of main stream economics (there is little emphasis on it at 'A' level) so the teacher may himself be uncertain about what to include. Few textbooks cover this topic adequately, and those that do rapidly become out-of-date with each new upturn or downturn in the birth rate. There is a danger too that the teacher's lack of interest in this topic will be reflected in the pupils adopting a similar attitude.

Content

Most syllabuses concentrate on the UK's population – its growth, trends in its birth rates and death rates, its age, sex, geographical, and occupational structure. Some syllabuses may require a knowledge of world population trends, and the differences in growth rates and life expectancy between the rich and poor countries. Indeed, it may be useful and interesting to add a section on this area even if it is not directly required by the syllabus. The relevance of Malthusian theory may also give rise to an interesting discussion because it is in essence simple enough for 13 to 16 year olds to understand.

Methods

11 Historical Approach
Most syllabuses require some background knowledge of eighteenth and nineteenth century trends in birth rates and death rates. These periods can be used in any case to demonstrate the reasons for population growth and why birth and death rates changed. The history department may well be able to assist with material here. Details of eighteenth and nineteenth century living and working conditions, medical treatment and contraceptive techniques all add interest to these topics which could otherwise become rather dry. A particularly good reference source here is the book *Human Documents of the Industrial Revolution* which gives contemporary accounts of conditions in the eighteenth and nineteenth centuries (see Resources). Extracts on the primitive conditions of eighteenth century hospitals, surgery and remedies for illnesses fascinate many fourth and fifth year pupils!

2 Population Models
With pupils who have some mathematical ability or who are taking computer studies courses, it is possible to construct some very simple demographic models. Pupils with an interest in statistics can become quite involved in working out future population sizes and trends. This all adds interest as well as understanding to the topic. One important discovery they should make, through the construction of such models, is how difficult it is to predict the future size of population.

The basis of more sophisticated economic models, varying one factor (e.g. birth rate) and holding all the other factors (e.g. death rate, immigration, emigration, etc) constant, can be introduced to the more able pupils by using simple population models.

Examples of possible exercises: (a) Assuming a present world population of 4000 million and a birth rate of 28 per 1000 population per annum and a death rate of 12 per 1000 population per annum (statistics from *The Economist*, 8 January 1977), what will be the population in 1980, 2000 and 2020? Show the results on a graph. (b) A comparison of the growth rates of population between the UK and a developing country to show how the 'gap' widens progressively (this is best shown graphically). (c) A demonstration of how a small change in the UK's birth rate can quite dramatically alter the predicted size of population for the end of the century.

The implications of these predictions, both on the particular country concerned and on the world, in terms of economic planning, growth and living standards should give rise to considerable classroom discussion.

The use of calculators and possibly a computer terminal is clearly desirable in these exercises so that the actual amount of mechanical mathematics required is kept to a minimum.

3 Surveys
It is quite possible to carry out a mini 'census' in the class based on the pupils' parents and grandparents (the teacher needs to be careful to avoid embarrassment here). Place of origin of parents and grandparents can be used to illustrate migration patterns (this very often shows how little movement has taken place and will depend to a great extent on social class). The number of children in their own family can be compared to that of their parents' families in order to illustrate changes in birth rate. Occupational categories of parents can be compared with those of grandparents to see if they reflect national trends. Very often such surveys will produce results which run contrary to the national trends but this in itself is useful as a basis of discussion about why this is so.

4 The Census of Population
Most local libraries will contain a copy of the census pertaining to that particular area. This will contain a mass of statistics which can easily form the basis of a large number of exercises and mini-projects on local population. To give but one example, age/sex 'pyramids' can quite easily be constructed for a number of districts. These can be compared to show how these distributions vary. It is especially revealing to do a cross-section in a city to show how the pattern varies between inner and outer boroughs. Alternatively, the pupil can be presented with different 'pyramids' and

asked to allocate them to a particular type of area and to give reasons for so doing. For example, the 'pyramid' for a seaside resort will have a high percentage of older women whilst a new town or housing estate will have a high percentage of people in the 20–30 age categories with young children.

5 Data Response

Population is a good area in which to use a data response approach. Indeed, Examination Boards have already set questions involving the interpretation of population statistics. Pupils frequently encounter difficulties with this type of question (see later) so it is appropriate to introduce statistical interpretation as a teaching method. The teacher might find the following type of exercise useful:

Age	1861 %	1911 %	1931 %	1967 %	1975 %
0–15	36	31	24	23	24
16–64	60	64	69	64	62
65+	5	5	7	12	14

Table 19.1 Age Structure of UK population. N.B. Due to rounding, totals do not always add up to 100%

Questions on Table 19.1:

1 Why do you consider that the particular age categories have been selected?
2 What main trends do the statistics show?
3 What are the possible causes of the trends shown?
4 What economic consequences might there be from the trends shown?

There is also a wealth of non-statistical material on population which could be used as a basis for exercises. Articles on the Third World's population problems frequently occur in the newspapers and elsewhere. Material supplied by Oxfam or its advertising could provide the basis for discussion or data response type exercises.

The following is an example of the type of material that might be suitable for use at this level:

'Figures published last week show that, for the first time since the First World War, in one 12-month period, our population level fell . . . .'

The answer to the question: 'Who wants children?' is simple: fewer and fewer of us. In ten years, our birth rate has dropped by one quarter, and is now so low that we are no longer replacing ourselves. Last year our total population fell.' (From *The Listener*, 27 January 1977.)

Questions:

1 Why might the birth rate be declining?
2 Is the decline in population solely due to the fall in the birth rate?
3 The extract claims that it is the first time since the First World War that the population has fallen, but people have been talking about a falling rate of population growth for some time. Explain.
4 What consequences might there be of zero population growth or even a declining population?

6 Project Work

Although the material is not quite so easily accessible for project work as in other syllabus areas, it is still possible for pupils to carry out some quite interesting work here. They will, however, need to be carefully guided. Suggestions here include the use of the local census of population, family surveys, studies of local commuting patterns and employment in the local area.

Areas where Pupils have Problems in Understanding

1 *Interpretation of statistics.* Pupils given population figures to discuss will very often make rather wild and exaggerated claims as to what they show. Interpretation of figures on population tend to be a common examination question. 'There must have been a recurrence of the Black Death' and similar statements are not uncommon from pupils asked to interpret birth and death rate statistics. Clearly, practice in handling population statistics in the ways mentioned above is essential and extremely useful for the pupil. Population statistics present an excellent opportunity for the teacher to illustrate what statistics can and cannot be used for.

2 *The difference between absolute and relative changes.* This is not a problem specific to demographic studies but it does tend to occur quite frequently in this syllabus section. Pupils will confuse a slow down in the rate of population growth with an actual decline in the size. Again, a percentage increase in the population in the tertiary sector of the economy may often be interpreted automatically as a growth in the actual size of the tertiary population. The use of a graph may help to illustrate the difference between a change in the rate of growth and the change in the total population size. Pie diagrams may help to show that the size of the 'cake' can remain the same but 'shares' in it can alter.

3 *Immigration.* Examination Boards have from time to time set questions on the nature and consequences of immigration. Answers to this type of question tend, not surprisingly, to be charged with highly emotive statements with their bias depending upon the political

viewpoint of the candidate. Clearly, this can only be overcome by a detailed discussion of the facts about immigration, so that pupils may make positive statements rather than value judgements on the subject. This can often be difficult and lead to embarrassing situations when the class contains pupils from different ethnic groups.

4 *The causes of population 'ageing'*. Pupils find it very difficult to understand why population 'ageing' can be caused solely by changes in the birth rate as is the case in the UK (many textbooks are misleading on this point). This is often best explained by taking an extreme model of population change. For example if there were 1000 babies born in 1977 and none born in the next 10 years then the population will age as this 'baby bulge' moves up the population pyramid. Extreme cases will often help explain other demographic phenomena as well.

5 *Unemployment*. This, like the topic of immigration, tends to encourage misunderstanding and prejudiced statements. It needs to be emphasised that there are other causes of unemployment besides idleness, and that the number of people out of work because they 'find it easier to scrounge off the State' is likely to be a very small percentage of the total unemployed, even though pupils can supply countless examples of such people living next door or quoted in the popular press! Another frequent misunderstanding is that unemployment is directly related to size of total population, i.e. 'Unemployment could be reduced if the total population size of the UK was reduced.' An example showing that unemployment was higher in the 1920s but that the working population was smaller than at present is useful here.

6 *Occupational distribution of population*. This is an important section in most syllabuses. A frequent examination question at this level is 'How has the occupational distribution of population of the UK changed in the last twenty years?'. In answer to this question, candidates will frequently become too involved in discussing the changes in individual industries and fail to discuss the overall trends. Pupils should be made aware of the main changes which have taken place in the occupational distribution of population between the primary, secondary and tertiary sectors before individual industries are considered. The problem here is that individual industries may well show the reverse trend to that of the overall sector and this may lead to some confusion amongst less able pupils. When asked to explain why changes have taken place in the occupational distribution of population, pupils will often automatically consider that there has been an absolute change in output and fail to consider relative shifts in output and changes in productivity. Pupils

need therefore to be given total output figures of various industries alongside the figures for employment. When a decline in a particular category is discussed, it should be made very clear to the pupil whether it is an absolute or a relative decline that is being referred to.

Resources

Books
Books dealing with the descriptive aspects of population have a tendency to be almost out-of-date when they are printed. They need to be constantly kept up to date by one of the statistical sources mentioned below.

Manchester Economics Project (Ginn, 1972). Study section 3. Although meant for 'A' level there are some good tables, diagrams, etc. which could be adapted for 'O' level.

National Institute of Economic and Social Research, *The UK Economy*, (Heinemann Educational, 1976), chapters 1 and 2. Demographic trends (figures up to 1975).

Nobbs, J., *Social Economics*, (McGraw-Hill, second edition, 1976), unit 25, 'World Population'. An interesting section with international comparisons of diet, population growth rates, etc. Unit 26, 'The Population of UK' deals with census, sex, age, geographical and occupational distributions (figures up to 1975). Future population trends.

Royston Pike, E., *Human Documents of the Industrial Revolution*, (Allen and Unwin, 1966). Human documents of the industrial revolution. Eye witness accounts of the conditions of hospitals, living conditions and working conditions in the eighteenth and nineteenth centuries.

Stanlake, G., *Introductory Economics*, (Longman, second edition, 1976), chapter 2. Quite good coverage of world population, UK, age, geographical and occupational distributions.

Annual Abstract of Statistics, (HMSO). Details of most recent population statistics of all kinds.

UN Statistical Yearbook and *UN Demographic Yearbook*. World population figures.

Pamphlets
The UK in Figures. (Press and Information Service, Central Statistical Office.) Available free in multiple copies for distribution to pupils. UK vital statistics presented on a pocket card.

An Economic Profile of Britain (Lloyds Bank). Small booklet giving large number of basic UK statistics including birth and death rates etc. Available free in multiple copies.

Other Resources
Population Problems. Tape and film strip presentation of world population problems. Available from Student Recordings Ltd (AVC 29).

Malthusiana (Longman, Schools Council General Studies Project). Simulation on population problems.

20   The Welfare State

A. G. Anderton

Many economics CSE and social economics 'O' level courses require a knowledge of:

(a) the National Insurance system – the way it finances its operations and the benefits available under the system;
(b) the social security system – the benefits available and the conditions under which they are given;
(c) other 'situation benefits' available like family allowances;
(d) other aspects of the welfare state like the National Health Service, education provision, housing, social services departments of local authorities, etc.

Skills demanded are mainly lower order knowledge skills – a great pity because application and evaluation will be the skills required in real life.

Pupils find difficulty in distinguishing between National Insurance and the social security system. A good way of distinguishing between the two is to emphasise the *insurance* nature of the National Insurance system and the *means-tested* aspect of social security. Only workers who have paid National Insurance contributions are entitled to benefits. If you haven't paid in, you can't get anything out. An excellent example of this is relevant to school leavers. A school leaver cannot technically go on 'the dole' when he leaves school because he hasn't paid National Insurance contributions. Hence he is unable to obtain unemployment benefit. But he can get social security payments. If this is emphasised every time a pupil cracks a joke about going on the dole when he leaves school, the message eventually gets through. The social security system should be dealt with in terms of poverty and its alleviation. The complicated structure of the health service poses problems. A study of the health

service in the area in which the school is situated is often more meaningful than talk about distant and nebulous regional health authorities. On housing, pupils are fairly knowledgeable about renting and buying and the advantages and disadvantages of both. They do find it difficult to accept statistics – like the one about one household in ten (1971 census) still living without a fixed bath or an internal toilet. A realistic appreciation of poverty and its effects should be aimed for whenever the welfare state is taught.

On benefits, there is an excellent source of raw material. The Department of Health and Social Security will provide quantities of leaflets explaining all the different benefits available. They are written in fairly simple language, often with application forms at the end. Pupils could be asked to make a complete list of benefits available and in what circumstances they can be claimed. They could also be asked to fill in an application form for a benefit, having been given pre-specified information about an imaginary person. Comprehension questions could be set. The benefits could be grouped according to the situation of potential applicants (poor, sick, unemployed, etc) or according to whether they are National Insurance benefits, means-tested benefits or situation benefits. For the hard-pressed teacher, there is an excellent summary of benefits available in *Money Which* magazine September 1974 entitled 'Social Security Check List'. This needs to be updated of course. Examples of the sort of work that could be set are given at the end of the chapter.

There is very little book material on the subject. Most 'O' level CSE texts mention the welfare state in passing but do little more. In fact, sociology/social studies texts like *Looking at Society* by Carpenter and Ruddiman and *People in Society* by North tend to be more informative. Two economics books which are better than most are *Social Economics* by Nobbs which has a rather patchy section entitled 'Social and Economic Services' and *Daily Economics* by Nobbs and Ames, a book aimed at low ability pupils, which has a very selective tour of the 'social services'. A specialist text on the subject is *The Social Services* by D. Whittaker, published in the Longman Social Science Studies series, though the material is put mainly in a historical setting. The Pelican *Consumer's Guide to the British Social Services* could be used by the teacher and the most able.

If text material is rather limited, newspaper material is plentiful. Articles are good for evaluation rather than information. Pupils have strong views – most of which can correctly be described as prejudices – on the social security system. Some of the more common prejudices are that most immigrants live off the State, workers who are unemployed don't want to work, social security payments are used mainly for gambling and drinking and most people would be better off on the dole than working. In the light of this, it is very dangerous to provide articles which will reinforce these views. It is far better to pick articles which put over a more balanced viewpoint. An example of an article with questions is provided at the end of the chapter. Newspaper articles can be used for comprehension or to stimulate discussion. In discussion, the teacher should have at his fingertips the latest statistics on who is getting what and when. The most recent edition of *Social Trends* is very useful in this context. It contains statistics on benefits and also has good sections on housing, education and health. Newspaper articles are also a good source for material on the health service. The newly established tiered structure is difficult to understand and is attracting regular criticism. Newspapers will also provide comparisons with other countries, and they will often suggest that the welfare state abroad has been far better organised than in the UK. This could lead into consideration of alternative ways of financing the system. One simple example which can be used is to discuss 'free' versus insurance health systems. Although this is not specifically related to most syllabuses, it does make pupils think about what is being provided for them. It is often useful to reproduce accounts from two newspapers of the same story giving two different viewpoints. Political bias can then be discussed.

Audio-visual material is fairly thin on the ground unless one tapes material from the television or radio. Student Recordings have produced a tape–slide sequence on the social services covering 'the multiple State contributions to both individuals and families under the headings of Education, the Health Service and National Insurance Benefits'. However, TV and radio can be an excellent source of material. With radio recordings, it is better to get fairly short items of perhaps 5 or 10 minutes since pupils find it difficult to concentrate on purely aural stimuli. Reports on news programmes such as *The World at One* or *The World this Weekend* can be very good. The only trouble with this of course is that the right equipment must be there at the right time, something which many teachers would not have. Video cassette recordings, however, can be planned a little more in advance.* Of particular interest are programmes like *World in Action*, *Man Alive* and *Panorama*, which occasionally discuss provision in this area. It is a little unfortunate that the subject for these programmes is usually only announced a few days in advance and misses the *TV Times* and *Radio Times*. Recordings can be used to put over facts, but most assume some sort of knowledge on the part of the viewer. Hence, they are better used to stimulate discussion and discussion-type work. The whole nature of reporting can be brought in and bias looked for.

Shelter produce a game called *Tenement*. Players are asked to take the role either of an occupant of a rented house or a worker in a relevant agency like the Rent Tribunal and the Department of Health and Social Security. Role cards explain what each person is trying to achieve. It is a very good simulation which goes down very well at this level, covering housing, employment and the social services. It is very difficult to construct simulation games on this topic, because it really only lends itself to role-playing exercises of a fairly complex nature. A game which might be used to illustrate the cycle of poverty is *Starpower* by Gary Shirts but it would have to be used with fairly mature groups who would be able to link the in-built bias of the game with the in-built bias in real life.

There is very little point in organising a visit to a local Department of Health and Social Security office since there is very little to see. Nor do the other topics covered lend themselves to meaningful visits. The local Department of Health and Social Security office will, however, send a speaker or speakers to talk in the school. His outlook on the system can be quite refreshing to pupils who think that the whole benefits system is one huge fraud.

It is difficult to collect resources on the welfare state, because it is not mainstream economics. The places where the economist would normally look first are not particularly helpful. As a result, resources and information have to be dug out of the sort of pool which the ordinary man in the street has to use too. In one way this is not such a bad thing. The teacher will have to use the sort of material in his teaching which the pupils themselves will have to evaluate and interpret if they want to find out about or use the system, when they leave school. The traditional textbook approach can be of little value here in preparing pupils as future citizens.

* Editorial note: readers are reminded that only education transmissions may be recorded.

Resources

Carpenter and Ruddiman, *Looking at Society*, (Pitman, 1971), pp 61–76.
Social Trends, (HMSO).
Nobbs, J., *Social Economics*, (McGraw-Hill, 1975), pp 177–90.
Nobbs, J. and Ames, A., *Daily Economics*, (McGraw-Hill, 1975), pp 135–48.
North, P. J., *People in Society*, (Longman, 1973), pp 166–73.

Tenement, (Shelter).
Shirts, G., *Starpower*, (Management Games Ltd).
Student Recordings, *The Social Services*, (AVC/146).
Tape–slide sequence published by Student Recordings Ltd.
Whittaker, D., *The Social Services*, (Longman, 1975).
Willmott, P., *Consumer's Guide to the British Social Services*, (Pelican 1971).
ILEA TV Library, Guild Sound and Vision. Video for hire or purchase, *The Role of the Government*, 900 972.3.

Appendix I: Why £600 Million Stays Unclaimed Each Year

Fraud on the welfare system is insignificant compared to the sum of unclaimed welfare benefits – at least £600 million every year. One reason why welfare abuse is contained is the battery of 'control pro-
5 cedures' which are now in force.

The unemployed, for example, face these controls. Many claimants have difficulty in registering their right to benefit. The Government's own surveys show that at any one time, one in five of all unemployed
10 persons are drawing no benefit at all. In addition, those people who are believed to have left their last employment or who have refused suitable employment 'without just cause' lose their unemployment benefit for six weeks.

15 The Supplementary Benefits Commission also follows up any tip-off about claimants who are supposedly committing fraud. A squad of 343 special investigators brought 15 362 prosecutions last year for alleged fraud. It also cut or withdrew the allow-
20 ances of large numbers of other claimants.

The Department of Health and Social Security reckons fraud costs £2 million a year on all social security benefits. The most common abuses are made against the supplementary benefits system.

25 The Government does not publish official figures on benefits that are not claimed. If we assume that those who had the right to claim did claim, and drew an average size benefit, the bill for only five of the major benefits would be close to £600 million.

30 Something like £160 million in supplementary benefit is unclaimed by pensioners and £271 million by families. About £110 million annually is unclaimed in rent rebates and allowances and over £40 million in rate rebates. Families who are unaware of their chil-
35 dren's right to free school meals or who are unwilling to claim, lose £13 million a year, while a little under £5 million is unclaimed by low wage earners with children who are entitled to the Family Income Supplement.

Adapted from the *Sunday Times*, 21 November 1976.

1 Explain the meaning of the following words or phrases:

(a) Welfare abuse (line 4);
(b) Battery of control procedures (line 4);
(c) Claimants (line 7);
(d) Allowances (line 19).
2 What proportions of unemployed people draw no benefit at all?
3 How can you lose unemployment benefit for six weeks?
4 How does the Supplementary Benefits Commission check on fraud?
5 How much is lost through fraud each year?
6 How much money is not claimed each year?
7 Do you think that fraud is a serious problem for the welfare system? Give reasons for your answer. Should the system be reformed? If so, how should it be reformed?

Appendix II: Family Income Supplement
(Leaflet FIS.1, April 1977)

Figure 20.1 Family income supplement leaflet

You can claim family income supplement (FIS) if:

- you are in full-time work, and
- you have at least one child in your family, and
- your total family income is below a certain level.

You can claim even if you are a single parent or are self-employed.

Full-time work

You must be, and must normally be, working for 30 hours or more a week. This applies whether you are employed or self-employed. In the case of a couple it is the man who must be in full-time work. If you are *not* in full-time work you may be entitled instead to supplementary benefit (see leaflet SB.1 from post offices and Social Security offices).

Children in your family

All children under 16, and those over 16 who are still at school, are included in your family if they live with you.

Your income

The level of income below which you can get FIS depends on the number of children in your family, and is the same if you are the only parent in the family.

You can claim FIS if your total income, which includes the gross earnings of yourself and of your wife, where appropriate, is below the level for your size of family (see table below). Gross earnings are your pay *before* deductions and not your 'take home' pay. They include any regular overtime or bonuses as well as basic pay.

The following items do not count as income:

- child benefit
- the first £4 of a war disablement pension
- payments for children boarded out with you
- children's income
- the whole of any attendance allowance and mobility allowance
- rent allowances

Number of children in your family	Income level below which you qualify	
	For claims made BEFORE 19th July 1977	For claims made FROM 19th July 1977
1	£39.00	£41.50
2	£42.50	£45.00
3	£46.00	£48.50
4	£49.50	£52.00

For each additional child the qualifying income levels shown here are increased by £3.50.

2

The amount you get

You will get half of the difference between your family's total income and the level for your size of family as shown in example A below. If half the difference is 10p or less, no supplement is payable. The maximum payment is £8.50 for families with one child, £9.00 for families with 2 children, £9.50 for families with 3 children, going up by 50p for each additional child.

Example A:	Before	From
Couple with two children	19 July 1977	19 July 1977
Income below which you qualify	£42.50	£45.00
Family income before deductions	£35.50	£37.00
Difference	£ 7.00	£ 8.00
FIS payable (half difference)	£ 3.50	£ 4.00
Example B:		
Single person with one dependent child		
Income below which you qualify	£39.00	£41.50
Income before deductions	£20.00	£20.00
Difference	£19.00	£21.50
FIS payable (maximum payment)	£ 8.50	£ 8.50

Other benefits you will be entitled to

If you get FIS you will also be entitled to the following benefits:
- Free NHS prescriptions, dental treatment and glasses
- Free milk and vitamins for expectant mothers and children under school age
- Free school meals
- Refund of hospital fares
- Legal aid and advice

Further information about these benefits will be given when your supplement is paid. See back page for more details.

How to claim

Complete the claim form, tear it off and send it to the Department of Health and Social Security, Family Income Supplements, Poulton-le-Fylde, Blackpool FY6 8NW. You can get a stamped addressed envelope at post offices or local Social Security offices.

With the claim form you should send pay-slips for the last 5 weeks if you are paid weekly, or 2 monthly pay-slips if you are paid monthly. **Don't delay** sending in your claim if you cannot send pay-slips, for example, if you have just started in your job. We shall send you a form for your employer to fill in.

If you are self-employed, you should send your latest profit and loss account. Don't delay sending your claim if this is not available.

Your claim will be dealt with by post and it will not usually be necessary for you to be interviewed. Any information you give will be treated as confidential.

What happens after you claim

You will be told the result of your claim as soon as possible. If you are not satisfied with the decision you can appeal to an independent appeal tribunal.

How you will be paid

You will be sent a book of orders which can be cashed each week at a post office of your choice. Usually the supplement is awarded for 52 weeks and is not affected if your circumstances change during that time.

Further information

If you need further advice or help in completing the claim form, contact your local Social Security office, whose address you can get from the post office. Or write to Family Income Supplements, Poulton-le-Fylde, Blackpool FY6 8NW.

Other benefits and services available

WHETHER OR NOT YOU QUALIFY FOR FAMILY INCOME SUPPLEMENT, you may be entitled to the following benefits on grounds of income.

Free milk and vitamins for expectant mothers and children (including foster children) under school age. For details get leaflet M11 from a post office or Social Security office.

Free dental treatment and glasses. For details get leaflet M11, from a post office or Social Security office and ask your dentist or optician for a claim form.

Free prescriptions. For details get leaflet M11 from a post office or Social Security office.

Free family planning advice and treatment is available to everyone from NHS clinics. A similar service is available for women from most NHS family doctors.

Free school meals. Your local education office or the local Education Welfare Officer can advise you (local District Welfare Office in Scotland).

Rent and rates rebates, rent allowances. You may be able to get your rent or rates reduced, or a cash allowance if you live in private accommodation. For details ask at your town hall or council offices.

This leaflet gives general guidance and should not be treated as a complete and authoritative statement of the law. The amounts shown in it were subject to Parliamentary approval at the time of printing.

Leaflet FIS.1: Issued by the Department of Health & Social Security.
Misc 329

3

Figure 20.1 – continued

1 Can a person who is unemployed claim family income supplement?

2 What are 'gross earnings'?

3 What items don't count as income?

4 In the following situations, would you be able to get family income supplement? Assume that you are applying on 1 August 1977, and calculate how much you would receive:

(a) Married man earning £45 a week with three children;

(b) Married man earning £48 a week with four children;

(c) Married man earning £30 a week with one child;

(d) Married man earning £30 a week with no children;

(e) Single woman with three children earning £26 a week;

(f) Married man with four children earning £25 a week.

5 Find out more about the other benefits you are entitled to if you are getting family income supplement.

Part Two
Teaching Economics to the 16–18 Age Range

Introduction to Part Two

'Sir, are you so grossly ignorant of human nature, as not to know that a man may be very sincere in good principles, without having good practice?'

Dr Samuel Johnson

The bulk of the economics teacher's time is still spent with the sixteen to eighteen year olds, and this is reflected in the length of Part Two. Increasingly, the teacher is called upon to run non-'A' level courses, and the problems that this brings are laid out by David Butler. It seems that no entirely satisfactory solution exists to the puzzle of how to meet the diversity of needs at this level. Philip Negus develops one strategy: the individualised learning approach, which he has refined at the college level. Other difficulties which are peculiar to colleges are outlined by Ann Cotterrell. Here the radical transformation of business studies courses is causing economics teachers to reappraise their syllabuses. Maurice Knights has gained expertise in running schools conferences over a number of years; a study of his experiences should ease the way for future organisers. Urban trails have been developed over the last decade by a number of subject specialists, but Jim Hough's is probably the first geared specifically to the needs of economics students. Similar trails could be developed from most urban study centres, the nature and functions of which are examined by John Rees. It was his enthusiasm and organisational enterprise which led to the setting up of the first such centre at Notting Dale in 1974.

Bill Jennings leads off Section 3 (22 chapters on teaching particular topics) with a simulation aimed to motivate a class at the beginning of the year, introducing at the same time a number of basic ideas. The detailed scrutiny of mainstream concepts begins with Andrew Maclehose's examination of the problems and pitfalls in teaching about supply, demand, and pricing, which is complemented by the first of Graham Loomes' games: *Monopoly, Demand and Supply*. Three further simulations are provided by Alain Anderton in his important chapter on the theory of the firm. The complexity of the game *Scale of Production* will not endear it to some practitioners, but it is included for those with the time to run it, perhaps in an Economics Society which meets at lunchtime. Myron Joseph's simulation about market pricing has been available for a long time, but deserves re-printing in this comprehensive Handbook. His oligopoly game has been extensively modified by Rick Helm: the revised version has greater flexibility, and more teaching points can be derived from it. One of the hardest subjects to teach sixteen to eighteen year olds is the theory of distribution, not least because the teacher has first to decide which theory to teach! Andy Leake steers a wary course through this minefield, and suggests a number of useful protective devices. Brinley Davies focuses on the benefits of small-group discussion work in making the subject of monopolies and restrictive practices livelier, whilst Stuart Luker recommends the use of role-playing simulations to enable students to come to grips with the problems of industrial relations. A major difficulty discussed in the chapter on money and banking is exactly what to cover, in how much detail, and at what stage during the course. The credit creation game which follows could succeed in reducing the number of fallacies which pervade this topic.

A substantial contribution for those who find their teaching of national income theory unsatisfactory is provided by Alistair Thomson and Sally Donovan. They show how confusing the topic is when terminology is inconsistent, and present new schematic models for improved understanding. Gordon Hewitt's simulation *The Economy of Oltenia*, which involves the Chancellor of the Exchequer making decisions about macro-variables, has surprisingly not been published before.

The chapter on international trade and finance is by that doyen of economics teachers, Maurice Willatt, who, in his inimitable style, puts us back on the right tracks. Two more games follow: a very simple balance of payments problem by John Wolinski, and one on world trade by Graham Loomes.

Keith Marder suggests historical and problem-solving approaches to the teaching of instruments and objectives of government policy, while John Rees takes a case study to demonstrate the teaching of social and environmental economics, and in an appendix by Z. S. Starnawski, a role-playing exercise illuminates some problems of cost-benefit analysis. Data response questions are rapidly becoming *de rigueur* at 'A' level; John Rees shows how well-organised collection and retrieval of current economics topics may provide the basis for stimulus material. Nigel Wright's chapter on values shows how they impinge not only on the syllabus content, but also on the teacher and his pupils. His notes should provide a number of fertile lines of approach, and an appendix by James Haywood will challenge pupils' perceptive powers. Finally, the simulation by Kenneth Neubeck on income distribution is easy to run, and should enable students to see that this is not just another topic to be learnt.

Section 3: General Problems

21   Teaching the Non 'A' Level Sixth Former
David R. Butler

Most sixth forms include pupils who are not pursuing a full 'A' level course, but who are staying on for a number of reasons: (a) To take only one or two 'A' levels with the rest of the timetable being 'filled' with 'O' levels; (b) To obtain more 'O' levels or higher grade CSEs to supplement those gained in the fifth year; (c) To convert CSEs into 'O' levels; (d) To avoid becoming unemployed or to spend a further year making up their minds what they want to do.

How many non 'A' level sixth formers stay on, and the reasons why they do, will clearly depend upon the policy of the school. The number of such pupils has, however, been increasing and is likely to go on increasing in the near future for three reasons. First, there are increasing demands for paper qualifications by employers, coupled with greater difficulty in finding employment. Secondly, comprehensive schools often have a policy, backed up by resources, of encouraging pupils to stay on to gain further qualifications. Such schools are now catering for the pupil who wishes to take a combination of 'A' levels and 'O' levels or who simply wishes to improve upon his existing 'O' levels and CSEs. Thirdly, the present employment market has meant that schools are being urged to retain pupils who would otherwise become unemployed.

The Problems

Assuming that all four categories of pupil outlined above are in evidence, and this may not be uncommon, the economics teacher is faced with a number of problems:

1 Some pupils may have already completed a two year economics course whilst others may be completely new to the subject. This may be more of a problem in economics than in other subjects since economics courses can be successfully completed within a year without any previous knowledge. The syllabus content is also frequently regarded as being particularly relevant to the non 'A' level pupil. It would be very unlikely, for example, for a pupil to opt for or be accepted on a physics course without having studied the subject before.
2 Pupils who failed to obtain grades A–C (the old pass grades) in the 'O' level or who obtained good grades at CSE in the previous Summer, may be entered for the November or January 'O' level. The needs of such pupils in terms of examination preparation and a programme of work will be very different from those pupils pursuing a complete one year course. There arises also the problem of what to do with such pupils between the taking of the examination and the publication of the results two months later. If they pass and stay on and are required to continue the economics periods in order to 'fill up their timetables' then this creates a further problem. If they fail and stay on to retake the examination in the Summer yet another programme of work needs to be devised.

3 Pupils who have gained low grade CSEs in their fifth year may not have the ability to cope with an 'O' level syllabus and an essay type of examination which 'O' level frequently demands. These pupils often have reading difficulties which will not be cured within the extra year, but a suitable course for such pupils must be found. The problem is perhaps greater for those pupils who have done economics or commerce before than for those new to the subject. At least with the latter group of pupils the economics teacher has something new to offer in the way of syllabus content.

Possible Solutions

Most schools will limit the non 'A' level sixth former to about two to three hours of tuition in economics a week and there will frequently be provision for only one such class. Given these restraints, there is no one perfect solution to the problems outlined. The economics teacher may find the following suggestions useful in overcoming at least some of the problems he will encounter with the non 'A' level sixth former.

1 *Certificate of Extended Education.* This looked like solving many of the problems of teaching the non 'A' level sixth former as it was designed specifically for this group of pupils. A number of syllabuses are available in economics and related subjects. (An example of one by the Metropolitan Regional Examinations Board is included in Appendix I.) They normally include course and project work and there is usually a wide choice within the syllabus and in the examination.

There are unfortunately several problems with CEE. First, at the time of writing, the Secretary of State for Education had still not given official approval to CEE. Although this by no means precludes its use and examination boards have gone ahead without official approval, its status as a qualification must remain in doubt for the time being. Secondly, because of these doubts, pupils are more likely to opt for the more certain 'O' level qualification if they have the ability. There then remains the problem of having pupils pursuing different syllabuses within the same class. Lastly, the nature of the examination in CEE may not be suitable for the less able as it is designed for pupils at about CSE grades 2 and 3.

2 *Individual learning programmes.* These might be particularly valuable where there are a number of pupils taking the November and January examinations and a number pursuing a course for the whole year. They might also be useful where there is a mixture of pupils, some of whom have done economics before and some who are new to it.

This enables the economics teacher to teach one group of pupils while another group are usefully employed outside the classroom. With four periods per week, the teacher might devote himself to each of the two groups for two periods in the classroom. Alternatively, if the numbers are small enough, he could work a tutoring system outside the timetabled periods.

Again, there are a number of problems to be considered. First, the policy of the school might prohibit pupils 'working in the library' when they are supposed to be in a certain lesson. Secondly, many of these pupils are exactly the ones who find studying by themselves difficult. Thirdly, it will undoubtedly involve the economics teacher in a great deal more work and may well involve a loss of free time in tutoring and supervising pupils.

3 *Compatible 'O' level and CSE syllabuses.* Clearly where there is a range of pupil ability within the same class it is advisable to choose 'O' level and CSE syllabuses which closely correspond to each other. The AEB 'O' level economics syllabus II (social economics) might well tie in with a current CSE economics or commerce syllabus. This syllabus is less conceptual than many and includes a project, which is a feature of many CSE courses but is rare in GCE. The main problem is that the economics teacher may not have complete freedom of choice as regards examination boards. There may be insufficient overlap between his current GCE and CSE boards' economics and commerce syllabuses to combine the two successfully.

4 *Mode III CSE course.* This could be a course which all pupils followed and which was sufficiently different from the courses pursued in the fourth and fifth years. Alternatively, it could be based on the existing 'O' level which is used so that more able pupils could sit this examination while the less able could take the CSE. The syllabus content could be identical for the two groups with only the format of the examination varying.

Bearing in mind that Mode III syllabuses do involve a considerable amount of work on the part of the teacher and need to be started about two years before the first pupils sit the examination, they may well offer a solution to a number of the problems outlined. (See also Chapters 6 and 53.)

5 *Link courses.* It may be possible to run a link course with a local college of further education. These have the advantage of increasing the available teaching time with the same amount of resources supplied by the school. The college may well offer a larger range of courses and equipment than the school. Courses might well be vocationally orientated and include subjects such as data processing and accounts. The school will be expected to provide support for the course with classes and teaching. There may well be a problem in fitting the lessons at the school and the college into the same timetable. Cut backs in expenditure have also threatened many link courses.

6 *Non-examination courses.* With less able pupils, the economics teacher may well find it more useful from the pupils' point of view to design a course completely outside the CSE and GCE examination systems without even the constraints of a Mode III. He could, of course, issue his own 'Certificate of Competence' to pupils who successfully completed the course. Such a course needs to be designed very much with the pupils' interests in mind. It could well be drawn up in co-operation with the careers department so that it relates to various aspects of employment (trade unions, taxation, social security etc). The course might well include visits, outside speakers, films and some small pieces of field work. The great advantage of such a course is its flexibility in terms of pupil requirements and interests, but it has some drawbacks. However interesting and relevant the course is, it is often difficult to motivate pupils when there is no official qualification at the end of it. The subject may well be looked upon as the 'poor relation' in comparison to subjects offering a CSE certificate at the end of the course. The course might also attract those simply looking for a 'soft option' with which to fill their timetables. There will continue to be the need to provide courses for those wishing to re-take 'O' levels or obtain more CSEs to meet the growing demands of employers, parents, Heads and pupils for 'paper qualifications'.

As stated earlier, there is no ideal solution to the problems of teaching the non 'A' level sixth former when the resources of time and money are both strictly limited. The suggestions made all have their 'opportunity cost' which the economics teacher needs to take account of in choosing the best possible course for these pupils.

Appendix I: Metropolitan Regional Examinations Board Certificate of Extended Education Syllabus for Economic Studies 1976*

Economic Studies CEE

The form of the examination will be

1 WRITTEN PAPER   70%
Time allowed – 2½ hours (Candidates may be allowed up to half an hour extra.)
2 AN APPLIED ECONOMIC STUDY   30%

The aim of the syllabus is to familiarise the pupils with the economic basis of our society and to give some understanding of the economic factors which help to determine the environment in which they live as producers and consumers.

A great emphasis is placed on the major developments in the British economy since 1945 (including changes in industrial structures and the growth of the public sector) and Britain's position in the EEC.

The treatment is to be descriptive and analytical as appropriate.

* Reproduced by permission.

1 Written Paper – Developments in the British Economy Since 1945

The examination paper will be divided into two sections.

Section A – Short answer type questions. There will be no choice.   30 marks
Section B – Essay type questions. Candidates will answer 4 out of 7. The questions may or may not be structured.   40 marks

The syllabus for the Written Paper will be as follows:

1 The Economic Problem
Allocation of scarce resources to alternative ends; choice; scarcity; opportunity cost; the exchange of goods and services – banking and money; various economic systems.

2 The Labour Market
Population – statistics and trends – education and

training – mobility; trade unions – collective bargaining and wages.

3 Management of the Economy

Aims of government economic policy:
(a) National Income and Government Finance (detailed analysis of National Income Accounts not required); the Budget.
(b) Full employment and Regional Planning.
(c) The Balance of Payments.

4 The Capital and Money Market

Sources of finance: the value of money – index of retail prices and inflation. Banking.

2 Applied Economic Study

The Applied Economic Study should be chosen from either (a) or (b) below.
(a) One aspect of London's economy such as:
     The City of London
     Your neighbourhood
     Transport
     Tourism
     A growth centre, e.g. Croydon, Thamesmead
(b) A study of one *major* industry.

Notes of Guidance

Notes of Guidance on the Syllabus for the Written Paper
The following notes are intended as an amplification of the Syllabus for the Written Paper.

1 The Economic Problem

Allocation of scarce resources among competing ends; choice and the nature of opportunity cost; the factors of production and the importance of division of labour. Exchange of goods and services; money and other means of payment – cheques, bills of exchange etc. Various economic systems – production and distribution of goods and services in free enterprise, planned and mixed economies. Rewards to the factors of production: wages, rent, interest and profits.

2 The Labour Market

Population; change in size, sex, age, geographical and industrial distributions. The working population: determinants of its size and efficiency; the contributions of education and training. Factors determining geographical and occupational mobility, including the role of Employment Exchange and other government agencies. Trade Unions: structure and functions; collective bargaining.

3 Management of the Economy

Determinants of the standard of living. Aims and consequences of government expenditure, borrowing and taxation.

The maintenance of full employment. Regional planning of the location of industry and population. The Balance of Payments: main components; deficits and surpluses and their consequences.

4 The Money and Capital Markets

Sources of short and long term finances: banks, insurance companies, building societies, the Stock Exchange, elementary account of Bank of England control.
The value of money. Index of retail prices; inflation and deflation – causes and results. Stability of prices and incomes.

Notes of Guidance for the Applied Economic Study
Each candidate is required to submit an individual study relating *either* to an aspect of London's economy *or* to one major British industry. It must be a record of individual and/or group investigation, approximately 1500 words in length, and including diagrams, maps and statistical tables as appropriate. Previously published material such as pamphlets, should not be included, but candidates may use extracts of such material where appropriate.
The Applied Economic Study can earn up to 30 per cent of the total marks of the examination and it is suggested that approximately one-third of the total course work should be allowed for its preparation. Candidates preparing for the examination at the end of a one-year course would be advised to devote a considerable part of the middle term to the Applied Economic Study.
Each candidate is expected to adopt his own particular approach to the subject chosen. However, it may assist candidates if the following framework is taken as a general outline:

An Aspect of London's Economy
1 Definition. General description of the subject chosen.
2 Geographical boundaries – reasons for location.
3 Scope of productive activities.
4 Sources and determination of income.
5 Main channels of expenditure.
6 Pattern of labour employment.
7 Organisation and control.
8 Development. Recent changes in the area of activity described above.
9 Problems and prospects.

A Major British Industry
1 *Size:* Economies and diseconomies of scale; Reasons for the survival of the small firm; its contribution to GNP.
2 *Location:* Economic factors; Government policy.
3 *Ownership and Control:* Type of firm; The question of power – is public or private ownership desirable?
4 *Labour:* Division of labour and specialisation; Training; Mobility/immobility of labour geographically and occupationally; Automation and unemployment; Trade Unions and working conditions.
5 *Wages:* Determination of wages – supply and demand, marginal productivity, bilateral monopoly or negotiated bargaining; Non-monetary advantages.

6 *Prices:* Determination of prices – perfect competition, monopoly, some form of imperfect competition.

7 *Finance:* How is the necessary finance obtained? How much money is spent on advertising, on the development of research, technology and efficiency?

8 *Critique or Appraisal:* Recent developments; Criticisms; Problems and possible resolutions.

Allocation of Marks for the Applied Economic Study
School may choose one of the following schemes of marking:

1 Marks are awarded to the work out of the maximum as shown for each of the following elements.
(a) Factual content/grasp of the subject matter and application of basic economic ideas/comprehension/summary   15 marks
(b) Evidence of individual observation/enterprise/originality   5 marks
(c) presentation (including relevant diagrams, photographs, maps)/care in compilation   5 marks

(d) development in depth and breadth of approach over the duration of the course.   5 marks

2 *30–25 marks.* Use of original material showing evidence of logical arrangement resulting in interpretative conclusions. Ability to illustrate chosen theme and apply basic economic ideas. First class standard of presentation. Variety of sources used. Ability to see subject in a wider context.
24–19 marks. Thorough knowledge of subject chosen. A high standard of work throughout with some attempt to draw conclusions from the evidence presented.
18–11 marks. Some evidence of original work but reliance mainly upon material copied from reference works. Evidence of care in arrangement and presentation of material.
10–5 marks. Straightforward treatment of the subject. Material mainly copied without attempt at orderly arrangement.
4–0 marks. Similar, but material poorly presented and little material.

22   How to Organise Individualised Learning at 'A' Level in Colleges of Further Education*

Philip Negus

Individualised Learning

Individualised learning has a variety of meanings but each is based upon the recognition that a class of students is a collection of individuals rather than a homogeneous group.[1] Individualising a course means preparing materials for students to use on their own or in small groups so that they learn from the materials and each other rather than directly from the teacher. With advanced level economics the traditional process is for the teacher to extract the basic ideas from a book and then to teach them to the class. He acts in the manner of a wholesaler of information and skills. Individualisation removes the wholesaler and brings the student into direct contact with the sources of information. The teacher remains important however since

* An earlier version of this chapter appeared in *Economics*, 12(2), Summer, 1976.

it is he who researches the sources and produces the learning materials. The development of individualised learning is closely bound up with the development of resources and resource centres.

In primary schools individualisation can take more extreme forms than in colleges of further education. What is taught in colleges is frequently determined by external examiners, leaving little freedom for the teacher, whereas what is taught in primary schools can be controlled much more by the teacher. Where there are few external constraints on the curriculum, individualisation can involve producing materials of varying degrees of difficulty on a particular topic. In addition, different students can be allowed to study very different topics according to their own interests. When designing an individualised course for an 'A' level subject, these freedoms are considerably reduced. Individualisation tends to take the form of students determining their own work rate with some slight variations in the level of the materials on particular topics. For those who teach students 'A' level economics in one year, as is the case in many colleges of further education, the constraints on curriculum innovation are so considerable that it might be wise to make a distinction between individualised learning and independent learning. The former implies that materials are designed to meet the needs of particular students, the latter that all students learn from similar materials but do so in their own way. Independent learning is one step towards individualisation and it may be as far as it is possible to go for many teachers in further education.

The Arguments for Individualisation

Individualising a course of learning requires considerable effort on the part of the teacher, so before embarking on the process, he needs to be certain that it meets the needs of his students more effectively than some other system of instruction. The basic reasons for individualising learning can be set out as follows:

1 It leads to more effective learning. With traditional classroom instruction it is too easy for the individual student to hide in the group and do nothing; individualised learning forces him to work and makes that work more fruitful. This basic justification of individualisation rests on the philosophical and psychological theories that stress the role of experience in learning.
2 It can be geared to meet the particular requirements of individual students.
3 It encourages self-reliance.
4 Students can work at a rate suited to their ability.
5 It fosters good relationships between teacher and students. The element of confrontation that can exist between teacher and class is replaced by contacts on a personal level.
6 There are also economic arguments for individualised learning. It is no longer necessary to buy class sets of textbooks since students will be working on different topics, thus a wider range of books can be obtained with the same amount of money. Individualised learning may also provide a means of coping with small groups at advanced level since different classes can be timetabled into one room under the supervision of one teacher.

An Example of Individualised Learning

Classes in further education often constitute groups of very mixed ability and attainment, thus some form of individualised learning would seem to be a particularly effective system to adopt. Some students may have studied 'O' level economics whilst others may have

Block	Unit	Title
I	–	Population
II	–	Basic concepts
III	a	Supply and demand
	b	Elasticity
	c	Utility
IV	a	Theory of the firm: cost curves
	b	Theory of the firm: perfect competition
	c	Theory of the firm: monopoly
	d	Theory of the firm: exercises
	e	Theory of the firm: oligopoly
V	a	British industry: division of labour
	b	British industry: large and small firms
	c	British industry: monopoly power
	d	British industry: location
VI	a	Company finance: stocks and shares
	b	The capital market
	c	The distribution industry
VII	–	Resource allocation
VIII	a	Distribution theory
	b	Wages
	c	Rent
IX	a	Money and barter
	b	Commercial banks
	c	Discount houses
	d	Monetary policy
	e	Recent changes
X	–	Quantity theory of money
XI	a	Price indexes
	b	Inflation
	c	Control of inflation
XII	a	Overseas trade
	b	Balance of payments
	c	Foreign exchange markets
XIII	a	Comparative costs
	b	Free trade and protection
XIV	–	Unemployment
XV	a	National income accounts and the circular flow of income
	b	Consumption and savings
	c	Equilibrium
	d	The multiplier and the accelerator
XVI	–	The trade cycle
XVII	–	Economic growth
XVIII	a	Government income
	b	Government expenditure

Table 22.1   Main divisions of the economics syllabus.

already studied 'A' level at school but failed to obtain the grade they desired. Not all students will have passed 'O' level mathematics, others will be taking 'A' level or have already passed at that level. Because of the practice of running one year courses, a class can contain a range of students, from those fresh from school with CSEs and 'O' levels to those already experienced in 'A' level study under conditions of further education. To add to the confusion there may be mature students, who often have very special problems, and day release students who cannot attend all the lessons.

Economics teachers in at least one college have developed an individualised learning scheme.[2] The scheme was developed on a very small scale, involved little expenditure and no structural alterations to classrooms. The economics syllabus was divided into blocks of work. Some of the blocks were further subdivided into units: Table 22.1 lists all the blocks and units together with a brief indication of the topics covered. Each block in the course contains all or some of the following: basic information about the topic being dealt with; references to textbooks, cassette tapes, tape–slide packs and newspaper articles; extracts from *Economic Progress Reports*; multiple choice questions; numerical exercises; essays and questions to prepare for discussion in tutorial. Although the content of each block varies, the basic aim is to provide a framework around which the student can build his own notes. Most blocks contain an assessment section. The content of a typical block is set out in the Appendix at the end of the chapter.

The students make use of the materials in a variety of ways. Some take the list of blocks given to them at the start of the course as the order in which they must be completed. Other students, after having completed blocks I and II, go on to blocks V and VI, leaving the theoretical content of III and IV until later. Students who have taken 'A' level economics before tend to head for their weak areas. Except for the first few days, when most students are working on blocks I and II, the whole class is rarely studying the same topic. The students however are not allowed complete freedom. There are many instances in economics where certain concepts have to be mastered before others can be coped with, hence when a student starts on a block made up of several units he has to work through them in the order shown. In block IV for example, on the theory of the firm, units (b) and (c) on perfect competition and monopoly will not be understood unless unit (a), on costs, has been dealt with first. Nor is complete freedom allowed when students are deciding which blocks to deal with.

Each week students have a tutorial with a member of staff. Work is marked and discussed, particular points emphasised and weaknesses probed. At the end of each tutorial the student's progress is summarised on his personal record card and the next week's work allocated. Students also have contact with staff between tutorials as some problems need to be cleared up as they arise; if students cannot gain access to staff they normally turn to someone else in the class for help.

This particular scheme is not to be considered as a perfect example of how an individualised course should be designed. It has weaknesses which its designers readily concede,[3] but it is really worth considering because it illustrates some of the practical problems involved in designing and managing a course of individualised learning.

Practical Problems

Experience has shown that students can find it difficult to adapt to individualised learning. With traditional classroom instruction they gain some idea of what they should be doing from the teacher; with individualised learning there is no such guide. As a result some students do very little, while others rush through their work too quickly. It is important during the first few weeks for the teacher to offer considerable guidance as to how fast students should be working. There is a case for introducing the first few topics at regular intervals by means of conventional lessons to set the appropriate pace.

Most of the students who have used the individualised economics course have commented favourably on the principle of individualisation whilst making criticisms of particular aspects of the course. The most frequent favourable comment has been that the scheme allows the individual to work at his own rate, the most frequent criticism that it is too easy to drift along without doing sufficient work. This last point emphasises the need to develop effective techniques of classroom management and accurate record keeping, although it should not be forgotten that many students drift in conventional lessons too.

Many students seem to feel that they cannot understand something unless it has been explained to them first by a teacher. Their lack of confidence is sometimes so great that they will request explanations of topics that it is manifest they understand. Whilst this may be good for the teacher's ego it is clearly not good for the students and a major problem is boosting their morale and self-confidence.

Regular private sessions between teacher and student are essential if individualised learning is to work well. This can mean that it may be harder to deal with large numbers of students when using individualised methods than it is when using traditional teaching techniques. Turning again to the economics course already described, this started the year with twenty-four students. The 'class' was timetabled for eight and a quarter hours per week, thus allowing approximately twenty minutes' tutorial time per student per week. When formal teaching took place or when students required help out of tutorial time, this reduced the twenty minutes available. At the start of such a course, when students require considerable support, twenty minutes is the minimum amount of time in which a tutorial will work, and this sets an important constraint when it comes to timetabling for individualised learning at 'A' level. Increasing the time by dealing with two or more students at once does not really work as students are rarely caught on the same problems at the same time.

Ideally, during a period of for example two weeks, a student should experience periods of private study, two tutorials and perhaps one organised group discussion. If care is not taken, individualised learning can become rather like a correspondence course lacking in guided verbal debate. It is important that the teacher aims to provide opportunities for discussion when designing the course, possibly through regular seminars, to consider such items as case studies, topical events, data response questions or even examination questions. If regular seminars are introduced, this reduces the time available for tutorials, so they should perhaps be reserved for later in the course when students have become accustomed to the individualised approach.

It is not only students who have to adapt to individualised learning. The teacher also has to acquire a new range of skills and adapt to a new range of pressures. He has to become a mixture of artist and writer, since preparing materials that will maximise the possibility of learning involves consideration of design as well as content. Ideas and concepts have to be carefully sequenced, since once in print they are fixed. The teacher who wishes to incorporate cassette tapes and tape–slide sets into his course will have to learn the techniques of scripting, editing, recording and photography, but all this will be very time-consuming.

It ought to be obvious that conducting a tutorial is very different from teaching a class. Again new skills are needed in building up the confidence of the student in what is for him a possibly threatening situation. For perhaps the first time in his life he is going to have to put forward rational arguments and justify his opinions. He can no longer wait for someone else to put up his hand and answer the question for him. Encouraging hesitant students to speak up in tutorials requires more tact and patience and fewer dramatic gestures than conventional classroom teaching. The teacher should establish a system whereby the student hands in work a few days prior to his tutorial so that it can be marked, and the teacher can plan his tactics according to the weaknesses revealed. The situation where the student proudly places a week's unmarked work in front of the tutor at the start of the session should be avoided if at all possible.

A new strain that falls upon the teacher with individualised learning is that he can find himself asked to deal with a diversity of problems within a single lesson. He is no longer able to prepare just the topics he intends teaching to the class since it is the class, or rather the individuals who make up the class, who determine what topics will have to be dealt with. Introducing individualised learning is not recommended for a teacher who is not 'on top' of his subject. In addition to this new strain some teachers may well experience symptoms of what might be termed 'pedagogical withdrawal'. Many teachers enjoy dominating a captive audience by putting on a dynamic display of anecdotes, funny stories and diagrams. This type of acting is not required with individualised learning. The teacher is no longer the centre of attraction, and it can be hard to adapt to this fact.

As well as producing resources, the teacher has to devise a system for managing them. He has to decide on how and where they are to be stored, how they are to be catalogued and how he is to ensure they are returned by students. If he is lucky, the college will already have a resources centre to handle these matters for him; if not, he will have to work out his own solutions. A starting point is to establish a subject room or area where all the resources can be stored and where they are accessible to students during the lesson. Obtaining such a room or area is a matter of internal college politics which may require considerable subtlety on the part of the economics teacher, especially as he is offering a subject which does not need any specialist equipment. One tactic worth considering is to produce the resources and establish a 'need' for resource facilities; another is to engage the support of a teacher of, for example, geography who already possesses a specialist room which he may be prepared to share. Storage facilities do not need to be elaborate; a few shelves and strong cardboard boxes are all that are required for a start. Other useful items are a cassette playback machine with headphones and two or three slideviewers for use with tape–slide packs.

Some consideration should be given to the physical arrangement of the classroom. The ideal situation is to have tables arranged in small groups plus some study carrels. A more important matter however is to find somewhere reasonably secluded for the tutorial sessions. Perhaps part of the classroom can be partitioned off by bookcases or cupboards; perhaps a storeroom can be utilised. It is helpful if this tutorial area can house a small white board for diagrams. Another area of the room can be used to store tapes, slides and playback machines. The best rule to follow when deciding on these arrangements is not to make any permanent changes until the course has run for at least a year: the most effective decisions are made in the light of experience.

A final practical implication of individualised learning is that of record keeping. It is no longer possible to keep a record for the whole class since the class no longer exists, but records for individual students must be maintained. These need to show the blocks of work completed by the student, the level he has attained and what he is working on at the moment. A summary chart of the progress of all the students can also be kept so that the teacher can see at a glance how many students are working on each block. This can be useful when considering whether to have a group discussion on a particular topic or whether extra copies of a book need to be brought up from the store. In short, the teacher has to be much more systematic in his recording and classroom management.

How to Individualise an Economics Course

The practical implications just considered raise a number of problems which need to be resolved early in the planning stage of an individualised course.

1 *Start Planning at Least a Year in Advance*

2 *Specify Audience and Objectives*
Successfully designing any course of learning involves being clear about the characteristics of the students who will be using the course and about the course's objectives. The relative permanence of some of the materials produced makes decisions on these matters even more important than usual. With regard to students it can be useful to know the likelihood of their having studied economics before and at what level. In a school where the curriculum below the sixth form is known to the teacher of 'A' level this likelihood can be calculated reasonably easily, but for the teacher in a college of further education each new batch of students is much more of an unknown quantity.

It can also be useful to know something about the mathematical background of students and how many will be studying 'A' level mathematics. The teacher will have to consider whether he needs to design parts of his course at different levels to allow for different student abilities. There could for example be two types of material on the theory of the firm, one for the mathematically oriented student who can use calculus and another for the less mathematical.

In further education the objectives of courses tend to be much narrower and more specific than in schools. The prime concern is to ensure that the student passes his examination. If a course fails to achieve this objective then it must be redesigned. Whilst examination success may be the prime objective, there is no need for all others to be forsaken. It is still possible to design materials to foster such objectives as the promotion of deductive reasoning and rational discussion without reducing the chances of examination success. A further point to be considered when deciding upon objectives is the extent to which their achievement can be assessed. 'To encourage rational discussion' is not an objective that lends itself easily to measurement; 'examination success' is. The teacher can of course develop his own tests of economic understanding to assess the new course but this does raise the problem of test validity.

3 *How Much Individualisation?*
Having specified target audience and objectives the teacher must now look at the question of whether he wishes to individualise the whole course or merely part of the course. There are two arguments for individualising the whole course. The first is that students have to learn how to use the system, and it takes them time to adapt to the new style of 'indirect teaching'. If for example only a third of the course is individualised, then the students will experience the problems of adapting to the new approach without having the time to reap its advantages. A second reason for individualising the whole course is that one of the strengths of the system is that students can progress at their own rate. Teaching part of the course in a traditional manner can limit this advantage, especially if the course is designed so that a period of individualised learning is followed by a period of traditional instruction. If the course were designed along the lines of scheme II in Table 22.2 then all students would need to have completed the units of work on elasticity by week IV in

	Scheme I					Scheme II				
Week	Conventional		Individualised							
	M.	Tu.	W.	Th.	F.	M.	Tu.	W.	Th.	F.
I			Supply and demand.			Supply, demand and elasticity				
II			Supply and demand.			by individualised methods				
III			Elasticity			of learning.				
IV	Applications of					Applications of supply, demand and				
V	supply and demand.					elasticity by conventional methods.				

Table 22.2   *Combining individualised and conventional instruction*

order for the teacher to use this concept in his lessons. The same problem may arise with scheme I. The teacher will have to 'fill in' with some unrelated topic in the first few weeks in order to enable the students to complete their work on supply and demand.

Individualising the whole course raises other difficulties. One problem is whether the whole of an economics syllabus is suited to individualised learning. Certain portions of any economics syllabus are concerned with deductive theories, such as the theory of the firm, whilst others are concerned with more complex areas such as the control of inflation: the Phillips' curve, for example, is based on inductive reasoning. It is possible that whilst deductive theories may lend themselves well to individualisation, more empirically based theories may leave the student drowning in a welter of contradictory hypotheses. A good teacher can recognise when a student has lost the thread of a complicated discussion, and alter his classroom tactics accordingly; an individualised work unit cannot. Exactly which aspects of economics lend themselves to individualisation is an important area for future research.[4]

4 How are the Materials to be Used?

Individualised learning can take a variety of forms, and the form taken will have a bearing on the design of the materials. Consider this by no means exhaustive range of options:

1 All students work together on the same units at the same time and are closely supervised by the teacher.
2 Students are set a number of units which they can work through in any order. All of the units must be completed by a set date.
3 Students work through the course with the minimum of teacher supervision.
4 Small groups of students are set the same units which they work through together.

With the first option there is little need for any explicit instructions to be incorporated in the units since these will be supplied by the teacher. Very detailed, explicit instructions will be required if the third option is adopted; the clarity of the written unit becomes vital. If the teacher wishes to incorporate opportunities for class discussion he will find this hard to achieve if he decides on option three, since students will soon be spread over a wide range of topics. In the case of option two then class discussion can take place on the date set for the completion of the units. There is no code of good practice for individualised learning but a basic rule must be that the teacher is clear about how the course will be managed before he produces his materials.

5 Content and Presentation

At 'A' level the content of an economics course is determined by the Board through its syllabus and examination papers. Using these, the teacher can decide upon what information and skills his students need in order to pass their examination. The teacher has more freedom when it comes to questions of presentation. A wide range of possibilities presents itself: written resources including textbooks; cassette tapes; tape–slide sequences; video tapes; games and films. The heart of any individualised scheme will be the teacher-written materials, and priority should be given to these in the early stages of planning and production. However, other techniques of presentation should not simply be treated as 'frills'; every attempt should be made to incorporate them into the main body of the course. There is little use for example preparing written material on Keynesian economics, without including in it a reference to the tape on Keynes' life it is planned to produce at a later date. No reference in the written material means that students will not use the tape and that means the teacher has wasted his time. The teacher planning to individualise his economics course should draw up a master plan of resources available.

6 Format

The written materials should follow a standard format such as:

(a) Statement of objectives or general introduction;
(b) Basic information;
(c) References to textbooks and tapes;
(d) Assessment section.

Not every block need follow exactly the same form but it helps the student if a pattern is established.[5] Blocks should be as short as possible to facilitate feedback from the assessment section. The product should look as professional as possible, so it is probably better to have the material typed than handwritten. (See Chapters 4 and 5 on presentation of material.)

A practical point to remember is that some aspects of economics date very quickly. In order to avoid excessive rewriting of material from year to year, the teacher should try to keep material that dates quickly on a separate sheet from material that does not. Consider for example a written unit on population. The law of diminishing returns and the concepts of optimum, age structure and dependency ratio do not change from one year to the next, but population estimates do and are best kept on a separate sheet of information. Information on basic concepts can be duplicated on a large scale for use several years ahead, 'perishable' information need only be reproduced in small quantities to allow for frequent updating.

7 Sequencing the Course
Before preparing a particular block its exact position in the overall course must be decided upon. One of the virtues of individualised learning is that it allows students to choose how, when and what they study, but the economics teacher clearly cannot allow students to choose to study devaluation before having studied the concept of elasticity. As far as economics is concerned a certain amount of structure must be built into the course. The problem is how to ensure students approach economics concepts in such a way that their understanding of them is maximised without excessively undermining their freedom to choose a particular course of study. Because economics is a very sequential discipline complete individualisation will not work.

References

1 Taylor, L. C., *Resources for Learning*, (Penguin, 1972), pp 171–81. Gagne, R. M. and Briggs, L. J., *Principles of Instructional Design*, (Holt, Rinehart and Winston, 1974), pp 186–7.
2 Negus, P. E., 'Individualised Learning and Economics', *Economics*, Summer 1976, 12(2), p 91.
3 *Ibid*. pp 94–6.
4 Oliver, J. M., *The Principles of Teaching Economics*, (Heinemann Educational, 1973), pp 1–33.
5 Noad, B., 'Student Contract Learning: An Australian Experiment', *Economics*, Winter 1973–74, 10(3), p 176.

Resources

Further Information
Any teacher wishing to individualise his economics course should consult Taylor, L. C., *Resources for Learning*, (Penguin, 1972). Chapters 8 and 9 are particularly useful and discuss in detail the advantages and problems of individualised learning. A very practical booklet is *A Handbook of Classroom Management for Independent Learning* by P. Waterhouse, obtainable from the 'Resources for Learning Development Unit', which, although written with secondary school teachers in mind, is applicable to further education. Waterhouse looks at such matters as basic techniques of classroom management, indexing, storage and how to make the best use of the teacher's time.

Meighan, R., 'Individual Study Folders', *The Social Science Teacher*, February 1976, sets out the basic forms the written components of an individualised course could take. A more theoretical account of individualised learning can be found in Gagne, R. M. and Briggs, L. J., *Principles of Instructional Design* (Holt, Rinehart and Winston, 1974). A comprehensive introduction to the whole subject can be found in Dell, H. M., *Individualising Instruction* (Science Research Associates, 1972).

There are a number of guides to the production of audio-visual resources. A good book to look at first is the second edition of Romiszowski, A. J., *The Selection and Use of Teaching Aids* (International Textbook Co, 1976). Romiszowski discusses a range of audio-visual aids and attempts to assess their usefulness in achieving educational objectives. Practical advice on the production of such items as tapes and slides can be found in: Goudket, M., *An Audiovisual Primer*, (Columbia University, 1973); Langford, M. J., *Visual Aids and Photography in Education*, (Focus Press, 1973); and Kemp, J. E., *Planning and Producing Audiovisual Materials*, (Crowell, 1963).

The Training Department of the National Audio-Visual Aids Centre runs frequent courses on the production and use of audio-visual materials.

For ideas on how to manage the storage and retrieval of resources the teacher should consult Beswick, N., *School Resource Centres*, Schools Council Working Paper No. 43, (Evans/Methuen Educational). An alternative book is Edwards, R. P. A., *Resources in Schools*, (Evans, 1973). (See also Chapter 56.)

New teaching methods ought to be evaluated. Ideas on how to do this at a very simple level can be found in two articles by Atkinson: Atkinson, B., 'Classroom Research in Economics Education', *Economics*, Autumn 1974, 10(5); and Atkinson, B., 'Classroom Curriculum Development in Economics', *Economics*, Winter 1974, 10(6).

There are several textbooks on the market on how to design and conduct basic psychology experiments. They explain such matters as the control of variables, the use of control groups, randomisation and matching, all of which need to be considered when designing a research programme to evaluate a new method of instruction. A good example of such a book is Robson, C., *Experiment, Design and Statistics in Psychology*, (Penguin, 1973). See also Pilliner, A., *Experiment in Educational Research*, Block 5 of E341, (Open University Press, 1973).

Appendix I: An Example of a Block of Work

Block IV: Unit (a)

Theory of the Firm: Costs of Production
In this part of the course we are concerned with the following sorts of question:

(a) How does a firm decide how much to produce?
(b) What is a firm's most profitable output?
(c) What is its most efficient output?
(d) When will it pay a firm to cease production?

A firm's costs of production can be classified as follows:

(a) *Fixed costs:* those costs which remain constant as output changes, e.g. rent of premises. Even when a firm is producing nothing fixed costs have to be met;

(b) *Variable costs:* those costs which vary with output, e.g. wages;
(c) *Average fixed cost:* fixed costs divided by output;
(d) *Average variable cost:* variable costs of 'x' units of production divided by 'x';
(e) *Average total cost:* total costs of 'x' units divided by 'x';
(f) *Marginal cost:* the total cost of producing 'x' units minus the total costs of producing 'x–1' units. Put another way, marginal cost is the cost of producing the last or marginal unit;
(g) *Total costs:* fixed costs plus variable costs.

Below is a table of costs for a firm over a range of output from 0 to 15 000 units. Complete the table. The first few entries have been made for you.

Output	Fixed costs	Variable costs	Total costs	Average fixed cost	Average variable cost	Average total cost	Marginal cost
0	250	0	250	–	–	–	
1	250	70	320	250	70	320	70
2	250	120	370	125	60	185	50
3		140					
4		160					
5		190					
6		230					
7		280					
8		350					
9		440					
10		540					
11		660					
12		800					
13		960					
14		1200					
15		1800					

Notice how fixed costs form an increasingly smaller proportion of total costs as output rises and how total costs, after a point, increase more and more rapidly due to diminishing returns.

Now plot total costs and fixed costs on a graph. Plot output on the horizontal axis and costs on the vertical. Choose a scale so that you get the largest possible graph. Use a pencil; graphs drawn in pen or biro will not be marked. If you wish to draw a straight line use a ruler. Label all lines clearly and make certain the graph has a title. From the graph calculate the variable costs of:

(a) 4600 units
(b) 8400 units
(c) 13 200 units

Now plot average total, average fixed, average variable and marginal costs on a separate graph. Once again plot output on the horizontal axis. The table of figures shows marginal costs at the half way points between particular levels of output, e.g. the first figure for marginal cost, 70, is shown between output 0 and 1. This is because marginal cost refers to the *change* in total costs as output *changes* from 0 to 1 and not to either of these particular levels of output. (Those of you familiar with differential calculus should be able to see how marginal cost can be derived from the total cost curve of the first graph.) When you plot marginal cost on a graph apply a similar rule, i.e. the marginal cost of increasing output from 0 to 1 should be plotted at 0.5; the marginal cost of increasing output from 1 to 2 at 1.5. (N.B. Your cost axis need only rise to £350.)

HAVE YOUR WORK CHECKED BEFORE
PROCEEDING FURTHER

Reading: *Understanding Economics,* pp 137–42
        Harvey: *Intermediate Economics*, pp 74–81

Make notes on:
(a) the relationship between average cost and marginal cost;
(b) optimum output (or optimum size);
(c) the relationship between average cost and increasing/decreasing returns;
(d) normal profit.

THERE IS A SLIDE–TAPE PACK ON THIS UNIT.

23   Problems Specific to Colleges of Further Education*

Ann Cotterrell

Colleges of further education are generally concerned with vocational and GCE courses.[1] One of the first problems of new teachers in further education is to become familiar with a whole range of examining bodies with their different curricula, examining methods and standards. Where the course has existed for some years, copies of examiners' reports and past examination papers may be helpful, and the most useful guidance is often gained from other teachers who have successfully taken students through the course in earlier years. The curriculum for business studies students has been redesigned by the Business Education Council and the changes introduced by the Council are due to take effect from September 1978.[2] The most important change for economics teachers is that economics is no longer a compulsory, discrete subject but has been integrated into the study of business organisation in its economic, legal, social and political environment.

Lecturers employed in further education may be required to teach more than one subject, sometimes in an integrated commerce or structure of business course. V. S. Anthony and B. R. G. Robinson, in a survey of advertised posts for the period 1 September 1973 to 31 August 1974, found that under one-third of the posts advertised offered a full Economics time-

table, which was similar to the situation in secondary schools.[3] Further education was found to differ in the scope of the subsidiary subject, as the emphasis in further education was more likely to be on commerce and generally within the social sciences. The requirement by the Business Education Council for integrated business studies subjects could cause a decline in the demand for pure economics teachers in further education.

The main differences between the students in schools and further education are differences in motivation, age, choice of subjects for further study, the range of ability to be found in one class of students, and in some cases the additional requirements of paid employment which concern part-time students.

Many students leave school at sixteen and opt for the full-time or part-time vocational courses provided by the further education sector. Students are attracted into courses which offer training in catering, bakery, building, engineering and secretarial work. On such courses the teacher will be teaching economics to students who are not specialists in economics but who are required to take a compulsory economics course. The students entering these courses are generally of a practical outlook. Their preference is for movement around workshops, kitchens, or building sites rather than the physical inertia of the classroom. It is essential to provide a varied range of activities with the minimum amount of 'chalk and talk'.

* Acknowledgements are due to Mr P. Fearns of Weston-Super-Mare Technical College who read an earlier draft of this chapter and made useful comments.

Teaching economics to non-specialists requires considerable industry and imagination on the part of the teacher[4] who must adapt his knowledge of economics to the construction industry, hotels and catering, the computer industry and many other fields. Students on vocational courses other than business studies or public administration commonly regard the economics course as being peripheral to their main studies. The teaching of such courses is often unpopular and there may be a legacy of poor teaching, frequent staff changes and a high failure rate. In some cases economics is a compulsory course, but not an assessed course which contributes to the students' final examination results. Some students on vocational courses like to obtain evidence of their study by taking 'O' level economics while others in the same class prefer to study a course which is oriented to their vocational studies or to their outside interests (the economics of the motor cycle industry and football are two favourites). There is normally a published syllabus but in some cases this is sufficiently open to allow the teacher a considerable amount of discretion. There are problems in developing a syllabus to meet the needs and stimulate the interests of students on non-assessed courses and some useful guidelines may be found in *Curriculum Development in Economics*[5] and *Economics in General Studies.*[6]

Many of the students in further education are older than students on similar courses in schools.[7] They have already acquired some knowledge or deep-rooted misunderstandings of economic concepts from the mass media or through trade union and political activities. Mature students tend to be more inclined to question simplified models and assumptions. In some cases they attempt to reason from the practical examples with which they may be familiar, back to concepts. The relevance and realism of every theoretical statement requires immediate explanation. This approach to the subject is a problem where students are required to cover a large syllabus in an intensive way over a short period of time in order to meet the requirements of external examinations.

In addition to a large proportion of mature students, some colleges attract a large number of students from overseas. The problems of the immigrant pupil with an inadequate knowledge of English are not confined to further education.[8] In further education, however, there are large numbers of students who have come to this country with the sole purpose of acquiring an English education and qualifications. On completion of their education the students generally wish, or may be required, to return to their home country. The presence of these students may be an asset where they are prepared to discuss the economic problems of their own countries, but it can be an extra cause for concern where much of the course is related to the United Kingdom and may not be obviously relevant.

The lack of ability in English is not confined to students from overseas and may be a particular problem where most of the student's time is spent on subjects which require practical ability or numeracy rather than the ability to write articulate answers in essay form.

A lack of numeracy may be a problem on some courses. Some students employed in public administration, for example, require very little numeracy, but they may be required to study economics as part of their course in a college of further education. Graphs may have to be explained in some detail and remedial work in such elementary techniques as the calculation of percentages may be necessary.

There are some students who move from school to further education to study 'O' levels, 'A' levels, or other courses which are generally offered in sixth forms. The reasons are varied. Many students prefer the adult environment of further education where the organisation tends to be more open and less disciplined. There are still some students who take 'O' levels in secondary modern schools with no sixth forms, and these students would have to move to another school or college to take 'A' levels. Other students are from schools where economics is not a sixth form option. Some students return to full-time education after a few years in employment, perhaps because of dissatisfaction with their prospects or because they generate ambitions which require higher qualifications. There are some students in further education who left school for financial reasons and others who had no wish to remain at school because of conflicts with the system of discipline. The further education sector thus includes some very highly motivated students and others who are, or feel themselves to be, inadequate or disadvantaged. The problems of coping with or assisting students who lack adequate motivation or self-confidence are similar in further education and in schools.

There are approximately twice as many part-time day students as there are full-time students in further education. Students who are engaged in a full-time job, sometimes with family responsibilities, have frequently very little access to libraries and very little time for private study. They depend to a greater extent than any student ought to, on the information and techniques imparted in the classroom. Many part-time students prefer conventional lectures accompanied by routine note-taking. The teacher may be under pressure to meet the wishes of the students. G. G. Bamford has suggested that 'There may well be a need to educate the student in how he should be educated!'[9]

The financial problems of the full-time students are not confined to further education. Discretionary grants are available for some courses but many students are required to support themselves with little or no help from their local authorities. Unlike many sixth formers, they are required to provide all 'consumable materials' such as paper themselves. In most colleges they are expected to buy their own textbooks. The price of a textbook is a major factor in deciding which book to recommend and it is difficult to insist that every student should buy a textbook if economics is a subsidiary subject for the students concerned. It is helpful to notify the students and the local bookshop of a recommended textbook before the course begins.

Some further education colleges, especially colleges serving a small population with a wide range of courses, do not have adequate numbers to make separate classes for each course. The lecturers therefore face the problem of teaching more than one syllabus simultaneously in the same classroom. Syllabuses generally overlap but do not always coincide. A core syllabus applicable to a range of courses may help to alleviate this problem.

The problems of mixed ability teaching are discussed in Chapters 3, 5 and 22. Unlike many courses in sixth forms, most courses in further education have entry requirements for students. In most cases, however, students are selected because of their ability to undertake the course as a whole, of which economics may be only a small part. The solutions include frequent assessment and individualised learning.

The purpose of this chapter has been to outline the special problems of further education. This is not to suggest that the problems are insuperable, or that they are any greater than the problems faced in schools. In looking for differences there is a danger of obscuring similarities. The fundamental problems of stimulating interest, providing motivation, imparting knowledge, and assessing attainment are common to schools and further education.

References

1 For useful summaries of the structure of courses in further education and recent developments, see Bamford, G. G., 'Economics in Further Education', in *Teaching Economics* edited by Norman Lee, (Heinemann Educational Books, second edition, 1975); and Curzon, L. B., *Teaching in Further Education* (Cassell, 1976), chapter 18.

2 Information about the Business Education Council and copies of recent policy statements may be obtained from the Business Education Council. A summary of recent developments is contained in 'TEC and BEC, An "Education" Digest on the Technician and Business Education Councils', *Education*, 18 March 1977.

3 Anthony, V. S. and Robinson, B. R. G., 'The Supply of and Demand for Teachers', *Economics*, Spring 1975, 11(1), pp 38–9.

4 Shackleton, J. R., 'Teaching Economics to Non-specialists', *Economics*, Summer 1975, 11(2).

5 Whitehead, D. (ed), *Curriculum Development in Economics*, (Heinemann Educational, 1974).

6 *Economics in General Studies*, A pamphlet prepared by the General Studies Association and the Economics Association.

7 For detailed statistics of the age distribution of full time and part time students see *Statistics of Education 1974*, (Department of Education and Science, HMSO, volume 3).

8 A textbook designed to prepare students for studying economics in the English language is McArthur, T., *A Rapid Course in English for Students of Economics*, (Oxford University Press, 1973).

9 Bamford, G. G., op. cit., p 27.

24   The Use of Visiting Speakers*
Maurice Knights

Schools are now much more open institutions and increasingly teachers make use of visitors who can bring into the classroom a new approach, interesting personal experiences and different opinions. They can be of particular use to teachers of economics, many of whom have not had much recent experience of industry or commerce. On a more ambitious level the teacher may organise a conference within his school to which he invites a number of speakers and involves colleagues in several different schools. To some extent the role filled by one visiting speaker is different from that of a number participating in a conference. Both situ-

* Quintin Brewer read an earlier draft and made valuable suggestions.

ations will therefore be considered separately. However, whether one is arranging a large conference or simply inviting one speaker, it is necessary to bear in mind the following points:

(a) the teacher's aims;
(b) preparation;
(c) the part to be played by the pupils before, during and after the event;
(d) the methods of evaluating whether the aims were achieved.

Inviting One Visiting Speaker

Teacher's Aims
The economics teacher must be quite clear in his own mind what it is that he is attempting to achieve by extending the invitation. One might, for example, invite the manager of a local office of the Department of Employment to talk about the retail price index and its compilation. This will be fine if the manager has worked in one of the 200 offices which collect information and has first hand experience of the everyday problems encountered. If, however, he merely outlines the procedure, the teacher could well be faced with the question why he has invited somebody to talk about a subject which is explained in the textbook.

One might invite a trade union organiser to talk about the negotiation of collective agreements. Here again, if the visitor concentrates on his own experiences, he will bring into the classroom descriptions not to be found in textbooks. If, however, he merely gives an historic account of the development of collective bargaining, it is unlikely that the pupils will feel that he has added anything to their course.

A teacher may not be too sure of recent developments in one field of economics and may find it very difficult to find straightforward accounts among published sources. Provided that he is really sure of the reliability of the visitor he can ask for a straight factual talk on the subject in question and learn with the pupils. In short, experience indicates that when a visitor can introduce the human factor and real life experiences into his subject matter, then his talk is most likely to be successful.

Preparation
When selecting a speaker, there is no substitute for having heard him speak to an audience, but this is not always possible. An alternative approach is to pay a call upon the intended visitor on some pretext or other. Suggest tentatively that he might, in principle, like to come and talk to the pupils. If, after further conversation, it is doubtful that the talk would be successful, there is no need to extend a formal invitation.

If a large organisation such as a political party is contacted, it may be more difficult to make a useful initial contact with the intended speaker. However, it is certainly worth making the effort. If the visit is not a success then you should feel quite justified in writing to the organisation concerned to say so.

Assuming that the speaker has been selected and he has agreed to visit the school, it is essential to make sure that he knows exactly what topic he is to discuss. If the aim is to have a coal miner talk about the dangers of having a productivity scheme, and the miner agrees to do this but insists that he will also need to talk about the history of the National Union of Mineworkers, do not expect too much from the talk.

Two other important points to be borne in mind are the length of the talk and the level at which it is to be given. Many people do not have much conception of the level of attainment in different types of school or of different groups of pupils of the same age. It is worthwhile going to considerable lengths to make sure that the visitor knows that a mixed ability group in a comprehensive school may range from the semi-literate to the potential Oxbridge double first and that a sixth form group in a selective school is likely to have a good knowledge of the Taff Vale and Osborne cases from their earlier work in history. Teachers often tend to assume that people outside the school are as familiar with what their pupils know as they are themselves.

Agreement upon the length of time for the talk is essential otherwise the teacher can be placed in a very embarrassing position. If the group in question is unlikely to listen attentively for more than half an hour there is nothing to be gained by inviting a speaker who insists upon talking for three quarters of an hour.

Related to this is the role of questions and pupil involvement. Most speakers prefer to have questions at the end of their talk. Occasionally some will say that they prefer to have a continuous dialogue. The latter is the better method provided that it is done well, but in the hands of an inexperienced or naïve visitor this can soon become a disaster calling for the teacher's intervention. Unless the teacher is really confident about the visitor's ability to handle the group, he should not agree to a continuous dialogue. Otherwise pupils will ride hobby horses or merely seek attention and the real purpose of the visitor's talk will soon be submerged.

Certain mundane details need to be carefully considered to avoid an unsuccessful venture. Ensure that the visitor has clear directions to the school and that he has somewhere to park if travelling by car. If he is arriving by train, it can be valuable to have him met by two pupils who are part of the group he is going to talk to. If he is an experienced speaker it will give him a chance to see if his expectations are likely to be borne out.

Find out in advance if the speaker will require any audio-visual aids and make sure that they are set up and checked some time before his arrival.

The Pupils' Role

If the pupils are not used to having visiting speakers, or if they are particularly lively, point out that the visitor is doing them a favour and that as he is not a teacher they must be prepared to accept that he may do things rather differently. It is essential that the pupils have some knowledge of the subject matter of the talk but not of the particular detail likely to be given by the speaker.

The pupils should be quite clear as to the role which they are expected to play during the talk. It is unwise to expect them to absorb information passively for thirty minutes or so. If they are in the sixth form it is reasonable to expect them to take notes, but below this age it may be as well to ask the speaker to use the blackboard occasionally or to dictate certain points to them. Make sure that all the pupils have the necessary equipment before the talk begins.

It is unfair to visiting speakers to expect them to cope with indiscipline even if they have been largely responsible for creating it. If the situation threatens to get out of hand the teacher must tactfully intervene and restore it, or else bring the talk to a premature conclusion. This problem is only likely to occur if the teacher has not given careful thought to the choice of speaker, topic and group.

As a matter of politeness the teacher should stay silent during the visitor's talk even if he feels very strongly about what is being said. Any bias or incorrect information can always be rectified during the next lesson.

When questions are taken at the end of the talk there is often a long pause before a pupil will venture into discussion. The teacher can generally expect to fill this void initially. Pupils can gain much from hearing their teacher having a dialogue with a visitor. However, it is important that he should not monopolise the question time, and if the pupils remain silent it is always worthwhile provoking one or two of the more extrovert by asking them outright questions. Pupils are often used to asking questions during a lesson and when preparing for the visitor they can be advised to write down questions during his talk as these occur to them. Planting questions in advance is not generally to be recommended as this becomes obvious and there is very little follow-up by the pupils. However, if pupils have questioned the teacher on something in advance of the talk then by all means encourage them to save up the questions for the visitor.

The question of payment and out-of-pocket expenses will have been discussed during the preparation for the visit and these should be attended to at once. If the visitor is staying for a meal make sure that he is properly looked after and made to feel welcome. He may like to be shown round the school and this is always best done by a pupil. Finally, it is only courteous to ask the visitor if he would like to meet the Headteacher.

Evaluation

The teacher should make sure that some follow-up work is undertaken in the next lesson. This depends upon his original aims in inviting the speaker. If it was hoped that the class would obtain some factual matter, the teacher must ensure that this has been noted and understood. If the aim of the talk was to give background impressions then these should be discussed with a view to relating them critically to economic theory or to the aspect of the syllabus which they were intended to enliven. The teacher who intends to make use of a number of visiting speakers must ensure that suitable follow-up work is done or else the pupils will gain the impression that such visits are merely the occasion for light relief.

Conclusion

In determining the success of the visit the teacher should be influenced by the views of the pupils only to a limited extent. A very witty talk with many anecdotes may well have amused the audience but its educational value may have been slight. The teacher will assess the talk in the light of his aims and its general educational impact. When writing a letter of thanks he should try to be as honest as possible. To praise a visiting speaker who did not do what he promised is unfair to colleagues in the profession who may enlist his services in the future. This is particularly important if the person concerned is on the speakers' panel of a large organisation.

Organising a Schools' Conference

It is becoming quite common for groups from several schools in a locality to come together at a conference held in one of them. Organising such a venture takes much time, thought and preparation but can be particularly worthwhile. It is not advised that a new teacher in a school should undertake a venture such as this until he has become established and gained some experience. It is impossible to run a conference successfully without knowing the school thoroughly and obtaining the willing co-operation of all those responsible for organisation within the school.

Aims

In deciding to hold a Schools' Conference for sixth form pupils the teacher must be quite clear in his own mind what it is that he wishes to achieve. It is important to discuss with colleagues in other schools who are likely to send their pupils exactly what they are expected to gain from it.

It can be useful to take a topic common to the syllabuses of all the Examination Boards and have it discussed in depth. The merit of this approach is that the students can see the subject matter explored from various angles and can be given the chance to debate with experts in the chosen field. The choice of topic is important both from the point of view of the availability of speakers and its suitability as a subject for a conference. It is most useful if the subject chosen is currently controversial or is one which has undergone recent changes. In the first case the chances of lively discussion are increased and in the second it will be possible for the students to obtain information unlikely to be included in their textbooks. Subjects which have been used successfully bearing in mind these points are given below:

1 'The World Monetary System and International Liquidity' (1973). With the gradual break up of the adjustable peg system and the development of managed floating, this subject seemed quite appropriate at the time.
2 'Competition and Credit Control' (1974). As the policy had been in operation for two years and had led to unexpected developments, this subject had appeal. A suitable booklet had been produced and an added bonus was to get its author to participate.
3 'International Trade Policies' (1975). This subject was chosen to coincide with the economic debate centred on the cases for and against a greater measure of import control. It was a subject which lent itself to economic analysis without undue attention to the political differences which surrounded it at the time.
4 'Investment Funds and Future Economic Growth' (1976). Here again this subject was topical and yet provided a clear opportunity for economic analysis against the political background of controversy. (See Appendix I for full details of the programme for this conference.)

Preparation
A great deal of time and thought must be given to the preparation of a Schools' Conference. Work should begin at least three months before the agreed date and even earlier if this is the first such venture.

Discussion with other teachers of economics, and more particularly, with colleagues in other schools who are likely to send pupils, is essential. It is also most important to get the agreement and support of the Headteacher, the Deputy, and last but by no means least the caretaker and kitchen supervisor.

The support of the Headteacher is vital because however well the conference is run his school is going to be a little dislocated on the day itself. Also the name of the school will be linked to the conference and he will want to be sure that a reasonably successful venture is being planned. It can be useful and is in any case courteous to invite the Head to open the proceedings and to receive the speakers. The latter should not be invited to spend the lunch hour with the Head as an essential part of their day should be in contact with the pupils attending the conference. In many schools it is the Deputy Head who makes sure that detailed administration is carried out and his support is necessary to make sure that the conference can operate in a quiet and orderly environment. The school caretaker's goodwill can be most useful in making the physical arrangements. A well cleaned and polished conference hall is much more appealing than a dirty and lack lustre one.

Careful thought has to be given to the catering arrangements at any conference. At the very least provision must be made for coffee and biscuits in mid-morning, although there is much to be said for making a full-scale lunch available to all participants to encourage intermingling. An extra burden will fall upon the kitchen staff and the support of the supervisor is therefore essential.

Having obtained the support, in principle, of the above-mentioned, one may proceed to hold discussions with colleagues on the nature of the conference. These must cover not only the subject, source of speakers, cost, and suitable date but also the basic structure of the conference.

Once the subject has been agreed and a range of suitable dates noted it is important to consider the speakers. Here the same considerations apply as with invitations to individual speakers, and in addition their cost, reliability and compatibility are important. If one is likely to have to meet large bills for travelling expenses and fees, this will affect the cost charged to the students. Secondly, if the speakers are supplied by organisations which operate speakers' panels, then if last-minute sickness afflicts the chosen nominee, there is likely to be little difficulty in getting a replacement. Thirdly, it is essential to have a good blend so that certain parts of the conference are not conducted at a level markedly different from that of the remainder. The use of an organisation such as the Bank Education Service is to be recommended because speakers do not even charge travelling expenses, one is always assured of a replacement and considerable attention is paid to the choice of participants.

Cost is an important factor which must be borne in mind. Students are not wealthy and everything should be done to keep the cost to a minimum. For example, by starting a conference in London at 10.30 a.m. or after, students can take advantage of cheap day travel. Participants' costs should be kept to a minimum in all respects.

It is worth noting that close attention to the local newspaper can be valuable in giving details of people visiting the locality and of others who have strong views on particular subjects. The 'Letters' page can be a fruitful source of names, organisations and addresses.

The structure of the conference must be well planned. It is important to provide variety and to allow for adequate student participation without making it seem that one session is more important than another.

Discussion with pupils can be most useful at this stage.

The basic format which has been found useful is to start off with either two half hour factual lectures or else one lasting roughly an hour. The use of two speakers can insure against a dull or inaudible opening but if the speaker's quality is assured then it is probably best to have a longer opening session. The merit of this approach is that the students arrive fresh, with alert minds and are keen to learn. Also the conference can be given some solid background material which can be drawn upon later in the day.

After this somewhat demanding opening the pupils then have a coffee break and return to a second session in which they again remain largely as observers. However, by staging a debate or a role-playing exercise it becomes possible to lighten the proceedings and to give ideas and material for the students' own activities later in the day. A debated motion should always be voted upon by those attending the conference.

Depending upon the day's timetable, the students either have lunch after the second session or else go on to their discussion groups. Opinions differ as to the way in which discussion groups should be organised. Some people argue in favour of groups containing a mixture of members from different schools attending the conference, for social reasons and to enable students to hear different points of view. This system suffers from the serious weaknesses that the leaders will know few if any of the group members and there will be a general reluctance on the part of most students to offer comments. If, however, the discussion groups are all made up of pupils from the same school, then the leader knows them and it gives an immediate opportunity for follow-up work to be undertaken. Furthermore, as the last session can usefully consist of contributions from the discussion groups, it is unlikely that individual schools will have little of merit to offer. On the other hand, groups identified only by a number or letter may not be so strongly motivated towards making worthwhile contributions.

The groups discuss questions related to the subject of the conference and to the morning session. It is useful to give group leaders some guidelines but not to limit them too severely. Participants from the previous two sessions should be freely available to visit groups upon request but it is essential to make sure that all groups have an equal chance of receiving such a visit if they require one.

The final session should involve the maximum of student participation. All the speakers from the first two sessions should be members of a panel, and representatives of each school group should put either a question or an expression of opinion to a named member of the panel. Other members can offer their comments and adequate time must be given for comments from the floor. A roving microphone can be a great help here. This final session can be very lively and

all schools become keen to put up a good performance. It is, however, essential to select a good chairperson who need not be an economist, but must be sympathetic to young people and able to get the best out of them.

The Pupils' Role

One of the benefits of making early preparations is that it gives the opportunity to make sure that the pupils are well briefed. If the same reading material can be recommended to all schools this is a great help. As so many different textbooks are used, it is best to recommend articles or booklets which are freely available and are not too long. The conferences in 1974 and 1975 relied heavily upon Bank Education Service booklets which proved to be quite adequate.

If a subject such as 'Competition and Credit Control' is chosen for a conference, it is essential that all the pupils have covered the 'Money' section of their syllabus. It is superfluous to try and anticipate the conference but the pupils must be aware of the working of monetary institutions, the money supply and its measurement together with the aims of monetary policy. They should also be familiar with monetary theory up to 'A' level standard.

In drawing up the topics or questions which are to be suggested to the discussion groups, there is some merit in the conference organiser listening to the ideas of his own pupils.

On the day of the conference the pupils of the host school should be full members able to give their undivided attention to the proceedings. Other pupils can easily be recruited to act as messengers and stewards. It is a great help to the organiser if he has a colleague from his own school who can look after his pupils who are attending the conference.

By providing an opportunity on the day for the subject matter to be discussed, the problem of a time lag between the conference and the necessary follow-up work is partly overcome. However, it is also necessary to do other such work in the lessons following the conference. This can take the form of the development of unusual themes which may have been raised or of particular points of heated discussion.

Evaluation

In assessing the value of a conference it is necessary to consider the comments of colleagues and pupils from other schools, those of the speakers and of one's own pupils. Administrative success or failure is important as well as the subject matter of the conference. The acid test over time is whether the same schools keep attending the annual conference. If they do, it is probable that a need is being met.

It is a mistake to think that a conference will necessarily give the pupils a corpus of knowledge which will be an invaluable aid to them in passing the 'A' level examination. Certainly one must hope for some benefit in this direction but the real value of a conference can lie in providing a stimulus to sixth form pupils who may have begun to feel jaded mid-way through the final year of their 'A' level course. Their awareness of the attitudes and opinions of similar students in other schools coupled with the chance to make contact with experts in different fields can encourage them to return to their studies with re-kindled enthusiasm. Contacts between teachers are also made and this is particularly important with economics as there may be only one teacher in each school teaching the subject. Further inter-school links may well be forged.

Conclusion

A carefully planned and well run conference can be a most worthwhile venture. Attention to detail and strict time-keeping are essential. In this connection the choice of chairpersons is most important.

The organiser should keep himself free of all responsibilities during the day so that attention can be given immediately to problems as they arise.

Finally, a pre-conference meeting with all the speakers can be invaluable in maintaining a consistent standard, punctuality and strict adherence to the published timetable. Too many conferences are spoilt in part or in total by a failure to bear these points in mind.

Appendix I: Programme for Economics Conference, Wednesday, 17 November 1976

Investment Funds and Future Economic Growth

09.30 Conference Assembles

09.35 Official Opening:
Mr J. Hodnett, M. A.,
The Headmaster,
Technical High School for Boys,
Tunbridge Wells.

09.45 'Investment Trends in Recent Years',
Mr G. Lipscombe,
Assistant Editor, *Lloyds Bank Review*.

10.15 'A Businessman's Investment Decisions',
Mr W. S. Muffett,
Director, S. H. Muffett Ltd., Tunbridge Wells.

10.45 Coffee

11.15 A Debate on the motion that:
'This house believes that nationalisation of the main financial institutions is essential for the future investment needs of the UK economy.'
Proposed by Mr A. Bartlett, Prospective Labour Party Parliamentary candidate for Royal Tunbridge Wells.
Opposed by Mr G. Lipscombe.

12.15 School Discussion Groups

1.15 Lunch

2.00 Open Forum
Chairman: Mr A. Bruce,
Head of Economics Department,
Hastings Boys Grammar School.

3.40 End of Conference

25 An Economics Trail*

J. R. Hough

Young people from ages five to sixteen, or more, spend the majority of their working day in school classrooms. There are a number of obvious reasons for this but in recent years many teachers have become concerned that pupils should be enabled to escape from the school environment and return to the world of reality: outside visits and excursions of many kinds have become popular and probably all schools make use of some form of such extra-mural activities at various times during the school year. One type of such activity that has been growing in popularity relates to a 'Trail' through some part of the local environment.

The essential idea of a 'Trail' is to help pupils to open their eyes to certain aspects of their local surroundings which they have not previously noticed. History Trails, Geography Trails, Nature Trails, Urban Trails, and Rural Trails, in addition to Trails of a non-specific nature, have all been produced in different localities – on all of them a pupil or a group of pupils is given a specific route to follow and a set of detailed instructions covering features to notice (e.g. contrasting types of architecture), things to do (e.g. count how many people want to cross the road at this point over a period of fifteen minutes), or questions to be answered (e.g. at what date was the parish church completed?). The Trail is a piece of self-instruction in that it should be so self-contained that no teacher accompaniment is required (although if a teacher is available he or she can often usefully supplement information provided, as might be desirable, for example, with a group of

Figure 25.1 Reproduced by permission from G. I. Barnett and Son Ltd.

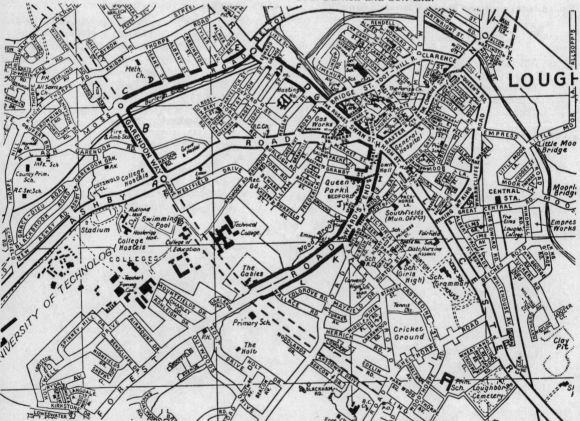

* An earlier version of this chapter appeared in *Economics*, 13(1), Spring 1977.

slow-learning pupils). It may be followed by one pupil alone or, preferably, by a small group of up to four or five pupils; once the group becomes much larger it may be less likely that useful work will be done, although this will obviously depend on the individual pupils concerned. The problems of fitting the excursion into the school timetable, obtaining the head's permission, and ensuring responsible behaviour by the pupils, are too obvious to need elaboration here.

The aim of such a Trail should be to develop pupil awareness of particular economic characteristics of an area, in this case parts of the town of Loughborough, as they are today and as they have changed over time. The emphasis would therefore be on changing land usage and land values (as evidenced by buildings of different types, roads and open spaces), town growth, and the localisation of different activities. The Trail should include sufficient work to be done whilst *en route* and/or subsequently to represent a reasonable learning component, but should probably not be as long as, for instance, a general interest Trail[1] which might occupy pupils for as much as a whole day. At least one introductory lesson, perhaps on the historical development of the locality, would have been required beforehand and subsequently follow-up work might include, for instance, a talk at the school given by a local businessman, or a look at local publications of interest.

Whilst the specific details of the Trail relate solely to Loughborough and will therefore be of little use to readers elsewhere, it is hoped that the general approach, and examples of the kind of material which may be included, will be of wider interest. Certainly any area will contain sufficient material for the construction of such a Trail if one looks hard enough. For readers not familiar with this locality, Loughborough is a prosperous small town of some 40 000 people, with a heavy investment in further and higher education but with also a 'clean' industrial sector. It is well served by both road and rail transport and the pleasant Leicestershire countryside is only a five-minute drive from the town centre.

Finally a plea: as it becomes more common for school pupils to study economic aspects of their local environment, would it be too much to ask that they should be given more encouragement to utilise such knowledge in external examinations, in much the same way as history examiners have for some years encouraged and rewarded material relating to local history? Doubtless this is already being done in some places via CSE Mode III.

Details of the Trail follow: the original version has a small sketch to accompany each point but these have been omitted for the purposes of this chapter. Also, the comments shown below do not appear in the original version. The capital letters are reproduced on the attached map so that the route may be followed.

Text	Comments	Text	Comments
A. Start (at Ashby Rd./Garendon Way roundabout): You are now on the site of the proposed Loughborough by-pass.		**B.** (i) Walk along Garendon Way. Why do you think that the new fire station and ambulance station were built alongside Garendon Way? How can these emergency services currently reach the southern part of Loughborough?	(i) To make use of the by-pass once built; only by making a long detour through Loughborough town centre.
(i) Can you identify the route that it will take?	(i) This is obvious, as evidenced by the Garendon Way dual carriageway (which serves little purpose until the rest of the by-pass is completed).		
(ii) What has happened to the land at the southern end of Garendon Way? Why?	(ii) Has lain waste for some years/been turned into allotments.	(ii) Why do you think new fire and ambulance stations were needed?	(ii) 'Demand' had grown so much that the previous premises proved inadequate.
(iii) Notice the nearest tennis court on the College of Education site. When do you think it was built? What do you think of its location?	(iii) It is obvious that it is very new; it is on the course of the proposed by-pass.	**C.** What is the land at the northern end of Garendon Way used for? Why?	Allotments; route of eventual by-pass.

Text

D. Turn right into Alan Moss Road. What do you notice about the width of Alan Moss Road and its grass verges? What effect would this have had on the cost of constructing this road? Then why do you think this was done?

E. Turn right into Derby Road.
(i) Count number of vehicles passing along (a) Alan Moss Road and (b) Derby Road (A6), over a period of fifteen minutes and compare the results. What will be effects on land usage and land values beside these roads?
(ii) Note names of Station Street and Station Hotel. Can you find any evidence of a railway station here? What has happened to the site? Why?
(iii) Can you find any evidence of the changing fortunes of the Station Hotel?

F. Note location of factories which front on to A6 and back on the canal. What caused them to be located there? Is this still an important factor? (Look at rear, by turning left down Canal Bank.)

Comments

Very wide – wide enough for building of a dual carriageway. Increased the cost substantially, but probably cheaper in long run if it becomes feeder road to the eventual by-pass.

(i) Derby Road is very much busier, and it is lined with motor vehicle dealers and service stations. Alan Moss Road is lined with council housing.

(ii) A few remaining signs indicate that the industrial site to west of Derby Road was formerly site of a railway station.

(iii) The large premises and the spacious stabling at the rear indicate a period of prosperity catering for rail travellers many years ago. Now a fairly ordinary public house.

Original reason for location was canal. But at rear of factories bricked up doors and exits and construction of high walls indicate that the canal frontage is now of no interest.

Text

G.
(i) Continue down The Rushes. Note the timber merchants and the building they occupy. What was this building formerly? Suggest an economic explanation for the change of use. Why was the site suitable for a timber yard?
(ii) Swan Street is right in the town centre. What dominates its use? Note the new multi-storey car park over Tyler's shop and comment on its location.

(iii) Notice Pickworth's shop. Can you see at a glance how its fortunes have changed over the years?

H. Turn right into Market Square, the heart of the town. Note usage of the shops in the Square. Who are they owned by? Can you find any owned by small independent retailers? Why is this the case?

Comments

(i) Was formerly a large toilet which presumably suffered a fall in demand. Large open space at rear.

(ii) The motor car (a very busy road). Built over the shops, this car park has an ideal location since it is right in the town centre but uses no scarce land (except for the small area required for the entry and exit ramps).

(iii) This firm has clearly declined, as one can see from the name-signs: formerly occupant of a whole block, it now has just one small shop.

All the shops in the Square are owned by large organisations with nationally known names. Only these, thanks to their large economies of scale and rapid turnover, can afford to pay the high rents and rates which in turn are caused by the pressure of demand.

Text

I. Turn into Granby Street.

(i) Notice the yard underneath the multi-storey car park and say what happens here. Why should this take place just here?

(ii) Notice the houses facing the park. What were they intended to be used for when first built (some 80 years ago)? What are they used for now? Why has this change come about?

J.

(i) Retrace steps down Granby Street and continue towards Bedford Square. What kind of shops do you find here?

(ii) Notice the Curzon Cinema. How many separate films are showing at any one time? Why? What do economists call this?

K. Continue along Wards End into Forest Road. Notice the large block of flats next to Emmanuel Church and say what they are now used for. How do you think this came about?

Comments

(i) A cattle market held every Monday: Loughborough a market town for farmers in the vicinity, but no longer any real need for this market to be right in the centre of the town. Re the car park, similar comment to G (ii).

(ii) The houses, originally private residences (this is obvious), are now mainly offices of various kinds. Change caused by their location close to town centre and need for further business premises as town grew: businesses can oust private residences from such relatively costly sites.

(i) Those with less need to be right in town centre, e.g. ones with slower turnover – jewellers, electrical goods, estate agents, wallpaper showrooms, (i.e. no supermarkets).

(ii) Three separate cinemas, from sub-dividing the former large one: product diversification.

As a university Hall of Residence. The university saw that purchasing a whole block of flats was an attractive financial proposition.

Text

L. Continue along Forest Road. This seems a strange place to find a piece of dual carriageway. Why do you think it was built?

Things to do subsequently:

1 Plot on a sketch-map (i) the main housing areas in the town and (ii) the main factories, and show the typical journeys to and from work. How do they compare with the site of the proposed by-pass? What conclusions can you draw? Suggest an alternative site for the by-pass. Why was this alternative not chosen? Try to list the various types of expense that would be involved in completing the by-pass and say who will pay for these. Who will reap the benefits? Does this seem right economically?

2 Find out when the proposed by-pass may be built. What will this tell you about the length of life of the new tennis-court at the College of Education?

3 Find out whether demand for allotments in Loughborough is high or low and increasing or declining. Discuss reasons for your findings.

4 Find out how many railway stations there were in Loughborough fifty years ago. How

Comments

To link with the proposed by-pass. (This should be fairly obvious from the way the site of the by-pass has been left idle for some years.)

1 Most people's journeys to work will go right across the by-pass, therefore latter seems badly sited. But only alternative route to east of the town centre would be much longer and would cross the canal at least twice, thus making it much more costly.

In short run costs met from taxes and rates whereas benefits fall primarily on motorists, but in longer run motorists pay extra taxes to offset the costs (new roads always generate additional traffic and so more petrol is used).

2 It was recently included in County Council's estimates for 1977–78. The tennis court will be short-lived.

3 It is high and increasing; there is a long waiting list for municipal allotments. Reasons to do with high costs of food and current inflation.

4 Were three, now one; two of the lines not economic to run, with insufficient demand.

Text	Comments	Text	Comments
many remain in operation now? Why have the others ceased to be used?	The remaining one badly located on outskirts of town.	population during term-time and express this as a percentage of the population of the town.	the large campus tends to divide the town geographically and the unevenness of expenditure which falls off during the vacations. Total students (of all the colleges) number about 12 per cent of the town's population.
5 Find about a dozen shops owned by small independent retailers and plot these on a map of the town. What can you say about their location? Give reasons for this.	5 All are located away from the town centre on sites where rents are cheaper, due to demand being lower.		
6 For some time there has been local discussion about whether Market Square should be made a pedestrian-only area, with traffic excluded. List the probable economic consequences of such a move and say why you think it is being considered.	6 The economic arguments revolve around whether Loughbrough will lose shopping trade to Leicester and Nottingham if access by car to the town centre is restricted, or whether the more attractive, traffic-free town centre would attract in additional shoppers. But main point relates to environmental pollution, more social than economic.	8 What evidence is there that Loughborough is a prosperous and expanding town?	8 This should be obvious with an expanding commercial centre and new shopping precinct, large new housing estates, new sports centre and swimming pool, new extension to Council offices, new police station.
		9 Use any standard economics textbook to check on the meaning of product diversification and explain how this applies in the case of the sub-division of the Curzon Cinema.	
7 Discuss the economic advantages and disadvantages (or 'benefits and costs') to the town of having the university and colleges in its midst. Find out the total student	7 Economic advantages relate to the additional spending-power of staff and students, together with official contracts placed by the university. Main disadvantages the way		

References

1 Such as the excellent one which greatly eased the writer's task: 'An Urban Trail through Loughbrough' produced by a panel of local teachers and published by Glebe House Teachers' Centre, Forest Road, Loughborough. Some of the points indicated above under G, H, and I, are mentioned in that publication.

26 Urban Studies Centres and the Teaching of Economics

John Rees

Economics tends to be taught essentially as a classroom subject, with only limited scope for work outside the walls of the school. Visits are often the cherries on the top of the cake, the treat for good work during the year. However, unknown to most economics teachers, the last five years have seen the emergence of urban studies centres, concerned to interpret the urban environment, either to local inhabitants or to visitors from other parts of the country.

Although Britain is an urban country, the fieldwork (i.e. out of classroom) movement developed along rural lines. The Field Studies Council, the YHA, local education authorities and even individual schools set up field study centres so that by the beginning of the 1970s there were over two hundred such bases, used by biologists, geologists, geographers and others who concentrated in large part on the 'natural' environment. The familiar environment is urban, yet it is not familiar to the young people who live there. The economics teacher will happily talk in general terms about housing, land values, patterns of employment, external economies and the location of industry, but will rarely go out into the urban field to test his pupils' understanding of these and other concepts against messy reality. The urban studies centre movement developed from a number of different directions, and was given impetus by the Skeffington Report (*People and Planning*, 1969) the establishment of the Education Unit at the Town and Country Planning Association (TCPA) in 1971, and the creation of a 'Council for Urban Studies Centres' (CUSC). The evolution of the concept has been comprehensively documented in the pages of the *Bulletin of Environmental Education*, published by the TCPA Education Unit, and indispensable to anyone interested in what has been called 'streetwork'.

In its first Report, CUSC put forward a number of potential roles for urban studies centres. The emphasis within each USC varies according to staffing and interests, sources of funding and a host of other factors including patterns of demand from users.

1 As a learning base for secondary school and other students visiting a town or city.
2 As a centre serving visitors to the area, and external to the formal educational process.
3 As a teaching resource centre, with staff and materials available for use by students and teachers.
4 As a learning base for local secondary schools (although note that Notting Dale Urban Studies Centre has already run residential courses for primary school children), providing both the base for local study of the home environment, and an alternative institution to the conventional school.
5 As a centre through which local authority (particularly planning) information may flow to the public.
6 As a venue for community forums of the kind envisaged by the Skeffington Report.
7 As a specialist institution, serving the needs of 'environmental professionals'.

Economics teachers can assess the possibilities for their own courses. Colin Ward and Tony Fyson wrote a book in 1973 which they called *Streetwork* and subtitled *The Exploding School*.[1] Although economists have visited the Bank of England, local tobacco factories and breweries for many years, they appear to have made little use of the urban study centres listed at the end of this chapter. It may well be that examination syllabuses for economics as at present constructed provide little incentive for work outside the classroom, and many teachers confronted by the additional demands on time, effort, and imagination of the widespread introduction of multiple choice and data response testing will plead for respite from yet further new directions for their energies. Chapters 24 and 25 discuss other external resources – it is to be hoped that economics teachers will look at urban studies centres to see what use can be made of the expertise and material resources in their own courses.

The Notting Dale Urban Study Centre was established in 1974 as part of the expansion of activities of the Harrow Club W.10, a classic nineteenth century public school Mission. It is located close to the White City in an area characterised by massive redevelopment, multifarious small industries, and a whole range of social and economic problems. The centre has catered for groups ranging from eight year old primary children to radical statisticians, from 'A' level economists to local tenants' associations. In a little over two years it has established a number of roles for itself, as a centre on which formal education is based, and as a point of reference to which local people can come to learn how to increase their control over their own urban environment. 'A' level economists have used the centre as a residential base to make the Grand Tour of

London's economic sights (sites?!), and more positively to study the patterns of employment in local industry. The danger of voyeurism is a problem, but where local groups have been involved it has been possible for them to make much more sense of their local social and economic environment than was possible in the classroom. The problem of values is a clear one when you get in the field and see the consequences of unequal income distribution, of unequal provision of public services, etc. It is clear that here the economist must discuss values, and must declare his own values; but at the same time he should not abandon his basic commitment to the use of economic principles to explain these and other situations.

Reference

1 Ward, C. and Fyson, A., *Streetwork*, (Routledge and Kegan Paul, 1973).

Urban Study Centres in the UK

An up-to-date list of urban studies centres can be obtained from the Education Unit, Town and Country Planning Association.

Details of Functioning Urban Studies Centres

Bedford	Michael Hopkinson Bedfordshire College of Higher Education Polhill Avenue Bedford MK41 9EA Tel: Bedford (0234) 51671
Bristol	Rev Mark Williams Advisory Teacher for Urban Studies Resources Centre 23 Great George Street Bristol BS1 5QZ Tel: Bristol (0272) 298244/5
Canterbury	Anthony Collier, Director Canterbury Urban Studies Centre Sydney Cooper Building St Peter's Street Canterbury, Kent Tel: Canterbury (0227) 54445
Chester Heritage *Centre*	Heritage Centre Manager Town Hall Chester CH1 2HN Tel: Chester (0244) 40144 ext 2287
Edinburgh	Walter M. Stephen Senior Adviser (Curriculum) Dean Education Centre Belford Road Edinburgh EH4 3DS Tel: Edinburgh (031) 343 1931
Faversham Heritage *Centre*	The Faversham Society Fleur-de-Lys Preston Street Faversham, Kent Tel: Faversham (079 582) 4542
Gillingham	The Warden Gillingham Teachers' Centre Gardner Street Gillingham, Kent Tel: Medway (0634) 53742
Notting Dale *(London)*	Chris Webb, Director Nottingham Dale Urban Studies Centre 189 Freston Road London W10 Tel: London (01) 969 8942
Saltburn	R. Howarth and E. Anderson College of St Hild and St Bede Geography Department Durham DH1 1SZ Tel: Durham (0385) 63741–6
Stevenage	Martin Cribb, Director Stevenage Urban Studies Centre The Education Centre Six Hills Way Stevenage, Herts Tel: Stevenage (0438) 66102
Stirling Urban *Visitor Centre*	The Director Stirling Visitor Centre The Esplanade Stirling, Scotland
Stoke-on-Trent	The Director Burslem Leisure Centre The Old Town Hall Burslem, Staffordshire
Wakefield	Ray Smith, Warden Wakefield Urban Studies Centre Thornhill Street Wakefield WF1 1NL Tel: Wakefield (0924) 76682
York Heritage *Centre*	The Director Castle Museum York Tel: York (0904) 53611

Section 4: Ways of Teaching Particular Topics

27 'Survival' – A Simulation to Introduce Students to the Study of Economics*

W. E. Jennings

It is always surprising that the students who select economics as an option seem to know virtually nothing about its true nature. They seem to think the course may help them save money when they buy their first car or that it is going to teach them how to make a million on the stock market. Little experience with economics, combined with a new bundle of assumptions, concepts and models of analysis, make the introductory months in an economics course difficult ones for the students.

This simulation has several advantages which the first chapters of standard textbooks lack. Because it is a game, it interests and motivates without being threatening.

Survival is a very flexible simulation, and it can be used with success to introduce students to ideas in ancient history and politics as well as economics and with students aged thirteen to eighteen. It has the advantage of being quickly played, usually taking up three forty minute periods. The materials required to play it are inexpensive and readily available.

With economics students, the simulation is used to introduce the concepts of:

1 *scarcity* which necessitates the making of economic decisions and choices;
2 *economic resources* – land, labour and capital;
3 *basic economic questions* of what to produce, how to produce it, and for whom goods and services are produced and the different ways in which these decisions can be made which leads to a discussion of
4 *different economic systems* such as the traditional, command and market models;
5 *economic interdependence and specialisation* and the advantages and disadvantages of both.

Although the simulation itself can take as little as two forty minute periods to complete, it can set the stage for several weeks' work.

Materials

The amount of materials needed depends upon the size of the class. Generally the following suffices: unlined white paper, paper of some other colour, cloth (which is easy to cut with blunt scissors), compasses, rulers, pencils, scissors, a washer, or bottle cap, etc (anything which is small and round), felt markers and staplers.

Assuming a class size of twenty five, the following proportions are suggested: a good quantity of white paper and cloth; several sheets of coloured paper; five compasses; six rulers; seven pencils; one washer or bottle top etc; three scissors; three felt markers and two staplers.

Day 1 – Round 1

First set the scene. The group has been lost on an Arctic island with little hope of rescue. Their objective is *survival*. At this point it must be established – either by telling them directly or asking questions – that in order to survive each of them must satisfy basic needs for food, clothing and shelter. Their objective in the simulation is to produce one unit of each basic need. If they fail, they perish.

Next, show them the items they must produce: a fish to satisfy the requirement for food; an igloo, the requirement for shelter; and a poncho, the requirement for clothing. These examples are posted at three different points around the room. A cautionary word: *their reproduction must be exact in every detail and no tracing of the models is allowed.* After they have completed a unit they must immediately hand it in to the teacher for credit. If it is not an exact reproduction, tear it up or send them back to improve it.

Complication 1
And now the complicating factors which make the game challenging and fun. *The students will not be able*

* An earlier version of this simulation appeared in *Economics*, 13(1), Spring 1977. It first appeared in *Rapport*, the Bulletin of the Canadian Foundation for Economic Education.

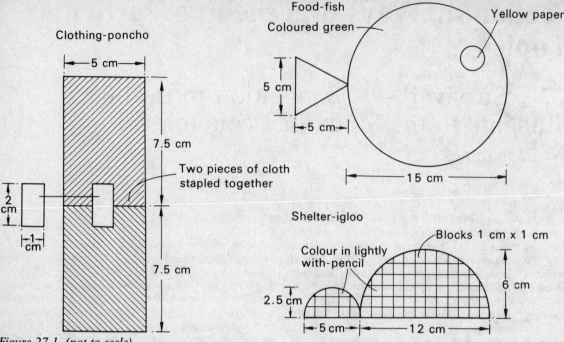

Figure 27.1 (not to scale)

to use any equipment or materials other than those supplied. (For this reason the pencils, rulers, compasses, etc. should be readily identifiable to prevent inventive students from increasing their resources. A standard trick is to break the pencils in two so inform them that all broken pencils will be removed from the game.) Show them all the equipment, leaving it in one pile.

Complication 2
Their tasks must be completed within a time limit, (fifteen to twenty minutes). Warn them that since some of the tools can cause injury (particularly the compasses), you will allow no roughhouse tactics. Start their time immediately. If questions are asked, answer them individually but make it expensive in terms of lost production time. This will help them realise the desperation in the situation.

The game having started, the teacher's role is simply to act as a policeman enforcing the rules, to listen sympathetically, and to encourage those who give up or who are slow starters. Record who successfully produces what during the round. On some occasions, the whole round breaks down in frustration as students become aware that they have no hope of completing the tasks. If this happens, end Round 1 at any time. The purpose of Round 1 is really only to have them experience the difficulty of producing a large quantity of goods with limited resources in a limited time. The last task is to collect all the materials and equipment, making sure everything is accounted for. Be sure any par-

tially completed units are destroyed. This introductory exercise can usually be squeezed into one forty minute lesson.

Day 2 – Round 2

Begin the second round by reviewing the results of the previous day's efforts and congratulate those who managed to survive (if any did).

Tell them that today they get a second chance to do better under the same conditions. They will be given the same amount of time and the same equipment and resources. They will, however, have a maximum of fifteen minutes to discuss the problem as a class to see if they can work out better solutions. At this point, the teacher should retreat from a position of dominance and make it clear that the students will have to work out their own solutions.

There is usually a minute or two of awkward silence but eventually every class comes to life. Note how decisions begin to be made. This is one of the most interesting periods in the simulation, for the group must decide whether decisions are going to be made on a democratic basis or whether it will follow the lead of a strong group or individual who makes decisions and gives orders. Every class eventually organises itself into three groups – each producing one item.

Further specialisation develops if the groups are organised so that each individual does just one step in the production process. Towards the end of the fifteen minute planning period, things become frantic as each group decides what resources it is going to need to complete its task and starts to negotiate with other groups for these items. If it is well organised, everyone will have an important role to play and the resources to accomplish that role. This is why it is important that there be a sufficient, but not an abundant, supply of resources and tools from the beginning. Some students can be efficiently employed as transporters of the finished goods to the teacher for his approval and credit.

After fifteen minutes, let them have the materials and begin the twenty minute production period.

Everyone is usually much busier and happier during this round. The teacher's main task is to keep a running total of approved units which have been produced. These units begin to flood in after the first ten minutes of the round and things become wild as the end of the production period approaches. When the twenty minutes are up, collect the materials and tally up the score.

Day 3

During these two days, students have not learned much about economics – at least they do not realise they have. They have had some fun and are interested. In this case, the medium is not the message. If the message is to get across, some very good teaching must now take place. The students should be questioned to help them relate the simulation game to economics. Listed below are some of the questions that might be asked and some of the points which can be developed from these questions.

1 What problems did you as a group face during Round 1 of the simulation?
Students will point out that there was a lack of paper, tools and time, thereby preventing them from producing enough to satisfy their basic needs for survival. This opens the way to introduce the concept of abundant human needs or wants and the problem of scarcity – the heart of economics, in other words.
2 Specifically, what did you need if you were to survive?
Students will say that they needed paper, pencils and rulers etc – the concept of economic resources. Go on to identify the major categories of resources – land, capital and labour. Interestingly enough, students often overlook their own labour as a necessary factor to survival.
Relate the items used in the game to the categories of land (the paper and cloth) and capital (rulers, compasses, pencils, etc). At a higher level of abstraction – some systematic organisation of production was also

necessary and can be related to the birth of an economic system. At this point, students should be able to give a definition of economics which is something along these lines: 'Economics is the study of how man uses his scarce resources of land, labour and capital to satisfy his wants and needs.'
3 What basic problem did you (try to) solve during the planning period prior to Round 2?
Students can easily comprehend that they were trying to determine *how* they could best produce the food, clothing and shelter they needed to survive. This leads to a discussion of the basic economic questions any economic system must solve:
(a) *What* to produce – in this case determined arbitrarily by the simulation which forced everyone to produce and consume fish regardless of whether they preferred meat.
(b) *How* to produce goods – the purpose of the fifteen minute planning session.
The third economic question – *for whom* goods are produced – is one that students never deal with during the planning period. It never seems to enter their minds and even if it did the shortness of the planning period would prevent them from arriving at a conclusion. This leads to some really interesting discussions. Assume that in Round 2 our class of twenty-five was able to produce the following units.

Food	Clothing	Shelter
34	17	22

How many students would survive? Eventually they will see that since every survivor needs at least one unit of each, only seventeen out of the twenty-five students will survive. Then comes the crunch – which seventeen? The question of *distribution* is one of the most difficult economists tackle.
4 Explain how you organised yourselves in Round 2 in such a way as to increase production greatly.
From the students' responses to this question can be developed some of the basic principles of economic life in modern times – specialisation, fostering interdependence and stimulating trade.
5 How did you decide what groups to form and what task each individual would do in the group?
This question leads to a discussion of the decision making process. It is also an excellent introduction to the concepts of market, planned and mixed economies and a discussion of the differences between them.

Perhaps the simulation offers other possibilities. No doubt, many of the things it accomplishes could be done in a more direct way and in a shorter length of time, but the experience does demonstrate some basic and important concepts and engenders interest in the subject as a whole.

Extensions

The simulation may be extended to introduce students to the effects of different economic variables such as the depletion of natural resources and innovation. These variations should be used when and where useful in the course of study rather than immediately after completing the basic rounds just described. In this way, previous learning may be reinforced while the simulation still provides a new problem to motivate the students.

(a) The Depletion of Natural Resources

Given plentiful resources – paper in this case – students will, as a rule, use a separate sheet for each unit of food and shelter they produce. For a class of twenty-five, that means a minimum of fifty sheets of paper. Begin this round by announcing that due to the previous reckless exploitation of the natural resources of their environment, the available supply of paper has been drastically reduced. The further supply is reduced, the more difficult the simulation becomes.

Allow the students a short time to plan how they can overcome this crisis. The most obvious ways are to use both sides of the paper and squeeze multiple units on each side. If this is done by a class of twenty-five, a *minimum* of sixteen standard sized sheets of paper measuring 210×297 mm (A4) will be needed. They may satisfy their need for food by using just twelve and a half sheets of paper drawing one fish on each side. Four units of shelter can be reproduced on each side of a standard sheet of paper so an additional three and a half sheets will be needed to produce enough igloos. It is a good idea to use thick paper or even cardboard in this round so students will not be able simply to trace what they have already done on the other side.

This variation forces students to re-organise their method of production and creates a situation in which much more careful planning and co-operation within the economy must exist if they are all to survive. Students will be surprised how, with more careful planning, they are able to reduce their consumption of resources when they must. This point may be reinforced with particular clarity if a total has been kept of the amount of paper used to produce the same output in an earlier round when resource depletion was not a factor in the simulation. It is also interesting to note how decision-making in this crisis situation differs from that in other rounds. Is it more centralised and authoritarian? What happens to the production of clothing where shortages do not exist? Are more or fewer resources devoted to its production than before? Does total output increase or decrease? Why? Does the simulation accurately reflect what happens in a real economy when it faces a shortage of some necessary resource such as oil?

(b) Innovation

The objectives of this extension are to allow students to develop new technologies and methods of production and see what effect these changes have on the total output capacity of their economy. In order to achieve these objectives, it is necessary to suspend the rules concerning the methods of production employed in the basic rounds although tracing of the original output models should again be forbidden.

It is important that the students be given the same materials and tools they received before. However, it should be explained that they may use these in different ways and for different purposes than previously. A planning session in which students are given time to develop their strategies should begin this round. The teacher's role at this point is to answer students' questions concerning the interpretation of the rules.

Under these circumstances there are a number of improvements that inventive classes will develop. They may decide to draw and cut out accurately one unit of each good and, using it as a master, cut out multiple copies of the three different goods to be produced. This will save the time of drawing the outline of each unit of output individually.

Perhaps some students might be able to devise some type of grid mask which, when placed over the igloo, would allow them to draw in accurately the lines representing the blocks of ice without taking the time to measure accurately.

Clothing may be produced more efficiently in the following manner: cut each piece of cloth 5 cm in width and 15 cm in length; fold it in half lengthwise and mark the centre of the width; around this centre cut out a square 1 cm by 1 cm and the poncho is complete with a minimum of measurement and no stapling.

This variation might be used to introduce the concept of productivity and the factors which affect it, or perhaps as an introduction to the study of modern technology such as transistors, computers and automated production lines and their effects. Using the simulation in this way creates a very positive frame of reference from which to study the topic which could be modified effectively later by discussing the economic costs of some of our modern technology such as automobiles.

28   Supply, Demand, and Pricing*

Andrew Maclehose

The biggest challenge facing the teacher of supply and demand as part of an 'A' level or equivalent syllabus is that of combining 'academic rigour' and a firm grasp of the theory with an understanding of how pricing decisions are arrived at in the 'real world'. Perhaps even more than in other parts of the syllabus it is necessary to make generalisations and assumptions which further study may reveal to have been unwarranted, in order to enable the student to understand the essential elements of the theory. Nevertheless, this topic provides a particularly good opportunity to relate the subject-matter to the student's experience, and it would in any case be an incomplete treatment of the subject to fail to deal with the applications of the theory to practical pricing problems. The suggestions made below are intended for someone who is about to teach an 'A' level course for the first time, and attempt to indicate the main topics which normally need to be covered, some suggestions as to suitable reading, and certain difficulties which seem to be most frequently encountered by students.

Supply and demand will have to be studied at least to some level by all those doing a course in economics, and as the students will differ considerably in ability, previous knowledge of the subject, interest, mathematical competence and ambition, the coverage suggested below gives scope for a certain amount of flexibility. It is recommended that the topics are covered in the order indicated, but the less able or ambitious group might wish to omit sections 8 and 9, and possibly also 10, and to go less deeply into certain topics and to omit the case-studies and project work suggested. In what follows, it will be assumed that students have no previous knowledge of the subject and are not taking 'A' level mathematics or its equivalent. Those whose mathematics is stronger will be able to proceed rather further within certain topics, but even for this group the most essential objective is a thorough understanding of the basic principles.

There seems to be a strong argument for dealing with supply and demand at the beginning, or at least in the early stages, of the 'A' level course, for the following reasons. First, almost every other topic makes use of the concepts of supply and demand in some form or other, and confidence in handling the basic theory will be of benefit in everything which follows. Secondly, it is relatively easy (compared, for example, to national income or the theory of the firm, two other possible choices for starting the course) to relate the subject-matter to the students' own experience and thus to create interest from the very beginning. Thirdly, it is at the basic level one of the easier topics; the more difficult parts can, as is suggested below, be returned to later in the course. Finally, it requires work on graphs; this has the dual advantage of ensuring that the student can handle graphical presentation of data from the beginning and delays the need to write essays until a few weeks after the course has begun (this is not to suggest that it is neither possible nor desirable to set essays on supply and demand, but that the type of essays set can be made appropriate to the beginning of the course rather more easily than with other topics). However, what follows is not dependent upon the position of the topic in the overall teaching order of the course. Within the topic, the following order is recommended: 1 The derivation of an individual demand curve (elementary treatment); 2 The derivation of a market demand curve; 3 The derivation of an individual supply curve; 4 The derivation of a market supply curve; 5 Equilibrium between supply and demand; 6 (a) Shifts in demand curves, (b) Shifts in supply curves, (c) Inter-related demand and supply; 7 (a) Elasticity of demand, (b) Elasticity of supply; 8 A more precise account of the derivation of a demand curve (including marginal utility and either or both of indifference curves and revealed preference); 9 Some applications of the theory; 10 Real-life pricing policies.

The justification for suggesting such an order is first that it proceeds from the direct experience of the individual (his own demand curve for a commodity) to more general concepts; secondly, it proceeds from easier to more difficult topics; and thirdly it ensures the repetition and development of important topics in something approaching a spiral manner. It would be possible, for example, to deal first with all those items related directly to demand, i.e. numbers 1, 2, 6a, 7a and 8, one after the other, as occurs in certain textbooks. This however is likely to prove less interesting to the student, as demand will seem to be taught in a vacuum, and it will no longer be possible to return

* The author is grateful to Vivian Anthony, Andrew Bennett, Chris Marsden and John Rees for advice on writing this chapter.

frequently to the demand curve, each time for a somewhat different treatment.

By the end of the topic the student will have been introduced to scarcity and choice as general core concepts and to the following specific concepts: value and surplus, equilibrium, the margin, and opportunity cost. He should also understand the significance of 'all else being equal' and the 'rational' behaviour of consumers and producers. Among the skills the student will have acquired, if he does not already possess them, will be the interpretation of simple graphs and the presentation of data in graphical form.

It is of course essential that each student thoroughly understands the principles underlying the topics covered rather than merely copying graphs or schedules prepared by the teacher (though this could be the first step) or from a book. The most obvious way in which the teacher can ensure that the student has fully understood the material is to check that he can produce his own schedules and graphs at each stage. This seems to be an absolute minimum. It also enables the student to produce schedules and graphs for commodities with which he is familiar. The use of multiple choice or other objective tests can ensure that the common errors have not been made. A number of suitable multiple-choice booklets are referred to elsewhere, but most teachers will wish to draw up their own set for each topic, drawn from the various published sources, aimed specifically at checking on and eradicating common misunderstandings. It is possible to make the tests both sufficiently easy to instil confidence and thorough enough to ensure that there are no gaps in understanding.

Alternatively, workbooks such as Stilwell and Lipsey's,[1] which accompanies Lipsey's textbook, may be used. Many teachers produce their own worksheets along these lines, partly for use as homework, and this has the advantage that they can be organised to accompany the development of the topic in class and to deal with particular problems which have been raised. The introduction of data response questions in 'A' level examinations (e.g. JMB and London Boards) has led to the production of at least four books of data response questions.[2] Even if they were not included in examinations, such exercises enable the teacher to apply theory to practical problems, not only bringing the subject-matter to life but also fostering the development of analytical skills in the student. There is plenty of material in newspapers and journals which enables a teacher to produce his own up-to-date set of data-response exercises.

Almost all sections of the syllabus give an opportunity for reinforcing previous work and providing practical examples of supply and demand theory. The theory of the firm, distribution theory, and international trade are obvious examples, and it may be decided to postpone the treatment of certain of the more difficult elements of supply and demand until later in the syllabus. Some suggestions are made in what follows, in which each of the suggested topics is briefly discussed.

1 The Derivation of the Individual Demand Curve

It is wise to choose for the first example a commodity which a student is likely to buy, which normally has a relatively low price per unit, and which has for most people a rapidly diminishing marginal utility – ice-creams, pints of beer, and cups of tea would all be suitable. It is necessary to choose commodities which are homogeneous – cinema tickets and meals in restaurants are obviously not, and add an unnecessary complication at this stage. A simple schedule can be drawn up and the following two points emphasised: first, that the schedule refers to the demand of one individual for a particular product over a specified period of time; secondly, that the schedule will be affected by such factors as the tastes of the individual, the prices and varieties of other goods available, the weather (in all three examples mentioned above), advertising, etc. At this early stage it is probably best not to attempt a precise definition of a demand function but to let the class work towards it, producing examples of their own. The schedule can then be transposed on to a graph and students asked to produce their own schedules and graphs. If this is the first time that they have drawn graphs in economics, it is wise to insist from the outset on their correct presentation (labelling of both axes and curves, for example).

It will be necessary at some stage to introduce the possibility of a demand curve sloping upwards for at least part of its length, the two cases normally identified being the 'Giffen good' and the 'ostentation good'. The only obvious problem in introducing them now is that students might think they are common occurrences, so it will be necessary to explain that this is not the case. It is difficult to find examples of a Giffen good in a standard textbook, so an imaginary one is offered here: a (mediaeval) man has 50 farthings per day to spend on small loaves of bread (the only form in which bread is available), the Giffen good in this case, and meat, the superior good. His pattern of expenditure might be as shown in Table 28.1.

The point is that when the price of bread reaches 5 farthings, his total food consumption would be too little if he were to spend anything on meat, so he devotes all his money to buying bread.

When drawn on to a graph, this schedule will give a curve which slopes up to the right at the top. Some students will naturally point out that they might have acted differently in the situation envisaged, and this is a good opportunity for a reminder that individual

Price per small loaf (farthings)	Loaves bought	Expenditure on bread (farthings)	Expenditure on meat (farthings)
$2\frac{1}{2}$	10	25	25
3	9	27	23
$3\frac{1}{2}$	8	28	22
4	7	28	22
$4\frac{1}{2}$	6	27	23
5	10	50	0

Table 28.1

demand curves for the same product might well differ significantly.

The other example of an upward-sloping demand curve is an ostentation good. There is plenty of scope here for drawing attention to a trend in advertising which emphasises the expensiveness of the product. Students could be asked whether they would be willing to buy as presents for their parents, boyfriends or girlfriends goods which have been advertised as being cheap.

Speculative goods of various kinds (e.g. shares) have sometimes been cited as examples of upward-sloping demand curves, but it seems clear that this is in fact a case of a series of upwards shifts in demand curves as expectations change.[3]

2 Derivation of a Market Demand Curve

This should present few problems. One method of introducing it might be to ask some or all members of the class to draw up a demand schedule for a particular commodity and to derive the class's aggregate demand schedule from the various individual ones. This would probably be a good time to introduce a more precise account of the demand function, i.e. $D_n = (p_n, p_1 \ldots \ldots, p_{n-1}, Y, T, etc)$.[4] This might present some difficulties at first, but it is worth persevering to get across the message that formulations of this kind make eventual understanding and communicating easier rather than harder.

3 The Individual Supply Curve

It frequently proves to be more difficult for a student to understand why a supply curve should slope upwards than why a demand curve slopes downwards, mainly because there is an initial tendency to reason that a supplier will need to supply more as price falls in order to maintain his revenue (as in a backward-sloping supply curve). It is therefore necessary to give a clear definition of a supply schedule and to relate it from the beginning to costs of production and to alternative production possibilities. A straightforward way of

making this latter point clear is to take the example of a farmer who has a field on which he can grow, say, either potatoes or cabbages. As the price of potatoes rises relative to that of cabbages, he will, all else being equal, shift some of his production from cabbages to potatoes. A full treatment of this topic will have to be delayed until cost curves are dealt with, but it will be possible to make it clear why the supply curve normally slopes upwards to the right. This would be a good moment to introduce the concept of opportunity cost.

The distinction between short-run and long-run supply is probably best left until the section on elasticity (see section 7b). The teacher may wish to introduce backward-sloping supply curves at this point but there is a case for postponing this until the treatment of the supply of factors of production (see Chapter 34 on the theory of distribution) on the grounds that it is generally more relevant there and that it will give a good opportunity for revising supply curves in general.

4 The Market Supply Curve

This topic can be treated in a way similar to the derivation of the market demand curve from individual demand curves, and, by introducing the possibility of the entry of new firms into an industry and their departure from it, as the price of the final product and production costs change, reinforces the points made in the previous section about the slope of the supply curve. Lipsey gives an extremely clear and concise account of the factors influencing supply and of the supply function.[5]

5 Equilibrium between Supply and Demand

It is important that the student understands clearly from the beginning the meaning of the term 'equilibrium', the most straightforward definition being 'a position from which there is no tendency to change'. Each student should work out for himself what will happen if attempts are made to sell at a price greater or lower than the equilibrium price. It is suggested that the problem of time-lags and interference with the equilibrium position be dealt with rather later (see section 6).

6 Shifts in Demand and Supply Curves and Inter-related Demand and Supply

(a) Shifts in Demand Curves
This is a relatively straightforward topic and is well dealt with in nearly all the textbooks though few, if any, mention all the possible factors causing a shift which a student at this level might reasonably be expected to

know. The first step is to ensure that the meaning of a shift of a curve is understood, as this is not immediately obvious. Easily the biggest problem arises from a confusion between a shift of a curve and a movement along it and in particular the idea that a change in the price of x will *cause* a shift in the demand curve for x. One reason for the confusion is the rather loose definition sometimes given of the term 'increase in demand'. Some textbooks[6] differentiate clearly between an 'increase in demand' and 'an increase in quantity demanded' and it does seem fairly generally agreed that the term 'increase in demand' should be reserved for shifts in the demand curve while a 'change in quantity demanded' refers to a new equilibrium position arising from a shift in either curve. It is relatively easy to check understanding of this with a few simple multiple-choice items and this will almost certainly need doing.

(b) Shifts in Supply Curves
The same general points about the distinction between a shift of a curve and a shift along a curve will have to be made in relation to supply curves. A particularly good summary of causes of shifts in supply curves can be found in the Manchester Economic Project, *Understanding Economics*.[7]

It is worthwhile to ensure at this stage that the student not only understands the distinction between shifts of a curve and movement along it but also realises that the demand and supply curves are independent of each other except in a very indirect way. An error often made is to assume that a shift in one curve will lead to a shift in the other – for example that a rightwards shift in the supply curve will lead to a rightwards shift in the demand curve on the ground that the commodity, being cheaper at each quantity offered to the market, is now relatively more attractive than it was.

(c) Inter-related Demand and Supply
This topic leads naturally on from the previous one and gives plenty of scope for the production of examples, possibly finishing up with each student producing a single example involving several commodities and illustrating each of the following relationships which are normally distinguished at this level: joint (complementary) demand, competitive demand, derived demand, composite demand, joint supply, and competitive supply. It is worth pointing out, as this is not always made clear in the textbooks, that each of the first two types can begin with a shift in either the demand or the supply curves. (See Figure 28.1.)

It is quite easy to construct an exercise in which students are given a graph with, say, three demand and three supply curves for a commodity, the intersection of the middle of each set being the original equilibrium point, and are asked to identify the new equilibrium point following various changes in the situation (e.g. an increase in income tax, improvements in technology etc).

Without yet going into the question of elasticities, it is worth pointing out here that the actual change in price and quantity following the shift of either curve will depend on their slopes. This will be covered again more fully by those who go on to section 9a. More capable students could discuss time-lags and the 'cobweb', which is very clearly treated in Lipsey,[8] and Samuelson,[9] though in view of the greater complexity involved than anything which has yet been dealt with, it might be thought more sensible to deal with this during a revision of the main course.

7 Elasticities

(a) Elasticity of Demand
Though it is beginning to come under fire on the grounds that the concept of slope is of more practical value than that of elasticity,[10] it is likely to remain important that every student understands how to measure arc and point elasticity of demand and the significance of elasticity for total revenue. The relationship between slope and elasticity must also be clearly understood. Students should be warned about different conventions on the use of the negative sign indicating price elasticities of demand and about the need for consistency in calculations.[11] Factors affecting price elasticity of demand are well dealt with by most textbooks though not all mention all the points which the student can reasonably be expected to know. An interesting discussion can be held on whether the extent to which a commodity is a necessity or a luxury is going to affect its price elasticity of demand. This is dealt with by Stanlake[12] and, in more detail, by Lipsey. It will also be necessary to deal with income elasticity of demand, which is particularly well covered in chapter 10 of Lipsey. This provides a good opportunity for introducing the concept of 'inferior goods'.

It is not easy to obtain sound figures for elasticities in the real world, but some examples, taken from Stone, are to be found in chapter 16 of Lipsey[13] and in Hewitt.[14] Good accounts of problems involved in calculating elasticities are given in Nicholson[15] and in the article by Baumol in the Open University Readings in Applied Economics.[16] There are also various articles containing estimates of elasticities, including some for tobacco, in Watson's *Price Theory in Action*.[17]

(b) Elasticity of Supply
Measurement of elasticity of supply generally presents little difficulty, though students are likely to be puzzled at first why all straight-line supply curves passing through the origin have an elasticity of 1.0. This is well worth discussing as it helps to clarify the method of calculation. Factors affecting elasticity of supply must

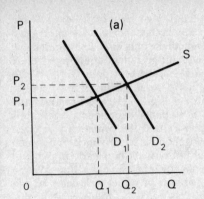

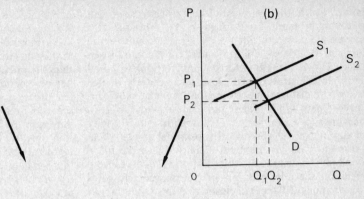

COMPLEMENTARY (JOINT) DEMAND

A and B are in complementary (joint) demand. Either of the two shifts on the right can lead to the position shown in the lower graph.

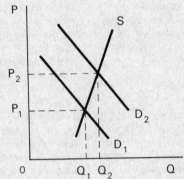

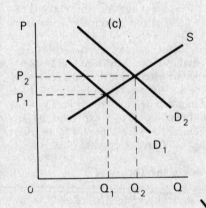

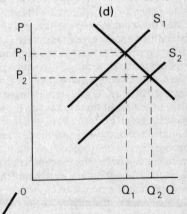

COMPETITIVE DEMAND

C and D are in competitive demand. Either of the two shifts shown on the right can lead to the position shown in the lower graph.

Figure 28.1

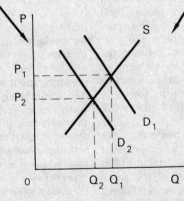

Care needs to be taken in the construction of multiple-choice items to make clear which kind of shift has caused the change in price in the first place. In the case of the joint demand shown above, a fall in the price of B will follow either a rise or a fall in the price of A depending on whether the change is due to a shift of the supply curve or of the demand curve.

be dealt with, though repeated reference to them will probably be made when long-run and short-run cost curves are covered. For a very clear account of the distinction between long-run and short-run, see Lipsey pages 218–19. It is easy for students to think up good examples illustrating high, low, and zero elasticities and of the distinction between long-run and short-run curves. Many kinds of agricultural goods – e.g. apples – provide good examples of very low short-run elasticity of supply (in the absence of substantial stocks). The sub-section on the element of time in chapter 14 of Benham[18] is useful on this. Chapter 10 of Lipsey, including the appendix, provides a particularly good explanation of all types of elasticity at this level, though it does not include a precise account of the measurement of point elasticity of demand, which can be found in Stonier and Hague.[19] Hewitt's *Economics of the Market* also gives a very useful account of elasticity of supply and demand.[20]

8 The Shape of the Demand Curve

The student will now be in a position to make a further study of the demand curve. This topic is one which gives scope to the more able student, and it is possible to divide it into various sections according to the capabilities of the class or different members of it. Three different approaches are possible: marginal utility, indifference curves, and revealed preference. A 1976 survey of economics departments at UK universities and polytechnics[21] in which respondents were asked to indicate what topics they would like those starting their undergraduate courses to have covered while at school (if they had taken the subject) revealed that the great majority thought that marginal utility should be dealt with, just under half wanted indifference curves, and rather less than a third, revealed preference. There would seem to be even less advantage for those not intending to study the subject further to cover indifference curves or revealed preference, but the benefits of studying one or both seem to be that they introduce the distinction between income and substitution effects which is useful for various purposes, both theoretical, such as an understanding of Giffen goods, and practical, such as in analysing the effects of taxation. They introduce an element of 'academic rigour' in the form of providing a sounder theoretical basis for what has gone before, for those capable of it,[22] and they provide a base for further work in microeconomics.

Of the three possibilities mentioned, marginal utility is the most straightforward and is well covered in most textbooks. The 'law of diminishing marginal utility' is perhaps best introduced with the aid of the same example as that used for the individual demand curve (see section 1). It is not always easy for students to understand 'units of utility' or 'units of satisfaction' and it is necessary to explain that they are 'psychological' and arbitrarily assigned, the only important point being that each successive unit gives less utility/satisfaction than the previous one, until after a point, zero or even negative marginal utility results. Pints of beer, cups of tea and ice-creams again provide good examples and are easily related to students' experience. Again, it is important to emphasise that the commodity in question must be homogeneous. The distinction between marginal and total utility must be clearly drawn and there may well be an advantage in extending this to a discussion of the paradox of value, well dealt with in most textbooks.[23] This could be followed by a discussion of the principle of equi-marginal utility per £ (price), which also affords a suitable opportunity to introduce the notion of 'rational' consumer behaviour, which Lipsey covers in the last section of chapter 15. As this may well be the first occasion on which the student has encountered the concept of the margin, it is worthwhile ensuring that it has been fully understood.

Indifference curve analysis is thoroughly dealt with in several textbooks,[24] though neither Cairncross, Harvey, Shafto nor Stanlake gives the topic a full treatment. Points which need emphasising are that the curve represents a series of combinations rather than indicating a relationship as in the graphs previously studied (a very obvious point but one which takes time to grasp) and the idea of the marginal rate of substitution.

The revealed preference theory, explained in chapter 15 of Lipsey, makes clear the distinction between substitution and income effects and can be understood by able sixth-formers. There is often, however, some initial difficulty in grasping how the various combinations (alpha, beta, etc in his explanation) are arrived at, a problem which will not arise if the student has already studied indifference curves.

9 Some Applications of the Theory

By this stage the student should understand clearly how a knowledge of the operation of supply and demand will enable pricing and production decisions to be made more rationally by sellers and purchasing decisions by customers. Many day-to-day examples will have been discussed in class and worked out by students, and it will have been explained that the firm's decision-making will be more fully dealt with in the forthcoming section on the theory of the firm. It is normally thought necessary to cover the following four applications of the theory: the incidence of an indirect tax; the effect of a subsidy; the legal imposition of a maximum price; and the legal imposition of a minimum price (or wage). Not only are these worth discussing for their own sake but they also help to bring out points already made. It is of course possible to deal with these during the main section on supply and demand, but it might be considered more sensible to defer their treatment to those sections of the syllabus in which they are more directly relevant. The effects of indirect taxes and subsidies are well treated in the MEP *Understanding Economics*,[25] and the effects of legal price controls and tax incidence in Lipsey chapter 11. Hewitt,[26] deals clearly with the effects of maximum and minimum price controls and Harvey[27] discusses an interesting example of cup-final ticket prices.

10 Real-life Pricing Policies

At some point it will be necessary to discuss the meaning of the term 'market'. In many textbooks this is done at the very beginning, but this is unnecessary. Students might do better to gain an understanding of the operation of supply and demand and thus to realise that transactions are not confined to a physical 'market-place' before attempting a precise definition. Shafto[28] gives a very thorough account of the various kinds of market, and a concise definition is suggested on page 72 of Lipsey. Stanlake, at the beginning of chapter 12, is also very clear on this. Discussion of markets also leads in to the notion of perfect and imperfect markets, to be dealt with more fully under the theory of the firm, and to the use which economists make of models.

For obvious reasons, the question of how prices are fixed 'in the real world' must be introduced at some stage. The problem is to achieve the right balance between theory and practice – it would be both dispiriting and misleading to leave a class with the impression that because a manufacturer or retailer fixes his prices with no explicit reference to the operation of supply and demand and quite probably disclaims any knowledge of the theory, there is no benefit in studying it. An excellent account of this topic, particularly for students who have already been introduced to the theory of the firm, is to be found in chapters 5 and 6 of *Pricing in Practice* by J. Davies and S. Hughes.[29] The book as a whole gives a clear picture of the difficulties of applying theory to reality. An extremely good, short discussion of how prices are determined in various industries in Britain can be found in chapter 6 of Turvey's *Supply and Demand*.[30] This chapter, and Baumol's article already mentioned, make it clear how difficult it is to carry out empirical investigations in this field. The article by Skinner in the Open University book of readings,[31] slightly more difficult than Turvey's chapter, would certainly interest the more able student, though both would be better understood after an introduction to the theory of the firm. The article entitled 'The Raw World' in the Economist booklet *The Uncommon Market* is useful on commodity prices.[32]

National newspapers and journals carry figures on the prices of shares, foreign currencies, and various commodities on a daily or weekly basis, and articles can be found in newspapers giving advice to shoppers on 'good buys for the day' which frequently include an explanation of, say, the sudden increase in coffee prices or fall in potato prices. For early risers there is the BBC farming news programme giving current market prices, while at the other end of the day the Financial News Tonight discusses commodity, share, and foreign exchange prices. All such articles and (recorded) programmes can be used to bring life to classroom work. This can be supported by visits to markets (at which price differences during the day can be observed) or factories where pricing policies can be discussed, though it is likely that only broad outlines will be revealed.

A more structured way of achieving similar objectives is with the use of case studies. Chapter 21 of Samuelson deals generally with the application of supply and demand to agriculture, but there are now a number of specialised books available, including C. V. Brown's *Economic Principles Applied*[33] of which the first chapter is relevant and very useful, Sandford and Bradbury's *Principles of Economics* (also chapter 1),[34] and *Price Theory in Action* edited by D. S. Watson.[35] No. 4 in the *Case Studies in Economic Analysis*[36] contains material relevant to this topic but will make sense to the student only after the treatment of the theory of the firm. The summer 1977 issue of *Economics* includes a number of very useful articles on the use of case studies; that by Maunder,[37] in particular, contains an example relating to agriculture which could well be used by students who have completed a basic study of supply and demand. Teachers can easily make use of cuttings from newspapers and journals, which can be used either to keep the studies topical or to build up a series; these will, of course, provide good practice in dealing with the data response questions discussed above. Teachers with able students looking for something more ambitious might make use of books such as A. J. Culyer's *Need and the National Health Service*[38] in which the provision of medical services is discussed in the context of socio-economics, or McKenzie and Tullock's *The New World of Economics*[39] in which the principles of economics, in particular those relating to rational behaviour and supply and demand, are applied to such topics as sex, the family, crime, and learning. A case study of a different kind is that called *Out of Control*, marketed by CRAC.[40] Though advertised as examining the problem of supply and demand in a manufacturing company, it deals with production problems which would more normally fit into the treatment of the firm. Nevertheless, the approach of confronting the student with practical problems is a very useful one. Another game which has been found useful in this context, as well as introducing students to many other economic issues, is *Economic Crisis*, available from Simulation Games.

There is also scope for project work, probably on a relatively small scale in the early stages, though it can be undertaken at various levels of difficulty and ambition. Almost all projects will first involve obtaining information, a task which is worthwhile in itself both because it brings the student into contact with the real world and because it calls for a substantial degree of thoroughness and zeal. Students must realise that the provision of information by individuals, firms, or government departments may well be both time-consuming and expensive, and it should therefore not be frivolously asked for. It may well be better to start with published sources, such as those already mentioned. At a simple level, it may be enough merely to record price changes over a period, particularly of those goods liable to seasonal fluctuations, but the more ambitious will probably wish to apply theory to the information obtained by attempting, for example, to calculate the effects of changes in prices on sales (e.g. of newspapers, for which circulation figures are available, or of petrol during a price war). These are likely to prove very difficult owing to the number of variables which will be involved, as Baumol's article warns.[41]

Among audio-visual aids available, the following may be found useful: Donaldson's *The Way of the Market* from his TV series *The Economics of the Real World* is also available in 16 mm. His programmes in the series *Illustrated Economics*, no. 9 *Your Place in the Economics Puzzle* and no. 10 *The Market at Work* may also be helpful in the early stages. The following films are available for hire: Training and Education Film Library *Demand Curves* 16″ (900 8078–6) and *Market Equilibrium* 17″ (900 8080–3); Institute of Economic Affairs *Man uses Markets* 30″ in which the price mechanism is applied to water, housing, and roads. Student Recordings Ltd produce a tape/filmstrip programme called *Supply, Demand, and Price* (AVC/142), and McGraw-Hill a filmstrip entitled *Supply and Demand*.

Everything in this chapter so far has assumed a free enterprise or a mixed economy. It is, of course, important to draw attention to the fact that many prices in a free enterprise and almost all in a centrally planned economy are determined in other ways. This is worth emphasising, perhaps, before one leaves a first treatment of supply and demand. Further work on comparative economic systems will afford opportunities to discuss the effectiveness and deficiencies of the market system.

References

1 Stilwell, J. A. and Lipsey, R. G., *Workbook to Accompany an Introduction to Positive Economics*, (Weidenfeld and Nicolson, 1967).

2 e.g. Perrow, J., *Economics Data Response*, (University Tutorial Press, 1977); Oliver, J. M., *Data Response Questions in AL Economics*, (Heinemann Educational, 1976); Livesey, F., *Data Response Questions in Economics*, (Polytech Publishers, 1976); Watts, M. and Glew, M., *Worked Examples and Data Response Questions for 'A' Level Economics*, (Heinemann Educational, 1977).

3 Nevin, E. T., *Textbook of Economic Analysis*, (Macmillan, second edition, 1963), p 54.

4 This is fully explained in Lipsey, R. G., *Introduction to Positive Economics*, (Weidenfeld and Nicolson, fourth edition, 1975), chapter 7.

5 Lipsey, R. G., op. cit., chapter 8.

6 e.g. Lipsey, op. cit., p 85; on Harvey, J., *Intermediate Economics*, Macmillan, second edition, 1972), p 17.

7 Manchester Economics Project, *Understanding Economics*, (Ginn, 1972), p 156.

8 Lipsey, R. G., op. cit., chapter 12.

9 Samuelson, P. A., *Economics*, (McGraw-Hill, tenth edition, 1976), chapter 20.

10 Robinson, J. N., 'A Comment on Elasticity', *Economics*, Spring 1977.

11 See Lipsey, R. G., op. cit., pp 103–4; and Samuelson, P. A., op. cit., pp 384–6.

12 Stanlake, G. F., *Introductory Economics*, (Longman, second edition, 1971), pp 123–4; and Lipsey, R. G., op. cit., pp 107–8.

13 Lipsey, R. G., op. cit., p 200.

14 Hewitt, G., *Economics of the Market*, (Fontana/Collins, 1976), p 74.

15 Nicholson, R. J., *Economic Statistics and Economic Problems*, (McGraw-Hill, 1969), chapters 9 and 10.

16 Wagner, L., and Baltazzis, N. (ed), *Open University Readings in Applied Microeconomics*, (Oxford University Press, 1973), chapter 10 by W. J. Baumol, 'On Empirical Determination of Demand Relationships'.

17 Watson, D. S. (ed), *Price Theory in Action*, (Houghton Mifflin Co, 1965), part I.

18 Paish, F. W., *Benham's Economics*, (Pitman, ninth edition, 1973), chapter 14.

19 Stonier, A. W., and Hague, D. C., *A Textbook of Economic Theory*, (Longman, 1964), p 234.

20 Hewitt, G., op. cit., chapter 3.

22 Schools Council 18+ Research Programme on N and F proposals, Report of the Economics Commissioned Group based on the Economics Association, Appendix (1976).

22 For example, Farquhar, J. D. and Heidensohn, K., *The Market Economy*, (Philip Allan, 1975), pp 25–47 might be very useful for this.

23 For example, in Samuelson, P. A., op. cit., pp 434–5.

24 For example, Hewitt, G., op. cit., chapter 4; Lipsey, R. G., op. cit., appendix to chapter 15 (fourth

edition only); MEP, op. cit., section 8, and Nevin, E. T., op. cit., chapter 3.

25 MEP, op. cit., section 11, pp 163–5.
26 Hewitt, G., op. cit., chapter 2.
27 Harvey, J., op. cit., chapter 26.
28 Shafto, T. A. C., *Introducing Economics*, (Nelson, 1971), chapter 6.
29 Davies, J. and Hughes, S., *Pricing in Practice*, (Heinemann Educational, 1975).
30 Turvey, R., *Demand and Supply*, (George Allen & Unwin Ltd, 1971).
31 Wagner, L. and Baltazzis, N. (ed), op. cit., chapter 8 by Skinner, R. C., 'The Determination of Selling Prices'.
32 Economist Brief *'The Uncommon Market'*, *The Economist* (1977), pp 13–14.
33 Brown, C. V. (ed), *Economic Principles Applied*, (Martin Robertson, 1970).

34 Sandford, C. T. and Bradford, M. S., *Case Studies in Economics: Principles of Economics*, (Papermac, 1971).
35 Watson, D. S., op. cit., part 1.
36 Barker, P. J., Blois, K. J., Howe, W. S., Maunder, W. P. J., Tighe, M. J., *Case Studies in the Competitive Process*, (Heinemann Educational, 1976).
37 Maunder, W. P. J., 'The Case Study Approach in Bridging Actuality with Theory', *Economics*, Summer 1977, pp 46–8.
38 Culyer, A. J., *Need and the National Health Service*, (Martin Robertson, 1976).
39 McKenzie, R. B. and Tullock, G., *The New World of Economics*, (Richard D. Irwin Inc., 1975).
40 Obtainable from Hobsons Press (Cambridge) Ltd.
41 In Wagner, L. and Baltazzis, N. (ed), op. cit., chapter 10.

29 'Monopoly Demand and Supply' – A Game

Graham Loomes

Teacher's Notes

Introduction

The purpose of this game is to familiarise students with demand and supply from the point of view of the firm.

Firms know their costs but they do not know the demand for their product – and must experiment to discover the most profitable quantity to produce.

There are two variations. In variation 1 firms are faced with a single demand schedule throughout. It is suggested that this variation should last for eight rounds – four before tax and four after. The purpose of variation 1 is to indicate the general properties of a demand schedule and show the effect and incidence of a tax.

Variation 2 alters the position of the demand curve at intervals during the game. The idea is to suggest the kind of factors that may affect demand, and the direction in which these factors are likely to shift the demand curve.

In both variations, the firm only sets the quantity and has to accept whatever price is necessary to clear all output. There are no stocks involved. Of course, this is an oversimplification, but appropriate to the simple theory it is illustrating.

Equipment

(a) Players' instructions (one per team);
(b) Scoresheets for firms (one per team);
(c) Rough paper;
(d) Tables 29.1 (one per umpire);

Also, but to be held back until the game has been played:

(e) Graph paper (two sheets per player);
(f) Tables 29.1 (one per player);
(g) Follow-up worksheets (one per player);
(h) Further worksheets (one per player).

Preparation

Each firm may consist of one to four players. There should be no more than eight teams unless there is more than one umpire – otherwise the pressure on the umpire is heavy.

The umpire is strongly advised to read through the players' instructions with the players, sorting out any difficulties that may arise. It is particularly important to make sure that teams understand how to calculate their costs. The most difficult part is that *extra* raw materials come at a discount, while extra workers not only cost more themselves but also raise the level of wages for all other workers.

The Actual Play

It is not necessary in this game for all firms to have completed one round before any can begin the next. It may speed things up to allow firms to submit each entry as soon as they have worked it out. However this requires extra care by the umpire, especially in variation 2, and could result in some firms finishing well before others. So firms should be encouraged not to be too hasty, nor too slow – it is suggested that each round might take about ten minutes.

Once the game has begun, the umpire's job is:

(a) To check each firm's calculation of costs and profit – Table 29.1 is the key – if profit is wrong, there is a mistake. If there is a mistake, the firm must take its scoresheet away and put right its mistake before it can proceed.

(b) When previous calculations are correct, the umpire fills in column F with the appropriate price. Since this is valuable information, any other players waiting to see the umpire should be asked to queue some distance away.

(c) The final task is to check the overall total profit at the end of each game.

Afterwards

When all variations have been played, hand out the follow-up and further worksheets to each student together with copies of Table 29.1. Below are the answers to questions, plus notes on possible problems.

Follow-up Worksheet

Q1 Something to the effect that *as price rises, quantity demanded goes down*.

Q2 They should have drawn a demand curve.

Q3 (a) quantity 900, price 86p.
    (b) quantity 800, price 91p.

Q4 (a) £72.80 – 10% of total revenue.
    (b) £40.00.
    (c) Previously consumers were paying 86p each. Now they are paying 91p each – 5p more on each of 800 goods.
    (d) The firm.
    (Some problems may be thrown up by this question – they are dealt with in Further Work Q1.)

Q5 After deletions, brackets should read:
    left to right; contract; rises; falls; part; part.

Q6 They should have drawn four demand curves.

Q7 (a) (i) shifts to right.
        (ii) rises from 96p to 104p.
        (iii) rises from 1000 to 1300.
    (b) (i) shifts to left.
        (ii) falls from 104p to 84p.
        (iii) stays the same.
    (c) (i) shifts to right.
        (ii) rises from 84p to 87p.
        (iii) rises from 1300 to 1500.

Variation 1

Quantity	Price (p)	Before tax profit (£)	After tax profit (£)
100	120	−175	−187
200	116	−108	−131.2
300	112	− 49	− 82.6
400	108	+ 2	− 41.2
500	104	+ 45	− 7
600	100	+ 80	+ 20
700	96	+107	+ 39.2
800	91	+118	+ 45.2
900	86	+119	+ 41.6
1000	80	+100	+ 20
1100	72	+ 30	− 49.2
1200	64	− 36	−112.8
1300	56	−118	−190.8
1400	52	−160	−232.8
1500	48	−210	−282
1600	46	−236	−309.6
1700	44	−266	−340.8
1800	42	−300	−375.6
1900	40	−338	−414
2000	39	−360	−438
2100	38	−437	−516.8
2200	37	−456	−537.4
2300	36	−477	−559.8
2400	35	−500	−584
2500	34	−525	−610
2600	33	−552	−637.8
2700	32	−581	−667.4
2800	31	−612	−698.8
2900	30	−645	−732
3000	28	−710	−794

Table 29.1

Q8 (a) 80p–84p.
    (b) 80p is the price of the new substitute. Above that price substitution effect outweighs income effect, so D3 is to the left of D1. Below 80p income effect is more important, so D3 is to the right of D1.

Q9 After deletion, brackets should read:
    (a) increase;
    (b) decrease;
    (c) increase.

Further Work

Q1 (a) £32.80.

Variation 2

Quantity	Rounds 1, 2, 3 Price (p)	Profit (£)	Rounds 4, 5, 6 Price (p)	Profit (£)	Rounds 7, 8, 9 Price (p)	Profit (£)	Rounds 10, 11, 12 Price (p)	(£)
100	116	−179	125	−170	110	−185	108	−187
200	114	−112	124	− 92	108	−124	107	−126
300	112	− 49	123	− 16	106	− 67	106	− 67
400	110	+ 10	122	+ 58	104	− 14	105	− 10
500	108	+ 65	121	+130	102	+ 35	104	+ 45
600	106	+116	120	+200	100	+ 80	103	+ 98
700	104	+163	119	+268	98	+121	102	+149
800	102	+206	118	+334	96	+158	101	+198
900	100	+245	116	+389	94	+191	100	+245
1000	96	+260	114	+440	92	+220	99	+290
1100	92	+250	112	+470	90	+228	97	+305
1200	88	+252	108	+492	87	+240	95	+336
1300	84	+246	104	+506	84	+246	93	+363
1400	80	+232	98	+484	80	+232	90	+372
1500	74	+180	92	+450	76	+210	87	+375
1600	68	+116	86	+404	72	+180	84	+372
1700	62	+ 40	80	+346	68	+142	81	+363
1800	58	− 12	72	+240	64	+ 96	78	+348
1900	54	− 72	68	+198	61	+ 61	75	+327
2000	52	−100	64	+140	58	+ 20	72	+300
2100	50	−185	60	+ 25	56	− 59	69	+214
2200	49	−192	58	+ 6	55	− 60	67	+204
2300	48	−201	56	− 17	53	− 86	65	+190
2400	47	+148	54	−212	51	− 44	62	−116
2500	46	−225	52	− 75	49	−150	59	+100
2600	44	−266	50	−110	47	−188	57	+ 72
2700	42	−311	48	−149	45	−230	54	+ 13
2800	40	−360	46	−192	43	−276	51	− 52
2900	38	−413	43	−268	41	−326	48	−123
3000	36	−470	40	−350	38	−410	45	−200

(b) £73.80.

(c) The difference is £41. This can be accounted for as follows. When the firm produced 900 instead of 800, the extra 100 sold for 86p each – a total revenue of £86 for that last 100 goods. The cost of producing that last 100 was £45. So the firm previously made £41 profit from that ninth hundred. However the imposition of the tax forced the firm to reduce output to 800. So besides paying £32.80 tax on that 800, the firm also lost £41 profit by not producing the ninth hundred – total deterioration in profit thus coming to £73.80p.

Q2 (a) No.

(b) It can only be explained by saying that simple demand and supply theory applies only to perfect competition. When a firm faces a downward-sloping demand curve, there is no single supply curve independent of demand.

Q3 (a) MR=MC.

(b) Because as long as MR is greater than MC, an increase in quantity will lead to extra profit. But as soon as MC exceeds MR, any increase in quantity will reduce profit. So maximum profit must be between these two situations, i.e. where MR is neither greater nor less than MC, but equal to it.

Players' Instructions

Aim
You are a firm producing jars of coffee. You produce in lots of 100 jars, up to a maximum of 3000 jars in any one round. Your aim is to make as much profit as you can over a certain period of time.

Preparation
Each firm needs:
one set of players' instructions;
one scoresheet;
some rough paper.

The Actual Play
1 After due thought, you decide on a certain quantity somewhere between 0 and 3000 jars. Enter this quantity in column A.
2 You can calculate the total cost of producing that quantity. Your costs are made up of three payments:

(a) *Fixed costs* – the costs of various overheads are fixed at £250 per round whatever quantity is produced. This amount has been filled in column B of the scoresheet.
(b) *Labour costs* – for each 100 jars produced, one worker must be employed. The first ten workers cost £20 each in wages. If eleven to twenty workers are employed, the wage rate for *all* the workers (including the first ten) rises to £22 each. And if twenty-one or more workers are employed the wage rate for all the workers is £25 each. Total labour costs should be entered in column C.
(c) *Raw materials* – for the first 1000 jars produced in any one round, the cost of raw materials is 25p per jar. If output goes above 1000 jars then raw materials for the *extra* coffee, up to and including 2000 jars, costs 20p per jar. If output goes above 2000 then raw materials for any *extra* coffee costs 10p per extra jar. Total raw material costs should be entered in column D.

Columns B, C and D are then added together to give total costs, entered in column E.
An example is given here.
Suppose you decide to produce 2800 jars. Besides fixed costs (£250) you need twenty-eight workers at £25 each (£700) and raw materials – 1000×25p plus 1000×20p plus 800×10p – which cost £530. Altogether, total costs of production come to £1480.
3 When you have filled in columns A – E, take your scoresheet to the umpire. The umpire will fill in column F, which shows the price you can expect to get for your output. You must sell all of your output. You cannot keep any stocks.
The price you get is valuable information. You should not allow other teams to see your scoresheet

Round	Quantity A	Fixed costs B	Labour costs C	Material costs D	Total costs E	Price F	Total revenue G	Post-tax revenue H	Profit J
1		250							
2		250							
3		250							
4		250							
From now on, firms must pay 10 per cent of their revenue in tax									
5		250							
6		250							
7		250							
8		250							

Overall total profit

Table 29.2 Firm's scoresheet (variation 1).

Round	Quantity A	Fixed costs B	Labour costs C	Material costs D	Total costs E	Price F	Total revenue G	Post-tax revenue H	Profit J
1		250							
2		250							
3		250							
The Chancellor of the Exchequer reduces the rate of income tax, thus increasing everyone's take-home pay									
4		250							
5		250							
6		250							
Another brand of coffee appears on the market, priced at 80p per jar									
7		250							
8		250							
9		250							
At no immediate cost to you, the coffee producing countries sponsor an advertising campaign									
10		250							
11		250							
12		250							

Overall total profit

Table 29.3 Firm's scoresheet (variation 2).

since the information may help them gain an advantage over you.

4 Now calculate the total amount you receive from selling your output by multiplying quantity by price. Put the answer into column G.

5 If you are playing variation 1, at a certain point a tax will be imposed. This tax will be 10 per cent of your total revenue. When the tax is in operation, deduct 10 per cent of your total revenue and put the remaining amount in column H.

But if you are playing variation 1 before the tax is imposed, or you are playing variation 2 where there is no tax, put the same figure in column H as in column G.

6 Now calculate profit in column J by subtracting total costs (E) from total revenue after tax (H). Do *not* take

this to the umpire – it will be checked when the next round's price is filled in.

7 Having calculated your profit, you must then decide whether to produce the same quantity again, or try a different quantity. Enter your decision in next round's column A, and begin the process all over again.

Please Note Well

A In variation 1, a certain quantity will always sell for the same price, whatever the round. But in variation 2 a certain quantity *may* sell for four different prices – one price in rounds 1,2,3, perhaps another price in rounds 4,5,6, another price in rounds 7,8,9, and possibly another price in rounds 10,11, and 12. You are given some information on your scoresheet which you should think about carefully – it gives you a clue about how prices may behave.

B Put your calculations in pencil first, in case you have made a mistake.

C Your first quantity is crucial – a wild choice to begin with can handicap you for several rounds after. Take care over all decisions, but take special care with your first decision.

Follow-up Worksheet

Variation 1

1 On a piece of graph paper, put price on the y-axis from 0–125p, and quantity on the x-axis from 0–3000. On the graph plot the different quantities you produced against their prices. Do *not* join these points up yet. What is the general relationship between price and quantity?_____

2 Using the copy of Table 29.1, plot *all* the price–quantity combinations for variation 1 and join up the points. You now have a *demand curve* which shows the different quantities that consumers will buy at various prices.

3 Look at the columns for variation 1 in Table 29.1.

(a) At what point is profit maximised when there is no tax?

quantity _____; price _____.

(b) At what point is profit maximised after the tax is imposed?

quantity _____; price _____.

4 Assume that, both before and after the tax is imposed, firms produce at the point of maximum profit.

(a) How much does the government raise each round from the tax? _____

(b) How much of this is paid by consumers? _____

(c) How did you work out your answer to part (b) of this question?_____

(d) Who pays the rest of the tax?_____

5 Delete the incorrect parts of the following paragraph:

A normal demand curve slopes down from (left to right/right to left) and this shows that if market price rises, quantity sold tends to (extend/contract). If a tax is imposed on the goods, the demand curve stays the same but the market price (rises/falls) and the quantity sold (rises/falls). The consumers usually bear (none/part/all) of the tax and the producers bear (none/part/all) of the tax.

Variation 2

6 On the other side of the graph paper, draw the four demand curves that correspond to the four periods in variation 2. Label the curve for rounds 1–3 D1, the curve for rounds 4–6 D2, and so on.

7 Assume that in all cases firms produce at the point of maximum profit.

(a) Comparing D2 with D1, what is the effect of an increase in consumers' income on:

(i) position of demand curve;

(ii) market price;

(iii) quantity sold.

(b) Comparing D3 with D2, what is the effect of a new substitute on:

(i) demand curve;

(ii) market price;

(iii) quantity sold.

(c) Comparing D4 with D3, what is the effect of a favourable advertising campaign on:

(i) demand curve;

(ii) market price;

(iii) quantity sold.

8 Compare D3 with D1.

(a) Over what price range do they cross? _____

(b) What, if anything, might be the significance of this price range?

9 Delete the incorrect parts of the following paragraph:

The position of a demand curve can be shifted by various factors: a change in consumers' income; or the behaviour of other goods; or a change in consumers' tastes; or a combination of these. In variation 2 we have seen that:

(a) An increase in consumers' income leads to an (increase/decrease) of demand at every price;

(b) The introduction of a new substitute leads to an (increase/decrease) of demand at every price;

(c) A favourable advertising campaign leads to an (increase/decrease) of demand at every price.

Further Work

1 Look back to follow-up question 4. If you take the total amount of tax raised by the government and subtract the part paid by consumers, you are left with the amount paid by firms. How much was this amount?

_____

Now look at Table 29.1. Take the firm's maximum profit before the tax was imposed and compare it with the maximum profit possible after the tax was introduced. How much profit does the firm lose as a result of the imposition of the tax? _____

The amount of profit lost is greater than just the amount of tax paid by the firm. How would you account for this difference? Where has the rest of the money gone?

2 Simple demand and supply theory suggests that equilibrium price and quantity are determined by the point where the demand curve and the supply curve cross.

The implication of this is that there is a distinct demand curve, a distinct supply curve, and demand and supply are independent of each other.

It is also assumed that unless supply conditions change, the supply curve will stay in the same place.

Now look at the four demand curves you drew in answer to follow-up question 6. On each curve, put a small circle round the point where profit is maximised.
(a) Can you draw a *single*, normal supply curve that goes through all these points?
(b) How would you explain this?
3 Take the four demand curves from variation 2. For each demand curve in turn, find the profit-maximising quantity and write that quantity into the box next to the * on the appropriate table in Figure 29.1.

Then in the quantity boxes above the * insert the three quantities that precede the profit-maximising quantity. In the bottom three boxes of each table insert the three quantities that follow the profit-maximising quantity. Table D1 is filled in as an example.

By multiplying quantity × price, fill in the total revenues for each table in turn.

Now calculate the *differences* between consecutive total revenues. That gives you six *marginal revenues* for each table. Write them in.

Using your players' instructions, calculate total costs for each quantity. By working out the differences between consecutive total costs, calculate *marginal costs* for each table.

Finally, plot the marginal cost curve (MC) and the four marginal revenue curves (MR) on a fresh piece of graph paper. *When you do this, it is important to remember that a marginal is the difference between one total and the next, so it should be plotted half way between e.g. the marginals between 700 and 800 should be plotted over the quantity 750.*
(a) What is the relationship between MR and MC at the point of maximum profit on all four curves?

_____

(b) Why does this relationship *always* apply at the point of maximum profit?

_____

30   The Theory of the Firm*

A. G. Anderton

A study of the various forms of competition has been entrenched in 'A' level economics syllabuses ever since they were introduced. The content core of monopoly, monopolistic competition and perfect competition (hereafter referred to as 'traditional' or 'neo-classical' theory) has remained almost unchanged. Because of this, there is a tendency for newer material in the area to be ignored or glossed over by the teacher. Examining Boards, however, are now increasingly demanding in essay questions a knowledge of more recent work in the area, whilst testing traditional content often in multiple choice question papers. In particular, they require an understanding of:

1 Cost and revenue curves, including marginal, average and total;
2 The assumptions underlying the main deductive

* I would like to thank B. Davies for very helpful comments on this chapter.

theories – profit maximisation, number of firms in the industry, perfect knowledge, freedom of entry into the market and product homogeneity;
3 How different firms reach price and output decisions in equilibrium – for instance, that in perfect competition firms will produce where MC = MR = AC = AR whereas in monopoly they will produce where MC = MR and price according to the average revenue curve. Equilibrium decisions for the main types of competition are covered in any standard textbook;
4 What happens in disequilibrium – what happens if a perfectly competitive firm is making abnormal profits or a loss? Why is it that a monopolist, to produce where AC = AR, would be going against one of the assumptions of the neo-classical theory of the firm?
5 Interesting corollaries of the deductive theories – an excellent exposé of the corollaries associated with mainstream neo-classical theory can be found in

Lipsey's *Positive Economics* written into the explanation of the main theories. These include why all perfectly competitive firms in equilibrium must have identical cost curves, how monopolists can profitably split markets and why monopoly is accused of being less efficient than perfect competition;

6 The main criticisms of the deductive theories – does it really matter that firms in real life don't know their marginal cost and revenue curves? Are the assumptions of 'perfect knowledge' etc realistic, and if not, does it affect the validity of the theory? Is it important that evidence shows that AC curves are L-shaped and not U-shaped?

7 An appreciation of the inductive theories and their particular contribution to the theory of the firm – the main work here is on theories of oligopoly, (see Appendix I for a game dealing with games theory), with Galbraith's ideas probably acting as a starting point, looking at the behaviour of the modern large public limited company and the multinational corporation.

Underlying the critical examination of theory will be an understanding of the firm in the UK economy and in the world economy with regard to concentration and behaviour in pricing, output and competition.

Methods

Neo-classical theory of the firm is particularly difficult for pupils to understand. When asked about what sections of the course they have found difficult, pupils will almost invariably mention this area, and for two main reasons. First, the theory is not intuitively obvious to them. The teacher can work through the theory, and the pupil may understand each step, yet he will often turn round at the end and say 'I don't understand'. Pupils don't seem to be able to see the wood for the trees. Secondly, the theory is taught mathematically and many pupils have a block about mathematics in general and graphs in particular. They see the mathematics as an (impossible!) end in itself, not as a means of understanding economics.

One of the best ways to increase understanding of traditional theory is to get the pupils to use it in individual questions. All the workbooks published at this level have sections on the theory of the firm. Working through these individually, pupils will be much more likely to understand the theory. Multiple choice question books are also a very good source of these questions. Harbury's *Workbook in Introductory Economics* has some particularly interesting exercises on industrial concentration in the UK, trying to relate the theory to the concrete situation.

Workbooks don't solve the problems of exposition, and most teachers probably approach this topic using

chalk and talk. The textbooks usually take the following path through the minefield: cost curves, perfect competition, monopoly, monopolistic competition. Strewn along the way is normally work on the short and long run. As mentioned above, it is very important for the pupils to have an overall picture of what they are doing at all times. What follows is a possible way of guiding pupils through the exposition with this in mind.

At this level, the theory tries to find out three things:

1 At what price will the firm sell its goods?
2 What quantity will it produce?
3 How much profit will it make?

At the start, pupils should be made to realise that pricing, output and profit all depend on costs and revenue. Average, total and marginal can then be introduced. The relationship between average, total and marginal tends to present comparatively few difficulties. Plenty of practice from a workbook is advisable though. If a pupil is failing to understand, always go back to a simple example – such as 'if you buy 3 apples at 5p each, what is the total cost to you?' or 'if a firm buys three sacks of material, one priced at £3, one at £4, the last at £5, what is the average price paid per sack?' Total cost curves are not required but the shape of average and marginal cost curves should then be explained to pupils. The law of diminishing returns gives rise to the upturn in the average variable cost curve. From average cost data, the marginal cost curve can be derived via total costs. A useful introductory exercise is to get the pupils to construct the cost curves from just the average cost data. Small points, like the fact that the MC curve cuts the AC curve at its lowest point, should be briefly explained. It is not worth spending a great deal of time explaining the mathematics of this since it tends merely to confuse the pupils. It is far better to press on and to return later on once the pupils have an overall view of the mechanism. It should be emphasised that these cost curves apply to ALL firms. (See also the Appendix to Chapter 22.)

Revenue curves can now be introduced. For all firms, output in equilibrium is where MC = MR. As with many proofs on this topic, the easiest way to approach it is to show what would happen if MC ≠ MR. MC = MR is a crucial landmark and every pupil should, when asked 'where does a firm produce in equilibrium' immediately reply 'where MC = MR'. A game to reinforce this is included in Appendix III. Once output is known, price is known because of the demand curve facing the firm. Work out the shape of the demand curve facing the firm, show that it is also its AR curve and then derive the MR curve from it. The differing assumptions for each type of competition will have to be introduced here. Profit is simply total revenue minus total costs. Pupils experiencing difficulties with profit should be taken back to an easy example of how to calculate total revenue and costs, and then asked to apply it graphically. Equilibrium output, price and profit depend on the freedom of entry assumption. If there is freedom of entry, no abnormal profits will be made in the long run. Pupils then work out what this means in terms of MC, AC, MR and AR curves. The concept of long and short run will have to be introduced here if it has not been explained before. Finally, the corollaries for each type of competition can be proved, preferably by the pupils.

All the time, the simplicity of the mathematics involved, the similarities between the differing forms of competition and what is ultimately going to be proved by the theory should be emphasised. If the pupils have a clear idea of where they are going, the exposition will not get bogged down in time-consuming minor points which merely clutter up and obscure the argument. The finer details can be set in place once the broad outline has been established. Table 30.1 could perhaps be written on to a wallchart for constant reference by the pupils.

Landmarks

1 We want to find out: (a) output;
                             (b) price;
                             (c) profit.
2 Remember that standard cost curves apply to *all* firms.
3 Output for all firms will be where MC = MR if profits are maximised.
4 Using the demand curve, output will determine price.
5 Total profit = total revenue – total costs.
6 Equilibrium: if there is freedom of entry, it will be where no abnormal profit is made;
if there are barriers to entry, it will be where there is maximum abnormal profit.

Table 30.1

The teacher can considerably improve his exposition by attention to his teaching skills. A very common source of misunderstanding arises from the use of poorly drawn graphs. Many textbooks are guilty of this. But, more important, the teacher may draw hasty diagrams on the blackboard which *he* can understand but the struggling student cannot. One simple way to improve the quality of a diagram is to use coloured chalk – using a different colour for each curve; or one colour for total cost and revenue curves, another for average cost and revenue curves and another for marginal cost and revenue; or perhaps putting all cost curves in one colour and all revenue curves in another. What system of colour is used depends on the purpose of the exposition. Carefully drawn curves and straight labelled axes should always be the rule, however quick the sketch. Simple drawing rules should be observed and passed on to the student. For instance, the MC curve cuts the AC curve at its lowest point. A downward sloping marginal revenue curve bisects the distance between the x = 0 line and the average revenue curve. One particularly difficult diagram to draw is the equilibrium position in monopolistic competition where the AC or MC curves should be drawn last, remembering that the MC curve cuts the AC curve at its lowest point and that AC = AR and MC = MR. It should also be remembered that many schools now teach modern maths, the terminology of which is different to traditional maths. The SMP course, for instance, uses the 'x = 0' line where most teachers would talk about the 'y axis'. It is well worth consulting the maths department in your school to see how they tackle the mathematics which economists use.

One way to get round drawing difficulties is to produce a set of overhead transparencies, each transparency carrying a different curve. These can then be built up as overlays to produce whatever situation is desired. Once completed in permanent ink, these transparencies can be used year after year (see Figure 30.1).

Resources

Virtually every textbook aimed at 'A' level covers basic neo-classical theory – cost and revenue curves and their derivation and the main aspects of perfect competition, monopoly and to a certain extent monopolistic competition. A good booklist with relevant chapter numbers can be found at the beginning of chapter 3 in Harbury's *Workbook in Introductory Economics*. However, certain books go further than others. Lipsey's *Positive Economics* has already been mentioned. Apart from a comprehensive list of corollaries, he also has a very good chapter on a defence of neo-classical theory. His section on oligopoly too is first-rate, simplifying the main ideas in this very difficult area. But his comments on a games theory approach to oligopoly are not really full enough to give pupils an understanding of what is meant.

The most readable critique of neo-classical theory is Galbraith's *The New Industrial State*. Written for the intelligent layman, it is well within the grasp of the sixth former. It is very well written in Galbraith's sardonic style. The other major attack on neo-classical theory comes from the Cambridge school. Robinson and Eatwell's textbook *An Introduction to Modern Economics* is not the lightest of reading. It is more a book about an alternative theory (or non-theory about the firm) than a coherent attack on the theory of the firm.

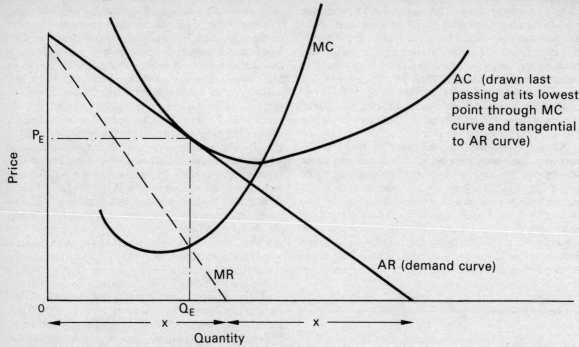

Figure 30.1   Equilibrium position in monopolistic competition

In Heinemann Educational Books' *Studies in the British Economy* series, *Pricing in Practice* by Davies and Hughes is well worth reading. It provides a summary of theory and a down-to-earth analysis of how firms price (and hence determine output of) their products. *Monopoly* by Lee, Anthony and Skuse is a summary of theory and practice in the area. *Industrial Concentration* by Utton is good background reading for the teacher and the more advanced student on how industrial concentration can be measured. The statistics are a little old, the book having come out in 1970.

There are some relevant cases in various case study books. *Case Studies in Competition Policy* by Blois *et al*. has an interesting study on tea and the oligopolistic nature of the tea processing industry in the UK. In Sandford and Bradbury's *Case Studies in Economics: Principles of Economics*, there are several good studies on cost curves and forms of competition.

The Open University radio programmes are well worth considering for audio material. Radio 3 occasionally has talks on economics as well. Otherwise the main educational tape publishers have various items on offer:

1 Sussex Tapes: *Monopoly and Competition* (E9) with speakers Barna and Cooke, both of Sussex University. Side One: Theory; Side Two: Practice.
Imperfect Competition (AE1), speaker Joan Robinson.

Side One: Development of the theory; Side Two: the Modern World.
2 Audio Learning: Tapes: *Monopoly and Competition* and *Issues in Monopoly Policy* (ECA001) with speakers Yamey and Hindley, both of LSE.
The Nature and Importance of Multinational Companies and *Effects and Politics of Multinational Companies*, with speakers E. Penrose of London University and J. Dunning of Reading University (ECA027).
Cassette/filmstrip programmes: *Production – Fixed and Variable Costs of Production* (ECO003).
The Law of Diminishing Returns (ECO010).
McGraw Hill produce a filmstrip entitled *Profits and Cost Equilibrium*.

In Peter Donaldson's television series *Economics of the Real World*, programmes 12 and 13 entitled *What's Left of Consumer Sovereignty?* and *The Firm in Theory and Practice* cover the theory of the firm. Donaldson is very much a critic of traditional theory and the programmes are valuable in that they open up many areas for possible discussion. But both they and the accompanying book are pitched at a fairly sophisticated level, assuming a fair amount of background knowledge and ability on the part of the viewer or reader. In his other television series, *Illustrated Economics*, Donaldson covers economies of scale and pressures to merge in programme 13 entitled *How Beautiful is Big?*. This could be used to try and explain how certain industries gradually come to have fewer and fewer firms in them and the consequences of this. The game entitled *Capitalist* would be suitable reinforcement for showing this urge to merge (see Appendix II).

The theory of the firm is an exciting topic to teach. Traditional theory is intellectually very satisfying, but without application to the real world it becomes arid and boring for students. Quite rightly they come to see cost curves and revenue curves and the margin as having nothing to do with British industry if these are taught as theory in a vacuum. For this reason, the teaching of the theory of the firm should be firmly grounded in a study of British and world industry.

References

Barker P., Blois K., Howe S., Maunder P., and Tighe M., *Case Studies in the Competitive Process*, (Heinemann Educational, 1975).

Davies J. and Hughes S., *Pricing in Practice*, (Heinemann Educational, 1975).

Donaldson P., *Economics of the Real World*, (Penguin, 1973), pp. 148–65.

Galbraith J. K., *The New Industrial State*, (Penguin, 1967).

Harbury C. D., *Workbook in Introductory Economics*, (Pergamon Press, second edition, 1974).

Lee D., Anthony V. S., and Skuse A., *Monopoly*, (Heinemann Educational, 1975).

Lipsey R. G., *Positive Economics*, (Weidenfeld and Nicolson, 1975), pp 213–339.

Sandford C. T. and Bradbury M. S., *Case Studies in Economics: Principles of Economics*, (Macmillan, 1971), pp 42–118.

Robinson J. and Eatwell J., *An Introduction to Modern Economics*, (McGraw-Hill, 1973).

Appendix I: Games Theory Game

Aim: To allow pupils to experience the sort of situation which games theory tries to explain, so that they can discuss possible optimum strategies, and their relevance to the theory of the firm.

Equipment: Paper and pencil for each player.

Playing numbers: Any even number.

Preparation before play: Pupils should be asked to split into pairs. The two matrices in Table 30.2 should be prominently displayed and the rules and objectives of the game carefully explained.

Playing time: About fifteen minutes, plus debriefing.

Play: One pupil is firm 1 and the other firm 2. About ten rounds should be played for each matrix. Each round the players are asked to choose one of the four strategies available. Firm 1 can pick strategies down the matrix, firm 2 across the matrix. So, if firm 1 chooses strategy 3 and firm 2 chooses strategy 4 in the first matrix, the result is −2. For the sake of simplicity, the game is assumed to be zero-sum – that is, the profits of one company are the losses of the other. So, firm 1 would score −2 and firm 2 would score +2. If firm 1 chose strategy 1 and firm 2 chose strategy 2, firm 1 would score +7 but firm 2 would score −7. Once they have picked their strategies, they simultaneously reveal their choice to each other, note down the result and pass on to the next round.

Winner: The two winners of the game are the firm 1 with the highest profit out of all the firm 1's playing, and the firm 2 with the highest accumulated profits (or lowest losses) out of the firm 2's.

Debriefing: Players could be asked to explain how they arrived at their strategy choices. What, in the light of play, would be an optimum strategy for matrix 1? for matrix 2? In what ways does games theory provide an explanation of oligopolistic situations?

Oligopoly – the Games Theory Approach

Games theory tries to explain how people or organisations react when placed in a position where their decisions will have a direct impact on the fortunes of their competitors or rivals. A zero-sum game is where the gain of one competitor is matched by the loss of the other.

Example	Firm 2 (−)				Zero-sum
	10	7	15	4	game
Firm 1 (+)	5	14	6	−3	*Profit matrix*
	19	6	7	−2	
	25	11	8	−1	

If firm 1 adopts strategy 2 and firm 2 strategy 4, firm 1 will make profits of −3 and firm 2 of +3.

[*continued overleaf*]

Example		Firm 2 (−)			*Zero-sum*
	6	20	−2	50	*game*
Firm 1 (+)	10	2	17	0	*Profit matrix*
	3	6	11	7	
	18	9	−4	21	

Games theory assumes that firms will want to maximise their minimum profit.

There will be equilibrium if one firm's max–min profit = max–min profit of rival (as at strategy 1, 4 giving profits of 4 and −4 in the first example).

If there is no equilibrium, firms will pursue the strategy giving maximum probable results (as in second example).

Table 30.2

Table 30.2 presents an example of the sort of explanation that could be used on an overhead transparency or handout on the theory which could be used in conjunction with the game.

Appendix II: 'Capitalist' – A Game

Capitalist is a game intended to show the effects of increasing returns to scale within an industry.

Materials Needed
The game can be played just using pencil and paper. However, it is suggested that the following physical materials be used:

1 a large map of Billshire – an imaginary county whose only important geographical characteristic is that it is split up into twenty five plots of land;
2 a set of different coloured counters for each team of players;
3 money denominated in units of £1, £2, £5, £10, £20, £50, £100 and £500. One of each type of note per team should be sufficient.

Number of Players
Any number of players can play. It is suggested that players be split up into between five and ten teams – depending on your own preference, teams can consist of one or several players.

Object of the Game
The winner of the game is the team which has the most assets at the end of play – units of land, labour and capital being valued at purchase price. Normally, if the game has been played long enough, there will only be one team left in play at the end anyway.

Preparation for Play
The map should be put on a table in the centre of the room, and since each team starts off with one unit of land and one unit of labour and capital, two of each team's counters should be put on a plot of land. Some of the plots of land therefore will remain unallocated at the beginning of play. The teams should be seated on separate tables round the outside of the room and each team should be given £10 and a bag of counters. Table 30.3 should be displayed in some fashion or be given to each team on a handout.

The object of the game and its rules should be carefully explained to the players. The following could be read out:

Billshire is at the start of its development. It is about to undergo an agricultural revolution due to newly discovered techniques. Each team represents a farming family which starts off with one of the twenty five plots of land in Billshire, with one unit of labour and capital, and £10 in money. Each counter represents either a unit of land or a unit of labour and capital. The winner of the game will either be the

		Units of land employed				
		1	2–3	4–6	7–11	12+
Units of labour and capital employed	1	3	9	18	30	45
	2–3	6	12	21	33	48
	4–6	12	18	27	39	54
	7–11	21	27	36	48	63
	12+	33	39	48	60	75

Price per unit of land 10
Price per unit of labour and capital 10

Table 30.3 Revenue matrix

team with the most assets at the end of play or the sole surviving team at the end. Each round, starting in round 2, the team will get an income from its land, labour and capital. The income *per unit* of land and labour and capital employed, is shown in the revenue matrix (Table 30.3). For instance, if a team employs one unit of land and one unit of labour and capital, then looking at the revenue matrix, the income *per unit* is three, i.e. total income is $(1+1)\times3$ which is 6. Say a team has five units of land and five units of labour and capital, then the income *per unit* is 27, i.e. total income is $(5+5)\times27$ which is 270. The cost of a unit of land or of a unit of labour and capital is 10. There is a fixed supply of 25 units of land in Billshire and once teams have bought up the empty plots of land, the only way to acquire more land is by takeover or merger. The supply of labour and capital is infinite however. Every time a unit of land or a unit of labour and capital is bought, a counter should be put on the board to signify ownership. Thus if in round 2 a team buys one unit of land and one unit of labour and capital, a counter should be put on an unoccupied piece of land and another should be put anywhere on the plots of land which the team owns. For revenue purposes, it does not matter where the labour and capital are situated.

Money may be borrowed by teams. The maximum amount allowed is 100 per cent of the purchase value of units of land and units of labour and capital owned by the team. So, for instance, if a team owns one unit of land and one unit of labour and capital, it may borrow up to £20. All borrowing must be done in the round of play *before* units of land, labour and capital are bought. Due to the fact that Billshire is a developing county, interest rates are high, standing at 50 per cent per round. Funds for borrowing are always available from the bank, but there is nothing to prevent teams borrowing and lending money between themselves on terms which are mutually acceptable.

All teams represent private companies. However, a private company may, if it wishes, 'go public' and issue shares. A team may only go public once in the course of the game. In return for going public the team will receive in cash 100 per cent of the value of its *net* assets – that is, the purchase value of its units of land and units of labour and capital, *plus* cash in hand, *minus* borrowing.

Teams may take each other over if they so wish. If the team being taken over is a private company then it is assumed that a bid of *twice* the value of its *net* assets is so tempting that the team must sell out. The money must be paid by the company which is doing the taking over to the banker, and all the assets and liabilities of the taken-over team are transferred to the team which has taken it over. If the team being taken over is a public company, then the team which wishes to take it over must be able to bring to the banker in cash 100 per cent of the value of the other team's *net* assets. If it is able to do so, then the takeover occurs and all the assets and liabilities of the taken-over team are transferred to it. However, it is assumed that the new team issues more shares to the value of the taken-over company's net assets and hence the cash paid for the takeover is returned to the team.

Teams may merge if they wish to do so. If a team merges or is taken over, the players from that team automatically join the players of the team they have merged with or been taken over by and have an equal voice in any decisions that are made.

Order of Play
Each round, the following order should be followed:

1 the income of each team is distributed (except in the first round);
2 teams may borrow money or go public if they so wish;
3 teams may buy units of land or units of labour and capital.
Mergers or takeovers may take place.

Time
The game should last no more than four or five rounds, each round lasting approximately ten minutes (less in the later rounds), assuming of course that the teacher is efficient at distributing income, selling units, etc. The game and the debriefing session can fit into a double period.

Role of the Teacher
The teacher acts as banker and umpire. He should keep a record of the state of each team either publicly – on the blackboard or overhead projector – or privately on a piece of paper, so that he can keep a check on income demands from the teams (teams for instance will often forget interest payments on loans), and also so that teams can know roughly the value of the assets of other teams. A simple record like the following could be used:

	Land	*Labour and Capital*	*Borrowing*
Team Smith			
Team Jones			
....			

Previous figures can merely be crossed out or written over. The rounds are very hectic and the umpire should be careful that teams don't collect revenue and buy twice during a round.

Mathematics
The only mathematics involved is an ability to interpret the revenue matrix and some multiplication. A calculator for the umpire and each team is useful for the multiplication.

Debriefing
The debriefing is one of the most important elements in any game. It could proceed on some of these lines:
1 At the beginning of the game, why was it more profitable to invest in land and labour and capital rather than keep your money and continue on with one unit of each?
2 At the beginning of the game, was it more profitable to invest in land or in labour and capital? Why?
3 At what size did the existing holdings of land and labour and capital cease to increase with the addition of extra units of land, labour and capital?
4 What were the reasons for teams either merging or trying to take over other teams (both on an economic and psychological level)?

5 When teams merged or were taken over, who in the teams actually did the decision making? Was there any loss of efficiency in the decision-making process in large teams?
6 How realistic is the game? In what industries are there increasing returns to scale like this?
7 Should there have been decreasing returns to scale on the revenue matrix? If there had been, what would have been the effect, if any, on takeovers and mergers?
8 How could the game be improved both from the aspect of greater realism and improved playability?

Variations
Like all games, this game should be modified to suit the needs of those playing it. Virtually every aspect of the game is flexible, from the revenue matrix to the number of plots of land in Billshire. As mentioned earlier, the game can be played with just pencil and paper – each team recording its purchases of land, labour and capital, borrowings and cash in hand. The teacher should also keep a record of all transactions and should take care not to sell more than twenty-five units of land in the game.

Appendix III: 'Farmer' – A Game

Objective: To reinforce the idea that for profit maximisation, firms will produce where MC=MR.
Equipment: Paper and pencil for each player.
Playing numbers: Any number, playing individually or in small teams depending upon the preference of the teacher.
Preparation before play: The production matrix should be prominently displayed or given to the pupils. The following could be read to the players:
'You are farmers, growing wheat. To do this on your farm, you have to use both labour and capital (or machinery). If you use more machinery with the same amount of labour, you will obviously expect to grow more wheat. The production matrix (Table 30.5) shows you just how much. If you use one unit of labour with one unit of capital, you can see that you will grow ten units of wheat. If you now take on more men and use three units of labour with one unit of capital, you will grow thirty-four units of wheat. If you use six units of labour and nine units of capital you will grow 118 units of wheat. At the beginning of each round, the umpire will tell you the price of labour, the price of capital and the price of one unit of wheat. From that, you must decide how much to produce. The winner of the game will be the farmer with the most accumulated profits. It is assumed that you can sell as much wheat and buy as much labour and capital as you want without altering its price.'
Playing time: About twenty to thirty minutes plus debriefing.
Play: The umpire must announce the price of labour, capital and wheat at the beginning of each round.

Reduce the time given to players to make their decisions from round to round, initially giving enough time to allow all pupils to work out their strategy carefully – possibly five minutes. Once the decision has been made, players calculate their profit and move on to the next round. In the first few rounds it is advisable to keep the price of labour and capital the same. Table 30.4 could perhaps be used.

Round number	Price of Labour	Price of Capital	Price of Wheat
1	9	9	1
2	12	12	1
3	2	2	1
4	2	2	2
5	6	6	2
6	9	2	1
7	8	9	1
8	24	25	4

Table 30.4

Winner: The farmer with the highest accumulated profit.
Debriefing:
1 How did players decide where to produce?
2 How did they calculate MC?
3 How did they calculate MR?
4 How was their strategy affected by being faced with

differing prices for labour and capital? How could this
be applied in the real world (e.g. to the increase in the
price of oil)?

5 How does the production matrix link in with the
concepts of increasing and decreasing returns to
scale?

6 How realistic is the game? How could it be
improved?

	+	1	2	3	4	5	6	7	8	9	10
					Units of capital employed						
1		10	21	34	50	62	72	81	90	98	106
2		21	34	50	62	72	81	90	98	106	112
3		34	50	62	72	81	90	98	106	112	115
4		50	62	72	81	90	98	106	112	115	117
5		62	72	81	90	98	106	112	115	117	118
6		72	81	90	98	106	112	115	117	118	119
7		81	90	98	106	112	115	117	118	119	120
8		90	98	106	112	115	117	118	119	120	121
9		98	106	112	115	117	118	119	120	121	122
10		106	112	115	117	118	119	120	121	122	122

(Left axis, reading down: Units of labour employed)

Table 30.5 Production matrix

31 Scale of Production
Graham Loomes

Teacher's Notes

1 Introduction
This game is intended to focus attention primarily on
scale of production, but a number of other topics –
profit maximisation, substitution between factors,
competition between firms etc – are involved, and can
be developed at the teacher's discretion. Some suggestions are given under Further Work.

2 Equipment
(a) Instructions for players (one per player, one per
umpire);
(b) Decision sheets (two per team);
(c) Factor cost–demand schedules (one per team, one
per umpire);
(d) Envelopes (one 10 cm×22 cm, one 22 cm×30 cm
per team);
(e) Rough paper;

(f) Umpire record.
   Also, but to be kept until the game is over,
(g) More rough paper;
(h) More factor cost–demand schedules (up to one per player);
(i) Follow-up worksheets (one per player).

3 Preparation

When reading through the players' instructions, it is particularly important to make sure teams know how to calculate and set down costs. Besides going through the example in the Instructions, it might pay to invent another and get them to practise on rough paper.

If there are more than four teams, it may help to have a second umpire, either to check decision sheets as they come in, or to be responsible for the blackboard grid and the umpire record.

4 The Actual Play

The ten minutes time limit is a rough guide, but generally adequate. On average a whole round – making and handing in decisions, checking calculations, working out price, revenues and running totals – takes fifteen to twenty minutes, depending on the number of teams and how quick or accurate they are.

The task of checking calculations is not as time-consuming as it might seem. Often teams use the same system – and a system only needs to be checked once in a round. Of course, a calculator may still help.

The two most convenient stopping points are (a) when all sheets are handed in, or (b) at the end of a round. Total playing time: about three hours.

5 Afterwards

Hand out the extra materials. The worksheet is intended to make students familiar with comparing systems. In a simple way, it brings out points about the relationship between fixed costs, variable costs and average costs, differences between optimum size and profit maximising size, as well as showing how the size of the market may limit the scale of production. It also prepares the way for some further work.

The answers to the worksheet follow.

Q1 The completed grid should look like that in Table 31.1.

(a) System A involves much lower fixed costs on machinery;
(b) £40;
(c) £4;
(d) Difficult to say – the *amounts* of materials rise faster, but the *costs* of labour go up more steeply. Look at umpire record to see what did happen;
(e) Yes, but only if wages or power become very expensive (wages £170 or power £6 per unit) or a fairly expensive combination of the two;

	System A	System B	System C	System D	System E
Total cost of machines	3600	4800	3200	3200	3000
Total cost of labour	960	480	640	160	120
Total cost of materials	1920	1440	1440	960	960
Total cost of power	480	720	960	960	480
Overall total cost	6960	7440	6240	5280	4560

Table 31.1

(f) A and B – but only if power became very expensive while material prices remained fairly stable – virtually impossible in the terms of this game;
(g) None of them, because none is more efficient than E in any department.

Q2 The table should look like Table 31.2.

	Output	Total cost	Average cost	Price (£)	Total revenue	Profit
(a)	200	524	2.62	8.00	1600	1076
(b)	400	870	2.175	7.00	2800	1930
(c)	600	1238	2.063	6.00	3600	2362
(d)	800	1414	1.78	5.50	4400	2986
(e)	1600	2928	1.83	4.60	7360	4432
(f)	2400	4548	1.895	3.80	9120	4572
(g)	3200	6336	1.98	3.00	9600	3264
(h)	4800	10 104	2.105	2.10	10 080	−24

Table 31.2

(i) 800 – up to that point, the firm adopts increasingly efficient methods. Beyond that point, there are no extra technical advances – but there are rising factor costs.
(ii) 2400 – because even though AC and TC are ris-

ing, total revenue is rising faster up to this point (i.e. marginal revenue exceeds marginal cost).

(iii) No – even though AC at capacity output of 4000 is only £1.696 per unit (nearly 10p lower than System E's best) the market is not big enough to take this System F – no output under System F in this market can give profits as big as System E operating at 2400.

(iv) The main limit in this game is the size of the market.

Further Work

1 One very interesting exercise is to reconstruct the game, in part or in full. A suggested structure for doing this is to have each team gathered round its decision sheets and ask the winning team to tell the rest what it did round by round. This is accompanied by the teacher putting up the appropriate factor costs and goods prices from the umpire record. In each round teams who differed in their play might be asked to discuss why they behaved as they did, and perhaps criticise their own or their opponents' play.

In the course of the reconstruction, many questions could be asked by the teacher. Here are a few:

Under what circumstances did teams choose to keep a lot of unused cash? Was this a wise move? (Incidentally, a more complex game might have allowed teams to earn 'normal' interest on spare cash – would this have affected decisions?)

Under what circumstances did firms use more than one system in the same round?

Did teams ever operate systems below maximum capacity? If so, why choose this instead of other options – like the ones above?

Were there rounds where production was unprofitable for some or all firms? Did this occur accidentally or deliberately? What were the reasons behind it?

Were there firms who chose not to produce in any round? If so, why?

Were there any alliances between firms? How did they operate? What was the result?

And so on, depending on the nature of the play.

2 The results of this exercise are somewhat unpredictable, but should reveal to students something about the concept of 'the demand curve facing the firm'.

Provide each student with a piece of graph paper and ask them to plot the market demand schedule. Then ask them to plot each of *their firm's* quantities against the prices they fetched, and draw a line (not necessarily a straight line) which is the best 'fit' of the points they have plotted.

Points to look for are:

(a) The nature of the difference between the market demand curve and the demand curve facing the firm, and the reasons.

(b) Any cases of similar outputs of firms selling for significantly different prices in different rounds, and reasons for this.

(c) Any points on a team's graph which are a long way from the 'fitted' curve – possible reasons for this.

3 Players might be invited to list criticisms of the assumptions made by the game. A possible one has been mentioned – no interest on spare cash. Others might lead into discussions of other economies of scale not dealt with by the game e.g. the ability of a large firm to offset rising material costs by getting a discount for buying in bulk, or the ability to increase its share of demand by advertising and differentiating its product.

Players' Instructions

Aim

The aim of this game is to produce and sell in such a way that your firm makes as much money as it can.

The game is played over a fixed number of rounds. The number of rounds should be decided before play starts.

Preparation

Players divide into a maximum of eight teams, each team representing a firm.

Each firm receives:

> copies of players' instructions;
> a factor cost–demand schedule sheet;
> two decision sheets;
> two envelopes;
> rough paper.

The umpire draws a grid on the board which will show current prices of factors and goods throughout the game. It may look like this:

Wages	Materials	Power		Goods

Firms have five systems of production to choose from, and may use any system or combination of systems in each round. A firm does not have to spend all its money in any round, and may choose not to produce at all in some rounds. However, firms may not spend more money than they have previously accumulated, i.e. no credit is allowed.

The five systems of production are as follows:

System A: Each machine costs *£300* and lasts two periods.

It requires *two workers per period* to run it, and can produce up to a maximum of *100 goods* each period.

It uses *4 units of materials +2 units of power per ten goods.*

System B: Each machine costs £400 and lasts two periods.
It requires *one worker per period* to run it, and can produce up to a maximum of *100 goods* each period. It uses *3* units of materials +*3* units of power per ten goods.

System C: Each machine costs *£400* and lasts two periods.
It requires *two workers per period* to run it, and can produce up to a maximum of *150 goods* each period. It uses *3* units of materials +*4* units of power per ten goods.

System D: Each machine costs *£800* and lasts two periods.
It requires *one worker per period* to run it, and can produce up to a maximum of *300 goods* each period. It uses *2* units of materials +*4* units of power per ten goods.

System E: Each machine costs *£2000* and lasts two periods.
It requires *two workers per period* to run it, and can produce up to a maximum of *800 goods* each period. It uses *2* units of materials +*2* units of power per ten goods.

The Actual Play

1 Firms begin with £600 each.

2 If a firm chooses to produce, it must produce in multiples of ten goods.

3 Each firm decides on the quantity to be produced and the method(s) to be used.

The first thing to buy is machinery. All machines last two periods, so whenever a machine is bought it should immediately be recorded in the current period *and* in the next period.

The full cost should be entered against the machine in its first round of life because that is when it is paid for. A dash should be put against the cost of the machine in its second period.

4 Firms buy factors of production at the prices marked up on the blackboard grid. Each firm may buy as many factors as it wishes and can afford at the prevailing prices – but this may affect factor prices for the following round. In the first round factor prices are always set at: wages – £20 per worker; materials – £2 per unit; power – £1 per unit.

5 Each different *system* should be entered on a different line of the decision sheets – *both* of the decision sheets. Then, when the firm's entry for the round is complete, costs in each column should be totalled up and a thick line drawn across underneath. One of the sheets should be put into the smaller envelope and handed in to the umpire. It is suggested that firms should be given about ten minutes to fill in their sheets each round and hand them in.

Example: This is what an entry might look like in a round where, let us say, the firm starts with £1200 and carries forward one machine from System C. Wages,

---

Factor Cost – Demand Schedule

Remember that factor prices in the current round are determined by total demand for factors in the round before.

Whereas goods prices in the current round are determined by total output of goods in the current round.

Finished Goods

Total number of goods produced	Price (£)
1– 200	8.00
201– 400	7.00
401– 600	6.00
601– 800	5.50
801–1000	5.20
1001–1200	5.00
1201–1400	4.80
1401–1600	4.60
1601–1800	4.40
1801–2000	4.20
2001–2200	4.00
2201–2400	3.80
2401–2600	3.60
2601–2800	3.40
2801–3000	3.20
3001–3200	3.00
3201–3400	2.80
3401–3600	2.70
3601–3800	2.60
3801–4000	2.50
4001–4200	2.40
4201–4400	2.30
4401–4600	2.20
4601–4800	2.10
4801–5000	2.00

and thereafter price falls 10p for every extra 200 or part of 200 produced.

---

materials and power happen to be £20, £2 and £1 respectively. *You should note that machines do not have to be used to capacity – see System B in this example – but if not used to capacity, machines still don't last longer than two periods.*

6 If any envelope comes in late, the umpire deducts a £50 fine.

When all envelopes are in, the umpire checks the calculations. If there are any errors on a sheet, the umpire deducts a £50 fine and corrects the sheet.

Decision Sheet

System	Number of machines	Cost	Number of workers	Cost	Number of materials	Cost	Units of power	Cost	Output	Total Cost	Unused cash	Revenue	Running total
C	1	—	2	£40	45	£90	60	£60	150	£190			
A	1	£300	2	£40	40	£80	20	£20	100	£440			
B	1	£400	1	£20	24	£48	24	£24	80	£492			
Total	3	£700	5	£100	109	£218	104	£104	330	£1122	£78		

Labour		Materials		Power	
Total number of workers demanded	Wage level (£)	Total number of materials demanded	Unit price (£)	Total units of power demanded	Unit price (£)
1 or 2	15.00	1– 200	1.60	1– 200	0.80
3 or 4	16.00	201– 400	1.80	201– 400	0.90
5 or 6	18.00	401– 600	2.00	401– 600	1.00
7 or 8	20.00	601– 800	2.30	601– 800	1.10
9 or 10	22.00	801–1000	2.70	801–1000	1.20
11 or 12	25.00	1001–1200	3.20	1001–1200	1.30
13 or 14	30.00	1201–1400	3.80	1201–1400	1.50
15 or 16	36.00	1401–1600	4.50	1401–1600	1.70
17 or 18	42.00	1601–1800	5.50	1601–1800	2.00
19 or 20	50.00	1801–2000	7.00	1801–2000	2.40
then every extra worker raises wage level by £5		then every extra 200 or part raises price by £2		then every extra 200 or part raises price 60p.	

Umpire Record

Round		Workers	Materials	Power		Goods	
1	Factor price demand	£20	£2.00	£1.00	Output price		
2	Factor price demand	↓	↓	↓	Output price		
3	Factor price demand	↓	↓	↓	Output price		
4	Factor price demand	↓	↓	↓	Output price		
5	Factor price demand	↓	↓	↓	Output price		
6	Factor price demand	↓	↓	↓	Output price		
7	Factor price demand	↓	↓	↓	Output price		
8	Factor price demand	↓	↓	↓	Output price		
9	Factor price demand	↓	↓	↓	Output price		
10	Factor price demand	↓	↓	↓	Output price		

If there is not enough unused cash to pay the fine(s) the umpire may deduct the money from revenue at the end of the round. On the other hand, if the umpire discovers that a firm has underestimated its costs so badly that correction raises costs to more than the money it has available, the umpire should deduct the fine and return the sheet to the firm, giving five minutes for the entry to be rewritten.

7 When the umpire has all the corrected sheets, he:
(a) Adds up the total demands for workers, materials and power, enters these figures on the umpire record together with the new factor prices read off from the factor cost schedules, and puts up these prices on the grid. These prices will apply in the next round.
(b) Adds up the total number of goods produced and reads off the price they will fetch. Quantity and price are entered on both the umpire record and the grid.
8 Firms and umpire then calculate the revenues, entering them on their respective copies of the decision sheets. Then they add the round's revenue to the unused cash to find the running total at the end of the round (any held-over fines being paid in the process).
9 The umpire puts his copies of the decision sheets back into their envelopes and returns them to the firms who check that the figures agree with their copies. There are no penalties for mistakes at this point, but the figures must agree. Then firms can begin to make their entries for the next round.

Worksheet

Q1 Using the table below, calculate the costs of producing 2400 goods by each system in turn. Assume throughout that wages, materials and power units cost £20, £2 and £1 respectively. Since machines last for two periods, assume that the cost of using machinery for one period is half its initial price.
Then answer the questions underneath.

	System A	System B	System C	System D	System E
Total cost of machines					
Total cost of labour					
Total cost of materials					
Total cost of power					
Overall total cost					

(a) Why is System A preferable to System B, even though System B uses fewer workers and materials per 100 goods?
_____
(b) To what level would wages have to rise (all other things staying the same) to make System B as cheap per unit as System A? _____
(c) To what level would the cost of materials have to rise (all other things staying the same) to make System B as cheap as System A? _____
(d) Out of (b) and (c) above, which do you think more likely to happen? Explain _____
_____
_____
(e) Could System B ever be preferable to System C? Explain _____
_____
_____
(f) Out of A, B and C, which if any could possibly be preferable to System D? Explain _____
_____
_____
(g) Out of A, B, C and D, which if any could possibly be preferable to System E? Explain _____
_____
_____

Q2 Now assume you are the only firm in the industry – a monopoly. Using a fresh decision sheet, calculate the cheapest way of producing the following quantities: (a) 200, (b) 400, (c) 600, (d) 800, (e) 1600, (f) 2400, (g) 3200 and (h) 4800.
    For the purposes of this exercise, assume that since you are the only firm, your demand for factors determines their cost.
    For example, if you were to decide (wrongly) that the cheapest way of producing 600 goods is to use four machines of System C together with eight workers, 180 units of materials and 240 units of power, you would consult the factor cost – demand schedule and find that wages would be £20, materials £1.60 and power 90p per unit.
    Fill the results in the table (page 175), then answer the questions alongside.

Output	Total cost	Average cost	Price (£)	Total revenue	Profit
(a)					
(b)					
(c)					
(d)					
(e)					
(f)					
(g)					
(h)					

(i) At which quantity are average costs minimised? Explain why it is this quantity _____

_____

_____

(ii) At which of these quantities are profits maximised? _____

Why is this not the same quantity as in (i)? _____

_____

(iii) Suppose there were another system of production – System F – where each machine cost £4000 and required four workers to run it, could produce up to 4000 goods, and used two units of materials and two units of power per ten goods. Would you want to employ System F? Explain _____

_____

(iv) What are the limits to increasing the scale of production? _____

32 Pricing in a Perfectly Competitive Market*

Myron L. Joseph

Aims

Students often have difficulty in accepting the concept of a price fixed by market forces. The root of this problem is not usually the algebra or geometry used to develop the model of a perfectly competitive market, but the apparent unreality of some aspects of the model, which emerge when the student compares it with the 'real world'. In particular, it is part of most students' experience that the seller sets the price at which his product is sold. Given this, he is likely to argue that it is unrealistic to assume that the firm must accept the market price as given.

Consequently, even though it may be accepted that the market price equates supply and demand and clears the market, the conclusion is likely to be drawn that the model is an intellectual exercise with no application outside the classroom. Thus, a foundation has been laid for a misunderstanding of, and a resistance to, elementary microeconomics.

* This is reprinted by permission from Sandford, C. T. and Bradbury, M. S., *Projects and Role-playing in Teaching Economics*, (Macmillan, 1971).

This simulation aims to avoid this barrier to understanding by giving students a chance to participate in the determination of market price in a highly simplified market. Subsequent comparisons of alternative market structures and analysis which assume price determination in competitive markets will then be based on a more solid foundation.

Level and Requirements

'A' level, first-year degree, HND and HNC in business studies and various professional courses.

About twenty-five to fifty students and at least two staff.

As the game can be noisy, an isolated classroom, or one which is available when other rooms are not in use, is ideal. To allow buyers and sellers to mix, furniture should be pushed back to the walls.

Materials needed are two packets of differently coloured 6 cm×3 cm index cards, for the buying and selling instructions, a duplicated sheet of general instructions for each student (optional), and a blackboard, or, better still, overhead projector.

The case can be completed within a one-hour teaching period, but more time is required for variants and follow-up discussion.

Necessary Preparatory Work

No particular preparatory work needs to be undertaken by the class; the game can precede or follow a conventional treatment of pricing in a perfectly competitive market.

The teacher will need to prepare in advance a set of buy and sell instructions. The instructions are based on demand and supply functions that intersect at a price of 180p per bushel. As can be deduced from Table 32.1, at the equilibrium price twenty-four transactions are possible and eight buyers and eight sellers are excluded from the market.

Price (p)	Buyers (not more than the price)	Sellers (not less than the price)
280	4	–
260	4	2
240	4	2
220	4	2
200	4	2
180	4	4
160	2	4
140	2	6
120	2	6
100	2	4

Table 32.1   Distribution of buy and sell instructions

The instruction cards will contain an order to buy 1000 bushels of wheat *at not more than* the specified price; or to sell 1000 bushels of wheat *at not less than* the specified price. To distinguish between buyers and sellers, the two packs of instruction cards should each be a different colour.

If required, copies of the following general instructions can be duplicated for distribution to participants:

You are about to participate in the operation of a commodity market. You will be given an order to buy or sell 1000 bushels of wheat under certain conditions. In general you should not reveal your instructions to any of the other dealers, unless you have a particular reason for doing so. You should consider yourself to be an agent, acting on behalf of a client who has given you specific instructions. You have an obligation to do as well as you can for your client, and you are not permitted to violate the instructions.

When the market opens, at the signal of the teacher, you may proceed to carry out your order. Buyers will be identified by a (red) and sellers by a (white) instruction card. A transaction is completed when a single buyer and a single seller agree on the terms of a sale. As soon as you complete a transaction, report to the teacher so that he may record and report your transaction. As soon as your transaction is reported, you should turn in your buy or sell order and receive a new one of the same kind. You may proceed immediately to complete a new transaction in accordance with your new order. If you are unable to complete a transaction within ten minutes, you may obtain a new order from your teacher.

When the market is closed, the teacher will determine and report whether the buyers or sellers have represented their clients more successfully.

The Case Study

Students are divided into buyers and sellers and given copies of the general instructions. One teacher, A, takes responsibility for distributing the buy and sell instructions and the other, B, records the prices at which transactions occur. Before starting the case, it is useful to run through the instructions verbally with students, stressing the importance of keeping to the rules and of acting in the best interest of their clients.

Once the game has started, students are free to circulate and make purchases and sales at any time, provided these are consistent with their client's instructions. On completion of a sale, it is reported to teacher B, who records it on the blackboard or the overhead projector, and announces the price. The two students concerned then give their old instructions to teacher A and receive replacements.

Some of the buy and sell orders should be retained initially and given out when instructions are returned. So that students will not know which transaction a particular order was used in, the instructions should be shuffled from time to time. This process minimises fluctuations in market conditions, although some shifts will inevitably be caused by the lag in reporting the sales and feeding orders back into the market.

After a short period of transactions at widely scattered prices, the market moves rapidly towards the equilibrium. In Table 32.2 a typical distribution of transactions over the range of possible prices is shown. It will be noticed that the prices which occur most often are clustered around the equilibrium price, which is what we would expect given our supply and demand functions.

It will be found that students take their roles seriously, bargain vigorously and are keen to know whether buyers or sellers have best represented the interests of their clients.

One way of following up the game is to ask students

Price (p)	Number of transactions
260	1
250	–
240	1
230	–
220	6
210	1
200	15
190	25
180	27
170	20
160	16
150	13
140	5
130	1
120	3
110	1
100	1

Table 32.2   Distribution of transactions

to discuss the differences between their market and that specified in the perfect competition model. Given the background provided by the case, students are more able to evaluate the importance of such influences as information, factor mobility and product homogeneity in the market process. Additionally they appreciate why a firm in a perfectly competitive market will not deviate from the going price.

Problems of Application

If many students complete transactions at about the same time, teacher A may become surrounded by students all clamouring for new orders. This disorder can be minimised by arranging the furniture so as to separate buyers and sellers wanting new orders.

Some students will, of course, have received instructions which cannot be met at the market price. It is to prevent such students from cheating so as to remain in the market that it has been found useful to allow an order to be replaced if no transaction is possible within ten minutes. To improve motivation and reduce cheating, every opportunity, including the wording of the buy and sell instructions, should be taken to stress the importance and nature of the broker relationship.

Variants

All the transactions for a ten-minute period can be recorded on a separate section of the blackboard or the projector. This enables students to see the changing distribution of prices over time, and tends to speed the movement towards equilibrium price.

A change in the equilibrium price can be introduced by having a further set of buy and sell instructions based on a shift in the supply or demand function. These can be introduced into the case at an appropriate stage, one or both of the original sets of instructions being withdrawn. If this is done, the new instructions should be colour-coded so as to avoid accidentally reintroducing an instruction from the previous supply and demand functions.

33   An Oligopoly Game*

R. Helm

The oligopoly situation lends itself less readily to diagrammatic representation than do the other market forms in the theory of the firm. It is less a study of individual firms than a study of interaction between firms. Students will better appreciate the strategies involved in this interaction once they understand the interaction process itself. The game described below allows them to experience this, and may thus be found suitable for use early on in the discussion of oligopoly.

* This game is an expanded version of 'The Oligopoly Game' by Myron L. Joseph, first published in *Role Playing and Case Studies in Economics*, (Macmillan, 1971).

Each student requires paper on which to record his pricing decisions (in the form indicated), a copy of the game instructions and either a Game A or a Game B profit outcome chart. Both games consist of two parts. The students need not know initially of part two, and should only be supplied with part two information once a stable position is reached in part one with their group. Part two information *complements* that of part one. The teacher should be free to regulate the game, issuing part two to the groups as necessary.

Instructions for the Game

Introduction – Oligopoly
In an oligopolistic market the total output is produced by a few large firms. Each individual firm must make pricing and output level decisions. The implementation of these decisions by, for example, firm X will not only affect the sales of firm X but also the sales of other firms in the market. Similarly the pricing decisions of other firms will affect the sales of firm X.

The result is that firms are sensitive to the pricing policies of other firms in the market, and continuous interaction takes place.

Aim of the Game
1 To demonstrate the potential instability of an oligopolistic situation.
2 To indicate the possible benefits to firms in endeavouring to stabilise the market.
3 To lead to a discussion of how the market might be stabilised by the firms in theory and in practice.

Play
Students are arranged in groups of three (Game A) or two (Game B). Thus, running both games at once, any number of students may be accommodated.

Each student acts as an individual firm. Each group represents an industry consisting of identical firms in oligopolistic competition.

The students study the profit possibilities resulting from alternative pricing policies. The price options are high (H) or low (L) in Game A, and high (H), medium (M) or low (L) in Game B. Each firm makes and records a price option for the first month having regard to what other firms in the market may do. The decisions must be concealed until all in the group have been recorded. When all firms in the group have recorded a price, the decisions are revealed and the monthly profits/losses each firm has earned by its price decision are read off the profit outcome chart and recorded by the firm.

The procedure is repeated for the second month, then the third, etc until the game is halted.

Objective
To maximise average profit, i.e. profit per month. The winner is the student who most successfully achieves this objective.

Background Information on the Game
The simplifying assumption of constant average variable costs has been made. As is normal in the theory of the firm, all output is assumed sold (i.e. output=sales).

The profit figures are calculated on the basis that each firm has fixed costs of £1000 and variable costs of 20p per unit of output. Revenues are total sales times price and profits are revenues minus costs.

Summary:

	Game A	Game B
Fixed costs	£1000	£1000
Variable costs	20p/unit	20p/unit
Prices	H = 80p	H = 80p
	L = 60p	M = 70p
		L = 60p

Game A – Three Firms
Part 1. (Price options: H = 80p, L = 60p)
The chart below indicates all possible combinations of prices amongst the three firms in the market. With each price combination, sales and profits are given for each firm's individual price decision. For example, if two firms in the group opted for low price and one for high the price combination would be HLL, the firm pricing high makes a loss of £400 and each firm pricing low makes a profit of £1000.

Price combination	Price decision	Firm's sales	Firm's profit (£)
HHH	H	3000	800
HHL	H	2000	200
	L	6000	1400
HLL	H	1000	−400
	L	5000	1000
LLL	L	4000	600

Record the game as follows:

Month	Price decision (H or L)	Price combination (HH, HHL, etc)	Your profit (+) or loss (−)
1			
2			
3			
etc			

N.B. Firms may enter into collusive decisions but such arrangements are *not* binding; they may be broken by firms, without warning, at any time.

Part 2. A further price option, very low (VL), is available.
(Price options: H=80p, L=60p, VL=40p)

HHVL	H	0	−1000
	VL	13 000	1600
HLVL	H	0	−1000
	L	2100	−160
	VL	11 000	1200
HVLVL	H	0	−1000
	VL	6600	320
LLVL	L	2000	−200
	VL	9300	860
LVLVL	L	400	−840
	VL	6500	300
VLVLVL	VL	4500	−100

Game B – Two Firms
Part 1. The operation of the game is as in A.
(Price options: H=80p, M=70p, L=60p)

Price combination	Price decision	Firm's sales	Firm's profit (£)
HH	H	3500	1100
HM	H	2000	200
	M	5500	1750
MM	M	3900	950
HL	H	1500	−100
	L	6500	1600
ML	M	2000	0
	L	6300	1520
LL	L	4300	720

Part 2.
(Price options: H=80p, M=70p, L=60p, VL=40p)

HVL	H	0	−1000
	VL	9200	840
MVL	M	100	−950
	VL	9200	840
LVL	L	400	−840
	VL	9100	820
VLVL	VL	4800	−40

Part one of both games is structured so that firms trying to maximise short term profits will stabilise the market at a uniform low price level. A particular individual in a group may prevent this, preferring the excitement of the unpredictable to a more stable, and profitable, position. In such cases it may be necessary to re-emphasise the profit objective. Alternatively, a group, with long term profits in mind, may successfully collude to establish a stable uniform high price level. In either case the results for the group should be educative.

Once a stable position is achieved in part one, the group should proceed to part two. Whereas in part one there was a stable outcome giving profits, in part two the stable position results in losses. Given sufficient time, however, the firms may readjust to a uniform low price, recognising that while short term profits may be made by a firm in deciding to price very low, the instability thus caused threatens themselves just as much as the other firms in the long term (i.e. once a firm moves away from the uniform low price to very low the next outcome is unpredictable).

Since groups will operate at different speeds it is necessary to make the objective that of maximising average profit per month rather than total profit. This facilitates the determination of a winner but means additional time will be required at the end to calculate averages. Overall timing for the game will obviously depend upon the ability of the students, the extent of debriefing etc, but at least one hour should be allowed. Groups should be encouraged to make at least twenty-five decisions in the game, although regard should be paid to the degree of stability they are achieving and even twice this number may be worthwhile.

Debriefing Points

(a) It is in the interests of the firms to act to stabilise the market whether there is inherent stability or not;
(b) Price wars are to be avoided as leading to unpredictable outcomes;
(c) Total sales figures increase as market prices fall;
(d) The price/sales figures reveal the effect of consumer brand preferences.

Further Discussion:

Price leadership – all firms follow the price changes of one major manufacturer as, for example, prices are pushed up by rising costs.
Non-price competition – advertising, quality differentials (e.g. the automobile market), retailer incentives (e.g. discounts to supermarket chains for product franchise).
Collusion – its advantages and disadvantages and the difficulties involved in sustaining collusive agreements.

34 The Theory of Distribution
A. M. Leake

General Approach

As a topic in sixth form economics courses, the theory of distribution attracts a mixture of interest and dismay from students. The interest is generated by subject matter that is often close to all our hearts, including, as it does, such matters as explaining the level of pay for a particular job, and the distribution of income between individuals. The dismay is occasioned by the terminology, and complications associated with what are essentially straightforward theoretical arguments.

To help students by encouraging their interest, and conquering their dismay, we need to consider the problems posed by the topic and construct a teaching approach to overcome them.

Which 'Theory'?
A first problem is inherent in the title, for often at sixth form level, we are seeking only to explain the behaviour of individual factor markets. This is largely familiar ground, dealing, as it does, with supply, demand, price, elasticity, etc. Certainly, an understanding of individual markets is required before going on to consider the distribution of income between factors at a macroeconomic level, but this more complicated use of the theory is usually only touched upon at sixth form level.

The only problem implied by all this is that, to avoid confusion, the purpose of each stage of the analysis needs to be explicitly presented. This can often by achieved by constructing the analysis in the form of answers to specific questions, such as 'What determines a firm's demand for a factor of production?' or 'How will a man decide to work in one job, rather than the next best alternative?' and eventually, 'What determines the price level of a particular factor of production at a particular time?'

Keeping the teaching structured and purposeful in this way should help to avoid some of the confusions that typically dog this topic. For instance, it will become clear that the conclusions

(a) MRP = MC, and (b) $\dfrac{\text{MP}_L}{\text{MC}_L} = \dfrac{\text{MP}_C}{\text{MC}_C}$,

come in answer to very different questions, i.e. (a) 'Up to what point will it be worth a profit-maximising firm's while to employ any particular factor, other things being equal?', and (b) 'How can a firm produce each output level as cheaply as possible?'

Similarly, the confusion over whether MP theory is built upon an assumption of only perfect competition arises because, while deriving an 'optimum' allocation of resources at national level does require perfect competition in factor markets, explaining the demand for an individual factor input, according to MRP, does not.

Déjà Vu?
The second problem in teaching the theory of distribution is one that is only too familiar to most economics teachers. With a subject which is as 'developmental' as economics, more complicated topics build upon principles encountered at an earlier stage. This characteristic seems to apply especially to the theory of distribution, and, incidentally, to provide one of the main arguments for the topic's inclusion in sixth form courses.

The implication as far as teaching the topic goes, however, is that this is a very mixed blessing. The topic presents an ideal opportunity to test the students' understanding of basic principles, by applying those principles to new problems and practical examples. On the other hand, the topic *can* only be taught to students with a sound grasp of these basic principles. Thus, and as an unrepentant act of 'passing the buck', the reader is referred to a consideration of earlier parts of the syllabus such as:

(a) the concept of 'a supply curve';
(b) the 'process of establishing an equilibrium price';
(c) the 'principle of variable proportions';
(d) the 'distinction between price-setting and price-taking'.

To those students suffering under such a reincarnation of the theory, it will be necessary to relate back to earlier ideas deliberately, and persistently. Thus, it is advisable to construct the whole exposition of the explanation of factor prices as an exercise in standard market analysis – demand and supply functions and curves, elasticities, shifts and moves, and equilibrium price. Building upon this framework, one can consider the complications of price-setting rather than price-taking behaviour, in the goods market, and for buyers and sellers in the factor market.

Finally comes the distinction between transfer earnings and economic rent, built upon a sound understanding of the nature of supply and demand curves, and relating economic rent as a 'suppliers' surplus' to the idea of 'consumer surplus' on the demand side.

Theory at Work

The third problem to be overcome in teaching this topic is perhaps the most difficult of all. While encountered in many areas of the syllabus, it is of particular concern in factor markets. It is that of reconciling the students' everyday knowledge and practical experience with the very different picture proposed in traditional theory. The fact that these markets are so often characterised by non-homogeneity, indivisibility, lack of knowledge, institutionalisation, and blurred distinctions between individual factors tends, understandably, to tempt students into considering theory and practice as two quite different worlds. Certain methods of teaching serve only to foster this distinction, and as Lipsey warns: 'one of the most unfortunate tendencies in the teaching of economics, particularly in Britain, is that of making a clear split between economic theory and applied economics.'[1]

There would seem to be two main ways to prevent this error. The first is in explaining the theoretical principles to present 'alternative conditions' rather than absolute assumptions, so that the full implications of such alternatives appear at each stage. For example, do not 'assume perfect competition', but rather consider 'price-takers' first, then 'price-setters'. This approach may introduce complications at an earlier stage, but it does forestall the ignorance of complications, which is a more irretrievable fault. After all, 'the more simple and absolute an economic doctrine is, the greater will be the confusion which it brings into attempts to apply economic doctrines to practice, if the dividing lines to which it refers cannot be found in real life.'[2] The second way to relate theory and practice is continually to present illustrations of principles from the real world. Students must understand that the principles they are being taught are so basic that even when well disguised, they are always at work in real life. Students must adopt the economist's habit of using terminology, which is, incidentally, rife in the theory of distribution, as shorthand for common sense ideas. Those that never make this transition will rely instead upon the superficial, short-lived security of rote-learnt definitions.

Thus, learning the law of variable proportions in terms of labour and capital – whose definitions are very difficult to apply in the real world – is much less satisfactory than understanding the principle in terms of variable and fixed 'inputs', and illustrating it from everyday experience.

Similarly, the absolute distinction drawn in some sixth form courses between wages theory and industrial relations is less satisfactory than a development from one to the other. Several examples of economic principles at work in the real world will be considered later. For now, let it stand as probably the major problem teachers of the topic will encounter.

As a final and very general point, it must be remembered that economic theory can be tackled in many different ways – algebra, diagrams, formal terminology, common sense etc, and conveyed inside, or outside, the classroom by as many different methods. Each student, as much as each teacher, will probably prefer a different approach, so in the theory of distribution – as in most other areas of economic theory – a variety of approaches is to be recommended.

Teaching the Major Concepts in the Theory of Distribution

Marginal Physical Product

The 'law of diminishing returns' is the fundamental economic principle underlying the whole of the theory of distribution and the theory of costs. It must be well understood. As a theoretical notion it is easy to portray in terms of the standard textbook illustration of marginal and total product from varying quantities of a variable factor. For example, see the extracts from Marshall's *Principles of Economics*[3] in Figure 34.1, Lipsey[4] and Stonier and Hague[5]. It can, however, prove difficult to find real life illustrations because, in practice, measurements are rarely taken either 'at the margin', or with 'all things being equal'!

The Law of Diminishing Marginal Physical Product

[1] An illustration from recorded experiments may help to make clearer the notion of the return to a marginal dose of capital and labour. The Arkansas experimental station (see *The Times*, 18 Nov. 1880) reported that four plots of an acre each were treated exactly alike except in the matter of ploughing and harrowing, with the following result:

Plot	Cultivation	Crop yields, bushels per acre
1	Ploughed once	16
2	Ploughed once and harrowed once	18½
3	Ploughed twice and harrowed once	21⅔
4	Ploughed twice and harrowed twice	23¼

IV, III, 2

This would show that the dose of capital and labour applied in harrowing a second time an acre which had already been ploughed twice gave a return of 1½ bushels. And if the value of these bushels, after allowing for expenses of harvesting, etc. *just* replaced that dose with profits, then that dose was a *marginal* one; even though it was not the last in point of time, since those spent on harvesting must needs come later.

continued overleaf

Figure 34.1 Theory of distribution; extracts from Marshall's Principles of Economics, *1890 (Macmillan, eighth edition, 1959), pp 129, 139, 420, 463*

The Marginal Revenue Productivity Theory of Wages

An arithmetical illustration is given in the following table. Column (2) represents the number of sheep that might probably be marketed annually, together with a due complement of wool, from a large British sheep run if worked by 8, 9, 10, 11 and 12 shepherds respectively. (In Australasia, where men are scarce, land is abundant, and a sheep of relatively small value, there are often less than ten men, except at shearing time, to each 2000 sheep; Sir Albert Spicer in Ashley's *British Dominions*, p 61.) We are assuming that an increase in the number of shepherds from 8 to 12 does not increase the general expenses of working the farm; and that it takes off the shoulders of the farmer as much trouble in some directions, as it imposes in others: so that there is nothing to be reckoned either way on these accounts. Accordingly the product due to each successive additional man, set out in column (3), is the excess of the corresponding number in column (2) over the preceding number in that same column (2). Column (4) is got by dividing the numbers in column (2) by those in column (1). Column (5) shows the cost for shepherds' labour at the rate of 20 sheep per man. Column (6) shows the surplus remaining for general expenses, including farmer's profit and rent.

(1) Number of shepherds	(2) Number of sheep	(3) Product due to last man	(4) Average product per man	(5) Wages bill	(6) Excess of (2) over (5)
8	580	–	72½	160	420
9	615	35	68⅓	180	435
10	640	25	64	200	440
11	660	20	60	220	440
12	676	16	56⅓	240	436

As we move downwards the figures in (3) constantly diminish; but those in (6) increase, then remain without change, and at last diminish. This indicates that the farmer's interests are equally served by hiring 10 or 11 men; but that they are less well served by hiring 8, or 9, or 12. The eleventh man (supposed to be of *normal* efficiency) is the marginal man, when the markets for labour and sheep are such that one man can be hired for a year for the price of 20 sheep. If the markets had put that hire at 25 sheep, the numbers in (6) would have been 380, 390, 385 and 376 respectively. Therefore that particular farmer would *probably* have employed one less shepherd, and sent less sheep to market; and among many sheep farmers there would *certainly* have been a large proportion who would have done so.

VI, I, 7

On the other hand, services which land renders to man, in giving him space and light and air in which to live and work, do conform strictly to the law of diminishing return. It is advantageous to apply a constantly increasing capital to land that has any special advantages of situation, natural or acquired. Buildings tower up towards the sky; natural light and ventilation are supplemented by artificial means, and the steam lift reduces the disadvantages of the highest floors; and for this expenditure there is a return of extra convenience, but it is a diminishing return. However great the ground rent may be, a limit is at last reached after which it is better to pay more ground rent for a larger area than to go on piling up storey on storey any further; just as the farmer finds that at last a stage is reached at which more intensive cultivation will not pay its expenses, and it is better to pay more rent for extra land, than to face the diminution in the return which he would get by applying more capital and labour to his old land.

But building land does give a diminishing return of convenience as increased capital is spent on it.

IV, III, 8

The Principle of Equal Net Advantage

Thus then the attractiveness of a trade depends on many other causes besides the difficulty and strain of the work to be done in it on the one hand, and the money-earnings to be got in it on the other. And when the earnings in any occupation are regarded as acting on the supply of labour in it, or when they are spoken of as being its supply price, we must always understand that the term earnings is only used as a short expression for its 'net advantages.' We must take account of the facts that one trade is healthier or cleanlier than another, that it is carried on in a more wholesome or pleasant locality, or that it involves a better social position; as is instanced by Adam Smith's well-known remark that the aversion which many people have for the work of a butcher, and to some extent for the butcher himself, raises earnings in the butchers' trade above those in other trades of equal difficulty.

The attractiveness of a trade depends not on its money-earnings, but its net advantages,

Of course individual character will always assert itself in estimating particular advantages at a high or a low rate. Some persons, for instance, are so fond of having a cottage to themselves that they prefer living on low wages in the country to getting much higher wages in the town; while others are indifferent as to the amount of houseroom they get, and are willing to go without the comforts of life provided they can procure what they regard as its luxuries.

subject to differences between individuals,

VI, III, 8

Nevertheless, memorable and realistic examples can be constructed in a number of ways:

1 A classroom game, involving as many complex productive processes and as much different fixed equipment as possible, can provide a vivid and pertinent exhibition of both division of labour and diminishing returns to labour. However, since students are notoriously capable of 'irrational' economic behaviour, teachers must beware of results that are (a) wrong, (b) forgotten in the general ribaldry.

2 For imaginative students, it may prove more suitable to describe a credible – or indeed incredible – example. This also has the merit of showing exactly *how* increasing and decreasing returns come about. For example, consider the situation of window cleaners, cleaning windows on a housing estate. More and more can join the team, bringing all their own equipment, *except* ladders. There is only one ladder for the whole team.

As the first two or three workers join the team, they can employ division of labour, until the best combination of factors is achieved. Possibly this will be with one man working on the ladder, cleaning upstairs, and another supporting the ladder turn and turn about, while a third man cleans downstairs. Adding more and more cleaners will yield diminishing returns, with cleaners knocking each other off the ladder, etc. For the less imaginative, a film might do just as well, but at some expense.

Notice, in all these illustrations, how it must be made clear that diminishing returns to the variable factor occur only because of the fixed amount of at least one other factor.

The Derivation of Marginal Revenue Product

If students are to understand why the MRP curve is the firm's demand curve for a factor, they must be able to derive it from its constituent parts (marginal physical product and marginal revenue). At a deeper level, if they are to predict shifts in this demand curve, and understand what determines the elasticity of that demand, they must be able to think in terms of this relationship.[6]

The three graphs concerned (see Figure 34.2) can be intimately connected, with axes in common, in a way

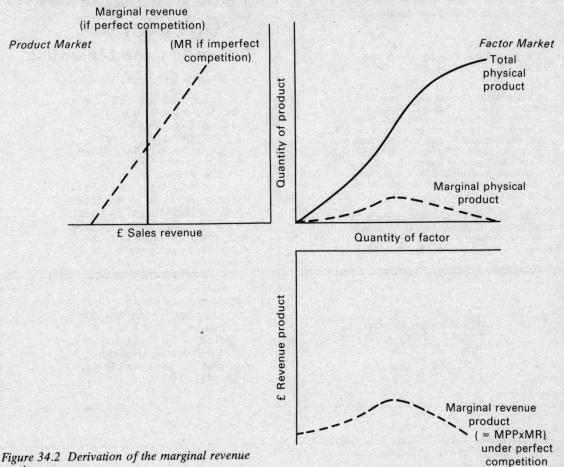

Figure 34.2 Derivation of the marginal revenue product curve

which the best students will implicitly grasp. For general consumption, however, it may prove useful to relate the three familiar graphs directly – as shown in Figure 34.2. With this framework, the differences can be traced between selling under perfect or imperfect competition, or the changes caused by increased productivity, or whatever.

With the added scope offered by an overhead projector, these alternatives can be superimposed upon the same diagram, to great effect.

The Principle of Equal Net Advantage and Disadvantage

This can be illustrated for most factors quite convincingly. In the case of labour, where students probably feel the most immediate impact, they can list the monetary and non-monetary advantages of alternative jobs, and build up the supply curves to different markets. Two examples of this approach are shown (see Figures 34.3 and 34.4).

In capital markets, where the monetary gains from investment have to cover the risk and the length of a loan, there is an opportunity for role playing. Some students propose investment projects, with the security they can offer, and others act as bank managers taking and explaining decisions on whether to grant the loan, at how much above base rate.

The financial sections of the Sunday press provide many suitable case studies – success stories and failures – for this type of exercise.

SALES DIRECTOR

c. £10,000 per annum

The Canned Goods Division of Lovell & Christmas Limited, a major subsidiary of the Fitch Lovell Group, is seeking a Sales Director.

Based at the Divisional Head Office in Liverpool, the successful applicant will be responsible to the Managing Director for the continuing profitable development of the Company's canned food products in the U.K., and must be able to clearly demonstrate a successful record of achievement in this field. Candidates (male or female) should ideally be within the age range of 35-45 years, with broadly based experience of sales and marketing management.

Salary will be negotiable and will reflect the importance of the position. Other benefits include, Company Car, Contributory Pension, Life Assurance Scheme, B.U.P.A., etc.

Please apply in writing, giving details of your career to:

The Managing Director,
Lovell & Christmas Limited,
Belle Vale Road,
Gateacre,
LIVERPOOL L25 2PF.

BWADD DATBLYGU CYMRU WLEDIG
DEVELOPMENT BOARD FOR RURAL WALES

Director

Promotion and Marketing

from £8,500

The Board requires a senior executive responsible direct to the Chief Executive for

- promotion of economic growth within Mid Wales
- attraction of industry to Mid Wales.

The Board is concerned with the economic and social develop-ment of Mid Wales. The post offers opportunities to apply a wide range of experience in industrial development and promotion.

Full details may be obtained from Secretary,
Development Board for Rural Wales;
Ladywell House, Newtown,
Powys, SY16 1JB.
(Tel: 0686 26965).

Applications should be received not later than Friday, 27th May, 1977.

Figure 34.3 Question: *Assuming that you are equally well qualified for, and have been offered both jobs, list all the points you would have to consider in choosing between them*

Reasons for Emigration	
Reasons for emigrating	Percentage mentioning
Low status for scientists in United Kingdom	14.1
Science in United Kingdom is demoralised	
Britain frustrating and depressing	12.5
Lack of facilities in United Kingdom	10.4
Dissatisfied with conditions (of scientific work) in United Kingdom	17.5
Greater professional opportunities in North America	38.6
Low salaries in United Kingdom	6.2
Higher salaries in North America	18.0
Higher standard of living in North America	10.6
Higher social standing of scientists in North America	6.5

Source: *The Brain Drain*
Cmnd 3419, HMSO, 1967

Last week's news that Hoover is to expand at Merthyr Tydfil, creating 3500 new jobs, brought dismay to the coal board. Hoover's will be a magnet. Miners will compare the advantages of a surface job with their dirty, dangerous and, in their view, underpaid life underground. The labour shortage is making life harder for colliery managers. They have to deploy their men like an army, ensuring that there are full teams of face workers to operate costly and sophisticated gear, and teams to supply them and to keep the workings safe.

The shortage of men is also a key part of the issue of absenteeism. On average in South Wales about a fifth of the mining work force do not turn up. There always has been an absenteeism difficulty in the coal industry. It is a complex and frequently misunderstood one. People in the industry say fairly that absence is a fact of national working life at all levels; the mining industry discusses it openly.

In many surface jobs men may go to work with injuries or minor ailments. But a miner who is less than fit is a hazard.

It all comes back to the conditions of mining. Men will endure them in the main when they find comradeship, achievement, involvement and high wages. Without those factors, morale sags, absenteeism increases, production falls, men leave and pits close.
Source: *The Times* 25 October 1973

Figure 34.4 Question: *Compare the advantages and disadvantages from employment that are of concern to scientists, and miners, respectively*

Economic Rent
The concept of economic rent is one that many students are tempted to learn in terms of a diagram or a standard definition, rather than to understand fully. By presenting the concept in different disguises, the teacher may help students to recognise it in any context.[7]

With labour we can consider the earnings of particular individuals, to assess their transfer earnings and economic rent payment. In terms of profit, students who have grasped the distinction between 'normal' and 'supernormal' profit will quickly identify these payments as transfer earnings or rent accruing to the factor of production, enterprise.

Finally, there are several useful applications of the concept when considering the effects of taxation in factor markets, invoking the disincentive effects that are of such concern to politicians, wage-earners, and economists alike.

The Theory of Capital
The marginal productivity theory of distribution has been challenged on many grounds, but perhaps more intensely over capital than any other of the factors. At sixth form level, the severe complications to do with the indivisibility and non-homogeneity of the capital stock, and the difficulty of distinguishing between loan capital and risk capital, should certainly be acknowledged, but that is about as far as it is possible to go.

Instead of constructing a marginal revenue product curve for all capital, it is more practical to take the closely related approach that business enterprises adopt each day, that is, to assess the merits of each particular investment project, so as to construct a collective demand curve for liquid capital.

To calculate DCF, the two main principles involved are quite simply (a) comparing costs and returns to assess profitability, and (b) discounting sums over time to allow for the cost of alternatives foregone. Confusions arise for two reasons: the first is that compound interest rates, rather than simple proportions, have to be calculated; the second that in order to compare thousands of projects simultaneously the conventional discounting approach is turned on its head. In fact, the same assessment of costs and returns goes on, but the particular rate of discount that balances them is taken as a measure of profitability.

From a teaching point of view, it is of concern that these complications mask the underlying marginal revenue product principle, and a much simplified exercise is greatly to be preferred. See the example in Figure 34.5.

A most satisfactory way to overcome the calculation problems, for the privileged teachers who have both the facilities and workforce available for such a project, is to do again as firms do, and construct a computer programme. The print-out from just such an exercise is shown in Figure 34.6.

Three Applications of the Theory of Distribution to Labour Markets

The applications suggested here are all from the labour market. This is partly because students relate most

Calculating the DCF Rate of Return on a Project: a Simple Example

Project:
Cost, now, is $90.
Return, at the end of one year, is $100.

Comparison with one alternative:
This is generally straightforward. Suppose the alternative is to invest the money, instead, in a deposit account paying 5% per annum (simple interest, at end year). Then depositing the $90 would bring $94.50 at the end of the year – less than the return from our project.

Comparison with a whole range of projects, some of which have not even been decided yet!
This is the sort of problem that usually faces investors. We need a measure of the profitability of our project ... its Discounted Cash Flow rate of return.

This is the particular rate of discount that makes returns just balance costs.

This project has a return of $100 at the end of one year. Discounting at a rate of 10% (simple interest rate, again) involves subtracting $10. This leaves $90, which just balances the cost of the project.

The DCF rate of return of the project is 10%, and this rate can now be compared with the rates on *any* number of other projects, to choose those that are profitable, or the most profitable.

Cautions:
These calculations will generally be much more complicated, taking returns and costs over several years, and requiring compound interest rates.
The whole exercise can only be as accurate as the original assessment of returns from the project.
Any change in the assessment of returns, due to changes in 'business expectations', will change the profitability, and DCF figure for every project.

Figure 34.5

```
RUN
WHAT IS INITIAL COST OF INVESTMENT?1000
YEARLY EXPECTED RECEIPTS(-1 IF CHANGING)        ?250
LIFE OF INVESTMENT              ?5

YEAR              ACTUAL        EXPECTED      MULTIPLIER      ACTUAL
                  COST          RECEIPTS      AT 7.931        YIELD
   0              1000
   1                            250           .926518         231.629
   2                            250           .858436         214.609
   3                            250           .795356         198.839
   4                            250           .736912         184.228
   5                            250           .682762         170.69
TOTAL YIELD IS 999.99
BREAK EVEN POINT AT 7.931        %
WHAT IS INITIAL COST OF INVESTMENT?2345
YEARLY EXPECTED RECEIPTS(-1 IF CHANGING)        ?-1
LIFE OF INVESTMENT              ?4
YEARLY RECEIPTS
YEAR 1            ?975
YEAR 2            ?476
YEAR 3            ?876
YEAR 4            ?734

YEAR              ACTUAL        EXPECTED      MULTIPLIER      ACTUAL
                  COST          RECEIPTS      AT 11.896       YIELD
   0              2345
   1                            975           .893687         871.345
   2                            476           .798676         380.17
   3                            876           .713767         625.26
   4                            734           .637884         468.207
TOTAL YIELD IS 2344.98
BREAK EVEN POINT AT 11.896        %
```

Figure 34.6

directly to it, but also, it must be admitted, because it is much harder to find satisfactory documentary material on other factor markets.

1 A test to see how well market forces explain the movements of wages in the labour market, subject, as it is, to major imperfections.[8]

Leading students through this exercise, perhaps presented in the condensed form shown in Figure 34.7, or trying to find similar statistics from a primary source, can prove extremely worthwhile – for a number of reasons.

First, it is a clear introduction to the everyday work of practising economists. Secondly, it shows how economic analysis, model-building and testing can be applied in 'real life'. Thirdly, it involves applying statistical methods to economic data, either at the simplest level, by using scatter diagrams to assess correlation, (as shown in the exercise), or even to the extent of calculating co-efficients of correlation.

Finally, it presents a realistic assessment of the role of the traditional theory of distribution in labour markets – so that students are no longer tempted to accept it uncritically, or to dismiss it out of hand, but rather to apply the theory as and when appropriate.

2 The economic influence of trade unions in labour markets. Trade unions themselves are usually prepared to supply ample material on their aims and activities. This may need careful editing in order to identify the economic, rather than the social or political, principles involved, and to prevent presenting what might amount to classroom recruitment campaigns! The national press will also often offer comment upon suitable issues.

The following extracts show the method, and results, of Reddaway's test to see how well market forces explain wage movements, or whether the labour market is so dominated by imperfections, that only through 'recruiting activity' can employers hope to attract extra labour.

Exercises: After reading the sheet,
(a) Plot the relevant figures from the table on to a graph with the same axes, and 'best-fit line', as graph (1).
Compare the results for 111 industries with those for the 14 industrial groups.
(b) Write a short paragraph to summarise Reddaway's conclusions.
(c) List the main imperfections that might inhibit changes in relative wages within industries.

Manufacturing Industries taken Singly
The first set of data presented relates to the 111 separate manufacturing industries covered by the Ministry of Labour's earnings inquiries.

Employment. The average change in numbers employed was an increase over the five years of 5.3%, but the individual industries showed very great variations – far greater, perhaps, than one might expect from some discussions of the rigidity produced by the welfare state and its full employment pledge. Without taking the individual extreme cases, we can note that 10 industries showed increases of over 30%, and 10 showed *decreases* of more than 15%. If we want a more conservative indicator of the variations, we can say that one-third (37) of the industries showed rises of 9.6% or more, and one-third showed falls of 2.5% or more. Whatever the mechanism, big changes in the distribution of labour were in fact effected.

Hourly earnings. The average increase in hourly earnings over the five years was 42.3% – measured, of course, in money. By comparison with the movements in employment, however, the variations from industry to industry were much smaller. If, as before, we exclude the top and bottom ten, the range is from 33% to 50%; if we exclude one-third at each end, we find that the middle third is in the narrow range from 40.8% to 45.2%.

How far, then, do the biggest increases in employment tend to go with the biggest increases in earnings? The diagram gives a general picture: there clearly is some tendency for this to happen – the points show some tendency to cluster round a line running from the south-west to the north-east. But the association is not very close.

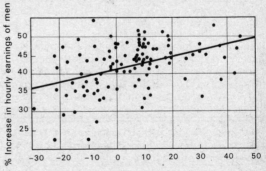

% Change in employment of males
Notes: 1. Each dot represents one industry

2. The line down (regression of y on x) has equation y = 41 5 + 0.165x

3. The aircraft industry had too large an increase in employment (62·3%) to include in the figure; its earnings increase was 52.3%

Percentage changes 1951-56 in employment and hourly earnings in 111 manufacturing industries

Figure 34.7 Extract from Wage Flexibility and the Distribution of Labour, *W. B. Reddaway* (Lloyds Bank Review, *54, 1959) – continued overleaf*

Table 2

Industrial order	Changes 1951–6 in number of males employed	Rise 1951–6 in average hourly earnings of men	
	%	% deviation from average rise	Actual % rise
Vehicles	+18.7	+12.0	47.0
Engineering, shipbuilding, electrical goods	+13.3	+15.9	48.6
Paper and printing	+10.8	+18.0	49.5
Chemicals, etc	+ 9.4	+ 4.4	43.8
Miscellaneous manufacturing	+ 7.8	+ 3.9	43.6
Metal manufacture	+ 5.5	+ 9.4	45.9
Food, drink, and tobacco	+ 5.1	+ 3.9	43.6
Precision instruments, jewellery etc	+ 4.8	+ 2.0	42.8
Bricks, china, glass etc	+ 3.6	− 3.0	40.7
Miscellaneous metals	+ 2.8	+ 5.1	44.1
Wood and cork	− 7.1	−19.4	33.8
Clothing	− 8.2	−15.6	35.4
Textiles	− 8.9	−18.0	34.4
Leather, etc	−17.2	−18.7	34.1
Average	+ 2.87		41.9

Manufacturing Industries by Groups

Before attempting to interpret these results, it is useful to see the picture as it emerges when the various industries are grouped into the 14 industrial orders used in the Standard Industrial Classification (i.e. when we have, for example, a single employment figure for 'textiles', instead of 15 separate ones for cotton spinning, cotton weaving, wool, and so on).

The result is shown in the table, in which the orders have been arranged according to the size of their change in employment. On this basis there is, as was to be expected, a smaller spread of movements in employment, though it is still considerable. The greatest increase shown by a single order is 18.7% (for vehicles), and the biggest fall is 17.2% (for leather,

etc). Without these two extreme cases, the range is from +13.3 to −8.9%. For *earnings* movements the spread is also somewhat reduced, but not very much: without the highest and lowest orders the increases range from 48.6 to 34.1%, which is not much less than we obtained for the individual industries, after cutting out ten at each extremity.

The most striking feature of the results is, however, the much more marked association between the two movements. All the highest increases in earnings come near the top of the table and all the lowest near the bottom. The orders were in fact arranged according to the size of their employment movement, but they are also roughly in the order of their rise in earnings.

Industries within the Groups

In view of the pictures revealed in the above two sections, it is of importance also to examine the movements in employment and earnings for the industries *within* each of the various orders. Unfortunately, this information is not so easy to present in detail, but the general conclusion is clear enough.

The engineering order (more strictly, 'engineering, shipbuilding, and electrical goods') will serve as a good illustration. The 17 industries comprised within this order show a very wide range of employment movements between 1951 and 1956, ranging from three decreases (including one of 17% for textile machinery) to two increases of over 40% (for wireless apparatus, etc, and valves, etc). On the other hand, the *earnings* movements are all grouped within a rather narrow range, from 40.2 to 52.9%; indeed twelve of them fall within the range 45 to 50%. Moreover, statistical analysis shows no real association between the movements. In effect, the industries all have much the same wage-movement but widely different movements in employment; and there is no significant tendency for such variations in wage-movement as there are to be associated with variations in the same direction for employment.

The other orders do not all show quite such clear-cut results, and many of them have too few industries within them to permit much of a conclusion. Nevertheless, it is a fair general summary to say that within an order the wage-movements are usually fairly similar, and that the association between wage-movements and employment movements is negligible.

A project on trade unions can illustrate their monopolistic behaviour in restricting supply, and trying to make the demand for their labour less elastic, as well as introducing wider issues.

The example in Figure 34.8 shows the type of stimulus material that can be prepared, in this case concentrating upon the question of shifts in the marginal revenue product curve.

3 The issue of 'equal pay'. There is plenty of source material in papers, pamphlets and official reports. Yet again, this must be employed with discrimination if the economic principles involved in the issue are to surface.

The example shown here (Figure 34.9) is particularly suitable for illustrating the influence of demand and supply upon women's wages, and could be used to lead on to a wider discussion of the issues involved.

Productivity Bargaining

A productivity bargain is essentially an agreement to pay higher wages in return for specific changes in working practices which lead to higher productivity.

Any change in an established practice can be the subject of a bargain as, for example, a change in the method of shift working; driving a passenger service vehicle and collecting fares by a single operative; or reducing the time taken on a job to eliminate overtime. It is for this reason difficult to lay down more than very general principles.

Here are five general principles:

1 *Saving labour*
The workers must be given a substantial share of the savings in the form of higher wages and better working conditions. There must be guarantees against redundancy and loss of job status, with re-training opportunities as necessary.
2 *When increases in productivity cannot be accurately estimated*
The trade unions set as a minimum basis a 33 per cent increase in earnings for transfer from time rates of working to piece rate intensity. The changes involved in a productivity deal, especially one that has involved a thorough study of the work process, should certainly be no smaller.
3 *Piece-work abandoned*
Employers often call for the ending of incentive working as part of a productivity bargain. They propose to bring in schemes like measured day work or high day rates as an alternative. By such an arrangement the advantages mentioned above will be lost. Such changes need to be compensated not only by higher wages, but by careful safeguards for the role of the trade union representatives in the workplace.
4 *No exclusion of other forms of negotiations*
Some employers assume that a productivity bargain makes any other type of wage negotiation inadmissible. This is unacceptable. Wages are influenced not only by factors internal to a firm. They respond to outside influences – the price level, wages in other firms, and so on. These outside influences may create the conditions for a further change.

Questions

1 Illustrate with a supply and demand diagram of the market for 'passenger service vehicle operatives,' the effect upon equilibrium wages and employment, of the introduction of single-operative working methods.
2 Under what circumstances will a productivity agreement cause (a) an increase, (b) a decrease, in employment opportunities?
3 Give three examples of jobs where you would expect that labour's Marginal Revenue Product 'cannot be accurately estimated.'
4 What are the economic arguments that explain why trade unions are so concerned to 'protect the role of their representatives in the workplace'?
5 Construct two supply and demand diagrams to help you explain the effect on equilibrium wages and employment, of a particular firm's labour market, if:

(a) there is an increase in the price level at which the final product produced by that firm is sold;
(b) there is an increase in wages offered by another firm competing for the same labour source.

Figure 34.8 Extract from a TGWU education and training pamphlet, The Union in Action; What it Does, How it Works *(March 1972)*

References

1 Lipsey, R. G., (see Resources), p xiv.
2 Marshall, A., *Principles of Economics*, (Macmillan, eighth edition, 1959), p viii.
3 Ibid., pp 129, 139.
4 Lipsey, op. cit., p 220.
5 Stonier, A. W. and Hague, D. C., (see Resources), p 273.
6 Lipsey, op. cit., pp 348–53.
7 For applications, and implications, of economic rent and transfer earnings, see Lipsey, op. cit., pp 369–74.
8 Reddaway, W. B., (see Resources).

Resources

Textbooks
Most basic textbooks cover this section of the sixth form syllabus, and several explain it clearly, thoroughly and accurately. Not all sources manage to overcome the problems considered earlier, however, and teachers need to recommend sources to their students with special care. The following can be treated with confidence:

Donaldson, P., *Economics of the Real World*, (Penguin, 1973), chapter 14. An excellent introduction to the topic, and one that is welcomed by students for its straightforward, readable style. Unfortunately, some tend to underestimate its content, and miss the qualifications and references that make the argument theoretically watertight. It will be especially useful to courses in other than main-stream economics, and in 'A' level courses as an introduction to more difficult sources, or to the discussion of issues involving the distribution of income that the book itself leads on to.

Lipsey, R. G., *Positive Economics*, (Weidenfeld and Nicolson, fourth edition, 1975), part 5. A com-

Women are walking into the future backwards. The last 20 years have seen dramatic increases in the number of women working; even in the 1970s despite growing unemployment, this number has kept rising. Legislation – in the form of the Equal Pay Act and the Anti-Discrimination Act – now provide at least potentially effective weapons against the raw deal which women have traditionally received at work. Despite these advances, however, most women remain deeply committed to a traditional view of themselves. They still seem anxious not to offend either the male ego or their own sense of the proper sexual order of things.

A National Opinion Poll specially conducted last weekend for the *Sunday Times* reveals the extent of this conservatism:

Three-quarters of working wives say that if unemployment gets worse, men should take priority over women in the job market;

Only 57 per cent of working wives would accept promotion involving more responsibility, compared with 81 per cent of men;

Even at a time when living standards are falling, three-quarters of working wives say their families could manage if they did not work;

Almost 90 per cent of both husbands and wives believe that housework should be shared – yet a large majority of wives willingly accept that they do far more than their husbands;

In one important respect attitudes have changed since 1971. Then, two out of three working wives considered themselves mainly as 'housewives with a job'. Today, almost half regard themselves first as 'working women who also run a home'.

In order to discover how husbands and wives have responded to the recent expansion of women's legal rights, NOP last weekend interviewed a quota sample of 422 working wives, 393 non-working wives, and 412 married men. NOP last surveyed attitudes on this subject six years ago.

Since then there have been substantial social and economic changes. The birth rate has fallen by more than a quarter.

Women today form a higher proportion of the workforce than ever before – 40 per cent. In the last six years their wage rates have risen one third faster than men's. Even so, women are caught in a vicious circle.

Their actual earnings and conditions are much worse than men's. In April 1976 the average weekly pay for full-time women was only £46, compared with £72 for men. And 43 per cent of women against 5 per cent of men earned less than £40.

But low pay and poor prospects are no guarantee of militancy. In 1971 only one third of women workers were in unions, though the number is rising and women are slowly developing the habit of voicing their discontents.

Underlying the different approaches to work by men and women is the continuing but anachronistic way families divide responsibility. The idea that a woman's work is secondary – to her family, if not to the economy – persists, and inevitably depresses women's wages. Women are not *expected* to earn a living wage.

Table 1

How necessary to the family budget are the earnings of working wives?

The only or main wage in the family	5%
Could not manage without her earnings	23%
Would have to cut down on luxuries without her earnings	51%
Would not be greatly affected by stopping work	14%
Would not be affected at all by stopping work	8%

Table 2

Do you think of yourself primarily as a housewife who has a job or as a working woman who also runs a home?

	Working wives 1971	1977
A housewife who has a job	67%	53%
A working woman who also runs a home	28%	43%
Don't know	4%	3%

Source: The *Sunday Times*, February 27th 1977

Figure 34.9 Equal pay. Question: *In terms of supply and demand, women's wages are generally lower than men's for any of these three reasons: (a) they enter a limited range of jobs in great numbers; (b) their productivity in any work they enter is lower than men's; (c) they are being exploited by monopsonistic employers in a way that men are not. Assemble the evidence, from the extracts below, for each of these three views*

prehensive and precise exposition of the standard theory. It may seem rather daunting to some sixth form students, but, in the case of this topic, should not be neglected.

Stonier, A. W. and Hague, D., *A Textbook of Economic Theory*, (Longman, fourth edition, 1972), chapters 10–16. A textbook that is thorough, reliable, and, in the fourth edition, well laid out. Most suitable for those really wishing to get to grips with the topic. The introduction of isoquants may, however, make it a little too ambitious for some courses.

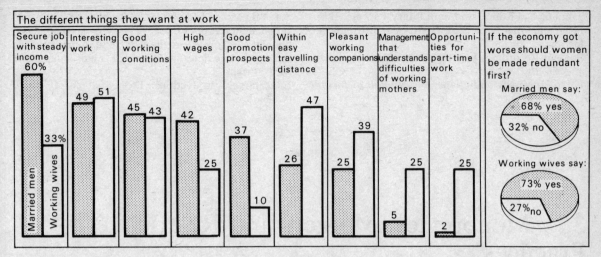

Figure 34.9 – continued

Harvey, J., *Intermediate Economics,* (Macmillan, third edition, 1976), section V. A more moderately paced, and less expansive explanation of the theory, that will therefore be suitable for the less high-powered sixth form student.

Nevin, E., *An Introduction to Microeconomics,* (Croom Helm, 1973), part 5. A heavily mathematical treatment of the topic, which will establish the theory more convincingly and quickly for those who can understand it.

Owen Smith, E., 'Income Distribution and its Place in the Sixth Form Curriculum', *Economics,* Spring 1977, 13(1). Most useful as a source of references. Notice that Pen, J., *Income Distribution* (Penguin, 1974) which was so strongly recommended in this article, went out of print in 1976.

King, J. E., *Labour Economics,* (Macmillan, 1972). A concise survey of the theory of labour economics, at an advanced level, but one that is more suitable for use by sixth form students than some others in the same series.

Applications
Most of the copies of multiple choice questions, data response questions and case studies published to supplement 'A' level courses have sections on the theory of distribution.

Unfortunately, it is difficult to find examples that illustrate directly the main economic principles underlying the topic. Teachers can make up some of this gap themselves, as suggested earlier, but otherwise a few suitable sources are especially valuable:

Turvey, R., *Demand and Supply,* (George Allen and Unwin, 1971), chapters 7 and 10. This provides applications of the theory to explain the earnings of laundry workers, contract cleaners, temporary secretaries, and university teachers; and the price of urban space.

Livesey, F., *Data Response Questions in Economics* (Polytech Publishers, 1976). It is one of the virtues of data response questions that they break across the standard categories of the syllabus, but here there are several questions that involve applications of the theory of distribution, especially in sections A and E.

Norris, W. K., 'Differentials in Pay', *Lloyds Bank Review,* October 1975, 118, p 27.

Reddaway, W. B., 'Wage Flexibility and the Distribution of Labour', *Lloyds Bank Review,* (1959), pp 32–48, reprinted in McCormick, B. J. and Owen Smith, E. (ed.), *The Labour Market* (Penguin, 1968, now out of print).

Powicke, J. C., Iles, D. J. and Davies, B., *Applied Economics* (Edward Arnold Ltd, 1972, now out of print), chapter 3. A brief exposition of the role of MRP in explaining wages, followed (pp 31–8) by applications of that analysis to teaching, acting, collective bargaining, etc.

It is important to remember, with all these applications, that, while the particular data involved become out of date, the general economic principles which they are being used to demonstrate do not.

Films, Tapes, etc
Training and Education Film Library, *Factor Incomes,* derives MRP curve, standard exposition, (16″, 900 8084–1).
Training and Education Film Library, *Population and Economic Growth,* (23″, 900 8100–8), Malthus, law of diminishing returns, production techniques in developing countries.

Training and Education Film Library, *Income: Where From and What For?*, (25″, D101 4), redistribution of income.
Student Recordings Ltd, tape/filmstrip, *Rent, Interest and Profits*.
Open University audio tape, *Distribution of Income*, (D101 06/12).

Audio Learning Ltd, tape, *The Problem of Wages* and supplementary booklet (1971). The accompanying booklet contains an excellent, concise summary of the theory of wage determination that is most valuable in its own right!
Educational Productions Ltd, one chart, *Profit* (C1243).

35   Monopolies, Mergers and Restrictive Practices
Brinley Davies

Introduction

The teacher new to this subject may well decide to use a narrative approach: 'In the 1930s and 1940s there was growing evidence of monopoly in the UK ... in 1948 the Monopolies Commission was set up ... in 1956 the Restrictive Practices Court ... a spate of mergers in the 1960s ...' and so on. One drawback is that this is rather boring, both for the student and the teacher. Another is that in the 'A' level examinations, particularly the data response section, the examiner may call for a 'slant' which is decidedly non-narrative.

Can monopolies policy be taught in a way which whets the analytical appetites of the students? Below is one approach which can be used as early as the second term in the sixth form, with students who have learned about economies of scale and the theory of the firm.

1 Revision of the Theoretical Case For and Against Monopoly

This part of the teaching sequence is intended to kill two birds with one stone. It provides useful reinforcement of the theory of the firm, and it introduces the theoretical background to monopolies policy.

The class is presented with an unlabelled cost diagram of an *industry* operating in conditions of perfect competition (Figure 35.1).

First the students are required to label the two curves, fill in the long-run equilibrium output OQ and price OP, and insert the market demand line in its correct position (Figure 35.2).

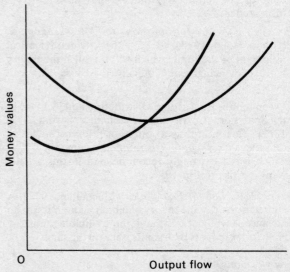

Figure 35.1

They are next asked to imagine that the multitude of firms in the industry are somehow instantly reconstituted into a unified monopoly, which sets about maximising its profits. The point here, of course, is that DD now becomes the monopoly's average-revenue line. Students will already have been taught the relationship between straight-line average and marginal revenue lines. They are now asked to draw in the marginal revenue line and mark the monopoly output OQ_m and price OP_m. We now have the following 'all-in' diagram (Figure 35.3).

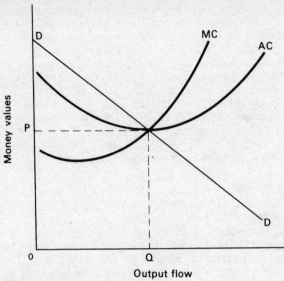

Figure 35.2

The theoretical case against monopoly is graphically explicit: restricted output, higher cost and price, and too large a profit.

Lastly students are reminded of the case *for* monopoly, namely that it may allow, through economies of scale, a lower cost structure. Consumers of the product may then face a price which is less than that which would rule under perfect competition. It is important for the students to realise, however, that it may be possible to reap the economies of scale without turning the industry into a monopoly; this depends on the type of economy of scale available and the size of the indus-

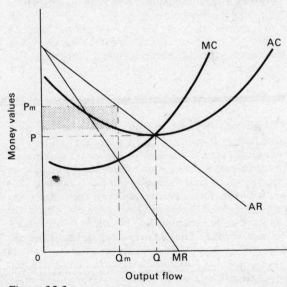

Figure 35.3

try. That is, it might be possible for a firm to reap all the economies and still only have, say, one-tenth of the industry's output. Galbraith's[1] view – that firms may need to expand beyond the 'optimum size' in order to plan future output policies – also needs to be considered. In essence then there is no theoretical proof that monopoly is necessarily harmful – it depends on 'things done'. The point may also be made that in practice, in an imperfectly competitive economy, the elimination of monopoly in one market may strengthen it in another.

2 Small-group Discussion Work

This part of the teaching sequence takes the form of discussion work in small groups of three to five students, each with its own teacher-appointed chairman who guides the discussion, takes notes of it and later reports back to the whole class.

Question 1 Each group independently discusses the question 'If you were a monopoly how would you protect high profits against potential competitors?'

Groups can be given different situations – a telephone company, a detergent firm, a multi-national pharmaceutical combine, a sweetshop in a village, a camping site proprietor in a busy tourist area.

These discussions are intended to elicit the significance of:

1 Natural entry-barriers (e.g. octopoid industries, control of a localised raw material, restricted size of market).
2 Artificial practices:
(a) general monopoly practices (e.g. fighting subsidiaries, suppressing competition by tied retail outlets, denying essential equipment to competitors).
(b) cartel restrictive practices (e.g. pooled tenders, gentlemen's agreements on selling areas, boycott sanctions on recalcitrant firms).

After a 'report-back' and class discussion, students are referred to textbooks and other sources from which they will shortly write up their own classification in their own time.

The teacher could get the students to draw up a classification based on their pooling of monopoly practices derived from the 'report-back' session, compare this with the textbook categories and discuss the differences.

Question 2 Each group discusses the question 'If you were a government setting up a monopolies policy from scratch, what methods would you adopt for finding harmful monopolies?'

With luck (and we all need that), many of the following points should occur.

1 The difficulty of uncovering a significant number of

monopolies among the thousands of major firms in the economy.

2 The two 'faces' of monopoly: the single-firm monopoly, which may be quite obtrusive; and the shadowy network of practices which constitute a cartel.

3 What criteria should be used for identifying firms worthy of further scrutiny?

(a) per cent share of the market. The 1973 Fair Trading Act reduced this from $33\frac{1}{3}$% to 25%; however 'market' is difficult to define.

Some of the remaining material thrown up by the discussion can be shaped by the teacher into categories which correspond to the provisions of the 1973 Act.

(b) Provisions relating to restrictive practices. The 1973 Act required restrictive agreements affecting goods or services in about one hundred industries to be registered at the Office of Fair Trading. The agreements related to four main areas: arrangements between firms to fix prices or commissions; agreements to standardise terms for customers; agreements between competitors to take orders only of a certain size; and agreements to 'share out' market sectors.

(c) Provisions relating to monopolies and mergers. The Office of Fair Trading has developed a 'screening' approach in terms of four 'conduct' and four 'performance' indicators.[2] The conduct indicators are complaints from firms and consumers, evidence of price dominance, a high ratio of advertising to sales, and high merger activity in the market concerned. The performance indicators are the ratio of capital employed to turnover, return on capital employed, profit margins and changes in relative price levels.

Students may mention:

4 The difficulty of identifying 'too high' a profit:

(a) high risk may justify a high return;

(b) a monopoly may earn low profit because of a 'cosy' high-cost existence;

(c) difficulty of using and interpreting company accounts.

Question 3 'How would you, as a government, deal with an identified harmful monopoly?'

This question should elicit several points, with the teacher contributing illustrations and references:

1 A legal ban on monopolies (the American attitude, which is reflected in the UK's Restrictive Practices Court).

2 Control of monopolies (the traditional German attitude), i.e. either (i) nationalise, or (ii) control indirectly (for example, the Monopolies Commission).

3 Maintain competition: tactical tariff cuts, government contracts to monopolists' rivals, support for small firms (Bolton Committee).

4 'Do nothing' (the teacher may need to suggest this one): Schumpeter's argument that private monopolies invite their own destruction, via the innovating effects of economies of research and growth.[3]

All four types of policy are seen to have drawbacks.

Each group could now consider an actual monopolies investigation, comparing its own assessment with that of the authorities. Or the class could 'act out' a case situation, with one group being the monopoly 'defence', another the 'prosecution' and the remainder of the class the 'judges'. The teacher might see in this an opportunity to introduce in a cartel context the Restrictive Practices Court and the role of the eight gateways and tailpiece.

Question 4 'How would you, the government, react to a spate of mergers among leading firms?'

This may elicit:

1 Motives for mergers: defensive stability through vertical integration; size and prestige; improved efficiency; and monopoly influence.

2 Mergers policy: how to encourage 'efficiency' mergers and deter 'monopoly' mergers. (Or is it better to leave merger decisions to market forces?) The teacher may refer to the 1965 Act; establishment of the IRC in 1966 (it fostered the AEI-GEC electrical merger); the 1975 Industry Act which set up the National Enterprise Board (Norton-Villiers-Triumph).

3 What are the actual after-effects of most mergers? Do they in fact improve efficiency? Often, no.[4]

3 Consolidation of the Learning Process

After the discussion sequence it is necessary for the students to use the above framework to understand and fix in their minds the UK's post-war experience of monopolies policy: the Commission, the Court, the IRC (possibly), the Office of Fair Trading, EEC attitudes, various case studies and so on. The teacher can hive this off for the students to do in their own time, for example, through essays.

It is clearly important that the students should have access to a range of recent case material and, if possible, some specialised books on monopolies (see Resources).

Conclusion: An Appraisal of the Method

The teacher who uses the above approach and finds (one hopes) that it works, should be careful not to over-do it – once a term is probably more than enough. In any case, there are not many areas in the economics syllabus which lend themselves to this treatment. But when this method can be employed there are some useful benefits. It helps to 'thaw out' a quiet class, for shy students are often willing to talk in a small group and may then also later do so in a large group. (This can be useful in a sixth form which collects its members from a number of feeder schools.) Students often find small-group work a refreshing interlude after being subject to what they may feel was a straitjacket of introductory theory in the 'A' level course. It is also satisfying for them to have the opportunity to contribute worthwhile ideas of their own – to be active rather than passive. The students obtain a useful insight into how theory relates to practice. Finally, they are required independently to research, classify and write up material; a foretaste of later study at college or university. From the teacher's point of view, the method is an opportunity to get the class working on its own, while he unobtrusively and selectively monitors and guides its activity.

Could a teacher with, say, a large class of robust students run into discipline trouble with this approach? Possibly; if the class was new and had not yet had time to assimilate enough economics to support the discussion. Apart from this there should not be any difficulties. It would, in any event, be made very clear to the students at the outset that it was entirely their own responsibility to work up the material which would shortly form the basis of their formal written work. The ball is in their court!

References

1 Galbraith, J. K., *The New Industrial State*, (Hamish Hamilton, 1967), chapter 3.
2 Livesey, F., *A Modern Approach to Economics*, (Heinemann Educational, 1977), p 249.
3 Allen, G. C., *Monopoly and Restrictive Practices*, (Allen and Unwin, 1968).
4 Maunder, W. P. J., 'Technical Progress, Competition and Mergers: Some Empirical Evidence for British Competition Policy', *Economics*, 10(4), pp 334–41.

Resources

Allen, G. C., *The Structure of British Industry*, (Longman, 1970). Barker, P. *et al.*, *Case Studies in the Competitive Process*, (Heinemann Educational, 1976), has two cases on the detergent industry and the retail grocery trade.
Blois, K. *et al.*, *Case Studies in Competition Policy*, (Heinemann Educational, 1976).
British Economy Series, (Oxford University Press), Summer 1976, p 7; Spring 1977, p 5, Summer 1977, p 5.
Maunder, W. P. J., 'The Glass Container Industry and the 1956 Restrictive Practices Act', in *Economics*, 9(4).
Monopolies Commission, *Household Detergent*, (HMSO, 1966).
Monopolies Commission, *Breakfast Cereals*, (HMSO, 1973).

Audio Learning Ltd tapes, *Monopoly and Competition; Government Responsibility and Industry*. Also a new cassette/filmstrip pack, *Types of Business Integration*, (ECO 005).
Sussex Tapes, *Monopoly and Competition*, (E9).

36   Industrial Relations
Stuart Luker

General Comments

Industrial relations is likely to be taught to three main categories of student in the sixteen to eighteen range: those following an 'A' level course, those following an 'O' level course and to students as part of additional or complementary studies lessons. For the first two categories of student there are general syllabus constraints which must be considered, and particular attention needs to be paid to the appropriate theoretical background. For students on additional studies courses, detailed analysis is probably inappropriate, but there is more opportunity for wider coverage and the inclusion of material which some teachers may consider to be beyond the scope of an 'A' or 'O' level economics syllabus.

Industrial relations is an area where there is likely to be considerable student interest, and it is important that the teaching methods adopted take advantage of this. There is quite a lot of basic factual material which must be learnt by students taking economics exams, and one way in which this can be made more interesting is to relate it to current industrial relations problems, a number of which are always in the news. However, the temptation to look at industrial relations solely as a current affairs subject, or to deal with it in a purely descriptive way, should be avoided.

A further consideration of general significance that arises from the nature of the topic and its coverage in the media is that the majority of students will start with a number of preconceived ideas, which are unlikely to be based upon objective information or understanding. It would be unrealistic to suggest that there will be a major change of attitude on the part of the student as a result of studying industrial relations practices and problems, but it is important to get them to recognise their own prejudices. A recognition of the fact that industrial relations problems are unlikely to be solved by purely rational analysis is sometimes difficult to get across but it is nevertheless important. Some of the participative exercises suggested are designed to generate 'feeling' in the classroom, and follow-up discussion of what happened can be used to emphasise the role of attitudes. This is an area of the economics course where value judgements play a big part, and it may be worthwhile to look, in a general context, at the relationship between normative and positive economics using this part of the course to illustrate some of the problems of treating economics as a science.

Content

The material has been selected bearing in mind the requirements of most 'A' level economics syllabuses and examinations, but it was not the sole criterion. The following industrial relations topics have been included and it is probable that they would form the major part of any 'A' level economics course: the structure of the trade union movement, employers' organisations, the structure and nature of collective bargaining, industrial disputes, and suggestions for the reform of industrial relations in the UK. Some teachers may also wish to consider incomes policy under the general heading of industrial relations, and although it has not been dealt with as a separate topic in this chapter, some resources have been cited. (See Resources 1, 2, 3, 5, 6, 9, 13, 35, 40.)

Teaching Methods

The Structure of the Trade Union Movement
The usual ways of imparting the necessary information for this part of the course are: by dictation, by the teacher preparing and duplicating a handout for each student, or by giving the students textbook references and asking them to make notes under a number of headings provided by the teacher. It is likely that one or more of these methods will provide the main way of

teaching this section. (See Resources 1, 2, 3, 5, 6, 7, 8, 9, 10, 14 for useful material.) However, these methods can be supplemented by:

1 The construction of a table of statistics by the teacher describing, for example, the number of unions, the total membership of unions and the distribution of membership between unions. The *Annual Abstract of Statistics* will provide this type of data in the form of a ten year series. Questions can then be asked which are designed to enable the student to discover for himself the main trends and important features of the current structure of the trade union movement.

2 Alternatively, the statistical sources may be given, and the students asked to find for themselves answers to questions such as:

(a) What is the total number of unions in the UK?
(b) What is the total number of union members?
(c) What proportion of the working population in the UK are members of a union?
(d) How many unions have less than 1000 members?
(e) What proportion of the total union membership is represented by unions with over 50 000 members?
(f) What has happened to the total number of unions between 1966 and 1976?
(g) What has happened to the total number of union members between 1966 and 1976?
(h) What has happened to the average size of trade unions in the UK over the same period?

Answers to all of the above questions can easily be obtained from the *Annual Abstract of Statistics*, which is likely to be available from most public libraries, and is also a very useful addition to any school library. Answers to questions such as 'How many unions are affiliated to the TUC and what is their total membership?' can be obtained from a variety of other sources. (See Resources 2, 6, 7, 8, 9, 14.)

3 There are also occasionally newspaper or periodical articles on the relevance of the structure of the trade union movement to collective bargaining in the UK. They can be duplicated and given to the student, together with a list of questions, and used as a case study or as a means of stimulating discussion.

4 There are two very useful information sheets which are produced by the TUC and which can be obtained free of charge. They are entitled: *Trade Union Organisation and Structure* and *Facts about the Trade Union Movement* (see Resource 14). They are clear, concise and fairly comprehensive and could be used instead of teacher-produced handouts or dictated notes.

Employers' Organisations
This is only a very small topic and there is not as much information readily available in the basic textbooks as there is for the trade unions. For most courses it will be

necessary to cover briefly the role of the CBI and the national employer organisations, such as the Engineering Employers' Federation. (See Resources 2, 6, 7, 8, 9, 45, 46.)

The Structure and Nature of Collective Bargaining

Again for this part of the syllabus there is some basic factual material which needs to be covered and there are a number of standard texts which deal with it reasonably well. (See Resources 2, 6, 7, 8, 9, 10.) However, the collective bargaining process is particularly suitable for participative exercises of various kinds. Also included in this section is some material designed to illustrate particular industrial relations problems which are likely to be subject to collective bargaining or the procedures which result from collective bargaining.

Role playing exercises. There are some role play situations which are commercially produced, (see Resource 42), but those produced by the teacher have the advantage they can be constructed to meet the teacher's precise requirements. The following example has been used successfully on a number of occasions.

A *Materials: Three duplicated information sheets*
1 General background to the negotiations. This is to be read by both the employer's and employees' representatives.
2 Employer's instructions.
3 Employees' representatives' instructions.

Sheet 1 – General Background to the Negotiations

(i) The firm produces components for the main car producers and is situated in Coventry.

(ii) The workers involved in the negotiations are toolmakers who belong to the AUEW.

(iii) Inflation is at present estimated to be about 17 per cent but the government has predicted that by next year it will fall to about 12 per cent.

(iv) Pay rises and increases in the Retail Prices Index during the past three years have been as follows:

	Percentage wage rise	Increase in RPI
1974	25%	16%
1975	10%	25%
1976	5%	14%

(v) A similar group of workers in Birmingham have recently negotiated a 28 per cent pay rise which includes a productivity deal.

(vi) A local firm that used to employ toolmakers has gone into liquidation.

(vii) The TUC, after agreeing to two years of severe wage restraint, now wish to see a return to free collective bargaining, but have warned of the serious consequences of a wages explosion similar to that which occurred in 1974.

Sheet 2 – Employer's Instructions

(i) You have recently received a very large contract, but as yet neither the employees nor the union are aware of this. The order would keep the firm fully employed for the next eighteen months. However, the contract is conditional upon the delivery dates, which have been specified, being met. The first consignment is due shortly.

The firm has other orders in the pipeline, but should this contract be lost then the firm will be in financial difficulties and redundancies will be inevitable. There is also the risk of bankruptcy should a strike result which lasts for more than a month.

(ii) You would prefer any wage increase to be tied to a productivity deal to help meet the cost of the settlement and to increase output to meet the new order.

(iii) Any payment in excess of 25 per cent will result in bankruptcy unless it is tied to an effective productivity deal. But even with a basic increase of more than 12 per cent profits will be severely squeezed.

Decisions to be made before the negotiations:

(i) Decide upon the wage settlement that you would like and the maximum that you are willing to accept in percentage terms.

(ii) You should also discuss your general strategy and try to anticipate union action under various circumstances.

Sheet 3 – Employees Representatives' Instructions

(i) Your members are somewhat disillusioned with union action over the past couple of years. They have seen a significant decline in their real living standards as a result of wage increases falling behind the rate of increase in retail prices. They may well take unofficial action if they don't receive a substantial increase this year.

(ii) You have heard that your firm has recently received a very large order which will keep the firm busy for the next eighteen months. The employers believe that you are unaware of this secret order.

(iii) You would prefer a straightforward wage increase and are not very keen on productivity deals, because in the long run they tend to lead to a reduction in the number of men employed and hence reduce the number of union members.

Decisions to be made prior to the negotiation:

(i) Decide upon your initial wage demand and the minimum increase that you are willing to accept (in percentage terms).

(ii) Decide upon the general strategy to be adopted during the negotiations. This should include the types of action you are willing to threaten should the employers prove reluctant to agree to your demands.

B *Procedure*

The class should be divided into groups of about six to eight, half of whom are to be employer's representatives and the other half trade union representatives. Alternatively, one group may be used, with the rest of the class as observers. Each member of the group is provided with the 'General Background' information sheet to read carefully, and they should then be asked whether there are any questions. One of the two 'sides' (e.g. the employer's representatives) is then sent away for five to ten minutes whilst the other 'side' are given their own instruction sheet.

The employer's representatives are briefed with the trade union negotiators out of the room, and at this stage time must be allowed for each group to prepare a general strategy before the bargaining session begins. If during the negotiations either side require an adjournment to discuss their position in private, this should be allowed.

A possible extension of the game could be the provision of a conciliator and/or arbitrator who may be used if both parties agree.

The game is fairly open-ended and it is difficult to predict in advance exactly what will happen, but it usually proves an enlightening experience for those involved and provides a basis for follow-up discussion. Reviewing what actually happened is very important. In selecting the students for the various roles it is often worthwhile to choose trade union representatives from those with 'right wing' views and vice versa.

Case studies. Surprisingly there are only a few case studies which are commercially produced. (See Resources 9, 43.) However, the teacher can devise case studies of his own, which may be based upon newspaper or journal articles. For example, there is an article in the *Department of Employment Gazette* (see Resource 19), which is entitled 'Industrial Relations in the Newspaper Industry' and is based upon the ACAS enquiry. This would prove ideal case study material. Similarly the industrial relations section in the *British Economy Survey* of Summer 1977 (see Resource 13) looks at the British Leyland Toolmakers' dispute and this too could be used as a case study.

Industrial relations discussion questions. It is relatively easy for the teacher to make up a number of short examples of possible industrial relations situations which can be duplicated and used as a basis for discussion. They are probably best used with small groups. The following examples are designed to highlight fairly common industrial relations problems.

1 You work for a firm employing 100 men on the factory floor. Ninety-seven of these belong to the union paying a weekly subscription of 40 pence.

(i) You are a member of the union and would like to see the union negotiate a closed shop with the management. Explain why.

(ii) You are one of the non-union members. Explain why you think that a closed shop would be wrong.

2 You are the supervisor responsible for a group of twenty-five men in a factory making shoes. You are on the day shift and it has been a very hot day. At 12 o'clock the shop steward comes up to you and says that at 2.30 the men are going out on an unofficial stoppage. This is likely to disrupt the factory's production. Outline the course of action you would take.

3 You are the Managing Director of a company producing car components, but which is part of a large conglomerate involved in a number of different product markets. Much of your machinery is outdated and needs replacing. Labour productivity is low, which is partly due to the obsolete equipment but also because of restrictive practices and demarcation disputes between unions which have resulted in overmanning. The Finance Director has informed you that he is willing to sanction the finance necessary to re-equip the factory over a period of four years, provided evidence can be provided that productivity can be increased substantially and hence a satisfactory return can be made on the investment. What would you do?

Films. There are some films available which illustrate the collective bargaining process. (See Resources 24, 25.) Films are particularly useful because they help bring a sense of realism into the classroom. Some films are suitable as case study material, (see Resources 23, 24, 25, 33, 35), and they have the added advantage that they involve student participation.

Visiting Speakers. It is usually possible to get speakers from both sides of industry to talk on a variety of industrial relations topics. For students to come into contact with someone with first hand experience of industrial relations problems and collective bargaining has obvious advantages. (See Chapter 24 for general comments on the use of visiting speakers.) (See also Resources 44, 45, 46.)

Industrial Disputes

Many of the methods suggested in the previous section can be used to teach this particular topic. Role-playing exercises, case studies, films and the use of outside speakers are particularly appropriate. Current information and stimulus material can be found in newspapers. Most of the main textbooks on the procedure for settling disputes are out of date, but there are other sources of more current information (see Resources 12a, 15, 16, 19, 45). Once more there is a certain amount of factual material to be absorbed and again questions involving the interpretation of data are one means of supplementing the usual methods. The source of the data for the following questions was the *Department of Employment Gazette*.

Days lost per 1000 people employed. Average for:

	1966–1970	1971–1975	1966–1975
Australia	608	1464	1036
Belgium	314	422	368
Canada	1836	1862	1849
Denmark	64	1006	535
West Germany	12	92	52
Finland	256	1410	833
France	263	342	303
India	1204	1553	1379
Irish Republic	1102	752	927
Italy	1822	1730	1766
Japan	166	328	247
Netherlands	34	90	62
New Zealand	326	384	355
Norway	18	104	61
Sweden	36	62	49
Switzerland	–	2	1
UK	404	1146	775
USA	1500	1173	1337

Table 36.1 Industrial disputes: international comparisons.
Source: Department of Employment Gazette, December 1976.

1 (a) Which of the major industrial countries in Table 36.1 has a better strike record than the UK?
(b) Which of them has a worse strike record than the UK?
2 What reasons would you give for the increase in the average number of working days lost during 1971–75 in the UK?
3 To what extent does the information in Table 36.1 support the claim that one of the most important reasons for the poor economic performance of the UK in relation to the other major industrial countries is due to her poor industrial relations record?

The *Department of Employment Gazette* is a useful source for other data on this topic. Two other examples of relevant statistical series which appear annually are:

(i) A summary of the main causes of industrial disputes in the UK during the previous year.
(ii) A ten year series of the number of working days lost due to industrial disputes.

They are usually accompanied by a short article which provides more detailed analysis.

Suggestions for Reforming Industrial Relations in the UK

Before considering the reform of industrial relations in the UK, it is necessary to highlight the problems. Most of these will have been dealt with previously and by looking at the suggestions for reforming industrial relations in the UK, material that has already been covered can be reviewed.

Recent attempts to reform industrial relations in this country have involved the passing of laws and many teachers would want to consider, at least briefly, some aspects of:

(i) The Donovan Commission Report;
(ii) The 1971 Industrial Relations Act;
(iii) The Employment Protection Act and the Trade Union and Labour Relations Acts passed by the Labour Government.

However, other reforms not included above are also important. Examples include picketing, the right to strike, and the structure of the trade union movement. The teacher may also wish to consider ideas such as worker participation and alternative methods of organising work as a means of improving industrial relations. (See Resources 8, 16d, 17, 31, 32.) Several basic texts include details of industrial relations legislation and suggestions for reform. (See Resources 1, 2, 3, 5, 6, 7, 8, 9, 10.) However, they are often out of date. Newspaper articles are an obvious means of keeping abreast of developments, but there are other sources of current information. (See Resources 12b, 13, 16, 19, 45.)

This section of the course can provide some interesting topics for a formal debate. Alternatively one or more of the students could be asked to give a prepared talk which can provide the stimulus for a fuller discussion of the topic. At this stage most of the students will have sufficient background to make discussion worthwhile. It is also an area where a visiting speaker may well have something interesting and controversial to say.

Other Teaching Methods

There are a number of other methods which can be used to teach industrial relations which have not been mentioned so far. Some of these include:

(a) Topic or project work. This enables the individual student to cover a particular section in more detail than might otherwise be possible.
(b) Pre-recorded tapes. (See Resources 38, 39, 40.) These can be used for individual study or played to a class. If the school has a language laboratory it is possible to use pre-recorded tapes much more effectively

by using them in the following way. First the tape should be played through the control and recorded on each of the individual tape recorders. This means that each student now has a copy of the tape which can be played back as required. Each student can be given an assignment which he can complete at his own pace.

(c) Industrial Society Conference. The Industrial Society will arrange two-day Conferences for fifth and sixth formers which are largely concerned with industrial relations issues. The students are divided into groups of about eight to ten and the Society recruit a number of managers and union representatives to act as group leaders. The two days consist of talks, films, case study exercises and small group discussions. They are well organised and in the writer's experience enjoyed by all who take part. The cost is £1 per delegate but with a minimum charge of £150.

The Industrial Society will also help schools to arrange their own conferences.

Resources

Books

The coverage of industrial relations in the basic economics textbooks is frequently inadequate, at least in some respects, for an 'A' level course. However, there are a number of more specialised texts which are good. One of the problems with the majority of textbooks currently in print is that they have not yet caught up with the recent changes in the law (i.e. the repeal of the Industrial Relations Act and the introduction of the Employment Protection and Trade Union and Labour Relations Acts). When new editions appear this should be rectified.

Some Basic Economic Texts

1 Stanlake, G. F., *Introductory Economics*, (Longman, third edition, 1976). Chapter 18 covers: basic theory of wage determination, description of the trade union structure and types of union, trade unions and the arguments used as a basis for wage claims. The coverage of all the above is very basic, but is of some use for the weak student.

2 Marshall, B. V., *Comprehensive Economics*, (Longman, second edition, 1975), part 2, 'Analytical and Applied'. Chapter 10, part 5 covers: aims and functions of trade unions, structure and organisation of trade unions, collective bargaining machinery, state intervention in industrial relations. The section on state intervention is out-of-date but the other topics are covered in detail and include a lot of useful statistics which are well presented. The section on the structure and organisation of trade unions is particularly well done.

3 Nobbs, J., *Advanced-level Economics*, (McGraw-Hill, second edition, 1976). Unit 6 covers the following: an outline of several theories of wage determination, trade union organisation, a glossary of a number of industrial relations terms, trade unions and the law, prices and incomes policy and equal pay. The presentation is clear and the information is reasonably up-to-date, but the coverage of most of the topics is rather superficial. However the book would be of use to the weaker 'A' level candidates.

4 Lipsey, R. G., *An Introduction to Positive Economics*, (Weidenfeld and Nicolson, fourth edition, 1976). Chapter 26 provides a largely theoretical analysis of the effects of trade unions upon the wage rate in a particular occupation.

5 Prest, A. R. and Coppock, D. J., *A Manual of Applied Economics*, (Weidenfeld and Nicolson, sixth edition, 1976). Chapter 5, section IV, is a short but interesting section on trade unions and industrial relations in the UK containing up-to-date statistical and other information.

More Specialised Books

6 Clegg, H. A., *The System of Industrial Relations in the UK*, (Blackwell, third edition, 1977). This book can probably be regarded as the standard text on the UK system of industrial relations. As one would expect it is comprehensive covering all the important issues. An additional advantage is that it incorporates the implications of recent legislation.

7 McCarthy, W. E. J., *Industrial Relations in Britain*, (Lyon G. and G., 1969). A good basic introductory text covering the main areas.

8 Grant, R. M., *Industrial Relations*, (Ginn, 1977). This is a Manchester Economics Project Satellite Text. A very useful book written specifically for 'A' level economics students. A brief but thorough account of the British system of industrial relations. The fact that it is short means that it is more likely to be read by the majority of 'A' level students than the previous two books.

9 Williamson, Hugh., *The Trade Unions*, (Heinemann Educational, fourth edition, 1977). A book in the *Studies in the British Economy Series*, so again it has been written with 'A' level students in mind and is short enough for a number of students to find time to read it. The book also includes three case studies and a list of past essay type examination questions.

10 Allan Flanders, *Trade Unions*, (Hutchinson University Library, 1968). A standard introductory text on trade union structure and functions.

11 Hawkins, Kevin, *British Industrial Relations 1945–1975*, (Barne and Jenkins, 1977). This book is different from the majority of other books on industrial relations in that it takes an historical approach. Very good background reading for the teacher, but it would be optimistic to suggest that it is likely to be considered worth reading by many students.

Other Written Material

12 Bank Review Articles

Recent examples of useful articles on this particular topic include:

National Westminster Bank Review, February 1976, 'Trade Unions, A role in Society' by David Warburton. This article gives the trade union point of view;

National Westminster Bank Review, May 1976, 'Continuity and Change in Recent Labour Law' by J. H. Beascoby and C. G. Hanson. This article compares the current legislation and institutions with those that existed in the period 1971 to 1974 as a result of the 1971 Industrial Relations Act. It is an excellent up-to-date summary of the present situation. The article could be given to students with a list of questions designed to extract important points such as the role and function of ACAS or the CAC;

Three Banks Review, September, 1976, 'The Political Economy of the British Trade Union Movement', by S. Brittan. A stimulating, if controversial article with some interesting suggestions for reform;

Lloyds Bank Review, June 1977, 'Participation by Agreement' by B. C. Roberts. The article argues against the recommendations of the majority report of the Bullock Committee of Inquiry into Industrial Democracy.

13 The British Economy Survey, (Oxford University Press). A termly journal containing articles written by teachers and hence very suitable for 'A' level students. There is a regular section on industrial relations which provides an easy way of keeping up to date. For example, the Spring 1977 edition had a section on 'Worker Directors and the Bullock Report'.

Some of the articles could also be used as case study material, for example, part of the article in the Summer 1977 issue on 'British Leyland and Phase Three Incomes Policy'.

14 TUC publications. The TUC education department publish quite a lot of information suitable for 'A' level students. Some of the materials produced are provided free, but most have to be paid for. Examples include:

(a) *Going to Work* (a short guide to trade unionism);
(b) *ABC of the TUC;*
(c) *Labour* (TUC's regular newsheet);
(d) *Facts about the Trade Union Movement* (free fact sheet);
(e) *Trade Union Organisation and Structure*

The fact sheets are particularly useful.

15 ACAS publications. Five short pamphlets are published and they include:

(a) *This is ACAS;*
(b) *An Industrial Relations Service for Industry;*
(c) *Arbitration in Trades Disputes.*

16 The Department of Employment also publishes various pamphlets some of which may be obtained from the local D of E offices. Examples:

(a) *Employment Protection Act (A General Outline)*. *Plus* a number of complimentary leaflets giving detailed information on certain sections of the Act, such as *Trade Union Membership and Activities*.
(b) *The Trade Union and Labour Relations Acts 1974 and 1976;*
(c) *Manpower Papers* on topics such as: *The Reform of Collective Bargaining at Plant and Company Level* (No 5), and *Industrial Relations Procedures* (No 14).

17 Jackdaw Folders. These contain largely historical information, but may be of general interest. The relevant folders are: *The Early Trade Unions* (No 35) and *The General Strike* (No 105).

A similar publication is the Times Topic Series. Number 3 is entitled *Strikes*. It is published by Times Education Services and deals exclusively with problems and ideas connected with strikes.

18 Schools Brief, 'The Market for Work', (*The Economist*). This is an article published in *The Economist* of the 30 October 1976 and has since been included in *The Economist*/Economics Association publication *The Uncommon Market*. The article relates the marginal productivity theory of wage determination to the realities of the UK labour market.

There are of course other useful articles appearing in *The Economist* quite regularly, some of which may be suitable as case study material.

19 Department of Employment Gazette. A very useful source of current statistics and up-to-date articles on a variety of industrial relations issues. For example the January 1977 issue contains a summary of the ACAS report on 'Industrial Relations in the National Newspaper Industry', which would make an excellent case study. Many of the large public libraries will keep copies of the *D of E Gazette* in their reference section.

20 'A' Level Business Studies Project Notes. The 'A' level business studies course includes a section on industrial relations and a series of notes can be obtained at a small charge from the 'A' Level Business Studies Project Office at the London University Institute of Education. In due course an up-dated version will be included in the course book *People and Decisions* which is to be published by Longman in 1978.

Films
The films have been divided into two sections;

(i) Those which are broadly within the scope of most 'A' level economics syllabuses.
(ii) Those which are of less direct relevance to 'A' level economics but which may still be of interest.

Section (i)
21 *Member of the Union*, (BBC Enterprises), 25 mins. A modern account of the work of a trade union on the shopfloor, produced for schools by the BBC.

22 *We are the Engineers*, (available from the AUEW), 40 mins. The film covers the history, current structure and activities of the Union.

23 *Strike Village*, (Concord Films Council), 50 mins. A study of a Nottinghamshire village in the 1972 coal strike, and its effects on trade unionists.

24 *Dispute*, (Concord Films Council), two part film, 50 mins each. This film shows two real disputes and a 'smoke filled room' controversy.

25 *The Space Between Words – Work*, (Concord Films Council), 55 mins. Concerned with a dispute in an electronics factory in 1973 and shows management and union strategies and goals.

26 *Democracy at Work* (from TV series 'The Risk Business'). (Concord Films Council), 30 mins. Looks at the organisation of work as a means of improving industrial relations. Some examples of job enrichment and the encouragement of worker participation including one long-established example of worker control. Companies shown include Meccano Ltd, Bristol Ship Repairers Ltd, ICI Ltd, and Scott Bader Commonwealth Ltd.

27 *Give Us the Works*, (Concord Films Council), 25 mins. Concerned with industrial relations and the reality of workers' control in the steel industry.

Section (ii)
28 *March*, (from the TUC), 17 mins. The film records the TUC demonstration against the Industrial Relations Bill held in February 1971. The commentary refers briefly to the TUC case against the Bill.

29 *What About the Workers?* (Rank Film Library), two films, 18 mins and 15 mins. On the history of the trade union movement. Part 1: 1880–1918, Part 2: 1918–1945.

30 *Do not Fold, Staple, Spindle or Mutilate*, (Concord Films Council), 50 mins. Concerned with obsoles-

cence, the depersonalisation of industry and the role of trade unions.

31 *Day after Day*, (Concord Films Council), 30 mins. An impression of the tedious routine in a paper mill.

32 *What about the Workers – Are they to Blame?* (Concord Films Council), 50 mins. An enquiry into the status and role of workers in the UK.

33 *Them and Us*, (Concord Films Council), 30 mins. Looks at the will to work in British industry and whether the class structure in the average factory has anything to do with our failings. Shows the sweeping changes introduced by Tannoy Ltd at Coatbridge in Scotland where the little things which differentiated between workers and managers at all levels have been swept away.

34 *The Industrial Worker*, (National Audio Visual Aids Library), 17 mins. Shows the day-to-day routine of two industrial workers, their problems and fears of automation.

35 *A Case Study in Incomes Policy*, (Training and Education Film Library), 16 mins. An Open University film concerned with the NBPI.

36 *Brickworker*, (Training and Education Film Library), 25 mins. An Open University film examining the attitudes towards monotonous jobs.

37 *This Automation Age*, (Central Film Library), 33 mins. Considers the meaning and challenge of automation.

Tapes
38 *The Morality of Strikes*, (Ref. IR 108 from Seminar Cassettes).
39 *Employment and Manpower*, (Sussex Tapes E.6.).
40 Side A: *The Problem of Wages*, (Audio Learning); Side B: *Applying an Incomes Policy;* by Lord Balogh and Derek Robinson.

Other Resources
41 Wallcharts.
(a) Pictorial Charts Educational Trust. One chart on *The Growth of British Trade Unions*.
(b) Educational Productions Ltd. Set of two charts: (i) *The Structure of the TUC;* (ii) *The Relationship between Trade Unions and their Individual Members*.

42 *The Supervisor and Shop Steward* (CRAC). A simple industrial dispute argued by pairs of players. The pack contains ten sets of materials plus a teacher's manual. It is obtainable from Dept. 953/54, Hobsons Press, as is Resource 43.

43 *The Alpha Complaint* (CRAC). A case study of an industrial relations problem in the road transport industry. Again the pack contains ten sets of materials plus a teacher's manual.

44 Talks on trade unions. The TUC will provide names and addresses of local trade union officers who are willing to give talks in schools and colleges.

45 *Understanding British Industry Project*. The UBI project is funded by industry with the support of the

CBI. A resource centre has been set up in Oxford which has collected and catalogued existing materials on a variety of topics connected with industry and commerce. Other services are also provided.

46 Information on individual trade unions and employers' associations. Addresses can be found in the *Directory of Employers' Organisations and Trade Unions* which is compiled by the Department of Employment and published by HMSO.

37 Money and Banking for 16–18 Year Olds*
David R. Butler

Content

The topic of money and banking is a very wide ranging syllabus section including not only the banking system but also aspects of inflation and the international monetary system. Some of these aspects are dealt with in other chapters so this chapter will limit itself to a consideration of the teaching of the development of money, the UK banking system and the Quantity and Keynesian Theories of money. Clearly, topics such as the Quantity Theory cannot be taught in isolation from their wider implications in macroeconomics, but it is necessary to impose some limits on the range of this chapter. The following 'check list' on money and banking may be useful to teachers, especially those embarking on the teaching of this topic for the first time.

Checklist on Money and Banking
Money: functions, development, credit creation, money supply, monetary theory and policy;
UK money markets: Interbank, Local Authority Bond, Certificate of Deposit, Treasury Bill, Commercial Bill, discount, finance house;
International money markets: Euro-dollar, Euro-bond, Petro-dollar;
Financial institutions: commercial banks, central banks, merchant banks, savings banks, building

societies, discount houses, IMF, IBRD (World Bank), Bank for International Settlements.

Teaching Problems

There are three main problems facing the teacher with this topic. First, when and where to include it in the syllabus. As indicated above, the topic can be wide ranging and it does not fall neatly into any particular 'slot' in the syllabus. Should it be taught before or after the main body of macroeconomics? Should the Quantity Theory be dealt with here or under a separate section on inflation or as an alternative to Keynesian economic theory? These problems may be common to other areas of the syllabus, but the many-sided nature of this topic makes these problems particularly acute here. The economics teacher might find that at least a partial solution is not to teach the topic in its entirety but to return to it at suitable intervals. For example, the basic descriptive material on banks and other financial institutions could be taught early in the syllabus while the role of the Bank of England in controlling the economy might be better placed after basic macroeconomics has been taught.

Secondly, there is the problem for the economics teacher in keeping up-to-date with changes in the bank-

* I would like to thank Alain Anderton for valuable assistance with this chapter.

ing system. Change seems to occur in this area more rapidly than in nearly any other topic. Textbooks in common use still refer to 'bank rate' rather than to 'minimum lending rate'. Very few textbooks mention the now very important 'Certificate of Deposits' and there is little discussion of the importance of the Euro-dollar market. Clearly the financial press and bank reviews are a useful source of up-to-date information but the hard pressed economics teacher may lack the necessary time to extract it. A particularly useful summary on 'The Sterling Money Markets' can be found in the centre page spread in *Barclays Bank Review*, February 1977. A speaker from the Bank Education Service could prove invaluable here. If the speaker is asked to speak on recent developments in banking and finance, a very useful synopsis should be provided of the most up-to-date changes in the banking system. (See Chapter 24 on visiting speakers.)

Thirdly, certain parts of this topic are apt to be rather 'dry', particularly those dealing with the more descriptive aspects of the banking system or with other financial institutions. This is often particularly true of institutions such as discount houses or merchant banks with which students are unfamiliar in their everyday life. At least with the commercial banks the student comes into contact with them and is able to see them in his local high street. A help here may well be student's apparent fascination with the large sums of money involved in monetary transactions in the City which the teacher could use to illustrate the workings of the various money markets. The financial institutions could possibly be made less dry by concentrating on the work of the money markets and explaining the functions of the various types of institutions rather than approaching it institutions first, markets incidental.

Pupil Problems

1 Credit creation. There is a good deal of confusion as to how banks create credit and what assumptions there are in the credit creation model. Pupils will often be under the misapprehension that a bank is able to loan out eight times its deposits. Possibly the best explanation of this is contained in R. G. Lipsey's *Positive Economics* (see Resources). A simple classroom simulation might be useful here in demonstrating how the system works (see page 79).

2 'The rate of interest'. Because textbooks refer to 'the rate of interest' pupils often gain the impression that there is a single rate of interest or confuse this with minimum lending rate. The pupil needs to know that there are a number of different but interrelated interest rates. The following type of exercise might prove useful here.

The following rates of interest were quoted in *The Times* on 7 April 1977:

building societies (investment accounts) 12%; clearing banks (deposit accounts) 5%; gilt-edged stock (Treasury $11\frac{1}{2}\%$ 1979) 11.2%; local authorities (yearling bonds) $10\frac{3}{4}\%$; National Savings Bank (up to £30 on demand) 7.7%; minimum lending rate $9\frac{1}{2}\%$.

Questions: (a) Why are there different rates of interest?
(b) What is the relationship between these rates of interest?
(c) What would the likely effects be of a fall in MLR (i) in the short term, (ii) in the long term, on the other rates of interest?
(d) What rate of interest approximately are commercial banks likely to be charging on overdrafts? Give reasons for your answer.

A useful source of information on interest rates is *The Financial Times* which publishes daily market rates for the inter-bank market, Treasury Bills, etc.

3 The velocity of circulation of money. Pupils frequently experience difficulty in understanding the relationship between the velocity of circulation of money and the other terms in the Fisher equation. A good explanation of this which could easily be developed into a classroom simulation is given in J. Nobbs' *Advanced Level Economics*, p 196.

4 The inverse relationship between the price of a bond and its rate of interest. A simple mathematical example is very useful in demonstrating this relationship. It is a small point which the economics teacher may assume the pupil to be aware of without explaining it properly, and this can cause a good deal of confusion in the pupil's mind when such topics as the Keynesian theory of money are dealt with.

5 The Quantity Theory. Because in its crude form it is relatively easy to understand, pupils tend to accept it without criticism. Whilst in an 'A' level answer it does not make any difference to the candidate's mark whether he adopts a 'Monetarist' or a 'Keynesian' approach, he should at least be aware of the arguments which are made against the two schools of thought.

6 Monetary policy. Pupils often experience real difficulty in understanding the operation of monetary policy. For a really searching question on this see Harbury's *Workbook in Introductory Economics* (Pergamon, 1974), chapter 6, p 123 problem 2. A good possible exercise might be to get pupils to work out all the effects on bank asset structures, discount houses' balance sheets, money supply etc of various changes in monetary policy.

For example, if the Bank of England sells £500m Treasury Bills over and above its expected weekly sale, but buys in long-dated government stock with over a year to run, what will be the effect? If the Bank of England calls in £1000m of special deposits, what will be the effects?

The question of the rate of interest and how

Government monetary policy affects it can also cause real difficulties of understanding.

Teaching Methods and Aids

1 The use of newspaper articles. This is one syllabus section where there is an abundance of 'live' material available from the Press. Such material used correctly must help to add stimulus to what could otherwise become a rather dull topic. Appropriate articles could provide the basis of a discussion or data response question. Table 37.1 is an example of the type of material which might prove useful:

	Barclays %	Lloyds %	Midland %	NatWest %
One year loan	16.65	16.4	17.48	16.44
Three year loan	16.65	16.5	17.51	16.53
Overdrafts	11½–13½	11½–12½	11½–13½	11½–12½

Table 37.1 The cost of personal loans (from the financial press, 14 May 1977).

Questions: (a) Is there competition between the banks?
(b) What determines the banks' interest rates?·
(c) Why are overdraft charges lower than personal loans?
(d) What factors would a customer take into account when deciding whether to take out a loan or an overdraft?

2 Debate. The Keynesian/Monetarist controversy is an ideal topic for a classroom debate. It is best here to divide the economics group into two sections, each representing a different side in the debate. A few days before the debate, the sections are given the appropriate literature to read (see Resources) so that they are well briefed on the arguments. It often works well if two staff take opposing sides in the debate. Possibly a debate could be organised in conjunction with a neighbouring school.

3 Outside speakers. The Bank of Education Service or the individual commercial banks will provide speakers. They will normally lecture on any mainstream economics topic although, as has already been suggested, it is particularly useful to have a lecture on recent developments in the banking system. This is obviously an area where they have expert knowledge and access to material not easily available elsewhere. Barclays Bank run a series of half day sixth form conferences at their training headquarters at Teddington. They consist normally of a lecture (not necessarily on a banking

topic) and then a debate amongst the various schools attending. Information on these can be obtained either from Barclays head office or through the local Barclays Bank manager.

4 Visits. Commercial banks do a great deal to encourage visits either to local branches or to main City branches. Details have already been provided of a visit to a local branch for younger pupils (see Chapter 13) and this could be adapted for older pupils, who might well be more interested in the securities and investment side of branch banking rather than the counter operations. National Westminster Bank provide excellent one day City visits for a small group of sixth form pupils. This normally includes a talk on banking as a career, a visit to one of the main City branches and two other financial institutions such as the Stock Exchange and Lloyds.

5 Games and simulations. Money and banking is a topic which lends itself to the use of games and simulation exercises. The simulation suggested in Chapter 13 for use with young pupils could easily be extended for older pupils. See also page 207 for a credit creation game which illustrates the oligopolistic nature of the UK banking system. National Westminster Bank have devised a simulation exercise where the pupils act the role of bank managers in deciding whether or not to give a loan to customers in various circumstances and under what terms the loan might be given. NatWest will lay this on for sixth form pupils on request.

6 Use of overhead transparencies. Banking lends itself to the use of transparencies which can be re-used each year. They are particularly suited to subjects such as the various money markets and the monetary transactions taking place between the financial institutions.

7 Multiple choice questions and workbooks. Objective test questions will quickly sort out those who do and those who do not understand the main concepts.

Resources

Books
Lipsey, R. G., *Positive Economics,* (Weidenfeld and Nicolson, 1976), chapters 41 and 42. Particularly good on credit creation in a multi-bank system.

Nobbs, J., *Advanced Level Economics*, (McGraw-Hill, 1976), units 15–18. Excellent on the Keynesian/Monetarist debate at a relatively simple level. Good explanation of the Quantity Theory and the velocity of circulation of money.

Harvey, J., *Intermediate Economics*, (Macmillan Education, 1976), chapters 12, 13, 14 and 25. Good on descriptive aspects of banking and other financial institutions.

Manchester Economic Project, *Understanding Economics*, (Ginn & Co, 1976). Section 6 is good on financial institutions, and section 12 on explanation of Keynesian and Quantity Theories of money.

Galbraith, J. K., *The Great Crash 1929* (Penguin, 1969) and *Money; Whence it came, Where it Went* (André Deutsch, 1975). Both for the more able sixth former. Extracts could be used as the basis for discussions.

The Economist, The Uncommon Market (Economist Newspaper Ltd, 1977), p 20. Britain's money supply. Methods and repercussions of monetary expansion.

The Economist, What's Going On?, (Economist Newspaper Ltd, 1976), p 4. Keynes and the Monetarists. Good summary of the debate. Page 14, 'Banking in Slumpflation'.

Bank Education Service. Series of up-to-date pamphlets available free of charge and in multiple copies; No. 4: *The Clearing System;* No. 8: *Banks and Overseas Trade;* No. 10: *How a Banker Looks at a Balance Sheet;* No. 12: *City of London and Its Markets;* No. 13: *Foreign Exchange and the Euro-Currency Markets;* No. 14: *Competition and Credit Control* (recently republished and up-dated); No. 15: *Recent Developments in the International Monetary System.*

Anthony, V., *Banks and Markets*, (Heinemann Educational, 1974). Excellent descriptive book covering the whole field apart from the Quantity Theory.

Williams, R. M, *Sample Studies of Financial Institutions*, (Ginn). Good coverage of the field. New edition to be published shortly.

Davies, B., *Business Finance and the City of London*, (Heinemann Educational, 1976).

Films and Tapes
Guild Sound and Vision, *Bank of England; History and Functions*, (20″, 5125 7177–2, free loan).

Royal Bank of Scotland, *Your Money and Your Life*, (20″, free loan). Guide to services provided by the bank.

Training and Education Film Library:
Money Supply Theory, (15″, 900 8083 4);
The Supply of Money, (16″, 900 8133 8). How money comes into existence, monetary institutions, constraints on control of money supply;

What is Money?, (25″, D101 11). History and development of money;
Banking, (25″, D101 12). History and development of banking.

Multilink Film Library:
The Curious History of Money, (16″). Also deals with functions of banks;
The Bankers, (27″). Daily life of a bank manager;
The Rise of Parnassus Needy, (13″). Bank overdraft and the finance of small scale business;
The Pilgrim, (11″). Bank aid for exports;
Bankers to the World, (32″). Role of banks in international trade;
Fly Me to the Bank, (23″). Shows services Midland Bank perform for customers;
The Bargain, (10″). Cartoon on why people use banks. All the above Multilink Films are free loan.

Student Recordings Ltd tape/filmstrips:
The Joint Stock Banks (AVC 14);
Finance and Investment (AVC 15);
Money and Banking (AVC 140).

McGraw-Hill filmstrip, *Banking and Monetary Control.*

Sussex Tapes, E3, *Banking.*

Wallcharts
Bank Education Service. Four charts: *The Role of the Banks; Life Story of a Cheque; How to use a Cheque; The History of Banking.* (All free).
National Westminster Bank. Six charts on various aspects of banking, (free).
Pictorial Charts Educational Trust. One chart: *Your Money,* (F16).

Other Material
Bank reviews. Published quarterly by Barclays, Lloyds, National Westminster and Midland, plus *The Bank of England Quarterly* and the *Three Banks Review.*

Birt, D., and Tinniswood, P., *Bank Loan – A Simulation*, (Longman/Lloyds).

The *Financial Times* contains daily reports on the money markets and often has excellent surveys on various aspects of the City and the international money markets.

38   Banks and the Creation of Money

A. G. Anderton

This is a game designed to show how banks can create money. Furthermore, it should also promote discussion about the oligopolistic nature of the UK banking system.

Equipment. Playing manual; one balance sheet for each bank; one record sheet for each bank.

Numbers of players. Any number can play. Each player is a director of a bank. It is suggested that four banks play, the players being assigned in roughly equal numbers to each bank.

Setting up the game. The room should be so arranged that the 'board of directors' of each bank sit together and the discussion of the board cannot be overheard by other boards. Ideally, each board should sit round a table at some distance from the other boards.

Each bank should be given a balance sheet and a record sheet. The 'background information' (see below) should be read out and the teacher should ensure that the players fully understand the rules of the game and how to fill in the balance and record sheets.

Background information. Each player is a director of a bank which has just been set up in the developing country of Baka. By the beginning of the game, each bank has managed to attract deposits worth £10 million which it is proposing to lend out in the form of loans to individuals. The interest on these loans is 10 per cent per annum, each round being one year. Throughout the game, it is assumed that the demand for these loans exceeds the supply and hence the banks have no difficulty in lending out all available funds. Due to government decree, no bank may charge more than 20 per cent per annum on its loans.

It has been found after long experience in other countries that a bank need keep only 10 per cent of total deposits in the form of cash. So, 90 per cent of total deposits may be lent out at a rate of interest of 10 per cent per annum.

Furthermore, it has been found that all money which is lent, after passing perhaps through several hands, comes back to the banking system in the form of new deposits over the period of one round.

Market research undertaken has shown that once money is deposited in a bank, then that money tends to remain in that bank, whatever the policy of the bank. However, new deposits created by loan money are placed amongst the banks according to four criteria:

1 20 per cent of new deposits are attracted by the amount of interest paid on the deposit. The bank which offers the highest rate of interest gains this share of the market. If two more banks offer the same, highest, rate of interest, then the market is split equally between them.

2 40 per cent of new deposits are attracted by the cheapness of the bank charges. Charges are quoted as a percentage of deposits, e.g. a bank may offer to charge 1 per cent of total deposits as charges. The bank offering the lowest bank charges gains this share of the market. If two or more banks offer the lowest charges, the market is split evenly between them.

3 30 per cent of new deposits are attracted by the convenience of branch banking. Banks may invest money (in £0.1 million lots) in new branches. The market is shared according to how much an individual bank has invested in relation to all other banks. For instance, if total investment by the banking system in one round has been £1 million and one bank has invested £0.2 million, then its share of the market won is $0.2 \div 1$ or 1/5. Or again, if total investment has been £2 million and one bank has invested £0.3 million, then its share of the market won is $0.3 \div 2$ or 15 per cent. If investment by a particular bank is b, and total investment by the complete banking system is s, then the market share won by the bank is b/s.

4 10 per cent of deposits are attracted by spending on advertising and promotions. Money may be spent in £0.1 million lots. As with investment in new branches, the market is shared according to how much an individual bank has invested in relation to all other banks.

Thus part of the market is offered to the banks offering the highest return on deposits or the lowest banking charges. The rest is split up according to how much each bank spends on investment in new branches and advertising.

At the beginning of each round, banks must decide on what rate of interest to offer on deposits, and so on, bearing in mind that the flow of new deposits to their bank, which in future rounds will be lent out at 10 per cent interest per round, will be affected by these decisions. The game is played in six rounds. The winner of the game is the bank which has the highest accumulated profit figure at the end of play. Banks may consult each other at any time if they so wish.

The play. At the start of each round, each bank must complete its balance sheet and then declare to the teacher how much money it is able to lend out, in addition to its existing advances – which in fact will be 90 per cent of the new deposits gained in the previous round.

Each bank then decides on what rate of interest (if

any) it will offer to depositors, how much their banking charges are going to be, how much money will be spent on investment in new branches and how much on advertising. The bank then works out its profit or loss on the round.

The share of the market won by each bank is then worked out by the teacher after each bank has openly declared its pricing and investment decisions. Each bank then fills in its new deposits won in the appropriate column on the record sheet. A new round of play can then start.

Duration of the game. It is suggested that a time limit be put on the part of the round where banks make pricing and investment decisions. (Perhaps of five or ten minutes.) Depending on how competent the teacher and the players are arithmetically, the preliminary explanation and the actual play should last from one to two hours or more. At least half an hour should be devoted in addition to this to the debriefing sessions.

The balance sheet (Table 38.1). Each bank must fill in its balance sheet at the beginning of each round. The only debit item for a bank is its deposits. On the credit side, 90 per cent of credit should be in the form of advances and 10 per cent in cash. Total credit and total debit should of course be equal.

The record sheet (Table 38.2). Each bank must keep a record sheet and fill in the columns from 1–19.

Column   1 – total deposits – these are as recorded for the round on the balance sheet.

Column   2 – total advances – these are as recorded for the round on the balance sheet.

Column   3 – per cent rate of interest on deposits – decision to be made by each bank.

Column   4 – per cent level of bank charges – decision to be made by each bank.

Column   5 – investment in new branches – decision to be made by each bank.

Column   6 – expenditure on advertising – decision to be made by each bank.

Column   7 – interest on deposits – columns 1×3 ($\div 100$).

Column   8 – total costs – columns $5+6+7$.

Column   9 – interest on advances – column 2×10 per cent.

Column 10 – revenue from bank charges – columns 1×4 ($\div 100$).

Column 11 – total revenue – columns $9+10$.

Column 12 – profit or loss for the round – column $11-8$.

Column 13 – profit or loss so far – column $12+$previous round's column 13.

Column 14 – total new deposits market possible – this is calculated by the teacher and is the combined totals of the individual banks' new loans for the round.

Column 15 – market from interest on deposits – the

bank or banks offering the highest rate of interest on deposits (in column 3) gain this share of the market (worth 20 per cent of column 14).

Column 16 – market from bank charges – the bank or banks offering the lowest percentage rate of bank charges (in column 4) gains this share of the market (worth 40 per cent of column 14).

Column 17 – market from investment in new branches – calculated by the teacher from column 5 (worth a potential 30 per cent of column 14).

Column 18 – market from expenditure on advertising – calculated by the teacher from column 6 (worth a potential 10 per cent of column 14).

Column 19 – total market share won of new deposits – columns $15+16+17+18$.

When all banks have completed column 19, the next round may begin by banks completing the balance sheet for the next round. The deposits (debit) are calculated by adding column 1 (existing deposits) and column 19 (new deposits attracted in the round) of the round just played.

Arithmetic. The game involves some arithmetic, both for players and teacher. It is therefore suggested that there be at least one player in each team who is arithmetically competent. It might help the teacher if he has an electronic calculator available. The teacher should work out what the total new deposits market (column 14) is, and from that work out 10, 20, 30 and 40 per cent of that for columns 15–18 whilst the players are deciding on columns 3–6. Or, if the teacher knows how many banks will be playing, he can work these figures out before the start of the game. It is very important for the success of this game, or indeed any similar game, that it doesn't turn into an arithmetical jamboree.

Variations. Like most games, this game can and should be altered to suit the needs of the players at the time of playing. Superficial changes can be made – such as altering the distribution of the shares for new deposits, or adding other reasons why depositors put their money into a bank, or assuming that banks have to compete for all existing deposits as well as just new ones – as well as more fundamental ones, such as altering the aim of the game or changing the oligopolistic nature of the game by increasing the number of banks. Teachers should make changes to make this a better game for their needs.

The debriefing. The debriefing is perhaps the most important part of any game. The following points could perhaps be usefully made:

Each bank started off with £10 million of deposits, yet ended up with more.

BANK

BALANCE SHEET (IN £ MILLIONS)

First Period

Debit	Credit
Deposits	Advances
	Cash
_____	_____
Total	Total

Fourth Period

Debit	Credit
Deposits	Advances
	Cash
_____	_____
Total	Total

Second Period

Debit	Credit
Deposits	Advances
	Cash
_____	_____
Total	Total

Fifth Period

Debit	Credit
Deposits	Advances
	Cash
_____	_____
Total	Total

Third Period

Debit	Credit
Deposits	Advances
	Cash
_____	_____
Total	Total

Sixth Period

Debit	Credit
Deposits	Advances
	Cash
_____	_____
Total	Total

Table 38.1

	1	2	3	4	5	6
Period	Total deposits (As from balance sheet)	Total advances	%rate of interest on deposits (20% of market)	%level of bank charges (40% of market)	Investment in new branches (£0.1 M's) (30% of market)	Expenditure on advertising (£0.1M's) (10% of market)
1						
2						
3						
4						
5						
6						

7	8	9	10	11	12	13
Interest on deposits (1×3)	Total costs (5+6+7)	Interest on advances (2×10%)	Revenue from bank charges (1×4)	Total revenue (9+10)	Profit or loss (11−8)	Profit or loss so far

Table 38.2

1 How have the banks 'created' this money?

2 Is there any limit to how much money the banking system can create? What is this limit?

3 In reality, banks do not create as much money as the game would imply. What are the limits on money creation? How much money does the British banking system create approximately?

4 If, within the context of the game, a central bank in Baka wanted to control credit expansion in the country, how could it do it? How does the Bank of England try to do it in the UK? What are the difficulties it faces when trying to implement this control successfully?

		14	15	16	
Period		Total new deposits market possible	Market from interest on deposits (Maximum: 20% of 14)	Market from bank charges (Maximum: 40% of 14)	
1					
2					
3					
4					
5					
6					

17	18	19
Market from investment in new branches (Maximum: 30% of 14)	Market from advertising (Maximum: 10% of 14)	Total market share won of new deposits (15+16+17+18)

Table 38.2 – continued

The game creates an oligopolistic market situation.

1 Is this representative of the UK banking scene? Why?
2 In the game, why did banks make the decisions on pricing and investment as they did?
3 Was collusion between banks profitable? Or, would it have been profitable if none took place?
4 The winner of the game was the bank with the most profits, and not necessarily the bank with the largest deposits. Is this realistic? In reality, what is the success criterion for a bank?

5 How realistic was the assumption that customers tended not to switch their existing deposits from bank to bank?
6 How realistic was the 'market research' which, for instance, said that advertising was not a very powerful way of attracting new deposits?

How could the game have been improved, both from a playing angle and also from the point of view of making it more realistic?

39 National Income Theory

Sally Donovan and Alistair Thomson

Introduction

This chapter attempts to cover a fairly broad topic area. It is assumed that most students in this age range will be attempting 'A' level. The material dealt with covers the syllabus requirements of most examining boards and is presented in such a way that elements may be drawn out for other types of course. The aim is to highlight the difficulties which may be encountered by the teacher and to suggest particular methods and materials which may be of help in surmounting them.

The initial difficulty faced by the teacher arises from the historical development of national income theory itself. Keynesian income/expenditure analysis has only relatively recently been adopted as a form of orthodoxy (unlike much of micro theory). Students rarely have to go far into the subject before encountering 'controversial' areas.

The textbooks reflect the problem. The section devoted to this subject has invariably expanded in relation to other topics in the last decade. Compare Nevin's[1] earlier editions with the present fourth edition[2] for instance. Stanlake[3] has brought out a text devoted solely to macroeconomics. There is only now some consensus emerging on the approach to adopt and there is still a lack of convention on the use of terms.

The macro approach involves the use of different and often more sophisticated analytical techniques and concepts. Micro analysis involves comparative static partial equilibrium whilst macro involves dynamic general equilibrium theory. A failure to identify and adapt to the differences can lead to considerable difficulty even at this relatively low level.

A number of basic concepts are brought together in order that those which are used in this area may be developed. It is not the task of this chapter to comment on how these basics may be taught (production, exchange, money, etc) but problems can often be traced back to more fundamental misunderstanding.

The position of this topic in the structure of the course and the ordering of the subject matter itself will have a considerable influence on teaching method and learning. The ordering adopted in teaching and textbooks offers a number of choices. Covering micro before macro is probably the most common, the advantage being that key concepts are developed first. There has been a move towards reversing this order[4, 5] on the grounds that the macro issues of inflation, unemployment, etc are often closer to the students' experience and interest. The distinction itself may be blurred by some other form of ordering[6] or the two strands may be taught simultaneously by different teachers. The type of structuring must influence the particular teaching approach which is chosen.

The topic itself may be split logically into three parts – the concept of national income, the measurement of its value and the determination of its value. This is in fact the order most often followed by the texts. It is argued here that a more appropriate ordering would place measurement last, after the discussion of the concept and an examination of the factors which determine its value. The linking of the concept to the dreaded 'national income accounting' often leads to the student being swamped with a flood of figures and terms which have little relevance and cannot be really appreciated until the underlying interrelationships have been developed more fully. The importance of theory being linked to practice is recognised but better left until the students are aware of the whole area. Lumping the concept and measurement together often means that little time is spent in developing the basic ideas. It is quite possible for students to be able to use the concept without needing to appreciate all the difficulties of measurement.

A lack of mathematical ability may hamper a student in his attempts to comprehend complexity. The introduction of analysis which is beyond the student may hinder progress even more. The premature presentation of Blue Book[7] figures may confuse the 'less numerate' as may the assumption that all are familiar with the concept of a geometric series and its summation.

A simple verbal or written prose approach is used by most teachers to introduce the topic. This can be supplemented by numerical, diagrammatic, algebraic or graphical methods. Each will have its own particular advantages and disadvantages in relation to the concepts and relationships which are being represented and demonstrated.

Having dealt with some general problems we now examine specific difficulties.

The Concept of National Income: its Meaning and Significance

The general idea of national income can be reached by way of an individual's income and aggregate income. Students ought, at this stage, to be familiar with the concept of income being made up of the returns or payments, whether in money terms or in real goods and services, to the factors of production. It should then be a simple step to arrive at aggregate income merely by summing a group of individuals' incomes. The national income can be seen as the sum of all incomes generated in one country.

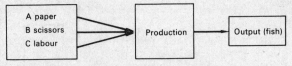

Figure 39.1 Simulation 1

This sequence does presuppose a knowledge of the production process, the meaning of wealth, the role of money and the distinction between stock and flow concepts. The idea of production can be reinforced quite simply by a simulation (see Figure 39.1) involving some resources (paper, scissors and labour) which consumers/workers transform into output (paper fish) giving increased utility.

An individual's income can then be seen to be the share of fish which he receives (as directed by one of the group) for providing his factor of production.

The role which money plays can be demonstrated by extending the simulation to a two-good monetary economy in which workers are paid a money wage which they use to purchase goods valued in money terms by the price system. The consumers/workers are divided into two groups (ABC and DEF in the diagram) and the second group now produces paper sheaves of corn from the same resources. (See Figure 39.2.)

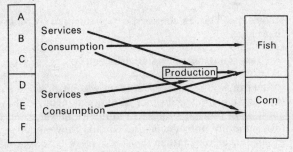

Figure 39.2 Simulation 2

It may be appropriate to clarify a common confusion arising from the distinction between real and money flows. In the first case, a rise in income is obviously synonymous with receiving more fish (*real* income) resulting exclusively from an increase in the output of fish. In the second case, a rise in the *money* income of all factor owners does not necessarily imply a rise in the quantity of real goods and services, fish and corn, which are available for purchase; a rise in prices could wipe out their monetary gain.

Before turning to examine the difference between stock and flow concepts, it is necessary to arrive at some understanding of net income. At some stage during the simulation, the supply of paper may run out (or the scissors 'wear out' by becoming blunt!). The question then arises as to how these capital goods are replaced. If they are not, then the national income must fall.

Continuing the simulation exercise, the scissors can be identified as the capital good which wears out. If the production of fish is to continue, the scissors will have to be replaced by, say, the producers of corn switching into scissor production. Now one production unit will have to purchase the output of the other and only the output of fish will be available for purchase by all income earners. This must result in involuntary saving. Hence, expenditure on investment in addition to consumption must be accompanied by positive saving (given this closed, no government system). Finally, the difference between replacing worn-out capital goods (depreciation) and producing extra capital (two pairs of scissors to replace one) can demonstrate net and gross measures of capital formation.

This bears directly on the question of stocks and flows. Since it is a difficulty which is generally encountered, it would seem worthwhile to give some attention to emphasising this point. Teaching by analogy is particularly useful in this context when a concept, that of a flow, is already familiar in everyday life.

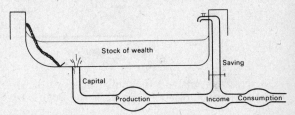

Figure 39.3

An explanation, using a bath of water to represent the stock of wealth, a tap as the flow of savings and the outlet pipe as the flow of capital which is used up in production and then becomes capital consumption or depreciation, can bring out most of the relevant points (see Figure 39.3). The flow of income pumps that part which is not consumed, saving, back into the bath to increase the stock of wealth, while the flow of capital which is used in current production decreases the stock of wealth in the bath. Thus the stock of water cannot rise unless the inflow is in excess of the outflow; new wealth must be created faster than old wealth is used up. As regards measurement, it can be demonstrated that the amount of water in the bath must be measured at *a* point in time while the savings tap and outflow pipe yield a flow *over* a particular period of time.

National income appears to be an area in which few

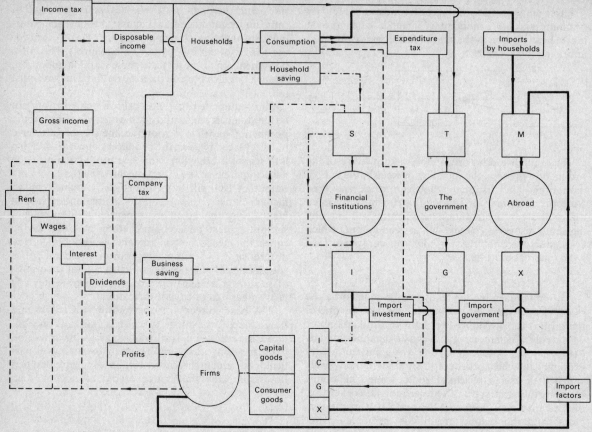

Figure 39.4

resources are available to help the teacher or the student. Most textbooks sadly neglect a thorough introduction to the concepts involved before using them in analysis. Many do, at some time, treat the points brought up here, such as money versus real income, but often in a rather piecemeal fashion. The majority of 'A' level texts launch far too rapidly into the circular flow and the equivalence of national output, income and expenditure. Harvey[8] does, however, commendably begin by examining the flow of wealth and approaches measurement by way of a simplified example of a 'small self-sufficient community' which he then represents diagrammatically. Thus it appears that teachers are very much left to their own devices when introducing the topic, though their approach will be governed by how they plan to develop the subject. However, it is hoped that the mere separation of the concept from its measurement will result in better understanding by the students.

The teaching of this section can be neatly rounded off and linked to the next by means of a discussion on the significance and usefulness of national income as a measure of standard of living and for comparative

studies etc. This, in contrast, is well covered by most textbooks.

The Determination of National Income

In the previous section the student was introduced to the meaning and significance of national income. The question of policy measures to influence its value follows naturally. Introducing the circular flow model as an analytical tool rather than as a mere description makes much of the detailed study which is required more meaningful. Before an economist can suggest appropriate policy he must have a theory.

The development of the circularity concept is fairly straightforward and most texts have a standard exposition. The simulations used to introduce the concept can easily be adapted and a flow chart developed from the basic idea of 'one man's expenditure is another's income'. The chart can show both real flows, factors and outputs, and money flows, incomes and expenditures, between the groups responsible for consumption, households, and those responsible for production, firms.

It can be argued that the students are introduced to two fundamental ideas which are essentially new to them. First, the idea of a system in which a number of decision-making units interact is central to the description of any economy. The interdependence of the actions which result from the millions of separate decisions can be demonstrated by calling the students' attention to the diverse origins of the goods and services they consume. Feedback is illustrated by the circle developed above and the concept of equilibrium demonstrated by referring to the water flow analogy. Secondly, it should be explained that the complexity of the real world system can be represented by a model. This involves abstracting the main concepts and relationships from reality. The aggregation of individuals into classes (in this case households and firms) involves assumptions. Many difficulties in understanding this area arise from these analytical concepts rather than from the economic content *per se*. Only Lipsey[9] deals with the system whilst Nobbs[4] deals with the model and refers the reader to Pen.[10] Ackley is also useful here.[11]

Texts differ in terms of the complexity which is introduced into the flow model. Most start with the closed economy with no government sector and some continue with this through most of their exposition. If the flow model is developed intuitively, i.e. by looking at the real world and abstracting from it, then aspects of the government and foreign sectors will almost certainly be introduced. A more fully worked out model is highly instructive for the examination of measurement in the next section and of policy later in the course, but can prove awkward for introducing the basic ideas of equilibrium and the multiplier mechanism. However, although it is important to start with a simple exposition, the omission of all flows apart from simple saving and investment can lead to considerable difficulties and confusion.

The principal failing is to ignore the import and indirect tax components of consumption expenditure (C). The marginal propensity to consume (c) is variously defined as the proportion of any change in gross income which is spent on consumption, the proportion of any change in disposable income which is spent on consumption goods and the proportion of any gross income increase which is spent on domestic consumption goods. The addition of another symbol to represent the proportion of any income which is returned to firms would perhaps simplify matters. Seddon[12] and Marshall[12] offer approaches which counter the import problem whilst the latter deals with all the 'multipliers' quite comprehensively including the 'compound multiplier' which takes into account induced injections. The advantage of this is that induced investment can be included quite simply in the model. Prest[14] offers a clear analysis and some figures for the UK values of the propensities and the multiplier itself.

Most of the above analysis can be carried through with the simplest assumptions about the behaviour of the groups in the system, e.g. households either consume or save. The effect of say a change in exports (X), or investment (I) of a given value will depend on the value of a given marginal withdrawals rate. In order to be able to predict the behaviour of a system one has to have an understanding of the factors which influence the decisions taken by the individual units which make up the system. Having established the general conditions for equilibrium and the mechanisms of change the next logical step is to tackle the question of why the variables involved take on particular values. The students are quite able to appreciate this and the texts usually slot in the theory of consumption behaviour and investment into the circular flow section. The former can be developed intuitively to give the consumption function but the latter can present difficulties.

In attempting to provide a simple analysis of a complex phenomenon many texts only manage to present the student with greater problems when he attempts to rationalise the analysis. A common confusion derives from the failure to distinguish between the desired stock of capital and the flow of investment. Lipsey[9] recognises the distinction between the marginal efficiency of capital and that of investment whilst McCormick *et al.*[19] go further and provide a thorough and useful analysis of the problem. An approach based on the links with micro marginal productivity analysis may be utilised to develop various strands of investment theory. It is important to bring together aspects which are often taught in isolation. The influence of changes in income may be seen as one of a number of factors which affect the level of desired capital stock. The accelerator may then be seen as a simple way of describing the relationship between a change in income, which affects the final demand for the product, and changes in desired capital stock (and hence investment) which are associated with the change in derived demand. The role of technology in determining the value of the capital/output ratio, on which the accelerator principle is based, can then be made clear. Highlighting the time dimension at this stage aids understanding and lays the foundations for future analysis of the multiplier/accelerator feedback mechanism, from which the instability associated with the trade cycle may be derived, and for discussions of growth. This is a very complex area of theory and simplification is obviously necessary, but it is important to avoid the possibility of students dismissing the model as irrelevant because of unrealistic assumptions. This can be avoided if the student is always made aware that it is logically possible to progress from the simple to a more complex model. A simple induced component $(I = i(Y))$ can be incorporated in either the graphical approach (sloping J function) or in the

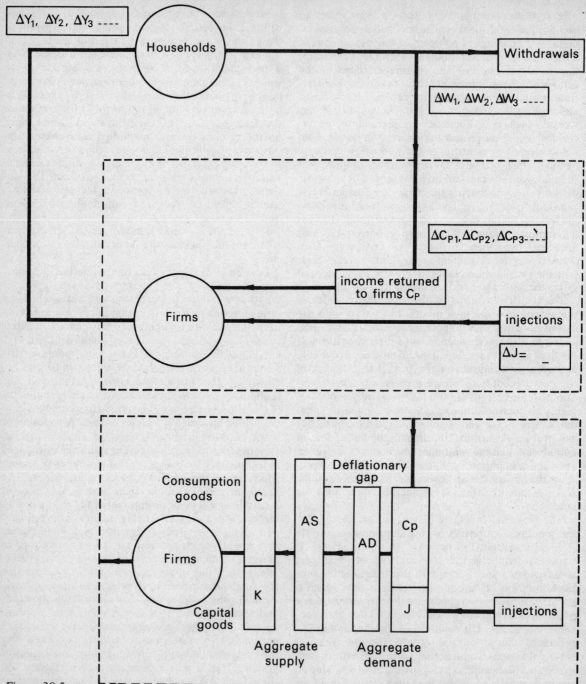

Figure 39.5

algebraic analysis (compound multiplier) without any great difficulty, but can be seen as a path along which the model can develop towards the 'real world'. Individual students will of course react differently in terms of what they are prepared to accept or question so the teacher must judge what is an appropriate level for a particular class. There is always a very thin line between unrealistic simplicity and confusing reality.

An important step in the analysis is the realisation that the total of individual spending decisions which contribute to aggregate demand need not correspond to the value of the output available from firms. Getting students to appreciate this is not made any easier by the treatment of the planned/realised spending distinction. Willatt[15] has commented on the plethora of terms which exist to describe planned decisions (intended, ex ante, etc). The practice of expressing aggregate demand in terms of expenditure symbols (C, I, X and G) adds to the confusion.

The flow chart can be used to demonstrate the direction of causality in relationships, the pattern of the interactions, and can also accommodate quantification. Wates[16] provides schematic representations of many areas of macroeconomics which are suitable for the initial presentation of ideas and revision. The overhead projector is particularly suitable for this sort of approach. Colour can be used to distinguish between different flows and separate transparencies can be used to build up the diagram or chart sector by sector.

The order of approach taken here really requires two flow charts. The purpose of Figure 39.4 is to build up the system with as much relevant detail as possible, without confusing the issue with a mass of lines. The conventional diagrams tend to exclude the possibility of business saving, indirect and direct tax, disposable income, and the import content of both investment and government spending.

The advantage of such a chart is that each sector can be added via different transparencies (i.e. the households and firms followed by saving and investment, then the tax and spending flows of the government, and finally the foreign sector's exports and imports). A simple households and firms transparency can form the basis for an introduction upon which the students' suggestions may be represented; the full diagram might then be introduced to codify their efforts. Figure 39.5a shows the simplification with just withdrawals and injections. This can be derived from the first chart and can be used as a basis for the discussion of how the system adjusts to change. Successive 'multiplier rounds' might be followed through by inserting numerical values in the ΔY, ΔW and ΔCp (that part of households' consumption which reaches domestic firms) boxes. The necessary quantification is thus linked directly to the causality shown by the flow chart rather than being shown separately in a table or calculation.

The most difficult idea to get across in this area is that of the series of changes which take place in the multiplier process. A simple numerical demonstration such as that which may be used in Figure 39.5 runs into the problem that the numbers rapidly involve fractions which the students find awkward to manipulate. A choice of an initial change in spending which is a power of two and using a withdrawals rate of $\frac{1}{2}$ is one possibility which avoids complex fractions (64, 32, 16, 8, 4, 2, 1, $\frac{1}{2}$, $\frac{1}{4}$) and will give a sum of demonstrably $1/w.dE$ (change in spending initially). There are obvious dangers in using such a constructed example; in this case

the sum of the withdrawals changes will be the same as that for the sum of all the incremental changes in income returning to firms after each round. Some texts assume that all students will be familiar with the summation of a geometric series. The example given here may take the student a step nearer accepting this piece of mathematics.

Some students will require a more concrete approach. The multiplier might be explained by means of a simple role-playing exercise. Students act as both consumers and producers/shopkeepers; they receive income when any other player purchases their product. The recipient of such income is allowed to spend some given proportion (e.g. $\frac{1}{2}$) on other players' products and they in turn spend the same proportion. The process may be started by one player receiving a gift of money (e.g. 32 pence in $\frac{1}{2}$ penny pieces or more ambitiously some amount in 'monopoly' money). The spending continues until every member of the group has spent the required proportion of new income. When all the individual incomes are summed then the total should approximate to twice the value of the original gift. The process can be repeated with different values for the marginal propensity to consume (e.g. $\frac{3}{4}$) and /or the injection. Students should then be able to see that the final figure for incomes created by a given injection will depend on the proportion not spent (saved). The simulation demonstrates the interdependence of economic decisions and makes the students aware of the fact that a given amount of money can finance different amounts of income generation.

Fluid analogies have formed the basis for a variety of explanatory models. Providing that care is taken not to push them too far they may provide valuable insights into the concepts of equilibrium, the stock/flow distinction and the role of money. Students are frequently unhappy with the idea that a certain quantity of money injected into the system can create income of a greater value. Future confusion between monetary variables (supply, velocity of circulation, etc) and real variables may be avoided by adhering strictly to terms like income, expenditure and demand rather than speaking more casually of, for instance, 'putting more money into the system'. A fixed stock of fluid in a system can be seen to be pumped round indefinitely, representing the stock of money which finances income generation, the flow. The obvious point to emphasise is that although the money keeps flowing round, each cycle of production is a finite process in which resources are used to produce output which is consumed.

Several texts employ block diagrams which may be used to give an alternative visual representation of the processes involved. Figure 39.5b may replace the marked section of the transparency part of Figure 39.5a to illustrate the concept of inflationary or deflationary gaps. Figure 39.6 on page 219 is an example of a block diagram used to demonstrate equivalence. Heilbroner[17] utilises such diagrams particularly well.

The graphical analysis of this area is fairly standard, although very few texts explicitly link the aggregate spending/income graph to the injections/withdrawals graph when discussing equilibrium. The limitations of the 45° approach have been recognised.[18] Authors of recent texts[2,3,19] have introduced the aggregate demand/aggregate supply (Z-curve) analysis. The advantage of this approach is that it becomes easier to progress from micro to macro and inflation as a process can be far more easily analysed.

The Measurement of National Income

It is hoped that the difficult area of measurement can now be tackled on the basis of a firm understanding of the meaning of national income and of the factors which determine it.

There are three main problems which need to be exposed and solved. The first, which has already been discussed, is that measurement is commonly treated at the outset, simultaneously with meaning, to the disadvantage of both. The ordering presented here will help to overcome this problem. The second point is that textbooks tend either to develop their own unique terminology or to make use of more established terms and define them differently, which is perhaps the thornier problem. This can lead to confusion among students who are encouraged to consult a variety of sources. In general, textbooks are not rigorous about the use of ' = ' and ' ≡ '. It may help students to understand the different meanings of an equation and a definitional identity if the appropriate signs are used. The final problem involves an attempt to make the difficulties encountered in measurement, such as double-counting, more than academic points or rules to be learnt without much real conceptual understanding.

Returning to the second problem, most confusion over the meaning of terms arises from the expenditure method of calculation. Textbooks introduce either the measure of Total Domestic Expenditure (TDE) or Total Final Expenditure (TFE) but not both. However, since both appear in the *Blue Book*, it might be advantageous to introduce both. Gross National Expenditure (GNE) is occasionally used for GNP by expenditure to distinguish it from GNP by output even though they are equivalent. The differences between these measures are summed up in Table 39.1.

These measures should be more readily understandable if emphasis is laid on each component having an import content which has to be removed if a measure of national output is to be arrived at. Lipsey builds up his identity for GNP by removing the import content from each component.

$$C^* \equiv C - C_m$$

where C is the conventional total consumption spending and C_m is that part spent on imported consumer goods. Thus C^* is consumption on domestically produced goods.

$$GNP \equiv (C-C_m)+(I-I_m)+(G-G_m)+(X-X_m)$$
$$\equiv (C+I+G+X)-(C_m+I_m+G_m+X_m)$$
$$\equiv C+I+G+X-M.$$

Prest also highlights this point in his table 'Domestic output content of total final expenditure at market prices' giving numerical proportions.

Another method of emphasising the import content and relating output to expenditure is given in Figure 39.6. Students should be able to work out the second column intuitively when asked: 'Who might purchase each of these four categories of goods?'

So far only expenditure estimates have been discussed, with the assumption of market prices, since the (tax – subsidy) component has not been removed. Students should be aware that GNP must be converted to factor cost to correspond with the income estimate which, by definition, is measured at factor cost. This point brings up the related one, namely, that the term National Income is used very loosely with a variety of meanings. Strictly, it is Net National Product (NNP) at factor cost but it is used to stand for almost every other aggregate measure and this should be made explicit.

However, exceptions to this general framework do exist. For example, Lipsey uses the term 'aggregate expenditure' for TFE. Aggregate Monetary Demand (AMD) is a common term which is not often explained in a clear and precise way. It should imply *planned* expenditure which is, of course, not measurable. But this is not made explicit, thus allowing for confusion when it is used in the determination of National Income. MEP uses the term AMD to equal C+I+G+X−S−M−T. 'These actually add up to the

	TDE	TFE	GDE
Spending:	domestic	domestic & foreign	domestic & foreign
Output:	domestic & foreign	domestic & foreign	domestic
Measurement:	C+I+G	C+I+G+X	C+I+G+X−M

Table 39.1 N.B. GNE=GDE+net asset/property income from abroad

Figure 39.6
Total output

Total output		TFE	TFE
domestically produced consumer goods Q_c	=	consumption ^CQ_c	C
		exports ^XQ_c	
		government ^GQ_c	
		change stocks $^{\Delta S}Q_c$	
domestically produced capital goods Q_k	=	private inv. $^{PI}Q_k$	X
		govt. inv. $^{GI}Q_k$	G
		exports ^XQ_k	
		$^{\Delta S}Q_k$	=
imports of consumer goods M_c	=	^CM_c	PI
		^GM_c	GI
		$^{\Delta S}M_c$	
imports of capital goods M_k	=	$^{PI}M_k$	ΔS
		$^{GI}M_k$	
		$^{\Delta S}M_k$	

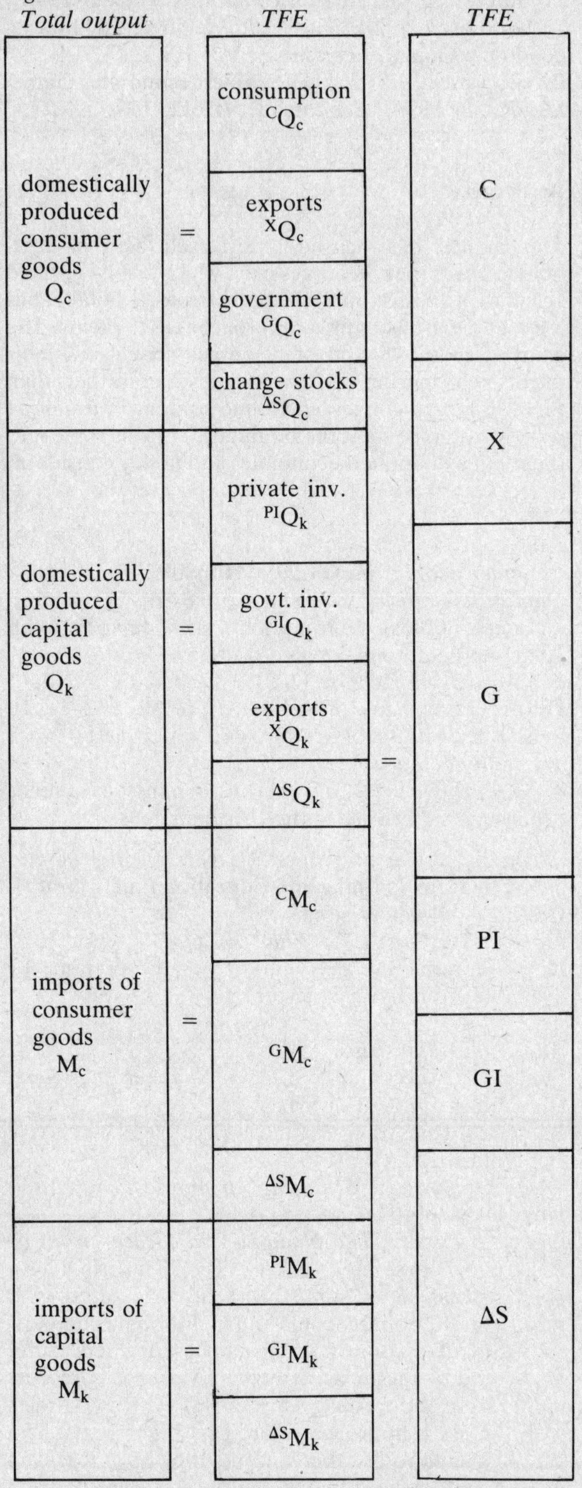

$$GDP+M=C+PI+GI+G+X+\Delta S;$$
$$GDP=C+PI+GI+G+\Delta S+X-M.$$

value of GNP, but in this section we shall use the term National Income to mean AMD. . . .'[6] If textbooks are unclear about what is meant, how can students be expected to have clear distinctions in their minds? Similarly, Harvey defines AMD as spending on consumer and capital goods. 'In a closed economy, aggregate demand is equal to GDP. It should be noted that "money National Income" is often substituted in general discussions on the subject.' There is not much evidence for what constitutes AMD in an open economy and no mention of planned spending. Therefore it is very important to develop a workable set of terms and definitions and to apply them rigorously.

The actual presentation of the information contained in accounting identities is an important consideration. The most usual treatment is by the use of symbols, but identities can of course be written out in full, or both may be used together.

$$\text{Gross National Product} \equiv \text{Consumption} + \text{Investment}$$
$$\begin{array}{ccccc} \text{GNP} & \equiv & \text{C} & + & \text{I} \\ \text{Y} & \equiv & \text{C} & + & \text{I} \end{array}$$

Information must be given not only about the relationships between variables but also about actual money values. The numerical values, distilled from the *Blue Book*, are most commonly given in tabular form. However, it is important to give an idea of relative sizes of the components of aggregates and this can be done by means of a block diagram. Harvey uses these to summarise the National Income calculations and to avoid the use of symbols for identities. Lobley[20] uses a histogram to give a visual display for relative size together with actual numerical figures. Stanlake has a numerical table as in the *Blue Book* as well as a flow diagram to connect all the various aggregate measures. Since one student learns nothing from a symbolic equation and another little from a block diagram, the best course is to present a number of different visual approaches. Also it can be useful to present some historical data, rather than just one year's current figures, for comparative purposes.

The final area to be discussed is the approach to presenting the economic difficulties in measurement. Most textbooks just list them rather unsatisfactorily. They could perhaps be made less dry and more intuitive by the further use of a simulation. If the class is divided into small producing units (a landowner growing trees, a timber producer, a furniture producer and a furniture retailer) each of whom sells his output to the next in the chain, it should become obvious that measurement of total output must be made by value-added or by final products only to avoid double-counting. If a government group is introduced into the simulation, whose only function is to redistribute workers' wages by taxing some and paying out to others (rather than to purchase real goods and services), then evidence should be provided that transfer payments cannot be included as additional income for the whole community. The problem of the import content of spending has already been dealt with. Finally, a general discussion should bring out what is and is not included by economists in production, that is, non-monetary transactions.

Conclusion

This topic is intellectually taxing and as such is difficult to present in a novel or stimulating way. The key to success may be to ensure that students fully appreciate the meaning and significance of their work rather than be led through a series of seemingly unconnected material. This involves careful structuring of the course. The published material makes this particularly difficult, but it is conceded that this only reflects the inherent difficulties which are encountered.

References

1 Nevin, E., *Textbook of Economic Analysis*, (Macmillan, 1967).
2 Ibid., (1976).
3 Stanlake, G. F., *Macroeconomics: An Introduction*, (Longman, 1974).
4 Nobbs, J., *Advanced Level Economics*, (McGraw-Hill, 1975).
5 Allport, J. and Stewart, C., *Economics*, (Cambridge University Press, 1972).
6 Manchester Economics Project, *Understanding Economics*, (Ginn and Co., 1972).
7 *National Income and Expenditure*, (CSO, annual).
8 Harvey, J., *Intermediate Economics*, (Macmillan, 1972).
9 Lipsey, R., *An Introduction to Positive Economics*, (Weidenfeld and Nicolson, 1975).
10 Pen, J., *Modern Economics*, (Pelican, 1965).
11 Ackley, G., *Macroeconomic Theory*, (Collier-Macmillan, 1969).
12 Seddon, V. J., 'More on the Value of the Multiplier: Limits to its Magnitude', *Economics*, Autumn 1971, pp 103–105.
13 Marshall, B. V., *Comprehensive Economics*, (Longman, 1975).
14 Prest, A. R. and Coppock, D. J., (ed), *The U.K. Economy: A Manual of Applied Economics*, (Weidenfeld and Nicolson, 1976).
15 Willatt, M., 'Economics Teaching: Some Lessons from Experience', *Economics*, Vol 10, Summer 1974.
16 Wates, C. J., *A Visual Approach to Economic Analysis*, (Longman, 1969).
17 Heilbroner, R. L., *Understanding Macroeconomics*, (Prentice-Hall, 1972).
18 Skouras, A., 'Recent Trends in Macroeconomics: a Bibliographical Review', *Economics*, Autumn 1971.
19 McCormick, B. J., *et al*., *Introducing Economics*, (Penguin Education, 1974).
20 Lobley, D., *Success in Economics*, (Murray, 1974).
21 Robinson, J. N., 'The Reading University Macroeconomic Game', *Economics*, Vol 10, 1974.
22 Robinson, J. N., 'The Macroeconomic Game: Lessons of 1974', *Economics*, Vol 11, 1975.

Resources

This chapter has focused almost exclusively on textbooks. Few other resources exist which can be applied specifically to this topic. Other media are available but they tend to utilise similar approaches to the texts. The gains from these type of resources arise from their intrinsic properties as teaching devices rather than their ability to convey economic content in a unique way. Most go beyond the boundaries of this topic into the realms of applied economics and policy considerations. Some resources which may be useful:

Films
National Income and Output, (900 8082–7), 20 mins.
Output, Income and Demand, (900 8129–7), 16 mins. Good use of block diagrams to illustrate links between AMD and National Income.
The Multiplier, (900 8130–7), 16 mins.
The Concept of Full Employment, (900 8132–1), 16 mins. Case study of Corby – re different types of unemployment.
Unemployment, (D101 01), 25 mins. Examines experience of two men who lost their jobs.

All the above are Open University programmes available from Training and Education Film Library – Guild Sound and Vision.
More Production . . . Of What? . . . and for Whom?, 25 mins. Economics of the Real World – Programme 17 available from BBC Enterprises.

Audiotapes/Filmstrips
Student Recording Ltd, *National Income* (tape/filmstrip, AVC/143).
Student Recording Ltd, *The Trade Cycle* (tape/filmstrip, AVC/147).
Open University, *Measuring Unemployment* (audio tape, D101 00/01).
Open University, *The Meaning and Measurement of Production* (audiotape, D101 10/11). This provides a good discussion of some problems associated with measuring National Income and makes some comparisons with other countries. This can be extremely useful at the end of the measurement section as it presents points from the whole area in a way which contrasts with the stark approach offered by many texts. The students have to use the concepts they have learnt in order to understand the commentary – a useful exercise.

Seminar Cassettes, *Roots of Inflation* (audiotape).
Audio Learning Tapes, *Keynesian Economics Today; Employment and the Balance of Payments; Inflation; Macro Analysis – Problems and Potential.*

Other Resources
Computer games and simulations have been developed but are not readily available. If the school has access to a computer terminal then the programmes available could be tried, but they are generally more orientated towards policy than towards the simple theory required. One obvious advantage is the power to perform the complex calculations required to analyse a model based on a number of behavioural equations. The problem is that often these 'workings' are hidden away in the programmes and are not always immediately available to the user. The expense and difficulty in obtaining access to these resources is rarely worthwhile in terms of returns to effort put in.

The Multiplier, Schools Council Computers in the Curriculum Project.
The Macroeconomic Game – operated by Reading University, described in *Economics*,[21],[22]. The students manipulate policy variables which are fed into the model. Four-country worlds compete with each other to maximise a utility function.

Programmed learning has a far greater hold in the United States than in the UK. The approach is of course suited to individual learning and can be incorporated into a teaching course. Two texts may provide a source of material:

Attiyeh, R., Lumsden, K. and Bach, G., *Macroeconomics – A Programmed Book*, (Prentice-Hall, 1970).
Attiyeh, R., Lumsden, K. and Bach, G., *Basic Economics – Theory and Cases*, (Prentice-Hall, 1973), chapters 13–16.
(Both useful for theory if students are not put off by dollar signs.)

Case-study material is rare. Once again it is usually linked to policy.

G. Kennedy, *et al.*, *Case Studies in Macroeconomics*, (Heinemann Educational, 1977). Some useful applied material.
Sandford, C. T. and Bradbury, M. S., *Case Studies in Economics: Economic Policy*, (Macmillan, 1970).
Sandford, C. T. and Bradbury, M. S., *Case Studies in Economics: Principles of Economics*, (Macmillan, 1971).

Educational Productions Ltd, *Understanding Our Economy*, wallchart, (C 1164).

40   The Economy of Oltenia* – A Macroeconomics Simulation†

Gordon Hewitt

The Oltenian Chancellor of the Exchequer is about to formulate his last budget before the General Election. He has received the following forecast from the Treasury and letter from the Prime Minister.

The Chancellor is expected to present his policy to the Prime Minister at this afternoon's Cabinet meeting.

Your task is to prepare the Chancellor for the meeting by providing him with the answers to each of the points raised in the Prime Minister's letter. You will probably find that you can best deal with the problem by dividing total demand into its components and cal-

* The national currency of Oltenia is the Lei, written as £.
† This version is derived from an original by J. N. Robinson.

culating the relationship between each component and total output.

The Oltenian Treasury

Chancellor of the Exchequer

Economic prospects for the next fiscal year

The Domestic Situation
Consumers' expenditure is likely to remain reasonably buoyant and can be expected to reach an annual rate of £1.1 million plus ⅗th of personal disposable income. We know that firms in Oltenia retain ⅛ of

(Continued overleaf)

---

gross domestic income (i.e. $\frac{1}{8}Y$) as retained profits, so that households receive $\frac{7}{8}Y$ as income. They pay 20 per cent income tax on their income (i.e. $\frac{1}{5}$) and hence personal disposable income is $(1-\frac{1}{5})$ of their pre-tax income. Therefore personal disposable income is $(1-\frac{1}{5})\frac{7}{8}Y$.

As you will recall, your party's success in the last election led to a massive increase in business confidence and hence in investment in plant and machinery. Our forecast is for a level of *gross investment* of £1.5 million.

Your 'Lame Ducks' policy has now been fully implemented so that all state subsidies, unemployment benefits, national insurance, etc have been abolished. Government activity in the economy is now limited to direct expenditure on goods and services and the raising of revenue through the taxation of incomes. Existing government programmes are likely to lead to an *expenditure on goods and services* of £2 million. Present levels of *taxation* are likely to yield to the Government a sum equal to 20 per cent of all incomes subject to tax. As a result of the adoption of the proposals contained in the White Paper *Tax Policy* (Cmnd. 3210), wages, salaries, dividends and retained profits will all be liable to this tax.

Productivity has increased a little since last year so that, if the economy were to attain a position of full employment, its gross domestic income would be £10 million.

The International Situation

The recent international monetary crisis has somewhat checked the growth of world trade so that *exports* are unlikely to exceed £1.4 million. *Imports* will represent about 15 per cent of gross domestic income.

Following the adoption of your isolationist policy, Oltenia's overseas assets have now been disposed of and foreign-owned assets in this country have been repurchased. As a result Oltenia will receive no property income from abroad and will pay none abroad; Oltenia will receive no transfers from abroad and will make none abroad.

The Chancellor of the Exchequer

1 You will note from the enclosed extract from Hansard that I had a rough time in the House yesterday. The Opposition have no clear idea about the state of the economy; but I do not like to see both parties united against us. The success of your forthcoming budget will be a crucial factor in the next election.
2 What will next year's level of national income be? Do you expect that this will result in a labour shortage or do you expect unemployment to occur?
3 If we have a labour shortage and inflation, I am not too worried. But if you forecast unemployment, it is imperative that we adopt a policy to produce full employment next year.
4 It seems to me that we have to choose between increasing government expenditure or reducing taxation. The Inland Revenue has threatened to stage a walk-out if we change tax rates again, so perhaps we should go for the required increase in government spending. You might also let me know whether such an increase would produce a budget surplus or deficit. (Did you see that the *Daily Post* has again called us 'this bankrupt government'?)
5 In the past, whenever we have gone for full employment we have had a wretched balance of payments problem to deal with. Can we achieve full employment without running into a balance of payments deficit this time?
6 I have arranged a Cabinet meeting for this afternoon at which you can present your budget plans.

Prime Minister

Enc.

Extract from Hansard

Mr Skive (National Radical, Grimesford):

Your government is committed to the most vicious policy ever contemplated since the War. You are trying to bludgeon the working man into submission by creating a high level of unemployment with all the human suffering that this entails. The people of Oltenia have long memories and when at last you pluck up the courage (interruptions from Hon. Members) to call an election your government will find itself out on its ear. The sooner this happens the better.

Mr Ffitch-Hamilton (National Reactionary, Milchester Spa):

By pandering to the unions and forcing up demand to boiling point, the government has sown the seeds of its own destruction. As the year goes by, we shall find an acute shortage of labour, inflation will be rife and once again the Lei will be the world's weak currency. Where is the government's sense of responsibility? Where is the dynamic leadership which we were promised? Lost in a welter of incompetence (jeers from Hon. Members).

Late Flash
Inland Revenue now say OK to tax change ... PM will prefer tax change in order to get full employment only if it results in a lower budget deficit than an increase in government spending ... what do you recommend?

Suggested Brief for the Chancellor

1 The expected level of GDP next year can be calculated as follows:

$$Y = C + I + G + X - M.$$

The Treasury forecasts can be substituted into this equation as follows:

$$Y = 1.1 + \tfrac{5}{7}(1 - \tfrac{1}{5})\,\tfrac{7}{8}\,Y + 1.5 + 2.0 + 1.4 - 0.15Y$$
$$= 6.0 + 0.35Y,$$
$$\therefore Y = 9.23.$$

Since the full employment level of GDP is 10, there will be unemployment in Oltenia next year.

2 The Prime Minister wishes you to take action to increase aggregate demand by raising government expenditure, so that next year's level of GDP becomes 10.

To calculate the required value of G, you can find what value G would have to take in the above equation to ensure that $Y = 10$,

i.e. $10 = 1.1 + \tfrac{5}{7}(1 - \tfrac{1}{5})\,\tfrac{7}{8}\,(10) + 1.5 + G + 1.4 -$
$$-0.15(10) = 7.5 + G,$$
$$\therefore G = 2.5.$$

3 If GDP is 10, tax revenue will be 2 (i.e. $\tfrac{1}{5} \times 10$) while government expenditure will be 2.5, so that the budget deficit will be 0.5.

4 If other policies remain unchanged, Oltenia will have a balance of trade deficit at full employment. If GDP is 10, exports will be 1.4, while imports will be 1.5.

Hence unless the PM is willing to consider other policies (e.g. export drives, import surcharges, quotas, deflation, etc) he cannot have full employment and a balance of payments surplus.

Late Flash

5 To calculate the required value of the tax rate, return to the original equation, this time leaving the value of G at 2 and estimate T – where T is the unknown variable whose value has to be calculated.

$$10 = 1.1 + \tfrac{5}{7}(1 - T)\,\tfrac{7}{8}\,(10) + 1.5 + 2.0 + 1.4 -$$
$$-0.15\,(10) = 10.75 - 6.25T,$$
$$\therefore T = 0.12.$$

So the tax rate must be reduced from 20 per cent to 12 per cent to ensure full employment.

6 If GDP is 10, tax revenue will be 1.2 (i.e. 0.12×10) when the tax rate is 12 per cent. Government expenditure is 2.0, so that the budget deficit will be 0.8. Hence, an increase in government expenditure will be the preferred policy, if the PM insists on minimising the budget deficit.

Appendix

You might like to point out to the PM that these two changes are not mutually exclusive. If he is seriously concerned about the budget deficit (which at the moment is $2 - \tfrac{1}{5}(9.23) = 0.154$), it is possible to attain full employment *and* balance the budget by changing government expenditure and the tax rate simultaneously.

There are now two unknowns in the equation, G and T,

i.e. $10 = 1.1 + \tfrac{5}{7}(1 - T)\,\tfrac{7}{8}\,(10) + 1.5 + G + 1.4 - 0.15\,(10)$
$$= 8.75 - \tfrac{5}{8}\,(T)10 + G.$$

But if the budget is balanced, government expenditure is equal to government revenue,

i.e. $G = (T \times 10)$.

Hence by substituting G for $(T \times 10)$ into the equation,

$$10 = 8.75 - \tfrac{5}{8}\,G + G,$$
$$\therefore G = 3\tfrac{1}{3},$$

and

$$T = \frac{G}{10} = \frac{10}{3} \times \frac{1}{10} = \frac{1}{3}.$$

Thus, in order to have a balanced budget and still ensure full employment, government expenditure will have to be raised to $3\tfrac{1}{3}$ and the tax rate simultaneously increased to $33\tfrac{1}{3}$ per cent.

41 International Trade and Finance; the Law of Comparative Advantage

Maurice Willatt

The Basic Problems

'I must give notice that we are now in the region of the most complicated questions which political economy affords, that the subject is one which cannot possibly be made elementary; and that a more continuous effort of attention than has yet been required will be necessary to follow the series of deductions.' Thus wrote John Stuart Mill in 1848; the tradition became established that everything to do with international economic relations is difficult and should be grouped together in a special section at the end, or very near the end, of any general course in economics. Nearly all textbooks commonly used with this age group follow the tradition: for example, Nevin[1] devotes pages 365–405 to the subject out of his total of 415 pages; Lipsey[2] pages 635–708 out of 812. A few writers, for example McCormick et al.,[3] treat comparative costs when discussing internal trade and location, and omit the rest; or like Stonier and Hague[4] leave it all out, presumably for the more able students to study in some special text on international trade.

The teacher has to decide whether to follow tradition; whether the problems involved in teaching international trade are different from, and more difficult than, those which the rest of 'political economy affords'; and whether detaching those problems from the main body of theory makes their solution easier or more difficult. The difficulties which led to the traditional separation may be considered under three main headings: first, the theory of value; secondly, nationalism; thirdly, accounting. First, Mill's main problem was reconciling two quite different theories of value: the one used in the main body of his work in terms of absolute or labour costs, and the other used in the theory of international trade in terms of comparative costs. Modern students should have no trouble here, but there seems to be a natural tendency to want value to be an absolute, inherent in commodities. As every examiner knows, beneath the apparent skill displayed in handling value as a ratio established by supply and demand, lurks an inveterate tendency to make it the result of cost alone. This compounds the difficulty which many people have in understanding ratios. They have to think hard when asked how much cloth will exchange for a litre of wine, if a metre of cloth exchanges for three litres.

Secondly, there is an inherent economic nationalism in the students, which makes them accept almost any fallacy, provided that it turns on doing down the foreigner. Perhaps the teaching of macroeconomics is partly to blame: does it ever deal with maximising *world* income, with exports and imports cancelled as internal transfers?

Thirdly, much of the treatment of international economic relations involves a balance sheet, called 'the balance of payments', which offers many difficulties to those unskilled in accounting, and may well clash with the treatment of national accounts adopted in teaching macroeconomics.

International Economic Relations as a Topic

Most of this chapter considers the problems of teaching students of this age group in the course of an attempt to present the whole of elementary economic theory incorporating appropriate factual material. But economic relations between the home country and others may also be singled out as a topic or focus of interest by itself or as part of some general studies or inter-disciplinary course. 'Britain in the red', or 'What price sterling?', would tap current interests. 'Britain in the Common Market' or 'Britain and the Third World' would bring in political science, demography, geography, etc.

Teachers and students of such topics will often have to make up by their enthusiasm for the lack of adequate time and materials, and of the salutary burden of an external examination. Very careful preliminary planning is essential. Factual material must be pre-packaged to be within the constraints of the students' time and ability, while still requiring from them genuine efforts to search, analyse and select. To avoid the ill-formed and intemperate discussion of ill-defined issues without encouraging the mere collection of information is perhaps the hardest task. A useful procedure is to arrange the syllabus as a series of items in ascending order of generality, with the material required indicated at each stage, as a kind of flow diagram. The teacher should be clear about the items of theory involved and have decided where they should be introduced; for example, where and for which students reference to books like Powicke[5], chapters 13, 14, 15, or Rogers[6], is appropriate.

There are many advantages in giving such topics a

definite historical slant: 'Britain in the modern world economy', or 'The decline of sterling'. Simple paperback books are available; a narrative interest is present; the incorporation of theory and fact is easier to achieve. Successful courses on these lines have been undertaken, not only with main-subject historians, but also with natural scientists who need and enjoy the contact with human affairs. All experience shows that, in all such 'general interest' or 'liberal studies' or 'minority time' courses, more planning and more expertise are required of the teacher than in the traditional treatment. But when successful, they come near to reaching that goal proposed by all the great economists: the intimate and fruitful union of fact and theory.

Comparative Cost and Comparative Advantage

The traditional treatment starts with two countries producing one or both of two commodities. There is a great temptation to plunge into this too readily. It seems easy to the teacher because he understands it already: it appears simple to the student as a detached event easy to memorise, the ability and eagerness to memorise being the strength and weakness of this age group. But some preliminary treatment is essential, if not covered at an earlier stage. 'Isolated exchange' between two persons or firms is now rarely treated in the introductory theory of price, perhaps because prices are so often clearly marked in the shops and 'administered' by large firms. Certainly some such device as Tom and Jack shipwrecked on a desert island, followed perhaps by East Lancashire selling cloth in exchange for food from West Lancashire, should be used to make clear from the start that trade based on comparative cost differences is not a mysterious feature of international trade alone.

Some thought should also be given to the form of the two-country model; is it to be a comparison of output per unit of factor, amount of factor per unit of output, or comparative price differences measured in money? It is better to avoid real countries and real currencies, lest the student should feed in what he knows about them as an attempt at premature realism. Some teachers and students seem to like fanciful names for the countries and currencies. The advantages of taking factor costs rather than prices are, first, that the beginner is happy to think in terms of real costs; secondly, that arithmetical problems can more easily be devised, presumably to give the student a sense of achievement and some 'fixative' effect. On the other hand, is it wise to indulge the innate love of real costs or to give the impression that elaborate sums based on bogus situations are of any value in themselves?

Most textbook writers and probably most teachers adopt a factor cost model of the form: 'Country A has 1000 units of factors which can be used to produce either 2000 units of X or 1500 units of Y, whereas country B ...' What is to be done when the students accept unquestioningly that, before trade begins, since 2000 is larger than 1500, A will produce only X? The teacher who uses this approach is responsible for making sure that demand is expressly brought in, perhaps by asking: 'What if people in A do not want X at all, or are unwilling to buy it except at a low price?' Similarly, teachers who prefer a model in terms of money prices must explore the conditions of demand and supply which underlie the differences in price ratios.

The restriction to two countries and two commodities seems rarely to excite doubts in the minds of this age group. Probably an attempt should be made to explain the importance of the complications caused by relaxing the restriction. An effective method is to set up a table of n countries and m commodities, measured in common (e.g. metric) units. In each country goods are arranged in descending order of price. Each difference in the order of goods between different countries represents a difference in comparative cost and offers a possible advantage. Most students can take a useful part in discussing the complexities: some might have the ability and opportunity to bring in a computer programme.

Possible and Actual Gains from Trade

There is an understandable but most regrettable custom of stopping short, once the demonstration has been made that if comparative advantages exist, both A and B may gain from starting trade. It is understandable, because everyone seeks to economise time; but regrettable because it leaves theory in the air. Students will recite the story of country A and country B, but their commonsense tells them that it does not apply to real life and they are thrown back on old mercantilism, the slaves of some seventeenth-century economist. Examiners in economic history, marking some question on commercial policy, cannot tell which, if any, of the candidates have been studying economics. A group of seventeen-year-old boys, all of whom got high grades in 'A' level economics, were asked to comment on a passage in Williams[7] (page 85): 'In 1846 British industrial supremacy was clearly established, and a policy of free trade was a useful means of exploiting this situation to her advantage; by 1932 it was equally clear that this supremacy had passed and that Britain's industry had at least as much need of protection as that of her rivals.' They agreed on the opinion that free trade is good for a country if, and only if, she has a clear technical superiority in manufacturing industry; also that, if such a lead is lost, it can be regained by taxing imported manufactured goods. Subsequent questioning showed that these students were competent performers in the usual exercises on comparative costs, which had evidently not been connected at all with real or historical situations.

Time saved here is a false economy. Students must be led to consider what costs in addition to the cost of transporting goods are incurred in changing the patterns of economic activity. No great depth of historical knowledge is required to comment on the fate of handloom weavers, in Britain and elsewhere, when Lancashire became the cotton manufacturer of the world. This, and similar examples of the side effects of cashing in on the gains from trade, should be linked with the earlier treatment of the hopes and perils of specialisation in general, but perhaps teachers have followed Adam Smith's example in treating the good effects in chapter one and leaving the bad effects to several hundred pages later. Opportunity should be seized to put the 'infant industries' argument correctly: it should be allowed to refer not to the protection of *any* industry but only to the overcoming of frictional obstacles to achieving a position nearer to the optimum use of comparative advantage. Harrod[8] (chapter 3) will be found helpful.

Another fundamental difficulty is the assumption that the cost relationships existing before trade begins may be expected to persist; hardly anything could be more improbable. Given the opportunity, students will readily point out that imports of Y and exports of X, by altering the quantities offered for sale, will alter the relative prices and tend to erode the comparative advantage. Concentrating on the production of one of the two commodities and cutting down on the other will alter average costs of production. Specific factors limited in quantity, learning effects and economies of scale should readily be adduced. Is there not something absurd in the common practice of calculating at great length the possible gains from trade, using cost conditions which are bound to alter the moment trade begins?

Breaking up the Package

In view of the difficulties outlined in the previous sections, an increasing number of teachers break up the detached package labelled 'international trade' on the grounds that it either duplicates or conflicts with earlier work, that it is time-consuming if done properly and dangerous if scamped; and that there should be a single theory of trade, whether within or across national boundaries. This may represent the path which progress will take, but there are obvious advantages in putting before students the traditional procedure because they are bound to meet discussion (and examination) couched in the traditional language and employing the traditional concepts. It should be possible to get round this by covering the general theory of trade thoroughly as part of the main course and then

adding a rapid perusal of the traditional treatment as a kind of savoury.

An increasing number of students will have been brought up on indifference curves and production possibility (or transformation) curves. A person, firm or country is assumed to be able to produce various alternative combinations of commodities X and Y as indicated by the area under the curve PP in Figure 41.1. By putting into the diagram an indifference curve map (which can be done very effectively using a transparency on an overhead projector), the optimum combination can be shown, where PP touches the highest possible indifference curve II. The common tangent HH expresses by its slope the ratio between the prices of X and Y. No apology is offered for rehearsing this elementary theory: the purpose is to introduce a useful simplification. When the closed economy shown in Figure 41.1 starts trading with the rest of the world in Figure 41.2, it is assumed that world markets for X and Y are so large that exports and imports made by this country have no effect on world prices, so that a constant world price line WW can be drawn on Figure 41.2. It is now easy to show that the country should

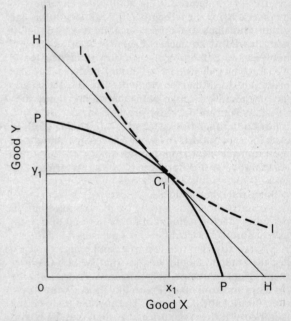

Figure 41.1

produce y_2 of Y instead of y_1 and x_2 of X instead of x_1. It can now exchange y_2 minus y_1 at the world price ratio for X, getting x_3 minus x_2 which is obviously greater than x_1 minus x_2 no longer produced at home. This is the gain from trade.

Assuming that the assumption is reasonable, as in most cases it surely is, certain advantages follow. Students will ask what assumptions about indifference

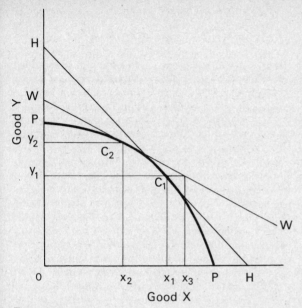

Figure 41.2

that the supply of broadcloth is the demand for linen, and vice versa. It will be noticed that most textbooks slide rapidly over the subject, never really dealing with the determination of the terms of trade, but passing on to the problem of *measuring changes* in the terms of trade. This is probably because looming up behind the two-country, two-commodity case is the complexity of real conditions. How can a set of n exchange ratios involving m different countries be added together in any meaningful fashion? One way out is to take historical examples as near to the two-commodity case as possible; another way is to own up and leave the matter as being too difficult for treatment at this level.

Measuring *changes* in the terms of trade is, however, possible and useful with this age group. Presumably index numbers, their construction, uses and dangers will already have cropped up in connection with prices, family expenditure and the cost of living. It is difficult to deal with the effects on welfare and employment of changes in exchange rates without their help.

curve patterns, (i.e. about demand for X and Y), have to be made if the new consumption position including x_3 instead of x_1 is to be significantly better than the old one; also whether the PP curve is likely to change: is it rigid, or a balloon, or a trampoline? All the considerations raised in the previous section suggest themselves naturally. Apparent complexity can be removed by the use of coloured lines, of course. A convenient discussion can be found in van Meerhaege,[9] pages 31–34. Teachers may well wish to experiment in suitable circumstances with more advanced techniques, remembering that many things now commonplace were regarded not so long ago as only suitable for good students at universities.

The Terms of Trade

The traditional two-country, two-commodity picture offers an unambiguous meaning for this phrase. As Mill says: 'When each country produced both commodities for itself, 10 yards of broadcloth exchanged for 15 yards of linen in England, and for 20 in Germany. They will now exchange for the same number of yards of linen in both. For what number?' Evidently to answer this question demand conditions in both countries must be known. So much attention is given to the theory of demand by most teachers that pupils of this age group are very ready to accept the proposition that the terms of trade depend on demand. But this is not demand as they understand it; apart from those who still think of 'demand' as the same thing as 'need', the rest think of it as an offer of money and cannot see

Exchange Rates and the Concept of Parity

After spending precious time on the difficult problems of the terms of trade, most people will move on eagerly to consider the theory of exchange rates between currencies, a topic in the forefront of current discussion. The obvious approach is to treat it as a special case of general price theory. Currency being a durable commodity with an important time dimension, its price is often dominated by anticipated future prices. Governments are usually eager to control it, but hampered by lack of power either over the buyers or over the sellers. But these special features should not prevent an effective application of the price theory previously learnt, as, for example, in Lipsey, pages 654–66.

The word 'parity' sometimes causes difficulty, which is not avoided by not using the word, since it crops up frequently in public and press discussion. It should be linked with the notion of equilibrium price. Some writers deny that equilibrium in exchange rates exists or is ascertainable. (See Robinson and Eatwell,[10] pages 261–2.) Students will accept the general proposition that, if the supply and demand conditions remain constant for long enough, a stable exchange rate ought to be reached, but have trouble in relating demand for currency to supply of goods, and vice versa.

The approach to equilibrium exchange rates used to be through the Law or Principle of Purchasing Power Parity, stating that an exchange rate must tend to bring internal price and income levels in the countries concerned into some sort of equality. This is easy to demonstrate with two countries whose economic relations are confined to the transfer of goods and within which all goods can be bought and sold and all incomes arise from such transfers. But long experience shows

Holidaymakers in Paris soon realise that entertainment that costs a pound in London costs far more than a pound's worth of French francs. The official rates of exchange state that the pound is equivalent in value to so many Deutsch marks or French francs. But once in West Germany or France the English traveller soon finds out the rates do not give a realistic measure of the worth of the pound.

The latest *Employment Gazette* publishes research by the statistical office of the European Communities showing how much currency is required in EEC countries to buy approximately the same basket of goods and services (vol 85, No. 5, HMSO, £1.20). For a traveller from London, prices in all the EEC countries except the Irish Republic are higher than in London.

In October 1975, £100 would buy in foreign exchange: 531 deutschmarks, 906 French francs, 139,418 Italian lire, 546 Dutch florins, 8,005 Belgian/Luxembourg francs, 100 Irish pounds and 1,238 Danish kroner. However, in order to buy the goods and services which £100 would buy in London, it would be necessary to spend: 686 marks in Bonn, 1,188 francs in Paris, 140,787 lire in Rome, 652 florins in Amsterdam, 9,785 Belgian francs in Brussels, 9,047 Luxembourg francs in Luxembourg, 98 Irish pounds in Dublin, and 1,821 Danish kroner in Copenhagen.

So the London holidaymaker would find that prices in Bonn were 129 per cent of the prices in London, in Paris 131 per cent, in Rome 101 per cent, in Amsterdam 119 per cent, in Luxembourg 113 per cent, in Dublin 98 per cent, and Copenhagen 147 per cent. These calculations are based on a wide range of services, including food, clothing, fuel, household furnishing, transport, and recreation. The table shows the comparative costs of the goods and services the holiday maker is most likely to want:

Costs in EEC capitals, London = 100

	food, drink and tobacco	transport and communication	recreation, culture etc*
Bonn	128	125	147
Paris	114	128	177
Rome	104	98	145
Amsterdam	109	124	136
Brussels	106	116	157
Luxembourg	110	104	129
Dublin	97	107	97
Copenhagen	147	146	176

*includes entertainment and education

Figure 41.3 From New Society, *2 June 1977, the weekly review of the social sciences*

that learning the principle is much easier than applying it, whether because students' commonsense revolts at the severity of the assumptions, or from the usual problem of understanding ratios. Hence the common practice today is to omit Purchasing Power Parity.

Starting from the facts, instead of the theory, has its attractions. Press cuttings, such as Figure 41.3, can be used to start discussion about the possible reasons for the well-known differences between the purchasing power of the pound at home and the purchasing power abroad of the amount of foreign currency obtainable for it. With careful handling, the gist of the principle can be reached without introducing the name.

Another approach, used with great success by some teachers, is by way of some particular historical situation. Older people, brought up in gold standard times when floating rates were regarded as an unnatural practice found among foreigners, will wish to start from rates tied to gold or to international agreements. This has the great advantage that attention is focused from the start on the impact of exchange rates on internal levels of prices, incomes and employment, and on government responsibilities to make the impact effective but tolerable. The situation in Britain in April 1925 is well documented in readily accessible, readable and short historical narratives and in Keynes' pamphlet: *The Economic Consequences of Mr Churchill*[11]. Similar possible situations, such as September 1931 or September 1949, could be used. Very successful simulation exercises have been created out of the events of 1925, with students showing not only gusto but also surprising accuracy in playing the roles of colourful characters like Norman, Churchill and Keynes. Care must of course be taken to structure the simulation so that the impact effects referred to above are clearly evinced.

A consideration often neglected in all economics teaching, but particularly in this area, is that people of sixteen (or for that matter of eleven) enter schools and colleges already soaked in the economic ideas current in the society in which they live. The problem is often that the received economic ideas are mythology and must be taken apart and rebuilt. The economic history teacher, in particular, has to spend much time cutting down to size the happy peasant, the miraculous intervention of trade unions, or the 'collapse' of agriculture in 1879. In this matter of exchange rates, pupils are already convinced that a rate may be too 'high', that a country may be 'living beyond its means', that if sterling is to 'look the dollar in the face', incomes must be reduced – not mine, but yours. It must be confessed that in this field the net effect of teaching is usually a very minimal improvement in the sophistication and accuracy of comment. Probably there are new ways, not yet thought out, of canalising and developing the elements of truth in popular thinking. Consider the following: 'The prices of our exports in the international market are too high. Why are they too high? The orthodox answer is to blame it on the working man for working too little and getting too much. In some industries and some grades of labour, particularly the unskilled, this is true; and other industries, for example, the railways, are overstaffed.' This is an extract, not from modern journalism, but from Keynes' pamphlet of 1925 referred to above. Is it feasible to cash in on the useful elements in popular opinion by starting with a selection of quotations from academic economists and trying to work back to the more formal analysis based on general price theory?

The Balance of Payments

Perhaps the most common error in teaching is to assume that a class knows elementary points which in fact it does not, and is too proud or shy or passive to ask about. Many people, remembering failure to grasp lists of figures when much younger, are allergic to balance sheets. Whatever experience they may have in clubs and committees, they appear confused between profit and loss accounts and cash accounts. Thus a class of boys who had 'done' the balance of payments all agreed with the definition: 'a statement of the gains and losses incurred by dealing with foreigners during a given year'. It took some time to convince them that in such a statement the plus side would include imports and investment abroad (the latter valued at the discounted sum of estimated future income accruing as a result) and that exports would go on the minus side. It is essential to make sure that the balance of payments with which governments and economists deal is a cash account, clearly understood as such, before going further. This may involve courting impatience or even mild derision by taking trivial examples from ordinary life. Why is expenditure on a new cricket pavilion shown as a debit item in one kind of account, but as an asset in another? It might be wrong to despise the childish device of an account for John Bull's holdings of dollars (see Table 41.1).

million dollars

Held by J. Bull on 1st January:	1000
Paid to Uncle Sam for goods and services:	500
Received of Uncle Sam for goods and services:	400
Loss on current account	100
Lent to Uncle Sam	50
Borrowed from Uncle Sam	150
Gain on capital account	100
Held by J. Bull on 31st December	1000

Table 41.1

Once this is clear, the model may be made progressively more realistic, until treatment with the more advanced students reaches the level of, for example Prest[12], where the section on foreign trade and the balance of payments by J. S. Metcalfe provides the ultimate target for students of this age group.

Two difficulties may perhaps be safely ignored, unless they are encountered in discussion: first, the fact that transactions undertaken in one year may be paid for in another, giving rise to variations in the timing of payment when exchange rates are expected to alter; secondly, the fact that official intervention is not confined to adding to or subtracting from a hoard of gold and foreign banknotes in the vaults of the Bank of England.

Government Policy

At this point the subject inevitably broadens. Whatever treatment has been adopted, whether international trade has been isolated in a single package, or brought in piecemeal as part of a general consideration of economic activity, governments in modern times must place their attitude to foreign trade in the pattern of general economic policy, and teachers must bring together the macroeconomics and monetary theory previously taught so as to take into the outside world. The changes in the different items in the balance of payments, for example the rise in imports of manufactures and the decline in invisibles, have to be related to changes (or lack of change), in British industry and British society. All that can be done here is to point out some ways in which specific and systematic treatment of international economic relations can assist the meaningful and productive handling of issues of policy. One theme to discuss is the remarkable concentration of attention on exchange rates, evident in the (rather misleading) prominence given by the media to monthly balance of payments figures. The public are convinced that the British balance has been 'in the red' continuously and that sterling has fallen continuously, for many years. The thesis should be considered, but not necessarily accepted, that inspiring anxiety about exchange rates is an important device for preserving social structure, as unemployment was forty years ago; before that, the Labour Laws; and before that, serfdom. The less inclined towards left wing views students may be, the more they should be brought to question the established right wing views on the causes of Britain's economic difficulties. In the process, the teacher will note to what extent the theory put before them has been absorbed, in a form in which it can be applied.

Another important subject is the restriction of the movement of commodities and factors across national boundaries. The main difficulty experienced in considering the pros and cons of restriction will usually be, (as suggested on page 224), the strong emotions roused, particularly in dealing with movement of persons. If the careful treatment of the gains from trade, advocated on pages 225–226, has been fully absorbed, the probable gains and losses caused by tariffs will be given a more moderate assessment than has been usual in popular controversy. A useful scheme of work in this field may be found in Lipsey, chapter 46. Students should be left with the impression that restrictions, whether quantitative or fiscal, are unlikely to help much, and unlikely to be as important as other causes of distortion and inefficiency in inflicting damage.

There may be some readers who feel that cooling down restrictions such as tariffs by playing down their importance is inadmissible. Such readers will presumably choose, in their own teaching, to devote a good deal of attention to the European Common Market, as a special case of attempting to get great economic advantages by removing restrictions. How much time can be spared for this subject, at this stage of a continuing general course in economics? The economic advantages claimed by the supporters of EEC can be explained briefly under the headings of fuller use of comparative advantages, increased competition, and economies of scale. But an examination of how far such advantages are accruing is a much more lengthy business. Moreover, it may well be true that the real purpose, and the ultimate results, lie outside the field of economics, or at least of 'positive' economics. In that case, particularly if the economics teacher has precise examination targets to meet, he will try to push the Common Market into some general studies or minority time assignment. But, in view of the widespread public interest and the importance attached by most people to the Common Market, there is a strong case for devoting some considerable time to it.

The same arguments apply to the treatment of another topic which arouses current interest, i.e. migration of people. If it is treated at all, it should clearly refer not only to New Commonwealth immigration into Britain since 1945, but also to the 'brain drain', 'guest-workers' in continental Europe and some reference to the USA. However, since the main issues are social, cultural and political rather than economic the subject may have to be passed over very briefly.

International Co-operation and Institutions

There is never time to give more than perfunctory attention to this topic; often all that can be done is to spell out the more important sets of initials – IMF, UNCTAD, OEEC, IPU, GATT and so on. Placed right at the end of the usual systematic treatment of the whole of elementary economics, it naturally gets crowded out in accordance with the Parkinsonian principle that everything takes more time than was allotted. But why is it placed right at the end; and why, even in specialised topical courses on international economics, does it not fare much better? There was a period in history when the economists of western Europe could concern themselves mainly with the household and the firm, treating the state as a disagreeable necessity left to the end of the book. Then, in accordance with the realities of economic development, macroeconomics emerged; there are now textbooks which start with the economy as a whole, and in which it is the household or the firm which tends to get crowded out. But where are the books which start with the *world* economy?

By the twenty-first century, when the present sixteen to eighteen age group will have come to control the world, economically independent national states will have joined the city states and the grand duchies in history books. If the object of education is to prepare people for life, is it right to set economics teaching in a framework of self-centred nationalism? Just as it now seems strange that the seventeenth century encouraged privateers and slavers and regarded international trade as war carried on by other means, so it will seem strange that the twentieth century allows beggar-my-neighbour policies, thinks it clever to put heavy taxes on foreign goods with an inelastic supply, tolerates flags of convenience, tax havens, brain drains and speculative attacks on particular currencies by international financiers, etc.

But until such time as the appropriate changes in the lay-out of economics courses arrive, the practical teacher has to make the best of the limited time available. It is important to decide when planning the syllabus how much time can be allotted and by what sacrifices earlier in the scheme he can ensure that there is enough elbow-room to allow a significant treatment of this subject. But this is not the place to suggest omissions, apart from those allowed by breaking up the traditional international trade package: the comment may be allowed that there are probably sacred but barren cows for slaughter, knick-knacks ripe for the jumble sale. The minimum treatment to be aimed at must surely include: emphasis on the extraordinary extent and variety of activities and institutions; consideration of the forces encouraging and those inhibiting the growth of supra-national institutions; examination of the structure, and assessment of the importance, of one typical example of each major type.

They can be classified either by their origin and structure, or by the kind of economic activity they affect. A classification, which has worked well with some kinds of student and enables most types of international economic organisation to be included, is as follows:

1 general political organisations in their economic aspects, e.g. agencies of the UN;

2 customs unions and trade agreements, e.g. GATT, EEC;
3 commodity and currency agreements, e.g. sugar agreements, the European currency 'snake';
4 agreements on commercial law and police;
5 'public utility' type agreements, e.g. IPU, safety at sea and in the air;
6 multi-national corporations and international banks;
7 organisations of firms and trade unions for action in industrial relations;
8 private or quasi-national welfare organisations.

The test of such a list is of course the number of items which do not fit neatly into one slot; just as a filing system can be judged by the thickness of the 'miscellaneous' file. In choosing examples to illustrate each type, the obvious plan is to use those which have already occurred in other connections: cocoa, tin, rubber or sugar agreements while dealing with the effects on price of supply conditions; multinational corporations when dealing with the control of monopoly; EEC in dealing with tariffs; international banks when dealing with money and banking.

It will require much self-restraint to confine discussion to purely economic aspects; whether with this age group such self-restraint is legitimate is doubtful. Here, as elsewhere, the usual assumption that economic activity is directed to maximising material welfare, specifically in this field the welfare of an abstraction called the 'national economy', is a fertile source of trouble.

Some General Considerations

Ideology
If we say we have no ideology we deceive ourselves. All the foregoing comments are based on the liberal tradition of Keynes, Marshall and Mill. Those teachers who start out from different assumptions will choose a different set of topics and emphasise the circumstances in which international trade is exploitation, and the political pressures which may tend to fix the terms of trade in the interest of the stronger power. Since economics is to them merely politics, the teaching of the theory of international trade is hypocrisy intended to deceive the masses. 'Liberal' teachers will be careful to make sure that the element of objective truth in the communist case is not glossed over, by explicitly considering possible and historical cases where one country gained from trade and the other lost, and where gains from trade accrued to certain people in a country at the cost of losses to the rest. See also *The Teaching of Economics in Schools*[13], page 16.

Theory
It has also been assumed in this chapter that theory is essential, in the sense not only that it *ought* to be included in any teaching of economics, but also that it *is* automatically present whether we wish it or not. The human mind – any human mind – apprehends the outside world by selecting and arranging, which is as good a definition of theory as any other. Attempting to teach purely factual or descriptive economics is illusory: the information is structured either by the teacher or the pupil. The choice is between explicit and, it is hoped, defensible theory, and unstated and therefore uncontrolled theory. It has also been assumed that the theory is the basic thing and the part that is difficult to teach. Get that right, and the rest will follow. Does experience not show that this is broadly true? Naturally the kind of theory and way of presenting it should be adapted to the maturity and academic skills of the learner. More will be said in the next section about the special difficulties of the theory of international trade for less academic pupils. In the present state of knowledge, when teaching is an art rather than a science, the fitting of intellectual tools to hands capable of handling them may be a matter of trial and error. Moreover, the sharpness of the tools must also be varied to suit the powers of the learner. On this, see Lee[14], page 43.

The Place of History
Many teachers say that they would like to teach a good deal of economic history as part of their economics teaching but that they do not get the time, or alternatively that only immediately current events and facts are of interest to their students. Four points could be made in reply. First, the alleged 'current' material is in fact fairly recent history and often wrongly stated history at that, which has to be corrected by official statements later on. Contemporary evidence tells us more about the persons concerned than about what actually happened. Secondly, teacher and student alike are themselves pieces of history and will select and interpret evidence in accordance with their past experience. Thirdly, they are all exposed to, and governed by, a kind of folk knowledge of economics, already referred to on page 228, and it may be necessary to correct views of the past before there is much hope of understanding the present. Fourthly, much of the theory can be illustrated better from the past. Examples can be selected which are simpler and less charged with emotion, with results which can be assessed more securely. Current examples can then be considered with less confusion and prejudice. In the larger textbooks, particularly the older ones like Haberler,[15] examples can be found which can be lifted by teachers like flowering plants, to be fruitful where required.

Handling Factual Information
It was assumed above that if the theory were properly taught, the handling of the facts would follow. Perhaps, however, a few words on the lessons of experience in

this field would not be out of place. Information about international economic relations is abundant, complicated and not as a rule directed at this age group. Public libraries, and the libraries of colleges and schools, are not always ideally provided with the relevant periodicals and handbooks on this subject. Free or cheap material, like the *Bank of England Quarterly Bulletin* and the bank reviews seem much more difficult on this subject than on others. Articles in the 'quality' press tend to be either too full of jargon or too 'popular' in treatment. The material issued by firms and departments for the general reader tends to be merely leaflets, useful for opening up a subject but not much else. One of the most important functions of the teacher is to act as intermediary, guiding, selecting, and often producing paraphrases of the more technical articles. An obvious method, where a group is of very mixed ability, is to set up teams or syndicates in which there is a relatively able leader directing the scissors-and-paste activities of the rest of the team.

The Less Academic Student

No doubt some readers have been getting rather restive: 'Not only does this writer talk about nothing but the teaching of theory; he also deals only with the teaching of highly academic students.' The reason for this is that the target has been to find ways of teaching what Mill thought 'cannot possibly be made elementary'. Only if it can be mastered by the more academic does the question of teaching it to the less academic arise.

'Less academic' covers two types of student. The first is lacking in intellectual qualities, in energy or in motivation, but has basically the same cast of mind as the academic 'high flyer'. The second type is non-academic in the sense that the method of precise definition, abstraction and artificial simplifying assumption has no significance for him. But he has his own kind of theory, using practical examples, analogy and metaphor and often reaches correct conclusions by a mysterious route of his own. The appropriate answer to the problems of teaching about international trade to both types is the same. Take specific examples covering a few main issues. Avoid technical language and the apparatus of geometry and algebra; do not aim at complete coverage even of the issues selected; be satisfied if some reasonable conclusions emerge.

Some examples of the issues which have been discussed successfully are: 'What benefits did we expect to get out of joining EEC and have we got them?', 'Could we reduce unemployment by limiting spending on imports?', 'Is it a good thing for the world as a whole if people are allowed to migrate freely?' The selection of issues requires a great deal of planning and preparation. Teaching about international trade to these types of student provides a challenge to the teacher; it calls for a highly structured and yet readily adaptable syllabus and for ample provision of time and resources.

References

1 Nevin, E. A., *Textbook of Economic Analysis*, (Macmillan, 1959).
2 Lipsey, R. G., *An Introduction to Positive Economics*, (Weidenfeld and Nicolson, 1975).
3 McCormick, B. J., *et al.*, *Introducing Economics*, (Penguin, 1974).
4 Stonier, A. W. and Hague, D. C., *A Textbook of Economic Theory*, (Longman, 1964).
5 Powicke, A. J., Iles, J. D., and Davies, B., *Applied Economics*, (Arnold, 1972).
6 Rogers, A. J., *Principles of Trade*, (The Dryden Press Inc., Hinsdale, Illinois, 1972).
7 Williams, L. J., *Britain and the World Economy 1919–1970*, (Fontana, 1971).
8 Harrod, R. F., *International Economics*, (Nisbet and Cambridge University Press, revised edition, 1957).
9 van Meerhaege, M. A. G., *International Economics*, (Longman, 1972).
10 Robinson, J., and Eatwell, J., *An Introduction to Modern Economics*, (McGraw-Hill, 1973).
11 Keynes, J. M., *The Economic Consequences of Mr Churchill, Essays in Persuasion*, (Macmillan, 1925, reprinted in 1972).
12 Prest, A. R., and Coppock, D. J., (ed), *The United Kingdom Economy*, (Weidenfeld and Nicolson, 1976).
13 Royal Economic Society *et al.*, *The Teaching of Economics in Schools*, (Macmillan, 1973).
14 Lee, N. (ed), *Teaching Economics*, (The Economics Association, 1967).
15 Haberler, G., *The Theory of International Trade*, (W. Hodge, 1936).

Resources

16mm Films
BBC Enterprises, Economics of the Real World, Programme 7, *Balance of Payments*, (25").
BBC Enterprises, Economics of the Real World, Programme 19, *International Constraints*, (25").
Concord Films Council, *The Exporters*, (50"), re those who export from UK, and those who try to. *Vicious Spiral*, (30"). Problems of overseas aid, international trade, and effects of these on developing countries.
Training and Education Film Library, *Economic Co-operation*, (24"), re gains from trade, specialisation and the division of labour (900 8071–7).

Tapes/Filmstrips
Student Recordings Ltd, *International Trade*, (tape/filmstrip, AVC/148).
Audio Learning Ltd, *Free Trade and Protection*, (tape).
Audio Learning Ltd, *The World Monetary System*, (tape).
McGraw-Hill, *International Trade*, (filmstrip).
Sussex Tapes, *International Trade*, (E5).

42   'Balance of Payments Problem' – A Game
John Wolinski

Aims of the Game

This game can be used in a variety of social science subjects – but a knowledge of economics is essential.

It presents the dilemma facing a government whose only economic consideration (for the purposes of the game only) is to retain a favourable balance of payments, and, at the same time, to remain popular in order to stay in power.

The aims of the game can be summarised as follows:

1 The major purpose of the game is to encourage analysis of economic policies by students. Ideally the students should be able to analyse the economic outcome of each policy, but must also calculate the probable effect on the political popularity of the policy.

2 By quantifying each policy, comparisons can be made between the relative effectiveness of the policies. The figures used are very subjective, and disagreements can provoke useful further discussion. If a student can successfully argue a case for changing them, then this should be done.

3 The game can be used to introduce or explain the phenomenon of 'stop–go'. Once players realise that unpopular policies are politically the most favourable when implemented well before a general election, whilst the most popular (but economically, invariably the most undesirable) policies are best presented just prior to an election, they will themselves employ a policy of 'stop–go'. 'Stop–go' has been heavily criticised, but by playing this game students can understand the reasons behind it, and the political factors leading to its adoption. Studying economics in isolation can often lead to intolerance of other, non-economic considerations. This game supplies an external influence, although it does not pretend to exhaust the number of considerations.

4 The various inter-relationships of the sectors of the economy can also be shown. The game can also be used to show the link between different branches of economics (theory of the firm, banking, etc) and the international sector, which may lead on to further study of links between other sectors.

5 The game can also be used to present the economic objectives of governments since the war. In this game the balance of payments is the only consideration, but the other objectives can be introduced in discussion after the game. Policies used during the game can also show the conflicts arising from these objectives.

6 Because students are playing the role of the government, they may gain an insight into the problems facing a government. This can encourage a greater tolerance and sympathy, and help towards an understanding of why policies are followed, even if they do not seem to be the most effective available.

7 Finally, the game can be used to provoke discussion on a variety of subjects.

It is vital to have feedback after the game. Particular attention should be paid to the most successful government: it is probable that this government followed a 'stop–go' policy. Discussions might also concern the quantifying of the policies; alternative policies not mentioned; and the dilemma of choice between different economic objectives.

Politically the game can lead to a discussion on the political system. Is it efficient when it appears to *cause* ineffective economic policies to be introduced, purely for political aims? How could this problem be overcome?

Rules

Each participant (or group) represents the government of a particular country, trying to improve its balance of payments – but at the same time aiming to stay in power.

The course of the game is for fifteen years (although this can be varied), and participants must make one policy decision each year. For the sake of the game, each policy must be taken from the list of policies provided and no policy can be used more than once.

Each policy has two effects: it influences the balance of payments and the government's popularity (measured by its balance of seats in parliament). A record must be kept of the policies used and their effect.

At the start of the game the government has just achieved a majority of *one* seat in parliament, with an even balance of payments. General elections are held every five years, and thus in the game they are held after years five, ten and fifteen. A continuous record is kept of the balance of seats in parliament but between elections this is merely a reflection of public opinion. Thus a government can have a negative balance of seats in a particular year, provided a majority has been achieved in the three years in which general elections are held.

After a general election the balance of seats is noted, and if the government has obtained a majority it can continue in the game. The size of the majority is unimportant – no benefit accrues to the government winning by the largest majority – because each participant represents a different country. If a government loses any of the three general elections it should be allowed to continue but be penalised £250m on the balance of payments (or £350m if it has lost the final election). Its balance of seats should not be changed.

The winner of the game is the country which has achieved the best balance of payments at the end of the game. The balance of seats in parliament is *not* considered (unless a majority has not been achieved).

The above is a straightforward version of the game. If desired, certain 'events' can be introduced to make the game more realistic. These 'events' show the possibility of further effects of policies that have already been used.

There are twelve possible events to be used (listed below). Six of these, chosen at random, should be introduced during the course of the game. These events occur two years and four years after each election, in order to give the government time to change its strategy, if necessary.

If *any* of the relevant policies has *already* been introduced by a country during the course of the game, then its balance of payments should be amended as indicated.

Before the start of the game it should not be indicated that the political popularity of a policy depends on the year in which it is used. However, after the first election it is advisable to hold a brief discussion on this subject. After this, governments that had not previously realised the connection will probably start using 'stop–go' policies.

It should be emphasised at the beginning of the game that the balance of payments is the government's *only* economic consideration. Other aims must be ignored for the purposes of the game (although they may affect political popularity).

Events

1 Avoidance of freeze on prices by businesses.
If policies (16) or (30) have been used, subtract £50m from the balance of payments.
2 Widespread strikes against wage freezes.
If policies (3) or (16) have been used, subtract £50m from the balance of payments.
3 Increased taxation discourages enterprise.
If policy (4) has been used, subtract £20m.
4 Change in currency valuation leads to international lack of confidence and trust in international trade.
If policy (20) has been used, subtract £100m.
5 Low inflation causes unemployment problems.
If policies (13) or (22) have been used, subtract £30m.
6 High inflation solves unemployment problems.
If policies (12), (21) or (31) have been used, add £30m.
7 Disagreement amongst countries of Free Trade Area.
If policy (29) has been used, subtract £20m.
8 Labour mobility improves.
If policies (7) or (9) have been used, add £20m.
9 Interest rates offset by inflation.
If policy (5) has been used, subtract £20m.
If policy (6) has been used, add £20m.
10 Retaliatory tariffs by foreign countries.
If policies (25), (26) or (34) have been used, subtract £20m.

11 Landlords hold back property.
If policy (8) has been used, subtract £20m.
12 African countries refuse to accept 'tied' aid.
If policy (32) has been used, subtract £30m.

Balance of Payments Problem: Policies

Copies of this list are to be given to each of the participants.

Participants must choose from the following policies, in order to solve their balance of payments problems.

No policy may be used more than once: fifteen are to be chosen during the course of the game.

For the sake of simplicity, the long-term effect on the balance of payments is taken – rather than short-run consequences.

1 Promote research into increasing industrial productivity.
2 Borrow from the USA.
3 Strict wage freeze.
4 Increase taxation substantially.
5 Increase the Minimum Lending Rate by 4 per cent.
6 Lower the Minimum Lending Rate by 4 per cent.
7 Give large subsidies to encourage firms to move to the development areas.
8 Freeze land prices.
9 Encourage industries to move to the South East.

Policies: Their Effects

This list (below) must only be seen by the controller.

10 Participate in World Trade Fair.
11 Introduce policies to reduce unemployment.
12 Lower the Commercial Banks' Reserve Assets Ratio by 5 per cent.
13 Increase the Commercial Banks' Reserve Assets Ratio by 5 per cent.
14 Introduce a selective subsidy/tax in favour of large firms.
15 Place a £50 limit on tourists travelling abroad.
16 Impose a strict prices and incomes freeze.
17 Sell many foreign investments.
18 Borrow from the International Monetary Fund.
19 Revalue your currency by 15 per cent.
20 Devalue your currency by 15 per cent.
21 Increase the money supply by 10 per cent.
22 Decrease the money supply by 10 per cent.
23 Encourage expansion of labour-intensive industry, by taxation on machinery and subsidies to employers for employing extra staff.
24 Encourage investment in capital-intensive industry, by taxation on employees and subsidies on machinery prices.
25 Increase tariffs on imports.
26 Subsidise exporting companies.
27 Subsidise agriculture.
28 Increase expenditure on social services.
29 Join a Free Trade Area with Canada and USA.
30 Impose a freeze on prices only.
31 Greatly reduce taxation.
32 Offer vast aid to African countries.
33 Set up free insurance scheme for exporters.
34 Charge heavy taxes on foreign firms in Britain.
35 Encourage high investment in industry, by use of tax concessions.

Policy	Balance of payments £m	Balance of seats				
		Year 1	Year 2	Year 3	Year 4	Year 5
1	+20	0	0	0	0	0
2	−30	0	0	0	−10	−10
3	+100	−5	−10	−20	−35	−60
4	+50	0	−10	−20	−30	−50
5	+50	0	0	0	−5	−15
6	−50	0	0	0	+5	+15
7	−70	+5	+5	+5	+10	+20
8	+10	+5	+5	+5	+10	+20
9	+60	0	0	0	−5	−15
10	0	0	0	0	0	0
11	−50	+5	+5	+10	+25	+40
12	−40	0	0	0	0	0
13	+40	0	0	0	0	0
14	+40	0	0	−5	−5	−10
15	+10	−5	−10	−15	−20	−30

Policy	Balance of payments £m	Balance of seats				
		Year 1	Year 2	Year 3	Year 4	Year 5
16	+200	0	−10	−20	−40	−60
17	−70	0	0	0	0	0
18	−20	0	0	0	−10	−10
19	−250	+10	+15	+20	+30	+40
20	+250	−40	−40	−50	−60	−80
21	−60	0	0	−5	−10	−20
22	+60	0	0	+5	+10	+20
23	−20	+5	+5	+10	+15	+25
24	+20	0	−5	−5	−10	−20
25	+40	0	0	0	−10	−20
26	+20	0	0	0	−10	−20
27	+10	0	0	+5	+5	+10
28	−30	+5	+10	+10	+15	+25
29	−30	+25	+10	0	−10	−25
30	+120	0	−5	−15	−25	−35
31	−40	0	+5	+10	+20	+40
32	+40	0	0	−10	−20	−20
33	+20	0	0	−5	−5	−10
34	+10	0	0	+5	+5	+10
35	+30	0	0	0	0	0

43 'World Trade' – A Game

Graham Loomes

Teacher's Notes

Introduction
This game sets out to increase students' understanding of the theory of international trade. Its central point is that no country can reach its target unless it trades, and playing the game raises ideas about opportunity costs, comparative costs and the gains of trade.

Equipment
(a) Progress charts (one per team).
(b) Envelopes (one 10cm×22cm and perhaps one very large per team).
(c) Production slips (enough for about twenty-five per team, although only ten need be given out initially).
(d) Money (at least £260 per team plus a banker's balance – with a good proportion of £1 notes and small change).
(e) Tokens – the banker should start with:

Red	50×1	50×5	40×10
Yellow	30×1	20×5	20×10
Green	20×1	20×5	20×10
Blue	20×1	10×5	10×10

(f) Pack of twelve production-target cards.

Preparation
In reading through the players' instructions, some attention should be paid to the role of the progress charts. It is worth going through the example given, emphasising the importance of these charts for further work. Draw attention to the fact that the times are very useful for reconstructing the game, and that watches should be synchronised. Also underline the final warning that no team can win unless its progress chart matches up with its tokens and money. Also suggest that where a barter occurs, it should be recorded in two columns on the same line, even if this involves leaving a space or two, because it will be easier to refer to later.

The Actual Play
The banker's job is mainly to deal with production slips. At the end, the values of any excess goods need to

Cost of producing each unit	Blue	Yellow	Red	Green
	200 p	120 p	70 p	180 p
Target no.	24	60	120	40

Cost of producing each unit	Blue	Yellow	Red	Green
	280 p	100 p	60 p	180 p
Target no.	30	48	120	40

Cost of producing each unit	Blue	Yellow	Red	Green
	240 p	100 p	70 p	180 p
Target no.	30	48	120	40

Cost of producing each unit	Blue	Yellow	Red	Green
	200 p	140 p	60 p	180 p
Target no.	24	60	120	40

Cost of producing each unit	Blue	Yellow	Red	Green
	240 p	120 p	70 p	150 p
Target no.	30	60	120	32

Cost of producing each unit	Blue	Yellow	Red	Green
	280 p	120 p	60 p	150 p
Target no.	30	60	120	32

Cost of producing each unit	Blue	Yellow	Red	Green
	240 p	100 p	60 p	210 p
Target no.	30	48	120	40

Cost of producing each unit	Blue	Yellow	Red	Green
	240 p	140 p	50 p	180 p
Target no.	30	60	96	40

Cost of producing each unit	Blue	Yellow	Red	Green
	280 p	120 p	50 p	180 p
Target no.	30	60	96	40

Cost of producing each unit	Blue	Yellow	Red	Green
	200 p	120 p	60 p	210 p
Target no.	24	60	120	40

Cost of producing each unit	Blue	Yellow	Red	Green
	240 p	120 p	50 p	210 p
Target no.	30	60	96	40

Cost of producing each unit	Blue	Yellow	Red	Green
	240 p	140 p	60 p	150 p
Target no.	30	60	120	32

Figure 43.1 Production – target cards

be calculated and winning progress charts checked. The recommended time limit is one hour *plus* about fifteen minutes for each team playing.

Afterwards

Teachers may wish to delay these exercises until all play has been completed; alternatively, it is possible to play the £260 game, do exercise 1, then play the harder game(s) and then do exercise 2.

1 Ask each country to write a report of how they played the game – the following headings (plus others) may be given as a guide:

Initial general plan;
How the team was organised – any specialist functions;
Problems that arose – and how the team responded;
What you would change with hindsight;
Any general rules of thumb for playing in future.

A couple of teams could read out their reports, and appropriate points be discussed.

2 The teacher should write up the contents of the cards drawn at the beginning of the game, listing the production possibilities on one side and the targets on the other side.

Then ask students to work out individually how these targets could most efficiently be met, i.e. with minimum amount of money being spent overall.

This may cause some discussion and disagreement, but when some consensus is reached, compare the theoretical result to the actual play, inviting reasons for differences (or similarities).

Finally, there might be some discussion of whether the simple predictions of the conventional textbook two-country – two-commodity example are borne out in a multi-country and multi-commodity situation like the game creates. Do, or should, countries specialise to a great extent? Do all countries stand to gain from trade, and if so, do they stand to gain equally? If there is inequality, what factors cause it?

Country _____		Time _____	
	Blue	*Yellow*	*Red*	*Green*
Quantity produced				
Cost per unit				
Total cost				

Overall production costs for this slip _____

Figure 43.2 An example of a production slip

Players' Instructions

Aim

The aim of this game is for a country to exceed the targets by as much as possible in a given period of time.

Preparation

The game could be played by two to thirty players, but probably the best number would be between six and twenty, plus one banker.

Players divide up into not less than three teams and not more than six, each team representing a country of its choice.

Each country receives:

> one progress chart;
> one envelope (about 10cm × 22cm);
> ten production slips (more can be obtained at any time).

Each country also receives the same sum of money. The size of the sum depends on how difficult the players want to make the game. It is suggested that the first time the game is played, each country should receive £260 to play with. To make the game harder, reduce the sum in subsequent games to £250, and then £240.

The final part of the preparation is for each country to draw a card from the pack which tells that country:

(a) how much it will cost to produce a unit of each of the four colours; and
(b) that country's target for each of the four colours.

Background Information

All players should be aware that:

(i) no two cards are identical as far as their costs of production are concerned: and
(ii) the only possible costs of production are:
> for Blue – 280p or 240p or 200p per unit
> for Yellow – 140p or 120p or 100p per unit
> for Red – 70p or 60p or 50p per unit
> for Green – 210p or 180p or 150p per unit

The Actual Play

Before play begins, the time limit must be set. Later on, players should be warned fifteen minutes and five minutes before the end. The banker decides which country's excess is worth most by valuing excess goods as follows:

Blue – 240p, Yellow – 120p, Red – 60p, Green – 180p.

Each country may try to win in any of the following ways:

1 *Produce and keep* – if a country wishes to produce some goods, it fills in a production slip, puts it in an envelope together with its card and the necessary money, and hands the envelope to the banker. The banker checks the calculations. If they are wrong, a £5 fine is deducted and the rest of the envelope's contents are returned for the necessary amendment to be made. If the original calculations are correct, the banker removes the production slip and the money, and replaces the card in the envelope together with the right number of goods, and gives the envelope back.
2 *Produce, sell and buy* – once a country has some

Blue	Yellow	Red	Green
a)	a)	a)	a)
b)	b)	b)	b)
c)	c)	c)	c)
d)	d)	d)	d)
e) _____	e) _____	e) _____	e) _____
f)	f)	f)	f)
a)	a)	a)	a)
b)	b)	b)	b)
c)	c)	c)	c)
d)	d)	d)	d)
e) _____	e) _____	e) _____	e) _____
f)	f)	f)	f)
a)	a)	a)	a)
b)	b)	b)	b)
c)	c)	c)	c)
d)	d)	d)	d)
e) _____	e) _____	e) _____	e) _____
f)	f)	f)	f)
a)	a)	a)	a)
b)	b)	b)	b)
c)	c)	c)	c)
d)	d)	d)	d)
e) _____	e) _____	e) _____	e) _____
f)	f)	f)	f)
a)	a)	a)	a)
b)	b)	b)	b)
c)	c)	c)	c)
d)	d)	d)	d)
e) _____	e) _____	e) _____	e) _____
f)	f)	f)	f)
a)	a)	a)	a)
b)	b)	b)	b)
c)	c)	c)	c)
d)	d)	d)	d)
e) _____	e) _____	e) _____	e) _____
f)	f)	f)	f)

Figure 43.3 A progress chart

units of a commodity (or even before) it may negotiate, in private or in public, to sell them at whatever price it can get. Correspondingly, a country with money may negotiate to buy from any other country.

3 *Produce and barter* – countries who have no money, or don't wish to use what they have for some reason, may negotiate a barter, either in private or in public.

There is no set order of play, but all deals, with other countries or with the banker, should be recorded on progress charts for future reference.

Progress Charts

You can see that every section in each of the four colour columns contains the six letters (a) to (f). Every time a deal is made, both sides involved must make entries in their charts. The information which should be given next to each letter is as follows:

(a) Whether the goods have been *bought*, *sold* or *bartered*;
(b) The number of goods, and whether incoming (+) or outgoing (−);
(c) Total value, either in money or in other goods;
(d) Name of other country involved, or banker;
(e) The time the deal was completed;
(f) Running total of goods.

Table 43.1 is an example of what part of a progress chart might look like.

BLUE	YELLOW
(a) Bought	(a) Bought
(b) +100	(b) +30
(c) £200	(c) £35
(d) Banker	(d) Erewhon
(e) 10.26	(e) 10.45
(f) +100	(f) +30
(a) Bartered	(a) Bartered
(b) −40	(b) +68
(c) +68 Yellow	(c) −40 Blue
(d) Utopia	(d) Utopia
(e) 11.03	(e) 11.03
(f) +60	(f) +98

Table 43.1

The Winner

To win, a country must at least have reached its target in *all four* goods. If a country has excess goods in three colours but has failed to reach the target in the fourth, it cannot be the winner. *And no country can win unless its tokens and money tally with the statements on its progress chart.*

44 Instruments and Objectives of Government Policy

Keith Marder

The role of government now extends into almost every part of Britain's economy, and aspects of government policy consequently enter into almost every section of the syllabus. A broad classification might distinguish the following main policy-making areas.

1 *Demand management:* the main macroeconomic areas of fiscal and monetary policy.
2 *Direct intervention in industry:* the nationalised industries; industrial location and regional policy; prices and incomes policy; industrial relations; monopolies and restrictive practices; the National Enterprise Board, National Economic Development Council, and other organs of industrial policy.
3 *External policy:* international trade; the balance of payments; international monetary relations.

Introducing Government Policy

Entering into the syllabus at so many points, government policy cannot be introduced to students as an independent topic but must be treated at appropriate

How banks were controlled

London clearing banks' advances:
percentage change on a year earlier

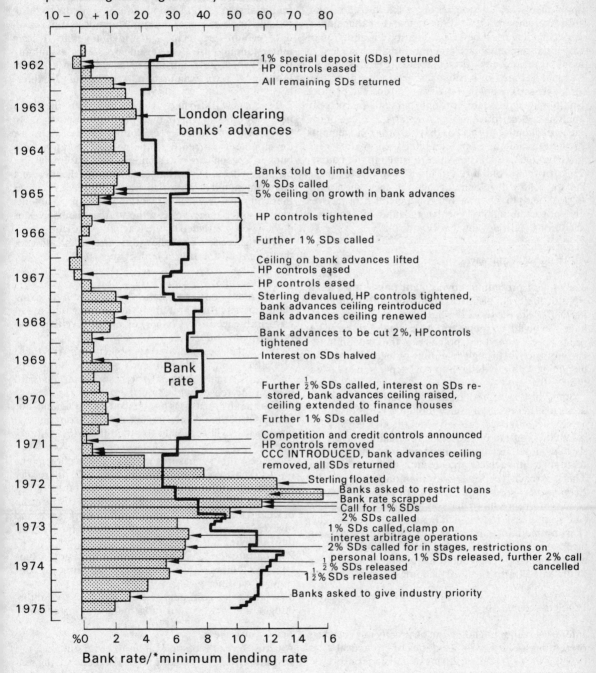

Figure 44.1 Reproduced by kind permission of The
Economist Newspaper Ltd

stages in the course. At each stage, policies can only be understood in the light of relevant economic theory. For instance, regional policy is only meaningful as an aspect of the location of industry, and the motives underlying monopoly policy logically stem from monopoly theory and a comparison of market situations.

In the important field of demand management, understanding must be based on a solid foundation of Keynesian and monetarist theories. In this connection, many teachers now prefer to make the study of national income flows and macroeconomic theory the effective starting point of their courses instead of more traditional approaches through demand and supply analysis or descriptive topics. A great advantage of the macroeconomic approach is that the broad movements of the economy and related policy measures become intelligible to students at an early stage in the course. Thus, by the second term, it should be possible for the class to follow developments leading up to the Spring budget and then view the Chancellor's objectives and proposals against the background of economic conditions and relevant theory.

An Historical Approach

Methods of presenting government policy must vary with the topic. An historical approach is often suitable, particularly in those areas where forms of intervention have evolved largely through legislation. The framework of regional policy can thus be built up chronologically through an outline of legislative action beginning with the designation of 'depressed areas' in the 1930s.

Some historical background is also helpful to students in other fields of policy though it is important to avoid the pitfall of excessive detail. Graphical representation often provides an invaluable means of showing broad developments in government policy in relation to underlying movements in the economy. This approach was effectively demonstrated in *The Economist*'s series of school briefs on macroeconomics, reproduced in its booklet *What's Going On* (see Resources), from which Figure 44.1 is taken. The charting method is also used to show the stages of incomes policy in the light of wage and price movements, and stop–go demand management in relation to the rate of growth of gross domestic product.

Problem-solving Approaches

Interest and understanding can be greatly increased by presenting students with situations of a practical kind in which they are required to make decisions or foresee and evaluate the consequences of alternative courses of action. Government policy is an area of the syllabus particularly suitable for such exercises.

Problem-solving exercises may be based on either hypothetical or real situations. Government activity provides abundant scope for real problems founded on either statistical data or written extracts from newspapers, journals, official reports, or the speeches of politicians. Problem-solving induces students to think out and apply rather than simply memorise and reproduce economic principles. Its advantages for testing understanding are recognised by some examining boards which have introduced data response papers into the 'A' level examination, (see Chapter 28, reference 2).

Teachers will also find it worthwhile to suit their own needs by devising their own problems, and this can frequently be done by exploiting policy issues or developments currently in the news. The report of a budget speech or other ministerial statement, an economic debate in parliament, or the publication of a government bill or white paper are examples of sources that can provide excellent working material. Students may be asked either to read the sources themselves or data may be extracted by the teacher to provide a basis for class exercises. The following is an example of work that might be set after a budget speech.

Questions on a Budget
1 Comment on the features of the underlying economic situation and any other factors that might have influenced the Chancellor of the Exchequer in preparing his budget.
2 What are the main budget objectives? Are these objectives compatible with each other?
3 Note the main financial forecasts or targets, and explain the reasoning behind them.
4 Outline the measures announced by the Chancellor and discuss their likely impact on the economy. To what extent will they help to attain the budget objectives?
5 Suggest other measures that the Chancellor might have taken to achieve his objectives. Are there any serious or surprising omissions from the budget?
6 How is the budget likely to affect (a) the distribution of wealth and income; (b) incentives to work, save, and invest; (c) the cost of living; (d) your own family standard of living?
7 What are the main criticisms of the budget? Comment on the reactions of industry, trade unions, consumers, or other groups.
8 What do you consider to be the main features of this budget, and what is your judgement of it in general?

News Coverage

An attraction of economics as an 'A' level subject is the scope it provides for linking textbook theory to the real life issues and problems that students currently read or hear about through the news media. Nowhere is this scope greater than in the realm of government policy.

The time lag in setting papers may prevent examiners from including questions on specific contemporary policies, but they certainly reward candidates who show up-to-date knowledge. In any case, teachers will always seek opportunities to introduce topical material in order to stimulate interest.

The ideal economics student should be an avid follower of current affairs, but perfection is rare and so teachers are forced to supply aids and incentives. In matters of government policy, even the most recently published books are likely to be out of date. The monthly *Economic Progress Report* published by the Information Division of the Treasury is invaluable, particularly since copies are supplied free, and teachers are advised to order these in sufficient numbers for each pupil to accumulate his own stock over the period of the course. Current policy developments are also well covered in the *British Economy Survey*.

Economics students should be encouraged to acquire the habit of regularly scanning journals and newspapers for relevant items, many of which will concern government policy. The teacher can help by displaying cuttings and bringing topical issues to the notice of the class. There are also ways of inducing direct activity by students:

1 *Economics diaries.* Each student keeps his own record of events in the form of news cuttings and/or notes. These should be classified, perhaps into the broad categories of government policy suggested earlier, and regarded as an integral part of the course work.

2 *Assignments.* Topics are allocated to cover the broad field of government policy, and each student is expected to keep abreast of developments in the sphere allotted to him. Periodic lessons may be set aside for individual reports to the class as a basis for questions and discussion.

Class Discussion

Government activity is manifestly a field in which economics cannot be divorced from politics, and value-judgements are unavoidable. On major issues, students should be aware of opposition party criticisms and proposals as well as the official line. Discussion of government policy enables differing views to be heard, encourages pupils to form and express their own opinions, and uniquely demonstrates the impact of value-judgements on economic decisions.

The basis of discussion may be a prepared talk, the report on an individual assignment, or a current news item introduced by the teacher. Tape or video recordings of topical broadcast programmes can also provide fruitful material. If the class is large enough, formal debates can be held, particularly on major policy statements such as a budget speech, the announcement of a counter-inflation package, or a party manifesto.

For instance, following a budget, the simple motion 'that this house approves (or disapproves) the Chancellor's proposals' can make an excellent starting point for a debate.

Interaction of Policies

A particular problem of teaching in the field of government policy is that students cannot initially perceive the extent of possible repercussions from particular measures and the consequent conflicts between different policy objectives. This difficulty stems from the interdependence of all parts of the economic system and the necessity for teachers to introduce each part in isolation. It can be most easily faced in the period of consolidation at the end of the course when students begin to see the economy as a whole. The role of government might then be usefully treated as a revision topic, linking together different parts of the system and drawing attention to the interaction of policies and the problems of reconciliation.

A major area of potential conflict is in the interaction of domestic and external policy objectives. Thus, policies designed to secure equilibrium in the balance of payments may have adverse domestic effects on employment, output, or prices. The problem can be put to students in the form of a simple diagram (see Figure 44.2).

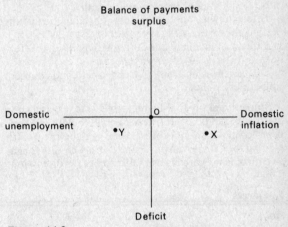

Figure 44.2

Points can be inserted on the diagram to show different combinations of domestic and external conditions, and students may be asked to select appropriate policies to move towards the origin O as a target point of both internal and external balance. For example, starting at point X – representing a trade deficit accompanied by inflation – it can be demonstrated that deflation is an appropriate policy but not devaluation or import controls, both of which have the effect of raising prices. Students may be expected to question the placing of unemployment and inflation as opposites on the domestic axis. By indicating that both X and Y could represent Britain's current position, it is further possible to focus attention on the problems of dealing with 'stagflation'.

The Treatment of Taxes

The structure of taxation raises difficulties because of individual complexities and the frequency of change. The relative importance of taxes as sources of revenue is shown by the table presented in the Chancellor's annual *Financial Statement and Budget Report*. Students can estimate the percentage of the total revenue obtained from each source.

It is unnecessary to memorise technical details or rates of taxation which are subject to alteration, but the characteristics of each of the principal taxes must be noted. In most cases, this can be done simply in the form of a list of salient features. Students can then be asked to consider the effects of individual taxes, and make their own judgements, on the basis of prescribed criteria such as the following:

1 Revenue-earning capacity.
2 Aspects of administration including the cost of collection, facility for evasion, problems of assessment, and convenience of payment by the taxpayers.
3 Social implications including the distributional effects on personal income and wealth.
4 Effects on the supply of factors of production including incentives to work, save, and invest.
5 Effects on resource allocation with particular reference to exports or other vital sectors.
6 Effectiveness in demand management and counter-inflationary policy.

Students are invariably interested in taxes, and class discussion can be controversial and stimulating. Proposals for innovation or reform such as Labour's wealth tax and the Conservative scheme for tax credits (negative income tax) are also suitable topics for discussion.

Resources

Books
Grant, R. M. and Shaw, G. K. (eds), *Current Issues in Economic Policy* (Philip Allan, 1975). Empirical treatment of various policy issues by different authors.
Lee, D., *Control of the Economy*, (Heinemann Educational, 1974). Sound description of management techniques.
Livingstone, J. M., *The British Economy in Theory and Practice*, (Macmillan, 1974). A theoretical outline followed by a substantial section on policy objectives and priorities.
Powicke, J. C., Iles, D. J., and Davies, B., *Applied Economics*, (Edward Arnold, 1972). Various topics in the field of government policy.

Sandford, C. T., *National Economic Planning*, (Heinemann Educational, 1972). Examines government planning attempts since the war.
Skuse, A., *Government Intervention and Industrial Policy*, (Heinemann Educational, 1972). An historical approach to government intervention and its effects.

Other Publications
Journals including *The Economist* and political weeklies comment on current government policies from different viewpoints.
Bank reviews including the Bank of England's *Quarterly Review* frequently contain relevant articles of high analytical standard.
What's Going On, (The Economist Newspaper Limited, 1976). School briefs on macroeconomics. A supplementary booklet, *Macroeconomics in Question*, published by The Economics Association, contains questions on the main policy areas covered by the briefs.
British Economy Survey, (Oxford University Press). Published three times a year. Articles cover current developments in all the main policy areas.
Government publications. The following HMSO publications supply statistical background to government economic policy:
Economic Trends. Monthly commentary, tables, and charts on trends in the UK economy.
National Income and Expenditure 'Blue Book'. Annual detailed estimates of the national accounts.
UK Balance of Payments, annual 'Pink Book'.
Financial Statement and Budget Report. Income and expenditure tables of central government and economic report including short-term forecast.

Films, Tapes, etc
Film programmes of Peter Donaldson's television series *Economics of the Real World*, are available from BBC Enterprises. The following deal with aspects of government policy: Programme 3, *The Budget;* 4, *Fine Tuning;* 5, *Who Cares for the Regions?;* 7, *Inflation;* 18, *Planning for a Change.*

The following are among films supplied by the Training and Education Film Library: *The Role of the Budget*, (16″, 900 8135–2), relating to fiscal policy since the 1960s; *Inflation* (25″, D 101 13), on causes and solutions; *Location of Industry*, (25″, 900 8088–9), case study of car industry, examining government influence; *The Balanced Budget*, (16″, 900 8131–4), relates to 1930s; *The Phillips Curve*, (16″, 900 8134–5), looks at the rate of change of wages and employment.

Discussion tapes on economics are produced by Audio Learning Ltd. Each provides about half hour discussion on each track at a standard suitable for 'A' level students. The following are suitable for revision or consolidation lessons on topics in government policy: No 7, *Government Finance/Nationalised Industry* by J. Wiseman and A. Peacock; No 10, *The British Economy – The Nature of the Problems/The Search for Solutions* by J. Hughes and R. Donaldson; No 26, *Government Responsibility and Industry/Control of Public Expenditure* by V. Bogdanor and W. Waldegrave; No 28, *Aims of Taxation/Economic and Social Characteristics – Different Taxes in the UK* by G. S. A. Wheatcroft and A. R. Prest. Also from Audio Learning Ltd., *Monetary Policy* by A. D. Bain and M. H. Miller.

Aspects of government policy are also covered by the following: Sussex Tapes: El, *Public Finance*, a discussion of taxation and government spending; E8, *Location of Industry*, a discussion of the labour market and regional policy.
Open University, *Taxation*, (audio tape, D1O1 13/20). Students Recordings Ltd, *Public Finance*, (AVC/144); *The Public Sector*, (AVC/30). Colour filmstrips with tape or spool commentaries lasting about 40 minutes. Filmstrip, *Business Cycles and Fiscal Policy*, (McGraw-Hill).

Wallcharts
Pictorial Charts Educational Trust, four charts: *Rates and Taxes* (D 715). One chart: *Taxation and Spending*, (C 32). Shows the average family's taxes and benefits within the framework of government income and expenditure.
P. Jay, *The Budget*, (Jackdaw).

45   Social and Environmental Economics
John Rees

In a recent Penguin, Allen Kneese wrote: 'The word environment is frequently used with a vagueness matched only by the fervour with which it is invoked'.[1] Although fervour should not be excluded from the economist's make-up, analysis and the dispersion of vagueness must be at the heart of what he is trying to do.

It is clear that if we were to ask our pupils which they considered to be the main social problems in Britain today, we would be given an enormous list, many of them with substantial economic implications. There would be disagreement over the relative importance of these problems, over what has caused them, and what can be done about them. The source of most of these ideas would be the mass media, so that perceptions of major issues are heavily influenced by presentations which emphasise conflict, sensation, and 'human interest.' Further, mass media consideration of many issues tends to be short-lived and grossly oversimplified, often distorting and denying the complexity of reality. There is a profound difference between social problems as they are perceived, and those problems as they exist, in particular because our perceptions are based on individual cases and 'problems' are in a sense generic. In our teaching we must ensure that our economic insights and models are applied to a wide range of these problems, partly because of the broad gains to be made from enlightened 'media suspicion', and partly because a major goal of our teaching must be to improve the ability of our students to apply familiar models to unfamiliar situations.

Some economics teachers may argue that there is a danger of the study of social problems deteriorating either into 'high class current affairs' or partisan polemic. The danger is there, and it is a major argument in favour of a *systematic* approach to key problems such as housing, the Third World, health and education. Further, since many of these issues will impinge directly upon the student's interest and self-interest, they should lead to greater commitment and greater understanding of the relevance of economic concepts to the bits of the world they know something about. Public expenditure and its control is hardly a subject to arouse enthusiasm – why '*your* mum has to wait two years for an operation and *your* mum can pay for it to take place next week' *is* likely to stimulate discussion and sustained interest. If we accept that economics is essentially a way of thinking, then serious consideration of such areas should present no greater problems than any other material in the construction of a coherent economics course. Almost any issue should therefore be grist to the mill, and may well give the daring teacher scope to discuss with his students which topics they would like to study in depth, on the clear understanding of course that they must play a major role in the necessary research and compilation of resource material.

The very selection of problems poses important questions. As J. B. Mays wrote 'who defines them, and in relation to what norms?'.[2] In our discussion of the particular problems we select, it should be part of our task to draw attention to this issue. Apart from the danger of 'bias', there is also a danger of stressing individual problems to the detriment of a general view. The key role of the teacher here is to bring his students to work towards generalisation and an understanding of the broad principles underlying the particular problem.

It has been said that the average person's study of social problems is a search for the villain, who may be identified and thus overcome. As economists we too may look for 'goodies and baddies', but only if we make it clear that few of the participants wear white hats or black hats. Rather they tend to wear hats of varying shades of grey, so that these are issues of marginal adjustment, of trade-offs and opportunity costs, played out against an ever-changing backcloth of scarcity. Further, the protagonists can be seen through different lenses, labelled micro, meso and macro. The issue of homelessness can be studied in terms of the individual family lacking the effective demand to operate successfully in the market; it can be viewed at the regional scale in terms of variations in housing quality, incomes, etc; or on a national scale in terms of income distribution, housing policy, etc.

Environmental problems emerge from a highly developed technology, and raise fundamental questions about the organisation of society. Many of the problems have a technological solution, but these are subject to often substantial economic constraints. Both social and environmental problems show that no single discipline can provide a sufficiently comprehensive approach. However, the necessary approach need not be interdisciplinary, but will certainly require the drawing of information from different disciplines. To understand environmental problems requires awareness of:

(a) the way in which decisions affecting natural resource allocation are made in public and private sectors;
(b) the importance of time lags in the response of systems to changes in price, social attitudes and technical knowledge;
(c) market failures, and attempts to overcome them through legal constraints, application of CBA, etc;
(d) the complex structure of interrelated legal, economic, technical and administrative factors.

Many of these issues are bound up with value judgements; yet economists have tended to fight shy of these dangerous areas on the proper grounds that their approach must be 'positive'. Yet it must be quite clear that at the heart of a whole range of social and environmental issues lie critical value judgements, and that in our teaching we are constantly confronted with the consequences of particular sets of individual and communal values. It may not be our job to teach values, but it is certainly our job to teach awareness of values. (See Chapter 47.)

Take two questions – 'Why do we have thousands of long term mental patients living in appalling conditions when a large proportion of our society can afford a colour television set?'; 'Why not build overhead power lines across the New Forest?'

We may say glibly 'Clearly the first question is concerned with resource allocation given the known constraints, etc, etc', but one would hope that neither the teacher nor his students would be content to gloss over such profound issues of social morality, in addition to a study of the market and extra-market forces at work. How can we make 'good' decisions about resource allocation amongst individuals, and between public and private consumption? What is the value of the concept of efficiency and Pareto optimality? Can we teach purely in terms of 'efficiency' and what dangers do we run if we don't? The second question illustrates the combination of technical possibilities and economic constraints, plus significant aesthetic factors of a kind which are extremely difficult to quantify. How much value should be attached to environmental deterioration (the writer is convinced that one set of powerlines with which he is familiar actually adds to the landscape)?

Both questions confim the essential truth of Buchanan's statement:

'The economist's stock in trade – his tools – lies in his ability to and proclivity to think about all questions in terms of alternatives. The truth judgement of the moralist, which says that something is wholly right or wholly wrong, is foreign to him. The win–lose, yes–no discussion of politics is not within his purview. He does not recognise the either–or, the all-or-nothing situation, as his own. His is not the world of the mutually exclusives. Instead his is the world of adjustment, of co-ordinated conflict, of mutual gains'.[3]

Teaching the Economics of Health

The financial stringencies of the 1970s have led to increasing public concern with the level of provision of communal services. An examination of the economics of health raises a number of key issues in an area with which most students ought to be familiar. The National Health Service has become a major element in the GNP and in public spending, and its operation exemplifies many of the problems associated with the intervention of the state in the economic system. The introduction of the Health Service implied that health was a good which should not be allocated on the basis of effective money demand. Zero prices would mean that no one would go without medical care because of lack of market power, and also that the quality of medical care should not be a function of income. At the same time it raised important problems as to how the 'proper' level of inputs and outputs could be determined without a market. The continuing operation of a private sector implied that health could be seen as a pure public good, a quasi-public good, or a pure private good.

The issue of clinical freedom and rationing of scarce resources is an important one and students may find it fascinating to discuss the wide variations in treatment times for identical ailments, and the problem of applying economic constraints of a general kind to areas of individual professional judgement. The difficulty of applying market considerations is clearly brought out in two opposing views of the best way of providing blood, on the one hand Cooper and Culyer[6,7] and on the other the classic *The Gift Relationship* of Richard Titmuss.[8] At the end of his book, Cooper lists the following 'questions for discussion':

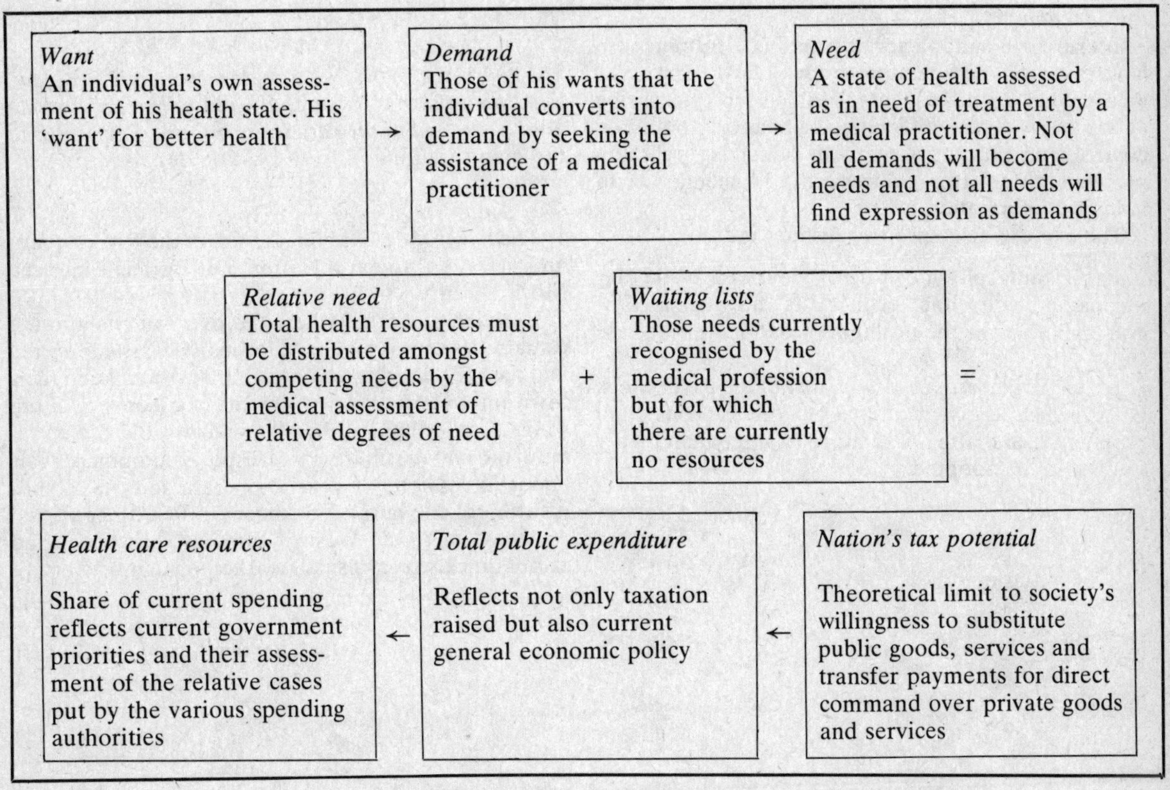

Figure 45.1 The accommodation of want to supply. Reproduced from Rationing Health Care *by M. H. Cooper[4]*

Health care brings together micro and macro approaches. Cooper in his fine book *Rationing Health Care*[4] and Culyer in *Need and the National Health Service*[5] draw attention to the distinction between what they term want, demand and need. This manifestation of need for health care has then to be fitted into the general availability of resources for health care, and for specific forms of health care in particular. Figure 45.1 is an excellent model from which to teach the economics of health care.

1 Can need be abolished?
2 How do we assess priorities for health care?
3 What is the role of the market versus the state?
4 Should private practice exist?
5 How can doctors be monitored?
6 What is the value of life?
7 Does the NHS exploit poor countries by its use of their skilled doctors and nurses?
8 Who should determine demand?
9 What does the hospital service seek to maximise?

10 Are income and wealth an irrelevance in meeting health care needs?
11 Is the regional allocation of resources 'fair'? If not, how can this be resolved?
12 Can shortages be assessed in terms of priorities?
13 How can the benefits of health care be measure?
14 Is it enough to see the costs of the health service in purely financial terms?
15 Who should die?

While it is extremely unlikely that the individual teacher would wish to cover all these questions many of them are of profound importance, and require careful consideration.

Appendix: Muck in the Mock: An Environmental Role-playing Exercise*

Introduction

This exercise is suitable for fifth and sixth formers who have done some preparatory study of how economists measure costs and benefits, problems of measuring pollution costs, the difficulties of financing pollution control, and alternative methods of solving pollution problems. (The latter requires a little elementary technological information.)

The exercise falls into two distinct parts:

1 Participants split into groups of four or five and play the part of consultant economists drawing up programmes to solve the problems described in the case study.
2 Seven participants act as member of the River Mock Board which receive submissions from the consultant economists, and attempt to move to agreement on the solution to be adopted.

The Muck in the Mock

The following details describe an economic problem. Read the information carefully and follow the instructions at the end of the case study information. Refer to the map (Figure 45.2) for location details.

Case Study

1 The River Mock is about the size of the River Severn and it flows through Ayleston and Burleigh into the Mock Estuary.
2 Burleigh is located where the river widens into the estuary. Its ratepayers have for many years supported and paid for filtering equipment that would keep their town and waterfront attractive and free from pollution. Their anti-pollution bye-laws have been strictly enforced and the filtering and disposal equipment costs about £1 million per year to operate and the administration of the laws costs about £250 000 per year.
3 Ayleston, to the West of Burleigh, has developed rather quickly from a small market town into an active

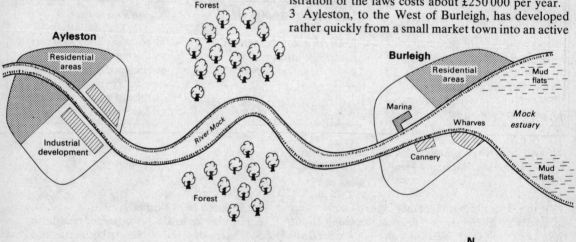

Figure 45.2

MOCKSHIRE

* This exercise was adapted by Nigel Wright for use in the UK, from the original by Z. S. Starnawski, published by the Victorian Commercial Teachers' Association.

industrial town. The whole of Mockshire has been an industrial development area for years. In fact, Burleigh has always been fairly lucky, thanks to a buoyant tourist trade, and partly to a substantial section of well-to-do residents. Ayleston, by comparison, has for many years been a depressed town, offering few employment (or other) prospects: young people from the town, and the surrounding country, have tended to drift away from the area. For Ayleston, then, the new industries have been the kiss of life long waited for.

4 Industries settled in Ayleston because of the fine water supply from the Mock and from nearby springs, and because of the fairly easy access to the motorway (it passes within five miles of Ayleston). The leading industries of Ayleston, attracted by the vigorous work of the local council, are: brick and tile, plastics, pulp and paper, and meat processing. Most firms are located near the river front.

5 Ayleston has neither anti-pollution bye-laws nor facilities because it grew too fast and the necessary planning was not done. Ayleston does not suffer too noticeably from pollution.

6 The industries of Ayleston deposit waste directly into the Mock. The natural flow of the river carries polluted waters towards Burleigh and the sea. Each of the industries discharges an equal amount of waste as a result of their production processes. Table 45.1 sets out the proportion of waste being discharged into the air and water:

Industry	% of waste discharged to the air	% of waste discharged to the water
Brick and Tile	50%	50%
Pulp and Paper	10%	90%
Meat processing	20%	80%
Plastics	70%	30%

Table 45.1

As a result of waste discharge many people now call the River Mock the 'River Muck'.

7 While ocean tides clean the Mock Estuary, the tidal flats that once supported shell (cockles, mussels, oysters, crabs, lobsters and shrimps) fishermen are now barren. Sixty men working in shell fishing are out of work. They are considering moving to Ayleston for factory jobs. There are no longer any fish in the Mock above the wharves. The river has become sluggish and smells very bad. The property on Burleigh's waterfront, once considered the best area in town to live, has lost much of its value.

8 A canning factory and a marina in Burleigh are facing problems. The yacht marina is expected to close down because few yachtsmen care to sail on the foul water of the Mock. Secondly, the demand for the products of the cannery is falling as the costs of production rise. Costs are increasing because:

(a) water treatment costs are increasing as the Mock becomes more polluted and more expensive filtering equipment is required;

(b) fishing boats are having to go farther out to catch fish. Fish within the upper parts of the estuary have a dangerous mercury level content.

9 Protests from Burleigh to Ayleston are politely listened to, but no action is taken. Say the Ayleston officials: 'It is too expensive to do anything about', or, 'The industries will close down or leave if we try to make them correct the problem. That would put our own town right back into the bad old days.'

10 Finally, local authorities of both towns have agreed on the forming of the River Mock Board, consisting of a chairman, two local community representatives, two representatives of firms, and two economists. The Board asks interested groups of economic experts to make submissions on the following matters:

(a) What should the two communities place first:
 (i) economic growth, increasing production and full employment? or (ii) no economic growth and stress on conservation of the environment?

(b) What social costs are being imposed on each community? Who should bear these costs?

(c) What are the alternative control measures that can be applied to the productive processes to reduce social costs?

Submissions to the Board must contain at least three suggestions as to what method or means can be used to reduce the problem. Submissions must also state the strength and weakness of each of the methods suggested.

Procedure for Group Discussions

1 Either on your own, or preferably in groups of four or five, play the part of economists making submissions to the Board as briefed in 10 above. One person is to act as secretary in each group so that the group's discussion can be recorded in writing. The same person should then present a short verbal report to the River Mock Board when it meets (see 2 below). Make sure that each point of the brief, a, b and c, is covered in discussion and allow time to discuss control measures.

2 Meeting of the River Mock Board. Seven people are needed to play the parts of the seven members of the Board. Instructions for each member are printed on separate cards. The object is for the Board to agree upon measures to resolve the problems and leave everybody satisfied.

Role 1: Chairman of the River Mock Board

The Board has been set up to deal with an economic and social problem as outlined in the case study. You will open the meeting and welcome members to the Board. A serious attitude is required as you need to show the qualities of leadership and of being able to handle people tactfully. After opening the meeting, the first duty is to ask the spokesman of each of the groups of consultant economists to give a verbal report of their group's recommendations. They should also be presenting a written report. After each of the spokesmen has made his report, you should ask for opinions from one member of the Board and then encourage others to state their opinions. You will have to make sure that each person on the Board gets a fair go and gets his/her say although this does not mean that others cannot interrupt. When they do interrupt, try to keep things going and smooth over disagreements. Your main objective is to steer the Board towards coming to agreement on what should be done about the muck in the Mock.

Role 2: Representative of Business Firms in Burleigh
You point out the problems being suffered by the cannery, by the fishing fleet (shell fishing included) and by the owner of the marina. You may bang your fist on the table to make the point that the cannery uses expensive waste treatment equipment because it is concerned about the community and the impact of wastes on the environment. You are convinced that firms in Ayleston are making profits at the expense of firms in Burleigh and that firms in Ayleston should be forced to use waste treatment equipment. You are most concerned about business problems and can see that the town of Burleigh will not survive for much longer unless something is done.

Role 3: Representative of Residents of Burleigh
You represent the general case of all residents, especially the more well-to-do ones. The pleasures of yachting, swimming and fishing no longer exist as the river is too polluted with waste. The marina, which brought a good class of person to the town and made Burleigh the social centre of the region, is in danger of closing. You are also concerned about the health problem, and about the loss of market value of properties of residents along the river front and elsewhere. Unemployment benefits for those put out of work are wasting a lot of the tax-payers' money and some families have moved to Ayleston for factory jobs because of the shortage of jobs in Burleigh. Do not be afraid to speak up and contradict the other representatives of Ayleston.

Role 4: Consultant Economist to the Town of Burleigh
You are a 'modern' economist, more aware of current thinking and believe that no one in their right minds would choose economic growth as the most important objective. You believe that production can be harmful and you point out examples to illustrate this. You are

adamant that the social costs of production must be paid for by the firms in Ayleston and by the consumers of Ayleston's products – the consumers living in heavily populated cities farther to the north. You contradict others but keep your self-control when the other economist gives his views. This does not mean that you cannot contradict him with an example or argument illustrated from problems suffered by Burleigh.

Role 5: Representative of Business Firms in Ayleston
You are a businessman/woman and you point out the fact that without increasing production and cheap production the town will not grow. You believe that businesses that cannot survive in the competitive world of today (like the cannery at Burleigh) should go out of business as it is wasting scarce resources. You are not very impressed by all the talk of social costs suffered by Burleigh. You point out that people can move to Ayleston for jobs if they cannot get one in Burleigh and that this will solve employment problems in both towns. You are a fairly tough character and believe that the objective of a firm is purely profit – not community aid. Do not be afraid to speak out about your views even if you interrupt others.

Role 6: Community Representative of the Town of Ayleston
You are Chairman of the lively Ayleston Trades Council. You are proud of the way your community has developed. You were partly responsible for encouraging industries to settle in Ayleston. The workers in Ayleston are doing quite well and your town is growing because of continuing and increasing demand for its products from heavily populated cities farther to the north. You will be standing as a candidate for the Council in the forthcoming local government elections so you will want to represent your town strongly on the Board. You will not be popular if you accept proposals which will place financial burden on Ayleston and lead to steep increases in the rates. You admit to town problems but consider these minor ones. You believe in higher standards of living for all in terms of material possessions. You regard Burleigh as a bit of an upper class preserve, with their yachting and high society. For you, Ayleston was a depressed area for generations until the new industries came. Do not be afraid to speak up and contradict the representatives of Burleigh.

Role 7: Consultant Economist to the Town of Ayleston
You are an older economist, more conservative and believe that free enterprise without government control results in a more efficient use of resources. As soon as the government sticks its nose in, more problems arise. Government bodies which control and enforce rules about environment protection are a waste of resources. You believe that if resources are no longer

required in Burleigh they should be moved to Ayleston. You are also a firm believer in economic growth and say this several times – how important economic growth is to our living standards. You are concerned that a reduction in the growth of industry in Ayleston will result in catastrophic unemployment. Absolutely catastrophic. Try to contradict the other economist.

Successful use of this role-playing exercise requires careful preparation by both teacher and students. Key concepts and techniques should be introduced beforehand, and when completed de-briefing must take place to ensure that the participants have understood the significance of particular courses of action, and to assist the teacher in evaluating the effectiveness of the exercise.

Teachers may be familiar with the game produced by Coca-Cola, *Man in His Environment*. In its raw, physically attractive state it has limited value for the 'A' level student, but the enterprising teacher can either set up a range of statistics and other factors, or can give his students the opportunity to create their own information.

References

1 Kneese, A. V., *Economics and the Environment*, (Penguin, 1976).
2 Mays, J. B., in Halloran, J. D. and Brothers J. (eds), *Uses of Sociology*, (Sheed and Ward, 1968).
3 Buchanan, J. M., in *Structure of Economic Science: Essays on Methodology*, (ed) Sherman, R. K., (Prentice-Hall, 1966).
4 Cooper, M. H., *Rationing Health Care*, (Croom Helm, 1975). Contains an extensive bibliography.
5 Culyer, A. J., *Need and the National Health Service*, (Martin Robertson, 1976).
6 Cooper, M. H., and Culyer, A. J., *The Price of Blood*, (IEA, 1968).
7 Cooper, M. H. and Culyer, A. J., *The Economics of Giving and Selling Blood in the Economics of Charity*, (IEA, 1974).
8 Titmuss, R., *The Gift Relationship*, (Penguin, 1973). See also Jones-Lee, M. W., *The Value of Life – An Economic Analysis*, (Martin Robertson, 1976), and Chester, T. E., *Health Service Reorganised*, (NWBR, November 1976).

Resources (Environmental Economics)

Books
Arvill, R., *Man and Environment*, (Penguin, 1969).
Barker, P. and Button, K., *Case Studies in Cost-Benefit Analysis*, (Heinemann Educational, 1975).
Barr, J. (ed), *The Environmental Handbook*, (Pan, 1971).
Barr, J., *Derelict Britain*, (Penguin, 1971).
Beckerman, W., *Introduction to National Income Analysis*, (Weidenfeld and Nicolson, 1972), chapter 3.
Beckerman, W., *In Defence of Economic Growth*, (Cape, 1976).
Black, A., *A New Radical's Guide to Economic Reality*. (Holt Reinhart Winston, 1971), chapter 17: 'Danger This River a Fire Hazard'.
Ehrlich, P., *Population Bomb*, (Pan, 1971).
Hines, L. G., *Environmental Issues*, (Norton, 1973).
Illich, I., *Energy and Equity*, (Calder and Boyars, 1974).
Jones, R., *Supply in a Market Economy*, (Allen and Unwin, 1976).
Kneese, A. V., *Economics and the Environment*, (Penguin, 1976).
Lecomber, R., *Economic Growth versus the Environment*, (Macmillan, 1975).
Mabey, R., *Pollution Handbook*, (Penguin, 1974).
Mackenzie R. and Tullock, G., *The New World of Economics*, (Irwin, 1975).
Meadows, D. and Meadows, D., *The Limits to Growth*, (Pan, 1974).
Mishan, E. J., *The Costs of Economic Growth*, (Penguin, 1969).
Mishan, E. J., *Elements of Cost-Benefit Analysis*, (Unwin, 1977).
Pearce, D. W., *Cost-Benefit Analysis*, (Macmillan, 1971).
Peston, M., *Public Goods and the Public Sector*, (Macmillan, 1972).
HMSO, *Royal Commission on Environmental Pollution*, (HMSO, 1974–76).
Schumacher, E. F., *Small is Beautiful*, (Blond, 1973).
Smith, P. J. (ed), *The Politics of Physical Resources*, (Penguin, 1975).
Victor, P. A., *Economics of Pollution*, (Macmillan, 1972).
Wagner, L. and Baltazzis, N. (ed), *Readings in Applied Economics*, (Oxford University Press, 1973).

Articles
Beckerman, W., Why we Need Economic Growth, *Lloyds Bank Review*, October 1971.
Mishan, E. J., Economic Growth: The Need for Scepticism, *Lloyds Bank Review*, October 1972.
Mishan, E. J., An ABC of CBA, *Lloyds Bank Review*, July 1971.
Richardson, H. W., Economics and the Environment, *National Westminster Bank Review*, May 1971.

Other Sources
The Open University publishes an enormous amount of material which is relevant to this and other parts of economics courses. Their student programme timetable for the year gives details of every radio and TV programme transmitted during the year, including

transmission times. Current courses which are relevant include:

Making Sense of Society (D 101);
Fundamentals of Human Geography (D 204);
Environment (S2–3);
The Earth's Physical Resources (S266);
Ecology (S 323);
The Man Made World (T 100);
Systems Behaviour (T 241);
Environmental Control and Public Health (PT 272).

In addition to the student timetable, the Open University publishes catalogues of TV and radio material which is available for hire, plus details of their excellent course texts.

Audio Learning have produced two tapes which are relevant; both are suitable for the teacher and better-than-average student.
Heal, G. M. and Dasgupta, P. S., *Economics and the Use of Resources*, (ECA 024).
Pearce, D. and Lecomber, R., *Pollution Problems*, (ECA 021).

Seminar Cassettes: tape on pollution and industry.

Films

There is a wide variety of film material available. Much of the best is heavily booked up for years ahead, and the challenge is to find material which is less popular (or be more efficient!).

The most comprehensive catalogue in the whole range of social and environmental problems is that published by Concord Films. Its comments on each film are very useful, and they hold film from an enormous range of sources.

Films are now expensive, particularly after one has paid return postage. Films should always be previewed by the teacher, and there is much to be said for worksheets to be completed during the showing of the film. From a cost point of view, films which can be watched with profit by geographers, environmental scientists, etc, would seem to be a sensible idea.

National Audio Visual Aids Library, *The Industrial City*, (16 mins). Case study of Detroit – problems of congestion, pollution, crime, etc.
Shell Film Library, *The River Must Live*, (21 mins, free loan). What happens when a river is overloaded with more waste than it can absorb and consequences to those who depend on it.
ICI Film Library, *The Choice*, (29 mins, free loan). Describes air, water and land pollution, and what is being done to combat it.
ICI Film Library, *The Shadow of Progress*, (27 mins). World's environmental problems; population, pollution, finite resources.

BP Film Library, *The Tide of Traffic*, (29 mins). Dilemma of car benefits and problems.
BBC Enterprises, Economics of the Real World, Programme 10: *Pollution: A Cost of Growth?* (25 mins).
Concord Films Council, *Trade It In, Throw It Away*, (50 mins). About planned obsolescence in USA.
Concord Films Council, *Limits to Growth*, (60 mins). 1972 Thames TV report on population, pollution, resources, etc.

Wallcharts

Dept. of the Environment. Four charts – *This is Our World*, (free). Problems of air, water, noise and land pollution.
Pictorial Charts Educational Trust. *The Motor Car*, (ten large photographs 15″×20″, 720). Considers the economic and social balance sheet of the effect of the car on our society.

Resources (Social Economics)

Books

There is a wealth of material and no bibliography could hope to cover all the ground and remain manageable.

Fontana have published four paperbacks which while not concerned with 'economics' in many cases provide many insights and much useful information. They are:

Butterworth, E., and Holman, R. (eds)., *Social Welfare in Modern Britain*, (1975).
Butterworth, E., and Weir, D. (eds)., *Social Problems of Modern Britain*, (1972).
Lambert, C., and Weir, D. (eds)., *Cities in Modern Britain*, (1975).
Weir, D. (ed)., *Men and Work in Modern Britain*, (1973).

An extremely valuable book for the teacher is:
Lawton, D., and Dufour, B., *The New Social Studies*, (Heinemann Educational, 1973), which covers an enormous amount of ground under five main headings:

1 Historical and Theoretical Perspectives;
2 Content of the New Social Order;
3 New Methods and Materials;
4 Topics and Themes;
5 Evaluation.

Other books include:

Anderson, R. W., *The Economics of Crime*, (Macmillan, 1976).
Atkinson, A. B., *The Economics of Inequality*, (Oxford University Press, 1975).
Barker, P. (ed), *A Sociological Portrait*, (Penguin, 1972).
Coates, K. and Silburn, R., *Poverty; the Forgotten*

Englishmen, (Penguin, 1973).
Field, F., Meacher, M. and Pond, C., *To Him Who Hath*, (Penguin, 1977).
Grant, R. M. and Shaw, G. K. (ed), *Current Issues in Economic Policy*, (Philip Allan, 1975).
Jackson, D., *Poverty*, (Macmillan, 1972).
Phelps, E. S. (ed), *Economic Justice*, (Penguin, 1973).
Roach, J. and Roach, L. (eds), *Poverty*, (Penguin, 1972).
Robson, W. A., *Welfare State and Welfare Society*, (Allen and Unwin, 1976).
Robson, W. A. and Crick, B. (eds), *The Future of the Social Services*, (Penguin, 1972.
Rawls, J. A., *A Theory of Justice*, (Oxford University Press, 1973).
Rowley, C. K. and Peacock, A., *Welfare Economics*, (Martin Robertson, 1975).
Williams, A. and Anderson, R., *Efficiency in the Social Services*, (Basil Blackwell, 1975).

Articles and Periodicals
The field of social policy receives much attention in the pages of periodicals such as *New Society*, *Political Quarterly*, *Socialist Commentary*, etc. Any university town will have a bookshop with an array of those fascinating but alas increasingly expensive little pamphlets about almost every subject. And as always the bank quarterlies contain many 'sound' articles about a number of major social policy issues. Articles of value include:

Ashton, R. K., 'The Housing Market', *National Westminster Bank Review*, August 1974.
Chester, T. E., 'Health Service Reorganised', *National Westminster Bank Review*, November 1973.
Economist Brief, 'What about Welfare?', in *The Uncommon Market*, (*The Economist*, 1977)
Harrington, R. L., 'Housing Supply and Demand', *National Westminster Bank Review*, May 1972.
Gripaios, P., 'A New Employment Policy for London', *National Westminster Bank Review*, August 1976.
Lees, D., 'Economics and Non-economics of Health Services', *Three Banks Review*, June 1976.
Llewellyn, D. T., 'The Individual in Economic Policy', *National Westminster Bank Review*, February 1970.
Maddison, A., 'What is Education for?', *Lloyds Bank Review*, April 1974.
Lydall, H., 'The Economics of Inequality', *Lloyds Bank Review*, July 1975.
Redwood, J., 'UK Housing Market', *National Westminster Bank Review*, November 1974.

Seldon, A., 'Thaw in the Welfare State', *Lloyds Bank Review*, July 1972.

In addition to this article by the Editor of the Institute of Economic Affairs, the IEA publishes a wide range of pamphlets on social policy, which represent an important contribution to any discussion of these issues. The Fabian Society also publishes a large number of relevant pamphlets which could be used in conjunction with IEA material.

Other Material
Audio Learning has published some tapes which include:

Atkinson, A. B. and Laidler, D., *The Rich and the Poor*, (ECA 013);
Harrington, R. and Smith, S., *The Economics of Housing*, (ECA 031);
Ramsey, J. B. and Steiner, P., *Basic Economic Insights*, (ECA 025).

The Open University has a number of courses which are of relevance (see Student Guide). Of particular value is Urban Development (DT 201).

Films
The key source of film material is the catalogue of Concord Films Council. No teacher wishing to use film for this area can afford to be without access to it.

Shell Film Library, *The Land Must Provide*, (24 mins, free loan). Population growth brings need for better farming methods – how traditional community methods may be changed.
Concord Films Council, *Rich Man, Poor Man*, (50 mins each). A five-part study of the relationship between rich and poor countries: *1 Industry; 2 Trade; 3 Education; 4 Medicine; 5 Food*. BBC TV 1972.
Concord Films Council, *Hard Times*, (50 mins). Thames TV report on poverty in UK in the 1970s.
Concord Films Council, *The Other Way*, (50 mins). Wisdom requires that science changes course to meet the *real* needs of mankind (see E. F. Schumacher's *Small is Beautiful*).

Wallchart
Pictorial Charts Educational Trust: One Chart: *Rich World, Poor World*. To stimulate discussion on underdeveloped countries. (S 27).

46   Teaching Current Economics Topics Through Data Response Questions

John Rees

The introduction of data response questions into public examinations seems to have come as a shock to many teachers, although one might have thought that this type of approach would long ago have been incorporated into economics teaching techniques. Economics is now tested by three different methods: essays, multiple choice and data response, and although we may quibble about the balance of marks amongst these different methods, we must surely accept that public examinations now place a heavy emphasis on understanding rather than memory as far as economics is concerned.

Most economics teachers would accept that there are two main reasons for studying the subject: that it is a rigorous mental discipline, and that it deals with key issues in the real world. There have been times when it appeared that one or the other element was emphasised almost to the exclusion of the other. It has become fashionable to criticise 'positive economics', yet data response questions would become a meaningless exercise if divorced from a sound understanding of the fundamental economic principles. The arguments for economics as an intellectual training centre on the view that economics is a way of thinking rather than a body of fact; an apparatus whose purpose is not simply to exercise the mind in some arid intellectual gymnasium, but to apply it in such a way that principles acquire flesh and become operational.

Economics has traditionally emphasised deductive methods of thought, but there seems no good reason why the subject should not be at least as concerned with inductive approaches. Indeed the average and below average pupil may well find economic principles easier to grasp if approached 'facts first' (not that you can become a good economist simply by diligent study of the *Financial Times* and *The Economist*!). However there is a clear danger that economists could fall into the trap from which geographers have only recently escaped – a contemplation of the unique rather than the establishment of sets of principles. The nature of multiple choice testing is such that the scope for inductive thought is limited; whereas the data response format lays great emphasis on this approach.

Like other methods of testing, data response questions enable teachers to test their pupils both in norm-referenced (i.e. against other pupils) and criterion-referenced (i.e. against absolute standards) ways. They also assist the wise teacher in evaluation of his own teaching method – nothing is more salutary at the end of an apparently successful attempt to teach a 'difficult bit of theory' than to be greeted with almost total silence when the concept is presented with the full trappings of the real world.[1] Sandford and Bradbury note that 'we cannot separate totally the procedure of illustrating generalisations from the particular and that of generalising from the particular'.[2] Equally, adding analytical problem questions adds another dimension to our ability to evaluate, diagnose and assess. Perhaps an additional advantage of the data response method is that it can be fully integrated into the teaching method – data response questions become the case studies from which the generalisations emerge. Most teachers use the technique without thinking: 'Did you see that TV programme last night?'; 'Have you seen that bit in the papers this morning?'; and it must be hoped that the introduction of data response questions into public examinations will not lead teachers to extract them from their natural place in the flow of teaching.

Data response questions may be used in a number of ways. As a teaching medium they may be incorporated into the general flow of teaching material. They may be used in an introductory way to raise new issues, to stimulate new directions of thought; equally they may be used to consolidate understanding. Alternatively their role may be to test the success with which a particular concept has been handled by the teacher or to assess individual pupil competence.

There are a number of ways in which data response questions can be employed in ordinary classroom teaching. It is quite clear that questions need to be chosen with great care, yet perhaps one of the most stimulating methods of approach is the DIY strategy (with all the advantages and problems known to the home handyman!). Two alternatives present themselves:

1 Pupils find their own piece for study from their own reading, e.g. article in newspaper or periodical – it can be an original experience for them to realise how limited is the conceptual content of much of what they read – and thus they are challenged to read more critically.
2 Pupils are presented with a piece which has been selected by the teacher, and are then asked to prepare their own questions, and may indeed be assessed simply on the questions themselves. After all it is often

the case that asking the right questions is as important as giving the right answers. This must act as a stimulus to the critical analysis of other questions, whether or not in the data response format, since they can see the range of possible questions on any piece of material.

Whether the approach is DIY or more conventional, we can identify a number of different approaches to their use in the classroom:

1 *Class discussion*
(a) as individual contributions to general discussion;
(b) use of syndicates to discuss parts of question and report back to teaching group as a whole.

2 *Written work*
(a) homework exercises;
(b) in-school tests;
(c) in-school practice of concepts under study.

The sources of data response material are legion – the teacher has to be aware of possibilities, and have a good filing system and card index! (see Chapter 56) – but four major categories of material can be found:

1 hypothetical data, aimed at those areas in which simple statistical information is difficult to obtain, e.g. supply and demand, theory of the firm, comparative costs;
2 interpretation of 'economic diagrams';
3 interpretation of 'real' statistical data, from official and other sources;
4 interpretation of articles and sections of prose from textbooks, periodicals, magazines and newspapers.

Many teachers have used newspaper articles of the sort to be found in the *Guardian*, or the Lombard column of the *Financial Times*, added half a dozen questions, and used the piece either as a test, or as a way of introducing a new topic.

Statistical interpretation involves the need for considerable groundwork, and without any doubt the need for basic work on the theory of statistics. Almost certainly we need to build into our courses work on:

(a) the compilation of statistics;
(b) basic statistical techniques – distributions, means and averages, calculation of index numbers, etc.[3]

In addition to the obvious government sources of material (*Annual Abstract of Statistics*, *Social Trends*, the *Pink Books* and *Blue Books*, and the monthly *Treasury Economic Progress Report*) there is a whole range of material published by nationalised industries, NEDO, boards and bureaux. The regularly revised Prest and Coppock contains a wealth of up-to-date material, and that book is outstanding for the way in which it interprets and incorporates the statistical material – a model of good practice.[4]

In addition to the official and quasi-official sources, almost every pressure group under the sun has 'give-away' material, which they use to advance their case with the public. While we must be aware of 'bias' in official material, we must be even more wary of the deliberate distortions which will be introduced by groups seeking to produce a strongly partisan case. Although it is unlikely that examination questions would ever ask pupils to elucidate bias in a particular piece of material, as part of our wider teaching responsibility we should illustrate the problems of information gathering and interpretation.

The serious newspapers and periodicals contain much useful material (note the problems of copyright); but rather more challenging is the task of finding material in the tabloids, or in periodicals not written with economists in mind. If two of the goals of data response questions are to eliminate the barriers between theory and its application, and to test the ability of pupils to recognise fundamental principles in ordinary situations, then this type of material is of particular importance. It is also worth comparing the treatment of particular issues in different media, including radio and television, perhaps operating on a class basis. The group can then study the assumptions which are made, the concepts used, the way in which 'facts' are used, and indeed the basic quality of economic argument put forward to the public. It may not be the purpose of the media to educate, but most people learn a great deal of economics from their papers. Our worry must be what kind of economics they learn, and what corrective filters we can give them.

A successful approach to the use of data response material requires flexibility and sensitivity on the part of the teacher. Contemporary material must be fully integrated into his teaching strategy, so that the 'real world' does not stand separately from the basic concepts of economics. Teachers should not fall into the trap of allowing economics to degenerate into a shapeless 'current affairs'. If we agree with Stonier and Hague that 'the value of economic theory lies in providing a framework of analysis which can be used by applied economists in interpreting facts about the real world',[5] then the inductive method and the linking of the particular and the general which characterises the data response approach should be seen as presenting further opportunities to the economics teacher.

References

1 See the useful paper produced by the Research Section of the Cambridge Local Board, Harvey Road, Cambridge, reviewed in *Economics*, 11 (2), Summer 1975, p 117.
2 Sandford, C. T. and Bradbury, M. S., *Projects and Role Playing in Teaching Economics*, (Macmillan, 1971).
3 Note the interesting material emerging from the

Continuing Maths Project, based on Sussex University, aimed at non-mathematicians who need maths in their 'A' level courses; material is being published by the Longmans Resources Unit, The Shambles, York. Also Davies, B and Foad, J. M., *Statistics for Economics*, (Heinemann Educational, 1977).
4 Prest, A. R. and Coppock, D. J., *The UK Economy*, (Weidenfeld and Nicolson, 1976).
5 Stonier, A. W. and Hague, D. C., *A Textbook of Economic Analysis*, (Longman, 1972).
See also Oliver, J. M., *The Principles of Teaching Economics*, (Heinemann Educational, 1973).

47 Values
Nigel Wright

The question of values has not been adequately dealt with in the literature of economics teaching. This chapter cannot, therefore, be a distillation of practical wisdom. Instead it is intended to sketch out some areas that economics teachers may want to consider further. We can examine the incursion of values under three headings: values implicit in the syllabus; the values the teacher brings to the class; and the values students bring to the class.

The Syllabus

It has become customary to draw a distinction between *positive* and *normative* economics. Positive economics has been supposed to be a value-free science. Thus in so far as the syllabus has consisted of elements of positive economics, teachers have been satisfied that there is no problem of values as far as subject matter is concerned.

Without entering into a lengthy discussion, it must be acknowledged that positivism is in the process of being discredited in the view of many economists,[1] as it has been by most modern philosophers of the social sciences. If the distinction between positive and normative economics is not valid, it follows that the whole subject matter must be reviewed for the hidden (and not-so-hidden) values implicit in it. A common view is expressed by an author of widely used textbooks:

'Beginners rarely need any encouragement to rush into normative ideas but rather require the hard discipline of positive analysis on which to base later, more mature judgements on what is desirable and attainable....'[2]

One problem, however, is that 'positive analysis' actually presupposes that certain questions of value have already been decided.* Thus you cannot use supply–demand analysis as a tool to criticise the free market system.[3] Similarly, you cannot use Keynesian macro-theory to make out a case against government intervention. Positive analysis cannot be seen as a neutral tool which one is free to use as one likes once one has learned how to use it. Neo-classical positivism will come to be seen as an historically located attempt to explain and justify a specific economic structure and a specific set of social relations.

If we examine the typical 'O' and 'A' level economics syllabuses (which dictate the pattern of most economics teaching in English schools) we find the problem exacerbated. It is not just that these syllabuses contain

---

* This point is crucial. The conventional story is this: 'Economic theorists have produced a set of analytical tools. Given an economic problem, these tools can be used to offer politicians, businessmen, etc a set of policy options. It is up to the politicians, etc to choose which policy option they want on the basis of *their* judgements about what is desirable.' In this story the value judgements come *after* the analysis. This is the reverse of the truth: in fact economic theorists cannot even begin work without making a host of value-laden assumptions which they may or may not be aware of but which pre-determine the kind of answers they are going to get.

many items which enjoy dwindling credibility amongst contemporary economists, but that they are built around some of the most controversial elements in terms of assumed values. From a value-laden corpus we teach a syllabus which consists of value-laden selections (such as the extraordinary emphasis on the free-market allocation of resources) from the total available corpus. A chief examiner when asked why there was no Marxian economics on the 'A' level syllabus replied that it would be 'politically unacceptable'. Whether this is true or desirable, or not, the point is that the decision to exclude elements of Marxian analysis is a *political* decision. Meanwhile in the USSR (for instance) students are being denied a fair opportunity to find out what Western economics has to say for itself.

This is not to argue that what we teach is wrong (though it sometimes is); just that we need to face the fact that our syllabuses are interest-laden, resting upon and justifying a particular belief system. We may decide that this is what we want: we may share the Black Paper view that schools have a duty to inculcate specific values – private ownership is good, competition is healthy, self-interest is praiseworthy, inequality is quite acceptable. But if so, let us not hide behind untenable claims of 'neutrality' or 'objectivity'.

If, by contrast, we wish to avoid a biased syllabus, we have a major task of reconstruction before us. A more balanced syllabus would have to include a comparison of various economic systems, and deliberate study of different value systems and the economic theories to which they give rise – in short the study of economic philosophy. And examiners will have to stop fighting shy of asking questions which involve assessment of different value positions.

In the short run we need to be aware that most of our syllabuses are hot potatoes, and try to use some of the little time we have left after 'doing' the syllabus to examine the question of implicit values and alternatives to them. This takes us on to the role of the teacher.

The Teacher

Paralleling the 'neutrality' of positive economics, teachers themselves have aspired to be neutral[4] in their presentation of the subject matter, in their interpretation of it, and in discussion. We do not know how many economics teachers succeed in this aim, or even how many try to, but a more fundamental question is: 'Is it possible?' Perhaps a quick test would be to ask oneself: '... if I invited a professor of economics from Peking into my classes and asked him/her to speak up as soon as I strayed from neutrality, how long would she/he keep quiet?' You may counter that this is unfair since such a person would be operating from an entirely different paradigm. But this is precisely the point: growing numbers of people within our own community are operating from different paradigms,[5] each resting upon a distinct belief system. It is because we live in a society without consensus that values have become such a burning issue.[6]

Probably our most serious biases are those of which we are unconscious. Does this matter? If our answer is to be 'No: there is a certain set of values to which we are committed and we are happy to put them across', then well and good. (But there might be an implication that other teachers have an equal right to put across contrary views.) But if bias *does* matter, further thought is needed.

Self-awareness

The first necessity is a high degree of self-awareness. This means not only knowing what your opinions are, but also knowing in what ways these opinions differ from those of others and understanding your own intuitions and motivations. Perhaps one day it will not be too far-fetched to suggest that economics teachers undergo some form of encounter or therapy group training. After all, it is often the case that beliefs such as 'competition is good' or 'profits are bad' spring not from some magnificent rational framework one has spent years developing, but from some 'in the guts' *feeling*. We need to recognise these 'guts' feelings, not necessarily so that we may avoid presenting them to our students, but so that at least we may be aware that we are doing so.

Being Explicit

Teachers who are aware that they cannot be neutral – particularly in ways of which they are not conscious – have to make a choice: whether or not to make it plain to students what their biases are. I want to argue that teachers ought to make it absolutely clear what their own opinions and dispositions are. If this is done, it makes it easier for students to discriminate, discount and compensate than when they face a teacher who leaves them continually guessing whether they are being offered a widely agreed fact or a value-ridden assertion. One teacher made no secret of his Monday Club affiliations and handed out photocopies of *Daily Telegraph* editorials; he was far less likely to confuse his students with his bias than others who felt confident that they were being neutral because they had left their politics at the door. Allowing students to argue with him, he left them free to accept or reject his views as they liked.

Indoctrination

Can economics teaching become indoctrination? The prevailing philosophy of education (from which one may well want to differ) has it that four, maybe five, conditions are necessary for indoctrination to take place.[7]

1 Content. Only one set of beliefs is presented even when it is known (to the teacher) that alternative sets of beliefs exist.*

2 Outcome. Students end up with a fixed allegiance to this set of beliefs and a resistance to alternative beliefs.
3 Method. The method used by the indoctrinator must be typically expected to present the content as in (1) and produce the outcome as in (2).
4. Time. Indoctrination is a relatively long-term process. A communist shop steward is not likely to indoctrinate his audience in a 40 minute talk.
5 Intention. It is a matter of debate whether intention to indoctrinate is a necessary condition.

'Positive economics' presents a nice example. Many of us taught it for years in the conviction that we were being quite neutral before we realised that it contained a whole set of implicit values which probably rubbed off on students in quite insidious ways. It is now appallingly clear that the typical school teacher of economics is in fact satisfying the first four conditions for indoctrination and that the only possible 'let out clause' is that we never had any intention of indoctrinating our students. On the other hand a Soviet economics teacher would equally vehemently deny any intention to indoctrinate, a denial which many of us might want to view with some scepticism.

An alternative way off the hook would be to ask whether indoctrination is necessarily a bad thing. If it is not, we have little to worry about. But if it is, economics teachers need to reappraise their approach with some urgency. The following steps could be considered:

1 Reconstructing the syllabus so as to give equal weight to as many sets of beliefs as possible.
2 Making positive efforts to introduce students to alternative points of view. So long as examination syllabuses retain their present bias, it seems fair to put considerable emphasis on alternatives of various kinds. This means giving as much consideration to ends as we do to means. (I say this without wishing to subscribe to the fallacy, springing from Robbins, that differences of value only arise in the consideration of ends.)
3 Students should be encouraged to be critical of what their teachers and textbooks say. To encourage open-mindedness will be a deliberate aim. A noted American professor writes:

'The economist is [in his training] drilled in the problems of *all* economic systems and in the methods by which a price system solves these problems. It becomes impossible for the trained economist to believe that a small group of selfish capitalists dictate the main outlines of the allocation of resources and the determination of outputs.... He cannot believe that a change in the *form* of social organization will eliminate basic economic problems.'[8]

It is one thing to claim that most trained economists do not believe these things, but something altogether more sinister to suggest that their training makes it *impossible* for them to believe them.
4 Authoritarian teaching methods seem particularly inappropriate. A packed examination syllabus which prescribes a fixed body of knowledge to be imbibed from unassailable experts – whether teachers or textbook authors – is a dangerous device. Students – and indeed teachers – who want to get on in life are left with little option but to concentrate all their attention on the conventional wisdoms and at least pretend to subscribe to them during the examination. It may be hoped that a recognition of the value-laden nature of economics will lead to further development of teaching methods away from those which are more appropriate for subjects like mathematics. An interesting side-question is the implications of multiple choice testing which presupposes that there is a set of questions which have only one right answer.[9] While such a set may theoretically exist, it may need to be conceded that given the present state of knowledge, and of society, it is an empty set.
5 From the point of view of avoiding imposition of values, departments which are lucky enough to have two or more economists might adopt a deliberate policy of employing teachers who have clearly distinctive outlooks, and arranging teaching programmes so that students are taught by all the teachers at one time or another.

Behaviour
On questions of values, what teachers *do* is just as likely to make an impression on students as what they *say*. If teachers say they want their students to be rational, and preach the virtues of rationality to students, they ought to behave rationally themselves. It will be of little use saying to students 'be critical' if one reacts with hostility and anger to criticisms levelled at oneself. Given the role that society imposes on teachers it is difficult to avoid behaving in a way that puts across a 'might is right' philosophy however much one may preach otherwise. Teachers should not only tell students what their beliefs are, but prove that they are committed to those beliefs by acting in accordance with them.

Students

There are two questions here: First, do the values

---

* As a corollary, teachers must make it their duty to find out what alternative sets of beliefs exist. Ignorance is no excuse.

students bring to the classroom affect their learning of economics? Second, should teachers attempt to influence or educate the students' value-judgements and, if so, how?

Most students have plenty of opinions, and these form part of the mental 'set' within which the student has to start fitting whatever he/she learns in economics lessons. Different sets will produce different learnings, and in some cases will result in a refusal of learning. (We are all familiar with the 'revolutionary' who believes that there is nothing at all to be said in favour of the capitalist mode, or the 'racialist' who refuses to believe that an increase in the working population through immigration could cause anything other than unemployment and general impoverishment.) We can help students develop their own self-awareness and show them how their own predispositions will affect how they see things. A number of perceptual exercises used by psychologists are helpful. (See the Appendix to this chapter, page 262.) The point of such exercises is to illustrate in a simple way how there are different ways of seeing things, and that our concentration on seeing them in one particular way may hinder us from seeing them in other equally valid ways. In some cases people cannot, however much it is pointed out to them, see things in certain ways.

Such exercises should only be thought of as an illustration of one aspect of the problem, because the question of values in economics is far more complex. Not only does it require far more than a few seconds' mental 'reconstruction' to 'see' other points of view, but the greater difficulties lie not in the perceptual 'blinkers' of the student but in the concealed bias of the subject matter and the way that certain elements are selected from it, and in the fact that belief systems are the product of a total social process.[10]

The social and cultural background of students has a marked effect on their response to economic questions. In one school in a traditionally Labour area all the students favour nationalisation; in another school in a prosperous middle-class area, all the students oppose it. These convictions remain regardless of the data and arguments that may be put before them. Should teachers attempt to alter or develop the value-judgements of their students? Those whose inclination is to answer 'no' should perhaps ponder whether they can really hope to *avoid* doing so. If not, there is much to be said for bringing one's attempts out into the open in a deliberate and systematic way. This does not mean that the teacher decides what are 'right' values and then proceeds by fair means or foul to get students to accept them.[11] Rather it requires that the teacher creates the preconditions under which students can examine and develop their own judgements, helping them to think rationally about them, pay due attention to the facts, recognise their own emotions and motivations, consider the interests of others, and so forth.

'To try to impose values is immoral, but to fail to create frameworks within which people can choose their own values is just as bad.'[12]

There are, then, a number of things an economics teacher can do.

Variety
Clearly students ought to be brought into contact with a variety of value-positions. The simplest way is to provide literature from a wide variety of sources (and allow students time to read it!). This could include fiction as well as non-fiction.[13] Textbooks present a thorny problem, since they tend to reflect examination syllabuses[14] and are held in even greater reverence by students than their teachers. In the absence of textbooks which 'come clean' on the question of values, it will be necessary to find literature which presents counter-viewpoints. Probably more effective than reading is meeting people who hold different viewpoints. The hoary practice of inviting a union official one week and the man from the Chamber of Commerce the next could certainly be improved upon. (For one thing full-time union officials and salaried managers usually have more in common than they care to admit.) A more exciting and provocative selection might include a Buddhist, a shop-floor worker (*not* a union official), a stockbroker, a one-man businessman, a radical feminist, a Chinophile, a real Christian, an ecologist or conservationist, a rastafarian.[15] (This is not, of course, an exhaustive list!)

Better still than reading or listening is to attempt to experience what it feels like to hold different beliefs. Role-playing or simulation exercises are valuable for this.[16] Field trips too can play a part.

Discussion
The most commonly used device will be discussion. Facing a packed syllabus, it is easy to be impatient with discussions that seem ill-informed, which stray endlessly from the point, and which produce few constructive insights into the subject matter. But the act of discussion is in itself useful to youngsters; what appears to us as a pointless ramble may in fact be a vital learning process in which students are discovering what constitutes a relevant point, what sorts of ideas are viable, what types of arguments are sustainable, how to listen, and so forth. None the less, there is much we can do to improve the quality of discussions.

First, the teacher must lay down strict ground rules.[17] One of the most difficult things is to prevent the discussion falling into the hands of three or four of the most articulate speakers. We need sensitive strategies for helping the more reticent students to make their contribution (which may include sending the most dominant ones off to the library for a period). We have a responsibility to stop the 'silent majority' being silent. The silent school students become the silent ones in university seminars, union meetings and so forth; school is the last chance that most such people will have of being helped to overcome this handicap.

Second, teachers have to work out exactly what their role in the discussion is to be. Making this decision and operating it in practice is a widely under-developed skill that could possibly be dealt with in teaching training and in-service courses.

Third, many intriguing topics are too complex for sixth-formers to have very useful discussions about them. Nationalisation is an example. It may be better to have topics which raise central questions of value but which do not depend upon familiarity with a mass of empirical matter. For instance, one might ask 'Supposing we in this room were stranded on a desert island with only ten cans of beans, in what ways might we distribute them, and which way would be best?' With one group the discussion on this lasted off and on for a whole term, and a lot of ground was cleared on many questions of value. (See also Chapter 48, page 264, for another example.) A number of role-playing exercises also supply just sufficient information to delineate the boundaries of debate and enable focused discussion to take place.

Fourth, the essential facts must be supplied by the teacher. It's too easy for discussions to degenerate into 'British Rail always makes a loss', 'No it doesn't', 'Yes it does', and so on. A certain number of fact packs and booklets are available,[18] and we must hope for more since producing them yourself is an onerous task. Some of the Humanities Curriculum Project packs are useful, though expensive.[19]

Finally, discussions with sixth-form groups can consume an inordinate amount of time. An hour or more may be spent tossing in all kinds of outlandish ideas and going up culs-de-sac. But for the teacher to cut short this stage by *telling* the students what is relevant and workable is not only to risk imposing value judgements on the discussion, but also to undercut a key learning process. (There are clearly many students who have difficulty in grasping the *concepts* of relevance and viability in the context of economics; they can learn from discussions which give them a chance to formulate, test and discard hypotheses for themselves.) It is important therefore to provide ample time, and this may involve setting up a forum for the continuation of discussions after allotted class time has been used up: an Economics Society for example.*

* We should not worry unduly if an Economics Society does not seem to be doing much economics, particularly if we want non-economists to join in. The answer to the question 'what is economics' may be far trickier than convention acknowledges, with plenty of scope for interest-laden answers. Thus neo-classical positivists with their distinctive belief-system insist that economics is not about ethics, psychology, politics, sociology or history. This isolationism has permitted all sorts of value-judgements to creep into the economic corpus

unnoticed. And it has prevented economics from providing useful answers to many pressing public problems. Perhaps we should allow future generations to decide for themselves what is, and what is not, economics.

Participation

It follows from a decision to help students develop their own values (as opposed to having them learn certain values) that student participation should be maximised at all stages of the learning process. Since this raises all sorts of questions which are beyond the scope of this chapter, I can take it no further here.

Is it all Worthwhile?

Everything I have suggested involves time and effort, and we will have to consider the opportunity cost. It has not struck economics teachers too forcefully in the past that we have a responsibility to grasp the nettle of values, partly because we have been able to hide behind the mask of positivism and reassure ourselves that values do not enter into it, rather as a mathematics teacher can. But it is not only economics teachers who have to face up to the problem. Just as English teachers have for over sixty years tried to share out their burden with the slogan 'every teacher is a teacher of English', we should recognise that every teacher is a teacher of values (not in the sense of inculcator but as an assistant in development, or 'enabler'). Since the kinds of value questions which arise in economics also arise in history and sociology, we could take a first step towards a 'values across the curriculum' scheme by getting together with teachers of those subjects. This could reduce by up to two-thirds the load of the measures I have proposed.

None the less, putting values 'in' necessarily involves cutting something else out, and this would need justification. My own justification would start from two points, (a) the student's right to know,[20] and (b) recognition of the social and economic crisis we are now experiencing and the failure of economists to have much of any use to say about it. An ultimate solution will only come when there is widespread consensus on a framework of values. If we reject an authoritarian solution which would *impose* such a framework, educators must take on their share of the responsibility for the creation of a voluntary consensus. If this means that students of elementary economics end up with rather less knowledge of the properties of the marginal cost curve and the role of special deposits, we must weigh up such short run costs against the long run benefits. The potential long run benefit is that future generations will be able to create a happy and just society, an objective which has notably eluded us hitherto.

References and Notes

1 See, for example, Ward, B. *What's Wrong With Economics?*, (Macmillan, 1972).
2 Powicke, J. C., book review in *Economics*, Vol. XI, part 3, Autumn 1975, p 186.
3 To be sure, one cannot attempt a rigorous critique of the market economy without *knowing about* supply–demand analysis, but this is not the same thing as using it as a tool with which to construct a critique.
4 It is interesting how the parameters of 'neutrality' are laid down in terms of the dominant issues of the day. Thus, because it appears that the dominant distinction in public political life is between Conservative and Labour, many teachers try to maintain neutrality on issues which divide those parties, such as the role of the state, nationalisation, the power of trade unions. Teachers are very much less circumspect when it comes to matters which are not at present major public issues, such as the rights or wrongs of usury or the virtues of small-scale production.
5 See note 15 below.
6 See Wilson, J., *Introduction to Moral Education*, (Penguin, 1967), pp 12–19.
7 What follows is derived from a lecture by R. F. Dearden given at the London University Institute of Education.
8 George Stigler quoted in Scott, James H. and Rothman, Mitchell P., 'The Effect of an Introductory Course on Student Political Attitudes' in *The Journal of Economic Education*, 6(2), Spring 1975, p 107.
9 For the results of a most revealing survey of leading economists on this question, see Brittan, S., *Is There An Economic Consensus?*, (Macmillan, 1973).
10 See Berger, P. and Luckmann, T., *The Social Construction of Reality*, (Penguin, 1967).
11 See Wilson, J., op. cit., part I.
12 Ibid, p 143.
13 The reader will of course be able to add to the following list of suggestions:
Dickens, Charles, *Hard Times* (Penguin, 1969);
Steinbeck, John, *The Grapes of Wrath* (Penguin, 1951);
Zola, Emile, *Germinal* (Penguin, 1954);
Tressell, Robert, *The Ragged-Trousered Philanthropists* (Panther, 1965);
Huxley, Aldous, *Brave New World* (Penguin, 1955);
Schumacher, E. F., *Small Is Beautiful* (Sphere, 1974);
Sahlins, Marshall, *Stone Age Economics*, (Tavistock Publications, 1974);
Robertson, James, *Profit or People?*, (Calder and Boyars, 1974);
Turnbull, Colin, *The Forest People*, (Pan, 1976);
Mandel, Ernest, *An Introduction to Marxist Economic Theory*, (Pathfinder, 1970).
14 Taking, as an example, the deliberate exclusion of Marxian analysis we find that of the thirty-seven introductory textbooks aimed at sixth formers, twenty-five make no mention of Marx or Marxian analysis. None of the other twelve contain more than a handful of *en passant* references to Marx, most often to note that this or that 'prediction' of Marx has turned out to be wrong. Not one textbook attempts to give the student a fair account of what Marx or subsequent Marxists have to say. This kind of hegemonic bias needs to be borne in mind when considering allegations that Marxism is becoming 'prevalent' (see Gould, Julius, *The Attack on Higher Education: Marxist and Radical Penetration*, (Institute for the Study of Conflict, 1977)).
15 The following organisations or groupings can put teachers in touch with speakers who can present distinctively alternative viewpoints on economic matters:
The Ecologist Journal, 73 Molesworth Street, Wadebridge, Cornwall. (The ecological viewpoint.) (London and South-West England only.)
Friends of the Earth, 9 Poland Street, London WC1.
Resurgence, Pentre Ifan, Felindre Farchog, Crymych, Dyfed, Wales. (Non-violent, 'small is beautiful', intermediate technology, consideration of individual needs.) (London, Southern England, North West England, and Wales only.)
Society For Anglo-Chinese Understanding, 152 Camden High Street, London NW1 0NE. (The Chinese experience.) (Most parts of the country.)
Turning Point, 7 St Ann's Villas, London W11 4RU. (A network of people with no doctrine and no manifesto but an interest in examining possible alternatives: 'do we have to have unemployment today, an energy gap in 15 years' time, and a burnt-out 'growth' economy by the year 2000?'.) (Most areas of Britain.)
Women's Information Referral and Enquiry Service (WIRES), 30 Blenheim Terrace, Leeds 2. (The feminist viewpoint.) (Most areas of the UK.)
16 Among simulations which centrally involve questions of value are: *The Coca-Cola Environment Game*, Coca Cola Export Corporation; the *Oxfam Development Game*, Oxfam Education Dept; *The Muck in The Mock* (See Chapter 46).
Other interesting simulation exercises are detailed in Taylor, John L. and Walford, R., *Simulation in the Classroom*, (Penguin, 1972).
17 Practical advice on organising discussions can be found in The Schools Council/Nuffield Foundation booklet *The Humanities Project: An Introduction* (Heinemann Educational, 1970), especially pp 16–29.
18 For example, certain units of the Schools Council General Studies Project (published by Longmans), particularly *Modern Britain* and *Population and Environment*, and the Longman Social Science Series booklets.
19 Particularly the packs on *Poverty, People and Work* and *Living in Cities*, all published by Heinemann Educational.
20 The case for which is argued in White, J., *Towards a Compulsory Curriculum*, (Routledge and Kegan Paul, 1973).

Appendix I: A Method of Showing Pupils That They Are Unlikely to Receive a Completely Unbiased Economics Education

James M. Haywood

Many economics teachers believe that it is important that pupils should know that they are not receiving a completely unbiased economics education. However, if the teacher just states that his own teaching is biased, pupils may lose faith in him but still treat the textbook as infallible. One way around this is to explain the following to them.

In order to be completely unbiased in one's understanding of economics one must, at least, be able to interpret reality accurately.

There are two sets of influences which determine interpretations of reality. There are perceptions, which may be accurate or inaccurate, that arise out of the biological structures of our sensory organs, and the habits that we acquire in using them. 'Perspective' is an example. There are, in addition, perceptions that result from our emotional and learned attitudes which guide us in the selection of information, and in the reassembly of information which we have. Racial prejudice is an example. The former type of misperception can be illustrated by reference to simple diagrams.

A major problem for the artist is to obtain realistic perspective. We are so accustomed to this representation of distance that when distant figures are drawn the same size as nearer ones we think that

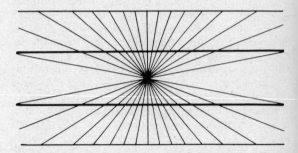

Figure 47.2 From 'Visual Illusions' by R. L. Gregory in Brian M. Foss (ed), New Horizons in Psychology (1972), page 79, reprinted by permission of Penguin Books Ltd

the distant ones are larger (see Figure 47.1). Another example shows how we are misled in our judgement just by reason of accompanying lines, e.g. all lines are straight in Figure 47.2 The effect of environment on our observations can be as distorting in economics as in the examples above. There is a good example of this in welfare economics. When one lives in a capitalistic economy one is likely to look at 'welfare' from an individualistic point of view, and thus accept the Pareto value judgement that if 'one person is better off, and no one is worse off, welfare is increased'. On the other hand, when one lives in a socialist economy one is likely to look at 'welfare' from a collective point of view very different to Pareto.

Figure 47.3 illustrates that we are capable of seeing the same thing in more ways than one. It is difficult to see one face in Figure 47.3 when you have first seen the other, but easy to see both when once you have looked hard and seen both. Many economists would argue that the debate between the Monetarists and the Keynesians is somewhat of this type (see V. Chick, *The Theory of Monetary Policy*, for an exposition of this view).

When we are ignorant about a situation, it makes no sense, and looks just a muddle. Figure 47.4 looks like ink blots, but if you look carefully you see parts fit into a recognisable pattern (see Figure 47.5) and a man's head appears. Examples of this sort of thing in economics are numerous (in fact all theories seem to be of this type) but the accelerator theory of investment shows this up well. The dramatic ups and downs in the demand for goods produced by the

Figure 47.1 The Hering illustration from 'Visual Illusions' by R. L. Gregory in Brian M. Foss (ed), New Horizons in Psychology, (1972), page 74, reprinted by permission of Penguin Books Ltd

Figure 47.3

same data on the economy, but one group is given a description of the theory of perfect competition and monopoly, whilst the other is given a description of oligopoly theory.

The errors we are likely to make as a result of false sensory perceptions are small compared with the errors we make as a result of the notions we already have when observing a situation. Thus, if we believe that inflation is caused by unions pressing for too high a wage we may notice the data on excessive wage claims, but fail to notice the data on firms' excessive price increases.

Figure 47.5 From The Anatomy of Judgement, *by permission of Hutchinson Publishing Ltd*

Figure 47.4 From The Anatomy of Judgement *by M. L. Johnson Abercrombie, by permission of Hutchinson Publishing Ltd*

machine tool industry make much more sense once one has studied the accelerator theory. However, Figure 47.6 illustrates how careful one must be in accepting help in sorting our information. Two groups of students were shown the same objects, but each group was given a different description of them. They were then required to draw what they had been shown. The effect the description had on the reproduced figure is quite startling. Similar results will probably occur if two groups of students are given the

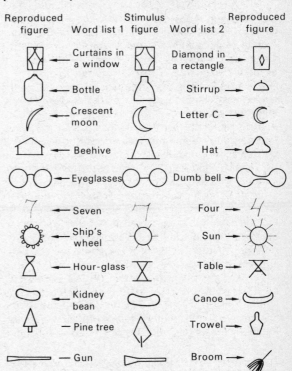

Figure 47.6 From The Anatomy of Judgement, *by permission of Hutchinson Publishing Ltd*

48　An Income Distribution Simulation: Economic Inequality and Cultural Values*

Kenneth J. Neubeck[1]

It is easy to demonstrate that economic inequality exists in the United Kingdom. Statistical data on the distribution of income, for example, are readily available. It is also fairly easy to show why certain redistribution mechanisms (e.g. taxation policies) and welfare state policies have failed to alter substantially economic inequality in the UK. But, perhaps due to its abstractness, the relationship between cultural values and inequality is more difficult for students to grasp. It is important for students of economics to have some basic understanding of this relationship.

The game below has been taught with class sizes ranging from twenty-five to forty students. There follows a brief description of the game, and then a discussion of some of the results of using it.

Conducting the simulation

The teacher begins the game by asking students to take a ten question test. The questions should have multiple-choice, objective answers. The topics covered by the questions do not really matter, for the test is merely a vehicle to move students into the heart of the game. But questions could bear on the facts of economic inequality in British society.

When the test is over, the teacher announces the correct answers. Students may mark their own papers, allowing ten points for each correct answer. It is helpful to assure students that this is only a part of the game, and that they should not feel worried or ashamed if they come up with a low score. Students who arrive in the class late and thus miss some of the test questions, and any who arrive after the test has been administered, must also calculate their scores. For the latter group scores would, of course, be zero. At times there may be some quibbling about the correct answers to the test questions. Students' concerns should be discussed, but for the purposes of the game the teacher's answers are to be taken as correct.

The next step is to add together the test score for all members of the class who are present. This is done by writing 100, 90, 80 .... 0, on a blackboard and asking how many students scored at each of these levels. As the teacher does this, students can be asked to keep a

* Reprinted from *Teaching Sociology* 4(2), January 1977, pp 167–76 by permission of the publishers, Sage Publications Inc. This American simulation has been 'anglicised' by the Editor, with the permission of the author.

running count of the total points class members have scored. This total is then also placed on the blackboard, and the students are advised that this number represents the total income in pounds 'earned' by the class through its 'work' (on the test).

The students' task is to decide how to distribute this total income among all those who are present.[2] It is this part of the game that encourages them to articulate and contemplate their values concerning economic inequality. It is useful to suggest some possible systems of distribution for students' consideration:

1 Equal shares. The total class income is simply divided by the number of students present. Everyone receives the same amount of income.

2 Productivity. The total class income is distributed in accordance with what each student earned by his or her 'work' (on the test).

3 Guaranteed minimum income. The total class income is distributed in such a way that no student receives below a minimum amount of pounds.

Other distribution systems are possible, and students should be encouraged to use their imagination.[3] That is, they need not feel restricted to choosing from among any of the possibilities suggested by the teacher. However, the students must be able to defend their choice and to provide reasons why they would choose one system over others.

At this point the teacher divides the class into small groups of seven to ten students. These groups are told to reach a consensus on one income distribution system and to choose a representative to put their views later on. So that the teacher's presence does not impede spontaneous discussion (i.e. it is not wise to hover over a small group before it can get started), a faked trip to the staff room is worthwhile. Afterwards, one can wander from group to group and hardly be noticed at all.

Finally, when the small groups seem to have finished deliberating (twenty to thirty minutes), group representatives are asked each in turn to announce the system of income distribution chosen and to defend it. Group members can fill in details of the defence if need be.

Results of Using the Simulation

In four years of utilising this simulation, the outcome

has rarely varied. In the small groups someone will cautiously or playfully suggest dividing the total class income equally. The students will stare at the blackboard, studying how many persons earned 100 or 90 pounds in the test, and how many earned little or nothing.

Next, someone will suggest that 'equality is not fair' – people should not be rewarded if they failed to contribute to the total pool of pounds. The issue of incentives will arise. If people are rewarded no matter how little they contribute, they will not work harder to do well in the future. Someone else will point out that dividing the money equally penalises those students who contributed the most (the high scorers on the test) and will reduce such students' incentive to perform to their greatest ability.

The above arguments against equal shares are frequently couched in terms of 'human nature,' or the 'natural' propensity of people to require material rewards if they are to work their hardest. Occasionally the view that 'some people are basically lazy' will be expressed, along with the belief that people should and usually do get only what they deserve. As students get into such discussion, the simulation often becomes secondary to allusions to the larger society: 'If refuse collectors were paid the same as doctors, who'd want to be a doctor?' or 'There are plenty of people who'd just sit around if they got paid anyway.' Such statements as these usually do not go uncontended within the small groups.

Depending upon the forcefulness and effectiveness of those willing to consider equal shares, a consensus of distributing the total class income on the basis of productivity may be adopted then and there. But typically the students – feeling some uneasiness at leaving several peers with few or no pounds – move to discuss the guaranteed minimum approach.

The ensuing discussion is at times framed in terms of guilt: 'You just can't let people starve.' More often, one is likely to hear demands for some sense of justice: 'Maybe the people who came in late and earned nothing had good excuses for being late?' or 'Maybe some people who earned a lot on the test studied these kinds of questions in other courses.' Thus students will consider the issue of handicaps versus advantages, and whether such matters should influence the distribution of material rewards. Some will say no: others will disagree. 'Inequality is inevitable.' 'It's less inevitable if you don't penalise people for handicaps over which they have no control.' The issue of equal opportunity to earn high material rewards in present day British society often enters the discussion at this point, along with differing views on the plight of minorities and the poor.

Ultimately, and almost invariably, a compromise occurs between the equality- and productivity-oriented within the small groups. An income floor is agreed upon in order to protect the students who would otherwise receive little or nothing under the productivity approach. Along with this, a graduated scale of income is proposed for those above the guaranteed minimum in order to handle the incentive issue. Students will sit busily calculating the exact number of pounds everyone in the class will get. In so doing, they will try to minimise the income taken away from the potentially affluent (high scorers on the test) that is to be transferred to the disadvantaged. The latter will be cared for, albeit rather reluctantly and begrudgingly by the productivity-oriented. Representatives, asked to announce the consensus that was reached by their groups, find that theirs is the class-wide choice of an income distribution system – and for similar reasons.

Only on rare occasions has the outcome of this simulation departed from what has been described. In one class, a group (all female) decided that women should receive all the money, and men should get nothing. The representative's announcement, after creating an initial period of turmoil among most students, provoked a spirited discussion of sexism in the economy. This led to the issue of 'reparations' for any groups that were economically disadvantaged due to systematic subordination over time. The few racial minority members in the class immediately supported the girls on the question of reparations, while most white males shuffled rather uncomfortably in their chairs.

On another occasion a small group decided to call itself a 'ruling class' and keep almost all of the total class income to itself. The group would, according to its representatives, be willing to pay a bare subsistence wage to those who pledged loyalty to its regime. Everyone else could starve. The shock of this announcement produced the verbal equivalent of fisticuffs within the classroom, as those who would be 'ruled' threatened to rebel.

On still a different occasion one student, who had been inflaming a more conservative classmate all term with his radical statements, argued for a productivity system of income distribution (he had scored well on the test). As students filed out at the end of the class period, the conservative shouted, 'You hypocrite! You've been mouthing all this radical stuff, but when it comes right down to it you're just like everyone else – out for yourself!'

It is possible to steer a group of students into taking a position that will be unpopular, just to generate more intensive discussion of the issues. One can conspiratorially ask a small group to back the equal shares system, advising them that no other group will tolerate it. While the conspirators will approach this task with some humour, the discussion that follows their representative's announcement rapidly becomes serious. The latter is likely to get really caught up in defending an income distribution system which, under most other circumstances, he or she would be unlikely to support.

Post-simulation Discussion

As was mentioned, in most instances all small groups within a class are likely to choose some variant of a guaranteed minimum approach to income distribution. At this point, the teacher may guide the discussion to a consideration of cultural values and economic inequality – using the small group deliberations as a base.

Why, the teacher might ask, did each group end up choosing a similar system? When asked, students are likely to explain such an outcome as due to their 'socialisation' – their choice was influenced by values they have been taught. But the teacher may then ask, where do these values come from? And why do they persist?

These last questions are best approached by asking yet another one. Suppose that students in the class had been permitted to co-operate in taking the test, sharing information, and turning in their answers only when widespread agreement had been reached as to their correctness. What kind of income distribution system would the students then have been likely to choose? Students will quickly respond, 'Equal shares'. The teacher may then point out that cultural values concerning economic inequality do not merely come from socialisation. Such values arise in response to the rules of the game. Change the rules (and thus the behaviour of the 'workers') and values are likely to change as well. This will make sense to most students, but any arguments to the contrary deserve to be pursued. If necessary, one can have the students play another round of the game under the alternative rules, and let them decide what system of income distribution seems to make the most sense then.

At this point it is also possible to move into a discussion of the 'rules of the game' in British society, wherein people are regularly competing with one another for a share of the total societal income. The labour market – to which most students are rather sensitive these days – may be used as a prime example of the competitive arena in which millions must strive for economic advancement. The cultural values to which such competition gives rise, it may be pointed out, make it difficult for many people to see great merit in programmes of income redistribution. One can bring up the antipathy towards 'welfare state scroungers' to illustrate the point. The values that arise in response to the 'rules of the game' in Britain, one may suggest, hinder public debate on economic inequality. Whether this is good or bad is, of course, also a value issue. In any event, it is a sociological fact.

Students can also be asked what system of income distribution might have resulted if only the high scorers on the quiz were permitted to make the choice. Following this, they can be asked what system might have been chosen if only the low scorers were permitted to make it. In considering such questions, students begin to see that material success or failure in a competitive arena can influence a group's values concerning economic inequality. Here they also begin to understand why welfare rights groups and economic élites might disagree on what should be done about such phenomena as poverty. It is not difficult to move from this to the questions of government economic policies, the economic class backgrounds of those who propose and vote on them, and the pressures which impinge on elected representatives.

Finally, students can be asked whether the values that they hold – as revealed during the simulation – help or hinder the reduction of economic inequality and the elimination of poverty in Britain. The question answers itself, and is likely to make many students thoughtful about their own role in the existing social and economic order.

The foregoing kinds of discussion regarding income distribution are, under classroom conditions, very free and academic. There are no continuing consequences for the students of choosing one or another distribution system once the simulation is over. Students should be reminded that this is rather unlike the real world, where we live in the company of millions who are affected by the distributive rules characterising Britain's economic system.

References and Notes

1 For the ideas necessary to play this game, I am totally indebted to Stevenson, G.L., 'A Simple Income Distribution Game', *Rev. of Radical Pol. Economics*, 3, Summer 1971, pp 107–19. Those examining his article will quickly see my modifications and will note that Stevenson suggests many of his own with which to experiment.
2 Stevenson suggests having students in the class distribute this income so that everyone present can 'buy' a letter grade for the test, and he offers a schedule of 'prices'. My experience in trying it this way is that students spend more time discussing the pros and cons of grading than they do the bases on which income might be distributed. The only advantage to doing it Stevenson's way is that students are forced to live with the consequences of their decisions when the game is over, should the teacher choose to count the test score toward their final grades.
3 Other possibilities offered by Stevenson are 'chance' (e.g. income distribution by lottery) and 'need'. The criteria for the latter would be left up to the students. I have found that students are not interested in discussing these possibilities.

Resource

A useful film on this theme is available from Concord Films Council, *All Work and Low Pay*, (30 mins), which deals with the problem of the lowest paid; dustman, policeman, caretaker and factory worker; problems of income distribution.

Part Three
Resources, Assessment and Organisation

Introduction to Part 3

'Change is not made without inconvenience, even from worse to better'.

Richard Hooker

The largest item of expenditure in the Head of Economics' budget is probably still 'textbooks'. All available textbooks may be viewed at the National Textbook Collection at the London University Institute of Education, but that is not possible for most teachers. Nigel Carr and Jonathan Bokor provide a substitute in the form of short reviews of each textbook coupled with up-to-date comparative information. Another chapter lists those economics resources which are not mentioned by contributors in Sections 2 and 4.

Linda Thomas is well-placed to explain current developments in methods of internal assessment, and she presents several new ideas which economics teachers might be interested to follow up. The chapter by Clive Baker on external assessment is replete with practical advice about the relationships between Examining Boards and teachers, and shows how a Mode III course should be presented if it is to stand any likelihood of acceptance.

John Rees offers the fruit of his experience in running a large, complex Economics Department; his comments are relevant to a departmental head in any type of school, since the organisational and managerial problems are universal. One of the decisions a Head of Economics has to take, even if he delegates its implementation, is how to classify his resources. Alain Anderton's system is workable, and not too time-consuming once established. Use of the Dewey system appended would provide sensible standardisation with public libraries. The list of 157 addresses was correct at the time of going to press (October, 1977). It might be advisable to transfer the addresses on to a card index so that alterations can easily be made.

Section 5 Miscellaneous

49 An Evaluation of 'O' Level and CSE Economics Textbooks
Nigel Carr

An evaluation of textbooks must surely be one of the most difficult tasks faced by the teacher when consider- ing how best to utilise a limited book allowance. This chapter attempts to ease the problem by providing an evaluation of the main textbooks in use at present. Since this evaluation is subjective, many of the judgements presented may be contentious. However the criteria considered important are described below, so that those ranking them differently can use the information provided to assist in their own evaluations.

With any book, its most obvious feature is its layout and presentation. If it is unattractive, readers are unlikely to be as willing to persevere as they would with a book which they found visually pleasing. Furthermore, a textbook which is enlivened by graphs, pictures, photographs or tables of data is preferable since, for some readers, the visual image will be more memorable than the written word. The use of language is equally important. Textbook writers must not assume a degree of literacy greater than that normally possessed by the CSE or 'O' level student. The information presented in economics textbooks gradually becomes out-of-date. This is inevitable with a subject such as economics, and teachers must be prepared, a few years after publication, to update the information provided in their textbooks. Therefore the only criticisms made, with regard to the data presented, are in those cases where the situation has changed drastically. It is not unreasonable to expect every book which discusses banking to do so in relation to the 'Competition and Credit Control' changes.

It is relatively easy to discuss the content of 'O' level textbooks since there is much similarity between the syllabuses of the examination boards offering 'O' level economics. Twenty topics have been selected (see Appendix I) and each book intended for 'O' level is given a score out of twenty. In some cases, such an exercise can be misleading because the degree of coverage can vary. Furthermore, it is also necessary to consider the price of the book and its 'value for money'. Appendix II therefore contains this information. No attempt has been made to score books such as *Understanding Industrial Society* and *Economics in Action* which are intended for different 'O' level courses. CSE books cannot be graded in this way because of the far greater difference between the examination boards in their syllabuses and also in their modes of assessment. Therefore these books have been evaluated in the light of their stated objectives. Some of the books attempt to cater for both markets and, where applicable, they have been awarded a score. In the same way that one would not attempt to use an 'O' level textbook with 'A' level students, it can be argued that those taking CSE and 'O' levels need their own specialised textbooks. However it is often the case that these two groups are taught together and follow a common course, possibly even up to the last term, and therefore a common textbook is necessary. This is a matter of personal preference, but where authors intend a book for joint use, an attempt has been made to assess its suitability.

The books have been reviewed on the assumption that they will be used as basic texts although, ideally, one would like to have copies of almost all of them available in economics libraries. Special features in the books reviewed, such as the inclusion of questions or a bibliography, are also mentioned.

CSE Textbooks

Production and Trade. B. Davies and D. Hender
This is one part of Longman's Social Science Studies which aims to provide an introduction to sociology, politics and economics for students at CSE level. The preface states that its aim is to introduce the basic concepts of the subject and the methods of enquiry employed. There is a second series which covers specific topics and a third consisting of shorter booklets dealing with contemporary issues.

The book is well produced, with ample illustrations, photographs and tables of data to supplement the text. Key economic terms are written in heavy type, defined in a glossary and, in addition, other important words are italicised to attract the reader's attention. Each chapter concludes with questions. However, in many cases these are too difficult for the average student, who will often require access to alternative sources of information (which might not always be available).

There are certain oddities in the text which teachers using this book might wish to correct. For example, how many economists would today regard the clearing banks as 'dangerous' as well as useful institutions? Furthermore, while there can be no objection to discussing 'John Brown' who borrows from a hire purchase company, the use of the name 'Alec Smart' to refer to a lender might give rise to connotations amongst pupils which, possibly, are unintentional.

In many cases, the book is too complicated for CSE pupils, and although well produced, the general impression gained is of a diluted 'O' level textbook. As such, it falls between two stools since it is unlikely to be used at 'O' level yet contains little upon which to base a stimulating CSE course.

Starting Economics. F. Davies
The aim of this book is to cater primarily for the CSE and, although it does not attempt to present a detailed picture of the UK economy, it sets out to provide an understanding of the workings of a modern economy. Much attention has been given to layout and the text is admirably reinforced by graphs, diagrams and pictures. Each chapter concludes with a summary of the main points and a series of questions. In order to maintain interest, many topics are illustrated by short stories. This is especially effective in the section on money where, through the exploits of Henry the Shoemaker, one realises the advantages of a common medium of

exchange. There are two other parts of the book which might have a wider appeal, namely the one explaining Keynesian economic theory and the chapters dealing with demand and supply where the key concepts are introduced, again through stories, and are clearly illustrated by half-page graphs and tables.

Despite its avoidance of the descriptive elements of many courses, (some might say because of), this is one of the best CSE economics books available and could be used as the basis for a variety of courses. It is possible, though, that some pupils might find the continued use of stories too juvenile.

Daily Economics. J. Nobbs and P. Ames

This is one of the few books intended solely for those taking CSE courses in economics or social studies and consequently the exercises at the end of each topic are all geared towards this group. The book is divided into twelve units. The first is called 'Starting Work' and the remaining sections progress logically through all the eventualities likely to befall the young worker, such as deductions from pay, trade union membership and use of a bank. After this, wider economic and social matters are discussed such as education and housing.

The book is excellently produced, with photographs, tables of data and cartoon illustrations reinforcing the text. There are CSE examination questions at the end of each topic as well as a large number of 'activities'. These are carefully chosen so that the majority of pupils will enjoy doing them. The only criticism is that some of the details of tax payments and social security arrangements have changed since publication, so that it is no longer necessary to obtain a National Insurance Card upon which stamps are stuck by one's employer, deductions now being made at source. However such a fault is to be expected since it will eventually befall any book attempting to provide up-to-date information.

Textbooks Intended for both CSE and 'O' Level Students

Economics: An Introductory Course. D. Baron (Score: 19)

The author suggests that this book will provide a year's course for those knowing no economics who may be intending to take either a CSE or 'O' level in the subject. However the former group may well find it too difficult in its use of language and the consideration of the concepts discussed. More advanced students are liable to find it extremely readable and it would be well-suited to providing the basis of a non-examined course for sixth-formers. Anyone using it for an 'O' level course might find it necessary to supplement and amplify the theoretical aspects since the emphasis is placed upon discussion of the British economy and the author's intention 'is to avoid wherever possible

economic theory'. Thus although demand and supply are discussed, the treatment is brief and there is no attempt to incorporate a diagrammatic treatment.

The text is divided into six parts, the first containing an extremely useful discussion of trade unions. Throughout, it is well laid-out and is interspersed with diagrams and pictures which serve to illustrate the main points. Each chapter concludes with questions, requiring both written and numerical answers, many of which might serve as the basis for longer pieces of work or projects. Answers are provided. There is also a comprehensive index and a glossary of terms.

Modern British Economics. J. Nicholson (Score: 19)

This is intended as an introductory course in economics and commerce for 'O' level and CSE students. It is well presented. Clear diagrams, short paragraphs and use of subtitles make it easy to follow. The descriptive side of the book is above average although much of the data only go up to 1973 and the teacher might wish to up-date it in places. At the end of each chapter there is a series of questions of different types with answers provided at the end of the book.

Unfortunately the treatment of the more theoretical elements is not up to the standard of the rest of the book. For example, the treatment of elasticity is such as to convey the impression that a 45° line has unitary elasticity over its length (page 159, figure 46). The general impression is that the theoretical sections are too short and it would have been better to sacrifice some of the more detailed elements in order to ensure a rigorous theoretical base.

Although intended for both 'O' level and CSE students, it is probable that its main use will be by the former, the latter requiring a more imaginative presentation. Commerce students will find this an especially useful book since it provides a sound guide to the British economy. However for the 'O' level student it falls midway between those books attempting a purely descriptive treatment and those managing to achieve a balance between theory and description.

Social Economics. J. Nobbs (Score: 19)

This book is particularly easy to follow, attractively written, with many good illustrations, graphs and tables of data. An attempt is made to enliven the subject matter by providing examples from the experiences of a hypothetical family, an approach which lends itself to further development by the teacher. Many might find the approach too detailed since 'social economics' is intended as a two year course leading up to either CSE or 'O' level. Those using it for one year courses or general studies schemes might wish to omit much of the information provided on such topics as savings institutions, concentrating instead on the more theoretical elements.

There are questions at the end of each chapter and

past examination questions at the conclusion of each section and, although there is no bibliography, there are occasional references to readings in the text. The index at the end of the book is extremely detailed, a useful feature since there might be those who wish to depart from the author's ordering. Overall, it is a high-scoring, relatively cheap book, appealing because of its suitability for both 'O' level and CSE classes.

Understanding Industrial Society and *Teachers' Guide.*
A. Sanday and P. Birch
Understanding Industrial Society is an attempt to provide pupils with an insight into the workings of a society such as ours in order 'to understand what happens to people in industry and commerce, and why they behave in the way they do,' (page 1). The book is intended to be used as a course-book for either a CSE (West Midlands Regional Examining Board Social Economics Mode III 'Understanding Industrial Society') or an 'O' level course, and the *Teachers' Guide* provides a suggested CSE Mode III syllabus as well as details of the 'O' level course.

The book is divided into three parts. Part 1 discusses the establishment of a firm, types of business, market research problems, and a small firm and the difficulties facing it in and after its creation, so providing students with an insight into the business world. Part 2 is concerned with ways of expanding the firm and increasing its profits and goes on to discuss the ways these activities might affect the individual as a consumer and worker. Part 3 is an attempt to study the macro implications of the firm's activities and also more general topics such as income distribution and population. An attempt is made to introduce a degree of social awareness of the firm's actions and the effect they have on the economy and the environment.

Because the course is orientated towards the practical, rather than the theoretical, areas of the subject, material in the latter category is introduced when required by the treatment of the firm's progress, so that, for example, banks are discussed when the firm is faced with the need to raise capital, the depth of coverage being determined entirely by the context. As a result, the degree of detail is such that the book would not be adequate for a standard 'O' level course (nor is it intended for such a use) but might form the basis of a general studies course in the sixth form.

The text is well set out with ample photographs, pictures, tables and cartoons. There is a strong emphasis on pupil involvement, through the collection of their own data, simulations, games and other exercises which are provided throughout the book. The case studies are of an especially high standard.

The only criticism is of part 3, which has alternative versions for CSE and 'O' level students. Both of these are brief and it might have been better to amalgamate them and allow the teacher to decide on the degree of

detail required. However the division makes this book especially suitable for mixed-ability classes since all students can follow the same course, differing only in the degree of detail in part 3.

The *Teachers' Guide* is useful, in suggesting approaches to be followed and providing answers to problems posed in the text. It also supplies information as to the available resources which can be used to supplement this or any other similar course.

Because of the special nature of the book and the course it is intended for, no score is given.

'O' Level Textbooks

Economics In Action. D. Christie and A. Scott
Christie and Scott's recent book is intended for students studying economics at 'O' level and also as an introductory text for 'A' level. However its content and intellectual level will possibly make it more useful for the latter group. It is divided into seven sections, the emphasis being on the theoretical elements and, furthermore, it is biased towards microeconomics. It is therefore unsuitable as a basic text for 'O' level courses requiring a detailed knowledge of the UK economy. Nevertheless as an introduction to the basic economic concepts it is first-class.

The approach is original, with considerable use made of imaginary case studies to illustrate key concepts. The authors have, incidentally, managed to escape from the Robinson Crusoe analogy to teach opportunity cost, replacing him with a marooned yachtsman. Some economics teachers might wish to amplify the text with definitions and terminology (such as the idea of elasticity which the authors present intuitively).

The book is admirably presented, interspersed with tables of data and clearly drawn graphs as well as occasional pictures which enliven the text. Throughout there are a large number of imaginative questions which the student will find challenging. Some of these are based on the text while others are more general. These questions are an integral part of the book and their solution is necessary for complete understanding. Like the text, many of these are highly original and, since answers are not provided, they will necessitate thought not only from the students but also on the part of their teachers.

Economics in Action is a text for the above-average student, although the approaches used, if expanded, could be employed with less able pupils. Even the former group will find it necessary to seek supplementary information when attempting the final section (on economic policy) which is difficult to follow, although the idea of using the advice of three economists to illustrate different approaches to economic problems is a good one. However it is unlikely that all readers will appreciate the significance of Professors Yensek and Narkip unless told.

Overall this is an admirable addition to the textbook market and it will be worthwhile modifying existing teaching techniques to make full use of it.

'O' Level Economics. L. Curzon (Score: 18)

This is intended as a book for those studying for 'O' level on their own, as an aid for revision and as a substitute for notes from the teacher. The format is of brief notes, sentences rather than paragraphs, with brief tests at the end of each chapter. It is totally geared towards the examination and there is a danger that people using it successfully will conclude their course with only a superficial understanding of economics. There are very few examples, merely principles and definitions, and it is impossible to conceive of this as a book which one might enjoy reading.

The lay-out is cramped and unattractive and the ordering is such that there are frequent references to definitions and principles not yet encountered, thus causing the reader much unnecessary searching. Furthermore, in a highly factual presentation such as this there is a tendency for the information given to become outdated. There is little attempt at discussion throughout the book; instead advantages and disadvantages are listed and the student is unaware of the emphasis to place upon each point.

The book covers more topics than those normally required for 'O' level including such theories as the Keynesian determination of the rate of interest. However the discriminating teacher might find a use for this book, possibly as a source of questions.

Economics from Square One. A. Davies and J. Coy (Score: 14)

The authors intend this book to provide the basis of a one year introductory course in economics, but possibly as a result of their industrial background, the treatment of accounts and businesses is too detailed for the economics 'O' level student. However, teachers of courses with a commercial emphasis might find the combination useful.

In many instances, the treatment is insufficiently rigorous for the examination student who might desire a lengthier treatment of opportunity cost or might be confused by discovering that deflation, as a cure for demand inflation, is found under a section entitled 'policies to encourage savings'. There is also a degree of confusion created by the distinction between fixed and constant costs.

Each chapter concludes with suggestions for further reading (necessary to update some of the tables and such things as the 28 per cent banking ratio). There are also questions and numerical problems for the student as well as a series of 'problem areas' on such topics as monopoly.

Illustrated Economics. P. Donaldson

This is not primarily intended as a textbook since it was written to accompany the television series of the same name and, were a score to be awarded, it would undoubtedly be a low one. Nevertheless, although the level of exposition makes it unsuitable for CSE work, it provides the basis for a general studies or possibly even an 'O' level course. The emphasis is on the current problems facing the UK economy and the sections on inflation, unemployment, growth and economic management are especially useful. There is also a comprehensive treatment of the theory of supply and demand which is linked to the real world, in the sections entitled 'Your place in the economic puzzle' and 'The market at work'.

There is a strong visual element, with cartoons and 'Batman' being used to express common economic fallacies which are then examined in the text. There is much information provided in the form of graphs, pie and block diagrams and tables of data, all of which are well-incorporated into the extremely readable, and at times amusing, text. The book concludes with a series of questions, with answers provided, which will test the reader's understanding of the subject matter.

Although not a book for use on its own, it would provide an excellent complement to the more theoretical textbooks as well as a guide to contemporary problems.

Descriptive Economics. C. D. Harbury (Score: 19)

This is intended to be an elementary textbook which provides readers with all the information they are likely to need. Implicit in the book is the author's view that a knowledge of the economy is a prerequisite for an understanding of theory. Many will disagree with this and prefer to use a textbook which covers both areas since, apart from an introductory chapter on 'The allocation of resources in a mixed economy', the treatment is descriptive.

It is intended to be of 'O' level standard and pupils at this level will find it easy to read. Very few tables of data are included, the information being presented in the form of charts, maps and graphs which enable the reader to comprehend the main points and orders of magnitude without having to wade through columns of figures.

Each chapter concludes with exercises, generally of a numerical nature, but there are no answers. Although there is no bibliography, there is a series of references to statistical sources. Even if not used in class, this book can serve as an excellent reference book for the teacher.

Elementary Economics. J. Harvey (Score: 20)

This is one of the more widely used basic 'O' level textbooks and therefore deserves close inspection. Its main virtues are its excellent coverage of the syllabus and its obvious value for money. Many, considering the former virtue, might argue that its coverage is too detailed since there is much that is unnecessary for the 'O' level pupil. It is unlikely that this book will appeal to the lower ability student who will find the language difficult in places and the presentation unattractive. One can describe *Elementary Economics* as an 'efficient' book, technically correct but unlikely to inspire many pupils with an interest in the subject. However, students with an historical bias are likely to find it stimulating since, in many cases, there are historical sketches provided as an introduction to the economic analysis.

The exception to the above criticism is the section on demand and supply which is well-presented and interspersed with easy-to-follow graphs and practical examples. In other sections, teachers might find the book lacking in its discussion of the current problems facing the UK economy. To remedy this, it could be used in conjunction with Peter Donaldson's *Illustrated Economics* (reviewed above) and, taken together, these two books would be adequate for 'O' level and possibly even more advanced students.

There are no questions in the text although there is an accompanying workbook (reviewed below).

Elementary Economics Workbook. J. Harvey

This workbook is intended to complement Harvey's *Elementary Economics* but can be used with any 'O' level textbook since it covers the topics included in the various 'O' level syllabuses and anyone using a different textbook can use the workbook in a different order.

Each chapter is divided into four sections. First there is a series of questions framed in a variety of ways which include true or false items, multiple choice items, and a number of ordinary questions which range from the very easy to some approaching 'A' level standard. Secondly there is a series of 'Things to do' which include local surveys and problems including many which could be expanded into projects. Thirdly, there are a number of 'Points to discuss', some of which could be incorporated into the last section which provides a number of past 'O' level questions on each topic from a variety of examination boards.

This is a book which teachers will wish to use selectively since there is considerable variation in the standard of the questions and much repetition. There is an accompanying *Teachers' Edition* which provides answers.

Economic Society. K. Marder and L. Alderson (Score: 15)

This book purports to provide an introduction, for those knowing nothing of the subject, to economics and social economics. It is orientated primarily towards the former and those using it for the latter purpose will find it deficient in important respects.

Although not completely satisfactory as a class textbook, since the treatment of topics such as population is limited, there is a place for it if only in economics libraries since its explanation of many topics is concise. Younger pupils might find it unattractive since the layout is uninteresting and the language too dry. Sixth-formers, especially those taking an 'O' level course in one year, are likely to find it useful.

The use of diagrams and other graphic features, especially those explaining relationships between variables, is excellent, and many of the latter could be adapted by teachers for use in the classroom. Each chapter concludes with past examination questions. However, in order to answer them adequately, it would be necessary for anyone using this book to supplement it with recent data, little being provided in the text. Unfortunately no bibliography is provided and the index is not as adequate as one would like.

An Introduction To Modern Economics. J. C. Powicke and P. May (Score: 15)

Although the latest edition of this book was published in 1977, little attempt has been made to consider the problems facing the British economy at present. Instead, the text has been rewritten to concentrate primarily upon the role of choice in economics. As a result, many teachers might find this too theoretical for an 'O' level course and might prefer a book more evenly weighted between the theoretical and descriptive elements, there being no attempt to cover the latter in great detail. The coverage of the former is full, indeed many might be unaccustomed to the inclusion at this level of such topics as the accelerator and the use of production possibility curves as an aid to analysis.

The book is well presented, adequately spaced out and the exposition is aided by the use of numerical examples, but some readers might find it unnecessarily complex. For example, with regard to the balance of payments, it might not be obvious that 'it is incumbent upon debtor nations to ensure that their current deficits should be matched by capital formation which will enable them to meet their debt service commitments without running into difficulties' (page 173).

Short exercises are provided in the middle of each chapter with further questions at the end. However the authors intend that this book should be used in conjunction with *Multiple Choice Questions for Economics* by Powicke and Turner to which there are references at the end of each chapter.

Introducing Economics. T. Shafto (Score: 15)

This book is divided into five sections: the standard of living and production, the market for goods, money and the financial markets, people in the modern economy, and international trade and the problem of economic choice. Within the book one would find sufficient information for all economics 'O' level courses except that it would be necessary to supplement the sections discussing the current problems facing the UK economy. The explanation of the idea of demand and supply is unclear but this is balanced by a series of examples which provide practical illustrations of the concepts involved.

The third section, on money and the financial markets, is presented in a stimulating manner with the text interpolated with newspaper cuttings, photographs, tables of data and graphs. However, the remainder of the book is unlikely to appeal to many pupils. This is unfortunate since, alternatively presented, it would be an extremely useful textbook.

There are review questions interspersed throughout the book and a series of past 'O' level questions at the end of the chapters. This is one of the few books to provide a list of statistical sources as well as some useful suggestions for further reading.

Introductory Economics. G. Stanlake (Score: 19)
The latest edition of this book represents excellent value for money and provides a comprehensive coverage of the subject, as is shown by its high score. Incorporated in the new edition are sections on the European Economic Community, recent developments in the international financial system and an expanded treatment of the role of the state. This is not a book intended for CSE students but would serve as a basis for economics courses at both 'O' and 'A' level.

The ordering of the topics is slightly unusual in that one is introduced to the theory of supply and then left in limbo for approximately a hundred pages until it is linked with demand but this can be easily remedied in use. There is an excellent discussion of taxes, the various types and their effect on the distribution of income, prices, consumption, savings, investment and incentives. There are no questions supplied but there is a book of objective test items by the same author, although this will be of more use to 'A' level than to 'O' level students.

Even if not used as a class textbook, it is strongly recommended as a source of up-to-date information for the teacher and it is easy to account for its widespread popularity.

Appendix I

List of Topics for 'O' Level

Demand and supply;
Production;
Large and small firms;
Specialisation amongst firms;
Private and public enterprise;
Stages in the flow of goods and services;
The location of industry;
Population – size, sex, age distribution;
    – occupational and geographical distribution;
The division of labour;
International trade;
Imports and exports – composition and geographical distribution;
Money;
The functions and operation of banks;
The Bank of England;
The Stock Exchange;
Taxation;
Public expenditure;
The National Income;
Inflation

Appendix II

Title	Author(s)	Publication date	Publisher	Price (£)	Number of pages	Score
Production and Trade	Davies and Hender	1974	Longman	1.30	105	—
Starting Economics	Davies	1977	Hulton Educational	1.20	144	—
Daily Economics	Nobbs and Ames	1975	McGraw-Hill	1.95	183	—
Economics: An Introductory Course	Baron	1975	Heinemann Educational	1.50	152	19
Modern British Economics	Nicholson	1976	George Allen and Unwin	1.95	184	19
Social Economics	Nobbs	1976	McGraw-Hill	2.35	224	19
Understanding Industrial Society	Sanday and Birch	1978	Hodder and Stoughton	2.25	192	—
Teachers' Guide				3.95	176	
Economics in Action	Christie and Scott	1977	Heinemann Educational	1.95	140	—
'O' Level Economics	Curzon	1975	Macdonald and Evans	1.25	223	18
Economics From Square One	Davies and Coy	1973	George Allen and Unwin	1.50	278	14
Illustrated Economics	Donaldson	1976	BBC	1.60	118	—
Descriptive Economics	Harbury	1976	Pitman	2.50	306	19
Elementary Economics	Harvey	1976	Macmillan	2.75	514	20
Economic Society	Marder and Alderson	1975	Oxford University Press	1.50	254	15
An Introduction to Economics	Powicke and May	1977	Edward Arnold	1.50	254	15
Introducing Economics	Shafto	1974	Nelson	1.50	269	15
Introductory Economics	Stanlake	1976	Longman	1.75	463	19
Elementary Economics Workbook Teachers' Edition	J. Harvey	1976	Macmillan	1.50	96.	
Pupils' Edition				0.70	80	

N.B Although the prices quoted are unlikely to be completely accurate on publication, they are intended as an approximate guide, since they usually maintain the same relative positions.

50   An Evaluation of 'A' Level Economics Textbooks

Jonathan Benjamin Bokor

A large number of economics textbooks are on the market, each covering the 'A' level syllabus, but at varying levels, to a different extent, and using different approaches. A thorough evaluation of these books can provide the teacher with information about the extent of syllabus coverage by particular books, and the methods used to explain topics. Each of the twenty-three textbooks available has different characteristics. Some are designed for the mathematical and some for the non-numerate. Others lay the foundation for a course of study, or concentrate on the higher reaches of an 'A' level course. Some have the exposition of economic theory as their goal, whilst others aim for an understanding of how principles may be applied. Most are written for a particular type of reader, and evaluation enables the book to be matched to the student harmoniously.

A three-part evaluation was carried out for each book listed. First the London University 'A' level syllabus was divided up into sixty topics. Each book was examined to see how much of this syllabus was covered. Each item covered merited one point. Thus complete syllabus coverage would gain sixty points.

The second part of the evaluation is a qualitative assessment of each textbook, including such aspects as method and level of treatment, lucidity, illustrations, lay-out, presentation of worked examples and questions, the presence and nature of the bibliography and a differentiated index.

The third part of the evaluation aims to judge whether the book is good value for money. The two criteria used are the actual price of the book, and whether it serves the needs of those students for whom it is intended.

After the evaluations is Table 50.1 (corrected up to July 1977). It includes information about the publisher, the latest available edition, the price and number of pages in the book.

Economics. J. A. Allport and C. M. Stewart (Score: 40)
This book begins with macroeconomics and ends with microeconomics. The earlier parts of the book deal with topics which many of the pupils would have heard of and this may inspire a feeling of assurance about the subject. However, the drawback of this arrangement is that the tools of analysis come later. The textbook features two sets of questions. Some appear every few pages and set out to test the understanding of the material and others are placed at the end of a chapter in order to test comprehension of the whole chapter. Answers appear at the end of the book so they can be cut out if desired. The book will be suitable for the non-mathematical but not for the non-numerate and will probably be updated in a new edition shortly.

Introduction to Economics. A. Cairncross (Score: 37)
This classic textbook has now been superseded by more useful works. The book is, in the main, discursive having few mathematical or numerical tables and few diagrams. No questions appear nor is a bibliography provided. Far from being an introduction from which further work would follow, the book appears as a self-contained work providing few skills for subsequent study. Because of all these limitations, this book is unlikely to have priority in teachers' budgets.

The Science of Wealth. C. F. Carter (Score: 33)
This book is designed to introduce the subject of economics. It is readable, thoughtful and thought-provoking. It provides no questions nor any bibliography but would stimulate the reader to go further into the subject. A minor criticism is that the drawings are rather small. The book could be usefully studied as a first term's textbook opening up the subject to pupils approaching it for the first time. It will be appreciated by the brighter pupil as a start to the course and by the average pupil as a conclusion to a course. The book would act as a means of tying the subject together. Because of the two-fold usefulness of this book, it would certainly be worthwhile to purchase a set.

Introduction to Economic Analysis. M. Fleming (Score: 32)
This Open University set book is mainly analytical in content and would strongly appeal to those doing mathematics at 'A' level because many ideas are expressed with the symbols of calculus. The text is rigorous and interesting, expressing assumptions very clearly. Although comparative economics is not in the syllabus, inclusion of this topic does provide insights to the pupil on the market economies of the West. The book is reasonably well produced and could be used as a second year sixth-form text or for 'S' level work. It possesses an analytical index and a small but advanced bibliography at the end of three of the four sections of

the book. It is really for the bright to very bright pupil, who would be greatly stimulated by it.

Economics for Students. J. L. Hanson (Score: 35)
This book is not a textbook as such but a crammer for examinations. Teachers would shun its use but it might provide much needed help to a pupil whose notes are not as useful as they might be. Whether one approves of such books or not, it is probably good to know that they exist for use in times of emergency. A new edition of this book will be appearing.

A Textbook of Economics. J. L. Hanson (Score: 44)
Despite the high score and low price, many teachers would be averse to using this book. No doubt students can pass exams with it but it is doubtful whether they can do well, for facts are stated but not explained well. It is written with a clear and definite world in mind, not the world where a wide range of possibilities exist. A bibliography and a set of essay questions are provided at the end of each chapter but no answers are included at the end of the book. This is common in books which contain only essay and not drill questions of the short type. If the book is used, it should only be given to those who would find a more reasoned book difficult.

An Introduction to Economic Behaviour. C. D. Harbury (Score: 31)
This is a high-powered introductory text and is part of a series of economics texts which provides a competent reader with skills of economic analysis which will hold him in good stead for further study. Algebra, diagrams and Keynesian terms are employed widely. Even macroeconomic problems are analysed first in terms of a market, then from the point of view of elasticities and lastly from an institutional stand-point. This is a sign of a rigorous textbook uniting macro with microeconomic analysis as much as possible. Several examples of application of price theory are included. Given its price and score, it is strongly recommended for the better pupil in the first year sixth form. It provides no questions or bibliography but does have a unique index, printing the main source in bold type.

Intermediate Economics. J. Harvey (Score: 44)
A useful textbook which, with its large number of questions at the end of each chapter, provides a thorough drilling in the nuts and bolts of the subject. The questions are not only for the mathematical geniuses but also for those with some numerical facility, but not for essay lovers. Answers are provided at the end of the book. It contains a good section on the EEC. This and the same author's *Modern Economics* are useful for the average but hardworking pupil.

Modern Economics. J. Harvey (Score: 49)
In his introduction, Harvey writes that this book comes half way in standard between his *Elementary Economics* and his *Intermediate Economics*. In the writer's opinion it is much more useful than *Intermediate Economics* and it has a guide and workbook written by Harvey and Johnson. It is comprehensive, and suitable for the average to above average pupil, stressing as it does a grasp of all the composite parts of the subject. It seems to aim at a similar market to that of Nobbs but on account of its greater syllabus coverage and its companion workbook, would have much to recommend it. A new edition is about to be published.

Positive Economics. R. Lipsey (Score: 38)
An attempt to review Lipsey is a formidable task since it has become a revered standard textbook. It is written primarily for first-year college economics rather than 'A' level which accounts for its relatively low score, the emphasis being on the theoretical elements of the course. Many teachers will find it too doctrinaire with its simple solutions to so-called simple problems which conceal the author's prejudices. The book is well presented with the important points set out in heavy type, which, from experience, facilitates easy revision. Although there are no exercises, there is an accompanying workbook. For its many good qualities several copies should be included in every economics department library.

Economics. F. Livesey (Score: 23)
This book, by a London University chief examiner at 'A' level, very much reflects the style of Paper 3 which has been set since June 1977. The text is followed by numerous data response exercises and work with this book should pay handsome dividends in the examinations. Its strength lies in the area of the firm to which about four-fifths of the space is devoted. In addition to the exercises which form an integral part of the text, additional essay and objective type questions appear at the end of the book. There is also a teachers' manual. Every teacher should certainly have a copy from which class exercises can be taken. However, because of its rather low score, multiple copies might be rather expensive. Nevertheless, several copies should be available for student use.

Success in Economics. D. Lobley (Score: 47)
This is very good value for money. The style is modern and the text is well illustrated with diagrams. Questions are set at the end of each chapter, but as they are of the essay type, no answers appear at the end of the book. One drawback is that data response type questions have been excluded. There is a bibliography recommending more advanced books and specifying useful chapters therein. This book could be widely used.

Understanding Economics. Manchester Economic Project (Score: 48)
This is the core text of a set of books. The text is replete with definitions, diagrams and exercises, answers to which appear at the end of each chapter. The diagrams feature multi-colour printing. A characteristic of the design, only shared by Nobbs, is the two column layout of pages. Eleven satellite texts have been produced on applied topics and are currently being revised, but the study-guide has been discontinued. This textbook is strongly recommended.

Comprehensive Economics. B. V. Marshall (Score: 54)
The 'Magnum Opus' of 'A' level textbooks is designed as an 'A' level and first-year undergraduate text. It thus deals with most topics at an elementary and advanced level, one chapter following on from the other. Each chapter concludes with numerous questions and an appropriate bibliography. Many diagrams are embodied in the text as are statistics, charts and drawings. Its 1163 pages suggest that it would be useful in the economics library, but it is too large and expensive to be used as a standard textbook.

Men, Money and Markets. J. Molyneux (Score: 29)
A cheap book, but not sufficiently comprehensive or rigorous to have much else to commend it. It has eight photographs that could be in a geography book as much as in an economics text and they are not integrated into the text, merely placed altogether. Although it claims to be more than an introductory book, one published in this decade should have a word for Keynes and his economics, and more than a passing concern for the role of the government. It does, at least, include 164 essay questions at the end of the book.

Economics. E. V. Morgan (Score: 39)
This book is more suited to a university economics course than to an 'A' level one unless the students are extremely able. The emphasis is strongly theoretical, although involving only simple mathematics, but is weak on the practical, descriptive side, creating the impression of a dry, unappealing book unlikely to foster interest in the subject. The use of graphs is clear and there are questions suitable for essays and discussions at the end of each chapter. Good value for money.

The Fundamentals of Economics. A. Morrice (Score: 42)
A well produced introductory textbook with sufficient diagrams, tables, charts and drawings to acquaint the reader with basic economic methodology. The book covers a lot of ground even including the kinked-demand curve. A lot of information is presented though not all of it is fully explained. Questions are provided at the end of each chapter but no answers are given. There is no bibliography. This could be useful as a first year sixth-form book which would be followed up by a more difficult book such as Harvey's *Modern Economics* or Perrow's *Economics*.

Textbook of Economic Analysis. E. T. Nevin (Score: 43)
This is a rigorous and high-powered textbook which is up-to-date. A short bibliography is placed at the end of each chapter, but no questions. There is a workbook on economic analysis to fulfil this role. However, this has not been revised recently. A book to be recommended for bright pupils or as a second year sixth-form textbook following on from Harbury.

Advanced Level Economics. J. Nobbs (Score: 41)
This book is designed for the average pupil. Analysis has been included but not at too great a depth. No one afraid of mathematics would be put off by the book, for very little has been included. It is laid out in two column format on very heavy paper. The style is terse with ideas in very short paragraphs. This commends the book for use by pupils unable to follow long, elaborate ideas. But because ideas are condensed, it is probable that much class discussion would have to accompany the book. Questions are included at the end of each of the main sections of the book. It definitely has a place in the textbook market, especially for the weaker to average achievers.

Benham's Economics. F. W. Paish and A. J. Culyer (Score: 40)
The emphasis in this book is on the 'micro' areas of the course and it is therefore unsuitable for a general 'A' level course book. However, although the order of topics is confusing, the coverage on the included topics is sufficiently interesting to make this a useful addition to a school economics library. The treatment is non-mathematical and as a result is sometimes excessively verbose; nevertheless it would probably appeal to an arts student studying economics as a third subject.

Economics. J. Perrow (Score: 38)
A well written textbook which should be in wider use than it apparently is. It is detailed in argument and reviews topics quite satisfactorily. The book is well laid out and colourful diagrams are used. The text is unmathematical. The book has no questions but the same author has published a book entitled *Examination Economics* in which several hundred test questions are set. It could be used as a two-year course book or as an introductory book for students who could then proceed to read more advanced texts in the second year. This will shortly be available in a new edition.

Economics. P. Samuelson (Score: 48)
This text is clear, comprehensive and comprehensible.

Definitions are printed in red, points to discuss and to review are to be found at the end of each chapter, as are questions. The accompanying workbook has now been discontinued. The data in the macro sections are all American. This is no disadvantage for exam purposes, as foreign data may be cited, and it is certainly educationally advantageous, giving pupils a grasp of another economic system. A great deal of space is devoted to agricultural pricing, income distribution per head, and even the government's role in collective bargaining receives treatment. The use of colour is unique amongst all the texts considered. Greens, blues, reds,

blacks and their shades are all generously used. It is an expensive book but worth including in any reference section of an economics library.

Introductory Economics. G. F. Stanlake (Score: 52)
This book represents excellent value for money and is a necessity for almost any economics course, either 'O' or 'A' level. The style is concise and issues are presented in black-and-white, something which the teacher might wish to amend when teaching. The balance between the theoretical and descriptive elements is maintained. However, the 'A' level teacher will find

Author(s)	Title	Publisher	Latest edition	Number of pages	Price* (in paper if available) (£)	Number of syllabus topics
Allport, J. A. and Stewart, C. M.	*Economics*	CUP	1972	405	3.60	40
Cairncross, A.	*Introduction to Economics*	Butterworth	1973	624	3.20	37
Carter, C. F.	*The Science of Wealth*	Arnold	1973	224	1.75	33
Fleming, M.	*Introduction to Economic Analysis*	Allen and Unwin	1969	500	4.95	32
Hanson, J. L.	*Economics for Students*	Macdonald and Evans	1973	240	1.25	35
Hanson, J. L.	*A Textbook of Economics*	Macdonald and Evans	1977	640	2.50	44
†Harbury, C. D.	*An Introduction to Economic Behaviour*	Fontana	1976	224	1.50	31
Harvey, J.	*Intermediate Economics*	Macmillan Education	1976	496	3.75	44
†Harvey, J.	*Modern Economics*	Macmillan Education	1974	557	2.25	49
†Lipsey, R.	*Introduction to Positive Economics*	Weidenfeld and Nicolson	1976	848	5.65	38
Livesey, F.	*Economics*	Polytech	1972	578	3.20	23
Lobley, D.	*Success in Economics*	Murray	1977	363	2.50	47
Manchester Economics Project	*Understanding Economics*	Ginn	1976	336	4.25	48
Marshall, B. V.	*Comprehensive Economics*	Longman	1975	1163 Vol. 1 Vol. 2	5.50 4.00	54
Molyneaux, J.	*Men, Money and Markets*	Hodder and Stoughton	1972	304	1.50	29
Morgan, E. V.	*Economics*	Pitman	1973	532	3.50	39
Morrice, A.	*The Fundamentals of Economics*	Heinemann	1972	256	1.90	42
†Nevin, E. T.	*Textbook of Economic Analysis*	Macmillan Education	1977	570	3.95	43
Nobbs, J.	*Advanced Level Economics*	McGraw-Hill	1976	249	3.25	41
Paish, F. W. and Culyer, A. J.	*Benham's Economics*	Pitman	1973	584	2.25	40
†Perrow, J.	*Economics*	University Tutorial Press	1975	640	3.25	38
Samuelson, P.	*Economics*	McGraw-Hill	1976	917	6.95	48
Stanlake, G. F.	*Introductory Economics*	Longman	1976	463	1.95	52

*See note to Chapter 49.

†These have accompanying workbooks.

Table 50.1   'A' level economics textbooks

it necessary to supplement this book in the second year since the theoretical treatment is not sufficient for the able student. The main strength of the book lies in its descriptive passages which are reinforced by excellent tables, diagrams and graphs. Even if not used as a class book, it would be invaluable for the teacher as a source of up-to-date information. The only criticisms are that there are no exercises and that the section on international trade theory is not up to the standard of the rest of the book.

51   Resources not Covered in Sections 2 and 4
David Whitehead

Books on Teaching Economics

Assistant Masters' Association, *The Teaching of Economics in Secondary Schools*, (Cambridge University Press, 1971).

Burkhardt, G. A., *Teaching Economics in the Secondary School*, (McGraw-Hill, Australia, 1976).

Committee on the Teaching of Economics in Schools, *The Teaching of Economics in Schools*, (Macmillan, 1973).

Lawton, D. and Dufour, B., *The New Social Studies*, (Heinemann Educational, 1976).

Lee, N. (ed), *Teaching Economics*, (Economics Association, 1975).

Oliver, J. M., *The Principles of Teaching Economics*, (Heinemann Educational, 1973).

Robinson, B. R. G. (ed), *Field Studies in Teaching Economics*, (Economics Association, 1975).

Sandford, C. T. and Bradbury, M. S., *Projects and Role-playing in Teaching Economics*, (Macmillan, 1971).

Whitehead, D. J. (ed), *Curriculum Development in Economics*, (Heinemann Educational, 1973).

An Unorthodox Reading List

Blaug, M., *Economic Theory in Retrospect. 'A Methodological Postscript'*, (Heinemann Educational, 1968).

Brittan, S., *Is There an Economic Consensus?* (Macmillan, 1973).

Coleman, J. R., *Comparative Economic Systems – An Enquiry Approach*, (Holt, Rinehart and Winston, 1968).

Friedman, M., *Essays in Positive Economics*, (University of Chicago Press, 1953).

Gree, F. and Nore, P. (eds), *Economics – An Anti-text*, (Macmillan, 1977).

Hutchison, T. W., *Knowledge and Ignorance in Economics*, (Blackwell, 1977).

Myrdal, G., *Against the Stream*, (Macmillan, 1974).

Phelps Brown, E. H., 'The Underdevelopment of Economics' in *Economic Journal*, March 1972.

Robinson, J., *Collected Economic Papers*, Volume 3, chapter 1, 'Teaching Economics', (Basil Blackwell, 1975).

Robinson, J. and Eatwell, J., *An Introduction to Modern Economics*, (McGraw-Hill, 1973).

Schumacher, E. F., *Small is Beautiful*, (Blond and Briggs, 1973).

Stamp, A. M., *Josiah Stamp and the Limitations of Economics*, (The Athlone Press, 1970).

Stigler, G. J., *The Intellectual and the Market Place*, (Collier Macmillan, 1963).

van Meerhaeghe, M. A. G., *Economics – A Critical Approach*, (Weidenfeld and Nicolson, 1971).

Ward, B., *What's Wrong With Economics*, (Macmillan, 1972).

Winch, P., *The Idea of a Social Science*, (Routledge and Kegan Paul, 1958).

Worswick, G. D. N., 'Is Progress in Economic Science Possible?', in *Economic Journal*, March 1972.

A List of Workbooks for Economics

Gensemer, B. and Shapiro, E., *Macroeconomic Analysis: A Student Handbook*, (Harcourt Brace).

Harbury, C. D., *Workbook in Introductory Economics*, (Pergamon, 1974).

Harvey, J., *Elementary Economics Workbook*, (Macmillan, 1976).

Harvey, J. and Johnson, M., *Introduction to Macroeconomics – A Workbook*, (Macmillan, 1973).

Lipsey, R. G., and Stilwell, J. R., *Workbook to Accompany 'Positive Economics'*, (Weidenfeld and Nicolson, 1975).

Marshall, H. A. and Mould, J. R., *Economic Analysis – A Workbook*, (Butterworth, 1972).

Nevin, E. T., *A Workbook of Economic Analysis*, (Macmillan, 1969).

Watts, M. and Glew, M., *Topics and Questions in 'A' Level Economics*, (Heinemann Educational, 1975).

Games and Simulations

Careers Research and Advisory Centre, *Esso Service Station Game*. Each team is allotted service stations with varying facilities in the town of Hemel Hempstead. They then compete with each other for a greater market share of petrol sales, car servicing and sales of tyres, batteries and accessories.

Careers Research and Advisory Centre, *Esso Students' Business Game*. Players experience the complexities of financing a company which manufactures and markets refrigeration equipment. Decisions have to be made for the finance, production and marketing areas.

Guardian Business Services, *Economy*. A simulation designed to reproduce aspects of the functioning of the national economy.

Kourilsky, M., *Beyond Simulation*. The mini-society approach to instruction in economics, from Educational Resource Associates.

Management Games Ltd., *Chancellor*. A simulation based on the management of the economy. Each participant has to maximise his GDP while maintaining political popularity.

Management Games Ltd., *Crisis*. A simulation of international relations in which six fictitious nations seek to resolve their conflicting interests for a high standard of living, national security and world peace.

Management Games Ltd., *Import*. A simulation in which six firms located in various ports around the world import and export the produce of those countries.

Management Games Ltd., *New City Telephone Company*. A business game concerned with the establishment of company objectives and reconciling the conflicting claims of customers, employees, shareholders and the community at large.

16 mm Films

Guild Sound and Vision (all free loan)
This is Lloyds, (126 1044–0), 40 mins, about insurance.
The Business Game, (300 2270–4), 22 mins, ICL game.
The World Assured, (126 0297–7), 23 mins, part played by insurance in economic and industrial history of UK.
Going Places, (292 3991–3), 30 mins, transport problems.
The Baltic Story, (138 2928–5), 40 mins, functions of Baltic Exchange.
City Port, (134 2893–0), 20 mins, the economy of London.
Adam Smith and the Wealth of Nations, (351 7627–5), 28 mins, produced by Liberty Fund of America.

Central Film Library
North Sea Strike, (UK 2637, free loan), 21 mins, natural gas, from 1959 to 1974.

Rank Film Library
Why we use Money: the Fisherman who Needed a Knife, (21.9030), 8 mins, US cartoon aimed at primary but suitable for other age groups.
Why People have Special Jobs: the Man who made Spinning Tops, (21.9031), 7 mins, aimed at primary but suitable for other age groups.

BBC Film Enterprises
A Growing Concern, (Economics of the Real World, programme 13), 25 mins.
Wealth and People, (Economics of the Real World, programme 14), 25 mins.

Multilink Film Library
Garbage In, Garbage Out, (free loan), 31 mins, uses of computers.
The Square Deal, (free loan), 13 mins, history of insurance, and how it works.
The Sure Thing, (free loan), 14 mins, cartoon on functions of insurance.

Wallcharts

Educational Productions Ltd
How Life Assurance Works, (C965), three charts.
Lloyds of London, (C1140).
British Industry, (C926/7), two charts.
The Baltic Exchange, (C1014).

Pictorial Charts Educational Trust
Energy-alternative Resources and How we can Reduce Consumption, (15″×20″, C721), ten large photographs.
Filling Up Your Income Tax Form, (D716), four charts.

Transport, (15″×20″, C722), ten large photographs.
British Farming, (A29).

Cassette/Filmstrips

Student Recordings Ltd
Mass Production, (AVC/33); *Industry At Work*, (AVC/35); *The Chain of Production*, (AVC/36); *The Social Services*, (AVC/146); *Insurance*, (AVC/149); *The Family Budget*, (AVC/150); *Buying Your Home*, (AVC/151).

52 Internal Assessment
Linda M. Thomas

Assessment is a global term used to describe a whole range of activities which are designed to produce answers to three main categories of question which classroom teachers ask. The teacher selects the appropriate techniques to fit each particular problem.

1 Teachers assess in order to monitor objectively pupil standards at strategic points in their educational progress, to provide a means of comparison with national standards and to provide a basis for prediction.
2 Teachers assess not only in order to measure their pupils' progress in the work which is undertaken but also to provide feedback for their pupils, to provide positive reinforcement and thus to motivate.
3 Teachers will assess as a diagnostic tool in order to identify pupils with special problems and in order to avoid presenting pupils with programmes of work which anticipate unrealistic levels of achievement.

In each of the above situations a different type of assessment procedure is required. Each one is considered in turn.

Objective Assessment

Testing
A single timed written test or assignment involves at least three kinds of sampling. The subject content is sampled; the skills and abilities relevant to the subject are sampled; the pupil's performance in the knowledge, skills and abilities which the test measures is sampled. The danger is that such sampling may produce a significant degree of bias.

Conventional tests. These consist of a relatively few items (questions) from which a choice may be made; the marking of scripts requires subjective decisions by markers. The reliability of such examinations by any measure of reliability tends to be lower than for 'objective' tests. Their validity is difficult to evaluate because statements about what they are designed to assess are not specific. The knowledge of facts learnt and the abilities developed cannot be comprehensively measured by such procedures.

Objective tests. These tests, more appropriately thought of as objectively marked tests, involve subjective decisions at the time the questions are devised but no such decision by markers.

Marker reliability is therefore high. Test items can be devised so as to make very specific demands on candidates, and the coverage of the table of specifications – i.e. the proposition that the test demands all the abilities relevant to the objective – can be examined. However, it is generally acknowledged that objective tests demanding 'higher' abilities are difficult to write, e.g. application, evaluation. Comprehensive coverage of the factual content of the curriculum is theoretically possible by the larger number of items included in such tests. However, the limitations of such tests in providing a comprehensive array of items to measure all the relevant 'abilities' must be recognised. It is certainly true that given sufficient ingenuity many 'higher' intellectual abilities can be tested in this way – but some cannot. The ability to produce an original written communication in either prose or equations cannot be so tested.

Continuous Assessment

There is a growing interest in this mode of assessment. In America, Bloom and Peters inquired extensively into teacher award grades as predictors of subsequent success at university, and found that under the circumstances in which they operated, teacher estimates compared favourably with the best predictors available.[1] Continuous assessment procedures are used in Sweden at primary school level. In this country some university departments, some colleges of education and some schools which submit candidates for the CSE are utilising in varying degrees forms of continuous assessment.

When continuous assessment is used to make an objective assessment of a pupil's achievement, it is essential that great care is taken to make it as valid, reliable and discriminating as possible. There are three fundamental requirements of any system of assessment used for this purpose.

First, it should be *reliable*, that is to say, the order of merit would have been the same if another teacher had made the assessment or if the assessment had been made at a different time. Secondly, it should be *valid*, that is to say, it should test what the examiner thinks it will test. Thirdly, it should *discriminate*, i.e. it should be able to sort out good pupils from average pupils and average pupils from poor pupils, by spreading them appropriately over the mark range available.

In this country continuous assessment may form part of the process of external assessment or it may be used to provide information purely for the teacher's use. Candidates may perform, at intervals during the course, a number of tests or assignments devised by their own teacher. Alternatively, all the work which a candidate does in a subject, e.g. classwork, homework, practical work, oral work etc, may be assessed.

Several good reasons can be advanced for considering the second form of assessment to be the best means of judging a pupil's attainment.

1 Assessments can be based on the pupil's work over a period of time rather than on his performance on particular days. This should provide a more reliable assessment of the candidate's attainment because it reduces the element of sampling, inherent in a one-day test.

2 Assessments reflect the normal activity of the pupil under everyday conditions and can therefore take into account many dimensions of his work. His written work, his oral work, his interest and enthusiasm and his creative and imaginative flair can all be assessed.

3 Assessments can be systematically planned to measure those specific skills and abilities which the course is designed to develop.

4 Assessments do not cause revision and the memorising of facts to be stressed more than is necessary for the development of the pupil's understanding of the subject.

Defects which Must be Avoided

1 The assessment may well be insufficiently objective.
(a) The teacher may be influenced too much by his attitude to the child, e.g. the pupil's characteristics such as effort, industry and perseverance may be rewarded.
(b) There exists the danger of awarding marks for the same few skills or abilities relative to a subject over and over again while some very important ones are omitted. It is recognised that continuous assessment by its nature involves the repeated assessment of certain skills and abilities but care should be taken not to concentrate on a small number and exclude others which are relevant.

2 Teachers' assessments are sometimes unreliable, that is to say they are variable, and particularly so over the range of average pupils.

3 While many teachers will be able to put pupils in the correct order of merit, they may well have difficulty in relating the internal standard to an external one.

4 There may be tendency for internally awarded marks not to discriminate well between the candidates.

Suggestions for Avoiding the Defects

The defects mentioned in the previous section may well be avoided if decisions are made about the following points before the assessment begins.

1 The precise educational objectives of the course should be stated. An example is given in Chapter 6.

2 The relative importance of the various objectives and the proportion of marks to be allocated to each should be decided. An example is given in Chapter 6.

3 A decision should be made about what is to be assessed. Will all the work which a pupil does in a subject during a specified period be assessed, or will the assessment be made on a number of specific tests or assignments? If so, how frequently will these tests be set?

4 The teacher should decide on the scale of marks to be used for each item to be assessed. If the assessments are to be frequent over a fairly long period, it may be advisable to use a five point scale using three as the average mark for the group.

5 If continuous assessment is to form part of the process of external assessment, all the intermediate

assessments will eventually have to be combined to give a final assessment and grade.

Decisions will have to be taken, therefore, on the following points:

(a) Is the final assessment to be an average of all the assessments? This is a method which is in use but the inherent danger in this is that the pupil who starts slowly/badly in the first year of the course may be penalised for this and one must bear in mind that the final assessment describes attainment at the end of the course, i.e. in the case of the leaving certificate it will be at the end of secondary education.
(b) If allowance is to be made for consistent improvement over the period, i.e. if the assessments are regarded as a progress chart, how subjective will the final assessment be? A compromise might be reached in that the final year, only, is taken into account.

Reinforcement

The effect of frequent and immediate feedback of results is often extremely beneficial to pupils. Psychological experiments on the effect of blame or praise on children show that improved performance results from either course of action whereas pupils who are not given any feedback at all do not display improvement.

When the main purpose of assessment is to provide motivation the usual criteria – reliability, validity, discrimination – are less relevant in the selection of the appropriate techniques, and the teacher is free to respond in a creative way. The Swindon RPA is one assessment scheme which is designed primarily as a system of motivation, of recording and of organisation. The RPA replaces teacher assessment by a factual record of whatever the pupil takes pride in having done.[2]

Its objectives are to offer an incentive to those pupils whose needs are not met by examinations, and to provide a means by which pupils gain a better understanding of their own interests, skills and general suitability for particular occupations. It is possible for an economics teacher to adapt the ideas contained in this scheme to his own use, and to encourage pupils to present evidence of interest in economics; for example, work undertaken, visits made, programmes watched, material collated, projects completed, interviews made, etc. Pupils may be interested in taking part in such competitions as Stockpiler or the Midland Bank general knowledge competition (this has an economics section). This record of the pupil's own personal achievement would be complementary to more conventional methods of assessment.

At a more mundane level, using assessment for motivation means structuring materials to provide built-in feedback, for example, by judicious use of such techniques as programmed learning; by setting realistic objectives and successfully communicating these to pupils; by commenting in detail on each piece of work; by fully discussing each piece of work with individual pupils.

Matching

The importance of using methods which fit the point which the pupil has reached is widely acknowledged by experts. A pupil can only use the ways of thinking and reacting which he has built up to help him to make sense of new experience. If the new experience is too far beyond the reach of his present ideas he not only fails to make sense of it but also misses a chance of advancing his ways of thinking. On the other hand, when his activities are at a level at which he can make sense of them, they enlarge his knowledge and help to strengthen, or perhaps modify, his abilities and ideas. An essential part of an effective teaching strategy is an attempt to match experiences to a pupil's development in the various skills, attitudes and concepts involved. The level at which activities are carried out by an individual pupil and the expectations set for him should take into account his unique set of strengths and weaknesses.

If this is not successfully accomplished there is no guarantee that students will gain more than a superficial familiarity with the subject. As Keith Drake wrote, 'A student of mainstream economics too often experiences a course which is not unlike a quick trip round a large and bemusing supermarket: at the cash desk (exam time) the contents of his trolley are no less prepacked and inscrutable than they were on the shelves – they have merely been handled'.[3]

Dr Wynne Harlen's *Progress in Learning Science* project distinguishes three separate sets of activities which are the essential components of the technique of 'matching'.[4] First, teachers must make and record observations about pupils. Secondly, teachers must consider how pupils learn, how they can be helped in their learning, and what factors influence development of various ideas and attitudes. Lastly, teachers must make decisions about the learning environment, and about the activities and approaches which are likely to be of most benefit at different points in development.

This chapter is concerned with the first set of activities listed above since these involve new forms of internal assessment which are playing an increasingly important role in the day-to-day teaching situation. Specially designed activities or tests are of little use to a teacher who has to make frequent decisions about 'matching'. Instead he must pick up evidence of development and progress through everyday observations. Dr Harlen advocates the use of checklists (see Appendix I). The main advantages of using this method are the following:

1 It encourages teachers to articulate precisely what they mean by learning economics; to list the abilities relating to 'learning how to learn' which can be strengthened through learning economics; and to list the economic concepts which enable pupils to make sense of the economic world (see Appendix II from *The Teaching of Economics in Schools*[5]).

2 It encourages teachers to develop criteria for making inferences from observations and to keep to the same criteria on all occasions for all pupils. These criteria enable teachers to be clear about what signs are acceptable evidence of the acquisition of skills or abilities.

3 It may help to reduce the subjective element in observation and enable teachers to interpret their pupils with greater accuracy.

4 It discourages application of the teaching technique in which a topic of work is presented; a few perfunctory questions are asked to test for understanding; an essay or assignment is set to provide evidence that students have fully grasped the point; and, in the case of failure on the student's part, the whole process is repeated.

5 It does not interfere with the ordinary teaching programme.

References

1 Bloom, B. S. and Peters, R. F., *The Use of Academic Prediction Scales*, (Longman, 1961).

2 A handbook describing the scheme is available from The Swindon Record of Personal Achievement Curriculum Study and Development Centre, Sarfort Street, Swindon, Wiltshire.

3 Drake, K., 'Economics: Cracks in a Monolithic Curriculum', *Educational Studies*, October 1977.

4 Harlen, W., Schools Council Project, *Progress in Learning Science*.

5 Economics Association, *et al.*, *The Teaching of Economics in School* (Macmillan, 1973).

Appendix I

One example of the application of the check list technique while teaching the concept of comparative cost in international trade.

Stage

1 The student is able to state the rule for working out opportunity cost ratios but makes mistakes which show that he has not used the inverse rule to check.

2 The student can work out opportunity cost ratios from output figures. He always uses the 'rule' to work out which country should specialise in which good and is unable to explain why.

3 The student is able to show the 'gain' from trade only by switching resources (usually units of labour) and calculating gains and losses in term of output.

4 The student is able to show the 'gain' from trade by applying the general case which involves substitution of units of output only.

5 The student is able to analyse for himself the assumptions which are made.

Appendix II

(a) The logic of choice in terms of opportunity cost and the marginal principle;

(b) the logic of specialisation and trade in terms of comparative advantage;

(c) the partial analysis of supply and demand in a single market;

(d) the determination of the rewards of factors of production; and

(e) the general analysis of aggregate national income, expenditure and activity.

(a) A capacity to follow and sustain an economic argument and to make logical inferences from given information;

(b) a capacity to set out and communicate to others a logical argument in economics;

(c) a capacity to be aware of assumptions made implicitly in the use of an economic model to assist a process of reasoning and to perceive how a modification of the assumptions might effect the conclusions;

(d) a capacity to understand the mutual interrelations

and interdependencies of the various elements in an economic system and to take account of them in handling economic problems;

(e) a capacity to understand and explain the economic effects of important economic institutions on economic policies;

(f) a capacity to make appropriate inferences from quantitative data;

(g) a capacity to apply to an economic problem the models of economic analysis that are most appropriate to it.

53 External Assessment

Clive Baker

What the Examining Board tells the Teacher

One of the major problems that an external examining body has is to keep in touch with its customers. A teacher requires two main items of information: what must be taught and how the material is to be examined. What has to be taught is set out in the syllabus. This is usually preceded by a section which states how it is to be examined.

Many teachers imagine that external examinations restrain them in what they are to teach. This is far from the case. The syllabus states the material which will be assessed but a teacher is not limited to just this material. The main constraints on what a teacher teaches are not the syllabuses that are provided by the examining boards but the amount of time available to teach the subject and the type of students taught.

The examining body provides five main types of information for the teacher.

The Aims and Objectives of the Syllabus

While these may not be set out exactly in the way that will be shown here, most syllabuses have an introduction indicating the aims and objectives that the board considers essential for those following the syllabus. In broad terms the aims will give the philosophy of the syllabus while the objectives will cover the educational skills which it is hoped that the candidate will have acquired by the time the examination is taken. The objectives tend to be set out in some form of table and often they follow the skills taxonomy of Bloom, starting with factual recall and following through comprehension, application, analysis, synthesis and evalu-

ation. These objectives are very often overlooked, and often too much emphasis is given to factual recall in the teaching, when in order to gain good marks in the examination it is necessary to create some synthesis from different parts of the syllabus in order to evaluate the information given. In looking at the aims and objectives it is necessary to see whether some kind of numeracy is required. If this is the case, the teacher will have to think how to present the material in such a way that the student is aware of the methods, for example, of calculating marginal cost and marginal revenue in order to arrive at an equilibrium point. For some classes this may be the obvious way of doing it, but for others the more natural way might be to use graphs (admittedly made up from the figures). For this second group some time will have to be spent in explaining and practising the purely arithmetical aspects of answering any problems that may be set. How much time should be spent on institutions and examples? There will be some indication of this in the syllabus itself. However it is worth looking at the introduction in order to see whether it is spelt out in greater detail there. Even if only theoretical concepts are set out in the syllabus itself, a sentence such as 'Candidates will be expected to show how the theory relates to the real economy in which they live' may appear. This implies that it is inadequate just to look at the theoretical concepts without relating them to practical examples if the student is to obtain a good mark in the examination.

The Assessment Methods

For 'A' level economics, most boards have now introduced some kind of objective test, all have some kind of essay question, and most have or are considering adopting some kind of stimulus material (data response questions). Since objective testing has been introduced, it has been necessary for the student to have an overall knowledge of all the items that appear in the syllabus – which was not the case when there were only two essay papers. The grid that the boards will issue for the objective test will give an indication of what bias there will be in the paper and what skills will be tested.

The teacher should carefully examine which methods of assessment are used in the examinations. The boards will have available documents which will indicate how they will assess the candidate. A new syllabus will have specimen papers or questions and old established syllabuses will have past papers. These are well worth looking at. The past papers will certainly give an indication of the way that a Chief Examiner is thinking. There is, of course, one snag. The term of office of a Chief Examiner is not indefinite and a teacher may get caught when a new one is appointed who does not ask such predictable questions.

The Syllabus

The syllabus is not an exclusive list of items that should be taught. It is the list of items that will be tested in the examination. Do not hesitate to introduce other material which can often be very useful to the student, as he can make useful comparisons or introduce off-beat examples which are always refreshing to the marker.

Do not think, either, that the way that the syllabus is set out means that it has to be taught in that order. It is important to think in terms of the students to be taught and the time available. What is necessary for the candidate to pass the examination (or get a Grade C at 'O' level or 1 in CSE)? If faced with teaching an evening class with two hours per week, it may be necessary to omit certain items or the student may have to cover less central topics himself. There may be some time left at the end of the course to go back and look at certain parts that were not covered earlier on.

In the layout of the syllabus, the designers will try to set out the material in what appears to them to be a logical order. But what is suitable for members of that group – and there is often much discussion about the order in which items appear – will not be suitable for all teachers. The teaching programme is something that is very personal to the teacher and also to the group that he is teaching.

The Chief Examiner's Report

This is provided by boards, more or less regularly, to help teachers. After the markers have done their work, they are asked to send comments to the Chief stating how well or badly the paper has been answered. In particular they are asked to highlight those parts that

were not well done and to indicate why this was so. From these reports, and the scripts that he has seen himself, the Chief will be able to sort out whether he should change his approach, and indicate to teachers where the candidates have fallen down in answering the questions. In some ways this can also be an indication to teachers that there are sins of omission and commission in their teaching. In the same way as there are many different types of teachers, there are many different types of Chief Examiners. Efforts are made to ensure that such unhelpful remarks as 'This question was badly done' do not appear unless there is an indication of the way in which the candidates' answers were lacking.

GCE boards do not issue model answers, mainly because it is felt that to do so would mean that some candidates would feel that if they had not answered the question in one particular way, they would not receive any marks. This is far from being the case, as anyone who has attended a standardisation meeting of examiners will know. However, a good Chief Examiner's report will outline the main points that were looked for and the main faults that were found in the answers. This report may well be hidden in the Head of Department's files – or even in those of the Headmaster or Principal. Do try to get hold of it. It should be helpful.

Notes of Guidance to Teachers

One of the best ways of trying to sort out the problems of a particular syllabus is to look at old question papers. But what happens when you are faced with a new syllabus or one that has been radically altered? As has already been mentioned, there will be a specimen paper or questions. For new syllabuses, as for old, there will be a suggested reading list if it is possible to provide one. This at least gives a guide.

But there are still likely to be certain questions unanswered. Some items in the syllabus may be a little vague, or the balance of the syllabus may not be obvious at first sight. If the information provided is inadequate, write to the body concerned and ask whether there is any extra information available in the form of notes of guidance to teachers. Very often this is provided in order to cover certain aspects of a syllabus that have not appeared before and to show where the emphasis should be in the syllabus itself. They may be supplemented by a reading list which may not only cover the textbooks that are appropriate for the syllabus but also additional reading which may be suitable for the library or for the teacher in helping him to prepare the lessons.

All this information may be useful, but there may still be certain items that are worrying. Once again it is worthwhile writing to the board in order to try and find out its view on the particular matter. It is quite possible that an acknowledgement will be sent in the first place as the subject officer may have to discuss the matter with the Chief Examiner and perhaps with a couple of people on the subject panel. Also it is advisable to send in questions early in the year. April to August are somewhat hectic and any enquiry is likely to take some time to resolve at this time.

Whilst not technically being notes for guidance, do keep an eye on the plethora of material that the boards send out to their centres in order to keep them up-to-date. There may be a tendency for this material to get stuck in the higher echelons of the school or college. However make certain that it gets to the person for whom it was intended and who is ultimately responsible for its implementation – the teacher at the chalk-face (or behind the OHP).

These circulars are likely to provide information on changes in syllabus and in the types of assessment that have been agreed. At this point it is a bit too late to do anything about it but normally some kind of advance warning is given in the form of invitations to meetings of teachers to discuss the matter, a questionnaire that needs answering or perhaps just the information that a new syllabus is in the offing and that teachers are invited to send in their suggestions. The boards very often face the criticism that they do not keep up-to-date with their syllabuses. But often when they try to do just this, they have to meet complaints that the whole syllabus has been altered. Basically they are there to help and they need the help of teachers when new ideas are being floated in order to ensure that the procedures and examinations are really what are required.

In short there is, or at least there should be, a dialogue between the boards and teachers. Unfortunately boards often find that the information does not get to the people concerned with its implementation. Heads of Department should make certain that the person concerned sees what applies to them.

What the Teacher can tell the Examination Board

Every subject officer worries about the mistakes that may get into an examination. If there should be a mistake in the paper try and get hold of the board in order to see if there is a correction available. This can be done by telephone. Alternatively, write to the board and set out the problem with the particular question. This will enable the board to take the matter into account at the various stages of the post-examination procedures. The letter should be addressed to the board at its offices, and not to the examiner.

Likewise if a candidate is off-colour on the day of the examination write to the board and tell them, with a medical certificate, so that special consideration may be given to the grading. Naturally the same would apply if there had been a serious problem in the candidate's family. However teachers should be careful not to try to claim special consideration for trivial matters. This tends to make it more difficult for the board's staff to consider those cases which are really worthy of some kind of extra help.

The same comments apply to questions which seem to be ambiguous. Write to the board immediately so that the facts can be taken into consideration when the Chief Examiner meets his assistants. Naturally the reasons why the question is considered to be ambiguous should be given.

The boards also welcome comments on the examinations if it is felt that something can be done to improve them. This may not be possible for the following year as the papers may already be in print, but the comments will certainly be taken into account when future papers are prepared and moderated. There are two routes for these comments. The teachers' unions have a joint committee which looks at the examinations of the boards in the light of teachers' comments. Alternatively, individual teachers may write direct to the board with their comments. A specific suggestion about content of papers or the rubric may be dealt with immediately. If it is a matter of policy, the matter will have to be referred to the subject committee and it may take longer to be implemented.

In spite of all the checks that the boards have, it may happen that occasionally a mistake is made. They have to deal with a very large number of candidates in a very short time. Among the results of hundreds of thousands of candidates that the major boards deal with a few mistakes are likely to creep in. Every care is taken that this does not happen. Marks and grades are checked and rechecked, but however careful one is, a grade may be awarded which does not make sense to the teacher.

If it is felt that a mistake has been made, please do not telephone the board – unless, perhaps, it is essential for a place at a university. State the case in a letter just as soon as it is realised that there may be something wrong. There may be something that can be done immediately to put the matter right. On the other hand it may take time to sort out the problem. Boards differ in what they are prepared to do in the case of an alleged mistake. They will normally want to be paid if they have to do a lot of work, though this can be refunded if a mistake is found.

First, the most obvious type of mistake is where there has been a miscalculation of the marks either within a question or in the totals of the paper. The markers are instructed to make certain that their addition is correct and the boards will check the scripts when they are received. However a slip can get through.

Secondly the school or college can ask for the script to be re-examined by another examiner. This will, of course, take time and is more expensive to carry out than a straight clerical recheck.

Both these are worthwhile for a small number of candidates. But it could be that the teacher wants to get an overall picture of where the candidates have been going wrong. It is possible for a teacher, even an experienced one, not to realise what is really being called for. In such cases a special report on the candidates may be requested. This is very much like the Chief Examiners' reports, but deals only with the work of the candidates from one centre. It may be cheaper to ask the board to do this when the scripts are being marked. This could be the case if a Head of Department is worried about the work of a new teacher. In such circumstances this would certainly be the best time to ask for the report. This service does not include a re-mark of the scripts but gives an overall impression of what the examiner feels is wrong – and right – in the work submitted by the candidates.

Each board has its own method of carrying out these checks and reports. If such a recheck or report seems to be justified, the regulations will state what services are available.

The Choice between Boards

In the case of the GCE examinations there is a choice between boards. Some people criticise this fact and feel that there is a duplication of effort. This may be true, but a competitive situation, while in some ways being wasteful of resources, does help to keep the people who work with the boards on their toes. This is particularly the case with reference to the various syllabuses that are available. If a teacher feels that the subject matter of the syllabus that he is teaching is not suitable for him or his students, he can have a look at the syllabuses of the other boards. It is possible that while the basic material may be the same, subjects on the periphery may be very different. The approach, too, can be different. Some question papers may call for a more practical approach while others will require a purely conceptual treatment. In addition the boards differ in their approach to methods of assessment. Some syllabuses call for objective testing, others for data response or stimulus material, others for an element of teacher assessment either through classwork or projects. The teacher should see what is available which fits in with his philosophy of teaching.

There is, of course, one difficulty. The school may not be a centre for the syllabus that the teacher wants to use. To overcome this problem it may be possible to persuade the powers-that-be to allow candidates for economics to be entered with the new board. However the basic fee will have to be paid to both boards if the students are taking the examinations of two.

In certain cases it may be possible to use the bor-

rowed subjects procedures. If the school's board does not offer a syllabus in the subject, permission may be given for the school to use another board's syllabus. Naturally, the work involved takes time and the applications have to be made in accordance with the regulations. The boards will not make the facility available if they offer a syllabus themselves in the subject. However, with new syllabuses coming into operation in the field of economics, this could be helpful.

The Choice between Methods of Assessment

One of the great changes that have come about in the examination scene over the last two decades has been the involvement of teachers in the assessment of their candidates. Chapter 6 covers the preparation of a Mode III syllabus for CSE. All three modes of assessment are also available for GCE examinations.

The following are the main characteristics of the different modes.

Mode I: This is the traditional examination in the United Kingdom with the syllabus being prepared by the board which also sets the papers and carries out the marking. More recently, some syllabuses, particularly at 'O' level and CSE, have introduced a teacher-assessed part to the examination. The N and F proposals also seem to be advocating some kind of teacher involvement in many cases.

Mode II. This, perhaps the most unpopular of the three modes, is where the school or college prepares the syllabus which is agreed by the board which then sets and marks the papers.

Mode III. Syllabuses in this mode call for the greatest teacher involvement. It is the teacher who prepares the syllabus, either as an individual or as a member of a consortium. The board will approve the syllabus and will also moderate the question papers and marking, both of which will be the teacher's responsibility. Mode III examinations will have, as a rule, a large element of course work or projects in their assessment.

The main advantage of Mode III is, or at least should be, the fact that the teacher will be able to tailor the syllabus to his style of teaching and also make use of result one would anticipate that the results that are obtained are going to be better than those for Mode I. There has been a great deal of criticism of Mode III in some quarters. It is often felt that it is a soft option. But if everybody is doing the job properly, this should not be the case.

In theory, Mode III syllabuses can be offered at 'A' level, and there is a small number of them at this level. The number is small because of the amount of work that is necessary to pass the Mode III through all its stages. In addition to having to pass through all the various committees of the boards, the syllabus will also have to be approved by the Schools Council. The whole operation is time-consuming and by the time that the syllabus has been approved, the originating teacher will have moved elsewhere and have to start the whole procedure again under different circumstances. However, it is worthwhile having a look at the possibilities of introducing a Mode III at any level. But make certain that the board will allow the development of Mode IIIs, and if they will, ensure that the fundamental concepts are agreed before going into too much detail. Show them a draft of the proposals in outline.

Before spending a great deal of time on a Mode III, it would be sensible to find out whether any of your colleagues have a similar idea. It could be time-saving, too, to see whether teachers in other schools in your area have similar ideas or whether they are offering a syllabus of a similar type. There can be financial advantages in being part of a consortium. Finally, check that the school is prepared to accept the additional cost that a Mode III will incur.

The boards have an obligation to ensure that the syllabus that is presented to them and its assessment are of a comparable standard to others that are being offered in the same subject area. It is possible that they will require a certain element of the Mode I to ensure this comparability.

The Syllabus and Assessment

In this section there will be a description of how a syllabus may be prepared from scratch. It is a case study of one which at the time of writing is under consideration and which, it is hoped, will be available by the time that this book is published. The idea started off as somebody's brain child. He suggested that he felt that there might be a market for a syllabus that took the basic needs of the family in the modern world and related them to the theory of economics. No syllabus seemed to do this and the subject matter seemed ideal for candidates who would be 17+ when they sat the examination. It was not aimed at the person who wanted to go on to 'A' level economics but at those who were appearing in greater numbers in the sixth form who did not have the ability or the desire to obtain an 'A' level in this subject.

The idea was taken to the economics subject committee and discussed in detail. It was agreed that there would be a number of schools and colleges for whom this subject would be suitable and useful.

A sub-committee was set up to examine the matter more fully. The fact that they had an outline syllabus made things very much easier, but the first decision that had to be taken was the possible candidates for the

subject. In discussions with teachers of sixth-form pupils, it transpired that they were enthusiastic about the idea, maintaining it would be of interest to their pupils. The sub-committee also discussed the matter with teachers in further education, and here it was felt that it would be a useful addition in general studies for the non-specialist student. The next question that had to be answered was what level the syllabus should be aimed at. After much discussion it was decided that the choice lay between 'O' (Alternative) level and CEE and eventually it was decided that in the first instance CEE would be the most suitable.

Before discussing the syllabus content in detail, the sub-committee had to examine the aims and objectives which would form the basis of not only the subject matter but also the assessment. The difference between the two caused some concern, but it was decided that in general terms the aims would set out what the teacher aimed to put over during the course while the objectives would be student-orientated and amongst other things would indicate what skills, educational or otherwise, the student would be expected to acquire during his study leading up to the examination.

The aims were quickly decided. There was a body of economic knowledge which could be useful to everybody in everyday life; there were concepts that really affected everyone whether they realised it or not. At the time the price of coffee was rising rapidly because there was a shortage of supply and the demand stayed the same. The price of strawberries was coming down rapidly as the season advanced. Why was this? What did someone have to give up if he wanted a holiday on the Costa Blanca? These concepts and many others should be useful for the person of sixteen or seventeen to know. They involved applying elementary economic theory and as a result were really educational. The principal aim was to point out the importance of economic concepts in everyday life.

Having defined the aims of the syllabus, the committee turned its attention to the objectives. These were important as it was on them that the eventual examination would be based. The sub-committee considered applying Bloom's cognitive objectives. At first sight, bearing in mind the candidates for whom the syllabus was being written, it seemed as though the last two, synthesis and evaluation, were not really suitable. But were students being asked to do anything more than they had to do in their everyday life, i.e. gather a certain amount of material or information together and make a decision in the light of what facts they had available? This is, after all, what the average person does when he goes out to buy a bicycle or a moped. Therefore it was agreed that if the questions were set with due regard to the level at which the evaluation would take place, it was reasonable to include them.

Another problem that faced the committee was whether to include a numeracy element. It was agreed that in view of the fact that it would be difficult to study the economics of everyday life without some kind of calculation and that much of the material which is presented in the media is shown in the form of tables and graphs, this should be included. The next stage was to discuss the subject matter. The main problem here was not so much what to include, but what to leave out so that the syllabus was balanced and at the same time did not include so much that it would be impossible to teach it in the time that was available. This section of the work, in spite of the fact that there was already a basic syllabus available, took two meetings, and there were rewrites and amendments even after it seemed that the syllabus was complete. If the committee had had to start from scratch, it is quite likely that this section of the work would have taken four or five meetings. It should be emphasised that a great deal of work was carried out by the members researching information between the meetings.

At the following meeting the committee started to consider assessment. In order to do this, the members had to go back to the objectives, check that these were met by the syllabus and then see what form the examination could take.

A check list of different types of assessment was provided and the committee went through all of the suggestions and discussed them in turn.

In order to test the breadth of the syllabus, either objective testing or short answer questions were felt to be suitable. It was considered that it would be possible to cover factual recall and comprehension. As it would be impossible to build up a bank of items until the syllabus was running, objective testing by multiple choice items was not feasible. So consideration turned to short answer questions, which it was felt would be very suitable at CEE level to test the broad areas of the syllabus. These questions would probably assess the candidates in the lower ranges of ability best but other methods had to be found to test the higher skills.

The committee was very interested in a suggestion that some kind of stimulus material of a practical nature should be used, and after much discussion it was decided that this should be used with the primary function of discriminating in the middle ranges of ability.

The next question to be answered was whether some kind of continuous writing should be introduced. It was felt that some kind of essay questions should be used, particularly as at the time it was suggested that two of the upper grades were to be considered comparable with 'O' level. Two types of essays were possible – one completely open ended, the traditional form of essay, and the other a structured essay which would guide the candidate through the skills. In both cases the committee felt that some kind of choice should be given, and finally a section incorporating this type of assessment was agreed upon.

For teachers to be able to consider the paper, it was necessary to prepare either specimen questions or a specimen paper. It was decided that the latter would be preferable if possible and the secretary was provided with a number of questions from which he was able to build up two papers, the first testing the lower skills and the second mainly to enable the board to assess and discriminate at the upper end of the scale.

The proposals were now submitted to the full committee and having been agreed it was decided that, rather than using a questionnaire to centres, a meeting of teachers would be held to discuss the final version. The teachers seemed to be very pleased with what was being offered, made some suggestions that were incorporated, and the subject committee was then in a position to take the syllabus to the board's education committee, which approved the proposal.

The syllabus was now ready to be offered to centres. Unfortunately there was a delay in the making of CEE into an official examination, so the syllabus, in the form in which it had been prepared, had to go into cold storage. However, the interest shown by teachers had been so great that it was decided that work would be started to convert the syllabus into an 'O' (Alternative) level. As most of the basic work had been covered in the seven meetings that it took to build up the CEE syllabus, this job was carried out comparatively quickly. Even so, a further four meetings were necessary to vary the objectives, rewrite the syllabus and prepare new specimen papers.

This description of how syllabuses are prepared has two functions. The first of these is to show the amount of work that is necessary to design a new syllabus, and a similar amount of work would also be necessary for a revised one. There are various checks throughout – the subject committee's discussions, discussions that the members will have had with colleagues, the teachers' meeting and the board's education committee. Had the syllabus been at 'A' level it would have been necessary to go one stage further, to the Schools Council, for approval. It should be pointed out that although 'O' levels do not have to be approved by this body, they are reported to it and it can and does pass comments on them.

Secondly, it will show people who are thinking of preparing a Mode III that there is a great deal of work entailed. A Mode III syllabus must be of an equal standard to a Mode I and teachers will find that a very great deal of work is involved, particularly if they are working on their own. In the syllabus discussed above, the number of man hours involved in meetings alone was at least 100 and much work was done outside, even though the outline syllabus had been prepared when the sub-committee started its discussions.

Some Tips on the Preparation of Mode IIIs

Preparation of the Syllabus

Look carefully at the Mode I syllabus of the board and examine carefully the way in which it is set out. Most boards have a house style which they will want followed in the Mode III. Apart from any other reason it will enable the board to assess how the Mode III compares with the equivalent Mode I. Before starting on the preparation of the subject matter, sort out the aims and objectives, to clarify the purpose of the proposed course. The board will also require these as part of the syllabus in order to be able to assess the syllabus.

Carefully examine the content in order to ensure that it is at a suitable level. Teachers should be able to assure the board that the amount of subject matter can be covered in the time.

Make certain that the syllabus in fact gives scope for the covering of the aims and objectives that have been set out. It must allow the setting of questions that will test the educational skills that are called for in the objectives and that will, in GCE and some CSE, permit all grades to be awarded. Set out the syllabus in a logical manner. Some kind of theme is normal in any syllabus and this should be followed through. Ensure that the syllabus is sufficiently detailed for the board, and for the specialists to whom it will send the work to ascertain whether it is of sufficient standard. It is quite possible that a teacher who prepares the syllabus will know what is meant but that another person who is looking at it will not. Make certain, perhaps by showing the work to a colleague, that what has been written is communicating what is required.

Normally Mode III syllabuses are only allowed when there is some considerable difference from a Mode I. Make certain that this is the case before submitting the work to the board. In some cases the board will perhaps look at the Mode III if the difference is on the assessment procedures, but this is not normally the case. There must be some fundamental difference, for example the introduction of a certain amount of economic history, that makes the Mode III different and perhaps unique.

Specimen Papers

The board will require a specimen paper to see that the teacher has been able to follow out the objectives of the syllabus. In deciding which methods of assessment to use, it is probable that there will be a written paper. The questions must be set so that there is no question of overlap, nor any chance of ambiguity, and so that the candidate will be able to answer them if he has done his work properly.

There are fundamentally five methods of writing questions.

1 *Objective test items*. These are for the specialist. It is impossible for an individual teacher to write year in and year out a series of multiple choice items that would be accepted. In addition they must be validated before the examination in some form of pre-test. Therefore, if these are available as part of the Mode I, use this paper. If not they may not form part of the assessment – or should not.

2 *Short answer questions*. These are ideal when the aim is to test a wide variety of different subjects. They should be so written that they can only have one answer. They will normally test knowledge, but on occasions they will be so constructed that they can test application. Ensure that short answer questions do not in fact call for an essay answer.

3 *Comprehension questions*. These are ideal in economics. Stimulus material is supplied which will enable candidates either to show that they understand a piece of continuous writing or alternatively that they have understood some statistics. However, the questions should be written, in the main, so that they cannot be answered without the material. It is a complete waste of time for the candidate to have to read the material and then have to answer general questions which he could have done without the material being presented.

4 *Structured questions*. These questions start at quite an easy level and by gradually introducing new material or concepts the candidate is moved from a straightforward factual recall question into making an evaluation either of the material presented or alternatively of work that has been taught during the course.

5 *Essay questions*. These are the traditional questions at 'O' level. They are very useful at testing the higher skills of evaluation after synthesis. However they can also be used in factual recall in such questions as asking the candidate to describe something. If they are being used to test the higher skills, make certain that they give pupils the opportunity to do so, and also that they are *required* to do so.

When preparing the specimen paper, make certain that there is reasonable coverage of the syllabus. It is probably impossible to do more than sample the knowledge of the candidate, but make certain that it is a reasonable sample. Make certain that all the skills that are set out in the objectives are covered by the paper, otherwise, however good the syllabus is, the material will be returned to the teacher. Make certain, too, that all the questions are covered by the syllabus. Very often it is when preparing papers that the teacher can see that certain items that are required have been left out.

Marking Scheme

In many ways the marking scheme is more important than the paper when trying to assess the syllabus. The marking scheme must be detailed, showing not only what the candidate is required to answer but also the weight that is being given to different parts of the question. Here again make certain that a question that calls for some kind of evaluation is not marked just on the basis of factual recall.

Make certain that all the information required to mark the paper is there. It is not enough just to put 'Definition of elasticity of demand'. A full definition showing exactly what is required should be given.

Conclusion

Carefully consider whether it is necessary to introduce a Mode III. Remember that it is very time-consuming – particularly if there is an element of coursework. This element of coursework, if introduced, should show certain skills being tested and should be marked just as carefully as the written paper, with a marking scheme. Follow any guidance that is available from the board or its officers. Before going as far as preparing everything in detail, make certain that there is a chance that the work will be acceptable by means of an outline scheme.

Finally, allow time for the Mode III to be accepted by the board. The checking and double checking are laborious for the board, and sometimes there are many Mode IIIs that have to be dealt with at the same time.

54 Running an Economics Department*

John Rees

Although most teachers aim to become Heads of Department, and many achieve this position, remarkably little attention has been paid in teacher training or in educational literature to the process by which an assistant teacher, competent (one hopes) as a classroom performer, is turned into a new and beautiful butterfly, assumed to have acquired omnicompetence in all matters departmental apparently as the result of a responsibility allowance and a summer holiday. It may be true that the induction of new teachers is neglected; it must be very unusual for Heads of Department to receive much guidance and support in a task which is quite different from and yet in addition to the need to be a competent subject teacher.

The organisation and management of schools has tended to be seen as boring but necessary. Unkind remarks are often passed about 'supernumaries', and the 'light timetables' of deputy heads and heads of subject, illustrating a failure to understand the positive and creative aspects of good administration within a school. This may account for the attitude that at worst sees the headship of a department as a reward for loyal service, rather than as a key appointment in the development of an effective school. The good academic is not necessarily suited to cope with a wide range of staff, pupils, needs and courses. Indeed one of the problems thrown up by reorganisation is that departmental heads have often had relatively little

* I am grateful to David Butler for comments on an earlier draft of this chapter.

experience of the full range of educational challenges offered by the comprehensive school. The grammar school was characterised by homogeneity of staff and pupils, and often relatively small size. The comprehensive is generally distinguished by the variety of backgrounds and needs of staff and of pupils, and by large units which are often difficult to 'know' in detail. The Head of Economics tended in the past to be faced with the relatively straightforward task of coping with academically motivated 'O' and 'A' level pupils. In many schools today, the task is not so simple, with the widening range of pupil needs within the department, and the proliferation of external examinations, itself creating the sometimes difficult job of deciding who should be entered for which examination.

It is extremely difficult to write effectively about running a department, to produce a guide for success. One must disentangle the peculiarities of one's own situation from the general statements which may be made. Clearly schools vary enormously, and departments within them. In addition there is a risk of stating the obvious. Finally, although this chapter stresses the managerial role of the teacher, it is patently clear that for a variety of reasons, teaching and administration of a department cannot be held separate.

The Head of Department should be the leader of a complementary team, the sum of which is greater than the parts. Diversity of interests and personality amongst the team is a strength which must be built on, whether this variety is inherited or deliberately created through appointments to the staff. Selection procedures are often poor – too little time and money are devoted to the appointment of staff who may be at the school for many years, and cause countless problems if badly chosen. Efficiency and courtesy pay off here as in most other areas of administration. The successful department requires a variety of skills, duties and responsibilities. The wise Head will seek to distribute the work of his department as far as possible not as necessary chores but according to the obvious abilities and interests of his staff. Provided that general policy is clear and that it is realised that delegation does not mean abdication of responsibility, many of the tasks for which the Head is responsible (issuing books, running a library, organising outside visits and speakers, etc) can be entrusted to other members of staff. Young teachers and teachers new to a school will benefit particularly from having a role, however minor, which means that other members of staff and pupils depend on them. Early integration into the team is to be desired if the full potential of each member of staff is to be achieved.

We are all familiar with the 'invisible hand'. In many ways the role of the Head is to create a system in which his manipulation and guidance are invisible – but although the invisible hand may be desirable, the invisible Head is not. He has prime responsibility for the academic standards of his department, which he will seek to maintain and improve by checks on performance – internal and external examination results, random examination of notebooks and other pupil work, discussions with individual members of staff, and even perhaps the occasional ear to the keyhole! As departments grow larger, and the range of courses wider, there is a risk that the Head withdraws to some inner sanctum, emergence from which means 'trouble'. Although the departmental Head has overall responsibility for discipline in his department, it is unfortunate if he is seen only as a source of retribution when indiscipline occurs. Support for the individual teacher with problems of control is a delicate but vitally important task – many a good teacher can be saved with the right support at the right time. He must be accessible to all members of his department, staff and pupils, not just at formal meetings but through the informal communications net of a thriving department. He must remember that people are the prime call on his time, and not retreat behind ever-growing and sometimes self-generated heaps of paper. Informal discussions are no substitutes for formal meetings – but the latter should be called (other than for routine administration) only when substantial issues need to be resolved. In addition, by making himself available in breaks and lunch hours, and by effective use of noticeboards and circulars, the Head can create a network of communication which ensures that he knows what members of his department feel, and they know what is going on. A departmental office, used by *all* members of the department is a notable instrument of cohesion. Divide and rule is *not* the best way to do things.

Large organisations have personnel departments, but the wise manager does not absolve himself from the problems of his staff, or from responsibility for their career development. In schools we do not have such ancillary services, although some Deputy Heads fortunately take a positive view of what can be done. Knowledge of the personal circumstances of each member of staff is valuable. It is not a matter of prying into personal affairs; rather that the effectiveness of teachers will be affected by their life outside the classroom. Although advice should not be forced on anyone, most of us like to feel that someone is concerned with difficulties we may be experiencing. Such guidance may simply bring the individual back to square one; but there is a second role for the Head which should be to enable the individual teacher to develop, to become more fulfilled and effective. Better teaching is in the interests of both department and individual. Thought about the pattern of teaching given to each teacher is one way of achieving this. The conscious creation of a range of expertise and specialisms is to everyone's advantage. Members of the department should be encouraged to go on courses, join their professional association, and to develop extra-curricular interests which enhance the life of the school and their own career prospects. It may be suggested that the Head's role is in part to build up a team all of whom are capable of moving on to better things, but who do not wish to.

Emphasis thus far has been on the welfare of the teaching staff – but however good the manpower, the resource base of the department will have a significant effect on the patterns and effectiveness of teaching. There are two key aspects of the use of resources:

1 What is available, and can this be increased?
2 How well are they used?

It is the departmental Head's responsibility to obtain adequate resources, to make decisions about capitation allowance expenditures, and to apply for central school funds or to specialist advisers where necessary. Efficient use of resources is partly his sole responsibility, partly a matter for discussion and delegation. Resource issues to be considered include availability of classroom, library and work space, equipment such as furniture, blackboards and audio-visual aids, and software, whether books, worksheets or filed newspapers and other material. Some of this responsibility can be delegated; more generally the head of subject should seek through discussion and encouragement to ensure that resources, once made available to his department, are used to the full. No economist should be content to see resources lying idle unless absolutely necessary – too often the Head of Department may be at fault, either because of a failure to discover the general value of something which he would like to have, or because he has failed to make known what is available, or indeed because some items are kept anonymously under his lock and key. Efficient resource retrieval is a major problem, especially as the range of subjects increases, as the piles of material grow deeper, and the number of people wishing to use the system expands. Certain questions pose themselves. Should there be a central index of all material? How thoroughly should material be cross-referenced? Should material for particular topics be organised in 'packs'? Should all material be available to staff and pupils alike? What can be borrowed and how can checks be kept? Are display areas available so that current topics can be illustrated and attention drawn to relevant material? The economic stringency of the late 70s seems unlikely to be relaxed in the near future; Heads of Department have a duty to make sure that they make the most of what they can get, and to ensure that losses are kept to an irreducible minimum.

This introduces another dimension of responsibility, that of relations with other departments, the Headmaster and the school at large. Subject status varies from school to school, and that can have a major effect on matters such as resource allocation on a discretionary basis, decisions about classroom occupation and priorities in the construction of the school timetable. The aim of the Head should therefore be to improve his department's standing, rather than build empires for the sake of it. Yet conflicts are inevitable with other subjects – the location of economics in the option groups will be of vital importance in determining the number and calibre of the pupils opting for it. It is in the interests of all members of the department that the subject is viewed favourably by the Headmaster, directors of studies, year tutors and the like. Successful operation in the political world of inter-departmental and faculty meetings, the communication of information from these meetings to members of the department and expression of their views at these meetings are of great importance. Status will be built up by successful subject teaching, positive parent and pupil reactions, and by a general feeling that the department knows what it is trying to achieve and how to set about it. Apparently unimportant efficiencies such as punctual return of reports, accurate knowledge of the disposition of manpower and possible alternatives, and many other forms of minor competence help to inspire confidence.

It may appear that pupils have been neglected so far; yet any improvement in the efficiency of a department must ultimately be measured in terms of pupil benefit. The Head cannot and should not expect to have the same relationship with all the pupils in his department that he has with the classes he teaches. As departments grow in size, so concern for the individual must be institutionalised. This can be achieved in a number of

ways, including an efficient card index system, regular discussions with colleagues on problem pupils, effective reporting at the end of each term or half term to the Head as well as parents, and perhaps the operation of a regular open house, when any pupil knows that his Head of Department will be available to discuss matters such as choice of subject combination, future careers, and individual academic problems. Records of attendance, marks, etc may also be important for reasons external to the department, e.g. attendance details may be required by courts, and marks have been known to be asked for by the Race Relations Board!

Parents should not be neglected. It remains obvious that social engineering cannot be achieved by school alone, and that parental support remains a key element in determining pupil success at school. Therefore apart from the general right of parents to be kept in the picture and what we can learn of the pupil from knowledge of the parents, we must seek to develop relationships with parents which will encourage them to support their children. The Head should ensure that reports give a full picture of the individual progress of each pupil, and should be willing to explain how the school works, the implications of particular courses, and how the individual fits in. If necessary he should be prepared to organise departmental parents' evenings.

The need for general concern for the welfare of other members of the department has been noted. In this section we suggest some specific responsibilities, beginning with one of the most difficult issues, the deployment of teaching staff. Should the least able classes have the least able teachers? Are able teachers equally able with all groups of pupils? Should the Head of Department take the best groups, worst groups, or spread himself widely across the department? There can be no set answer to this since so many variable factors are involved. The only rule of thumb can be that given careful consideration of courses, abilities and other constraints, the Head seeks to provide the best possible teaching for each pupil, and seeks to gear each teacher's programme as closely as possible to his own skills, interests and needs. It makes little sense to force the highly academic teacher to work with groups for whom his approach will have little meaning – although it may be possible in various ways to increase the flexibility with which individual teachers may be used – team teaching, tutorial systems, etc. Staff deployment may be further complicated where more than one subject is taught by the same person, or where pastoral and departmental roles require conflicting time. Economic stringency again makes it unlikely that some of the more enlightened schemes for the induction of new teachers will be implemented, but much can be done by a thoughtful Head of Department to ease inexperienced teachers into what is after all a taxing and challenging profession. A similar responsibility applies to the supervision of student teachers, who are unlikely to return to the department, but whose career can gain enormously from successful teaching practice sessions.

Finally there are the subject responsibilities of the Head of Department. It may be argued that this is primary, yet if we get people right we will get the subject right. However much we know about the subject itself, and of theories about teaching the subject, all is wasted if we cannot lead a team effectively. Yet having said this, there are many subject-related issues which provide departmental Heads with difficult decisions, irrespective of subject. We may start with the courses to be followed; today these may include CSE, CEE 'O', 'A' and 'S' levels (plus non-examination courses) and an incredible array which may come under the umbrella of economics including economics itself, business studies, commerce, European studies, economic history, politics and sociology. Much depends on how organisational structures have evolved, and the will and ability of schools to widen the range of courses. Courses offered are often intimately related to the abilities of particular members of staff, creating considerable difficulty when they move on, or are unavailable in particular areas of the timetable. Departments can become overstretched by the desire to provide a wide range of courses, and sometimes hard decisions have to be made to ensure that existing courses are adequately resourced.

Policy on grouping pupils is often laid down centrally, but in many schools Heads of Department may find themselves with substantial discretion over blocking or setting work, or whether team teaching schemes should be operated. In many cases this is simply a matter of judgement as to which course of action is best suited to the needs of pupils in the department. However, an external issue is movement of pupils between ability bands – again, accurate information on all members of the department must be available, if effective guidance is to be given on such decisions. Other important decisions concern courses for the non-specialist sixth-former and similar general needs. Whatever the course, whatever the subject, the Head of Department must ensure that a syllabus is available, and followed. Properly constructed syllabuses should not significantly interfere with individual teaching styles, particularly if they have evolved out of discussions, and if parts of the course and relevant course material have been prepared by members of the department. More positively, the syllabus reflects agreement on the ground to be covered, ensures continuity over the period of the course, and provides the basis on which resources such as books, worksheets, games and audio-visual material can be provided.

In conclusion, the job of Head of Department requires that a whole range of managerial skills be added to whatever classroom skills the teacher may have. The latter remain important since they set standards for the rest of the department, and ensure that the purpose of teaching is never forgotten. Management is both science and art – some people are better at it than others, but much can be done to learn the skills required.

55   Cataloguing Economics Resources

A. G. Anderton

Every teacher to some degree catalogues his resources. For the majority of teachers, the catalogue that they keep is mostly in their head. They know that there are fifteen multiple choice books in the cupboard in the corner with a section on demand and supply. For a teacher with few resources, the memory catalogue is perfectly adequate and requires little effort to maintain. However, as soon as the number of resources expands, then a more systematic approach is needed if those resources are not going to gather dust. For instance, many economics teachers must at some stage have collected newspaper articles. Most of them quickly gave up because they could never find the article they wanted quickly or easily enough, and anyway they completely forgot the existence of most of them because they had only read them once. The memory catalogue here breaks down.

The next stage beyond the memory catalogue is to develop some sort of filing system. What sort of filing system is developed depends upon particular needs.

However, the following questions should be asked before the system is developed:

1 Who is going to use the system? It could be just one economics teacher or other members of the department, or even more radically pupils as well.
2 How many resources are likely to be stored? The larger the number of resources, the more sophisticated the filing system must be.
3 How much time will the user have to spend retrieving resources? On the whole, the more sophisticated the filing system, the easier it is to retrieve resources but the more time has to be spent on filing. There is a trade-off between retrieval time and time spent on maintaining the system.

One of the first problems that presents itself is what cataloguing system should be used. There are two main choices, namely using Dewey or developing a personal system. If Dewey is used, the advantages are that it gives a good training in the use of libraries, the system is there already and it only has to be interpreted. The disadvantages are that it is inflexible to personal requirements, it is sometimes difficult to interpret and if the catalogue is to be used in any detail (say to distinguish between oligopoly and monopoly) the most modern edition of the Dewey catalogue is needed. Most libraries carry outdated catalogues where the detail is not great and many of the numbers are out of step with the most modern catalogue. (See the Appendix at the end of this chapter for Dewey classification numbers for economics.)

Another problem is how to store resources. One way is to put everything to do with one topic into one box or one file. The other way is to keep all the newspaper articles together, all the cassettes, all the bandas, and so on. If the latter course is chosen, there must be some way of cataloguing each type of resource into sections – all the newspaper articles on monopoly are put together but they come just after the articles on oligopoly for instance. Whichever alternative is used, trouble is encountered when items such as bank reviews and books are catalogued where the item contains several different sections of interest. Trouble also crops up if the item is relevant to two or more subject areas. The only solution to that is to start leaving notes in the box or whatever is used, saying that such and such an item might be useful. As soon as the teacher starts to cross reference, he will need to go a stage further and start a full economics catalogue – that is, keep a list of all the resources available on one topic. Again, ask the three questions that were asked at the start. If it is just for personal use, then very cryptic entries can be made.

If it is going to be used by other people, then more care must be taken over references. The system must be simple to use if pupils are going to use it. A teacher might be willing to spend five minutes retrieving an item. Pupils are not. The more resources there are, the greater the number of categories that should be used. It makes little difference when filing and cataloguing whether an item is filed under 'the firm' or under 'monopoly.' It certainly does make a difference for retrieval purposes if there are 100 items under 'the firm' but only ten items under 'monopoly.' Twenty to thirty items is the optimum number of items to have under any one category. If more items appear, then the category should be subdivided. The amount of detail about the item put on to the catalogue is very important. For instance, one could have a reference to a bank review or the title of the articles could be written down as well. Or one could even write a short abstract about the item. It would be sensible to use Dewey for the catalogue if the books are classified under Dewey. Pupils will learn to use the Dewey system and this will be useful in libraries, at university, etc.

On a file catalogue, the actual title of the resource is given. For instance, *Lloyds Bank Review* published an article in their January 1972 issue on insurance. On the catalogue the entry might be '"Britain's Insurance Industry," article, *Lloyds Bank Review*, January 1972.' It is worth the trouble putting the title of the resource on to the catalogue, because retrieval is more frustrating than cataloguing. It is essential if pupils are to use the system because they will not use the system if it is difficult to operate.

When cataloguing, give four pieces of information: the title of the item, what type of resource it is (e.g. article, wallchart, a chapter in a book), where to find the resource, and how old the resource is. Taking the insurance article, the entry 'article' gives its location in the library because all articles are kept on the same shelf. To give another example: '"Borrowing money from a bank", sheet, 332.14. 1975.' All single sheet copies are kept in a file, the sheet is stored under 332.14. The sheet was written in 1975.

For two types of resource, namely newspaper articles and commercial leaflets, the time spent cataloguing far outweighs any benefit to be gained. So for these, simply put a catalogue number on them and file them in order so they are quickly retrievable. On the catalogue, write on each page in large capital letters 'newspaper articles' and the pupils are generally willing to sort through them if nothing else is available. Any important newspaper article can quickly be put on the main catalogue and be put into the sheet file.

It may sound very complicated, but in practice it is not very difficult to construct a catalogue. Initially, it is time consuming. To get a school catalogue off the ground, with possibly 200 individual resources to go on the catalogue and 100 separate categories, would take about forty hours of individual work. Maintaining the file would take possibly a couple of hours every term. Once it has been started, it really takes little time to maintain. The advantages are great. For a start, it means the teacher can constantly see all the resources available on a topic, from printed material to cassettes and film strips. It can quickly reveal where there are gaps in resources. It will probably encourage a more varied approach to teaching. Some teachers may use chalk and talk because they have not organised their resources effectively. They do not remember that there is a worksheet on a particular topic, or that they cut an article out six months ago because it would make an ideal case study. If the catalogue is constructed with the pupils in mind as well as the teachers, and it is presented in such a way that they can easily use it, then it makes possible a more pupil-centred approach to learning. The pupils can see what resources there are and organise their learning round that. Work could be set based on resources listed in the catalogue. Pupils could be encouraged to sift through the material available and decide what is useful for themselves.

Whatever happens, they have a guide to resources independent of the teacher. Without a catalogue, most of the resources would essentially be 'dead' because nobody would use them. That is justification enough for the work involved in constructing a catalogue.

Appendix: Dewey Classification – 18th Edition*

330 Economics

.122 Free-enterprise economy
    Usually synonymous with capitalism
.124 Planned economies
    Class socialism and related systems in 335
.126 Mixed economies
    Interventionism, welfare state systems
.153 Classical economics
    School of Smith, Malthus, Ricardo, Bastiat, Say.
    Class neoclassicism in 330.155
.155 Miscellaneous schools
    Neoclassicism; welfare economics
.156 Keynesianism

331 Labour Economics

    Class here industrial relations
.118 Labour productivity
.127 Mobility of labour
.128 Obtaining employment
    Including employment agencies, labour exchanges
.137 Unemployment
.21 Wages
.252 Pensions
.257 Hours
.8   Labour unions (trade unions) and labour–management bargaining
.892 Strikes

332 Financial Economics

.041 Capital

.041 54 Sources of capital
.1   Banks and banking
     Class here comprehensive works on money and banking, on financial institutions and their functions
.11   Central banks
.12   Commercial banks
.15   International banks and banking
     Example: IMF
.17   Banking services of commercial banks
.38   Insurance companies
.4   Money

.401 Theories
     Examples: quantity theory, circulation and velocity equation, equation of exchange theory
.41   Relation to economic conditions
     Class here inflation and deflation
.64   Exchange of securities and commodities
     Operation and activities of securities and commodities markets; trading procedures
.67   Investment and investments
.7   Credit
.8   Interest and discount

333 Land Economics

.012 Economic rent
.7   Land utilisation
     Class here pollution
.72   Conservation

334 Cooperatives

.5   Distribution (consumers' cooperatives)
.6   Production

335 Socialism and Related Systems

336 Public Finance

.2   Taxes and taxation
.34   Public borrowing and public debt
.39   Expenditure

338 Production

.04   Entrepreneurship
.1   Agriculture
.2   Mineral industries
.21   Coal
.282 Petrol
.285 Gas
.3   Other extractive industries
.4   Secondary industries
.51   Costs
.514 4 Size of enterprise
     Economies and diseconomies of scale, use of technology
.516 Profit
.52   Prices
     Determination, effects of changes
.521 2 Price–demand relationship

Including law of diminishing marginal utility
.521 3 Price–supply relationship
.522 Determination in free markets
Free markets: markets comprising a number of sellers large enough that no individual seller can affect the price, selling either homogeneous, standardised products (pure competition) or similar but not standardised products (monopolistic competition)
.523 Determination in controlled markets
Oligopoly, monopoly
Including price leadership
Class organisation structure of combinations and monopolies in 338.8
.54 Economic fluctuations (business cycles)
.544 Business forecasting
.604 2 Location
Proximity to sources of power, raw materials, markets, labour supply, transportation
.604 6 Specialisation
Including law of comparative advantage
.7 Organisations and their structure
Private firms. Class government corporations under 350.0092
.8 Combinations
Organisation and structure for mass production and control of production
.83 Mergers and amalgamations
.87 Informal arrangements
Interlocking directorates, pools, cartels
.88 International
Including international cartels, foreign-owned subsidiaries
.9 Production programmes and policies
Examples: control, subsidies, grants by government, nationalisation

339 Macroeconomics

Behaviour and functioning of the economy as a totality; national income, saving, investment, consumption. For economic fluctuations, see 338.54
.21 Functional distribution of income
Compensation of employees, proprietor's income, rental income, corporate profits, payments for use of invested capital
.23 Input–output accounts (interindustry accounts)
Accounts and analysis of goods and services provided by each industry for all other industries and consuming units
.26 Flow-of-funds accounts
Sources of funds paid to and use of funds by various sectors of the economy
.3 Measures of national income
.4 Factors affecting national income
For economic stabilisation, see 339.5
.41 Income consumption relations
Marginal propensities to consume and save at various levels of income; multiplier effect, consumer response to decreases and increases in income
.43 Savings and investment
.46 Economic causes and effects of poverty
.47 Consumption
Including standard of living, control of consumption
.5 Economic stabilisation and growth
.52 Use of fiscal policy
Taxation, spending, public debt, debt management.
Including economics effects of taxation, of expenditure
.53 Use of monetary policy.

350.0092 Government corporations – nationalised industries
360 Social welfare
382 Foreign trade
382.7 Tariff policy
382.91 Multilateral agreements and customs unions

List of Useful Addresses

Access	Public Relations Dept, The Joint Credit Card Co Ltd, London Regional Office, 30–31 Newman Street, London W1P 4LJ
Advertising Association	The Information Division, 15 Wilton Road, London SW1V 1NJ
Allen and Unwin	40 Museum Street, London WC1
Amalgamated Union of Engineering Workers	110 Pelham Road, London SE15 5EL
Arnold (Edward) Publishers Ltd	25 Hill Street, London W1
Associated Examining Board	Wellington House, Station Road, Aldershot, Hants GU11 1BQ
Associated Lancashire Schools Examining Board	77 Whitworth Street, Manchester M1 6HA
Audio Learning Ltd	84 Queensway, London W2 3RL
Baltic Exchange	The Secretary, St Mary Axe, London EC3A 8BU
Bank Education Service	10 Lombard Street, London EC3V 9AT
Bank of England Quarterly Review	Economic Intelligence Department, Bank of England, London EC2
Bank of England	Schools Liaison Officer, Staff Division, Threadneedle Street, London EC2
Bankers' Clearing House Ltd.	10 Lombard Street, London EC3
Barclays Bank Review	Economic Intelligence Dept, 54 Lombard Street, London EC3
Barclays Film Library	25 The Burroughs, Hendon, London NW4 4AT
BBC Enterprises	Villiers House, Haven Green, London W5 2PA
BBC Schools Radio and Television	School Broadcasting Council for the UK, The Langham, Portland Place, London W1
Board of Inland Revenue	Press and Information Officer, Somerset House, Strand, London WC2R 1LB
BP Film Library	15 Beaconsfield Road, London NW10 2LE
British Gas	Education Liaison Officer, Room 414, 326 High Holborn, London WC1V 7PT
British Insurance Association	Public Relations Officer, PO Box 538, Aldermary House, Queen Street, London EC4P 4JD
British Rail	Controller, Public Relations and Publicity, British Railways Board, 222 Marylebone Road, London NW1 6JJ
British Standards Institution	2 Park Street, London W1
Building Societies' Association	Information Officer, 14 Park Street, London W1Y 4AL
Business Education Council	76 Portland Place, London W1N 4AA
Business Studies Project (AL)	Institute of Education, Bedford Way, London WC1H 0AL
Butterworth and Co (Publishers) Ltd	88 Kingsway, London WC2
Cambridge University Local Examinations Syndicate	17 Harvey Road, Cambridge

Cambridge University Press	Bentley House, 200 Euston Road, London NW1 2DB
Careers Consultants Ltd	12–14 Hill Rise, Richmond Hill, Richmond, Surrey TW10 6UA
Careers Research and Advisory Centre	Bateman Street, Cambridge CB2 1LZ
Central Film Library	Government Building, Bromyard Avenue, Action, London W3 7JB
Central Office of Information	Hercules Road, Westminster Bridge Road, London SE1
Central Statistical Office	Free Publications, PO Box 242, London SE1 0DE
Centre for World Development Education	Parnell House, 25 Wilton Road, London SW1
Coca Cola Export Corporation	7 Rockley Road, London W14
Commission of the European Communities	Information Office, 20 Kensington Palace Gardens, London W8 4QQ
Committee on Invisible Exports	The Secretary, The Stock Exchange, Throgmorton Street, London EC2
Community Service Volunteers	28 Commercial Street, London E1 6BR
Concord Films Council	201 Felixstowe Road, Ipswich, Suffolk
Confederation of British Industry	21 Tothill Street, London SW1H 9LP
The Conservation Society Ltd	12a Guildford Street, Chertsey, Surrey KT16 9BQ
The Conservative Party	32 Smith Square, London SW1
Consumers' Association	14 Buckingham Street, London WC2N 6DS
Co-operative Banks	Public Relations Department, Head Office, PO Box 101, New Century House, Manchester M60 4EP
Corporation of the City of London	PO Box 270, Guildhall, London EC2P 2EJ
Daily Express	Fleet Street, London EC4
Daily Mail	Carmelite House, Carmelite Street, London EC4
Daily Mirror	Production Dept (Visits), 33 Holborn, London EC1
Department of Health and Social Security	Alexandra Fleming House, Elephant and Castle, London SE1
Department of the Environment	Directorate of Information, 2 Marsham Street, London SW1P 3EB
Department of Trade and Industry	Room 707, Information Division, UK Publicity Section, 1 Victoria Street, London SW1
East Anglian Examinations Board	'The Lindens,' Lexden Road, Colchester, Essex
East Midland Regional Examinations Board	Robins Wood House, Robins Wood Road, Aspley, Nottingham NG8 3NH
Economic Journal	Royal Economic Society, Marshall Library, Sidgwick Avenue, Cambridge
Economic Progress Reports	PDSD Distribution Unit, Central Office of Information, Hercules Road, London SE1
Economics Association	Room 340, Hamilton House, Mabledon Place, London WC1H 9BH
The Economist	Subscription Dept, 54 St James's Street, London SW1 1JJ
Educational Foundation for Visual Aids	33 Queen Anne Street, London W1M 0NL
Educational Productions Ltd	Bradford Road, East Ardsley, Wakefield, Yorkshire WF3 2JN
Educational Resource Associates	1100, Glendon, Suite 945, Los Angeles, CA 90024, USA
EFTA Bulletin	EFTA Information Centre, 1 Victoria Street, London SW1

Encyclopaedia Britannica	Dorland House, 18 Regent Street, London SW1
Export Credit Guarantee Dept	Public Relations Section, Head Office, Aldermanbury House, London EC2
Fabian Society	11 Dartmouth Street, London SW1
Finance Houses Association	14 Queen Anne's Gate, London SW1H 9AG
Fontana Paperbacks	14 St James's Place, London SW1A 1PF
Friends of the Earth	9 Poland Street, London WC1
Ginn and Co Ltd	Elsinore House, Buckingham Street, Aylesbury, Bucks HP20 2NQ
Guardian Business Services Ltd	21, John St., London, WC1
Guild Sound and Vision Ltd	Woodston House, Oundle Road, Peterborough PE2 9PZ
Harrap (George A.) and Co Ltd	182/4 High Holborn, London WC1V 7AX
Heinemann Educational Books Ltd	22 Bedford Square, London WC1B 3HH
Hobsons Press	Bateman Street, Cambridge CB2 1BR
Hodder and Stoughton	Mill Road, Dunton Green, Sevenoaks, Kent TN13 2YA
HMSO	Publicity Section/PEC, Atlantic House, Holborn Viaduct, London EC1
ICI Film Library	Thames House North, Millbank, London SW1P 4QG
The Industrial Society	Peter Runge House, 3 Carlton House Terrace, London SW1
ILEA TV Service	Tennyson Street, London SW8 3TB
Inland Revenue	The Press and Information Office, Somerset House, London WC2R 1LB
Institute of Chartered Accountants	PO Box 433, Moorgate Place, London EC2 2BJ
Institute of Economic Affairs	2 Lord North Street, London SW1P 3LB
Joint Matriculation Board	Manchester 15. Regulations and syllabuses from: Messrs Sherratt and Sons, St Ann's Press, Park Road, Altrincham, Cheshire
The Labour Party	Transport House, Smith Square, London SW1
The Liberal Party	1 Whitehall Place, London SW1
Life Offices Association	The LOA Information Centre, Buckingham House (2nd floor), 62/63 Queen's Street, London EC4R 1AD
Lloyds	Information Officer, Lime Street, London EC3M 7HA
Lloyds Bank Ltd	Schools' Liaison Officer, PO Box 215, 71 Lombard Street, London EC3P 3BS
Lloyds Bank Review	71 Lombard Street, London EC3
London Central Markets	Clerk and Superintendent, West Smithfield, London EC1
London Co-operative Society	Education Department, 129 Seven Sisters Road, London N7 7QG
London University School Examinations Council	66–72 Gower Street, London WC1
Longman Group Ltd	Longman House, Burnt Mill, Harlow, Essex CM20 2JE
Longman Group Resources Unit	35 Tanner Row, York (General Studies Project)
Macdonald and Evans Ltd	Estover Road, Plymouth PL6 7PZ
Macmillan Ltd	4 Little Essex Street, London WC2R 3LF
Management Games Ltd	63B, George Street, Maulden, Bedford MK45 2DD
McGraw-Hill Book Company (UK) Ltd	Shoppenhangers Road, Maidenhead, Berks SL6 2QL
Metropolitan Regional Examinations Board	Lyon House, 104 Wandsworth High Street, London SW18 4LF

Middlesex Regional Examining Board	53–63 Wembley Hill Road, Wembley, Middlesex
Midland Bank Ltd	Schools' Liaison Office, Suffolk House, 7th Floor, 5 Laurence Pountney Hill, London EC4R 0EU
Midland Bank Review	The Manager, Public Relations and Advertising Dept, Midland Bank Ltd, PO Box 2, Griffin House, Silver Street Head, Sheffield S1 3GG
Multilink Film Library	12 The Square, Vicarage Farm Road, Peterborough PE1 5TS
Murray (John) Publishers Ltd	50 Albemarle Street, London W1X 4BD
National Audio-Visual Aids Centre	254 Belsize Road, London NW6 4BY
National Audio-Visual Aids Library	Paxton Place, Gipsy Road, London SE27 9SR
National Coal Board	Schools' Service, Hobart House, Room 342, Grosvenor Place, London SW1X 7AE
National Farmers Union	Agriculture House, Knightsbridge, London SW1X 7NJ
National Giro	Freepost, National Giro Centre, Bootle, Merseyside G1R 0AA
National Savings Committee	Education Branch, Alexandra House, Kingsway, London WC2
National Westminster Bank Ltd	Advertising Dept (Wallcharts), 200 Pentonville Road, London N1
National Westminster Bank Review	41 Lothbury, London EC2
National Westminster Bank Ltd	Schools Liaison Office, PO Box 297, Drapers Gardens, 12 Throgmorton Avenue, London EC2P 2ES
Nelson (Thomas) and Co Ltd	Lincoln Way, Windmill Road, Sunbury-on-Thames, Middlesex TW16 7HP
North Regional Examinations Board	Wheatfield Road, Westerhope, Newcastle upon Tyne NE5 5JX
North Western Secondary School Examinations Board	36 Grunby Row, Manchester M1 7EB
Office of Fair Trading	Field House, Bream's Buildings, London EC4
Open University	Marketing Division, PO Box 81, Walton Hall, Milton Keynes MK7 6AT
Open University Film Library	Guild Sound and Vision Ltd, 85–129 Oundle Road, Peterborough PE2 9PZ
Oxfam Education	274 Banbury Road, Oxford OX2 7DZ
Oxford and Cambridge Schools Examining Board	Elsfield Way, Oxford, or Brook House, 10 Trumpington Street, Cambridge
Oxford Delegacy of Local Examinations	Summertown, Oxford
Oxford University Press	Education Dept, Walton Street, Oxford OX2 6DP
Pictorial Charts Educational Trust	27 Kirchen Road, London W13 0UD
Pitman Publishing Ltd	39 Parker Street, London WC2B 5PB
Polytech Publishers Ltd	36 Hayburn Road, Stockport SK2 5DB
Post Office	Schools Officer, Postal Headquarters, St Martin-le-Grand, London EC1A 1HQ
Rank Film Library	PO Box 70, Great West Road, Brentford, Middlesex TW8 9HR
Resources for Learning Development Unit	Redcross Street, Bristol BS2 0BA
Routledge and Kegan Paul Ltd	39 Store Street, London WC1E 7DD

Schools Council	160 Great Portland Street, London W1
Scottish Centre for Social Subjects	Jordanhill College of Education, 76 Southbrae Drive, Glasgow G13 1PP
Seminar Cassettes	218 Sussex Gardens, London W2 3UD
Shell Film Library	25 The Burroughs, London NW4 4AT
Shell UK Ltd	PO Box, No 148 Shell-Mex House, Strand, London WC2R 0DX
Simulation Games	12 Kenilworth Avenue, Manchester M20 8NA
Small Firms Information Centre	Small Firms Division, Department of Trade, Abell House, John Islep Street, London SW1P 4LN
South East Regional Examinations Board	Belroe House, 2/4 Mount Ephraim Road, Tunbridge Wells, Kent
South Western Examinations Board	23–29 Marsh Street, Bristol BS1 4BP
Southern Regional Examinations Board	53 London Road, Southampton S09 4YL
Southern Universities Joint Board for School Examinations	Cotham Road, Bristol BS6 6DD
Stock Exchange	Public Relations Department, Offices of the Council, London EC2N 1HP
Student Recordings Ltd	King Street, Newton Abbot, Devon
Sussex Tapes	Educational Productions Ltd, Bradford Road, East Ardsley, Wakefield, Yorkshire WF3 2JN
Three Banks Review	7 Copthall Avenue, London EC2R 7HB
Town and Country Planning Association	17 Carlton House, London SW1
Trades Union Congress	Education Department, Congress House, Great Russell Street, London WC1B 3LS
Treasury	Information Division, Parliament Street, London SW1P 3AG
Understanding British Industry Project	Sun Alliance House, New Inn Hall Street, Oxford OX1 0QE
University Tutorial Press	9 Great Sutton Street, London EC1
Viscom Ltd	6–7 Great Chapel Street, London W1V 3AG
Weidenfeld and Nicolson Ltd	11 St Johns Hill, London SW11 1XA
Welsh Joint Education Committee	245 Western Avenue, Cardiff CF5 2YX
Welsh Office	Press Office, Cathays Park, Cardiff CF1 1PQ
West Midland Examination Board	Norfolk House, Smallbrook Ringway, Birmingham
West Yorkshire and Lindsey Regional Examining Board	Scarsdale House, 136 Derbyshire Lane, Sheffield 8
Yorkshire Regional Examinations Board	7–9 Cambridge Road, Harrogate, Yorkshire

Index